D1346131

ESTUARY BIRDS OF BRITAIN AND IRELAND

# ESTUARY BIRDS

## of Britain and Ireland

*by* A. J. PRATER

*Illustrated by* JOHN BUSBY

T & A D POYSER

Calton

ISBN 0 85661 029 1

A Report of the Birds of Estuaries Enquiry
conducted under contract from the Nature Conservancy
Council by the British Trust for Ornithology
with the help of the Royal Society for the Protection
of Birds and the Wildfowl Trust

First published in 1981 by T & A D Poyser Ltd,
Town Head House, Calton, Waterhouses, Staffordshire, England

Text set in 9/11 pt Linotron 202 Sabon, printed and bound
in Great Britain at The Pitman Press, Bath

# Contents

# List of Plates

# List of Figures

*Note:* Figures for Chapter 17, The Species Accounts, are by species arranged in Voous order.

# List of Tables

        *Note:* Tables for Chapter 17, The Species Accounts, are by species
        arranged in Voous order.

# Introduction

'It is nice not to have large exposed mudflats.' This comment, made in December 1978 by Sir Herman Bondi, the Chief Scientist of the Department of Energy, when talking in favour of a tidal barrage on the Severn Estuary, exemplifies the lack of appreciation and understanding of the ecology of intertidal areas by those wishing to remove more of our steadily diminishing estuary habitats.

To the one million or more birdwatchers, and to many other people, estuaries are magnificent places. Despite being a relatively simple habitat with a limited flora and lacking great contrasts of height, they are wide and uncluttered, quiet and tranquil, yet they are bursting with life. The life does not thrust itself upon you, since the invertebrates are mainly in the sand, and other life is in the water; it is only when the birds are forced to retreat up the shore as the tide floods in that they become really noticeable. For most of the tidal cycle, birds are scattered, individually or in flocks, across the intertidal flats. They use this time profitably to find their food before the incoming water once again covers it; at low water on our major estuaries, feeding birds are usually inconspicuous. It is presumably this which has given the impression that estuaries are empty places and has in part led to so many development threats to this habitat. We shall see later that estuaries are extremely productive and support very large numbers of birds, but what of the habitat? Is it a vast resource which can stand a considerable amount of reduction without serious damage?

The length of coastline of Britain has been estimated at 4,390 km in England and Wales, 3,860 km of mainland Scotland and 6,250 km of Scottish islands, giving a total of 14,500 km. In Britain there are 133 estuaries and bays with one km² or more of intertidal flats. There is a total of approximately 2,600 km² of mud and sand flats in these and smaller estuaries, plus an undetermined area along beaches and rocky coasts. The area of saltmarsh in Britain was estimated to be 448 km² during the late 1960s. All of the intertidal areas counted are shown in the map overleaf.

After barrage schemes had been suggested for the Solway and Morecambe Bay during the mid-1960s, it was realised that estuarine birds, particularly waders, could be threatened by habitat loss. The wader research initiated under the Morecambe Bay Barrage Feasibility Study was the first extensive professionally co-ordinated census study on this group of birds in Britain. However, it was immediately apparent that knowledge from elsewhere was fragmentary. In 1969, G. Thomas of the Royal Society for the Protection of Birds searched through the available literature for wader census data and highlighted its inadequacies. In the meantime, in 1968, Dr W. R. P. Bourne had put forward a proposal to the British Trust for Ornithology's Populations and Surveys Committee that a survey of estuary birds, particularly waders, was desirable. After some discussion, it was agreed that it was not only desirable but also practical and that a joint BTO/RSPB project should be started. Initial contacts during the first half of 1969 enabled almost half of the major estuaries to be counted during the 1969/70 pilot year. The organisation of the pilot survey was undertaken by D. E. Glue of the BTO and Dr P. J. K. Burton of the International Waterfowl Research Bureau's Wader Research Group.

It was soon apparent that the survey could produce the information required and the Nature Conservancy (now separated into the Nature Conservancy Council –

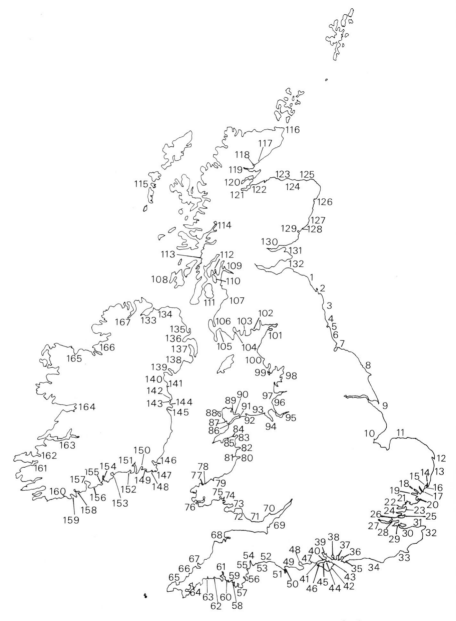

Fig. A. The intertidal areas counted– see opposite page for key.

| | | | | | |
|---|---|---|---|---|---|
| 1 | Tweed | 57 | Kingsbridge | 113 | Loch Crinan |
| 2 | Lindisfarne | 58 | Avon | 114 | Loch Linnhe |
| 3 | Northumberland coast | 59 | Erme | 115 | Uists |
| 4 | Whitley Bay | 60 | Yealm | 116 | Caithness coast |
| 5 | Tyne | 61 | Plym/Tavy/Tamar/Lynher | 117 | Brora/Golspie |
| 6 | Whitburn coast | 62 | Looe | 118 | Loch Fleet |
| 7 | Teesmouth | 63 | Fowey | 119 | Dornoch Firth |
| 8 | Whitby coast | 64 | Fal | 120 | Cromarty Firth |
| 9 | Humber | 65 | Hayle | 121 | Beauly Firth |
| 10 | Wash | 66 | Gannel | 122 | Moray Firth |
| 11 | North Norfolk coast | 67 | Camel | 123 | Spey |
| 12 | Breydon Water | 68 | Taw/Torridge | 124 | Deveron |
| 13 | Blyth | 69 | Severn | 125 | Philorth/Rosehearty |
| 14 | Alde | 70 | Taff/Ely | 126 | Ythan |
| 15 | Butley River | 71 | Glamorgan coast | 127 | Dee/Don |
| 16 | Ore | 72 | Swansea Bay | 128 | North Esk |
| 17 | Deben | 73 | Burry Inlet | 129 | Montrose Basin |
| 18 | Orwell | 74 | Gwendraeth/Tywi | 130 | Firth of Tay |
| 19 | Stour | 75 | Taf | 131 | Eden |
| 20 | Hamford Water | 76 | Milford Haven | 132 | Firth of Forth |
| 21 | Colne | 77 | Gwaun | 133 | Lough Foyle |
| 22 | Blackwater | 78 | Nyfer | 134 | Bann |
| 23 | Dengie Flats | 79 | Teifi | 135 | Larne Lough |
| 24 | Crouch | 80 | Dyfi | 136 | Belfast Lough |
| 25 | Foulness/Roach | 81 | Afon Tywyn | 137 | Strangford Lough |
| 26 | Leigh/Canvey | 82 | Mawddach | 138 | Dundrum Bay |
| 27 | Inner Thames | 83 | Traeth Bach | 139 | Carlingford Lough |
| 28 | North Kent marshes | 84 | Afon Wen | 140 | Dundalk Bay |
| 29 | Medway | 85 | Pwllheli Harbour | 141 | Boyne |
| 30 | Swale | 86 | West Menai Straits | 142 | Rogerstown |
| 31 | Minnis Bay | 87 | Afon Cefni | 143 | Malahide |
| 32 | Pegwell Bay | 88 | Inland Sea | 144 | Baldoyle |
| 33 | Rye Harbour | 89 | Traeth Dulas | 145 | Dublin Bay |
| 34 | Sussex coast | 90 | Red Wharf Bay | 146 | Wexford Harbour |
| 35 | Pagham Harbour | 91 | Conwy Bay | 147 | Lady Island's Lake |
| 36 | Chichester Harbour | 92 | Conwy River | 148 | Tacumshin |
| 37 | Langstone Harbour | 93 | Clwyd | 149 | The Cull |
| 38 | Portsmouth Harbour | 94 | Dee | 150 | Bannow Bay |
| 39 | Southampton Water | 95 | Mersey | 151 | Waterford Harbour |
| 40 | Beaulieu River | 96 | Alt | 152 | Tramore |
| 41 | North-west Solent | 97 | Ribble | 153 | Dungarven Harbour |
| 42 | Brading Harbour | 98 | Morecambe Bay | 154 | Youghall |
| 43 | Wootton Creek | 99 | Duddon | 155 | Ballymacoda Bay |
| 44 | Medina | 100 | Esk | 156 | Ballycotton |
| 45 | Newtown River | 101 | Solway Firth | 157 | Cork Harbour |
| 46 | Western Yar | 102 | Rough Firth | 158 | Courtmacsherry Bay |
| 47 | Christchurch Harbour | 103 | Kirkcudbright Bay | 159 | Clonakilty Bay |
| 48 | Poole Harbour | 104 | Wigtown Bay | 160 | Rosscarbery |
| 49 | Wey/Lodmoor | 105 | Luce Bay | 161 | Castlemaine Harbour |
| 50 | Portland Harbour | 106 | Loch Ryan | 162 | Tralee Bay |
| 51 | The Fleet | 107 | Ayr coast | 163 | Shannon/Fergus |
| 52 | Axe | 108 | Islay | 164 | Galway Bay |
| 53 | Otter | 109 | Inner Clyde | 165 | Killala Bay |
| 54 | Exe | 110 | Bute coast | 166 | Sligo Bay |
| 55 | Teign | 111 | Arran coast | 167 | Lough Swilly |
| 56 | Dart | 112 | Loch Riddon | | |

NCC – and the Institute of Terrestrial Ecology – ITE) agreed to fund a five year project. The aims of the 'Birds of Estuaries Enquiry' were threefold. Primarily it was to document the species and numbers of birds using each of Britain's estuaries. These data could be combined to give overall totals, so providing a conservation assessment of each and a comparison between them. Thus, should a development be suggested, it would be possible to assess, in general terms, its impact at a local, national or international level.

Secondly, annual counts could monitor bird population levels and keep a check on natural or man-induced changes. The third aim, which to some extent is a by-product of any regular comprehensive count, was to document seasonal population fluctuations which could be combined with ringing studies to help describe the migration and local movements of birds. This was achieved through the 'Wader Study Group' by including some of the wealth of information obtained by the specialist wader ringing groups around the country. The counts were designed to assess estuary bird numbers, but it was realised that quite large numbers of some species were found on rocky or sandy coastlines. Some data were collected from these habitats as part of the 'Estuaries Enquiry', but there remains to be much learnt about birds here.

A. J. Prater was appointed as National Organiser in June 1970. The 'Birds of Estuaries Enquiry' was organised and administered from the BTO but maintained a close relationship with the RSPB through wardens and regional officers counting or organising counts, through undertaking the printing costs of the annual reports and through invaluable advice. In February 1969, an Advisory Committee was set up, under the chairmanship of the Deputy Director Conservation of the RSPB, to aid and supervise the 'Birds of Estuaries Enquiry'. Its membership was drawn from a wide range of informed parties and its assistance has been extremely valuable throughout. The members of the committee are set out below.

BTO: Dr J. J. M. Flegg, 1969–75; M. Shrubb, 1969–79; R. Spencer, 1976–79; Dr R. J. O'Connor, 1978–79

RSPB: D. Lea, 1969–1972 (Chairman); I. J. Ferguson-Lees, 1972–75 (Chairman, independent member 1975–79); J. L. F. Parslow, 1975–79 (Chairman); Dr C. J. Cadbury, 1972–79; J. Andrews, 1976–78

WILDFOWL TRUST: Dr G. V. T. Matthews, 1969–70; M. A. Ogilvie, 1970–79

NATURE CONSERVANCY (Nature Conservancy Council/Institue of Terrestrial Ecology): Dr D. S. Ranwell (NC), 1969–74; Dr R. Mitchell (NCC) 1974–78; Dr J. D. Goss-Custard (ITE) 1975–79; Dr D. R. Langslow (NCC)1978–79

JWRB: Dr P. J. K. Burton, 1969–71; E. Carp, 1969–70

MAFF: Dr. P. J. Dare, 1969–71

SEABIRD GROUP: Dr W. R. P. Bourne, 1970–79

SPNR/SPNC: R. A. O. Hickling, 1969–79

WAGBI: B. Bailey, 1969–71; J. Swift, 1972–79

WASH WADER RINGING GROUP: Dr C. D. T. Minton, 1969–78

ORGANISERS: Dr P. J. K. Burton, 1969–70; D. E. Glue, 1969–70; A. J. Prater, 1970–79

During January 1971 A. J. Prater and A. Grieve (RSPB) counted waders on some Irish estuaries. Subsequently, the Irish Wildbird Conservancy launched the 'Wetlands Enquiry' with the aim of documenting waterfowl on both coastal and inland sites. Close liaison has been maintained since with their organisers who were C. D. Hutchinson (1971–76), L. Stapleton (1976–78) and P. Smiddy (1978–79). Results of their counts have been published recently (Hutchinson 1979). The Wildfowl Trust became a co-sponsor of the 'Birds of Estuaries Enquiry' in 1972 and has continued through G. L. Atkinson-Willes, M. A. Ogilvie and D. Salmon, to write the section on wildfowl in the annual report, incorporating information gathered by the 'Estuaries Enquiry', the 'Wildfowl Counts' and the goose counts. Following the change in structure of the Nature Conservancy, the 'Estuaries Enquiry' continued to be financed by both NCC and NERC through the agency of ITE until 1977; subsequently all of the funding came from the NCC.

Although this book describes the results of the 1969–75 counts, it must be emphasised that counts have continued and will be continued in the future. From June 1975, the official count dates were restricted to December, January and February (coinciding with international counts); other counts were still received and were welcomed, but were not essential for the main purpose of monitoring population levels and distribution.

This book is divided into two sections. The first part covers general estuarine ecology with special emphasis on aspects which are relevant to the distribution and abundance of birds. Additionally, it includes an outline of the migration and distribution patterns of the main groups, discusses in some detail the criteria used to assess the ornithological importance of an estuary, and looks at the many threats facing estuaries and their birds. The second part describes the results of the counts. There is an introductory chapter on the organisation and methods used; this is followed by two major sections. The first is a brief sketch of each area, describing its essential features and what aspects of its bird populations make it of significance. The second section looks in more detail at the distribution and numbers of the principal species of birds found in estuaries.

# Acknowledgements

Any project which spans six years and gathers data on a national scale must involve an enormous number of people. Unfortunately, it is not possible to thank all 1,000 observers by name, but I hope that the very production of this book will be taken by them as being a fitting tribute to the very many hours of help given, often in far from ideal weather. Without such a body of expertise, this study could never have been contemplated.

I would like specifically to mention the regional organisers who took up the burden of organisation, sometimes with the support of organisations, but most without help. Their efficiency greatly aided the Enquiry. Within each county the names are given in chronological order:

Cornwall – Rev. J. E. Beckerlegge, P. Fronteras; Cumbria, north – N. Hammond; Cumbria, south – J. Wilson; Devon – P. F. Goodfellow, S. Griffiths, the late P. T. Coard; Dorset – Dr D. J. Godfrey; Essex – Dr P. J. K. Burton, R. M. Blindell, D. Martin, J. Thorogood; Hampshire – G. P. Green, Dr N. H. Pratt, D. Steventon;

Humberside, north – D. B. Cutts; Humberside, south – A. Grieve, R. N. Goodall; Isle of Wight – J. H. Stafford; Kent – Major G. F. A. Munns, Capt. J. N. Humphreys; Lancashire, Cheshire – Dr P. H. Smith helped by the late R. H. Allen (Mersey) and R. A. Eades (Dee); Northumberland – B. Galloway; Suffolk – the late G. B. G. Benson, J. Shackles; Sussex – M. Shrubb, R. F. Porter; Teesside – E. Crabtree, M. Blick; Wash – M. Allen, Dr C. J. Cadbury; Severn, English – K. Fox; Severn, Welsh – P. Landsdown, C. Titcombe, Dr P. N. Ferns; Dyfed, east – D. H. V. Roberts, C. Street, E. Smith; Dyfed, west – J. H. Barrett; Glamorgan, west – R. J. Howells; Gwynedd, north – A. J. Mercer, Dr P. J. Dare; Gwynedd, south – P. Hope Jones, D. Brown; Ayr and Wigtown – A. G. Stewart, W. R. Brackenridge; Bute – I. Hopkins; Firth of Clyde – E. T. Idle, I. Gibson; Firth of Forth – Dr D. T. Parkin, J. Ballantyne, then jointly with Dr L. Vick and Dr D. Bryant; Moray Firth Basin – jointly A. Currie, C. G. Headlam, Dr M. Rusk; Solway Firth – J. G. Young, Miss J. Martin; Firth of Tay – R. W. Summers, N. K. Atkinson, R. Macmillan; Northern Ireland, overall – J. S. Furphy, B. Coburn; Londonderry – A. Bennett; Strangford Lough – National Trust (A. Irvine and P. P. Mackie); Republic of Ireland – C. D. Hutchinson, L. Stapleton, P. Smiddy.

Much assistance in writing this book was given by my colleagues, especially Dr R. J. O'Connor who has contributed the two chapters on estuarine ecology, and C. D. Hutchinson who wrote the chapter on estuaries in the Republic of Ireland. In addition, R. J. Fuller, P. A. Hyde and J. H. Marchant gave valuable help with preparing the text.

Throughout the 'Birds of Estuaries Enquiry' its Advisory Committee has given much needed advice and guidance; to the members, already named in the introduction, I would like to extend my thanks. These also go to many colleagues who have helped; these include Dr J. J. M. Flegg, R. Spencer, Dr R. J. O'Connor, R. A. O. Hickling and J. M. McMeeking of the BTO; D. Lea, I. J. Ferguson-Lees, J. L. F. Parslow and Dr C. J. Cadbury of the RSPB; Professor G. V. T. Matthews, G. L. Atkinson-Willes, M. A. Ogilvie and D. Salmon of the Wildfowl Trust; C. D. Hutchinson of the Irish Wildbird Conservancy and Dr R. Mitchell and Dr D. R. Langslow of the Nature Conservancy Council. There are many other staff members of these organisations who have also helped in many ways, including commenting on the draft text.

The many evocative vignettes and sketches which complement the text were drawn for the book by John Busby. Additional illustrative material was prepared by K. Baker. To them I offer many thanks, as I do to temporary assistants employed to assemble and prepare data on generous grants from the Worshipful Company of Grocers. These include J. Atherton, M. Davies, R. Hicks and C. Walker; Mrs E. Murray and Miss G. Watts also helped with this. The bulk of the typing of the manuscripts was carried out by Mrs E. Murray, who also undertook the formidable task of preparing most of the artwork for the maps and diagrams, Miss S. M. Woodman, Mrs G. D. Marriott and Mrs M. Millner.

The project was funded by a grant from the Nature Conservancy Council, formerly shared with the Natural Environment Research Council.

CHAPTER 1

# The nature of an estuary

by R. J. O'CONNOR

## PHYSICAL CHARACTERISTICS

An estuary is a more or less enclosed area in which freshwater from the land is mixed to some degree with salt water brought in by tides. Estuaries differ from other aquatic habitats in their exposure to a cycle of continuously changing salinity, water level and temperature within an area endowed with shelter, soft sedimentary deposits and a constantly renewed supply of energy and nutrients (Barnes 1974). The most spectacular estuaries form where large volumes of fresh water meet the sea across a coastal plain. With small volumes of flow estuaries tend to give way to salt marshes cut by creeks up which the tide flows freely, but where the coastal plain is absent the water enters the sea too precipitately to develop estuarine conditions.

McLusky (1971) has summarised the physical factors of most importance in estuarine environments. These are (1) the type of bottom (or substrate) (2) the extent of tidal influence (3) wave size (4) current strength (5) sedimentation patterns (6) salinity distribution patterns (7) the presence of interstitial water in the sediments (8) the supply of dissolved oxygen (9) temperature and (10) the concentration of certain ions. Not all of these are of equal import for the distribution of birds within an estuary and only the major factors in this respect will be discussed.

### Mudflats

The striking feature of the British estuaries of importance for birds is the presence of extensive intertidal flats. The origin of these intertidal sediments has not been established for most estuaries. In some cases the sediment is brought down by the river but in others, and probably most, such as the Mersey, Thames and Morecambe Bay, the majority of the deposits are brought in by the sea. In general, the amount of time sediment remains in the water flow depends on the energy of the water movement concerned. Nearer the mouth of an estuary wave action imparts considerable energy to the water and only the heavier sediment settles, creating flats of clean sand or shingle, whilst the finer particles of silt are carried further up the estuary to form mud banks. Similarly, near the head of an estuary the rate at which river-borne particles settle out is determined largely by the rate of flow of the river, usually leading to a gradient of increasingly finer sediment towards the centre of the estuary. In some estuaries, such as the Severn, strong water movements over a large range of tides lead to very turbulent conditions.

Mudflats formed by the deposition of sedimentary particles of intermediate size are more attractive to invertebrates – and therefore to the waders that feed on them – than are flats of either larger or smaller particles. This is because invertebrates concentrate onto the deposits of high organic and nutrient content (Fig. 1:1) normally formed by fine particles, but in beds of very fine mud they find their feeding and respiratory apparatus clogged and the oxygen supply depleted or poisoned (by hydrogen sulphide production) by bacteria and other micro-organisms.

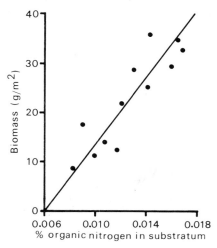

Fig. 1:1 Biomass of lugworms *Arenicola marina* in relation to the amount of organic material in the sediment (from Barnes 1977 after Longbottom 1970).

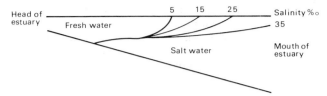

Fig. 1:2 Distributions of constant salinity lines in a 'salt-wedge' estuary, showing how the denser seawater penetrates up-river below the outflowing fresh water.

A very few estuaries are predominantly sandy; as, for example, in Cardigan Bay. In general they occur where the rivers drain hard igneous ground and where the off-shore deposits are of sand, stone or shell. Such estuaries are relatively poor in invertebrates.

### Tides

Tides, waves and currents shape the pattern of water movements about an estuary but not to equal effect. Waves are rarely important, given the semi-enclosed character of the typical estuary, and currents chiefly influence only the pattern of sedimentary deposition (see above). Tidal influence is the major factor affecting estuarine birds, for the regular ebb and flood of the tide determines their access to inter-tidal feeding grounds. Within some estuaries the nature of the tidal rhythm may be modified by narrow or shallow entrances reducing the speed and the amplitude of flood and ebb. Birds may thus be able to feed at different times on the open shore and in the estuary. Similarly, in some funnel-shaped estuaries, such as the Severn or the Kent Estuary in Morecambe Bay, the tidal range may be amplified by the funnelling effect, so that sea and fresh water are unusually mixed as a tidal 'bore' surges upriver (McLusky 1971).

### Salinity

The average salinity of the sea is 35‰ (parts per thousand) but in fresh water the equivalent value is always less than 5‰. Between the head and the mouth of an estuary mixing of water results in a gradient of salinity. This gradient of 'brackish' water is not static within the estuary: it moves seawards in the wet season when river volumes are high and there is more dilution than usual, and conversely moves landwards in the dry season. It may also move up and down the estuary under the influence of the tide. Sedentary animals resident in the estuary are, therefore, exposed to a fluctuating salinity, which physiologically is very demanding. This has important consequences for the distribution and abundance of estuarine species.

Estuaries also show a vertical variation in salinity. This occurs because salt water is about 3% denser than freshwater; so salt water tends to sink below the fresh water coming down from the river, forming the so-called 'salt wedge' (Fig. 1:2). An animal on the upper shore in the mid-reaches of the estuary encounters more or less saline conditions when covered by the tide, and is exposed to air when the tide ebbs. For organisms further down the shore, however, the animal is initially covered by salt water but, as the tide retreats down the shoreline and down the estuary, fresh water flows over the organism. Thus animals in the intermediate and lower reaches of the shore undergo greater extremes of salinity than do animals further up the shore, conditions not encountered by marine organisms elsewhere. However, most animals avoid the worst rigours of these salinity changes by dwelling in the interstitial water

– the water trapped between the sand grains and other particles of the sedimentary deposits. This has a very low exchange rate with that of the overlying waters and thus provides a less severe environment for invertebrates. On the other hand, organic sediments may have such a high bacterial content as to deplete significantly the oxygen supply available within the deposits, thus replacing one rigour with another.

### Oxygen

The majority of the important shorebird prey species respire aerobically, i.e. by consuming oxygen. In estuaries the oxygen supply is renewed by the regular flow of the tides. Few animals have evolved effective means of living anaerobically in estuaries, the *Tubifex* worms forming a notable exception. Most animals can reach the oxygen supply by emerging from their burrows in the mud when the substratum is covered. In some areas, such as those covered by algal mats or where the estuary receives locally heavy concentrations of certain pollutants, fresh oxygen supply is not available and only anaerobic species prevail.

### Temperature

The shores of estuaries are subjected to wide fluctuations in temperature when exposed at low tide. Mudflat temperatures are liable to be highest during the day-time low tides in summer and lowest during night-time low tides in winter. Indeed, in the coldest winters the surface may freeze, particularly on the upper shore (which is longest exposed to the air). Most invertebrates tolerate the twice daily exposure of the shore to ambient air temperatures but they are vulnerable to freezing temperatures. The 1962–63 winter, for example, killed invertebrates in considerable numbers and shorebirds died in consequence (Pilcher, Beer and Cook 1974).

### ESTUARINE PLANTS

Few plants have colonised the estuarine environment successfully. Marine species such as seaweeds are hindered by lack of anchorage points and by the reduction in photosynthesis consequent on turbid conditions while few land plants accept periodic submersion by salt water. McLusky (1971) provides a concise review of estuarine plants and much of the following is based on his account.

There are two major categories of estuarine plants: first is the truly marine species that grow whilst permanently covered with water (to the extent that the tides permit); second is the maritime species, land plants with specific adaptations for living in salt-laden environments. The former are predominantly algae but include one genus of angiosperm (the true flowering plants), the eel-grasses *Zostera* spp. These grasses have long dark green leaves and grow on sandy or muddy substrates, both in the intertidal and sub-littoral zones. They are of major importance as a food for Brent Geese and Wigeon. Of the algae the most important are the *Enteromorpha* species, which grow as long tube-like strands of green vegetation, usually on muddy substrates. They are eaten by a number of ducks and Brent Geese; in some areas, such as Chichester Harbour, *Enteromorpha* is the main food of the Brent Goose. The brown wracks of the genus *Fucus* are the most important estuarine algae. They occur only on rocky outcrops and boulder-strewn shores, since they need a hard substratum for attachment by their root-like 'holdfast'. They are not important as food for birds but a number of species, notably Turnstones, may forage amongst them for the invertebrates they contain. As one of the few sources of cover in estuaries the seaweeds frequently contain significant assemblages of the more mobile species of the intertidal, such as crabs, gammarids and winkles (Boaden, O'Connor and Seed 1975).

Maritime plants are found almost exclusively within the salt marshes which form above the neap high tide mark of the upper intertidal area, where they are covered, periodically, by spring high tides. Such plants trap accumulations of mud carried in by the tide and accumulate dead plant material with the annual cycle of growth and regression. At Scolt Head accretion rates of 1 cm of mud per year have been recorded and values of up to 20 cm have been recorded in France (Barnes 1974). These rates are far above those of the intertidal mudflats. This steady accumulation of material raises the saltmarsh area above the tide levels, so that only plants at the edge of the marsh receive frequent submersion and the plants further away on the higher ground are submerged less frequently. This leads to a succession of different plants as colonisers of the saltmarsh (Fig. 1:3).

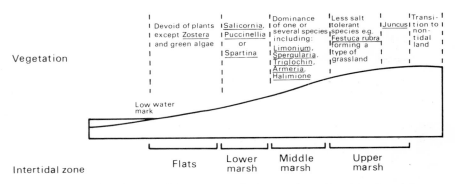

Fig. 1:3 Simplified diagram of the zonation of estuarine plants. Transition from left to right represents succession both in time and shore elevation due to sediment accretion (after Fuller in prep.).

Algae may aid the accumulation of mud, having mucilaginous sheaths to which particles adhere, thus stabilising the sediment. Mucus secreted by benthic diatoms is also of importance, mud contents in diatom-rich areas being much greater than otherwise expected. Macroalgae are also involved in increased accretion rates. In the Wash the presence of *Enteromorpha* can increase sedimentation by up to 33% and reduce tidal scouring, but the effects are short-lived since *Enteromorpha* is easily torn away during storms (Coles and Curry 1976). Stabilisation of intertidal areas is also frequently aided by the presence of *Zostera nana* which grows around mid-tide level on muddy shores. The subsequent accumulation of mud in its roots is colonised initially by seeds of the marsh samphire *Salicornia*. *Salicornia* has a distinctive dispersion at the edge of a developing saltmarsh, a dispersion which reflects the time sequence of the formation of the marsh. At its seaward edge the *Salicornia* area is covered with isolated plants whose density increases shorewards and eventually either become a dense monospecific 'sward' or merges with colonies of the grass *Puccinellia maritima*. With further accumulation of mud (or equivalently, as one moves further inshore) a mixture of *P. maritima*, the sea aster *Aster tripolium* and the annual sea blight *Suaeda maritima* appears. The next stages are formed by areas dominated by sea lavender *Limonium vulgare* and behind that by sea pink *Armeria maritima*. These species occur in the upper half of the saltmarsh. On the highest parts the marsh may be dominated by *Atriplex* species whilst the upper limit of the saltmarsh itself is provided by the red fescue grass *Festuca rubra* and sea rush *Juncus maritimus*. The exact composition of the vegetation stages depends in detail upon the successional history of the saltmarsh (Fig. 1:3).

Some saltmarshes are grazed and this may change the composition of the plant community. Sea aster and sea pink are frequently absent and the communities are dominated by *Glyceria* and *Festuca rubra*.

### Spartina

*Spartina* is the generic name of a group of species of cord-grass or rice grass. Several species are present on British estuaries but one hybrid form – that between *Spartina maritima* and an introduced North American species *Spartina alterniflora* – has become particularly important because of its vigorous growth. It has spread around the British and Irish coasts since its first appearance in Southampton Water about 1870, partly by natural processes but also through deliberate planting in coastal reclamation plans.

The plant develops by horizontal underground rhizomes across bare mud and also sets seeds. Lateral development of rhizomes is inhibited by the presence of root systems of other plant species, so *Spartina* grows over the bare mud of estuaries, both on the main mudflats and on the salt pans within the typical saltmarshes. Few waders are psychologically adapted to feed in close proximity to dense vegetation within estuaries, so *Spartina* marshes are poorly used by birds. In addition, the accumulation of *Spartina* detritus alters conditions for the microfauna beneath the plant, so that invertebrate food of the waders is gradually destroyed.

*Spartina* has been widely introduced onto mudflats in the belief that it will help claim back the estuarine land from the sea or that it will provide a measure of coast defence against erosion. Economically viable returns have been obtained from *Spartina* salt marshes in some instances, principally through grazing. *Spartina*-produced soils have not proved ideal for agricultural production. The most serious problem encountered with *Spartina*-based reclamation of coast defence has been an inherent instability in *Spartina* salt marsh as a component in successional sequences. The problem arises from the dense and vigorous growth of the hybrid form (now generally referred to as *Spartina anglica* – with the older name *S. townsendii* being reserved for the non-fertile hybrid) which acts as a silt trap as well as a retainer of its own litter. In the resulting eutrophic conditions a soil develops which is incompatible with colonisation by the normal pioneering species of salt marsh communities and in the oldest *Spartina* fields large scale die-back (the cause of which is uncertain) of the rice grass leaves the soil exposed and open to increasing erosion. Die-back is particularly prevalent in the Hampshire and Sussex marshes where it was first 'introduced'. *Spartina* salt marshes thus provide only a short-term solution to problems of coast defence, are not ideal for reclamation purposes, and destroy the character of the most valuable estuarine habitats for shore birds.

### ESTUARINE ANIMALS

As one progresses up a long estuary the proportion of purely marine fauna decreases slowly. Below about 10‰ salinity the number decreases sharply and few occur below about 5‰. Conversely, as the river enters the estuary the number of freshwater species falls steeply and few tolerate salinities above 5‰. A small number of brackish-water animals are also present, particularly at lower salinities but they rarely occur above 20‰. Estuaries have thus a rather impoverished fauna, dominated by species tolerant of low (and probably, more importantly, fluctuating) salinities. Animals which will accept variations in salinity are technically described as euryhaline. Common wader prey with this capacity include the polychaetes *Arenicola* and *Nereis*, the crustacean *Corophium volutator*, and the molluscs *Cerastoderma edule*, *Scrobicularia plana* and *Hydrobia ulvae*. As few species have this ability, interspecific competition is reduced and those that do colonise the mudflats can occur in enormous numbers. The tiny gastropod *Hydrobia ulvae* has been recorded in densities of over 25,000/m² on the North Bull Island in County Dublin (West 1977). However, it is worth noting that the structural diversity of an estuary is well below that of the marine environment, so that rock-dwelling species, for example, are seldom found.

Many marine species are smaller in estuaries than in the more saline open sea (Fig. 1:4), but as wader prey items their smaller size is offset by their far greater abundance.

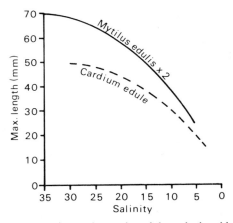

Fig. 1:4 Decrease in size of mussels *Mytilus edulis* and of cockles *Cerastoderma edule* with decrease in salinity through an estuary (after Remane, A (1934) *Verh. dt. zool. Ges.* 36, 34–74, after Barnes (1977)).

On an evolutionary scale estuaries are short-lived. Consequently, their faunas are dominated by marine species pre-adapted to estuarine life rather than by specifically estuarine species. Silting raises the level of a typical estuary at perhaps 2 mm a year, so its life-span is to be measured in tens of centuries at most. Few estuaries are older than about 8,000 years (Barnes 1974). Natural selection has thus little time to produce specifically estuarine forms. Many marine forms colonising estuaries may therefore survive less well or grow more slowly (Fig. 1:4) than in fully saline conditions. Their major problem appears to be with the speed of change of salinity within the estuary. Figure 1:5 shows that the lowest number of species in the Tay Estuary in Scotland occurred where salinity levels changed most rapidly, not where the variation was greatest. Thus, it is the speed of response to changes, rather than the average or the range of salinity which is the more critical to the animals concerned.

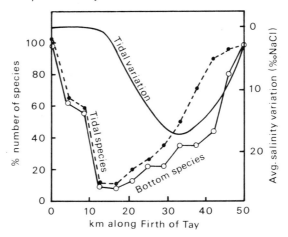

Fig. 1:5 Variation in species number with salinity variation along the Tay estuary (redrawn from McLusky 1971 after Alexander et al 1935).

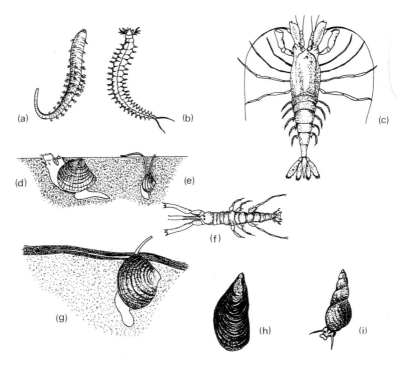

Fig. 1:6 Some important shorebird prey (a) lugworm *Arenicola marina* (b) ragworm *Nereis diversicolor* (c) shrimp *Crangon crangon* (d) cockle *Cerastoderma edule* (e) tellin *Tellina tenuis* (f) the amphipod *Corophium volutator* (g) the bivalve mollusc *Scrobicularia plana* (h) the edible mussel *Mytilus edulis* (i) the gastropod mollusc *Hydrobia ulvae*.

Table 1:1 lists the more common species in British estuaries, those important and
those unimportant as prey for shore birds. The more significant are illustrated in Fig.
1:6. Their densities vary greatly between estuaries, depending on the patterns of
sediment distribution (and, therefore, of available invertebrate food). Table 1:2
shows some densities found in British estuaries. For *Hydrobia ulvae* the densities in

Table 1:1  *Characteristic species of the macrofauna of British estuaries (after
Barnes 1977). Asterisk indicates important prey species for waders, two asterisks
especially important species. Certain other prey species such as Tellina, are not
strictly characteristic of estuaries in Britain but may occur in sand flats in the lower
reaches of certain sites*

COELENTERATA (hydroids, etc)
*Tubularia indivisa*
*Obelia* spp.
*Diadumene* spp.
*Cordylophora caspia*
*Sagartia* spp.

NEMERTINI (ribbon worms)
*Lineus ruber*
*Tetrastemma* spp.

ECTOPROCTA (sea-mats)
*Membranipora crustulenta*

ANNELIDA (segmented worms)
*Harmothoë spinifera*
** *Nereis* spp.
 * *Nephtys hombergi*
*Phyllodoce maculata*
*Eteone longa*
 * *Scoloplos armiger*
*Pygosio elegans*
*Heteromastus filiformis*
*Notomastus latericeus*
** *Arenicola marina*
*Ampharete grubei*
*Melinna palmata*
 * *Lanice conchilega*
*Manayunkia aestuarina*
*Clitellio arenarius*
*Tubifex costatus*
 * *Peloscolex benedini*

MOLLUSCA (molluscs)
** *Hydrobia ulvae*

 * *Littorina* spp.
*Retusa alba*
** *Mytilus edulis*
** *Cerastoderma* spp.
** *Macoma balthica*
** *Scrobicularia plana*
*Mya arenaria*

CRUSTACEA (crustaceans)
 * *Balanus* spp.
*Elminius modestus*
*Praunus flexuosus*
*Neomysis vulgaris* (= *integer*)
*Cyathura carinata*
*Eurydice pulchra*
*Idotea chelies* (= *viridis*)
*Sphaeroma* spp.
*Jaera* spp.
** *Corophium* spp.
*Gammarus* spp.
*Marinogammarus* spp.
*Melita palmata*
*Hyale nilssoni*
*Orchestia gammarella*
*Bathyporeia pilosa*
*Palaemonetes varians*
 * *Crangon vulgaris*
 * *Carcinus maenas*

INSECTA (insects)
*Bledius spectabilis*
*Heterocerus flexuosus*
*Bembidion laterale*
*Hydrophorus oceanus*

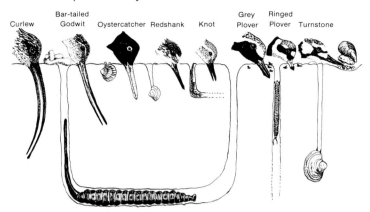

Fig. 1:7 Bill sizes of various waders in relation to the depth of some common prey species (after Goss-Custard 1975).

this sample range from 36,000/m² in the Dyfi Estuary, through 14,000 on the Tamar and 5,000 on the Exe, to only 24/m² on the Dee Estuary. On the other hand, *Corophium volutator* reached densities of over 22,000/m² on the Dee but only 312/m² on the Exe, and was infrequently found on the Mersey.

Typical densities recorded by Tubbs (1977) include 100–500/m² for *Nereis diversicolor* and 5,000–9,000/m² for *Hydrobia ulvae*; maxima include 96,000/² for *Nereis diversicolor* and 5,000–9,000/m² for N. diversicolor, 63,000/m² for C. volutator, 56,5000/m² for Macoma balthica and 220/m² for *Arenicola marina*. The species were slightly more alike in terms of biomass densities (grammes wet weight/m²) since the most numerous species tended to be of smallest size: for *Hydrobia ulvae*, the smallest of the detritus feeders listed, this density corresponds to 237 g/m² whilst the much lower density for *Arenicola* is equivalent to almost the same biomass density, at 200 g/m².

These prey are not equally important to all waders, each bird species tending to concentrate on particular groups. To a large extent prey size and burrowing depth are correlated with the bill size of the birds concerned (Fig. 1:7). Plovers have the shortest bill of the estuarine waders and tend to feed mainly by surface pecking, taking *Hydrobia* and other species on the surface. Dunlin and other waders with a moderate bill length are able to probe the top 4 cm of the substratum, the zone inhabited by many of the invertebrates, including many worms and bivalves, as well as *Corophium*. Only the longer-billed birds can cope with the deep burrowing prey such as the lugworm *Arenicola* and the ragworm *Nereis* and even some of these are accessible only when they surface in the course of their activity cycles.

### DISTRIBUTION OF ESTUARINE INVERTEBRATES

Table 1:3 shows the distribution of various invertebrate groups across the different habitats on the North Bull Island in County Dublin and demonstrates the relatively high value of the mud- and sand-flats. But even within the inter-tidal flats prey distributions can be markedly patchy: Fig. 1:8 shows concentrations of invertebrate species in different parts of Morecambe Bay. These differing concentrations reflect the effects of environmental gradients – of substratum particle size, tidal cycle, salinity, etc – and decide the densities of prey species available in any particular spot.

### Mudflats
Intertidal flats are only one of several habitats found within estuaries but they are by far the most important habitat for birds. This is because the sediments provide an

Table 1:2   Density ($\#/m^2$) of detritus-feeding invertebrates in various estuaries*

| | Mersey | Dee | Dyfi | Bristol Channel | Tamar | Exe | Colne | Ythan |
|---|---|---|---|---|---|---|---|---|
| Nereis diversicolor | ca. 20 | 12 | — | 2,000 | — | 132 | 234 | 340 |
| Corophium volutator | infrequent | 22,560 | 4,397 | — | — | 312+ | 1 | 3,890 |
| Hydrobiae ulvae | infrequent | 24 | 36,120 | 2,500 | 14,160 | 5,000 | — | 20,050 |
| Scrobiculariae planae | — | 280 | — | — | 1,094 | 404 | 59 | — |
| Macoma balthica | 4,736 | 600 | — | 320 | 28 | 32 | — | — |
| Mya arenaria | 3,872 | 100 | — | — | — | — | — | — |

Density of *Corophium arenarium*
Data from various authors

Table 1:3   Relative abundance and species richness (in parentheses) of common invertebrate groups and fish in different habitats on the North Bull Island, Co. Dublin. The relative abundance index is the sum of abundance ranks (0–4) for individual species within each group and of significance for shorebirds. Enchytraeids were treated collectively as one species (data from West 1977)

| | Mudflats | Sandflats | Salicornia flats | Channels | Beach | Littorial-terrestrial interface |
|---|---|---|---|---|---|---|
| ANNELIDA (segmented worms) | | | | | | |
| Oligochaeta | 9(3) | 3(1) | 9(3) | 1(1) | 0(0) | 0(0) |
| Polychaeta: Sedentaria | 2(2) | 8(4) | 0(0) | 2(1) | 6(4) | 0(0) |
| Polychaeta: Errantia | 5(3) | 9(4) | 0(0) | 2(1) | 6(3) | 0(0) |
| MOLLUSCA | | | | | | |
| Gastropoda | 5(2) | 4(2) | 6(2) | 4(2) | 0(0) | 8(4) |
| Lamellibranchia | 6(4) | 5(2) | 0(0) | 1(1) | 6(3) | 0(0) |
| CRUSTACEA | | | | | | |
| Ostracoda | 5(2) | 7(4) | 0(0) | 0(0) | 1(1) | 0(0) |
| Isopoda | 0(0) | 0(0) | 0(0) | 0(0) | 2(1) | 1(1) |
| Amphipoda | 4(1) | 2(1) | 4(1) | 1(1) | 7(4) | 3(2) |
| Decapoda | 1(1) | 1(1) | 0(0) | 2(2) | 1(1) | 1(1) |
| CHORDATA | | | | | | |
| Pisces | 0(0) | 0(0) | 0(0) | 5(3) | 0(0) | 0(0) |

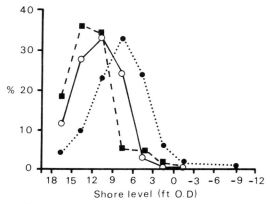

Fig. 1:8 Percentage of population of *Macoma* (●), *Hydrobia* (○) and *Corophium* (■) at different shore levels in Morecambe Bay (after Prater 1972).

enormously rich source of food for many invertebrates, yet their only anti-predatory defence is by burrowing. Moreover, because the filter-feeding invertebrates need to be near the surface of the flats, the extent to which they can burrow to escape is necessarily limited and can be 'broken' by predators using specialist devices, such as the long probing bills of godwits and Curlews.

A defence against predators is, of course, not the only concern of burrowing animals when the flats are exposed: they also face the problems of aquatic animals exposed to the atmosphere — obtaining oxygen, avoiding dehydration, temperature regulation, and so on. For these reasons many of the intertidal invertebrates are bivalves, whose shell morphology allows them to lock together the two halves of the shells to provide a 'life support capsule' in adverse conditions whilst exposed to the air. The majority of the remaining species are worms which escape these conditions by burrowing. Morphological, physiological and behavioural adaptations allow the invertebrate to cope with the physical environment but provide relatively limited defence against predators, once the latter have located the prey. Consequently, birds are the major killers of intertidal invertebrates. For some species, such as the cockle *Cerastoderma edule*, fish returning with the tide are a significant though smaller cause of mortality; first year cockles, for example, are hardly taken by birds but are severely depredated by plaice *Pleuronectes platessa*.

The cockle is probably the mollusc best known to bird watchers since its commercial importance has occasionally led to a controversy about depredation by Oystercatchers, as in the Burry Inlet. Figure 1:9 shows the size distributions found in one study, showing how the larger second and third year classes — the groups of economic importance — are most at risk to predatory Oystercatchers. As with other bivalves, *Cerastoderma* collects food by straining water across a series of gills: since it has a particularly short siphon it is therefore confined to a few centimetres of the surface, chiefly in sandy areas.

Another important bivalve is *Scorbicularia plana* (Fig. 1:6), a deposit feeding species largely concentrated into shallow beds of soft mud within the estuaries. About the size of a cockle it is taken by Oystercatchers with some regularity but it was severely affected by the cold winter of 1962–63 and it is not everywhere

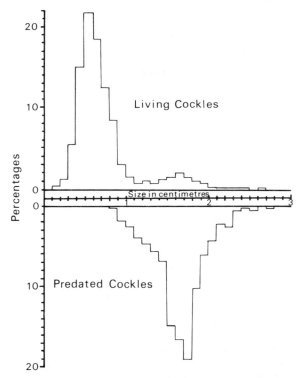

Fig. 1:9 Size frequency distribution of cockles *Cerastoderma edule* in Strangford Lough, Northern Ireland (above), with (below) size distribution of cockles predated by Oystercatchers in the same area. Predation falls proportionately on second-year and older animals (those above about 11–12 mm) but small first-year cockles are not taken. From Brown and O'Connor (1974).

abundant. A smaller thinner-shelled bivalve, *Macoma balthica*, is far more wide-spread, reaching densities in excess of $50,000/m^2$ within the top 5 cm of mixed sand/mud areas on some estuaries and is a major food item for Knot, Redshank, and Dunlin. A related bivalve, the tellin *Tellina tenuis* (Fig. 1:6), is more numerous in areas of clean sand where it is a supplementary prey of Knot and a significant item for Common Scoter. On rocky shores the well-known edible mussel *Mytilus edulis* (Fig. 1:6) is the only bivalve important to waders (especially Turnstone and Oystercatcher).

The tiny gastropod *Hydrobia ulvae* (Fig. 1:6) is the only other mollusc of great importance for waders. Although less than 7 mm long the animal may occur at great densities ($35,000/m^2$ or more in some areas) in mud or sandy mud. Emerging from the mud it floats inshore with the flow of the tides and feeds seawards on the fresh organic deposits on the newly exposed mud. Its huge densities attract several of the smaller wader species but the Shelduck's mud surface sieving action also makes it an effective predator.

Two crustacean species are particularly important to Redshank. The amphipod *Corophium volutator* is a small (about 1 cm long) invertebrate (Fig. 1:6) living in shallow burrows in estuarine mud and emerging to scrape organic material into its burrow. With densities of 50,000/m² recorded in places the species has become the preferred prey of Redshank. In spring and autumn, however, Redshank also take the brown shrimp *Crangon crangon* in numbers, from the pools and channels in which it swims. Curlew also take the shrimp seasonally but the shrimp migrates southwards for the winter and thus escapes mass predation. Similarly, the shore crab *Carcinus maenas* falls prey to Curlew and Turnstone only seasonally.

Various worms (predominantly those of the Phylum Annelida, especially the classes Oligochaeta and Polychaeta) form the second major category of wader prey. The two most frequently taken are the large (20 cm length 1 cm diameter) and well-known lugworm *Arenicola marina* (Fig. 1:6), which lives in burrows in areas of mixed sand and mud (Fig. 1:1), and the ragworm *Nereis diversicolor*, the commonest estuarine annelid. The highly predacious ragworm is widespread within estuaries, reaching densities of 2,000/m² or more locally, and at 15 cm length is, like the lugworm, an important prey for such large birds as Curlew and Pintail. The sandmason worm *Lanice conchilega* is a smaller (10 cm) burrowing worm which caps its 30 cm burrow built in clean sand with a characteristic crown of radiating 'twiglets' of mucus-bound sand grains. It occasionally appears in the diet of Grey Plover and Bar-tailed Godwit.

Other invertebrate species, of worms and mollusc alike, appear in shorebird diets but do not warrant extended description here. Some estuaries, however, support quite large populations of fish and in certain cases these are significant competitors to birds as predators of invertebrate stocks. The plaice *Pleuronectes platessa*, for example, is an important predator of first year cockles, thus reducing the second and third year stocks for Oystercatchers. Fish themselves appear only occasionally in the diets of shore birds. Estuaries are perhaps important as a source of fish only for Cormorants, Mergansers and Goosanders, and perhaps to a lesser extent for Herons. Greenshank, however, take small fish in autumn.

### Sandflats

Sandflats are characterised by the rather larger particles and lower organic contents already mentioned. Nevertheless, they are suitable habitats for invertebrates provided these are able to construct burrows or otherwise get down into the sand, the animals feeding on the organic material present. These features lead to rather lower densities of invertebrates than is the case on mudflats but there are still substantial numbers of certain species, particularly the shallow-burrowing bivalves such as *Cerastoderma* and *Macoma*. By the same token, beaches have an even lower faunal concentration, largely in consequence of the mobility of the sand there.

### Channels

Many estuaries are dissected by runs of freshwater channels across their surface. At low water these channels contain almost purely fresh water whilst at high tides they are filled by the sea, which may penetrate up the channel into parts of the estuary not otherwise reached by seawater. Consequently, animals living in the channels themselves are euryhaline. Common species are lugworms *Arenicola*, ragworms *Nereis*, cockles *Cerastoderma*, the amphipod *Corophium*, and the molluscs *Hydrobia* and *Littorina saxatilis*. Some swimming animals also occur, particularly those that can bury themselves in mud where necessary, such as the shrimp *Crangon*.

*Rocky shores*

Rocky shores on estuaries form a completely different habitat from the intertidal flats and have a correspondingly different fauna. The main characteristic of the rocky shore fauna is the prevalence of attached forms, dominated by such species as barnacles, principally *Chthamalus* and *Balanus*, limpets *Patella* spp., and mussels *Mytilus*. Rocky shores are also frequently covered with attached plants, such as the fucoids *Fucus* spp. When not covered by the tide these plants collapse onto the shore and provide cover over rocks and within rock pools for such species as shore crabs. They are also grazed by species such as the flat winkle *Littorina littoralis* and topshells *Gibbula* spp.

ESTUARINE FOOD CHAINS

Why do estuaries support such an enormous concentration of wildfowl and waders? Part of the answer can be obtained by considering what the ecologists call 'food chains'. Figure 1:10 shows a very simple food chain. Energy is provided to the plant by sunlight and with this energy nutrients in the ground are absorbed and turned into so-called 'primary production' – new vegetable material. This vegetable material is typically grazed by animals at the next level – usually referred to as a 'trophic' level (Greek 'trophos' for food). These grazers use the energy and material consumed from the primary production for so-called 'secondary production', in the form of additional growth and fat storage by the herbivore and for reproduction of further grazing individuals. The grazers may themselves be consumed by carnivorous species which form a still higher trophic level, and these may in turn be consumed by a top carnivore. Thus in a terrestrial situation photosynthesis of the sun's energy may produce an oak tree, part of whose vegetation is eaten by a caterpillar (the grazer here). The caterpillar may be eaten by a Blue Tit, acting here as a carnivore, which may itself fall prey to a Sparrowhawk, the top carnivore in this example. A general feature of food chains is that reduction in energy transfer of an order of magnitude, i.e. ten-fold, typically occurs as one progresses up the chain. This means that ten times as much energy has to be available to support an animal at the carnivore level as is necessary to sustain a herbivore.

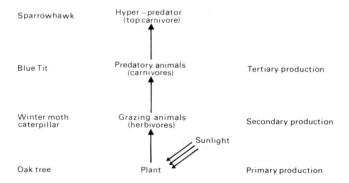

Fig. 1:10 A simple food chain showing how energy derived from photosynthesis passed through successive 'trophic levels'.

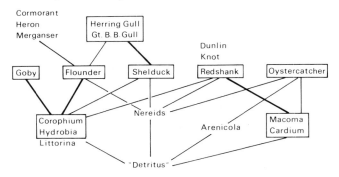

Fig. 1:11 An example of a mud flat food web based on detritus in the Ythan estuary (Milne and Dunnet 1972).

Such a simple food chain rarely occurs in nature, though it may occur in the Arctic and other simplified ecosystems. Normally the pattern would be more in the form of a food *web*, as shown in Fig. 1:11. Here the main features are that several species at the primary production level can contribute to the support of a single herbivore and more than one species may feed on a species at a level below it. In a slightly more complicated model a carnivorous species may feed at more than one level. For example, Wigeon ducklings may behave as carnivores consuming aquatic insects but later may feed by grazing on grasses. Thus in reality a food web is more complex than the simplified example presented here. Finally, in considering food webs one must examine the role of decomposers. These form a separate group aside from the main food chains within the web. Decomposers feed on dead material from each trophic level, be they dead oak-leaves in woodland litter, caterpillars killed by early frost, or the remains of a starved Blue Tit. The consumption of this organic material by the decomposers provides a sort of compartmental model for the ecosystem, such as is shown in Fig. 1:12, providing for the full recycling of the nutrients and other materials taken from the soil and cycled through the system.

Estuarine ecosystems differ from this simplified model mainly in the enormous importance of the decomposer compartment and in the transfer of energy in from other systems. Within estuaries one has the straightforward food chain component (Fig. 1:10) through the sequence algae consumed by grazing geese and ducks possibly consumed by Peregrines or, more likely, by wildfowlers; or through such sequences as algae consumed by grazing Littorinidae (winkles) which themselves are consumed by Turnstones which perhaps themselves eventually fall to predatory birds. But algae and fucoids are relatively minute sources for primary production within estuaries, which lack grasses and trees, the major channels of production in terrestrial systems. For estuaries it is the enormous importation of organic material brought in by the tides which forms the major source of energy and nutrients. This material is consumed by suspension and sediment feeders such as polychaete worms and bivalves and transformed into invertebrate biomass, which in turn supports the huge numbers of estuarine birds described in this book. Much of this transformation is performed by detritus feeders who consume the imported material as detritus and thus benefit in an unexpected way. The unusually small particle size of organic sediments deposited in estuaries render these deposits particularly prone to bacterial attack. Animals ingesting these deposits, therefore, ingest not only the detritus but

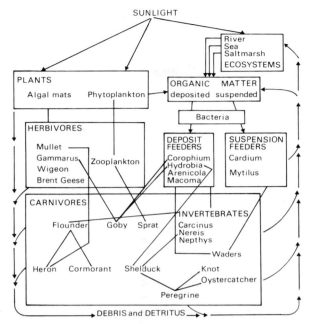

Fig. 1:12 Energy flow diagram for the intertidal flats of North Bull Island, Co. Dublin (from Jeffrey 1977).

also the bacteria feeding thereon, so that bacteria-rich detritus is nutritionally a better food source than the original organic material!

(In passing one may also note than another advantage of the detritus as a food source is that it is available during the winter when plant material provides little in the way of food supply.)

Figure 1:12 shows the resulting compartmental model for the North Bull Island intertidal flats on the east coast of Ireland (Jeffrey 1977). The diagram reveals the parallel food chains which ultimately interlock in the carnivore compartment dominated by birds. It is this parallel chain of energy and material flow which allows the relatively simple structure of the estuarine habitats to sustain such enormous numbers of birds. As yet there has been no major study quantifying the energy flow through the various compartments of estuarine models such as that of Fig. 1:12, so we lack a quantification of these flows which might be compared with terrestrial systems. Milne and Dunnet (1972) have, however, constructed a preliminary compartment model for mussel beds within the Ythan estuary, an important sub-habitat of their study area. They found that of the summer production of 1,300 kcal/m² (i.e. expressing the biomass produced only in terms of its energy content when metabolised) some 600 kcal was expended by the mussels for their own metabolism, 480 kcal was consumed by shorebirds (275 kcal by Eider, 112 kcal by gulls and 93 kcal by Oystercatchers) and 240 kcal was taken by fishermen. Thus the entire 'crop' of mussel flesh produced during the summer was consumed in winter, with 37% going to shorebirds. Such figures bring out more clearly than do absolute numbers the major role of estuarine birds as consumers of invertebrate biomass in estuaries.

CHAPTER 2

# Patterns of shorebird feeding

by R. J. O'CONNOR

Shorebirds can feed on intertidal animals only whilst the flats are exposed by the tide. They are therefore under pressure to feed efficiently. How birds achieve this has been the subject of much biological research in recent years and a body of theory (generally referred to as 'optimal foraging theory') has been developed (e.g. Pyke et al 1977, Krebs 1978). This theoretical work shows that an understanding of shorebird feeding efficiency must focus on three main questions (1) on what do estuarine birds feed, (2) when must they feed, and (3) where should they feed?

## WHAT TO EAT

### Prey spectra

Table 2:1 shows how different shorebirds concentrate upon various prey species. Several patterns are clearly evident from this Table. First, a small number of extremely numerous invertebrates, notably *Hydrobia* and *Nereis*, are important in the diet of many estuarine birds. These excepted, most prey species are the target for a relatively small number of estuarine birds, each species having its own feeding niche. By thus reducing competition the different species can co-exist.

The feeding methods used by the birds are closely linked to their morphology. With its short bill a Dunlin, for example, would have little chance of capturing a lugworm except on the surface. On the other hand, a Curlew has the length of bill needed to reach the lugworm in its burrow. This factor can also account for species-specific size-selection of individuals of a common prey. Large *Macoma balthica*, for example, bury themselves more deeply than do smaller individuals, thus lying beyond the reach of short-billed Knot but still vulnerable to Bar-tailed Godwits and Curlews (Reading and McGrorty 1978). The burrowing depth is largely determined by the siphon length of each *Macoma*.

The stoutness or otherwise of the bill is also important, and slender billed species cannot turn stones in search of crabs in the way that a Turnstone can. The innervation of the bill tip is significant too: for an Oystercatcher, hammering open cockles, a sensitive bill tip would be a disadvantage. The Curlew, on the other hand, relying on probing to obtain its prey, has a bill tip rich in nerve endings. Striking evidence for the reality of these differences comes from intra-specific variation within the Oystercatcher. Norton-Griffiths (1969) found that the bill of young Oystercatchers was initially soft and fairly sensitive for probing, but that this sensitivity was lost with increasing practice in hammering open cockles. The small number of Oystercatcher young that learned to take polychaete worms in preference to cockles retained the bill's sensitivity, a clearly adaptive situation.

### Prey profitability and size selection

Several studies have shown that waders tend to concentrate on the most profitable prey available (Goss-Custard 1977). In this context profitability has to take account of variations in prey density: it is no use a wader specialising on a large but rare prey. Figure 2:1 shows that Redshank feeding on two species of polychaete worm (ragworms, *Nereis* and catworms, *Nephthys*) took the more profitable large worms in proportion to their availability at all times but took small worms only when large worms were less abundant. Similarly, Redshank feeding on preferred prey

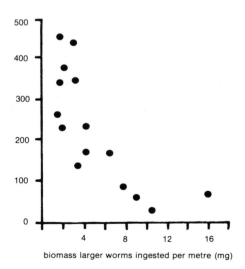

biomass larger worms ingested per metre (mg)

Fig. 2:1 Relationship between the number of small (0·5–9·9 mg) polychaete worms taken by Redshanks per metre searched and the biomass of large worms (10 + mg) captured and ingested during the transect. From Goss-Custard (1977a).

*Table 2:1    Correlations between feeding intensity (hours feeding per km²) of various wader species and the densities of invertebrate prey species in the Firth of Forth. Asterisks indicate the wader concerned was dependent on the prey indicated in ways not revealed by correlation analysis. After Bryant (1979)*

|  | Oystercatcher | Curlew | Bar-tailed Godwit | Redshank | Knot | Dunlin |
|---|---|---|---|---|---|---|
| *Hydrobia* | 0·61 | 0·58 | 0·55 | 0·53 | 0·62 | 0·54 |
| *Nereis* | — | 0·66 | — | 0·82 | — | 0·85 |
| *Nephthys* | 0·60 | — | * | — | 0·77 | — |
| *Macoma* | 0·79 | — | — | * | 0·53 | — |
| *Cerastoderma* | 0·57 | — | — | — | 0·78 | — |
| *Mytilus* | 0·84 | — | — | — | — | — |
| *Corophium* | — | — | — | 0·59 | — | — |

*Corophium* concentrate on the largest individuals they can readily handle but compensating for density variation (Fig. 2:2): note how the size difference between those available and those taken reduces as the average size available approaches this optimum. Similar results have been obtained with the Oystercatcher (O'Connor and Brown 1977). These findings are not as trivial as they may first appear, for the birds concentrate on those prey or size classes of prey yielding the maximum return on average, and not merely on the largest prey.

One would also expect to find a correlation between the size of prey taken by waders and their body size (since waders take prey items individually) and this does

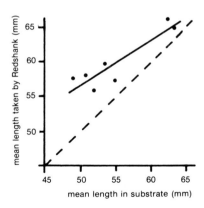

Fig. 2:2 Mean length of *Corophium* taken by Redshank in relation to mean length of those available in the mud. Solid line shows calculated regression equation: $Y = 2·56 + 0·622X$, $P < 0·01$ and dotted line shows line which would have been obtained had birds taken prey in proportion to their availability in the mud. After Goss-Custard (1969).

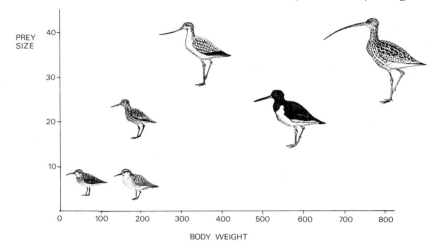

PREY
SIZE

BODY WEIGHT

Fig. 2:3 Prey size in relation to body weight for various waders at the Wash. Prey size taken as the mean of modal weights of major prey species. Data from Goss-Custard, Jones and Newbery (1977).

seem to exist (Fig. 2:3). This correlation does not apply to wildfowl, which have evolved a bill structure allowing them to handle large quantities of minute food items. Certain species, such as Wigeon and Brent Goose, feed almost exclusively by grazing but other species feed by a dabbling technique, sieving seeds and small invertebrates from the surface of the water. Such a strategy demands considerable densities of food if they are to support birds of significant biomass. For this reason the dabbling technique tends to be used only against species such as *Hydrobia* and *Corophium* and not against the individually larger but lower density invertebrates taken by waders. Shelduck provide an example of a large shorebird specialising on *Hydrobia* in this way.

We may note that certain foods may be profitable for the birds only seasonally. As already seen, most invertebrate species breed in spring or in summer, after most shorebirds have gone. Even the early spatfall is largely inaccessible to estuarine birds. Nevertheless, during the spring low tides large quantities of mussel *Mytilus* spat may become available to Knot and these apparently form an important component of their diet during pre-migratory fattening for the journey to Iceland and Greenland. By late autumn, however, when the birds return from their breeding areas many mussels may have grown to a point where they are too large to be liable to significant predation by the Knot, though still small enough to be taken by still larger birds such as Oystercatchers. This 'escape by growth' from predation appears to be an important defence strategy on the part of these shellfish (Seed and Brown 1978).

*Prey recognition time*

Waders learn by experience which prey items to take and to concentrate on the profitable size classes, but may spend time assessing and recognising each item for what it is. Redshank feeding on mudflats containing mixed populations of the amphipod *Corophium volutator* and two polychaete worms *Nereis diversicolor* and *Nephthys hombergi* appeared to have this problem (Goss-Custard 1977b). Had the

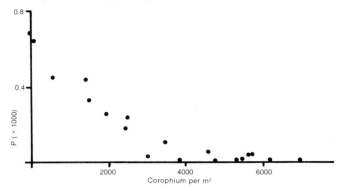

Fig. 2:4 Probability of worms being taken as prey in relation to simultaneous density of preferred prey, the amphipod *Corophium volutator*. Risk is calculated as ratio of worms eaten and those available in the area searched. From Goss-Custard (1977b).

birds taken worms alone their energy intake would have been about 214 cal/min but by concentrating on *Corophium* it averaged only 84 cal/min. Figure 2:4 shows that worms were taken in large numbers at low densities of *Corophium* but decreased as *Corophium* abundance rose. Goss-Custard suggested that the birds were more sensitive to cues provided by the activity of *Corophium* (the most abundant and preferred prey of Redshank in many estuaries) so that it became harder for them to recognise worms as the density of *Corophium* increased.

An increase in recognition time can reduce foraging success in other ways. Bar-tailed Godwits take considerable numbers of lugworm (*Arenicola* sp.) as the latter come to the tail-shaft of their burrows to defaecate. Defaecation takes only a few seconds so the worms are vulnerable for very short periods, but slowness of recognition by the Godwits may allow the worm to descend beyond reach of the birds' bills. On a newly exposed piece of sandflat the surface is initially relatively smooth and newly created tail-shafts of the lugworm burrows are particularly conspicuous as the animal goes through its irrigation/defaecation cycle. Bar-tailed Godwits can quickly spot a newly surfaced lugworm by this means and have high feeding rates. As time progresses, however, the density of such shafts increases to the point where the background 'noise' proves too distracting for Bar-tailed Godwits to keep pace with the appearance of prey individuals, their recognition times slow and their feeding rates decline (Smith 1975).

WHERE TO FEED

Some estuaries are able to support more wintering birds than others. For certain species these differences reflect the amount of specific habitat present in the estuary: Lapwings can use coastal fields and Snipe can use salt marshes only if these habitats are in an estuary in the first place. More subtle effects prevail also. On the Firth of Forth, Knot and Dunlin spend more time in the more inaccessible bays – those with least shoreline for their area and thus least disturbed by humans – and spent least time on the accessible small linear shores (Bryant 1979). The exposure sequence of the shore also influences the feeding time, for Bryant (ibid.) found that Redshank and Knot – both of them mid- and upper-shore feeders – spent most time in those

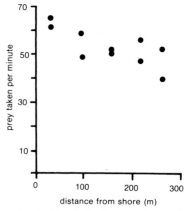

Fig. 2:5 Prey capture rates for Redshank feeding at different shore levels on the Ythan Estuary. From Goss-Custard (1977c).

bays exposed earliest on the Forth, doing so even at low water and after allowance for the greater prey capture success of Redshank close to than remote from the shore (Fig. 2:5). In contrast, Bar-tailed Godwits and Dunlin tended to follow the receding tideline even between bays, whilst Curlew and Oystercatcher fed predominantly on the mid-tide flats and abandoned the shore to feed in nearby fields when the tide submerged them once more. Nevertheless, as shown in Table 2:2 the habitat tolerances of most common waders are fairly broad so one must look elsewhere than to differences in habitat representation on an estuary for an explanation of winter wader densities.

Food seems to be the major determinant of shorebird distribution, for there exists a general relationship between the density of birds counted at any one time of the year in different estuaries and the amount of food available for the particular species. Figure 2:6 shows a strong correlation between the density of Curlew and the combined density of two of its common prey species. Similar correlations have been

Table 2:2   *Feeding scores of each species in eight habitat categories on the Gann Estuary (percentages in parentheses). From Edington et al (1973)*

| | Submerged sites | | | | Exposed sites | | | |
|---|---|---|---|---|---|---|---|---|
| | Tide edge fucoids | Tide edge sand and mud | Standing water | Running water | Exposed fucoids | Exposed sand and mud | Entero-morpha | Shingle |
| Curlew | 61(13·1) | 50(10·8) | 30 (6·5) | 2 (0·4) | 167(36·0) | 154(33·2) | — | — |
| Oystercatcher | 59 (9·4) | 100(15·9) | 26 (4·2) | — | 120(19·1) | 322(51·4) | — | — |
| Greenshank | 5 | 8 | 7 | — | 6 | — | — | — |
| Redshank | 13 (2·9) | 175(38·7) | 128(28·3) | 7 (1·5) | 23 (5·1) | 106(23·5) | — | — |
| Dunlin | — | — | 5 (5·0) | 11(11·0) | 1 (1·0) | 34(34·0) | 12(12·0) | 36(36·0) |
| Ringed Plover | — | — | 2 (1·3) | 1 (0·6) | 7 (4·4) | 48(30·2) | 41(25·8) | 60(37·7) |
| Turnstone | — | — | 5 (1·8) | — | 196(72·3) | 23 (8·5) | 10 (3·7) | 37(13·7) |

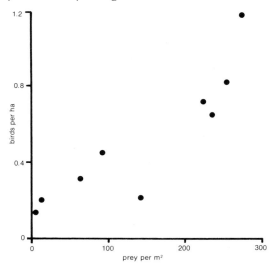

Fig. 2:6 Curlew densities on nine estuaries in south-eastern England in relation to the combined density of two major prey species, the polychaete worm *Nereis Diversicolor* and the bivalve *Scrobicularia plana*. From Goss-Custard, Kay and Blindell (1977).

shown in the cases of Redshank and Oystercatcher in south-east England (Goss-Custard, Kay and Blindell 1977). Dunlin densities in the south were similarly correlated with the density of ragworms, one of its prey species. Interestingly, research in both the Firth of Forth and the southern estuaries showed coincidence of the wader-prey density relationships. Even within a single estuary individual wader species are aggregated where their prey are unusually common (Fig. 2:7).

Table 2:3   *Risk\* of waders being found dead along a 5·63 km section of the Wash in winter (November–March) and at other times of year (August–October and April–May). Adapted from Goss–Custard (in press–IWRB Symposium)*

|  | 1969 | | 1970–1974 | |
|---|---|---|---|---|
|  | *Winter* | *Autumn/Spring* | *Winter* | *Autumn/Spring* |
| Oystercatcher | 0·21 | 0·07 | 0·08 | 0·05 |
| Dunlin | 0·16 | 0 | 0·02 | 0·01 |
| Knot | 0·15 | 0·02 | 0·04 | 0·02 |
| Redshank | 9·37 | 0·05 | 0·34 | 0·04 |
| Turnstone | 1·35 | 0 | 0·34 | 0·07 |
| Curlew | 0·72 | 0 | 0·22 | 0·08 |
| Bar-tailed Godwit | 0·15 | 0 | 0·08 | 0·02 |
| Grey Plover | 0 | 0·19 | 0·07 | 0·05 |
| Mean | 1·51 | 0·05 | 0·15 | 0·04 |

\*Risk was calculated as: $\dfrac{\text{number of corpses found per period}}{\text{total number of birds present on the Wash}} \times 1000$

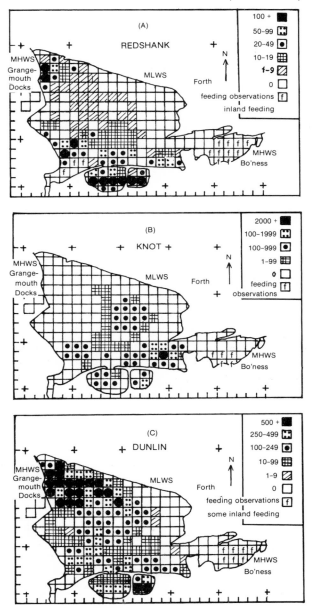

Fig. 2:7 Intensity of feeding by Redshank, Knot and Dunlin over a study area on the Firth of Forth, showing relatively patchy distribution of feeding effort. From Bryant (1979).

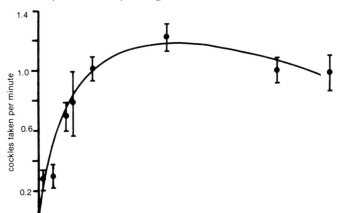

Fig. 2:8 Feeding patterns of Oystercatchers in relation to numerical density of cockles 16–42 mm long. Vertical bars show standard errors of each data point. From Goss-Custard (1977d).

The fact that birds are distributed over a large number of estuaries more or less in proportion to the density of prey implies a remarkable orderliness of dispersion. The birds must be responding to local densities and moving on from crowded areas. Goss-Custard (1977c) found that, within the Ythan Estuary in Aberdeenshire, Redshank preferred to settle in places with the highest density of *Corophium* but that this was counteracted by a tendency to avoid places of high bird density (Goss-Custard 1977c). Similarly, O'Connor and Brown (1977) found that Oystercatchers settling in the many small bays and inlets of Strangford Lough in Northern Ireland settled initially in a very dispersed manner but as the season progressed

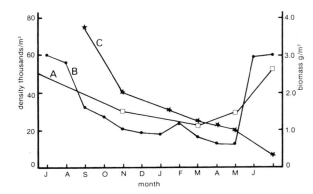

Fig. 2:9 Winter depletion of invertebrate stocks in estuaries: (A) biomass of *Neresis* and *Nepthys* worms in 1–10 cm size classes on the Wash. (B) *Corophium* densities on the Ythan Estuary, and (C) densities on the Ythan Estuary. *Corophium* and *Mytilus* data re-drawn from Milne and Dunnet (1972), *Nereis/Nepthys* data from Goss-Custard et al (1977).

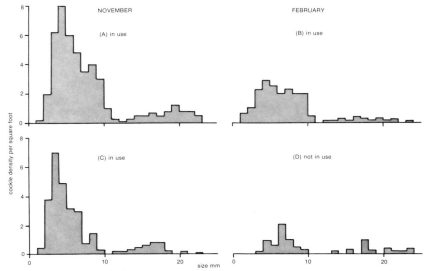

Fig. 2:10 Size-frequency histograms of cockles available to Oystercatchers in different parts of a study area in Strangford Lough. Each transect station was sampled for cockles in November and again in February, and each November samples was classified in February according to whether or not that station was still hunted over. Top row shows cockle sizes (A) in November and (B) in February, for areas still hunted over in February. Bottom row shows equivalent data for (C) November and (D) February for areas hunted over in November but abandoned by February and shows that depletion of the prey was already apparent at these stations the previous November. From Brown and O'Connor (1977).

crowded more and more into the richest areas which had first attracted large numbers of Oystercatchers.

At what point should a steadily depleting food patch be abandoned? Figure 2:8 shows how prey capture rates for Oystercatchers varied, falling steeply at low densities. Optimal foraging theory predicts that a bird does best if it remains feeding until its feeding rate falls to the average (allowing for the cost of searching for fresh patches) for the estuary as a whole, then leaves in search of another better-than-average patch. Consequently, the richer food patches should be selectively eaten down to some standard density so that birds must tolerate steadily falling densities of prey (Fig. 2:9). Schneider (1978) has shown that invertebrates on the Massachusetts coast are subjected to this type of frequency dependent selection by the four common shorebirds there (Sanderling, Semi-palmated Sandpiper, Short-billed Dowitcher and Black-bellied Plover).

Figure 2:10 shows that equalisation of prey numbers between patches is not a universal phenomenon, Oystercatchers at Strangford Lough depleting poor patches unexpectedly (on optimal foraging grounds) heavily before abandoning them. The reason was probably that the dominant birds on the estuary took possession of the best cockle beds, forcing the subordinate birds into the poorest areas which were then depleted to exhaustion of the second year and older cockles. Redshanks visually hunting *Corophium* are similarly intolerant of crowding, apparently because the amphipods are highly sensitive to surface vibrations which might signal the approach of a predator (Fig. 2:11), even to the point of retreating down their

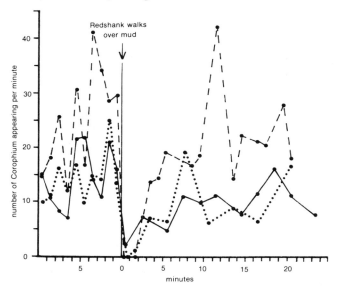

Fig. 2:11 Responses of the amphipod *Corophium* to a Redshank walking over the mud containing *Corophium* burrows. From Goss-Custard (1970a).

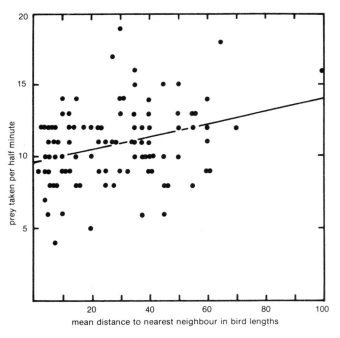

Fig. 2:12 Feeding rates of Redshank in relation to their separation from conspecifics, showing decreased feeding success as the birds were crowded together. From Goss-Custard (1976).

burrows on sensing falling rain! Consequently, Redshank hunting close together are less successful in catching prey than are birds further apart (Fig. 2:12), aggressive interactions between birds are common, and feeding is in loose dispersed flocks by day. By night, when feeding is apparently by probing and touch rather than using visual cues the inter-individual spacing within the flocks decreases significantly.

### WHEN TO FEED

Waders feed with the tidal ebb and flow of the estuary and Fig. 2:13 shows the feeding cycle of activities by Knot. At high tide the birds roost on the shore but as the tide begins to fall feeding commences, initially outside the main low water feeding grounds. By low water, increasing numbers of birds move on to mussel beds and scars, probably because their prey on the intertidal flats have burrowed deeper. As the mussel beds and flats are covered feeding resumes on secondary feeding areas before the birds finally return to the roost.

There are big differences between species in the details of these activity cycles. Some birds, such as Redshank, begin to feed on the saltmarsh and later move onto the mudflats. Turnstones use different feeding sites at different stages of the tide, with the more hungry birds going to feed immediately on areas ignored when less hungry (Harris 1979). The larger species, such as godwits and curlews, are the slowest to leave the roosts. This may be partly because the main concentrations of their prey are still underwater. However, there are theoretical grounds (Calder 1974) for the larger birds being more efficient at feeding and at storing fat reserves. Curlew and the like may therefore be more efficient feeders, with less need to spend time foraging (Fig. 2:15 below).

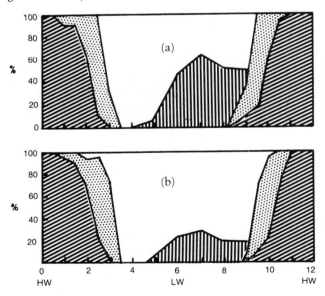

Fig. 2:13 The tidal cycle of Knot activity in Morecambe Bay, showing period spent roosting (cross-hatched), feeding carried out on low water feeding grounds (open) feeding carried out at other shore levels (stippled) and feeding carried out on mussel beds (vertically hatched). (a) Spring tides (b) Neap tides. From Prater (1972).

The intensity of feeding through the tidal cycle also varies seasonally since by mid-winter invertebrate stocks have fallen (Fig. 2:9), daylight hours are short, and low temperatures require greater heat production (and thus food intake) by the birds. In the case of Redshank and Oystercatchers it has been suggested that the increased occurrence of birds inland during winter in Britain has been caused by their inability to meet their dietary requirements on the estuaries, forcing them to move inland in search of earthworms in pastures during daylight hours when their estuarine food sources may be underwater (Goss-Custard 1969, Heppleston 1971).

In the light of the above points it is not surprising that research has shown that a significant proportion of the invertebrate stocks available within the typical estuary is taken in the course of each winter. Figure 2:9 shows that the season depletion varies between the invertebrate species and estuaries concerned. For the Wash, Goss-Custard (1977d) estimated that between 14% and 34% of the initial 'standing crop' of the prey were removed during the winter. For Oystercatchers similar estimates of their impact on cockle stocks have been made (Drinnan 1957, Brown and O'Connor 1974) which suggest that about 40% of the total production is removed in the course of the winter. The energy web presented in the previous chapter (Fig. 1:11) for the Ythan Estuary similarly showed that almost the entire annual crop of mussels was taken by predators (including Man), Oystercatchers taking 7·2%, gulls 8·6% and Eiders 21·2%. The evidence thus indicates that a significant or major part of estuarine invertebrate populations may be taken by shorebirds in the course of a winter. It follows, of course, that prey will be correspondingly scarce in spring since most invertebrates do not breed until late spring or summer (cf. Fig. 2:9).

Diagrams such as Fig. 2:9 illustrate only the broadest of trends in prey availability for shorebirds, for the behaviour of the invertebrates may significantly influence the moment-to-moment prey densities. Thus, at low temperatures invertebrates burrow more deeply than normal and may become largely inaccessible (Fig. 2:14). Other species such as the lugworm *Arenicola* and ragworm *Nereis* normally live at depths beyond the reach of wader bills but they are accessible as they surface to feed or to defaecate or to irrigate their burrows. Surfacing is less frequent on cold days, thus reducing their availability to waders. Lugworms have also been shown to defaecate less frequently on windy days, so denying Bar-tailed Godwits one of their usual prey items. As noted earlier in respect of Redshank disturbing *Corophium* (Fig. 2:11), rainfall can reduce the feeding rate of the amphipod and hence their availability to the birds. In this way, environmental conditions may, by altering prey behaviour, bring about significant variations in its effective density.

FEEDING SUCCESS

*Prey microhabitat*

Prey behaviour may differ between different parts of the prey's habitat, such that shorebirds can more easily take them in one than in another. Limpets, for example, are taken from pools and from rocks by Oystercatchers. On bare rocks the limpets sit out the low tide with their shells clamped to the surface to avoid desiccation but in pools the limpets are either grazing on algae or resting, and with no risk of desiccation the shell needs to be pulled down only during disturbance. Feare (1971) found that attacks by Oystercatchers on the limpet *Patella aspersa* were always successful in pools but were only 73% successful when the limpets were on bare

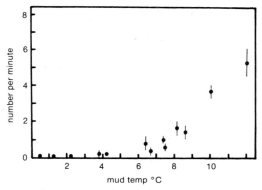

Fig. 2:14 Frequency of appearance of *Corophium* on the mud surface in relation to temperature of the mud, showing cessation of emergence at low temperatures. From Goss-Custard (1969).

rock. A second limpet species, *Patella vulgata*, had a harder and rounder shell, so that the anterior or head end of the shell – the weakest part because the horseshoe-shaped adductor is not attached to the shell at this point – could not be readily identified by the birds, and was less successfully attacked; even so, here too limpets in pools were more frequently killed (44% success) than were more tightly clamped rock-attached individuals (30% success).

### Feeding and age

One important factor determining the foraging success of a wader is its experience. During autumn migration along the Massachusetts coast of North America juvenile Turnstones were found to feed considerably less efficiently than adults (Table 2:4). The birds usually feed on barnacles attached to rocks scattered over the tidal flats and adults and juveniles were equally successful (about 81%) in their attacks, but the juveniles were considerably slower in locating suitable barnacles, needing an average of 11·3 per minute of foraging time, about 85% of the adult's rate. That this is due to the juveniles' inexperience is suggested by a comparison of adult and juvenile foraging on tide-wrack. Occasional autumn storms deposit large quantities of marine algae and eel grasses on the high tide line, providing an

Table 2:4   *Feeding rates of adult and juvenile Turnstones Arenaria interpres foraging on two different substrata (Groves 1978: Auk 95:95–103), expressed in means and (SD)*

|  | Barnacled rocks | | Significance | Tide wrack | | Significance |
|---|---|---|---|---|---|---|
|  | Adults | Juveniles | level* | Adults | Juveniles | level* |
| Foraging rate, movements/sec | 0·222 (0·070) | 0·188 (0·069) | 0·001 | 0·375 (0·281) | 0·246 (0·140) | 0·05 |
| Capture rate, prey items/sec | 0·185 (0·069) | 0·156 (0·069) | 0·01 | 0·258 (0·203) | 0·158 (0·106) | 0·05 |
| Success rate, prey per movement | 0·814 (0·137) | 0·812 (0·196) | n.s. | 0·645 (0·253) | 0·603 (0·230) | n.s. |

*From Mann-Whitney U-test between age-groups.

invertebrate-rich food source for the Turnstones. Adult birds with experience of such deposits had learned the technique required to flick over the weed and run down any mobile prey uncovered, and did better in such habitat than on barnacles (15·5 versus 13·3 prey per minute). Juveniles lacked this experience and were no more successful on wrack than on barnacled rocks (Table 2:4). Such results point to the need for young waders to start independent life in areas of easily accessible food. In some groups, particularly amongst geese and swans, family structure is a feature of wintering life, though the family bonds decline through the winter. The young birds are thus afforded a measure of protection against other adults and can feed in relative peace.

### Feeding and shorebird density

We saw earlier (Fig. 2:12) that Redshank were less successful when hunting close together than when further apart. Amongst Oystercatchers, too, feeding rates on mussels declined as the local density of the birds increased (R. H. Drent, in press). Drent found that feeding rates also declined when he increased the apparent density of birds by placing model Oystercatchers on the mud flats, though to a lesser extent than when real birds were involved. Zwarts (1978) similarly concluded that Curlew suffer reduced food intake with increase in local density.

Why such reductions occur is poorly understood. Part of the explanation lies in a greater frequency of fighting at high densities but, in a study on the Wash, Goss-Custard found that even the most aggressive species (the Knot, with 4·3 encounters per bird-hour) lost too little time fighting to account for the reduction in food intake. Klepto-parasitism, the stealing of food from one animal by another, also offers only a partial explanation, for food intake rates decreased with density even for flocks in which no such encounters took place. A third explanation may be based on the idea of prey renewal rates. Some invertebrates – for example, lugworms – can be captured readily only whilst at the surface point of their irrigation-defaecation cycle. Smith (1975) found that Bar-tailed Godwits took lugworms only if they surfaced whilst the bird was scanning the area concerned. Thus, the greater the Godwit's searching area the greater number of surfacing lugworms and the higher the feeding rate. Conversely, when each bird had only a small foraging area, the number of available worms was reduced.

This density-dependence of feeding rate is particularly significant in assessing the likely impact of estuarine development proposals on waders. The reductions in feeding rate described above were not due to depletion of the local food supply: the prey were still there but were being captured less successfully by competing birds. Consequently, reclamation of areas of an estuary may result in the displaced birds crowding onto the remaining food patches and reducing individual feeding success, even though the prey are still present.

Shorebirds hunting by touch or taking foods unresponsive to bird behaviour are not affected by crowding in this way. Instead, the pattern is of density-independent cropping of the prey to effective depletion, followed by dispersal to less preferred foods or feeding areas. Brent Geese for example, feed almost exclusively on the *Zostera* beds in southern England at Foulness and Leigh, Essex. In late autumn their food density is extremely high, with 60–70% of the mud surface covered with plant material. Exclosure experiments (building cages of netting over parts of the *Zostera* beds to exclude geese) showed that the feeding rate of individual geese was not reduced until nearly three-quarters of the available food had been removed. At this stage most of the birds moved to *Enteromorpha* beds elsewhere in south-east England. The few geese that remained on the depleted *Zostera* beds spread out, walked faster, and spent longer feeding. The *Enteromorpha* beds were similarly treated and, on depletion, were abandoned, with further dispersal to other sites in England or with birds moving on to cereals on adjacent land.

## SHOREBIRDS IN MID-WINTER

### Body size and energy reserves

There are theoretical reasons for believing that larger birds have proportionally greater energy reserves against food shortages than have smaller species (Calder 1974) and smaller birds do in fact feed more intensively than larger species (Fig. 2:15). The figure shows also that birds of a given size hunt about twice as intensively in mid-winter as in autumn, with birds lighter than about 150 g feeding for nearly all of the time available. Birds have higher metabolic rates at low temperatures and need more food as fuel, and their problems are compounded by the shorter days of midwinter and by the reduced activity (Fig. 2:14) and deeper burrowing of potential prey. The bivalve *Macoma balthica* in the Wash, for example, undergoes a vertical migration annually, to the upper layers of the mud in June and to deeper levels in December. Consequently, only 4% of the *Macoma* are accessible to the bills of Knot in December and hardly more than 25% at any time between September and April, the major period for Knot on the Wash. The migration is apparently triggered by day-length but its function is unknown (Reading and McGrorty 1978).

The shortness of winter day-lengths may be more important to shorebirds than the low temperatures. Bar-tailed Godwits have been shown to carry more fat in December, when days are shortest, than in January, when days are on average coldest (Evans and Smith 1975). It is, however, very difficult to separate the effects of one weather or seasonal factor from another in the face of normal seasonality, for the foraging success of shorebirds is also affected by wind and tide conditions (Evans 1976). Strong winds can cause wind chill (by forced ventilation of the body surface) and alter feeding conditions (by drying the substrate, forcing prey deeper, and by disturbing the water surface). In consequence, the birds may move to sheltered but less food-rich bays. Similarly, feeding rates may fall if low tides coincide with darkness. Grey Plover taking ragworm *Nereis diversicolor* averaged only 3·5 pecks/minute at night compared to 5·5–5·8 pecks/minute by day on the same mudflat (Evans 1976). The seasonal variation between neap and spring tides also influences the availability of prey.

### Adverse weather

These effects are six-fold, (1) reduction in feeding time due to ice covering the upper shore, which is the first to be uncovered and last to be covered by the tide, (2) fewer available prey on the unfrozen areas since invertebrates are less active at the surface in low temperature (above), (3) killing the prey and so eventually reducing their abundance (Hauser 1973), (4) perhaps increasing the density of birds in the reduced feeding area, so increasing interference between them (Goss–Custard 1976, 1977a), (5) reducing supplementary feeding in the coastal fields at high water (Dare 1966, Goss-Custard 1969, Heppleston 1971), and (6) increasing energy demand. These points have been discussed fully in a recent review (Goss-Custard 1980).

Severe winters with prolonged periods of frost are few in Britain, the most memorable recently being the 1947–48 and 1962–63 winters, though less severe spells of frost occur approximately every five years. Waders are killed by such severe winters (Dobinson and Richards 1964, Heppleston 1971, Goss-Custard et al 1977); the smaller species such as Dunlin, Knot and Redshank are especially vulnerable (Ash and Sharpe 1964, Pilcher et al 1974), and emaciated birds are frequently found, whether as a result of starvation or of starvation exacerbating a disease condition being unknown (Pilcher et al 1974). Heppleston (1971) estimated that 25% of Oystercatchers on the Ythan Estuary died during a cold spell lasting 22 days. Juveniles were much more likely to die than adults, perhaps because they were less effective at feeding or because they were forced by the adults to feed in a less profitable part of the shore (O'Connor and Brown 1977). On the other hand even brief cold spells have been uncommon in the last ten years, and mortality from severe weather is not normally a winter hazard on British estuaries. Even the 1962–63 severe winter depressed the population of the species most affected for only a few years (Pilcher et al 1974, Tubbs 1977).

*Winter mortality*

Few studies have estimated winter mortality rates in waders. However, Goss-Custard (in press) concluded that wader deaths on the Wash must normally be well below 10%. He found that waders were ten times less likely to be found dead during mild winters than in the 1968–69 winter when there was a cold spell lasting several days (Table 2:3). Unless normal mortality had been below 10% an increase of this magnitude during a moderately cold winter would have wiped out the entire population in the absence of extensive movements. Simulation studies of wader populations have, however, shown that even quite low levels of winter mortality may have quite profound effects on the longer term population size, particularly if this mortality is brought about by density-dependent competition for food (Goss-Custard 1980).

SUMMARY

Estuarine birds in Britain forage mostly on the exposed intertidal flats. A few common invertebrates are taken by many shorebirds but most are taken by those species with appropriate adaptations. Shorebirds generally concentrate on the most profitable prey (food gained per unit time) rather than on the largest available prey but this may be modified by the time required to locate and/or to identify prey. The density of shorebirds within and between estuaries is largely determined by the distribution of prey though physical characteristics of the estuary and interactions between birds may have some influence. Feeding routines vary tidally and seasonally and may be modified by prey behaviour. Young birds are less effective at foraging than adult birds but may be supported by living in family groups. Foraging success amongst shorebirds hunting live prey by visual cues is reduced by flock densities but touch feeders and grazers are unaffected. Energy demands, particularly on the smaller species, are greatest in midwinter, and most severe when icing occurs. Winter mortality is generally low but is sensitive to reduced feeding rates.

# CHAPTER 3

# Migrations and Distribution in Western Europe

## MIGRATORY PATTERNS

Estuarine birds undertake prodigious migrations. Several species which regularly reach British and Irish coasts in large numbers breed in the Arctic and sub-Arctic as far away as 130°E (the longitude of Japan) and 90°W (western Ellesmere Island). These long distance migrants include Knot, Sanderling, Turnstone and Brent Geese. The extent of the known breeding ranges for our migrant and wintering waterfowl is shown in Figure 3:1. There have been a few recoveries of British ringed birds (Mead 1974) further to the east and south of this line, including Ruff and Pochard. It is possible that a proportion of these species come from outside this range. Excluded from this map are vagrant birds from the Nearctic which, although occurring regularly, are only seen in very small numbers. Large numbers which have come from the distant Arctic breeding grounds migrate further south. Many winter in West Africa but some, especially terns and certain populations of Knot and Sanderling, continue their migration as far south as South Africa. A wader holds the longest recorded journey for any bird other than a seabird; this was a Ruff ringed in Cape Province, South Africa in winter and recovered 18 months later in the USSR just a few hundred miles from the Bering Straits, approximately 17,500 km away.

The breeding distributions of many species of waterfowl are discontinuous. There has, therefore, been a tendency for geographically separated groups to form sub-species (or races as they are more usually called). Where there has been inadequate time for evolution to have resulted in clear morphological separation (which is necessary before races can be described), a species can still be divided into different breeding populations. The races or populations have sometimes developed noticeable differences in the timing of their breeding seasons, moult or migration

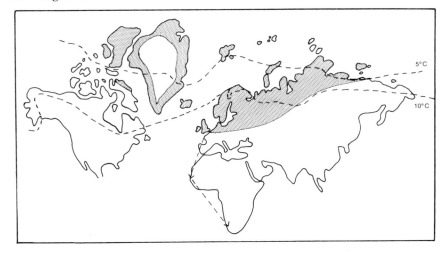

Fig. 3:1 Normal breeding ranges (hatched) of estuarine birds which migrate to or through Britain and Ireland. The July 5°C and 10°C isotherms and direction of migration to Africa are also shown.

strategies, and often in the wintering areas used. It is, therefore, possible to recognise different groups of some species migrating through the country. Comments on the details of these movements are included in the species accounts later in this book.

Before considering the many patterns of migration it is worth examining the development of racial separation and probable migration patterns. The separation of different populations of tundra breeding birds can be traced back to the refuges of ice-free breeding grounds during the Ice Ages of approximately 18,000 years ago. Figure 3:2 shows that refuges remained in northern Greenland, around the south of the present North Sea, between 40°E and 60°E in northern USSR and around the mouth of the Ob at approximately 70°E–80°E also in the USSR. The last two were almost contiguous (Moreau 1972, Ploeger 1968). A moderately wide zone of tundra existed south of the ice caps in the Palearctic but in the Nearctic the ice penetrated into coniferous forests. As the ice retreated, the breeding ranges of the Palearctic groups extended north, west and eastwards while most of the Nearctic birds extended their ranges southwards. The migration routes, however, probably remained traditional and so the northern Greenland birds still crossed the Atlantic to winter in the western Palearctic in the areas which were closer to the original refuges than were the coasts of the southern USA. This helps to explain the apparent anomaly of those birds now migrating south-eastwards rather than being involved in the much larger southern movement of the slightly more southerly populations in the Canadian archipelago.

Three groups of birds can still be recognised. The north-western group (Knot, Sanderling, Turnstone, Pale-bellied Brent Goose) despite having spread southwards are limited to Ellesmere Island and adjacent islands, eastern Baffin Island in Canada and to northern Greenland. The western European group have spread northwards, probably aided by a small refuge in Iceland, to colonise Iceland, parts of Greenland and much of Scandinavia. The species involved here are the sub-arctic and boreal birds such as Oystercatcher, Ringed Plover, Dunlin, Redshank, Golden Plover,

Pink-footed Goose and White-fronted Goose. The Siberian zone provided breeding areas for, amongst others, Knot, Sanderling, Bar-tailed Godwit, Grey Plover, Dark-bellied Brent Goose and Bewick's Swan. The great majority of dabbling and inland diving ducks and many of the *Tringa* sandpipers and snipes have always bred in the contiguous sub-Arctic and boreal zones and as a result have shown little racial differentiation.

There are no consistent similarities between the wintering areas for birds breeding in each region, even though the migration routes may be the same. For example, while Greenlandic and northern Canadian Knot and Turnstone winter in north-west Europe, primarily in the British Isles, the principal wintering area for Sanderling is further south in west Africa. Conversely, the Sanderling wintering in western Europe come mainly from the USSR, while the Knot and Turnstone from the USSR migrate to Africa (Branson and Minton 1977, Branson, Ponting and Minton 1978, Prater and Davies 1977).

A general pattern that emerges about the migration movements of all species is that a series of estuaries or wetlands is used in the course of each year. These can be considered as stepping stones. We do not really know why individual estuaries are chosen but it does appear that the same ones are utilised each year. Waders, swans and geese occur in predictable places; not only do ringing returns indicate that they return (both on passage and in winter) to the same estuary, but they also tend to occur on the same section of that estuary. The food supply is directly related to bird density in winter and, although we have little evidence about the migration period,

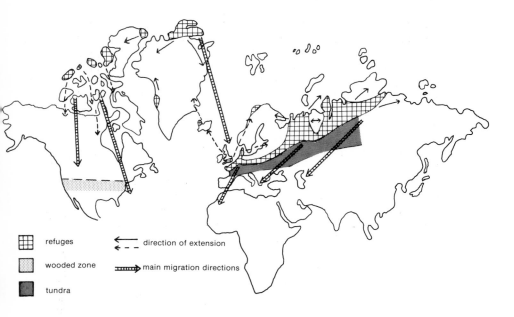

refuges   ⬅--- direction of extension

wooded zone   ⟹ main migration directions

tundra

Fig. 3.2 Schematic representation of the isolation of estuary bird populations due to the Pleistocene Ice Ages and subsequent extensions of ranges. Hatched areas are refuges at height of the Ice Age.

bird density at that time may also be partly correlated with food. Additional factors, in particular security of feeding and roosting grounds, may operate during the moult. During this process, birds not only require an abundant and readily available food supply, but because flight is impaired (either partially in waders or completely in wildfowl) they need to minimise this activity. Possibly the presence of adequate concentrations of certain minerals such as sulphur, which are important constituents of new feathers, may be another factor influencing the choice of moulting grounds.

Within Britain and Ireland there are regular migration routes which are used by waterfowl. These have been most clearly documented for waders. Visual observations of birds moving south along the east coast in autumn and east along the south coast in spring are well known. Oystercatchers were observed by Andrew (1959) to leave the Firth of Forth and head for the Solway Firth. Visual observations, however, only provide information on a small part of wader migration but two other techniques – radar tracking and ringing – have revealed most of the information. From radar tracking Evans (1968) showed that wader migration exhibited a high degree of site specificity and accurate navigation. His study area was from the Firth of Forth to Teesmouth; within this zone, apart from low level coasting movements, there were four main directional trends. Three of these originated from the outer Forth and were aimed primarily at the Solway and Morecambe Bay and at East Anglia; the least frequented of these three routes was to the Ayr coast. The fourth group of birds moved from Teesmouth towards the Ribble estuary. Significantly no movements took place from the west coast towards the east. Evans assumed that the east to west movements were of Scandinavian (and Russian) birds, but we now know that Greenlandic species may also migrate to Britain via Norway.

Ringing by the Wash Wader Ringing Group has revealed that a high proportion of Knot, Dunlin, Ringed Plover and other species present on the Wash in autumn move away after moulting. There is a very strong movement north-westwards both along the east coast to the Humber and Teesmouth and across the Pennines to the Irish Sea estuaries; many birds from here also move in the sector between south-west and south. Several other ringing studies, for example on the Dee, Morecambe Bay and the Thames, have confirmed the pattern of subsequent onward movement in early winter by a proportion of the moulting birds. Many of the estuaries of importance in winter support relatively few birds in autumn. However, the monthly counting procedure used in the Birds of Estuaries Enquiry could not estimate the number of birds moving through estuaries in the autumn. At this time of the year many birds may rest as little as one day and rarely (unless moulting) for longer than three weeks.

Clearly emerging from this is the question 'What would happen to the migration pattern or survival of birds if a massive development took place?' It is almost impossible to answer this question yet it is a basic one. In Britain in autumn migrants probably could make do with smaller feeding grounds; certainly birds do not normally have to feed all the time and there are no large demands made by low ambient temperature. The loss of autumn feeding areas, however, may still have serious effects, since it would result in a higher density of birds and hence high utilisation of the food supply in the remaining areas. But would the increased depletion of the food supply in autumn increase the difficulties in winter? From the evidence in Chapter 2 this seems likely. Spring poses yet another problem because only a few estuaries support large concentrations of birds on their way to Greenland and Iceland. These birds arrive with relatively low weights and then add large fat reserves to enable them to make the long crossing of the North Atlantic Ocean and to arrive in a reasonable enough condition to start displaying and breeding. The loss of these refuelling areas could also seriously affect the populations involved. Thus the removal of any major link, or of several numerically less important links, in the chain of estuaries could have consequences far greater than apparent at first sight. Additionally, each estuary has its own role and, therefore, should be considered separately.

*Migration patterns of waders*

In waders the autumn migration takes place in many stages with different timings for females, males and juveniles. Characteristically, females, having incubated the eggs and tended the small young, leave first, leaving the male to attend the older unfledged young. She then moves away from the breeding grounds. For species such as the Spotted Redshank, this may be as early as mid-June but for the majority it is not until early or mid-July. The females join with non-breeding birds (either immatures, non-breeding adults or failed breeders) to form the early migrants. Once the young have fledged, the males start to gather away from the breeding areas and form a second wave of migrants. Finally the juveniles, having remained around the breeding area for a further one to three weeks, migrate southwards. The influx of juveniles is perhaps the most noticeable feature of autumn wader migration for not only are they relatively tame, but they occur widely inland as well as on the coast. For many arctic breeding species, the arrival of juveniles in Britain and Ireland takes place between the last week of August and the third week of September.

Initially, the Siberian species move south-west along either the Arctic Ocean shoreline or across the tundra. Very large numbers pass through the White Sea and down into the Baltic Sea, finally arriving at the North Sea. A smaller but distinct movement of eastern birds takes place along the Norwegian coast. Greenlandic birds either stop in Iceland or make a direct flight to Europe. Clearly there can be major differences in the rate of migration – Siberian birds can migrate at a leisurely rate and from the steady daily turnover of birds on the Baltic coasts this appears to be the case, while the Greenlandic birds need to make either two considerable sea crossings or one very long one, in either case involving the prior deposition of considerable fat reserves.

Therefore, even for species with relatively simple patterns, the actual timing of influxes into Britain and Ireland is not entirely dependent on when they leave their breeding grounds. The clearest patterns emerge in juveniles and in those species which winter and moult in southern latitudes, as these pass through western Europe pausing just long enough to deposit fat reserves for the onward journey. The 'southern' Dunlin *C.a. schinzii*, Curlew Sandpiper, Little Stint, Spotted Redshank are good examples of this group. The waders which winter in Britain and Ireland show a much more variable pattern. Most of the Greenlandic birds moult here and, therefore, show a simple pattern, but the adults of most of the Siberian species pause on autumn migration to moult. As this process takes between two and three months, this age group does not disperse from moulting grounds until October or November.

In western Europe there are only a few estuaries which support large moulting flocks of waders (Fig. 3:4). The Wadden Sea (Denmark, West Germany, Netherlands) is pre-eminent, with up to 2,000,000 waders present in autumn, but over 100,000 are present in each of the Dutch Delta region, the Ribble, the Wash and Morecambe Bay. The main late autumn or early winter influx into estuaries all along the coast of western Europe is due primarily to the dispersion of Wadden Sea birds, although all of the above-mentioned estuaries contribute some birds. By mid-December a fairly stable situation has been reached which lasts well into February (Fig. 3:3) with just small fluctuations due to cold weather movements. The early spring (March) movements are more or less the reverse of the early winter ones, with birds withdrawing from the estuaries utilised in mid-winter and concentrating again on the estuaries favoured in autumn, particularly the Wadden Sea.

From mid-April there is the return movement of African wintering birds (especially Ringed Plover, Dunlin and Sanderling) which reaches its peak usually between the 10th and 20th May, although the last birds may depart as late as the end of the first week in June. These birds are found only on a handful of estuaries (Fig. 3:4). In Europe, the Wadden Sea receives most of the Bar-tailed Godwit and Grey Plover which join the very large numbers of other waders already present. In Britain this passage in May can be seen all over the country, but about three-quarters of all birds

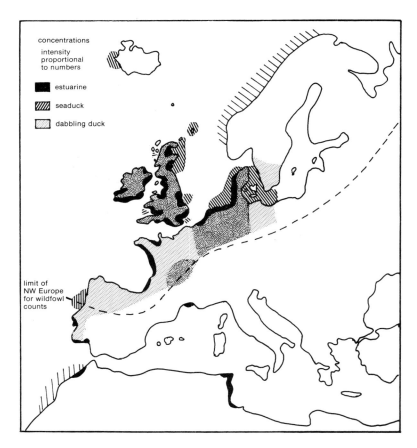

Fig. 3:3 Schematic representation of the ranges of wildfowl in Western Europe and north-west Africa in midwinter.

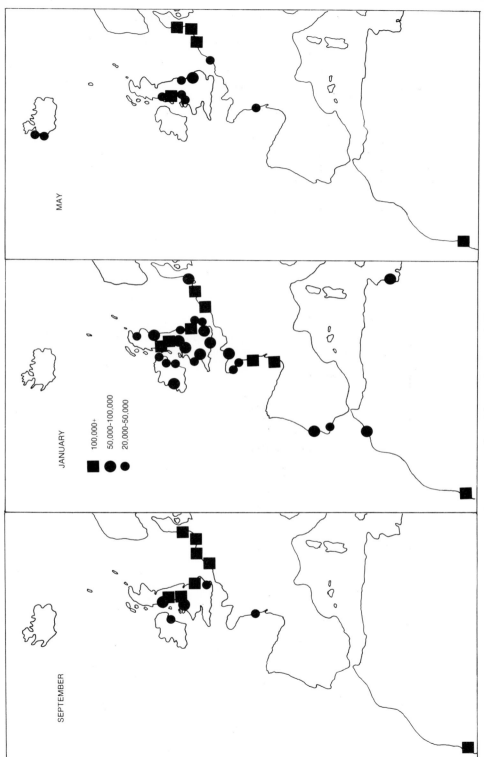

MAY

JANUARY

100,000+
50,000-100,000
20,000-50,000

SEPTEMBER

Fig. 3:4 Major estuaries for waders in Europe and NW Africa in September, January and May.

involved may be only in five major Irish Sea estuaries. These are the Dee, Ribble, Morecambe Bay, Duddon and Solway. Therefore, relatively few are seen in eastern England where a strong autumn passage occurs. Much more surprising is the apparently very small number recorded in Ireland in May. Although this may be due partly to the lack of observers in the west, Sanderling, Ringed Plover and Dunlin are scarce even on the east coast of Ireland only 190 km from the large estuaries of north-west England.

### Migration patterns of wildfowl

There are a number of major differences between the migratory patterns of wildfowl and waders. With few exceptions, such as Pintail, Shoveler, Common Scoter and Garganey, wildfowl rarely migrate further south than the countries bordering the Mediterranean. This is particularly true of the wildfowl which occur in Britain and Ireland; for them Iberia can reasonably be considered as the limit to migration. They do, however, breed well to the north and occur over the range shown in Fig 3:1.

The migratory patterns of geese and swans differ considerably from those of ducks. Geese and swans have developed strong family ties which last throughout the autumn migration and winter periods. Thus there is no separation in migration timing between adults (at least of the successful breeders) and juveniles. The successful adults moult their flight feathers on or near to the breeding grounds. In many species the non-breeding immature birds and some of the failed breeders however have developed a special moult migration. Unlike most immature waders these birds do not remain in the wintering grounds for the summer. Instead they migrate northwards with or slightly after the adults and go directly to traditional moulting areas. These areas are usually north of the breeding grounds and are characterised by many islands where the birds can find protection against ground predators, since the birds become flightless for a period of three or four weeks.

The Icelandic and Greenlandic Geese tend to arrive in Britain and Ireland suddenly during late September and October, but those from the Soviet Union build up slowly, usually not reaching a peak until forced westwards from the continent by severe weather in late December or early January. Very many geese, however, remain to winter in West Germany, the Netherlands and Belgium.

Ducks show some characteristics of the geese and swans; a few, such as Shelduck, undertake moult migrations. Generally, however, the adults or immatures gather on certain lakes or shallow tidal areas (either south of or within the breeding zone) to moult. Within Britain and Ireland there are a number of important moulting grounds such as Bridgwater Bay for Shelduck and Carmarthen Bay for Common Scoter. The subsequent arrivals in Britain do not appear to be separated into waves of age or sex groupings, nor however, does the family unit appear to operate in winter or during migration. The main influx of ducks takes place, like the waders, from late October through December and the exodus starts in February and is usually completed by late March. Unlike waders, there is a minimal onward migration in autumn and therefore virtually no northwards passage from southern latitudes in spring. The only exception to the latter is a movement of seaduck, especially Common Scoter, through the English Channel in April.

INTERNATIONAL COUNTS

The need to know more about the numbers, migration and feeding ecology of waterfowl at the international level has been recognised for a long time. International co-ordination on these subjects is achieved by the International Waterfowl Research Bureau (IWRB). This body was set up by the International Council for Bird Preservation (ICBP) in 1954 and its aim is 'to stimulate and co-ordinate research on the conservation of waterfowl and their wetland habitat, particularly where international co-operation is necessitated by the migratory nature of waterfowl'. At present the IWRB is based at the Wildfowl Trust at Slimbridge. Its members are drawn from 32 countries; initially they were mainly European, including many from Eastern Europe, but now many Third World countries are participating actively in its work.

The international wildfowl and wader counts are co-ordinated through two of the fifteen research groups of the IWRB. The counts are carried out between specific dates and are organised by national organisers and the results summarised centrally. The initial aims of the counts were to estimate total numbers in mid-winter (Atkinson-Willes 1976, Prater 1976a) and to look at trends in population size; however, data are now being gathered in other months in order to provide a more complete picture of distributional changes. This overall view provides the possibility to assess the numbers present in each estuary or inland wetland, in relation to the total numbers. The criteria used in this assessment will be considered later.

Waterfowl populations move along fairly well-defined routes (Shevareva 1970). The original concept was of 'flyways'; this, although still useful, perhaps gives the impression of strictly adhered-to routes. Therefore the term 'flyway' has tended to be dropped in favour of broad geographical terms, for instance, Western Europe. The direction and extent of migration tends to be influenced by geographical features such as mountain ranges, seas and river valleys. Because the counts require many observers, they have been most comprehensively carried out in western Europe. This area includes all of the Atlantic seaboard of western Europe and therefore its estuaries. Ducks and geese occur widely elsewhere in southern and eastern Europe in winter, but at this time of the year there are few waders away from the Atlantic coast. Therefore, the winter wader counts can be regarded as referring to the whole of Europe.

Britain and Ireland have been fortunate in having a large number of skilled birdwatchers; the information obtained through the national schemes of the 'Birds of Estuaries Enquiry' and 'Wetlands Enquiry' respectively and of the Wildfowl Trust's 'Wildfowl Counts', is more comprehensive than it is for any other country. However between 1967 and 1975 many mid-winter counts have been made elsewhere. All of the available figures have been averaged for each wetland to find out the number of birds regularly wintering on them and then added together to obtain the total number wintering in west Europe. Data exist for other regions but they are nowhere nearly so comprehensive as for West Europe.

The numbers of the principal species of ducks, swans and waders wintering in western Europe are shown in Table 3:1. As geese have discrete breeding and wintering grounds and the numbers of each group are known, the details of their population levels have been summarised separately in Table 3:2. On the information presently available there are two species of duck, Eider and Mallard, which exceed the one million level and if adequate counts were available, there can be little doubt

Table 3:1   Numbers of swans, ducks and waders wintering in western Europe
1969–75

| | W. Europe | Britain | Ireland | % Britain | % Ireland |
|---|---|---|---|---|---|
| Mute Swan | 120,000 | 18,000 | 6,000 | 15·0 | 5·0 |
| Bewick's Swan | 10,000 | 1,800 | 2,000 | 18·0 | 20·0 |
| Whooper Swan | 17,500 | 3,000 | 5,000 | 17·1 | 28·6 |
| Shelduck | 130,000 | 60,000 | 7,500 | 46·2 | 5·8 |
| Wigeon | 400,000 | 150,000 | 105,000 | 37·5 | 26·3 |
| Gadwall | 5,000 | 2,000 | 350 | 40·0 | 7·0 |
| Teal | 150,000 | 75,000 | 40,000 | 50·0 | 26·7 |
| Mallard | 1,500,000 | 300,000 | 35,000 | 20·0 | 2·3 |
| Pintail | 50,000 | 20,000 | 5,000 | 40·0 | 10·0 |
| Shoveler | 20,000 | 5,000 | 4,000 | 25·0 | 20·0 |
| Pochard | 500,000 | 40,000 | 40,000 | 8·0 | 8·0 |
| Tufted Duck | 250,000 | 45,000 | 40,000 | 18·0 | 16·0 |
| Scaup | 150,000 | 22,500 | 1,500 | 15·0 | 1·0 |
| Eider | 2,000,000 | 60,000 | few | 3·0 | — |
| Long-tailed Duck | 500,000+ | 10,000 | 150 | 2·0 | 0·03 |
| Common Scoter | 450,000 | 35,000 | 4,000 | 7·8 | 0·9 |
| Velvet Scoter | 175,000 | 3,500 | 20 | 2·0 | 0·01 |
| Goldeneye | 200,000 | 12,500 | 5,000 | 6·3 | 2·5 |
| Smew | 20,000 | 50 | — | 0·25 | — |
| Red-breasted Merganser | 40,000 | 7,500 | 3,000 | 18·8 | 7·5 |
| Goosander | 50,000 | 4,000 | — | 8·0 | — |
| Oystercatcher | 560,000 | 200,000 | 32,000 | 35·7 | 5·7 |
| Avocet | 23,100 | 100 | — | 0·4 | — |
| Ringed Plover | 25,000 | 10,000 | 7,500 | 40·0 | 30·0 |
| Golden Plover | (800,000+) | 200,000 | 250,000+ | 25·0 | 31·3 |
| Grey Plover | 30,000 | 10,000 | 1,000 | 33·3 | 3·3 |
| Lapwing | (1,000,000+) | ? | ? | ? | ? |
| Knot | 500,000 | 300,000 | 35,000 | 60·0 | 7·0 |
| Sanderling | 15,000 | 10,000 | 2,000 | 66·7 | 13·3 |
| Purple Sandpiper | (20,500+) | 18,000 | ? | NA | NA |
| Dunlin | 1,200,000 | 550,000 | 115,000 | 45·8 | 9·6 |
| Ruff | 1,600 | 1,100 | 20 | 68·8 | 1·3 |
| Black-tailed Godwit | 40,000 | 5,000 | 9,000 | 12·5 | 22·5 |
| Bar-tailed Godwit | 90,000 | 44,000 | 18,000 | 48·9 | 20·0 |
| Curlew | 200,000 | 63,000 | 25,000 | 31·5 | 12·5 |
| Spotted Redshank | 400 | 100 | 40 | 25·0 | 10·0 |
| Redshank | 125,000 | 80,000 | 15,000 | 64·0 | 12·0 |
| Greenshank | 800 | 300 | 350 | 37·5 | 43·8 |
| Turnstone | (32,100+) | 22,000 | (5,000+) | NA | NA |

Data for wildfowl based on Atkinson-Willes (1976, 1978, pers. comm.) and for waders on Prater (1976a, unpublished data), for Ireland on Hutchinson (1979) that Lapwing would join Dunlin, the only wader at the moment in that abundant category. The only other species which may possibly reach one million is the Long-tailed Duck; up to two million of which are thought to move westwards from the Soviet breeding grounds in autumn but, if this is correct, only a small percentage is picked up subsequently in winter (Atkinson-Willes 1978).

Waterfowl are not spread uniformly throughout western Europe in winter. The principal areas utilised by dabbling ducks and geese and seaducks are shown in Fig. 3:3. Coastal waders are shown separately in Fig. 3:4; also included are the autumn and spring concentrations of special importance. Waders are concentrated around the North Sea and the Irish Sea, each with a total of approximately one million birds in winter. There are smaller numbers in north and west France and south-west Iberia. Geese and the dabbling and freshwater ducks are also concentrated in the north-western parts of the region, particularly in countries bordering the North Sea. Sea-ducks concentrate in the ice-free shallow waters of the south-western Baltic Sea and parts of the North Sea but, with one or two exceptions, are scarce elsewhere.

Of the waders which migrate through western Europe in autumn, a considerable number winter on the Atlantic coasts of Morocco and Mauritania. The Banc d'Arguin in Mauritania supports the largest concentration of wintering waders known in Europe or west Africa. A detailed census in October 1973 revealed 730,000 birds (Knight and Dick 1975) and it is possible that even more could have arrived during the following two months. A number of waders which winter south

*Table 3:2   Numbers of geese wintering in western Europe\* 1969/70–1976/77*

|  | Origin | Population size | Number in Britain | Number in Ireland |
|---|---|---|---|---|
| Bean Goose | USSR/Scandinavia | 65,000 | 150 | — |
| Pink-footed Goose | Iceland | 75,000 | 75,000 | — |
|  | Svalbard | 15,500 | — | — |
| White-fronted Goose | Greenland | 13,000 | 5,500 | 7,500 |
|  | USSR | 107,400† | 7,600† | — |
| Greylag Goose | Iceland | 65,800 | 65,600 | 200 |
|  | Scotland | 2,000 | 2,000 | — |
|  | USSR/Scandinavia | 30,000 | — | — |
| Canada Goose | Britain | 19,500 | 19,500 | — |
|  | Scandinavia | 15,000+ | — | — |
| Barnacle Goose | Greenland | 28,600 | 23,600 | 5,000 |
|  | Svalbard | 4,900 | 4,900 | — |
|  | USSR\* | 41,600 | — | — |
| Brent Goose (pale) | Greenland/Canada | 12,800 | — | 12,800‡ |
|  | Svalbard | 2,500 | 500 | — |
| Brent Goose (dark) | USSR | 68,500 | 33,150 | — |

\* Based on Ogilvie (1978)
† Counts only to 1975–76
‡ Only to 1974–75 (excl. 1971–72)

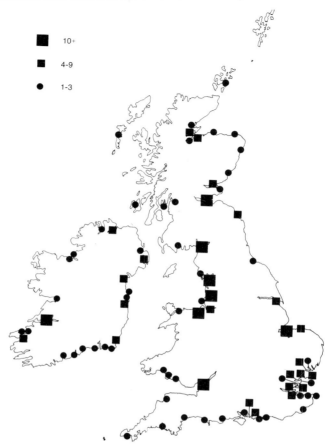

Fig. 3:5 Number of species of waders and wildfowl of international importance on each estuary in Britain and Ireland.

of Mauritania, and even some which penetrate as far as South Africa, migrate through Britain or along the Atlantic coast of Europe. Unfortunately it is not possible at the moment to estimate this number, but for some species (Sanderling, Ringed Plover and Turnstone and to a lesser extent Grey Plover and Knot) numbers could be significant. None of the western European wildfowl really migrate beyond Europe; the Pintail, Garganey and Wigeon which occur in west Africa appear to be drawn mainly from the central European area. Very few seaducks, with the exception of some Common Scoter, reach the west African coast.

DISTRIBUTION IN BRITAIN AND IRELAND

Many species of birds use the estuaries of Britain and Ireland throughout the year. Some are summer visitors, breeding here before returning to southern latitudes – terns and passerines such as the Yellow Wagtail are typical examples. Others, such as gulls, breed on estuaries but the largest numbers occur in winter when swelled by

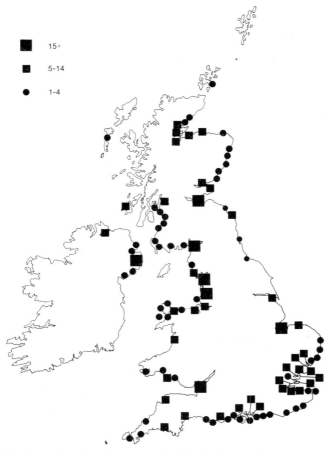

15+

5-14

1-4

Fig. 3:6 Number of species of waters and wildfowl of national importance on each estuary in Britain and Northern Ireland.

winter visitors from northern latitudes. The most characteristic estuarine birds are, however, the waders and wildfowl. The former occur in three waves – during spring and autumn migration or in winter; the last period provides the largest numbers. At this time of the year Britain's coastline supports about 2,000,000 waders. Wildfowl too are mainly winter visitors but many species in this group are found widely inland or at sea. Details of the migration and distribution patterns of waders and wildfowl will be described later in this book.

Few species are confined to estuaries but for many this habitat supports the majority of the population. It can be difficult to look objectively at the importance of estuaries, or indeed any site, unless there is a clear set of criteria against which to measure the bird numbers present. Although we have progressed a long way towards it we are still far from having an unequivocal set of criteria. Those used in the assessment and the method of presentation of the data gathered by the 'Birds of Estuaries' Enquiry' will be discussed in Chapter 6. For a general overall view of bird distribution within Britain and Ireland the information is presented here as the number of species of international (Fig. 3:5) and national (Fig. 3:6) importance occurring at each site. Figure 3:5 covers the whole of Britain and Ireland since the criteria used apply equally to each country but in Fig. 3:6 only Britain and Northern Ireland are illustrated because a different set of national criteria will apply to the Republic of Ireland.

Unfortunately our knowledge of the international or national numbers of gulls, terns, divers, grebes, cormorants, passerines etc, is still largely incomplete. Assessments based on the importance of waders and wildfowl only are, therefore, also incomplete and may result in some biased judgements. They are, however, all that we have at present and being the dominant bird group in most areas they are likely to provide the best estimate. It must also be remembered that numbers change, some species are increasing, others are decreasing, and international knowledge is still incomplete. These factors will result in the need for continual reassessment of the importance of sites.

This method of assessing the importance and relative importance of sites provides only a broad outline. In Figs. 3:5 and 3:6 the numbers of species on estuaries are separated into three groups. These represent, in ascending order, estuaries which are of (inter)national importance, of considerable (inter)national importance, and of outstanding (inter)national importance. Like all categorisation systems it has the drawback in that estuaries with different species, a different number of species or a different order of numbers for each species will be present within each category. For example Strangford Lough in early winter supports two-thirds of the European wintering population of Pale-bellied Brent Geese from Canada and Greenland; however, later in the winter three of the nearby Dublin estuaries each support over 1% of the geese. In terms of importance for that species they would be similarly classified although clearly their roles and importance are very different. However, this ever present difficulty does not invalidate the system of classification, but careful thought is required before using it. Similar problems exist when using a simple league table of numbers: should one use total waders only, shore waders only, total waders and wildfowl, or what? Does 12,000 Grey Plover (40% European wintering numbers) really equal 12,000 Dunlin (1% European)? It is also undesirable to provide a fixed league table for numbers change each year, in contrast to the international or national status which is much more stable. Also there is a tendency for its position to be quoted without qualification. If an estuary is eighteenth in a list might it not be argued that it is *only* eighteenth, or that there are seventeen which are 'better'? Undoubtedly as we know more about our bird numbers we will have to look more critically at species criteria and requirements if we are to maintain a diverse community. This provides yet another reason why the species approach should be used here.

Figure 3:5 shows the internationally important concentrations. It is not surprising that the largest estuaries have the most species in this category. In Britain there are large numbers around the Irish Sea, East Anglia, southern England and east Scotland but relatively few internationally important sites in Wales, south west England and west and north Scotland. In Ireland coastal sites are well scattered but apart from the Shannon and north Co. Kerry there are few sites on the west coast. The use of criteria for defining importance means that site boundaries too have to be described. Coastlines which support large numbers in total may be too difficult to delimit. For example, in Shetland, Orkney and the rocky coast in east Scotland, numbers of waders such as Turnstone, and possibly Purple Sandpiper, or duck such as

Long-tailed Duck or Eider, can often add up to important concentrations but no real site exists. It is much easier to define relatively short stretches of coastline which are of national significance since the numbers needed to qualify are lower, see Fig. 3:6. In a study in east Scotland Summers et al (1975) showed that the density of waders on the relatively productive rock shelf was nearly as high as on estuaries in the same area. Beach length and area are important considerations in the assessment of non-estuarine coastal bird populations. At a national level there are many more of the smaller estuaries and coastal stretches in southern England, Wales and Scotland which are of importance.

Details of the numbers and the international and national percentages involved are set out in the regional chapters later in this book. Species accounts also include further information. When looked at in terms of species of importance the major Scottish estuaries emerge as being more significant than their total wader numbers might indicate. The inner Solway Firth heads both lists with 15 internationally and 26 nationally significant species, the Moray Firth basin has 15 and 23, while the Firth of Forth has 11 and 19 respectively. Their importance is greatly swelled by the sea duck and goose numbers. In national terms the other estuaries with twenty or more species of importance are Morecambe Bay and The Wash, although the Firth of Forth, Ribble and Strangford Lough are close behind. Two other areas have been considered in their separate sections, these are the Thames and Chichester/Langstone/Portsmouth Harbours. Although there is some movement between sections of them the latter's birds are mainly separated while the Thames was not subjected to completely standardised counting, especially in parts of Kent. If the totals for each of these complexes are obtained, each rates alongside the estuaries mentioned above.

In the annual reports of the 'Birds of Estuaries Enquiry' league tables of wader numbers have been published. For reasons mentioned above this practice is not continued here. For this group of birds Morecambe Bay is outstanding with between 225,000 and 250,000 being present – and this does not include many Lapwing and Golden Plover, complete censuses of which were not attempted. The Ribble, Solway and Wash have between 150,000 and 200,000, and Dee and Thames over 100,000.

Wildfowl numbers are much lower, not surprisingly, since the individuals are larger. Seven estuaries did, however, have more than a total of 20,000 present. These were, in alphabetical order, the Firth of Forth, Lindisfarne, Mersey, Moray Firth Basin, Solway Firth, Strangford Lough and the Wash. If all wildfowl data available were incorporated the list would also include the Firth of Tay and Islay, and the Thames complex. With numbers in excess of 10,000 there are the Cromarty and Moray Firths (both within the Moray Firth Basin), Foulness and Medway (within the Thames), Morecambe Bay, the Ribble and the Severn.

### Density of waders on British estuaries

The number of birds using each estuary depends on several factors. Probably the more important are the density and availability of food and the area of feeding grounds, although possibly factors such as disturbance and position in relation to migration routes may cause slight modifications. Unfortunately, apart from one or two studies, few data are available for the first two of these and even they do not take into account the area of intertidal flats available.

The density of birds is frequently used when assessing the relative importance of an estuary. While in general it is probably true that areas of high density merit special conservation effort, the actual numbers present must be a more important factor in the assessment. In small estuaries high density may be partly influenced by unusual patterns of feeding and by roosting areas so that numbers at high tide could be misleading. For example in this survey the two highest densities of birds were on the Roach (Essex) where the 60 ha had supported a winter average of 49·4 waders/ha, and the Plym (Devon) where the figures were 97 ha and 30·9 waders/ha respectively. The first of these areas was influenced to some extent by birds from the channels around Foulness Island, while the feeding grounds for many of the Dunlin on the Plym estuary were not known but were considered to include some rocky coastline in Plymouth Sound.

The areas of all estuaries and major bays with 50+ ha of intertidal flats were measured as part of this survey. The information was obtained from tracings made of the intertidal areas, excluding saltmarshes, shown on the standard 1:50,000 Ordnance Survey maps. While there will undoubtedly be errors due to the small scale of the maps used, these are thought to be small and not likely to influence greatly the conclusions from this general overall survey. The average wader numbers from September, January and May were extracted from each site and densities calculated. Lapwing, Golden Plover and Snipe were excluded from the analysis since they rarely used the intertidal flats as feeding grounds. The densities given most closely represent those present when the intertidal flats were fully exposed on spring tides. The area available on neap tides may be very different, with the lower shore continually inundated and areas of the upper shore likewise exposed; in these circumstances the flats are either unavailable or unsuitable as feeding grounds for waders. In general the neap tide feeding zone is about 75–80% of that of spring tides. Experience in Morecambe Bay, the Wash, Dee, Solway and Severn has shown that most large sandbanks which are exposed only on extreme spring tides are not used by waders. These areas have been excluded from the bird density calculations but have been included in the description of the intertidal resource in Chapter 1. Thus the figures given here should be considered as minima since the feeding grounds measured include many smaller creeks, channels and areas of unsuitable substrata.

To look further at the relationship between size of estuary and wader density, data for the estuaries of eastern England were extracted and are summarised in Fig. 3:7. The data used were average highest annual counts, obtained by adding together the highest average monthly counts of each species, regardless of which month was involved. The region was chosen because it had full range of estuary size, a reasonable number of estuaries (23) and the estuaries are largely subjected to similar tidal, weather and migrational factors. The density of shore waders and of all waders was significantly negatively correlated with estuary size. A similar pattern is apparent for estuaries in other regions but a full analysis of these remains to be completed. The effect of the inclusion of inland waders is proportionately greater on smaller estuaries; due no doubt to a much greater edge effect operating to increase the likelihood of (especially) Lapwing occurring on the estuary. Perhaps, too, observers are more likely to have time to observe and include Lapwing on adjacent habitats on smaller estuaries where total numbers of birds is less. There was surprisingly a slightly better correlation for all waders than for shore waders only.

Very high densities occur in virtually all regions of Britain, with the one exception of north western England. This seems surprising since the region supports in excess of 500,000 waders at that time of the year. The reason probably lies with the size of

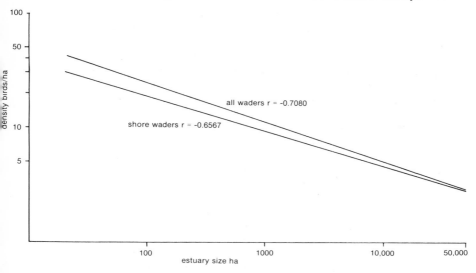

Fig. 3:7 Relationship between density of waders and estuary size in eastern England.

estuaries involved. Of the twenty-three estuaries which have more than ten shore waders per hectare only three were over 1,000 ha, the 1,600 ha of the Stour (Essex/Suffolk) being the largest. The largest estuaries, i.e. those over 10,000 ha, had densities ranging from 8·4 waders/ha in Morecambe Bay down to 1·9 waders/ha at Foulness. No doubt the inclusion of many unsuitable feeding areas is the main reason for this apparent decline in 'attractiveness' as size of estuary increases.

A summary of the regional and seasonal variations in densities is presented in Table 3:3. Since total numbers present in winter are much higher than in autumn and spring it is not surprising that densities follow this trend. In general the winter

*Table 3:3 Seasonal variations in the average number of shore waders per ha occurring in the regions of Britain*

|  | Total area (ha) | September | January | May |
|---|---|---|---|---|
| South-western England | 18,160 | 1·95 | 3·96 | 0·68 |
| Southern England | 10,749 | 2·65 | 7·95 | 0·63 |
| Eastern England | 80,403 | 3·16 | 4·55 | 1·13 |
| North-western England | 57,875 | 5·98 | 6·48 | 1·87 |
| Wales | 26,166 | 2·14 | 4·03 | 0·97 |
| Eastern Scotland | 25,131 | 2·08 | 3·75 | 0·40 |
| Western Scotland | 22,249 | 2·50 | 3·18 | 0·64 |
| Britain, whole | 240,733 | 3·44 | 4·86 | 1·12 |

densities are between 1·3 and 2·0 times the autumn figures, whereas in spring they are rarely more than 20–40% of the numbers present even in autumn. It is perhaps interesting to speculate as to why numbers should be lower in autumn than in winter. After all, the invertebrate biomass is at its peak in autumn and at its most available. In autumn very large numbers of waders are found over the Wadden Sea but the relatively severe winter weather there forces them westwards to Britian and Ireland. The birds may, therefore, be maximising their energy intake by using the very productive shallow wetland in autumn and then using our estuaries in the relatively mild winters. We could no doubt support more waders in autumn (assuming inter- and intra-specific territoriality and aggression does not limit them at the present time) but an increase in autumn may well reduce the winter food level and lead to a lower holding capacity. If this is so we should be concerned about the effect of the many reclamation plans put forward for the Wadden Sea. The great majority of estuaries follow the national pattern of supporting more waders in winter than in autumn; most of these are, with a single exception, small estuaries in south-west England, Wales and Scotland. The exception is the Ribble which supports twice as many in autumn as in winter. The reasons why this estuary should stand out are not apparent. Only the Dyfi (Gwynedd/Dyfed) supports more birds during the May passage than it does at other times of the year; again, why is unclear.

The regional variations in wader densities show a number of trends. North-west England not only supports a large percentage of the total numbers, but, despite the size of estuaries, stands out clearly as having a high density of birds at all seasons. The importance of passage populations in eastern England is also shown. While it is not surprising that Scottish estuaries are, on average, fairly poor for waders (they make up with their wildfowl), it is perhaps remarkable that the south-western

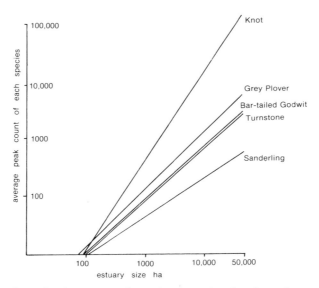

Fig. 3:8 Relationship between numbers of each species of wader and estuary size in eastern England. Correlation coefficients (r: Bar-tailed Godwit (0·7637), Black-tailed Godwit (−0·05905), Curlew (0·7283), Dunlin (0·8332), Grey Plover (0·8592), Knot

estuaries should show similar wader density characteristics.

Of considerable conservation interest is the relationship between the number of each species and the area of the estuary. Again eastern England was chosen to examine this aspect and the resulting relationships are shown in Fig. 3:8. All species, except Black-tailed Godwit, have highly significant positive correlations with estuary size. This is to be expected since generally the larger the estuary the more likely it is to include areas of habitat which each species prefers. Of the ten species which show this trend three – Turnstone, Sanderling and Ringed Plover – and possibly a fourth – Oystercatcher – might have been expected to have shown a less strong relationship. This is particularly true for the first two species, and all are species which occur in moderate or even large numbers on sandy and rocky coasts. The inclusion of coastal sites which are not estuarine may result in some modifications to the pattern. In Fig. 3:8a five species are shown which all apparently need estuaries – or at least intertidal areas. They also require substantial areas before they occur even in small numbers, in fact it appears that an estuary of 70–110 ha is needed before they regularly occur. The slope of the lines also indicates further the degree of relationship, the steeper the line the proportionately greater will be the increase in numbers with increasing estuary size. Knot show the strongest dependence and Sanderling the least; the variation in actual numbers on each estuary is least in Knot and greatest in Sanderling – hence the highest correlation coefficient for the former and the lowest for the latter.

In contrast, Fig. 3:8b shows species which are slightly less than totally dependent on estuaries or those which when they occur on small areas of mud are found in flocks. Ringed Plover and Dunlin have the latter characteristic, especially during migration periods. Oystercatcher is the slight anomaly, having an intermediate

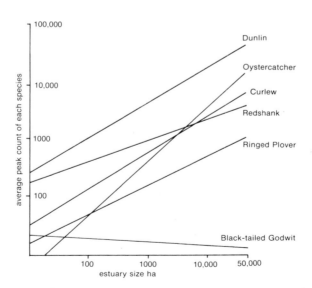

(0·9427), Oyster-catcher (0·8730), Redshank (0·6770), Ringed Plover (0·7144), Sanderling (0·6206), Turnstone (0·7945). All except Black-tailed Godwit are significant at least p = 0·05.

regression line between the strictly intertidal and more flexible species. In eastern England it does not feed in fields to the extent it may on the western coasts; probably here the relatively small estuary size needed for some birds to be present is related to the pre- and post-breeding concentrations of 30–60 in many of the small estuaries, particularly in Suffolk. Very few are found there in winter. The other two species, Curlew and Redshank, are commonly found on saltmarshes, pastures, plough or drainage ditches away from the intertidal flats. This leaves us with the anomalous Black-tailed Godwit which shows no relationship with estuary size. The species is highly clumped in its distribution and indeed relatively scarce in eastern England. Factors such as a specialist food supply on mudflats or suitable wet inland pasture probably play dominant roles in determining distribution and abundance.

CHAPTER 4

# Threats – barrages and reservoirs

For many years the wide open spaces of estuaries have attracted engineering proposals for barrages. Certainly, serious consideration was given to a barrage on the Severn estuary as long ago as 1933. The reasons put forward for development have been many, such as water storage, tidal power generation and improvement of road or rail links. Between 1960 and 1974 the main aim was to provide adequate supplies of fresh water, but this was usually allied, at least initially, with road crossings. The only proposals for generation of tidal power have been for the Severn estuary. While estuarine reservoirs and tidal barrages have many principles and problems relating to nature conservation in common, there are also many differences between them. They are, therefore, considered separately here.

## FRESHWATER RESERVOIR PROPOSALS

There is no shortage of water falling on England and Wales, but its distribution is uneven, with the bulk of it falling where there are fewest people. The authorities have traditionally used three main sources for water supply. Straight abstraction from rivers and groundwater accumulations were the original sources, but increasingly a constant water supply was needed and many reservoirs were built. These involved either the damming of a stream in a valley or, particularly in south-east England, the building of an embanked reservoir and filling it with pumped water. Valleys where flooding was practicable or desirable were relatively few and as the demand for water increased during the twentieth century so the alternatives left decreased. The conflict between water authorities and environmental interest inevitably became more serious.

*Table 4:1  Population forecasts to 2001 (in millions)**

| | 1965 | 1971 | 1972 | 1975 |
|---|---|---|---|---|
| Date forecasted | | | | |
| 2001 population | 66·0 | 58·5 | 55·5 | 52·1 |

* Based on estimates by the Office of Population Censuses and Surveys (from Water Resources Board 1973 and Central Water Planning Unit 1976)

In the mid-1960s concern about the water supplies likely to be available by 2001 were based on two related and predicted values, the population level and the total demand.

The estimates of future population size have steadily decreased during the last ten years to such a degree that 14,000,000 fewer users are now anticipated (Table 4:1). Demand, even when based on the 1971 population estimates, is now estimated to be about 7% down. This means that the short-fall of supplies is reduced by 53·3% from 1,800 megalitres per day (Ml/d) to 840 Ml/d. Such a decrease lessens the immediate prospect of massive water storage schemes at all sites, though obviously increased demands will still need to be met. Projections are, however, at best a guide and at worst wholly misleading, so it is quite possible that subsequent patterns of demand or population changes would materially alter them. Equally, regional patterns may differ and priorities change.

Initially, plans for estuarine storage were expansive. Barrages were considered for the Severn, Solway, Morecambe Bay and the Wash, but were soon ruled out on several counts. In each case a barrage would have meant a massive initial expenditure on a technology which was not yet proven in Britain. The Wash barrage was considered too difficult even by the more experienced Dutch engineers. In the Severn and Solway schemes the costs of transporting water were also considered to be prohibitive. By 1970 it was realised that the projected demand would be lower and attention was switched to smaller and ecologically less, though still significantly, damaging bunded reservoir projects. Indeed by the time of the second review of storage in Morecambe Bay the bunded reservoirs then proposed were very much smaller than in Schemes II and III.

It is perhaps worth looking with hindsight at the whole process of design changes. The first proposals involved very large barrages, then large bunded reservoirs, now perhaps much smaller ones seem suitable. There will be design changes, of course, as

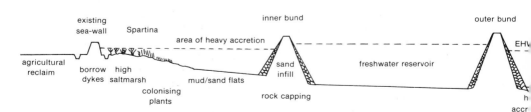

Fig 4:1 Cross-section of a typical estuarine pumped storage reservoir with no further development.

further hydrological studies reveal new features of sediment deposition. This should, however, not deflect a relevant question. Why were the smaller, less costly, schemes not considered first? Perhaps they are less interesting from an engineering viewpoint. The developers may have thought that suggestions for barrages would make the public aware of the need for large schemes while the conservation movement would object to the massive environmental impact. Then when a smaller scheme is proposed the opposition will be less!

Bunded reservoirs are simply reservoirs which are enclosed by an artificial bank (or bund). They have no natural freshwater inflow and depend on a pumped supply, hence their alternative name of pumped storage reservoirs. At Morecambe Bay they would be placed at some distance beyond the existing sea-wall to ensure that any back seepage would not affect present agricultural areas. A cross section of a typical bunded reservoir is shown in Fig. 4:1. Experimental bunds incorporated into the feasibility study on the Wash have shown that it would be technically possible for such a reservoir to be built on the higher intertidal flats. Between the inner bund and the existing sea-wall there would be an area of high level flats, which may already support a saltmarsh. Increased sedimentation would be expected to occur if no development of the area took place. In practice, in order to allow full access to the reservoir, some development is likely. This zone is called a polder, a Dutch word for reclaimed land. It may be used for agriculture, industrial development, nature reserves or for leisure activities, or any combination of them, depending upon the local priorities. The bunds themselves are likely to be relatively uniform to facilitate maintenance and to have quite steeply sloping sides. The water inside would be deep. The general implications for birds are considered later in this chapter. First the three major water storage schemes (on the Dee, Morecambe Bay and the Wash) under consideration at present are briefly summarised, followed by the tidal power schemes on the Severn. The schemes for the Solway are not considered since it is unlikely that they could proceed.

### Dee

The Dee crossing and reservoir scheme was one of the first full feasibility studies undertaken (Binnie and Partners 1971) although the work was primarily on the technical feasibility of the project. It was not until six years later that a detailed appraisal of some of the ecological implications was published (Buxton, Gilham and Pugh-Thomas 1977). A major attraction for this scheme was the opportunity for a new road link across the Dee as the present bridge at Queensferry is severely congested. Much of the initial debate centred on the very large area of intertidal flats proposed for reclamation (Figs 4:2 and 3) and the line of the road crossing. Two routes were put forward, either from Burton to Flint (Figs 4:6 and 7) or from Gayton to Greenfield (Figs 4:4 and 5). Nature conservation bodies and the Cheshire County Council strongly recommended that, should the development take place, the former route would be preferable on conservation grounds. Subsequent to the publication of the feasibility study, some of the assumptions made have been invalidated. The shape of the reservoirs was shown not to be ideal by a hydraulic model and secondly, plans for an extension of the Shotton Steelworks by British Steel had been shelved.

Accordingly, Binnie and Partners (1974) published a supplementary report incorporating new features. In particular (Figs 4:4–7) one or two small reservoirs were proposed for part of the estuary which had been set aside for the expansion of the steelworks. The bund shapes of the now reduced (but still large) reservoirs in the

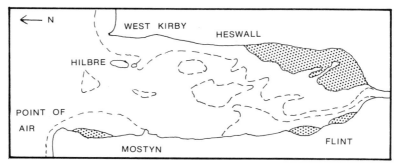

Fig. 4:2 Dee estuary showing main features, including mid-tide level (dotted line).

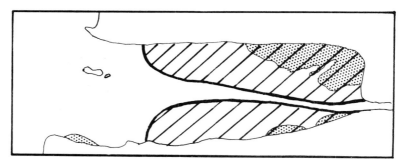

Fig. 4:3 Preliminary residual estuary shape plan for reservoirs on the Dee.

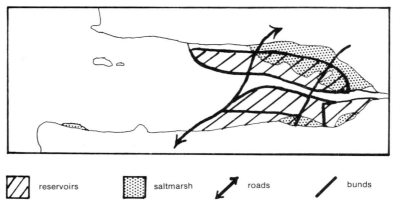

Fig. 4:4 Extended shape plan for reservoirs with Gayton-Greenfield road crossing.

middle of the estuary were realigned to preserve a conventional estuary shape. The only exception to this latter principle was the Gayton-Greenfield modified scheme (Fig. 4:5); in this, slack water in the angle of the constructions on the Wirral shore would inevitably lead to massive siltation and saltmarsh encroachment over the intertidal flats. The new schemes would allow for a start to be made with a road

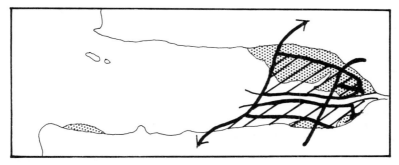

Fig. 4:5 Contracted shape for reservoirs with Gayton-Greenfield road crossing.

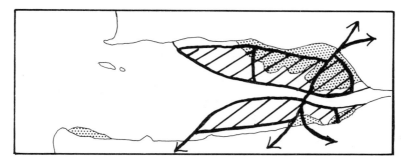

Fig. 4:6 Extended shape for reservoirs with Flint-Burton road crossing.

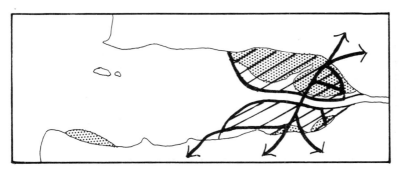

Fig. 4:7 Contracted shape for reservoirs with Flint-Burton road crossing.

crossing and one or two small reservoirs, the other reservoirs could be built in stages as dictated by the revised projected demand.

Although the inner section, above the line of the Burton to Flint crossing, includes a substantial area of saltmarsh, the mud flats between this and the present training wall along the river Dee are of high ornithological value. Many birds roost on the marsh and feed across this area on the rising and especially falling tides. It is also the area where virtually all of the Black-tailed Godwits and many of the Pintails feed, both species of international significance. If the reservoir covering Parkgate, Heswall

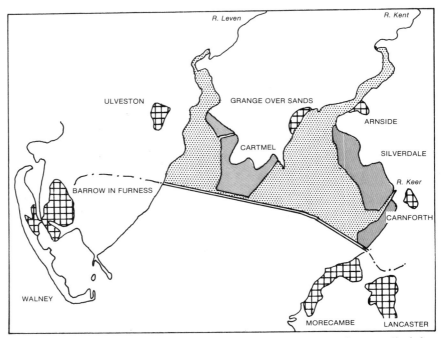

Fig. 4:8 Morecambe Bay Barrage – Scheme I: involving a main barrage. Shaded area = stored water; cross-hatched = polders; double line = barrage with road; dot-dash line = possible road.

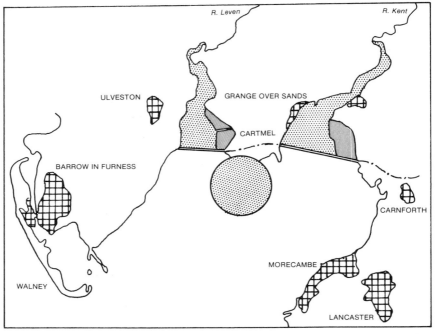

Fig. 4:9 Morecambe Bay Barrage – Scheme IIa: involving twin barrages with a Cartmel reservoir. Key as Fig. 4:8.

76

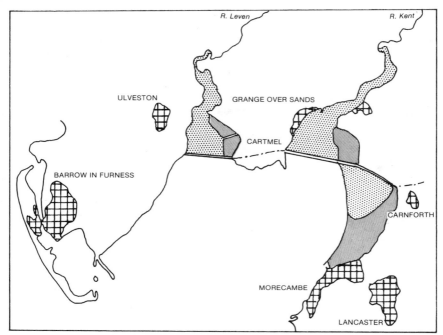

Fig. 4:10 Morecambe Bay Barrage – Scheme IIb: involving twin barrages with a Silverdale reservoir. Key as Fig. 4:8.

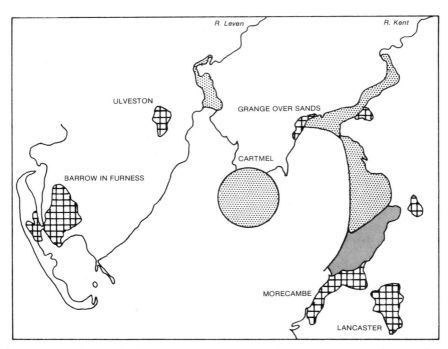

Fig. 4:11 Morecambe Bay Barrage – Scheme III: involving river barriers with Cartmel and Silverdale reservoirs. Key as Fig. 4:8.

77

and Neston Marshes and adjacent intertidal flats were to be built, the scheme would have a still greater impact on the birds of the estuary. Major feeding grounds for many species of waders and most of the wildfowl lie in a midshore zone off the saltmarshes. Numbers of birds are particularly large in autumn when Burton Marsh may support up to 32,000 waders, and the Parkgate complex up to 27,000 waders, although average numbers of birds roosting on the inner and middle estuary are 30,000 waders and 5,000 wildfowl in autumn and 25,700 and 2,000 in winter.

The report by the Water Resources Board (1973) recommended that staged development of the Dee should be part of the national water strategy. The implementation of the first stage should take place by 1990.

### Morecambe Bay

This embayment, incorporating the estuaries of the rivers Wyre, Lune, Keer, Kent and Leven, was the second British estuary to come under scrutiny for water storage in recent years, although suggestions had been put forward for a barrage from Morecambe to Barrow as long ago as the 1890s. The first was the Solway Firth, a desk study of which was completed in 1964. In 1965 the Water Resources Board was asked to undertake a feasibility study for a barrage across Morecambe Bay. The initial phase was a desk study (Water Resources Board 1966) which was followed by a full feasibility study between 1967 and 1970. Many aspects were considered, ranging from engineering studies, through economics to the biological implications.

Although the original terms of reference related to a complete barrage, other designs, in particular involving pumped storage reservoirs, were considered during the feasibility study. A summary of the four main schemes is shown in Figs 4:8–11. Schemes I, IIa and IIb provided alternative possibilities for water storage, plus various road crossings from the M6 to Barrow-in-Furness. Scheme III, however, was designed more specifically for water storage.

Clearly, the potential impact on the wildlife of the estuary differs considerably with each scheme. On the debit side, differing areas and types of intertidal flats and saltmarshes would be removed, reducing the feeding or breeding grounds of many species of birds. On the credit side, there could be gains from the newly created polders or the open water areas. The immediate result of these losses and benefits are fairly easy to predict, at least subjectively, but the net result is much more difficult to determine, as indeed are the many indirect effects on the birds as a result of changes in the sedimentation or hydrological patterns. Several species are unlikely to be seriously affected by any scheme; Bar-tailed Godwit, Grey Plover and Pink-footed Geese are virtually restricted to the Lune estuary, while Eiders occur only in the Walney region. It is thought improbable that serious indirect effects would be felt in these areas even if a full barrage were built. The full scheme would directly affect internationally important numbers of 11 species, while Scheme IIa would affect six, IIb seven and III also seven. In each case, Knot would suffer most with a minimum of 1·2% of the European population directly affected, while as many as 6·2% could be affected by a full barrage.

After the submission of the report on the feasibility study (Water Resources Board 1972) relatively little was heard of the possibility of development of water storage at Morecambe Bay. This was mainly because alternative estuary storage sites, the Dee and the Wash, were being considered by detailed feasibility studies. However, since the re-organisation of the water industry in 1974, further plans have been proposed and a reappraisal undertaken by the North Western Water Authority. The suggested designs involve much smaller bunded reservoirs, although still sited in the feasibility study areas. It should be remembered that water storage is not the only threat to Morecambe Bay; recently outline proposals have mentioned the possibility of a gas terminal being sited in the Lune/Wyre estuary. This will be covered more fully in Chapter 5.

*Wash*

Although a storage scheme involving a complete barrage across the Wash from Bennington to Snettisham was an alternative considered in the mid-1960s (Binnie and Partners 1965), the desk study (Water Resources Board 1970) concentrated on smaller bunded reservoirs which could be built on the foreshore of the inner Wash. The designs of these and some alternatives subsequently investigated during the feasibility study (Central Water Planning Unit 1976) are shown in Figs 4:12–16. Initially the plans were for a four stage development (Fig. 4:12) but on many grounds (primarily cost and a decrease in the projected demand for water) the proposals were restricted to the south-east of the Wash. As a result of tests on the hydraulic model, the shapes for the first stage of the original reservoirs (Fig. 4:13) were modified (Fig. 4:14) to reduce sedimentation and obviate the need for training walls to contain the river channels. All bunded reservoirs would be sited 1–3 km away from the present sea-wall. This polder area between the bund and the seawall

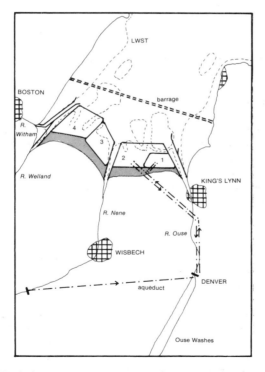

Fig. 4:12 The Wash showing reservoir positions for stages 1–4 and a possible barrage line from the Desk Study. The aqueducts are simplified from subsequent reports. Hatched areas = reclaimed land.

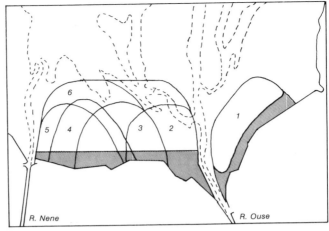

Fig. 4:13 Wash reservoirs: preliminary layouts for alternative reservoirs. 1 = Bulldog, 2 = West Stones, 3 = Breast, 4 = Westmark, 5 = Wingland, 6 = Walpole, 7 = Terrington.

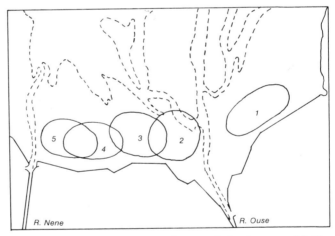

Fig. 4:14 Wash reservoirs: modified original proposals for first stage: labelling as Fig. 4:13.

could have an area of 3–10 km² depending on which design was implemented. The investigations narrowed down to assessing alternatives for a two-staged development with a smaller first stage and a larger second stage. Figures 4:15 and 16 show the two main contenders; the recommended scheme is shown in Fig. 4:16.

The biological studies for the Wash feasibility study were the most intensive yet made for any such investigation. As a result, many of the processes involved and the descriptive and predictive aspects are known in detail (Goss-Custard 1977d, Goss-Custard et al 1977, Goss-Custard, Jones and Newbury 1977). Of the single reservoirs, only one, West Stones, would not directly affect an internationally significant number of any species. Bull Dog, Breast Sands and Westmark reservoirs,

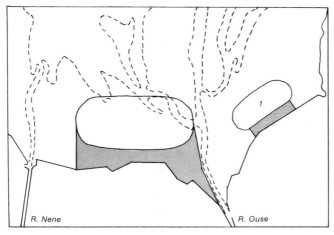

Fig. 4:15 Wash reservoirs: two reservoir layout involving Bulldog (first stage) and Breast Sand schemes. Numbers as Fig. 4:13.

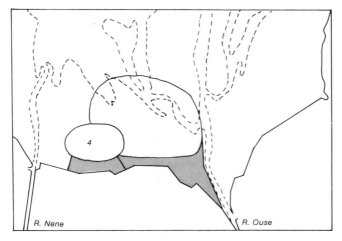

Fig. 4:16 Wash reservoirs: preferred two reservoir layout involving Westmark (first stage) and Hull Sand schemes. 4 = Westmark.

each covering approximately 6.5 km², would each affect between 15,000 and 17,000 waders and involve one or two internationally important concentrations. When stage one and the larger (an additional 10 km²) stage two are combined, however, there would be a much greater effect. All schemes, including the preferred Westmark and Hull Sand reservoirs, would displace 45,000 or more waders and involve at least five species of international importance. The numbers of birds involved are somewhat smaller than in the Morecambe Bay reservoir proposals, but so is the area.

The intertidal area is, ornithologically, the most important aspect of either a one or two phase Wash reservoir. There are, however, potentially related problems concerning the water regime of the Ouse Washes. This area of low grazing land between the New and the Old Bedford Rivers depends on winter and spring flooding to maintain its importance for wintering and breeding waterfowl. The Ouse Washes has been designated as one of the 13 United Kingdom sites under the Ramsar Convention. Figure 4:2 shows that these rivers would supply some water, via underground pipes, to the pumped storage reservoirs on the Wash. It is, however, possible with a careful management programme to prevent a serious decrease in water availability for flooding and especially for topping up dykes during the breeding season, at least with a stage one reservoir scheme. If, however, a much greater abstraction was required, then significant repercussion might follow.

The conclusion of the feasibility study was that despite the practicability of building bunded reservoirs on the Wash, they would not be needed before the end of this century nor would they, at this stage, present a viable economic alternative to other methods of obtaining water.

TIDAL POWER PROPOSALS

*Severn*

Tidal power generation was first put forward for the Severn in 1933. Elsewhere tidal power has been harnessed on the relatively small Rance estuary in north-west France, starting in 1966. No insoluble technical problems were encountered although perhaps the much larger scale of the Severn proposals may pose some. In Canada, a study was made between 1966 and 1969 of potential sites in the Bay of Fundy, the area with the greatest tidal range (up to 15·5 m — 48 ft) in the world. It was considered then uneconomical to embark on a massive tidal generation plant; however, a reassessment made recently by the Bay of Fundy Tidal Review Board reached the conclusion that it was practical and economical to build a power

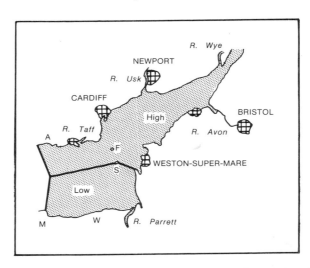

Fig. 4:17 Severn Estuary Barrage: Martin (1974) scheme. A = Aberthaw; F = Flatholm; M = Minehead; S = Steepholm; W = Watchet; H = High water level; L = Low water level.

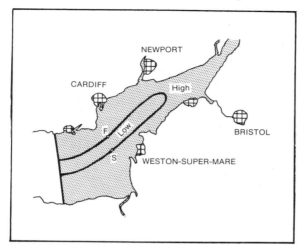

Fig. 4:18 Severn Estuary Barrage: MEL scheme. Key as Fig. 4:17.

generation plant on Cumberland Bay. This is an area supporting about 20,000 waders during the autumn migration. Similar economic doubts have been expressed about a tidal power project at Secure Bay, Western Australia.

Many schemes have been put forward for the development of the Severn estuary although here we are concerned with the barrage proposals, and six of these are illustrated in Figs 4:17–22. The original simple barrage from Sudbrook–Redwick along the line of the present Severn Tunnel has been omitted from this diagram since it is no longer a serious contender for power production. Almost innumerable alternative combinations of lines for the barrage(s) and reclamation of the foreshore have been proposed. Each of these schemes bring a different set of environmental problems, although all have some in common. Most barrage lines run from Lavernock Point (South Glamorgan) to Brean Down (Somerset) or sometimes Sand Point (Avon) and incorporate the islands of Flatholm and Steepholm in their structure. They embrace all of the intertidal flats of the Taff/Ely estuary, parts of the South Glamorgan coast and all of the Gwent, Gloucester and Avon coasts. However, Martin's (Fig. 4:17) and the original MEL (Fig. 4:18) schemes would extend approximately to Aberthaw in the north and Watchet in the south. Thus a much larger area of South Glamorgan and Somerset would be directly affected, including the important area of Bridgwater Bay. An account of the birds of the Severn was given by Ferns (1977).

There are three barrage designs for generating electricity from tidal movements. They are: (i) a simple barrage with turbines driven by the ebb tide; (ii) a simple barrage with turbines powered by both the flood and ebb tibes; and (iii) a complex barrage with a secondary basin kept at a different water level so that continuous generation of power is possible. The 1933 scheme and Wilson's (Fig. 4:20) involved the simpler patterns, but the production of electricity would be periodic; in the case of (i) perhaps as little as eight effective hours per day, while in (ii) there would still be two slack periods per tide around low and high water. The power would only periodically be available at the time of peak demand and, unless power could be stored elsewhere, the scheme would be relatively inefficient.

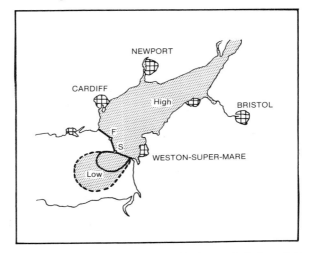

Fig. 4:19 Severn Estuary Barrage: MEL reduced scheme (dashed) and Shaw scheme (solid line). NEDECO scheme similar to Shaw scheme but with a small outer basin back to Steepholm, not Brean. Key as Fig. 4:17.

Most of the recently proposed schemes (MEL Fig. 4:18, MEL reduced Fig. 4:19, Shaw Fig. 4:19, CWPU Fig. 4:21 and Nedeco double scheme) however, include the concept of two basins. A high basin would fill at high tide and could empty into a low basin at low tide. The energy generated by this system could also be used to pump water into the high level basin during periods when demand for conventional electricity is low (e.g. at night); it would therefore incorporate a system for storing energy. Generally, the low and high basins would each generate electricity on both the flood and ebb tides as well as having this extra facility. Inside the high level

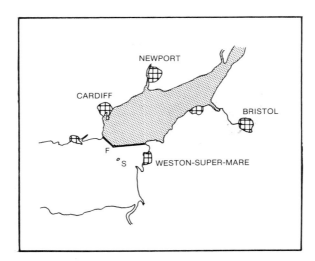

Fig. 4:20 Severn Estuary Barrage: Wilson Scheme.

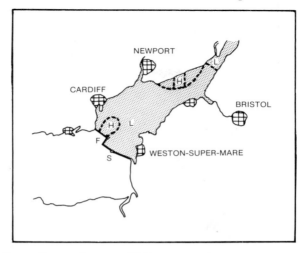

Fig. 4:21 Severn Estuary Barrage: CWPU (1977) scheme incorporating freshwater reservoirs. Key as Fig. 4:17.

reservoir, which invariably occupies the largest area, this would result in a more stable water level with the water fluctuating over the upper part of the present tidal range. The tidal range at Avonmouth would be reduced from about 12 m to 3–6 m on spring tides. In Shaw's scheme, the tidal pattern would be altered additionally to a 24 hour frequency. The net result would be a reduction in the area of the intertidal flats, which would affect the feeding regimes of many waders, although in ways that cannot yet be established. Mudge (1979) has shown that many birds would be displaced by Shaw's scheme. The impact on wildfowl, excepting Shelduck, may not be

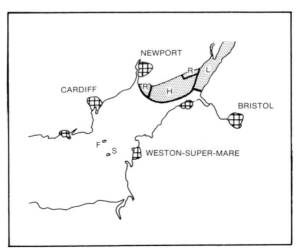

Fig. 4:22 Hooker scheme for an airport and industrial development on the Severn. Key as Fig. 4:17; R = reclaimed area.

detrimental, as they feed mostly on adjacent land. They could be affected, however, by changes in water regimes (as pumping would become necessary to remove excess water from drainage ditches that now discharge at low tide) which may allow arable crops to be grown where present drainage is inadequate, or which may encourage industrial reclamation (Owen 1975).

The relatively stable water level will have many other implications for the biology of the system. The reduced flow will allow sediment to settle, alter the sediment deposition characteristics of the exposed intertidal flats and reduce the oxygen dissolved in the water. In turn, the high nutrient load entering the estuary from sewage, agricultural run-off and industrial effluent, will increase the danger of algal blooms and eutrophication. The already high heavy metal release into the estuary would be trapped within the finer sediments of the barrage and would be more likely to be taken up into the food chain (Firth 1975, Little 1975). Another potential problem is the warm water inflow from the three nuclear and two conventional power stations already operating within the estuary. A reduction in water flow could result in some thermal stratification within the reservoirs.

A final aspect of these schemes of relevance to nature conservation, is the potential for reclamation of the remaining foreshore and the massive expansion of industry on to the low 'levels' that surround the estuary. Several schemes have been advanced for an airport and although that from Atkins and Partners makes no barrage proposals, the other two do. These are from Hooker (Fig. 4:22) and from Underwood and Snow. A proportion (unfortunately unknown) of waders and ducks may be able to remain after the reservoirs are built, but the further development of the foreshore or adjacent land is likely to impose additional serious problems.

At this stage very little hard data are available to enable an environmental impact statement to be drawn up, but a committee has been formed by the Department of Energy to supervise a feasibility study which will include ecological research. It is hoped this will lead to a much clearer assessment.

OVERALL IMPLICATIONS

There can be no doubting the massive environmental impact of barrage or reservoir schemes (Prater 1978). Three separate detailed effects need to be considered – the disruption caused by the construction, the sudden loss of the intertidal flats on its completion and finally the long term effects of habitat changes.

Most of the comments in this book refer to the effects of the various schemes on the estuarine birds. Of course such developments would influence many other aspects of natural history as well as having a social impact. After birds, the most clearly documented interests are fisheries, seals and plants. Fisheries are particularly important economically. The Morecambe Bay and Severn proposals would each obstruct major salmon rivers; there are extensive shrimping operations in the Wash and Morecambe Bay, and the former has one of the largest cockle industries in Britain. All estuaries are hatching grounds and provide food and shelter for young marine fish – especially flatfish such as flounders, soles, dabs and plaice, although others also occur. The loss of a major part of one of these estuaries could, therefore, have ramifications not only for fishermen within the estuary, but also for stocks at sea or in inflowing rivers.

Common Seals form a significant constituent of the fauna of the Wash; this area supports up to 7,000 individuals which is more than any other site in Britain. For plants, the impact would be considerable as a large area of saltmarsh would be enclosed by each scheme. Few of the marshes involved are of outstanding international importance, although several support species of plants which are at or close to the edge of their range. Surrounding areas, too, will have problems arising from schemes of the size proposed. Of special significance is the amount of construction traffic and the source of building materials such as stone; local sources are usually preferred and this can put pressure on nearby geological formations, which themselves may be of special value.

When assessing the impact of any scheme, there are a number of general implications which need to be considered. Birds have complicated patterns of usage of estuaries, and simple calculations based on single or even monthly counts may not reveal the necessary details. Seven broad aspects are briefly discussed here in order to illustrate some of these major points.

### (i) *Total numbers of birds using each estuary*

Anyone who has watched an estuary in detail will know that although there may be some degree of stability to the number of birds using the areas, there are always birds moving through it. This is especially true during the main migration periods but, to a lesser extent, it also happens in winter.

Counts which are made on a single day each month cannot expect to quantify such throughput. Equally, the average highest monthly count (the measure used here to detail and compare the bird numbers of all estuaries) does not describe the total number of birds occurring. Some information is available from the Wash, where intensive ringing by the Wash Wader Ringing Group has enabled calculations to be made to answer this question. These indicate that about a third more birds use the Wash than is revealed by the counts. This still does not adequately describe birds only present for less than a week, since the chance of their capture is very low. The Wash is known as an extremely important estuary for passage birds, but other estuaries too would show similar patterns if data existed. On west coast estuaries such as Morecambe Bay, estimates result in a 15–20% increase over the highest count aggregate figure.

### (ii) *Use made of different estuaries by one bird*

Numbers vary between months, so it is clear birds use each area for only part of the year. The understanding of the interrelationship between estuaries is a fascinating and vital aspect when considering conservation actions for birds. A simple example is shown by Ringed Plovers on the Wash. A nationally important number breeds here and after starting moult, the birds migrate to other British estuaries, especially Morecambe Bay, where they winter. Thus two estuaries are used by, and are vital for, the Wash population of this species. Both the Wash and Morecambe Bay are important staging posts in spring and autumn for other populations of Ringed Plover which breed in Iceland, Greenland and Scandinavia. Other species, such as the Knot, show a much more complex pattern involving estuaries in several countries. For example, a Knot breeding in Greenland will spend three weeks in May and again in July on coastal areas in Iceland building up fat reserves for crossings of the Atlantic. In the autumn after leaving Iceland, it arrives in the German or Dutch Wadden Sea where it moults; as the winter approaches, it migrates to the Wash where it may remain or may move to estuaries in northern or western Britain. In March it moves back to the Dutch Wadden Sea and, as the weather improves, into the German Wadden Sea, where the main deposition of fat takes place to enable it to reach Iceland again. Each estuarine area plays a specific role in the cycle and is therefore a link in the chain. Every species uses a chain of sites, and the loss of any unit may have far wider implications than may be immediately apparent.

### (iii) *Site faithfulness*

There is a considerable body of evidence to show that birds tend to return to the same breeding, wintering or migration areas each year. This happens in waders and many species of estuary birds, e.g. Bewick's Swan (Evans 1979). Clearly, experience of feeding conditions or patterns of predator activity in an area can aid survival, so the phenomenon of recurrence might be expected. Similar reasoning also applies to encourage birds to be sedentary once they have found or returned to a good food source. Minton (1976) showed that several species of waders (especially Dunlin, Redshank, Turnstone and Sanderling) were highly sedentary on the Wash, hardly ever moving away from one section of the embayment during the course of a winter. This might be expected of the last two species because they use a specialised habitat, but Dunlin and Redshank are adaptable species. Some others are relatively mobile even within a winter; the Knot is typical of this group. Its movements may be due to the variable nature of the food supply, *Macoma* and *Cerastoderma* having irregular spatfalls. Here there could be an advantage (see Chapter 2) in moving around to locate food sources.

### (iv) *The localised nature of different populations*

Most species of waders and several species of waterfowl have discontinuous breeding ranges; this results in separate populations which show different characteristics in the timing of their movements or distribution. Even with a country as small as Britain, many differences exist. For example, Scottish and Icelandic Oystercatchers winter mainly on the west coast, while on the east coast Norwegian birds predominate. Similar but more pronounced patterns are evident when looking at international distributions. Britain and Ireland are extremely important for Icelandic birds – Redshank, Golden Plover, Oystercatcher, Black-tailed Godwit, Whooper Swan – while populations of these species from Scandinavia and the rest of Europe tend to winter in eastern Britain, the coasts of continental Europe or in Africa. The loss of just one critical estuary could seriously affect one population of a species, even though not necessarily threatening the existence of a whole species. From an evolutionary point of view (as well as the loss that the country on the receiving end would suffer) such local reductions or even extinctions are highly undesirable.

### (v) *The patterns of age distribution*

The age of geese can be seen in the field by reference to plumage characters. Adult Brent Geese without young and adults with families tend to occur in different areas. The successful breeders are those most likely to resort to feeding inland or on the higher intertidal flats, while those feeding well out on the mud are mostly flocks of adults. In most species, the differences between adults and immatures is not as clear, so observations are more difficult to make. Other studies indicate that separation of ages may be widespread.

In the Oystercatcher, most birds feeding inland are immatures or deformed adults, while virtually all on the main feeding grounds are adults. In the summer, when the adults are breeding, the immatures come onto the mussel beds, but are actively displaced by adults on their return in the autumn (J. D. Goss-Custard pers. comm.). A separation of ages could be inferred from the ratio of adults to juveniles in birds caught in Morecambe Bay by the Morecambe Bay Ringing Group: very many more juvenile Knots were caught where feeding grounds and numbers of birds were small, and disturbance at high tide was considerable compared with large, disturbance free areas.

Perhaps the clearest age segregation takes place during the summer months when the adults are on their breeding territories. Most waterfowl are relatively large and do not breed in their first summer. There are exceptions, such as Dunlin or Little Stint, but virtually all estuary birds of one hundred grams or more show delayed maturity. Most medium-sized waders, for example Knot and Turnstone, are able to breed in their second summer, while large ones, such as the Oystercatcher and many gulls, may be four or five years old before breeding. The older immatures may be physiologically capable of breeding, but social factors prevent it. As a result, many immature birds remain south of the breeding grounds throughout the summer. They are not as widespread on British and Irish estuaries as wintering birds. Indeed only a handful of the larger areas support more than a hundred or two. Of particular significance are the Wash, Ribble, Morecambe Bay and the Dee. There is also a tendency for only relatively small areas of these estuaries to be used, respectively the east Wash, the Crossens/Banks Marshes, the Lune estuary and the inner Parkgate/ Burton/Shotton Marshes.

The concentration of immature birds on just a few sections of a few estuaries certainly deserves the close attention of conservationists. The fact that one age group could be displaced by a major development and that there are few apparently suitable summering areas, indicates a potentially weak link in the life cycle of many species. For example, there have been plans put forward for a reservoir on Bulldog Sands on the Wash. This would affect directly the summering birds in the east Wash. Similarly, and perhaps more immediate, are the plans for bunded reservoirs on the Dee discussed earlier in this chapter. If any of these were built, the head of the estuary would be destroyed and with it the main summer feeding areas. Fortunately, in this case, the RSPB recently bought a substantial area of the inner Dee and may have partly averted the threat for the moment.

There is age segregation of waders, too, during migration, when temporal and spatial separation occurs. If the adults winter south of Britain they migrate through first, the juveniles one to three weeks later; if they winter in Britain, the juveniles tend to arrive in relatively larger numbers slightly earlier than adults. The spatial separation is slightly complicated in that different populations occur in different habitats, but even so there is a trend for juvenile birds to occur more frequently in inland or brackish wetlands rather than on the coast.

### (vi) *The patterns of sex distribution*

There is very little information on the differences in the distribution of sexes compared with the previous section. This is not surprising since, with few exceptions, sexes do not differ greatly in size and therefore in feeding techniques or foods taken. In some species of waders, the sex ratio of wintering birds differs markedly from equality. For two species, the males outnumber the females in Britain — in the Bar-tailed Godwit, the ratio is about 2:1, and in wintering Ruff it is a staggering 9:1. In the former species it is not known whether the trend is seen throughout its range, although samples from West Africa indicate that it is. In the

Ruff, however, the ratio in southern Africa is almost exactly reversed, with females outnumbering males by 9:1. Perhaps the larger size of male Ruff makes very long migrations less attractive and their larger size allows them to winter in colder more northerly areas. In the Bar-tailed Godwit, there is a difference in the feeding areas utilised by males and females, with the smaller legged and billed males feeding on dryer areas, while the females can feed efficiently in shallow water as well.

There are small variations in the timing of migrations of males and females in many waders. Generally, in waders of the genera *Calidris* and *Tringa*, which breed in arctic and sub-arctic zones, females depart the breeding grounds soon after the hatching of the eggs, leaving the males to look after the young; thus there tends to be a two to three week gap between the peak migration periods of the sexes. The gap is more obvious nearer to the breeding grounds and is often difficult to detect in Britain.

### (vii)  *Patterns of roosting*

Most estuary birds form flocks, although these may range from well dispersed to highly aggregated. There have been many publications which discuss possible advantages in flocking. In flocks, birds need spend less time looking out for danger and can give more time to feeding. Also, an approaching predator finds it difficult to pick out one bird in a flock as the rest confuse it. In an open habitat, such as intertidal flats, a feeding flock may also focus information for others, indicating available food.

Inevitably, flocks join together at the edges of estuaries to form roosts at high tide when the intertidal feeding grounds are covered. These roosts provide protection against predators (see above) and perhaps also enable an exchange to take place of information on feeding grounds in the estuary (Ward and Zahavi 1973). While in the roost, the birds are able to rest, so saving energy while food cannot be gathered.

Roosts are therefore important for estuary birds, and their availability and quality can determine the status of the intertidal feeding grounds. A wide range of habitats is used by estuary birds, and they are particularly important for waders. Waders need dry land and cannot sit out high tide on the water like some other species. The range of habitats used is indicated below.

(a)  *Sandbanks.* Only usable on neap tides, when they provide relatively good roosts; if disturbance occurs, there are usually several alternative sites. Locally, however, disturbance can still be severe (for example in autumn at Hest Bank on Morecambe Bay, or West Kirby on the Dee) and force birds off these roosts.

(b)  *Sand/shingle beaches and spits.* Found on the outer estuary and not especially favoured at neap tides or in spring and autumn. On neap tides, waders (excluding certain specialist species – Sanderling, Ringed Plover, Turnstone, Oystercatcher) tend to be further inside the estuary. In spring and autumn, beaches and spits, unless they are nature reserves or very large, may be heavily disturbed by holidaymakers. However, the spits are often relatively high and are not inundated by spring tides; in winter, they can provide sites for major roosts (e.g. Thornham and Gibraltar Point in the Wash, or Walney in Morecambe Bay).

(c)  *Islands.* These vary enormously in type from shingle beaches to saltmarsh or reclaimed. Some offshore islands can provide good nocturnal roosts for inland feeding Curlew etc (e.g. Horse Island near Ayr or Cardigan Island, Teifi). Their isolation restricts the number of casual visitors but should disturbance occur (landings from yachts, wildfowling) the island is vacated as there is no real alternative area.

(d) *Saltmarshes*. These also are variable in nature, but tend to be in inner parts of estuaries where the mud has accreted over the years; they are close to feeding grounds of most species and there is usually a steady gradation in mudflat height towards them. Feeding can be carried out for most of the rising and falling tides. Saltmarshes tend to be formed at or above the level of mid-high water neap tides. On the lowest neap tides saltmarshes are little used and on extreme highwater spring tides they are completely inundated; so they are used for intermediate (most) high tides.

Saltmarshes have several advantages for roosting; most notably they have a good creek structure, making access by man difficult to dangerous at high water. Wildfowling is probably the only major disturbance on large saltmarshes. They provide sites for most of the main roosts on Britain's major estuaries. Different types of saltmarshes are used differentially by birds. The typical ungrazed marshes of eastern England have a rich flowering plant flora and are less desirable in autumn when the vegetation is high, but by midwinter the dieback of plants and high tides will have flattened them to make them highly attractive. Grazed saltmarshes of western Britain (especially in north-west England) are much more attractive for birds throughout the year.

*Spartina* marshes are far less attractive than others. Unless heavily grazed, this grass grows much too tall for small waders; only Curlew and, to a lesser extent, Godwits and Redshank, roost here. Many waders do roost on the mud where advancing clumps of *Spartina* are found, giving quite good shelter against wind and rain.

(e) *Fields*. Fields can be good roost sites although in most places they are only occupied when spring tides cover the saltmarshes. Some wetter grazing fields may provide feeding all the day, or high tide feeding for birds from the mudflats. Although fields are available at all seasons, they are not used when crops are more than a few inches high. Ploughed, burnt or recently seeded arable fields or well-grazed pasture are preferred. In eastern England, the harvesting of peas in mid-July coincides with the return of waders to their moulting grounds, and disturbance can be severe from harvesting or other agricultural operations and from scaring devices.

(f) *Man-made structures*. Waders will roost on many man-made structures, mainly on spring tides when alternatives are unavailable or in areas where all alternatives have been destroyed. Perhaps the most used sites are fly-ash lagoons at power stations, but docks, sea-walls, airfields and industrial sites are also used. Moored boats or buoys are used by Turnstones and Redshanks in several areas. In general, the best man-made areas are those which are protected against public disturbance.

(g) *In flight*. The last resort for birds is to 'roost' on the wing. In estuaries where there is a combination of very severe disturbance, high spring tides and no alternative roosts, some species may be forced to fly for the whole (up to an hour) of the high tide period. It is most noticeable in Bar-tailed Godwits, which will do this at times at the mouth of the Dee and in the Lune (Morecambe Bay). Clearly, much additional energy is used and if it occurred frequently, especially in winter, it could be very disadvantageous.

Large estuaries can be divided up into a series of subdivisions, each having a number of roost sites. These are used in a predictable way as indicated by earlier comments, and depend on tide height, time of year and disturbance. Essentially, the low level neap tide roosts on sandbanks or off saltmarshes, are used as sub-roosts on rising and falling spring tides. After two or three days of spring tides, the birds may move directly to the high level saltmarsh roosts rather than form an intermediate sub-roost. When the spring tides series starts to fall, the now available sub-roost is not, or hardly, occupied on the first day; but on subsequent days the habit is resumed. The birds appear to adapt continually to changing patterns of tides, and will fly the shortest distance possible between feeding areas and roosts to conserve energy.

Disturbance is the one factor, apart from tide height, which modifies greatly the distribution of roosts. Many comments have been made, but few detailed studies of disturbance have been carried out. Furness (1973) concluded that the roost site quality (essentially habitat type plus freedom from disturbance) modified the numbers and distribution of waders of Musselburgh on the Firth of Forth; indeed, he believed that the numbers of Oystercatchers and Redshanks might actually be limited by disturbance. There is a very large range of disturbance factors from wildfowling to birdwatching, from sailing and exercising dogs to industrial and agricultural operations. In certain circumstances, each can have an important influence, but further work is needed to show its effect quantitatively.

SPECIFIC IMPLICATIONS

### Construction effects

At present there are few data on disturbance caused by estuarine engineering works. Waders, and probably to a greater extent wildfowl, will move away from the immediate vicinity of active workings. No long-lasting adverse effects were noted on the intertidal flats of Lavan Sands, Conwy Bay when an oil pipe was laid from Anglesey to the mainland, but this operation only took a few weeks and involved a narrow route. A much greater impact was, however, seen where the pipe crossed a saltmarsh (Rees 1978). The bund construction schemes, particularly if they involve the extraction of sand or gravel deposits in the vicinity of the barrage line (such has been suggested on the Severn), will be on a very much larger scale and then effects may be noticeable. This will be especially true for roost sites or when small discrete feeding areas are used by one or more species. On the Dee, the very large saltmarsh roosts and feeding grounds of Pintail and Black-tailed Godwits on the inner estuary are particularly likely to be affected, as would be considerable saltmarsh breeding populations of birds on the Wash and Morecambe Bay. Construction effects may be significant locally, as the building of any major bund or reservoir could be spread over up to eight (or even more) years.

Because construction will take a long time, there will be changes in sedimentation patterns during its course. In some areas much stronger currents will occur with scouring taking place, especially when the gap in the bund or barrage is relatively small. In other areas there will be considerable silt deposition due to decreased water flow. Although taking place from the start, these changes are even more dramatically felt in the long term after closure and will be dealt with in more detail later.

*Immediate effects on closure*
Immediately the bunds are completed there will be a sudden massive change in environmental characteristics of the enclosed area. If a freshwater reservoir is envisaged, there will be large salinity changes, while a tidal barrage will result in substantial but more subtle hydrological variation. In any case, the effect is bound to be dramatic. Intertidal feeding grounds of waterfowl will become unavailable, and saltmarshes will either become inundated or be left to dry out above the water level. This latter process would take several months, possibly even years, before this habitat was greatly altered. With the absence of a tidal influence and large decrease in salinity, virtually the entire invertebrate fauna will be killed within a few days; so even if the bottom sediments do become exposed again due to draw-down, there will be little of the original food available to the birds.

The net result will be that immediately, at least if closure occurs between the end of July and the beginning of the following June, large numbers of birds will have to find other feeding grounds. The alternative is to die; but it is unlikely that this would happen over the few ensuing months.

A considerable amount of research on the feeding characteristics and the factors controlling numbers of waders has been undertaken over the last ten years. Two particularly important series of papers have been published by Dr J. D. Goss-Custard on work on the Ythan, Wash and several south-western and south-eastern estuaries, and by Dr P. R. Evans on Teesmouth and Lindisfarne. Many of the aspects of these and other studies have been outlined already in Chapter 2 on estuarine bird ecology. Despite the detailed work, we do not yet fully understand the implications of large scale loss of feeding grounds. Questions that need to be answered are: What would be the lasting effect of increasing the density of birds on existing grounds? Would the birds be able to obtain enough food to survive the winter or to migrate in a good condition and to ensure successful breeding? What would be the effect on birds already on those 'safe' feeding areas? In short, what is the role and carrying capacity for each estuary? The one thing that is certain is that each estuary is unique, having its own physical, chemical and biological characteristics. Each of the major reservoir schemes will have a different effect due to variations in conditions, design of the development and the species affected and the way that each uses the estuary. Inevitably, even when we have a good working knowledge of estuarine systems, we will still need detailed ecological surveys and research to provide the most accurate assessment possible.

The feeding studies have shown that:

(i) The numbers of birds studied to date are positively correlated with the biomass of food available both within an estuary (Goss-Custard 1970b, O'Connor and Brown 1974) and between estuaries (Goss-Custard, Kay and Blindell 1977).

(ii) There are preferred feeding areas which fill up first (Goss-Custard 1977d, Zwarts 1976).

(iii) The feeding distribution of birds can be modified by sediment characteristics (Prater 1972, Tjallingii 1972).

(iv) That intraspecific aggressive encounters over food items increase as bird density rises (Goss-Custard 1977d).

(v) Prey availability may decrease due simply to the presence of more birds in an area (Goss-Custard 1970b).

(vi) The food value of each bivalve mollusc decreases during the winter (Goss-Custard et al 1977).

(vii) Already between 14% and 34% of the initial standing crop of prey may be removed during the winter (Goss-Custard 1977d).

(viii) In winter, most species feed for virtually all of the time available (Buxton 1977, Goss-Custard et al 1977).

(ix) Prey availability and/or its detectability decreases in cold weather (Goss-Custard et al 1977, Smith 1975).

(x) In severe weather (Pilcher et al 1974) or even in an ordinary winter (Goss-Custard et al 1977) mortality rates of waders may increase by an average of tenfold.

The conclusions that one is forced to make on the points summarised very briefly above are, firstly that at present waders find sufficient food difficult to obtain in mid- and late winter. Secondly, that on being displaced, birds will go to feeding areas which are already occupied, any difficulties in finding food that exist already are likely to be enhanced – whether they go to optimal or sub-optimal areas. Thirdly, birds and their food supply are affected detrimentally by increasing the density of birds.

When the tide is excluded from a large area of an estuary by a barrage, the sea water will be redistributed around the coastline. In areas where the tidal range is small the effect elsewhere may not be particularly dramatic. Where, however, large tidal ranges and, therefore, volumes of water are involved, such as on the Severn, a considerable effect may be seen. In this example, a barrage from Lavernock Point to Brean Down would displace enough water to increase the tidal range on the Burry Inlet by 10–20 cm and a small (a few centimetres) increase in high tide levels would be detectable as far away as Morecambe Bay and western Cornwall. The effect of this increased water will be to inundate high level flats and saltmarshes more frequently, possibly to the detriment of some feeding birds and almost certainly of the breeding birds.

### Long-term effects of barrage schemes

The results of the disappearance of intertidal feeding grounds which would be lost to a reservoir development have already been discussed. There would also be considerable habitat changes outside the reservoir due to new sedimentation patterns being established on its seaward side and artificial management of the area on its landward side. A freshwater reservoir itself would introduce a new habitat component, so diversifying further the estuarine complex.

### (a) Gains due to the reservoir

As described earlier, the idea of a bunded reservoir is that the water should be deep, and shallow water avoided. Most of the productive wetlands for birds are shallow, often no more than 2–3 metres deep. In these conditions, emergent vegetation can occur at the edges and, in places, in the middle, with the potentiality of secure breeding areas. There would be plenty of food for dabbling duck, while diving duck could feed on the bottom. Deep water is much less favourable. It can, however, provide a secure roost from which birds can make nocturnal feeding forays into neighbouring areas. Such a reservoir could be used in this way by dabbling ducks and gulls, depending on the wildfowling pressure, although gulls may create public health problems. The species involved are relatively ubiquitous and are unlikely to figure significantly in any revised assessment of the site. Fish and invertebrates would colonise the reservoir through the water supply or other agencies, the former also are likely to be deliberately introduced. Food would, therefore, develop and encourage fish-eating birds such as grebes to come in.

Just as there will be pressures for recreational activities on the polders, so will there be many demands for the water space. These will come from sailing, angling and power boating clubs, to name but a few. Provided care is taken in the allocation of different zones for different activities, there is no reason why most cannot co-exist. Care needs to be taken to ensure that not only is there an enforced nature reserve area, but also that there is a buffer zone of sufficient width to prevent continual minor disturbance.

The bunds of the reservoir, even if seeded with grass, are unlikely to provide particularly good grazing conditions for ducks, although if disturbance can be kept to a minimum, some species, such as terns, may be able to breed there.

(b) *Changes outside the development to seaward side*
The design of the reservoir or barrage and the local tidal patterns will affect sediment deposition. In general, silt will be deposited in all sheltered corners, for example in the Severn the MEL reduced design (Fig. 4:19) would probably lead to a massive accumulation of soft mud in Bridgwater Bay because it virtually encloses it. Hydraulic models and mathematical models can be constructed of any estuary and its developments; from these a reasonable idea of areas and the extent of deposition can be gained. To date, however, only the outline of the changes can be shown. It is the detail which is of more significance for biological projection. Equally undeveloped is the ecological understanding of the consequence of sediment alteration. We know that the distribution of many species of invertebrates and plants are related to sediment characteristics and the closely related phenomenon of tidal height, see Chapter 1. Food distribution and abundance is also related to bird distribution. Altering the sediments outside the reservoir is, therefore, bound to alter the species occurring and their abundance. Observations indicated that among the waders an increase in silt would be more likely to reduce numbers of Oystercatcher, Knot, Bar-tailed Godwit and Turnstone, while it may enhance numbers of Grey Plover or Black-tailed Godwit.

It is realised that accretion will result in the formation of new sandbanks. Some of these at higher levels will be colonised by saltmarsh plants, while the lower ones will be invaded by invertebrates, thus providing new feeding grounds. However, two characteristics of lower level sandbanks are that they are made of coarse particles and that they have steeply sloping sides into often deep channels. By removing large sections of the more gently sloping upper shore, it would need massive or at least a very long period of accretion before a similar area of lower shore was converted into equivalently rich feeding areas, if indeed it were possible at all. It is probable too, that the profile of the beach will become steeper with two consequences. Firstly, the flats available for the invertebrates, which occupy distinct zones, will be compressed, so reducing bird feeding areas. Secondly, the steeper profile will make the flats more susceptible to marine conditions, especially wave and current action, which will hinder further sediment deposition.

Although these changes in sediment accretion patterns are partly hypothetical, recent researches on patterns of deposition on the Wash indicates that, at least in some areas, they are valid. It has been shown here that the rate of accretion, as measured by the area of intertidal flats based on the position of the low tide mark, has slowed down over the last hundred years. This is despite continued reclamation of the saltmarshes, which was previously assumed to be a catalyst for further silt deposition. The reason appears to be that there is little marine-borne silt now being brought into the Wash; the only accretion being of coarse sand.

Saltmarshes will be formed on the higher deposits, particularly in the sheltered corners outside the bunds. Quite how fast they will appear depends partly on the design of the outer bund. Artificial acceleration of accretion could be achieved by providing breakwaters. However, it must be recognised that this may affect birds too, and not necessarily advantageously. The most interesting saltmarshes botanically are often the most ornithologically valuable. If the pioneer plant was *Salicornia*, and it was followed by a wide range of grasses and flowering plants, then the marsh would no doubt support many feeding wildfowl, passerines and some waders; and it would, in time, also act as a good breeding ground. If, however, as is only too likely, *Spartina* were to invade, then there would be a large area of very poor habitat for birds. The colonising species will vary with what is present in the area already, but there are either active or sometimes relatively quiescent colonies of *Spartina* in all areas considered for reservoir development.

(c) *Changes between the reservoir and existing sea wall*

This is the only area in the proposed schemes which could be managed to produce a new and possibly exciting habitat for birds. It would include large saltmarshes and relatively small areas of existing upper mudflats but regular tidal inundation would be excluded by bunds running from the reservoir to the shore. Saltmarsh flora can withstand some desiccation for several years although it slowly changes its nature. Extensive studies on these changes have been made in Lake Veere in the Dutch Delta region (Beeftink 1975). If no active management took place to maintain salt or brackish water on the marshes, there would be a steady build up of salt tolerant, halophytic, terrestrial plants. Then, as leaching through rainwater occurred, a 'normal' land flora would become established. Management has the potential for mixing freshwater (from the reservoir) with sea water (pumped in or through a sluice), so maintaining the area at any water depth or salinity thought desirable. Of course, internal bunds could be built to ensure a diversity of conditions within the whole polder area. Discussion on the desired habitats have taken place with brackish marsh/shallow water pools for passage waders and ducks, grazing marsh for geese and Wigeon and dense reed beds with scattered willows receiving considerable support. One only has to think of the diversity of interesting breeding, passage and wintering birds at sites like Minsmere, Walberswick, Cley or the Ouse Washes to see the interest that this potential could realise. Birdwatchers would certainly be delighted to see a consolidation of our breeding Avocets, Black-tailed Godwit, Ruff, Savi's Warbler, Marsh Harrier or tern populations; equally no doubt, several species not yet breeding here could be persuaded to stay – such as Spoonbill, Purple Heron or Little Bittern.

We should perhaps temper our euphoria with a few other thoughts. Firstly, polders are not necessarily created for birds or conservation. Other interests such as agriculture or many leisure activities may wish to develop part or even all. Secondly, the size of the proposed areas are not especially large, definitely they are not on the massive scale of the Flevoland polders reclaimed from the Ijsselmeer in the Netherlands. On the Wash, the first stage Westmark reservoir would displace 210 ha of saltmarsh (CWPU 1976) and in total perhaps 300 ha could be included as polder. The expansive first thoughts on a Morecambe Bay barrage would have included 6,000 ha of polders (Corlett 1972) but it would be unrealistic to imagine that we could be talking on this scale now. So with the relatively limited areas, we could not expect to see massive increases in species. For example, there are only one to two pairs of Marsh Harriers and six to eight pairs of Bitterns in the 200 ha reedbed of Minsmere, so a further reedbed on a similar scale is not necessarily adding vastly to our limited stock. Thirdly, we should consider the relative international importance of the losses and gains. It would be unlikely that more than 1,000 pairs of Black-tailed Godwits could breed on a Wash polder even if all of it were suitable for the species. Mülder (1972) estimated 120,000 pairs bred in the Netherlands alone. The loss of the intertidal area within the Westmark reservoir, however, would affect a substantial proportion of Knot and quite large numbers of Shelduck, Redshank, Dunlin and Curlew. From a conservation point of view, therefore, the loss of mudflats sustained is greater than the gains from the polder areas.

# CHAPTER 5

# Other threats to estuary birds

Barrage and reservoir proposals have provided the main stimuli for research on the conservation of estuary birds, due to the scale of reclamation necessary. However, there are many other significant threats to the estuarine system which could, and indeed do, affect birds. The most serious are undoubtedly the large scale reclamation of upper shore for industrial development and the continual attrition from many small reclamations. Although the word reclamation is used here to describe the process of converting intertidal land to terrestrial land, it is an incorrect term. Reclamation of the estuarine habitat should only be used for the recovery of land lost to the sea; virtually no intertidal flats fall into that category, except on a geological timescale. The correct definition is really the claiming of land. There should be a different philosophical approach to taking something one never had from recovering that which was lost! Pollution too can have a noticeable affect, as can the multitude of leisure activities. We must also remember that natural and man induced patterns of erosion and accretion may be working to change existing estuaries.

Figure 5:1 summarises the main threats to British and Irish estuaries.

### RECLAMATIONS

Coastal sites appear to be attractive propositions to industrial developers. The adjacent reclaimed land, saltmarsh and upper intertidal areas are relatively flat and there is easy, or relatively easy, sea access. The rapidly rising prices of land make reclamation financially a viable proposition. A number of large developments, particularly involving the petro-chemical industry, have already made a noticeable impact on existing estuaries. Storage or refining plants have been built on the Thames (Canvey, Isle of Grain), Southampton Water (Fawley), Milford Haven, Teesmouth, Firth of Forth (Grangemouth), Cromarty Firth (Nigg Bay) and the Shetlands (Sullum Voe). The policy of fully developing facilities at a few sites has certain advantages but nevertheless can have an immense impact on the chosen sites.

Construction of maintenance yards for offshore oil developments have become a problem over recent years, especially in Scotland. In several cases little consideration has apparently been given to the environmental effects that they can cause. The yard at Ardesier on the Moray Firth for example was given planning permission but then there was a prompt attempt to reclaim a larger area than was agreed. This was, however, discovered before reclamation was completed. Subsequently, however, planning permission was sought for an extension into the area which had already been excluded on environmental grounds. Other heavy industries have utilised coastal land, examples such as gas developments (present proposals for which in the Irish Sea include the Dee, Ribble or Morecambe Bay), steel (Dee, Severn), docks (Thames, Teesmouth, Southampton Water), and airports (Maplin and Severn) have or could have significant repercussions on the estuarine bird populations. The potential pollution problems will be considered separately later.

A concept in favour in the early 1970s was of integrated industrial development at coastal sites. No fewer than 13 estuaries were mentioned as possible Maritime Industrial Development Areas (MIDA) these included the Burry Inlet, Medway and the Severn estuary. Fortunately little active pursuance of this policy has taken place although the possibility remains. For instance one of the proposals for the Severn includes an airport and industrial complex inside a reservoir.

The best documented case of industrial reclamation in Britain is that of Teesmouth. This estuary has been subject to just about all possibilities and exemplifies the problems that conservation and environmental interests face with national policies, political preferences and sweeping powers of harbour authorities. Seal Sands is the main feeding area for most species. It is used by almost all of the Shelduck and most Curlew, Redshank, Dunlin, Grey Plover and Bar-tailed Godwit. There are, however, other areas which support many birds; in particular Coatham Sands is of importance, although most of its principal species also occur in smaller numbers on North Gare sands. These include Sanderling, Turnstone and Knot, the latter feeding on the rocks uncovered at low tides. The recent history of its reclamation is shown in Fig. 5:2. The area of mud flats on Seal Sands has decreased from 655 ha in 1967 to a minute 149 ha by 1976. Initially reclamation, carried out by the Tees and Hartlepool Port Authority, was in response to the increase in size of ships; they were too large to penetrate the relatively narrow river channel. The inner part of the, then, large central mud bank of Seal Sands formed the first area. Steadily, but much more rapidly, during the last ten years, more and more of Seal Sands and Bran Sands were taken, the latter having already been virtually depopulated of birds due to effluent discharge in the 1950s. The development of North Sea oil fields provided a further impetus for reclamation during the 1970s. The petro-chemical industry, associated port facilities and steel expansion led the way.

The plan was for a three stage reclamation of Seal Sands. This started when a porous reclamation wall was built across Seal Sands in 1970. From a bird's point of view this was initially attractive. It separated an inner section of mud from the

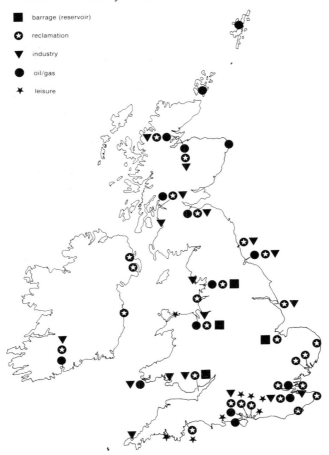

Fig. 5:1 Summary of main threats to British and Irish estuaries.

standard tidal inundation, water entered it much more slowly so that it was still uncovered as high tide approached, enabling valuable additional feeding time to be obtained. Once the water inside was high, that outside was being uncovered in the ebb, so once again birds could feed almost immediately. This was not, however, the purpose of the wall! Sand was being pumped in and by 1974 it had been reclaimed, restricting feeding grounds considerably. Since its size was less, not surprisingly, the importance of the site decreased.

The implementation of the second and third stages of the reclamation of Seal Sands was proposed in 1974, as by now it was considered that North Sea oil would require more storage and dock facilities. An Examination in Public of the Teeside Structure Plan, which included these proposals, was held in 1975 after which the Inspector recommended that the need for reclamation was not yet adequately shown and that in view of its conservation value no further reclamation should take place at the present time. Any relief that was felt by conservationists was short-lived as the recommendation was overruled by the Secretary of State for the Environment. He did, however, indicate that there was no immediate need for facilities but tempered that by giving the Port Authority power to reclaim when necessary. It was suggested that an 'alternative' reserve should be created if Seal Sands were to be reclaimed. The first suggestion was for the flooding and excavating of the inner western marshes. This was impractical both because of cost and because the landowners were not willing to sell. North Gare Sands, already designated as SSSI by the NCC, was then put forward together with Greenabella Marsh and Greatham Creek. In 1978 the Hartlepool District Plan was published; after a public inquiry the inspector recommended that part of the area of North Gare Sands SSSI should be designated as an industrial and port development area. Objections to this were voiced by a consortium of all local and several national conservation bodies. In his recent judgement the Secretary of State reversed this recommendation and so, at least for the foreseeable future, gave a most welcome reprieve for this valuable area for wildlife.

Throughout the period 1969–77 counts of the birds have been made monthly by the Teesmouth Bird Club. In addition a detailed research programme on wader feeding distribution and food supplies has been undertaken by Durham University.

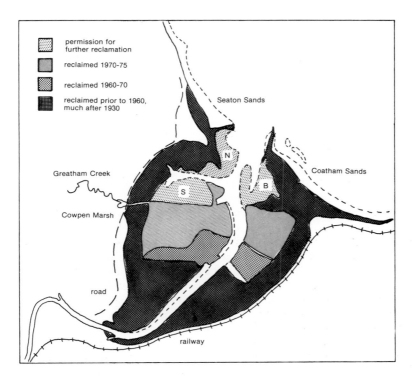

Fig. 5:2 Teesmouth and areas recently reclaimed. Key: B = Bran Sands; N = North Gare sands; S = Seal Sands.

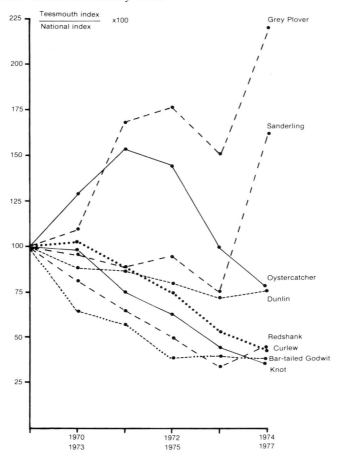

Fig. 5:3 Changes in numbers of main species of waders at Teesmouth between 1969–77 in relation to national fluctuations. The Teesmouth and national indices are based on three-year running average peaks with the period 1969/70 to 1971/72 given the value of 100. The Teesmouth index is plotted as a percentage of the national index.

Figure 5:3 shows the trends in numbers of the main species of waders at Teesmouth and in Britain over these years; they are presented as three year running averages of the annual peak numbers and this damps down the variation due to annual fluctuations. To ensure that the trends can be compared all numbers have been converted into indices with the first period of 1969/70–1971/72 having the value of 100. Up to 1972/73 there was relatively little change, although the majority of species decreased slightly. However, subsequently there was a steady, and in some species a quite dramatic, decrease in numbers. Two species, Oystercatcher and Grey Plover, did not completely follow the pattern, partly because the former is mainly found on the sea beaches outside the estuary anyway, but even these species had started to decrease by 1975/76, the time by which the reclamation of the southern part of Seal Sands had been completed. Of the other species only Sanderling has remained fairly stable, no doubt because they are mostly confined to the relatively unaffected Coatham and North Gare Sands. Unfortunately, even these areas are not secure, for a substantial part of Coatham Sands is included in a proposal for an extension of the British Steel Corporation plant and some of North Gare Sands has been set aside for development. The future of Teesmouth is indeed bleak with these development proposals in addition to the probable loss of Seal Sands.

*Agricultural reclamation*

This process has been happening for a long time. On the Wash, where it has been a particularly important factor, 470 km$^2$ of land has been reclaimed since Saxon times (Central Water Planning Unit 1976). This is a larger area than the 314 km$^2$ of intertidal flats and saltmarsh that remain. The process of saltmarsh development has already been summarised in Chapter 1. Accretion of sediment occurs when the intertidal flats are not stable; thus if the hydrology of an estuary were to remain similar or, as is more likely, to fluctuate within small limits, there would eventually be a balance between accretion and erosion. Reclamation has traditionally involved the enclosure of high level saltings by a seawall, then an interval of a few years for the leaching of salt from the ground, followed by crops. The land so gained has a high silt content, although it may grade to fairly sandy at the limit of reclamation, which provides a fertile soil. Much of the intensive agricultural belt of East Anglia has been reclaimed from marshland and estuary. Be reclaiming the higher salt-marshes, i.e. those which would be covered by higher spring tides, an imbalance is again introduced into the dynamics of sediment deposition. The result, if there is sufficient material in the system, is further deposition on the remaining lower marsh and previously uncolonised mudflats. Thus the process of reclamation might provide the right conditions for further reclamation in fifty or more years time. Quite how far this process of reclamation can go is not clear as deeper water and more marine influences are approached. Recent studies on the Wash have shown two alarming developments; firstly, the low water mark is now no longer moving seaward and all reclamation is a net loss of intertidal habitat. Secondly, very little organic sediment is being brought in from the North Sea. Concern is also felt as new techniques enable reclamation to be extended further down the shore than has hitherto been possible.

To date in most cases such reclamation had not caused great concern to conservation bodies. Two instances recently have, however, rather modified attitudes. Firstly, new techniques enabled large reclamation projects to be carried out on the Wash in the mid 1970s and others are projected for Gedney Drove End and other Lincolnshire marshes for the near future. Secondly, a proposal was put forward for a massive reclamation on the Ribble Estuary. Although saltmarshes seem to be extensive on our major estuaries they only cover about 410 km$^2$ in total, thus they are a relatively scarce natural habitat. Their value to birds has already been described in Chapter 2. Briefly, they support high densities (and nationally significant numbers) of many breeding species, provide valuable feeding areas for many wildfowl in winter (and especially in spring for Brent Geese) and are good roosting areas for waders. They are also essential in providing organic material on which intertidal invertebrates feed, so providing the food for waders. We cannot be complacent as to their future by simply saying more will accrete, especially if immature marshes can be reclaimed by modern methods. In the past a change of land use for saltmarsh to reclaimed arable appeared to be outside the planning laws and could, therefore, take place when the owner wished. Now, however, as a result of the Ribble proposal, it is apparent than an order signed by the Minister of State for the Environment can be obtained under Article 4 of the Town and Country Planning Act; this places reclamation plans under the constrains of local planning authorities. Thus important areas can be given a degree of extra protection. However, if an application is refused, the local authority could be liable for compensation. This is unsatisfactory in that it puts the burden on local ratepayers and indicates the need for some changes in the Town and Country Planning Acts. In fact, on the Ribble in 1979, a compulsory purchase order was initiated by the NCC in view of its outstanding international importance. It was never taken out because the dispute was settled without it. Land valuation is calculated from the development potential and this causes difficulties; on the Ribble, the putative developers claimed £4–7 million while the district valuer varied between £0.6 million and £3.5 million.

Of course, few estuaries have vast saltmarshes where such dramatic reclamation can take place. In many smaller ones limited reclamations have been made although subsequently the land is usually only suitable for rough grazing. Indeed, many attempts have been foiled by the sea breaking back through the defences and the areas reverting to saltmarsh. Good examples of this can be seen on Hamford Water and the Crouch in Essex, Newtown Harbour on the Isle of Wight, and Tramore and Dungarven in southern Ireland.

Saltmarshes can profitably be grazed by cattle or sheep and this may be essential for grazing species such as Brent Geese, although seed-eating birds tend to be scarce. Good grazed marshes are found in the Severn, Burry Inlet, Dee, Ribble, Morecambe Bay and Solway. In several areas the close grazed grass is cut commercially for turf; when this happens additional fertilisation and cutting regimes may be implemented.

*Small reclamations*
So far we have considered the effects of large developments. Few massive schemes have gone ahead, no doubt primarily due to the huge expenditure needed rather than to prevent the loss of wildlife. Perhaps much more insidious are the many small developments which beset virtually all estuaries. An example, Langstone Harbour, is illustrated in Fig. 5:4. Such reclamations take many forms, from the infill of a creek for a road, housing, small industry, a refuse tip or sewage works, to the siting of a yachting marina, slipways, quays, etc. It may be that only a few hundred square metres are involved although small creeks of up to a hundred hectares can be included. It is rare that such a development can be opposed successfully on the grounds that it supports x% of the international or even national population. Each removal, however, goes towards reducing the total area available as feeding grounds. The cumulative effect may be considerable and no doubt the same problems of bird feeding, outlined in the previous chapter, will still apply to the reclamation of many small sections although the details will vary with the species and areas involved.

One special area that could be considered separately is that of the need to dispose of dredged mud from navigable waters or waste fly-ash from power stations. In both cases a frequently used method is to build large bunded lagoons on low ground immediately adjacent to the estuary, or in some cases reclaim upper shore areas for the purpose. Power stations are found widely around our coasts and many are on estuaries. The ash is pumped in semi-liquid form into lagoons and the water allowed to drain away. The sediment can be deep and very dangerous to cross. Birds are able

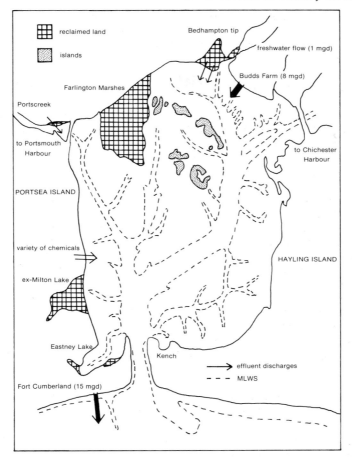

Fig. 5:4 Langstone Harbour showing reclaimed areas and main effluent discharges.

to use many of these areas as high tide roosts where security is maintained by restricted access and the difficult terrain. Roosts such as occur at Longannet and Musselburgh on the Forth, West Thurrock on the Thames or Uskmouth on the Severn can be very large. Similarly, the dredged material pumped into lagoons at Rainham or Cliffe on the Thames, Dibden on Southampton Water, Frodsham on the Mersey or Tivoli on Cork Harbour provide excellent conditions for roosting birds. This type of lagoon has a steady progression of invertebrate and plant colonisation with subsequent development of its own avifauna. The various changes at Dibden Bay have been summarised by Glue (1971). The lagoons do not support enough invertebrates to make good feeding grounds; certainly they never could be considered as alternatives to the intertidal flats. Unfortunately with all of these lagoons there comes a time when they are full. Unless kept deliberately immature and unless seawater is pumped in, they will dry out and become, at best, a roost area.

Frequently their final reclamation involves grassing over for industrial, agricultural or leisure activities. Now the once very interesting areas of Dibden Bay and Frodsham have degenerated greatly.

POLLUTION

Like every other part of our environment, estuaries are subjected to many types of pollution. Some are already showing noticeable effects while others remain as potential threats for the moment. Here four of the main types are considered – organic nutrients, heavy metals, oil and thermal.

Discharges involving a high level of nutrients – organic compounds, nitrates, phosphates, ammonia – come from three main sources: domestic sewage, industrial effluent and agricultural run off, although there are differing background levels in the waters due to the types of rocks in the watersheds. A high nutrient level may lead to an enrichment of the bird fauna through increased growth of invertebrates or plants. It is noticeable that there are concentrations of gulls and diving ducks at the end of discharge pipes. A survey in Scotland (Pounder 1976) showed that many Goldeneye, Scaup etc, found good feeding areas where sewage or distillery effluent was released into the sea. Perhaps the most striking case of the benefit of organic discharge to birds was at Seafield on the Firth of Forth. Here the sewage of Edinburgh and much grain from distilleries was discharged into the Firth of Forth and attracted up to 20,000 seaducks, mainly Scaup. Waders too could be found feeding in good numbers on the mud around discharge pipes.

The beneficial effect occurs when organic material is released into a sufficient volume of water to dilute it and provide enough oxygen for the bacteria to break it down. When these conditions are not met the results can be very different. There are several estuaries where there is a potential problem, none more so than Langstone Harbour. Portsmouth Polytechnic (1976) studied this relatively enclosed bay in depth and attempted to predict the effects of continued and projected organic discharge. Figure 5:4 illustrates the relevant features of the area. The present effluent inflow into the inner harbour, virtually all from Budds Farm, is about 9 million gallons per day (mgd) while the freshwater inflow is only about 1 mgd. The discharge from Fort Cumberland is much larger, about 15 mgd, but this goes into the sea during the ebb flow. There is also a significant inflow of nitrogenous compounds due to rain percolating through the rubbish tips, the large Bedhampton tip contributing almost a quarter as much as Budds Farm. Although the Fort Cumberland discharge is made outside the harbour some material returns on the flood tide. It was estimated that the concentration of effluent within the harbour is almost 3·5 times the daily flow (c. 84 million gallons) on neap tides and two times (c. 48 million gallons) on spring tides.

The nutrient enrichment thus obtained has apparently encouraged the growth of *Enteromorpha* on the mudflats, in places to such an extent that when the plants decay in winter the mud becomes deoxygenated and greatly reduces the diversity or abundance of other plant and invertebrate foods for birds. This process of eutrophication where the nutrient load so stimulates algal growth that its subsequent decay results in the whole system eventually becoming anaeorbic and so unable to support bird life, is one that rarely happens in estuaries. It has, however, occurred in a number of lakes and could happen in Langstone and several other south coast harbours with their restricted water circulation and high organic input. In fact, the report from Portsmouth Polytechnic considered that Langstone Harbour already has an excessive pollution load and that it should be reduced. From the bird's point of view the harbour probably has reached its maximum bird numbers after twenty years of steady increases in most species. Now a few are decreasing, especially Shelduck which is only half as abundant as it was in the late 1960s. Redshank, Curlew and Bar-tailed Godwit are somewhat down in numbers even though nationally they have been increasing slightly. These species have not decreased in the adjacent Chichester Harbour where the spread of *Enteromorpha* has been much less. Tubbs (1977) points to these coincidences and suggests there may be a causal relationship, but that there needs to be further research into this problem.

Rubbish tips have already been mentioned as a contributory factor to increasing nitrogenous loads in estuaries. This particular aspect is of widespread concern, for not only do chemicals leach out but the tips themselves are used to reclaim intertidal flats. Throughout Britain and Ireland rubbish is being used as an infill in reclamation schemes. Such projects may be very large indeed, as suggestions for reclaiming Spurn Bight in the Humber with colliery waste or Stoke Ooze on the Medway with the Greater London Council's rubbish bear witness. Rubbish tips also frequently form a most unpleasant mess, as can be seen by anyone visiting the northern shore of Rogerstown estuary near Dublin.

Agricultural run off bringing leached fertilisers down lowland rivers is not known to be a problem in estuaries at the moment, probably because of the dilution factor. Potential problems from this source arise mainly in estuarine storage schemes where water is abstracted from rivers. In these schemes the nitrates and phosphates could lead to algal blooms, anaerobic conditions and therefore to changes in the invertebrate and plant foods available. Equally, there have been few cases where industrial effluents or heavy metals are known to have affected bird populations. The effluents that contain very high proportions of cellulose from paper mills can result in anaerobic conditions and very few birds, as happened for a time near the Kemsley mill on the Swale in Kent. Here the problem was compounded by the unusual tidal conditions on a narrow creek which failed to flush the waste material adequately. On Teesmouth pollution from a different source, this time industrial waste of uncertain composition, virtually eliminated the invertebrate fauna of Bran Sands in the mid to late 1950s. Thus a feeding area which had held large numbers of waders was rapidly made barren. In Britain we have been fortunate that pesticide levels in estuary birds have been relatively low but the habitat should not be considered free of risk. In the Dutch Wadden Sea the Sandwich Tern breeding numbers slumped by 87% between 1959 and 1961 and breeding success was very low. The cause of this was the chlorinated hydrocarbons which had been brought down the Rhine from the local agro-chemical industry to enter the North Sea in the Delta area and drift north-eastwards along the Dutch coast.

Heavy metals occur naturally in geological strata and some estuaries have a considerable natural load. However, many industrial processes can release considerable amounts of lead, zinc, cadmium etc, into the atmosphere or as fluid effluents. These metals tend to be concentrated to varying degrees by different invertebrates which may then be consumed by birds, fish or even man. A good example of this problem is the Severn estuary. Here the aluminium smelter at Avonmouth releases some cadmium in its discharge. The invertebrates collected downstream show a gradation in concentrations: for instance in the limpet *Patella* it grades from 550 ppm at the mouth of the Avon to 500 ppm at Cardiff, and it is even detectable as far west as Hartland Point, Devon, where 30 ppm were found (Butterworth et al 1972). To date no adverse effects have been shown to occur as a result of heavy metal accumulations but we must bear the risk in mind. Indeed, in the winter of 1979/80 over 3,000 birds of a wide variety of estuarine species were found dead on the Mersey estuary. It is too early to be sure of the cause but, since many had lead concentrations of up to 100 ppm dry weight in the liver and the highly toxic organic lead compounds have been detected, it seems probable that this heavy metal is implicated.

Oil pollution has been an increasing problem over the last twenty years. In most cases oil has been deliberately (washing out tanks) or accidentally (due to major disasters) released at sea, with only a small proportion finding its way onto the shore and even less into estuaries. There is additionally a chronic problem of frequent small oil losses from shore-based activities such as oil terminals, industrial premises, power stations and dock yards. At sea, oil is known to kill many birds, especially auks, sea ducks, divers and grebes; in estuaries there are concentrations of the last three of these plus other ducks, geese and waders. Large spills on the coast such as the *Amoco Cadiz* (Brittany, 1978) and *Cristos Bitos* (Milford Haven, 1978) have rarely affected estuarine birds seriously, although the *Tank Duchess*, Dundee 1968, (Greenwood and Keddie 1969) off the Tay estuary killed many sea duck. Smaller spills in estuaries, such as that at an industrial premises in Leith (Firth of Forth, 1978) or from the *Esso Bernicia* in the new 'ultra safe' terminal at Sullom Voe (Shetland, 1979) have affected many birds. In the former there were 200 Great Crested Grebes among 740 birds found dead, while on the latter occasion over 3,000 birds are known to have died, including over 500 Black Guillemots and 110 Great Northern Divers. The only spill in Britain which caused serious damage to breeding communities was from the *Seestern* in the Medway estuary. This incident has been fully summarised by Harrison and Buck (1967). The *Torrey Canyon* experience has shown that some detergents used in cleaning up may be highly toxic to marine communities; indeed, some coasts cleaned in 1963 had not recovered fully by the 1970s. In general, waders have been little affected by oil spills, but should oil settle on the mudflats, or if toxic dispersant chemicals are used in estuaries, the loss of their invertebrate foods could be serious.

Thermal pollution is the last type that is considered here. Large power stations require prodigious amounts of water for cooling and for this reason tend to be sited on the coast. Water is taken from the sea, pumped round and then returned to the sea a few degrees warmer than before. So far power stations have, if anything, increased the ornithological interest of the surrounding areas. The warm water outfalls encourage a higher production of food organisms and the movement of the water brings food to the surface, attracting large numbers of gulls and terns. Some estuarine power stations which are beneficial for birds are at West Thurrock on the Thames and at Burry Port on the Burry Inlet. Others, potentially at least, could be detrimental. On the Severn, for example, there are five large power stations – Berkeley, Oldbury, Portishead, Uskmouth and Portskewett. Behind the barrage the warm water outflows could provide a thermal barrier to salmon migrating upstream to breed. Equally it is possible that with lowered water oxygenation due to restricted flow and the projected organic discharge into the reservoir, the increases in temperature may play a role in partial eutrophication of the reservoir. This would be to the detriment of birds as well as fish.

LEISURE ACTIVITIES

As prosperity and mobility have risen during the twentieth century, there has been a progressive increase in the numbers of people participating in various sports. Table 5:1 shows that activities such as sailing, angling and, more recently, water-skiing have increased along with more passive activities such as birdwatching or, no doubt, walking. Birdwatching can now be described as one of the most popular activities. Trends in wildfowling are more difficult to discern. Each of these activities is likely to have a different effect on different bird species although the subject has hardly been investigated in any systematic way. Despite the lack of data a few general comments can probably be made.

Yachting has increased rapidly in south and south-eastern England and, to a lesser extent, on north-western and north-eastern coasts. It is still a relatively minor activity in Scotland and Ireland. Figure 5:5 shows the distribution of the clubs on each estuary and along the coast. Clearly the impact of sailing varies with its scale, the areas used and the time of year. In most cases it is a summer activity, when duck numbers are fairly low, so causing relatively little disturbance. Equally, as it takes place on water, it probably does not greatly affect waders. However, its effect on breeding birds has caused concern. Unauthorised landings on the Medway saltmarsh islands, for example, are thought to be contributing towards a lack of breeding success in some species, due partly to disturbance which allows crows or gulls to predate eggs and partly to accidental fires (Harrison, Humphreys and Graves, 1972). Similarly, landings at Colne Point in Essex have caused nest losses of Little Terns.

The greatest problem from yachting is the building of marinas on intertidal flats. The gradual attrition of the estuarine habitat has been commented on earlier, but it is worth repeating in this context here. A marina may be relatively small but if sited on a sensitive area — as was proposed for a Brent Goose and Wigeon feeding zone on the Exe — its effect could be out of proportion to its size. Boats may be moored in special marinas or they may be anchored on intertidal moorings. Some waders and Brent Geese are willing to feed among boats lying on the mud but will move away if

---

*Table 5:1 Membership of some national organisations involved in recreation and conservation*

|  | 1965 | 1970 | 1971 | 1972 | 1973 | 1974 | 1975 | 1976 | 1977 |
|---|---|---|---|---|---|---|---|---|---|
| Royal Yachting Assoc.* | 21·6 | 31·1 | 32·2 | 33·7 | 36·1 | 39·5 | 36·4 | 49·2 | 52·1 |
| British Waterski Fed.* | NA | 3·3 | 3·4 | 4·0 | 4·1 | 4·4 | 5·7 | 6·8 | 7·8 |
| Nat. Fed. Of Anglers* | 394·6 | 354·4 | 354·4 | 360·8 | 383·4 | 407·7 | 451·1 | 461·8 | 448·2 |
| Wildfowl Trust* | 7·4 | 8·9 | 9·3 | 9·8 | 11·0 | 12·0 | 13·0 | 14·0 | 15·0 |
| BTO | 3·8 | 4·3 | 5·1 | 6·0 | 6·9 | 7·0 | 7·3 | 7·1 | 7·3 |
| RSPB | 29·7 | 65·7 | 71·2 | 122·0 | 139·0 | 166·0 | 181·0 | 204·0 | 216·0 |
| WAGBI* | NA | 21·3 | NA | 28·0 | 28·0 | 29·0 | 30·8 | 31·7 | 34·4 |
| SPNC (now RSNC) | 21·0 | 55·7 | 63·9 | 74·8 | 84·4 | 97·1 | 100·7 | 111·1 | 115·2 |

Note: figures presented in thousands

* Mainly from Sports Council (1977), Water Space Amenity Commission Annual Report 1977–78, Digest of Countryside Recreation statistics 1977.

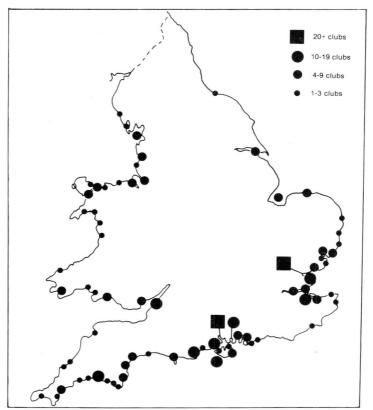

Fig. 5:5 Number of clubs in 1970 affiliated to the Royal Yachting Association on English and Welsh estuaries. Based on Tanner (1973).

anyone is working on them; there remains much to be learnt about the effect of these swinging moorings on bird numbers and diversity.

Fortunately only the more sheltered estuaries can be used by water skiers but the noise intrusion and, therefore, disturbance is considerable. Quite large areas of water, as in eastern Langstone Harbour, have to be set aside for this activity, which involves few participants. It is to be hoped that strict controls will be maintained on areas where water-skiing can take place.

Angling is a relatively passive activity on estuaries and as such appears rarely to disturb feeding birds for long, unless the number of anglers is particularly high. Bait digging, however, does give rise to some concern among birdwatchers. Bait digging is really more than a leisure activity, for quite large numbers of people obtain a living or at least some income from it. No detailed studies have been made but its effect on birds is likely to be twofold. Firstly, the presence of bait diggers can keep the birds from some potential feeding areas. One only has to see the numbers of people involved in places in north Kent, south Essex, north Norfolk or in some of the south coast or north-eastern estuaries to appreciate this possibility. Secondly, there is the reduction of the invertebrates themselves. Although a scarcity of larger *Nereis* and to a lesser extent of *Arenicola* has been reported locally, it is not known whether the reduction is due to digging, or if their removal permanently reduces their population. Equally it is possible that turning over of the mud could have harmful effects on non-desired species, either by burying them or by exposing them to excessive cold, heat, desiccation or predation. If this activity is increasing, as it appears to be, then its implications should be considered further.

Wildfowling, in contrast to many other activities, has been carried out for many decades. Throughout that time there have been many fluctuations in the numbers of birds present; weather conditions and hence wintering distribution, breeding success and habitat available have all varied. There is no information on how these factors have combined and, therefore, whether changing patterns that we have observed are related to any one of them. At the end of the nineteenth century and the beginning of the twentieth many waders that we now regard as wintering species in Devon – Knot, Bar-tailed Godwit, Grey Plover – were known only as passage migrants (Prater 1976). Did the heavy shooting pressure at that time force them either to move southward or to large estuaries where they were relatively secure? Tubbs (1977) suggests that shooting may have been partly responsible in the past for low numbers of waders on Hampshire estuaries in winter. The relatively enclosed nature of these estuaries could have increased the disturbance to waterfowl. Similarly Roberts (1974) indicates that on the Solway Firth the Barnacle and other geese were under severe pressure from shooters up to the Protection of Birds Act of 1954. The worst effects from wildfowling undoubtedly come from uncontrolled shooting. Nowadays many wildfowling clubs, affiliated to WAGBI, have done much to control the number of shooters or even to introduce bag limits. As a result, for example, at Caerlaverock the mean bag as a percentage of birds wintering varies from 2·6% for Pink-footed Goose to 17·2% for the Greylag Goose, with most ducks being between 6·0 and 8·0% (Kerr 1974). Unfortunately, even now many estuaries still have 'marsh cowboys' who cause a great deal of disturbance and, since they are quite unable to identify which are quarry or non-quarry species, attempt to shoot virtually anything that flies. It is probable, in most instances, that the major problems with shooting on estuaries relate to disturbance rather than mortality.

Shooting is not restricted to Britain and can be much more intense elsewhere. Southern Europe is well known as a danger area but so are some parts of north-western Europe: Denmark, in particular, has to be singled out in this context (Meltofte 1978). In Britain, until recent X-ray studies were carried out, the size of the shooting problem was not fully appreciated. No fewer than 24% of Pintail, and 19% of Pochard examined at Slimbridge in winter had been hit (data supplied by the Wildfowl Trust) while even in the protected Bewick's Swan a remarkable 34% carried lead shot (Evans, Wood and Kear 1973). On the Wash 23% of dead birds from the tide line examined by Pilcher et al (1974) had died directly from, or had been wounded by, shot. This is in addition to the birds retrieved by hunters. No adequate data exist for waders but it is likely that some of them, particularly the larger species, may also carry shot. The shooting season starts on 1 September and this may cause the break up of roosts when it is excessive.

The main impact of passive leisure activities occurs between May and September, thus affecting two important periods of the birds' year – breeding and moulting. Breeding birds are most threatened on the sandy beach and dune complexes on the outer parts of estuaries. Terns and some waders, especially Ringed Plovers, are particularly liable to be disturbed. Little and Sandwich Terns are very susceptible to disturbance. Blindell (1974) summarised twenty-five years of data on the former species from Essex; he showed that in 1974 egg collecting accounted for 61% of all nests lost and 30% of all clutches laid! While deliberate egg stealing is the major problem with this species, it is also vulnerable to disturbance from walkers, including inconsiderate birdwatchers. A colony of Little Terns was virtually exterminated by disturbance and accidental nest trampling at Bradwell, and breeding success at others was low until the colonies were fenced off and wardening introduced. There has been a tendency for the most susceptible species to concentrate in reserves or in the less inaccessible areas such as islands, or, as in the case of Ringed Plovers, on to adjacent farmland and industrial sites (Prater 1975).

Moulting birds are slightly less prone to disturbance since they tend to roost on the very large saltmarshes of our major estuaries. It is unclear whether this is a result of excessive pressure on them elsewhere or due to the patterns of food availability. While in moult the birds require a good food supply as the process of feather replacement increases energy requirements, also flight is impaired so if forced to fly unnecessarily even more energy will be needed. In winter few estuaries have serious disturbance problems from the general public. On spring tides, when available roosting areas are few and the birds concentrate at the top of the beach, dog-walking can sometimes have an impact. For example, it is severe at times on the Dee (at West Kirby and the Point of Air), the Ayr coast and on several sandy beaches in Essex. Inconsiderate birdwatching can also cause disturbance but there are few coastal areas where it is regular or severe enough in winter to cause a real problem although, with increasing popularity, it may become one.

SHELLFISH FISHERIES

Commercial exploitation of shellfish in Britain is limited to a few species and a few areas. Three species are involved – the cockle *Cerastoderma edule*, the mussel *Mytilus edulis* and oysters *Ostrea edulis*. Cockles are (or were) found in considerable quantities on the Wash, Thames and Burry Inlet, although other estuaries such as Morecambe Bay and the Dee have had small industries in the past. Problems for estuary birds can come from two directions; firstly, since shellfish are a cash crop anything feeding on them represents an apparent threat, leading to occasional pressure to kill the competing birds; and secondly, the techniques for gathering shellfish may be harmful to the other invertebrates in the sand. Looking at the latter problem first, we have to consider the methods used for gathering. In the Burry Inlet and to some extent the Wash, relatively unsophisticated hand-raking of cockle beds is employed. The cockles are gathered in heaps then raked and/or sieved into baskets. This method may leave a number of smaller individuals on the surface of the sand and increases their chances of predation, but it is thought that relatively little additional mortality to them or other species takes place. Modern methods, however, are much less satisfactory. On the Thames suction pumps are used to take in the surface 2–4 cm of sand, it is filtered and larger items retained. This damages a considerable percentage of both cockles and other invertebrates.

There is pressure from fishermen to reduce the numbers of cockle predators. As a result of their lobbies the Oystercatcher, the major avian predator, has been placed on the Second Schedule of the Protection of Birds Act. This allows it to be shot on specified areas (in North Norfolk, Morecambe Bay and the Burry Inlet) under the order of the local Sea Fisheries Authority if the species poses a threat to the fishery. In the last two of these estuaries this order has been invoked, on Morecambe Bay

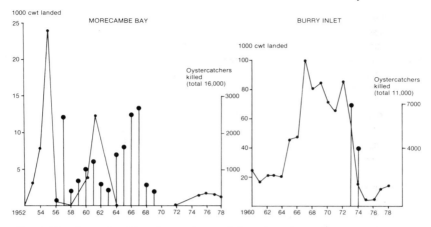

Fig. 5:6 Landings of cockles (*Cerastoderma edule*) and numbers of Oystercatchers shot in Morecambe Bay and the Burry Inlet. Data based on Driver (1977) and Franklin (1977).

between 1956 and 1969 and on the Burry Inlet between 1972 and 1974. The numbers of Oystercatcher killed and the weight of cockles harvested are shown in Fig. 5:6. Culls were introduced after concern had been shown by local fishermen at decreasing catches of cockles. Conservationists were alarmed at this situation. No one disputed that Oystercatchers were a major predator of cockles but the critical question was what is the relationship between numbers of Oystercatchers, numbers of cockles, and the yield? The Ministry of Agriculture, Fisheries and Food initially were satisfied with the answer, based on few data, that Oystercatchers were the prime predators, taking up to 90% of the second winter cockles and therefore decreasing the available catch. However, a recent review of the information available for the Burry Inlet (Horwood and Goss-Custard 1977) demonstrated that:

(i) there was no relationship between the size of the cockle population in early winter and the number of birds feeding on it

(ii) in years of high second year cockles stocks (400+ per m²) an average 46% was the maximum that theoretically could have been removed by Oyster-catchers

(iii) in most years with less than 210 per m² the theoretical consumption of cockles by Oystercatchers was well above the number available – in fact up to 25 times too high – indicating the birds must have fed on other items

(iv) regardless of the winter density of cockles it was found that cockles reached a relatively constant number and uniform distribution by spring. This indicated that Oystercatchers must have switched to other prey when the density of winter cockles decreased to around 50–100 per m². That this level was regularly reached also indicates that fishermen too restricted their catch or, at least, were constrained by the poor return at low cockle densities.

The one generalisation that does come through is that factors other than Oyster-catcher predation play important, if not dominant, roles in determining the cockle crop. Franklin (1977) mentions that changes in the river channel, an increase of fine sediment being deposited on the main cockle grounds and an increase in *Spartina* have all contributed towards the decline of the industry. The extremely variable spat settlement also appears to play an important role. The very good 1963 and reasonable 1965 and 1967 settlements resulted in a large crop available to the early 1970s but the combination of factors mentioned above, plus Oystercatchers, fish and fishing predation, have resulted in a very poor fishery at the present time.

There are a number of important lessons to be learnt from the Burry Inlet controversy. Perhaps the main one is that before any cull is started detailed scientific investigations should take place to see if it is justified. The results of these studies should also be assessed independently. Great care must be taken to ensure that a vociferous outcry from one group or another does not result in hasty action. Figure 5:6 shows that in two separate areas it is only when cockle landings have crashed that Oystercatchers are shot. Equally, careful monitoring needs to take place subsequent to any action in order to assess the patterns of any recovery in numbers. Since 1963 there has apparently been a steady increase in Oystercatchers in the whole country; as a result no lasting effect on their numbers has been detected in the estuaries where culls were implemented. Although relatively low numbers have occurred in the Burry Inlet it is not clear whether this is a function of little food, little immigration or even low production of young. There are indications that 1978 and 1979 have been good years for spat settlement so we may see some interesting developments.

Mussel fisheries are found in several Irish Sea estuaries, especially Conwy Bay and Menai Straits which are supplied with seed mussels from Morecambe Bay, and the Wash. Although Oystercatchers also take mussels this appears to have very little effect on mussel numbers. Some artificial fisheries have been established in sea lochs in western Scotland where mussels are grown on ropes hanging from floating platforms. Eiders have been shown to take 3–6% of these (Dunthorn 1971); at present they are not an important predator although perhaps the potential is there. A problem of similar proportions occurs in some fish-eating birds on estuaries. At times Red-breasted Mergansers, Goosanders and Cormorants have been accused of taking large numbers of fish. Here too there is lack of adequate data on standing crop predation rates and other mortality factors. Birds are not important predators of the few oyster fisheries which have been established in southern England, partly because of the size of the mollusc but also because they are not exposed at low water. New stocks of *Crassostrea gigas*, however, are being laid inter-tidally but little predation is yet apparent.

NATURAL PROBLEMS

So far we have considered direct threats from man. This is not the complete story since there are many natural changes taking place, some for the benefit of birds while others can be detrimental. The potential changes associated with accretion of sediments in inner estuaries have been described in the previous chapter and the pros and cons of the different saltmarsh types in Chapter 2. The balance of accretion and erosion determines the presence of intertidal mudflats. Typically there are currents running parallel or diagonally to coastlines. The net result is that in places there are erosion and in others accretion zones. As we have seen, many estuaries have sand bars partly closing off their mouths. Behind these bars finer sediments accumulate forming good feeding areas for waders. Good examples of these are Spurn Point in the Humber and Dawlish Warren on the Exe. On open coasts similar conditions may prevail although here sand bars form embayments with little freshwater inflow. Again such areas can be very productive; one only has to look at the complex area of spits and sandbars on the north Norfolk coast or along the Moray/Nairn shore of the outer Moray Firth. The system is dynamic with the sea building up the spit until at some stage it breaks through the middle, isolates a small island which it then erodes away and so repeats the process. Spurn Point has seen this chain of events happen on approximately a 250 year cycle. The sea broke through in 1849 and before that in about 1608; it threatens to do so in the near future despite artificial strengthening. Concern is felt for the loss of yet another area where shingle-breeding species occur, but also there is the danger that an eroding channel would be opened up well to the north of the present river channel, sweeping away considerable areas of Spurn Bight. This is a major wader and Shelduck feeding area.

In the inner estuary the movement of river channels, usually in their mid reaches, has two effects. Firstly, the sediments can be so mobile that a diverse invertebrate fauna never has a chance to build up to become an important feeding ground. On Morecambe Bay the Kent channel has moved a great deal over the years and parts of it are relatively poor areas; similarly, many of the sediments above the Severn Bridge on the Severn Estuary are very impoverished indeed. This is reflected in their bird populations. A second consequence of this mobility is that saltmarshes can be undermined with the resulting loss of breeding, roosting or wildfowl feeding areas. At Slimbridge, for example, the saltings called the Dumbles have been eroded for many years; the average annual loss of the 40 ha marsh during the last twenty years has been 0·4 ha, with a maximum of 2 ha in 1966–67. Here the area is primarily a grazing site for up to 4,000 Wigeon and several thousand White-fronted Geese.

THE FUTURE

The overwhelming majority of the population would be aghast if tens of thousands of birds were deliberately killed so that another development could be erected or more land created. This is precisely what will happen if we do not build conservation consideration into our actions. Change is inevitable, but surely progress should be on all fronts, so embracing cultural, aesthetic as well as economic grounds. The natural world is our only real resource; if we heedlessly exploit it, ignoring the forces by which it has evolved, then we shall all be poorer and will have introduced an automatic instability into the whole structure.

The conservation movement (and here I am using conservation in the natural context) operates on three planes. In alphabetical order they are amenity, educational and scientific. Individuals react in different ways depending on the balance of their interests. So a great range of attitudes exist from the 'everything must be protected' attitude up to the maximum compromise which is 'even a tiny concession means that not all is lost'. It is the duty of those professionally engaged in conservation to assess the impact of any proposal in an objective way and to advise and/or influence those weighing up the needs of the whole community. Conservation cannot always be judged by commercial criteria and so it is vital that co-ordinated plans are drawn up to deal with situations that arise. So how can this be done? Firstly, we need to know what natural resources we have and we must understand how they work. This is the scientific side of conservation but it is not confined to professional scientists, amateurs can and do play an important role. Perhaps because a preponderance of money goes towards research on birds, the input by birdwatchers through national or local societies has been immense; without it we would not be in the well-informed position we are today. The understanding of how the systems work is usually best carried out by professionals who can study a few examples in depth, but even here the broad survey approach which the amateurs can provide enables us to see if the conclusions from very detailed studies can be related to a wide range of conditions.

From the knowledge thus obtained we can decide what priorities there should be, which habitats or species are particularly vulnerable, how the amenity value can be enhanced without destroying the habitat, or at what stage we have to say 'enough'. In an ideal world this would be difficult enough but in reality the problems are much greater. Adequate data cannot be gathered on all habitats simultaneously; also different environmental factors will operate in differing ways on the various studies that can be carried out. To achieve all together would cost an enormous amount and the budget available would never suffice. We are left, therefore, with no alternative but to attempt a rationalisation with fragmentary knowledge.

Fortunately, birds form a group which is better known than most. This is not surprising since there are probably more people interested in birds than in any other single group of animals or plants. Indeed this may be a perfectly valid reason to concentrate a disproportionate amount of scientific conservation effort on them for surely conservation must be, at least partly, related to the value and interest to man. That is not to say that habitat or species maintenance should not be an end in its own right, only that some priorities may be needed and if so its relationship to man is, perhaps, the most immediate one.

Turning back to the estuarine habitat we have seen that there are many threats, some large, some small, but taken together they form a massive assault. The pressures are now just as great on the intertidal flats as they are on saltmarshes and reclaimed land. The counts of birds for the 'Estuaries Enquiry', the 'Wetlands Enquiry' and the 'Wildfowl counts' have provided detailed information as to what is where, and when, in Britain and Ireland. The international counts have achieved similar information for other European countries. We have seen clearly that in winter Britain and Ireland supports in the order of half of all waterfowl in western Europe. As a result, our conservation efforts for this habitat must rank among the national priorities. Certainly the Nature Conservancy Council, Institute of Terrestrial Ecology, Natural Environmental Research Council and the Science Research Council, have recognised this by providing funding for both additional survey and detailed ecosystem research.

Are we doing enough? Or to put it another way – are we allowed to develop a reasonable approach to estuarine conservation? Often the feeling persists amongst amateur and professional conservationists that each development scheme has to be fought off in isolation and that far too little thought is given to alternatives by developers. A national strategy is needed. Already an attempt has been made by the NCC in 'A Nature Conservation Review' (Ratcliffe 1977) to catalogue and describe the importance of all British habitats and sites. It does represent, however, only the absolute minimum number of outstanding or key sites, but nevertheless it provides a most valuable overall view. The relative importance of sites can change with changing habitat; more extensive data or the destruction of less good habitat may increase the importance of what is left. The NCC also operates the system of Sites of Special Scientific Interest (SSSI's) by which sites can be designed as being of importance. This, however, has the drawback that legal control remains with the owners and the NCC only have to be consulted if a change of land use is proposed that would involve a planning application. The NCC does operate a series of National Nature Reserves which are much more secure; similar, but usually smaller, reserves are operated by many voluntary bodies such as the RSPB and the county trusts. Surprisingly, despite the apparent massive array of reserves and documentation there are really very few estuaries which are securely protected.

Bridgwater Bay, Dyfi, Lindisfarne and the north Norfolk coast were included in the UK Ramsar list. The RSPB has recently bought sections of the Dee (2,040 ha), Langstone Harbour (554 ha) and Morecambe Bay (2,428 ha). Most of the other major estuaries are covered by SSSI orders. The Ribble estuary will soon be declared as a NNR. In virtually all of these cases, substantial areas have little effective statutory protection, even of the protected estuaries.

The framework does exist for a national policy to protect estuaries but it needs to be developed further. Some of those wishing to develop estuaries have shown appreciation of the national significance of the habitat. The Water Resources Board (1973) recommended that 'not more than two estuary sites should be developed in this century and not more than one at a time'. In fact their preferred strategy only involved the Dee. However, even here the Regional Water Authorities have considerable independence from the central organisation – now renamed the Central Water Planning Unit. The ad hoc assessment should be changed so that everyone can be more certain of the status of each estuary. Inevitably this will mean that money will have to be found, but the alternative of piecemeal loss with prime conservation areas being isolated and then destroyed, would present a much greater loss to the country as a whole.

CHAPTER 6

# The counts

Fortunately, as a result of a few earlier studies, especially on the Wash (Ballance and Scott 1965) and the Morecambe Bay Feasibility Study in 1967 and 1968, we already had some pilot studies to help formulate techniques and organisation. The pilot survey in the winter of 1969/70 provided more useful information for the full survey which then ran from August 1970 to May 1975.

ORGANISATION AND METHODS

A three- or four-tier system was found to provide the best combination of advantages. This consisted of counter, estuary organiser, regional (usually county) organiser, and national organiser levels. There were many cases where it was more efficient for individual counters or the estuary organisers to deal directly with the national organiser, particularly where there were few estuaries within a county.

The whole survey depended on the willingness and co-operation of the individual counters and their efforts cannot be praised too highly. They dealt directly under the individual estuary organisers. The immense advantage brought by the latter was their local expertise; they also acted as a focal point for organising effort. Thus there was someone who could be contacted at short notice if a counter was unable to turn out. He could then modify the counting procedure or find someone else able to stand in. In any event it reduced the problem of finding that a site was not counted because of illness, or because the counter had moved elsewhere, or was otherwise unavailable. The other job of the estuary organiser was to distribute and collect the recording cards, with local knowledge an assessment and continual check could be made on the quality of information.

From the estuary organiser the counts usually went to a regional organiser; this person tended to be at a county level and, apart from being the main distributor and collector of cards, was able to extract data for use within a local context. The national organiser was then left with a relatively small job. He was involved in deciding the counting dates, circulating cards and instructions, checking, adding and summarising the data, writing reports on and assessments from them, and developing and maintaining the counting network. Virtually without exception I was helped along by a keen, informed and able network of organisers; the job would have been much more difficult, if not virtually impossible, without them.

The counts were carried out during two hours either side of high water on spring tides. Experience from counting the larger estuaries had shown that this was the only way to ensure that birds were within reach of the observers. Since spring tides occur at two weekly intervals the actual date of the count had to be related to them. Whenever possible a date towards the middle of the month was chosen but frequently in autumn and spring this proved to be impossible. The count had to take place at a weekend, and Sunday was chosen to enable as many people as possible to participate. Counts were carried out on a range of dates over the six years and, therefore, the data provide a broad picture for the month and cannot be used to separate differential age or sex migration patterns. The dates recommended are presented in Table 6:1. To reduce the possibility of duplication or omission of birds due to local movements or migration, as many estuaries as possible were counted on the recommended day. Due to a number of factors not all estuaries (estimated to be about 20%) could be counted on that day. These included those whose high water occurred during the hours of darkness, or when there was stormy or foggy weather, illness or other unavailability of the counter, or difficulty of counting the estuary on spring tide. The last was a problem encountered on many small and long estuaries where access was difficult. These estuaries were counted on a date as close as possible to the official day, usually within a week. Whenever counts took place the whole estuary was counted on the same date and at the same tidal state to eliminate, as far as possible, any further duplication. Only occasionally did this prove to be impossible. The errors that this procedure involved could not be estimated but were thought to be small. Counts were returned through the local organisers to the national organiser on standard recording cards; these had space for comments on disturbance, weather or other factors which may have affected the counts. The card is shown in Fig. 6:1.

Table 6:1  *Dates for the co-ordinated counts of the 'Birds of Estuaries Enquiry' 1969/70–1974/75*

|  | 1969–70 | 1970–71 | 1971–72 | 1972–73 | 1973–74 | 1974–75 |
|---|---|---|---|---|---|---|
| July | — | — | 25 | 30 | 29 | 21 |
| August | 3 | 2 | 22 | 27 | 26 | 18 |
| September | 14 | 13 | 19 | 24 | 16 | 15 |
| October | 12 | 11 | 17 | 22 | 14 | 13 |
| November | 9 | 8 | 21 | 19 | 11 | 17 |
| December | 14 | 13 | 19 | 10 | 9 | 15 |
| January | 11 | 10 | 16 | 21 | 13 | 12 |
| February | 8 | 7 | 13 | 18 | 10 | 2 |
| March | 8 | 7 | 5 | 18 | 10 | 29 |
| April | 5 | 4 | 2 | 8 | 7 | 27 |
| May | — | — | 14 | 6 | 5 | 25 |
| June | — | — | — | 3 | 23 | 23 |

| OBSERVER | | COUNTY | | AREA COVERED |
|---|---|---|---|---|
| ESTUARY | | GRID REFERENCE | | DAY / MONTH / YEAR |
| COUNT Start    Finish   TIMES    B.S.T.    B.S.T. | | ACTUAL HIGH TIDE | | STATE OF TIDE |

| Species | Code | | Species | Code | | Species | Code |
|---|---|---|---|---|---|---|---|
| Gt.Cr.Grebe | 008 | | Oysterctchr. | 182 | | G.B-b.Gull | 258 |
| Cormorant | 035 | | Lapwing | 185 | | L.B-b.Gull | 257 |
| Mallard | 072 | | Ringed Plov. | 191 | | Herring Gull | 256 |
| Teal | 075 | | Grey Plover | 187 | | Comm.Gull | 255 |
| Wigeon | 080 | | Gldn.Plover | 188 | | Blk-hd.Gull | 263 |
| Pintail | 078 | | Turnstone | 218 | | | |
| Shoveler | 083 | | Com.Snipe | 221 | | | |
| Pochard | 086 | | Jack Snipe | 222 | | | |
| Goldeneye | 090 | | Curlew | 202 | | | |
| Com.Scoter | 098 | | Whimbrel | 200 | | | |
| Eider | 095 | | Bl-t.Godwit | 203 | | | |
| Rd.-br.Merg. | 106 | | Bar-t.Godwit | 204 | | | |
| Shelduck | 071 | | Green Sand. | 211 | | | |
| G.Lg.Goose | 059 | | Wood Sand. | 213 | | | |
| White front G. | 060 | | Common Sand. | 214 | | | |
| Pink foot G. | 062 | | Redshank | 206 | | | |
| Barnacle G. | 067 | | Spotted Red. | 205 | | | |
| Brent G. | 066 | | Greenshank | 208 | | | |
| Canada G. | 068 | | Knot | 225 | | | |
| Mute Swan | 057 | | Dunlin | 235 | | | |
| Whooper S. | 055 | | Sanderling | 224 | | | |
| Bewick S. | 056 | | Ruff | 239 | | | |

**BRITISH TRUST FOR ORNITHOLOGY:
ESTUARY BIRD COUNTING CARD**

Please consult instruction leaflet for method of completing card.

A few reminders:

1. Complete sections below concerning weather, disturbance and remarks.

2. Record only what you observe. Accurate counts are required. Estimated numbers must be written in square brackets thus [350]

3. GULLS. Where direct counts impossible please estimate.

WEATHER

DISTURBANCE

REMARKS

When complete, return this card to the regional organiser, alternatively to the central organiser:
A. Prater, B.T.O., Beech Grove, Tring, Herts.

Fig. 6:1 Count card used for the 'Birds of Estuaries Enquiry'.

*Waders*

Each estuary and each species has its own characteristic so that no precise method of counting was laid down. Techniques which had been found to be successful in Morecambe Bay were summarised by John Wilson and included in the instructions provided for observers. The essence of successful counting is to know the area and know all of the roost sites, the few exceptions to this will be considered later. Roosts are traditional although some may be vacated seasonally depending on disturbance or habitat quality factors, these aspects have been expanded in Chapter 3. Spring tide roosts can be discovered by visiting the estuary on neap tides when disturbance is usually less severe and noting the roosts used and the directions of flight lines. The neap tide roosts are usually used as sub-roosts on spring tides. By following the flight lines from these sub-roosts and by searching likely spits, areas of saltmarsh or adjacent fields, all birds should be located. Roosts are rarely monospecific but nevertheless species usually separate out to a certain extent.

With large roosts two approaches can be used to aid accurate counting. They are to position one or more observers around a roost, each counting different components, or to split flocks by a very careful approach. The former is much more successful. It is almost never practical to attempt to count all species in the same way; anyone who has stood on the Wash and watched a vast swirling mass of perhaps ten species flying on to an adjacent field will appreciate the difficulty. Equally it is very difficult to count massed roosting flocks of the smaller waders such as Knot and Dunlin. The more accurate method is to consider the behaviour patterns and conspicuousness of each species and count at the best time for each. At a large roost, which can be easily observed, counts can be spread over three or four hours. Some species can be counted as they enter the roost from sub-roosts. To do this the observer needs to be in a position almost two hours before high tide, when the incoming tide steadily moves birds past a stationary observer. Knot and Dunlin are often easier to count this way, for small flocks enter the main roost during a period of almost an hour. Even with these species there tends to be mass arrivals towards the end of the gathering period. Most species have gathered on the roost half an hour before high tide and will remain there for an hour. At this time most of the large and distinctive species can be counted. Oystercatchers, Curlew, Grey Plover, Bar-tailed Godwit and all of the wildfowl fall into this category. Repeat counts can be made. Then as the tide starts to fall and mud is uncovered some birds commence feeding almost straight away. Redshank, Ringed Plover and often Dunlin can be counted now. During the high tide period it is usually possible to check several others areas where different species roost. For example, Turnstone, Ringed Plover, Sanderling and Oystercatcher can be expected to separate out and roost on shingle or sand spits, while Curlew, Redshank and others, especially in south-eastern England, can be found roosting on inland fields. After checking these places it is possible to get back to the main roosts to count on the ebbing tide.

On large saltmarshes where it is impossible to find a suitable vantage point the alternative method has to be used. With a careful approach, usually diagonally or nearly parallel, it is possible to split up roosting flocks. Birds can then be counted as they fly behind the observer. A careless approach will put all birds up together and present immense difficulties.

It was found that small estuaries, particularly the long narrow ones of south-west England, were best counted at low water or on an intermediate high tide. On these estuaries trees reach down to the level of MHWS making visibility and often access poor, while the birds roost either on small saltmarshes or adjacent fields. By careful approach at low tide it was relatively easy to count all birds on their feeding grounds.

Although rocky shores were not included in the original proposals for the 'Estuaries Enquiry' counts of this habitat were encouraged. In areas where offshore rocks remained exposed at high tide the counts were best carried out by walking the beach at about mid-tide level during low tide. This allowed fairly close approach to all feeding birds and they could be counted as they flew behind the observer (Summers, Atkinson and Nicholl 1975). Da Prato and Da Prato (1978) estimated that up to 20% of Turnstone and 35% of Purple Sandpiper roosted on outlying rocks and could not be counted at a high tide visit. In areas where this roosting habitat was not present counts could be made at high water. A general problem, however, still exists where species such as Oystercatcher, Curlew and Redshank may feed inland but come to the shore to feed at low water. The problems of counting the inland waders such as Lapwing and Golden Plover are similar but greater – they also appear in greater numbers when the fields are frozen.

*Wildfowl*

The main aim of the counts was to record wader numbers, but much information was also gathered for wildfowl. Most of the duck found on estuaries during the day are best counted at high spring tide, when they sit on the water at the edge of the tide. Birds which had been grazing the marshes or had been tucked away in creeks and gutters are also conspicuous. Any birds still on the saltmarshes should be relatively close to the observer and within view. Of course the presence of duck does not necessarily imply that they are feeding on the estuary; many dabbling ducks, especially Mallard and Shoveler, will roost or loaf on the intertidal flats or the sea by the day and fly inland to feed at night. Usually, duck concentrate in a few areas, particularly where large creeks leave the marshes, and can be counted from one or more vantage points, but walking along a saltmarsh may be necessary at times. Ducks rarely fly during high water, making counting relatively simple. It is essential to make counts of duck on large estuaries at high tide, otherwise they can be widely scattered. Our counts were supplemented by those from the Wildfowl Trust's 'Wildfowl Counts'; these results were kindly provided by G. L. Atkinson-Willes.

Seaduck pose considerable problems although most Eider, Goldeneye, Scaup and Red-breasted Merganser are found in inshore waters. Again, high water counts provide the best counts but because these birds feed actively many repeat counts may be necessary. Scoter and Long-tailed Duck occur further offshore and can only be adequately counted from the shore in calm conditions; they also dive frequently. Our data were supplemented by data from the 'Wildfowl Counts' and that obtained from special studies; in particular L. Campbell and E. Milne – East Scotland; P. Kinnear – Shetland; D. Lea and P. Hope-Jones – Orkney; R. Lovegrove – Carmarthen Bay; and G. Mudge and D. Allen – Moray Firth to Spey Bay. Many of these studies involved the use of aerial surveys.

The grey geese pose yet another set of counting problems. Mainly, they use estuaries as nocturnal roosts and can only be adequately counted by counters positioned on flight lines before dusk as the birds come in. Most of the data on grey geese in this book are from special counts organised by M. A. Ogilvie for the Wildfowl Trust. Brent Geese behave and are counted in a similar way to most duck.

*Gulls*

The counts were not designed to obtain gull numbers and they are, therefore, poorly recorded. Gulls loafing on upper marshes or flats, or those feeding on the upper shore, often form daytime roosts near the main wader roosts and can usually be counted at the same time. However, many large gulls will be on the outer sand banks of the large estuaries and are never seen from the shore. Even so, the largest numbers in many estuaries occur in nocturnal roosts; these birds are drawn in from a wide area, including inland. Birds on the mudflats need to be counted an hour or two before dusk and then a network of observers will be needed to count birds coming in on the several flight lines. By counting many smallish flocks reasonably accurate counts can be made of the birds seen. The worrying aspects of all gull roost counts is the number entering the roost after dark, the difficulty of identification in bad light (usually only small and large gull categories can be used then) and the impossibility of finding out how many (if any) birds come to the roost from the outer banks. Some efforts were made to count this important group of birds but special counts are necessary before comprehensive data can be obtained.

*Other birds*

The techniques for counting other waterbirds such as grebes, divers and cormorants are quite straightforward although the main problem is to find the birds. Grebes and divers may be spread thinly over large areas but they usually concentrate in particular areas at certain tidal states. Preliminary investigations need to be made to locate these areas. Cormorants have a fairly complex tidal and diurnal pattern of activity and their local patterns of behaviour need to be known for accurate counting. However, they are large, conspicuous and often sit on sandbanks or constructions to dry their wings.

Examination of county bird reports and direct contact with county bird recorders and other observers with specialist knowledge provide estimates of the number in Britain for species not always well covered by estuary counts. The problems and errors in these data are discussed in the relevant publications and are summarised in the species accounts later in this book.

ACCURACY

Counting estuary birds is not easy, especially in winter, and counts are liable to a number of potential errors. These can be separated under two headings – those due to the observer's inability to count accurately all birds on the estuary, and those which subsequently involve an incorrect interpretation of results. Two factors contribute towards the former; they are errors in estimating the number observed and the inability to find all birds in the area due to variations in coverage or changes in weather conditions. Total population assessment involves inaccuracies due to the incomplete coverage of all estuaries or the species use of habitats not examined by the counts.

There has been much discussion of variations in the assessment of numbers by different observers but few detailed analyses have been made (e.g. Matthews 1960, Prater 1979). Most tests have involved a known number of birds in flocks on photographs, the observers being asked to estimate numbers in, usually, 30 seconds. The photographic tests indicate that there is little difference between the abilities of keen birdwatchers and experienced counters (Matthews 1960). There was, however, considerable variation in the estimates made but the average of all counts provided a fairly close approximation to the correct total, at least up to a flock size in the low thousands. There is a tendency for observers slightly to over-estimate (10–20%) flocks of 100–400, but to under-estimate larger flocks. With flocks of about 3,000 birds the average under-estimate was 24 ± 25% (Prater 1979).

The ability of observers to count birds accurately in the field is likely to be different from their ability to count from photographs. They are likely to gain by counting over a period of several hours as flock shapes continually change; also, species show different characteristics of dispersion, conspicuousness or behaviour which enables a much better 'feel' to be obtained. On the other hand adverse weather conditions are not infrequent in winter and these can affect the observers ability as well as affecting the birds' behaviour. Its effects on feeding have been considered earlier but a few words on the effectiveness of the counts under different conditions are appropriate here.

There were only a few counts which were hampered by stormy weather, when roosts may be difficult to find due to a combination of disruption from the 'normal' pattern by higher tides and the birds choice of sheltered areas such as the lee of saltmarsh plants or embankments. When birds fly in strong winds they are especially difficult to count because flock adhesion is less and at times they are even difficult to identify. In addition, November and December counts were frequently disrupted by fog. During the period 1969–75 no extended period of really severe weather occurred but such weather can affect counts in that roosts may develop on ice-floes and be quite inaccessible from the shore. This happened in the 1962–63 winter. A summary of the weather conditions during the period of the counts is presented in Table 6:2. Partial counts caused by bad weather have been omitted from the figures used when calculating average monthly numbers.

Counts are also affected by the tide height and the time of high tide. A moderate or high spring tide is desirable for counting on all major estuaries. On several large estuaries there are no really high spring tides in daylight in December, January or February. This problem is most acute from the Wash northwards on the east coast; and the further north one goes in midwinter so the shorter the days become, aggravating this situation. This difficulty with high tides occurs, although less

*Table 6:2   Differences in average temperature for England and Wales from the 1931–60 long term average for the winter months of the 'Birds of Estuaries Enquiry' counts*

|         | October | November | December | January | February | March |
|---------|---------|----------|----------|---------|----------|-------|
| 1969–70 | +2·5    | −1·3     | −1·4     | +0·1    | −0·7     | −2·1  |
| 1970–71 | +0·5    | +0·9     | −0·5     | +0·9    | +0·9     | −0·7  |
| 1971–72 | +1·3    | −0·7     | +1·7     | +0·2    | +0·5     | +0·6  |
| 1972–73 | +0·4    | −0·6     | +1·0     | +0·9    | +0·5     | +0·5  |
| 1973–74 | −1·0    | −0·8     | NA       | +2·5    | +1·9     | 0·0   |
| 1974–75 | −3·0    | 0·0      | +3·2     | +3·2    | +1·0     | −0·9  |

NA: not available

*Table 6:3 Percentage contribution of different roosting zones to the number of waders wintering on the Colne Estuary 1973–74 and 1974–75*

|  | Known main roosts* | Rest of larger areas† | Rest of smaller areas | Av. total |
|---|---|---|---|---|
| Oystercatcher | 99 | 1 | ‡ | 400 |
| Ringed Plover | 60 | 27 | 13 | 120 |
| Grey Plover | 58 | 41 | 1 | 170 |
| Turnstone | 37 | 60 | 3 | 170 |
| Curlew | 66 | 22 | 12 | 815 |
| Redshank | 58 | 23 | 19 | 1,605 |
| Dunlin | 47 | 31 | 22 | 6,430 |
| Sanderling | 77 | 23 | 0 | 135 |
| Mean | 63 | 28 | 9 | |

\* Colne Point and Fingringhoe
† Above plus East Mersea and Langenhoe
‡ Present

seriously, in south-western England and South Wales. Because counts have to be made at weekends, suboptimal tides may have to be chosen. Low spring tides affect April, May and, especially, June counts in some years. Midsummer counts are, therefore, particularly difficult. The effects of different tide heights combined with disturbance pressures has already been discussed.

Some species are particularly easy to count on their feeding grounds. Shelduck and Oystercatcher are in this category, being large, conspicuous and not in dense feeding flocks. On the Wash, Goss-Custard (in litt) found that low water and high water counts of Oystercatchers were closely correlated, even when the latter were made by observers for the 'Birds of Estuaries Enquiry'. A series of comparisons was made of Oystercatcher on feeding grounds on the Burry Inlet by observers from the BTO, RSPB, NCC, and MAFF. The difference in the counts between observers of flocks ranging from 50–1,000 birds varied between 0·5% to 3·0%, with the majority less than 1%.

Once the birds have been located they can generally be counted fairly accurately. Probably the greatest potential errors are from failure to find them on the estuary in the first place. Most of the major wader roosts around the country are reasonably well known; equally it is not difficult to guess from maps where most of the medium concentrations may be. There will, however, still be groups of birds scattered elsewhere which are difficult to find without a thorough search. We had the opportunity to gauge the scale of the problem on the Colne estuary during the Maplin studies. The two major roosts were known (at Colne Point and around Fingringhoe Wick), but some other areas were believed to hold moderate numbers (East Mersea shore and Langenhoe Marsh) and there were several small creeks, saltmarshes and adjacent fields. Table 6:3 shows the percentage of the main species of waders roosting on each of these categories. There were clearly differences between species but, overall, almost two-thirds were on the known roosts and only

9% were on the small peripheral areas. Predictably the species least well represented on the larger roosts are the more ubiquitous ones, i.e. Dunlin, Redshank, Curlew and Ringed Plover. From this it seems likely that unless each area is carefully examined up to 20% Dunlin and Redshank may be missed but only a small percentage of other species. However, the Colne is one of the more complex estuaries and smaller problems are likely elsewhere. Complete standardisation was not possible on all estuaries and no correction factors were included to take account of problems such as that described.

Incomplete coverage affects estimates of numbers in two ways. Firstly, if observations are made only on part of an estuary, or not on all estuaries, then the estimates regardless of other potential errors of total numbers cannot be made accurately. Secondly, each species has its habitat requirements and unless all habitats are thoroughly surveyed a full picture will not be obtained. In the 'Birds of Estuaries Enquiry' counts were obtained for almost all estuaries and there were co-ordinated counts for all of the larger ones. A number of small west coast Scottish intertidal areas were not covered but since the density of waders there is the lowest in Britain, and the areas are mostly under 60 ha, the error is almost certainly relatively small.

A number of rocky coastal areas in north-east England and eastern Scotland were included in the counts. The lack of cover of all habitats is potentially a much more serious difficulty.

Waders, wildfowl, gulls, divers and grebes occur in other areas. Where there are special problems of interpretation they are considered in the species accounts. There are a number of general difficulties affecting, in particular, species which occur on rocky coasts (Purple Sandpiper, Turnstone), sandy beaches (Sanderling, Ringed Plover), inshore waters (divers, grebes, Red-breasted Merganser) or inland (most geese, gulls and a proportion of waders such as Curlew, Oystercatcher, Golden Plover and especially Lapwing). For most of these species the proportion counted of the total number in Britain could not be estimated. Some special surveys have been undertaken and informed estimates are available for others; the magnitude of the omissions can be seen in Table 6:4. Of the total, the percentage on estuaries is between 10% and 25% for birds which really prefer rocky coasts (Purple Sandpiper), inland freshwater (Mallard) or the outer sections of inshore waters (Common Scoter). For many dabbling ducks, inshore ducks and sandy coast waders about half are found, while a much higher proportion of intertidal flat feeders is seen. Even for Pintail, which does occur regularly and in some numbers inland, almost nine-tenths were counted while 'guesstimates' of more strictly shore birds (Shelduck, Brent Geese, Knot, Grey Plover, godwits, etc) indicate that the counts revealed at least 90% of the total numbers.

CRITERIA OF IMPORTANCE

In order to assess the conservation importance of any site or the significance of concentrations of any species we need to have criteria which can be applied widely. Although the search for usuable criteria has spanned almost two decades, there is still no simple system available. The difficulties arise on a number of fronts, particularly because of the variety of circumstances which may apply. Some criteria refer to the world, European, national or even regional status of a species. Others relate to site protection, while still others are concerned more with the aesthetic, recreational, educational or scientific aspects of an area. Overlaying the whole

*Table 6:4 Percentage of total number of some species of waterfowl in winter which were counted by the 'Estuaries Enquiry'*

| | Total in Britain | Total in 'BOEE' | % recorded*† | Sources |
|---|---|---|---|---|
| Mallard | 300,000 | 40,000 | 13 | |
| Wigeon | 200,000 | 118,000 | 59 | |
| Teal | 75,000 | 29,000 | 39 | Wildfowl |
| Pintail | 20,000 | 17,000 | 85 | Trust |
| Goldeneye | 12,500 | 6,500 | 52 | |
| Common Scoter | 35,000 | 8,200 | 23 | |
| Red-breasted Merganser | 7,500 | 3,000 | 40 | |
| Golden Plover | 200,000 | 88,000 | 44 | Lloyd 1978 |
| Sanderling | 10,000 | 6,000 | 60 | Prater & Davies 1978 |
| Purple Sandpiper | 18,500 | 1,950 | 11 | Atkinson, Davies & Prater 1978 |

* 1969/70–1974/75 inclusive
† Figures are average January counts of the standard 'Estuary Enquiry' counts and do not include results of special surveys

problem is the dynamic nature of the habitats and the species involved. Some species are increasing rapidly, some are stable, while others are decreasing. The instability of population size means that any numerical criteria must be reviewed periodically and averaged over several years, but the basis for them should be fixed to prevent confusion. Detailed discussion on many of the criteria is to be found in the NCC's *A Nature Conservation Review* (Ratcliffe 1977) and Ratcliffe (1976a), and an outline of those specifically dealing with waterfowl and their habitats in Annex II of the 5th International Conference on the Conservation of Wetlands and Waterfowl, Heiligenhafen 1974. Further refinements to the latter are being considered.

Before we can look at the diversity, typicality or rarity of the different estuarine types we need a much more detailed national investigation into the intertidal habitats available and their invertebrate populations. Most of the criteria in Ratcliffe (1977) are used to define the importance of the habitat itself, such as diversity, rarity, naturalness, typicalness, and fragility. These are not subjects that can be enlarged upon by counts or birds, although the first two criteria can have their own more limited relevance for birds. Many botanical, physical and other faunistic features need to be included for a complete assessment. Estuarine flats are noted in the *NCR* to be a particularly fragile ecosystem. It is relatively scarce and highly disjunct and, therefore, subject to steady attrition. It is also particularly prone to pollution.

The 'Birds of Estuaries Enquiry' counts were aimed at documenting the abundance and distribution of waders and wildfowl, with the emphasis on the former. Some data were gathered for other groups of waterfowl but these were incomplete; very little information was obtained for passerines and other groups of birds. Certain aspects of species diversity, rarity, abundance and dispersion patterns can be obtained from the counts. Diversity can be calculated from them but the results have limited value because of the incomplete cover for all species. If restricted to waders and wildfowl only, there are still difficulties since it is more likely that an individual of another species will be detected amongst a small flock of waders than, for instance, in a 20,000 roost of mixed waders on Morecambe Bay. Abundance and distribution patterns can be obtained directly from the available counts and criteria have been developed to allow an objective assessment from them.

### International criteria

The Heiligenhafen conference recommended, and this was confirmed by the Cagliari meeting in November 1980, that two simple numerical criteria should be used to describe international importance. Firstly, to enable the whole community to be considered, a site with a total wildfowl population of 10,000 or a wader population of 20,000 would be of international importance. A species criterion was also agreed. This was that if a site held 1% or more of the numbers in a geographical population (for Britain and Ireland this is defined as western Europe from Norway to Iberia) then it, too, was of high international conservation significance. One important qualification was built into the species criterion — because the site criterion for wildfowl was 10,000 this, too, had to be the upper limit for the species criterion. For example, in Mallard and Eider, for which the total numbers certainly exceed one million, the 1% level is lowered to ten thousand. Similarly for the waders, 20,000 would be the limit for any species. However, none of the shore waders reach this level, and possibly only Lapwing would exceed it.

Common sense has to prevail in dealing with species which winter in small numbers in Europe when large numbers winter further south. Among the waders, species such as Greenshank, Spotted Redshank and Ruff are good examples with only 500–2,000 wintering in west Europe. It would be inappropriate to describe, automatically, 1% of the European wintering numbers as being of international importance. Of course some of these outlying small wintering groups may represent a relatively separate breeding population and be of special value. An example of this is the Greenshank, where it is possible that those wintering in Britain and Ireland may be predominately the small population of Scottish breeding birds. If isolated populations are involved then they deserve special consideration.

### National criteria

National criteria are less critically defined than international ones. No set of guidelines has been laid down by an international committee, since their application and relevance has to be considered in the light of the individual countries' requirements and priorities. In Britain we have tended to follow the international logic of the species criterion in that a site with 1% of the British population is of national importance. Because there have been detailed counts in Britain throughout the year for waders and from September to March for wildfowl, it could even be possible to assess national significance for most months. For this book calculations are based on the winter levels (November to March) although the exceptionally large numbers of some species, mainly Ringed Plover and Sanderling, during migration periods are noted.

The total number criterion is less easy to use at the national level and has not been included here. Logically it might be 10,000 waders because we have about half of the European wintering birds. The wildfowl figure is much less easy to define, but would be less than 5,000.

*The basis and use of criteria*

Before using criteria we need to examine their relevance a little further. What would the total population criterion reveal that the species criterion does not? Its main use is to reveal sites which are either rich in species of waterfowl but, perhaps because of limited habitat, do not support very large numbers of any one of them, or when several species just fail to reach the necessary level. For both waders and wildfowl a typical example of the former would be Pegwell Bay which, due to its position, has an extremely high diversity of species. This area does not reach the level of any present international or national criteria. There are no estuaries in Britain which would qualify as being internationally or nationally important on the total criterion which do not have at least one species reaching the 1% level. The total number criterion lacks clear information and is therefore a particularly difficult one to use well.

The species is, however, a much clearer concept and, if the population is known or can be reasonably estimated, then it can be used precisely in many situations. Thus the 1% can relate to moulting or migrant birds as well as wintering ones. Care still has to be taken because complete censuses take place in winter but heavy mortality, mainly through shooting, can occur during the autumn and early winter before the counts are made. By using the 1% criterion we are looking towards the requirements of the individual species.

Throughout the book the 1% international (see Appendix 2) and 1% national (see Appendix 3) levels have been used to assess importance. Total numbers have not been applied. It is worth repeating that levels of importance change with population level and comprehensiveness of surveys. The period considered here is 1969–76. The total population of several species has changed since then and different criteria need now to be applied. This is particularly true of the geese, complete international censuses of which take place in western Europe every winter.

The criteria themselves are simple but how the figures on which they are based are reached is less well defined. The European population is obtained by averaging the January counts for each species at each site. Then they are added together. In some countries only limited data exist, perhaps for December or for only one year. Until further information is obtained these are the best available and are therefore used.

Similarly, problems exist as to which figures one uses for comparison with the recommended standard. There are almost innumerable possibilities – peak count, average peak count, highest average monthly count, regular winter count (the average of the average December–February counts, or the average of the average of three highest counts each year, etc). Also, should these be averages over three, five or ten years? Each of the alternatives has certain advantages, except for peak count which is a highly artificial figure and which probably does not relate to the carrying capacity. The average peak count perhaps provides a figure which indicates average maximum usage of the site; it may be closest to a real maximum figure but even it cannot take into account the number of each species which move through an estuary. In the Wash the average peak count was only two-thirds of the total usage as calculated from ringing returns used to study the transitory populations (Minton 1976). The difficulty about using the average peak count is that exceptionally large numbers may occur annually at certain migration points but the value of the site for the species may not be particularly high. Also, complete and comparative cover is needed before sites can be compared using this figure.

The regular winter count provides more of a long-term comparison. It overcomes the problem of occasional exceptional numbers but results in a lower figure, particularly if three set months are chosen rather than the three highest months. The measure chosen for use in this book is the highest average monthly count. This is obtained by averaging all counts for each month and taking the highest figure, at least the highest within the appropriate season of the criterion. If there is partial cover of an estuary in any year, or if different sections are counted in different years, the total is obtained by averaging the monthly totals for each section and then adding the sectional averages together. This approach allows a better comparison between all estuaries than any other method. Another reason for using this approach is that total counts are based on the estimates made in the single month of January; this does not allow for variations in count efficiency which could alter the estimate.

The highest average monthly count is about 5% higher than that of the regular estimate, even if this is based on the three highest counts each year. It averages about 15% lower than the average annual peak. The highest average monthly count represents the number that can be expected in a given month each year, and although not a perfect method it provides a slight under-estimate of the significance of a site. Its use, therefore, cannot be open to criticism on the grounds of excessive claims. In individual cases of estuary assessment it can still be valid to look at average peak counts and although not presented here the data are stored at the BTO.

# CHAPTER 7

# The estuaries – an introduction

One of the main aims of the 'Birds of Estuaries Enquiry' was to document the birds of all estuaries. This was achieved although some inter-tidal areas in north and west Scotland were not visited. Similarly the IWC's 'Wetlands Enquiry' also had incomplete cover on the west coast. This section considers briefly each estuary and discusses its habitats, problems and bird populations. Larger and more important estuaries are described in more detail and, for many, maps are included in the text showing the main areas for waders and wildfowl. The estuaries are summarised by region starting with the Tweed and proceeding clockwise around Britain. Britain and Ireland have been divided into eight regions – eastern England, southern England, south western England, Wales, north western England, Scotland, Northern Ireland and Ireland. The accounts of Northern Ireland and Ireland differ slightly in their format since their estuaries have already been documented in detail in *Ireland's Wetlands and their Birds* published by the IWC (Hutchinson 1979).

Each region has a few introductory paragraphs which try to draw out the most important aspects of its estuaries and birds: these summarise the characteristic habitats, the main pressures on the coastline, the most comprehensive sources of literature about the birds, the main species and the migration patterns, and finally the principal estuaries. The Criteria used are discussed in Chapter 6 and detailed in Appendices 2 and 3.

For each estuary a similar but more abbreviated account is given, the species of international significance are included in the introduction but the national status of birds is summarised here. A number of abbreviations are used to describe the conservation status of whole or parts of estuaries. These are discussed in Chapter 5 and are:

NCR                      – *A Nature Conservation Review* published by the NCC

Grade 1\*, 1 or 2 site – A key site of prime conservation importance. If Grade 1\* it is of considerable international importance.

SSSI                     – A 'Site of Special Scientific Interest' designated by the NCC.

NNR, LNR             – National or Local Nature Reserve.

Of course much more detailed information has been gathered and it is simply lack of space which prevents a more expanded format. The full data are stored at the BTO.

# CHAPTER 8

# Eastern England

There are many contrasts in the form of the coast of eastern England, which stretches for almost a thousand miles from Kent to Northumberland. It can perhaps be divided into four basic types. South of the Humber the dominant habitat is a complex of sand-dune systems, extensive saltmarshes and sand or shingle beaches behind which lies reclaimed agricultural land. This is characteristic of the coast from the Humber to north Norfolk and again from south Suffolk to north Kent. Separating these two zones in east Norfolk and Suffolk, and between Flamborough and the Humber, are areas of eroding mud cliff above sandy beaches interspersed with shingle. In north Kent there is a small area of sandy cliffs. North Yorkshire, Durham and parts of east Kent have the only major cliffs in the Eastern region, those in Yorkshire having a number of bays with sand, shingle and rock shelves under the cliffs. Flat rock shelves interspersed with relatively small sandy beaches and backed by low grassland are typical of the fourth habitat type and are found widely in Northumberland, Tyne and Wear and Cleveland.

From Norfolk northwards there are just a few estuaries, although they are major ones, but coincidental with the appearance of the rock shelf stretching from Yorkshire to Northumberland quite large numbers of waders occur on the open coastline. South Suffolk, Essex and north Kent are almost entirely estuarine in nature, particularly the last two areas, and together with the Wash and north Norfolk have extensive and interesting saltmarshes. Very little grazing occurs on these marshes, consequently they have developed a clear zonation of plant species and exhibit considerable diversity. This has advantages for several saltmarsh breeding birds. The presence of many dicotyledenous flowering plants and even small shrubs provides a rich supply of food for passerine birds in autumn and winter.

Moderately large tidal ranges occur in the North Sea, usually of about 7 m on spring tides and 5 m on neap tides. The beaches and most of the outer parts of estuaries in eastern England are sandy but in the southeast, particularly the enclosed estuaries of north Kent, Essex and Suffolk, the tidal flow is small enough to allow considerable accumulations of silt. Similar conditions are found in corners of the Wash and Teesmouth and more extensively in the Humber.

### Urban and industrial development and recreation

The estuaries of eastern England have been affected more than most by man's activities. Large areas have been reclaimed for urban development, industry and agriculture, and for protection of the reclaimed land raised sea defences are widespread. The close proximity of large numbers of people in major cities has stimulated a continuing growth of leisure activities which form, potentially, a major threat to bird populations breeding and even wintering on this coast.

The three major centres where there has been massive urban growth and expansion of industry are the Thames, Teesside and the county of Tyne and Wear. On the Thames the greatest reclamation has been of coastal marshes for a wide variety of purposes; in its outer section, particularly Canvey Island in Essex and the Isle of Grain in Kent, oil refineries and storage have 'swallowed' considerable areas. Further upstream losses have resulted from docks and warehousing, and a large development at Thamesmead, and several marshes have been used as chemical or rubbish dumps. At Teesside and in Tyne and Wear there has not only been major loss of adjacent habitats but intertidal flats have been reclaimed as well. Teesside has the unenviable record for this (discussed in Chapter 5) but Jarrow Slake, the only major area of mud in the Tyne, has been largely reclaimed in the 1970s with working continuing to 1977. There are, of course, many other smaller industrial zones in eastern England and where appropriate they will be mentioned in the individual estuary accounts.

Agriculture has played a significant role in shaping the present estuaries. Extremely large areas of the fens which originally made up the Wash have been reclaimed during the last thousand or so years. About 32,000 ha have been reclaimed since the 16th century, and the 12,500 ha since 1800 has reduced the area of the Wash by about 30%. This reclamation is a continuing process which depends to a considerable extent on the maturity of the saltmarshes. In Essex, on the Humber and in north Kent, land has been gained at the expense of intertidal flats and marshes. Behind the sea wall, especially in the south-east of the region, there has been a trend towards draining wet pasture and turning it into arable; the results of this process are not yet known. However, it will undoubtedly adversely affect species such as Redshank and most ducks, unless the dykes and fleets with emergent vegetation are retained. The protection afforded against disturbance and tidal inundation has already encouraged Ringed Plovers and Oystercatchers to breed in this habitat.

Leisure activities along the east coast of England have developed greatly during the last decade. Many marinas have been built and other moorings laid down, particularly in north Kent and Essex; they pose conservation problems by their physical intrusion into the estuarine system and by disturbance of breeding or roosting birds on islands and saltmarshes from inconsiderate landings. Public access, wildfowling and even occasionally birdwatching all cause local problems. The frequent use of beaches and sand-dunes by holiday makers during the summer months has had a massive effect in modifying the distribution of terns and waders, often lowering breeding success, though this disturbance is rarely deliberate.

*Main literature on the birds of eastern England*

The principal recent county avifaunas for this region which summarise the records are: Kent – Harrison (1953) and Gillham and Homes (1950); Thames area – Harrison and Grant (1976); Essex – Hudson and Pyman (1968) and Blindell (1976); Suffolk – Payn (1978); Norfolk – Seago (1977); Lincolnshire – Smith and Cornwallis (1955) and Cornwallis (1969); Yorkshire – Chislett (1954); Northumberland – Galloway and Meek (1978) (first volume of a three volume work).

Additional records are available in the annual bird reports published by the Kent Ornithological Society, Essex Birdwatching and Preservation Society, Suffolk Naturalists' Society, Lincolnshire Naturalists' Union, Yorkshire Naturalists' Union, Teesmouth Bird Club, Durham Bird Club, Tyneside Bird Club, and the Northumbria Natural History Society. Other publications of a local nature are included in the accounts of individual estuaries.

*Principal species and migration patterns*

Eastern England is of considerable importance for most estuarine species of birds. It is a major passage and breeding area as well as being used by many birds in winter. Table 8:1 presents the highest monthly counts of the principal species of wildfowl and waders. By far the most numerous species are the waders Dunlin and Knot but in terms of international importance the Brent Goose (with up to 39% of the European population of the dark-bellied race at peak times and in severe winters up to 80% of the Svalbard pale-bellied race) is the most significant; Knot, Grey Plover and Redshank each constitute over 20% of the European winter population.

The North Sea coasts of eastern England and the Wadden Sea form a natural funnel for water birds migrating from northern latitudes, see Chapter 3. The autumn

---

*Table 8:1    Average highest monthly counts of the principal species of wildfowl and waders in eastern England, 1969–75*

| | | | | | |
|---|---|---|---|---|---|
| Wigeon | 45,717 | Dec | Dunlin | 181,015 | Jan |
| Brent Goose | 32,000 | Dec* | Knot | 116,178 | Jan |
| Mallard | 17,659 | Dec | Redshank | 32,013 | Sept |
| Shelduck | 17,343 | Jan | Oystercatcher | 31,885 | Sept |
| Teal | 9,308 | Dec | Curlew | 21,754 | Aug |
| Pintail | 2,883 | Jan | Bar-tailed Godwit | 10,265 | Jan |
| Eider | 2,387 | Feb | Grey Plover | 7,381 | Sept |
| Mute Swan | 1,632 | Feb | Ringed Plover | 5,678 | Aug |
| Goldeneye | 1,360 | Feb | Sanderling | 2,085 | Sept |
| Shoveler | 647 | Jan | Black-tailed Godwit | 1,182 | Sept |

* Includes average counts of 31,000 dark-bellied and 1,000 pale-bellied Brent Geese

Table 8:2   The percentage of the international populations of wildfowl and waders wintering on estuaries in eastern England based on highest average monthly counts

| | Whooper Swan | Pink-footed Goose | Brent Goose (dark) | Brent Goose (pale) | Shelduck | Wigeon | Teal | Pintail | Shoveler | Oystercatcher | Ringed Plover | Grey Plover | Knot | Sanderling | Dunlin | Black-tailed Godwit | Bar-tailed Godwit | Curlew | Redshank |
|---|---|---|---|---|---|---|---|---|---|---|---|---|---|---|---|---|---|---|---|
| Swale | – | – | – | – | – | – | – | – | 1·1 | – | – | 2·4 | – | – | – | – | – | – | – |
| Medway | – | – | – | – | 1·8 | 1·9 | 2·6 | 1·3 | 1·1 | – | * | 1·9 | – | – | – | – | – | – | 1·0+ |
| N. Kent Marshes | – | – | – | – | – | – | – | – | – | – | – | – | – | – | 1·5 | – | – | – | 1·0 |
| Leigh Canvey | – | – | 3·5 | – | – | – | – | – | – | – | 1·0 | 1·1 | – | – | – | – | – | – | –+ |
| Foulness | – | – | 13·5 | – | – | – | – | – | – | 1·1 | – | 1·9 | 1·3 | – | – | – | 2·6 | 1·5 | – |
| Crouch | – | – | 1·1 | – | – | – | – | – | – | – | – | – | – | – | – | – | – | – | – |
| Dengie | – | – | 1·9 | – | – | – | – | – | – | – | 1·0 | 2·4 | – | – | – | – | – | 1·0 | 1·5+ |
| Blackwater | – | – | 6·7 | – | 1·5 | – | – | – | – | – | – | 1·9 | – | – | 1·1 | – | – | 1·2 | 2·1 |
| Colne | – | – | 2·5 | – | 1·0 | – | – | – | – | – | – | – | – | – | – | – | – | 1·2 | 2·3 |
| Hamford | – | – | 4·9 | – | – | – | – | – | – | – | 1·2 | 2·5 | – | – | 1·0 | – | – | – | 2·8+ |
| Stour | – | – | – | – | 1·7 | – | – | 1·2 | – | – | – | 1·3 | – | – | – | 1·7 | – | – | 1·9 |
| Orwell | – | – | – | – | – | – | – | – | – | – | – | – | – | 1·7 | – | – | – | – | 1·0 |
| N. Norfolk[5] | – | 3·5 | 3·1 | – | 1·3 | – | – | – | – | – | – | – | – | – | – | – | – | – | – |
| Wash | – | – | 4·3 | – | 6·7 | – | – | – | – | 3·2 | * | 11·2 | 13·5 | 2·1 | 3·3 | – | 6·2 | 3·0 | 2·3+ |
| Humber | – | 3·0 | – | – | – | – | – | – | – | – | – | 2·0 | 4·4 | 1·3 | 1·5 | – | – | 1·1 | 1·8 |
| Teesmouth | – | – | – | – | 1·0 | – | – | – | – | – | – | – | 1·5 | 3·1 | – | – | – | – | – |
| Lindisfarne | 2·0 | – | – | 4·2 | – | 5·5 | – | – | – | – | – | – | 1·8 | – | 1·2 | – | 4·9 | – | – |

(1) * passage numbers in autumn or spring exceed 500 and are probably of international significance

(2) – numbers do not reach 1% of international level, does not imply absence

(3) The highest average monthly counts may occur during different months at different estuaries

(4) Some species of passage migrants and some seaduck may also occur in internationally significant numbers, the average count may be inadequate to reveal this so individual estuary accounts should be examined

(5) Estimated totals, see text

(6) + = many more in autumn

is the time of greatest diversity and abundance of most species of waders in eastern England; here many undertake their annual moult, especially in the Wash, or fatten up for onward migration to southern and western Europe and Africa. By the end of September or early October most of the migrants which are destined for southern wintering grounds have departed and birds in moult have almost completed the process. However, between October and December there is an influx of waders which have moulted on the Wadden Sea. Dunlin, Knot and Bar-tailed Godwit are the principal species in this movement. These birds, particularly the first two, are very numerous and their advent increases the total of waders to 300–400,000, 50% more than the autumn figure. There is a major return to the Wadden Sea during February and March, and the spring movement between late April and early June is relatively small.

Wildfowl, almost without exception, build up steadily to winter maxima, the peak occurring between December and February. These birds have used continental wetlands, coastal and inland, until the colder weather forces them across the North Sea.

The extensive saltmarshes and sandy spits of eastern England also provide some excellent breeding areas for waterbirds. The saltmarshes of Essex, the Wash and the Humber support approximately 2,500 pairs of Redshank, about 5% of the British and Irish total, and at least 1,200 pairs of Shelduck (10% of the British total). There are several large Black-headed gulleries, most notably on the Wash, and terneries; the latter include all five principal species, plus Ringed Plovers, concentrated now on areas which are either wardened bird reserves or inaccessible to the general public. Conservation societies have been active in preserving these breeding areas.

The inshore waters of north-eastern England in particular support quite large numbers of more marine species of birds. Wintering Eider, Red-throated Divers and Slavonian Grebes are significant in a regional context; the first also breeds in northern Northumberland and the colonies there amount to almost 90% of the English breeding birds.

*Principal estuaries of eastern England*

Seventeen estuaries in eastern England regularly support internationally important numbers of wildfowl or waders (see Table 8:2). Not surprisingly the Wash, the largest estuary in the region, stands out as being of greatest significance internationally with important numbers of three species of wildfowl and nine of waders. Virtually all sections of the Thames and all the Essex coast estuaries are also prominent, with the Medway, Leigh/Canvey Island, Foulness Island, Blackwater, Colne, Hamford Water and the Stour having each at least three species in significant numbers.

North of the Wash there are few large estuaries (Humber, Teesmouth and Lindisfarne) but each is of importance. Despite the loss of habitat caused by reclamation and industrial development at Teesmouth, three species managed to remain in important numbers, although as has been shown in Chapter 5 recent declines do not suggest a particularly hopeful future.

A further eight areas not listed in Table 8:2 support nationally important concentrations of waders or wildfowl. Details of these are summarised in the following individual estuary accounts.

*Table 8:3   Species of national importance found at Lindisfarne, 1969–75*

|  | Highest average monthly count | % British |
|---|---|---|
| Whooper Swan | 360 | 12·0 |
| Pale-bellied Brent Goose | 640 | virtually all |
| Shelduck | 605 | 1·0 |
| Wigeon | 21,900 | 11·0 |
| Eider | 1,710 | 2·8 |
| Long-tailed Duck | 160 | 1·6 |
| Common Scoter | 600 | 1·7 |
| Grey Plover | 150 | 1·5 |
| Knot | 9,250 | 3·1 |
| Sanderling | 130 | 1·3 |
| Dunlin | 13,900 | 2·5 |
| Bar-tailed Godwit | 4,380 | 9·7 |
| Redshank | 1,080 | 1·1 |

*Northumberland*

*Lindisfarne.* The legends and monastic traditions that surround Holy Island provide a perfect backdrop for this interesting area. A series of sand dunes runs along the outer shore of Goswick sands, Holy Island and between Fenham Flats and Budle Bay. Virtually all of the intertidal flats are protected by the dunes giving a relatively sandy shore although with some silt. A small amount of mud occurs on the upper shore but only small areas of saltmarsh have developed. The whole of the intertidal area is used by waterfowl, but wildfowl tend to concentrate on the upper shore, Fenham Flats and Budle Bay. The area was declared a National Nature Reserve in 1964, but there can be intense public pressure during the summer months and this does affect the breeding birds.

Lindisfarne supports internationally important numbers of six species (see Table 8:2); its national significance is summarised in Table 8:3. It is of outstanding interest for many species having the largest number of English wintering Greylag Geese, Whooper Swans, Eider and Long-tailed Duck. Additionally it is the only site in Britain where the Svalbard breeding population of Pale-bellied Brent Geese occurs, indeed this population amounts only to about 2,500 birds. Thus Lindisfarne supports over a quarter of the British population and in severe weather as in 1978/79 up to 80% may be present. The autumn Wigeon peak of around 22,000 is a notable feature, surpassed only by the 30,000 or so wintering on the Ouse Washes. For its size the numbers of waders, too, are large but lower than for the massive estuaries further south and west. A feature known to many birdwatchers is the wealth of birds on the sea, as indicated in Table 8:3. Additionally, Red-breasted Mergansers, Velvet Scoters, all three divers and Slavonian and Red-necked Grebes can be seen in good numbers. Perhaps due to summer pressure the area is not outstanding for its breeding birds although having an interesting community, including over 30 pairs of Ringed Plovers.

*Coastline.* Northumberland's 100 km of coastline has only a few small estuaries but, as mentioned, an area of intertidal flats has developed at Lindisfarne behind Holy Island. For most of the coast the habitat is sandy beach alternating with flattish rock shelves, backed by pasture or low sand dunes. Offshore, Coquet Island and the Farne Islands provide other significant habitats for birds.

The Farne Islands are owned by the National Trust and are SSSIs, as are Beadnell shore, areas either side of Lindisfarne, and Coquet Island. The last is also an RSPB reserve. Table 8:4a shows the average number of waders on the Northumberland coast, excluding Lindisfarne, based on detailed counts organised by the Tyneside Bird Club. A summary of early ringing recoveries and migration patterns is given by Evans (1966). Three species which occur in nationally and two at internationally important numbers are shown in Table 8:4b. A number of seaduck, especially Eiders, and a wide variety of divers and grebes occur offshore. The relative numbers of waders on each section are given in Fig. 8:1, which shows that the coast between the Aln and Budle Point supports the most birds and has the greatest diversity. The Tweed has important numbers of Mute Swans, up to 2% of the British population in autumn, and up to 3% of British Goldeneye in winter. In summer the Farne Islands and Coquet Island are excellent for breeding terns, all except Little Tern being in nationally significant numbers, and both areas have important Eider colonies (1,240 and 500 pairs respectively); the one on Coquet being at the south-eastern limit of the species in Britain.

*Table 8:4a   Wintering populations of the main wader species on the Northumberland coast, excluding Lindisfarne, 1969–75*

| | | | |
|---|---|---|---|
| Oystercatcher | 820 | Dunlin | 3,160 |
| Ringed Plover | 500 | Bar-tailed Godwit | 40 |
| Grey Plover | 30 | Curlew | 230 |
| Knot | 380 | Redshank | 740 |
| Sanderling | 140 | Turnstone | 1,300 |
| Purple Sandpiper | 780 | | |

*Table 8:4b   Important species of waders wintering on the Northumberland coast, 1969–75*

| | Regular number | % British | % W. European |
|---|---|---|---|
| Ringed Plover | 500 | 4·2 | 2·0 |
| Purple Sandpiper | 780 | 4·3 | *2 |
| Turnstone | 1,300 | 5·2 | *1 |

(*) Total numbers not known
(1) Probably of importance
(2) Possibly not of importance

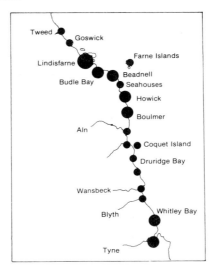

Fig. 8:1 Main concentrations of waders on the coast in Northumberland, 1969–75. Large circle = 20,000+; Medium circle = 2,000+; small circle = 100+.

### Tyne and Wear

*Coastal sites.* The short coastline of this county is intensively developed but there is a number of rocky and sandy bays. The main areas for waders and wildfowl are the Whitburn coast and the section from Tynemouth to the northern border at Seaton Sluice. The Tyne estuary is so heavily developed that at the start of the Estuaries Enquiry only one small area of mud flats, Jarrow Slake, remained and it has since been reduced. The Wildfowl Trust's Washington refuge by the tidal River Wear attracts migrant and inland waders, including some rarities, and reasonable numbers of wildfowl.

The total number of birds is fairly small although Purple Sandpipers (with a winter average of 100 and a spring peak of 150), Turnstones (average of 200), Sanderling (winter average of 130) are close to being of national significance, while about 1,000 Knot are also of interest. Few wildfowl except small numbers of Goldeneye, Eider and other seaduck occur off the coast. The most important remaining area is that north of Tynemouth, especially Whitley Bay, although Jarrow Slake formerly held over 2,000 waders.

### Cleveland

*Teesmouth.* The once fairly large estuary of the Tees is now greatly changed and is altering so quickly that any description of it is soon out of date. Originally the main intertidal flats of Seal Sands were sandy in nature but changes in sedimentation caused by development and dredging have covered it with a deep layer of fine mud. The outer beaches of North Gare and Seaton and Coatham Sands remain sandy. The rocks and breakwater at South Gare and the complex of pools on flooded rough grassland at Cowpen Marsh and adjacent areas are of particular interest.

The threats and changes to the Teesmouth complex are many and have already been discussed in Chapter 5. Although under great pressure it should be remembered that four areas are classed as Grade 2 sites in *NCR*; they are Seal Sands, Seaton Sands, Seaton Dunes and Common, South Gare and Coatham Sands and Cowpen Marsh. There is a thriving field centre near Seaton Carew run by the Teesmouth Bird Club.

Like the habitat, bird numbers have changed steadily during the 1970s (see Chapter 5). During the period 1969 to 1975 three species were of international importance – see Table 8:2. National levels of significance are summarised in Table 8:5. Several other species are found in numbers only slightly below this level, namely, Redshank (1,000+ in autumn), Grey Plover (90), Bar-tailed Godwit (350) and Ruff (15 in winter). More recent counts indicate that Sanderling are more numerous in winter, 620 being the regular figure but over 1,000 at times. Shelduck too are interesting, occasionally over 4,000 being seen, usually in early winter. Teesmouth regularly attracts rare waders and seabirds, as indicated by 30 wader and 23 wildfowl species seen during the counts.

### Yorkshire

*Filey – Whitby coastline.* This coast has a number of bays with sand or flattish rocks separated or backed by cliffs. Although many areas are popular with summer holidaymakers they are relatively quiet in winter. Counts did not start until towards the end of the Estuaries Enquiry but these and subsequent ones indicate the high interest of the area. Few wildfowl occur except in extreme weather but there are good numbers of waders. The whole coastal section is of national importance for Purple Sandpipers (385, 2·2% British) and Turnstones (490, 1·9% British) with Redshank (600) closely following. Of the individual sections Filey Brigg, for Purple Sandpipers, and Cornelian/S. Scarborough Bay, for Purple Sandpiper and Turnstone, are both nationally significant at times.

### Humberside/Lincolnshire

*Humber.* The Humber stretches 80 km from Spurn Head to Goole, making it one of the longest estuaries in Britain. For this survey the southern outer limit was Donna Nook but the sand dune system and wide sandy beach continues south to Theddlethorpe. To the north the shingle spit of Spurn Head forms another

Table 8:5   *Species of national significance wintering at Teesmouth, 1969–75*

|  | Highest av. monthly count | % British |
|---|---|---|
| Shelduck | 1,360 | 2·3 |
| Knot | 7,370 | 2·5 |
| Sanderling | 485 | 3·2 |
| Dunlin | 5,719 | 1·0 |

important habitat. There are few large saltmarshes, the most extensive being at Grainthorpe and Tetney with smaller ones on Cherry Cobb sands and Spurn Bight. Apart from the RSPB reserve at Blacktoft Sands, an area of reedmarsh and occasionally flooded marsh, the Humber is lined mainly by grazing and arable land with some freshwater pits behind the sea wall on the southern shore. There are two large ports at Hull and Grimsby. The intertidal flats are sandy on the outer estuary but further inland, and especially in Spurn Bight, there has been an accumulation of silt. In a number of areas the mud is unstable. A detailed study of the biological characteristics of the estuary is being undertaken by the University of Hull.

Part of the intertidal area of the Humber plus Read's Island and the Spurn peninsula is a Grade 1* site in *NCR*, this, the Barton and Barrow Clay Pits and Grainthorpe Haven are SSSIs. There is a National Wildfowl refuge near Broomfleet which forms part of the *NCR* site, and the RSPB has a reserve at Tetney. An active bird observatory, administered by the Yorkshire Naturalists Union, is sited at Spurn and the whole peninsula is managed as a reserve by the Yorkshire Naturalists' Trust.

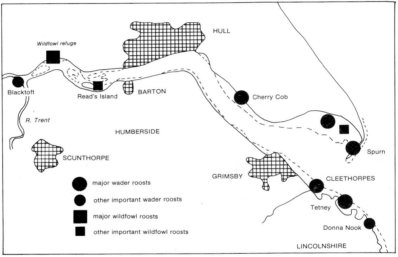

Fig. 8:2 Main concentrations of waders and wildfowl in the Humber estuary, 1969–75.

Like most larger estuaries the area is threatened by a number of developments, the most serious being a plan to reclaim an area of Spurn Bight with colliery spoil. Spurn Bight is the largest area of intertidal flats of the estuary and supports internationally important numbers of several species. Other areas of importance for birds are the Wildfowl Refuge in the inner estuary, the sands and marshes between Cleethorpes and Donna Nook, and the Cherry Cobb Sands. Read's Island and associated mudflats are of some importance but have not been well documented in recent years. In general the birds of the inner estuary roost at the Wildfowl Refuge or Blacktoft Sands, while other roosts develop at Cherry Cobb, in Spurn Bight, on Spurn Head and on the marshes at Tetney and Grainthorpe Havens (Fig. 8:2) Smallish roosts of the more ubiquitous waders, Dunlin, Curlew and Redshank, occur on adjacent

*Table 8:6   Nationally important species occurring on the Humber, 1969–75*

|  | Highest av. monthly count | % British |
|---|---|---|
| Pink-footed Goose | 2,390 | 3·2 |
| Shelduck | 1,090 | 1·8 |
| Mallard | 6,050 | 2·0 |
| Pintail | 200 | 1·0 |
| Ringed Plover | 325* | 1·1 |
| Grey Plover | 585* | 5·8 |
| Knot | 22,060 | 7·4 |
| Sanderling | 200† | 2·0 |
| Dunlin | 17,450 | 3·2 |
| Curlew | 2,100 | 2·1 |
| Redshank | 2,020 | 2·0 |
| Turnstone | 300* | 1·6 |

* Autumn peak
† Part of an average of 450 wintering from Theddlethorpe to Cleethorpes and on Spurn. (Prater and Davies 1978)

pasture. There is a movement across the mouth of the estuary of birds which feed on Spurn Bight and roost between Tetney and Grainthorpe, the frequency of the conditions for this movement to take place are being investigated.

The seven species of international importance have been shown in Table 8:2, the nationally significant species are summarised in Table 8:6. Of the wildfowl the Mallard deserves special mention since the Humber is the best site for them in Britain. Two other ducks Teal and Wigeon are numerous and the former exceeds the 1% level on occasions each year, but not at a consistent time of year. There has been a large decline in Pink-footed Goose numbers on the Humber refuge; although the area is still of international importance counts now are only about 6% of early years. The changes are summarised in Table 8:7. During the period of the survey a small group, up to fifty or so, of Dark-bellied Brent Geese started to feed on Spurn Bight, the northernmost regular feeding are for the species. The Humber's position on the

*Table 8:7   Changes in peak counts of Pink-footed Goose on the Humber since 1955*

|  | Average winter peak |
|---|---|
| 1955/56–1958/59 | 13,000 |
| 1963/64–1967/68 | 4,200 |
| 1969/70–1971/72 | 3,430 |
| 1972/73–1974/75 | 1,560 |
| 1975/76–1978/79 | 890 |

North Sea migration routes is demonstrated clearly by the large numbers of many waders in autumn but small numbers in winter. On the other hand there is a massive influx in winter of Knot and Dunlin which have moulted in the Waddensea and the Wash.

### Lincolnshire/Norfolk

*The Wash.* This major embayment incorporating the estuaries of four rivers, the Ouse, Nene, Welland and Witham, has one of the largest areas of intertidal flat and saltmarsh in the British Isles. For the purpose of this survey the limits of the bay are Gibraltar Point in Lincolnshire and Gore Point at Holme in Norfolk, although on high spring tides areas further east on the north Norfolk coast may be used for roosting. The intertidal area is predominently sandy, particularly the outer banks, but the higher flats which grade into saltmarsh have a high silt content. Gibraltar Point to the Witham channel is the second largest continuous sandflat in Britain. Saltmarshes are a feature of the inner and west Wash; in places they extend for a kilometre outwards from the sea wall. They are, however, botanically uniform and relatively immature due to continuing reclamation of the higher levels for agricultural land. The outer lips of the Wash, Gibraltar Point and Holme, are made of two

*Table 8:8   Species of national importance on the Wash, 1969–75*

|  | Highest av. monthly count | % British |
|---|---|---|
| Bewick's Swan | 30 | 1·5 |
| Pink-footed Goose | 3,150 | 4·2 |
| Dark-bellied Brent Goose | 2,970 | 9·0 |
| Shelduck | 8,660 | 14·4 |
| Wigeon | 3,680 | 1·8 |
| Common Scoter | 460 | 1·3 |
| Goldeneye | 260 | 2·1 |
| Oystercatcher | 14,820 | 7·4 |
| Ringed Plover | 600* | 2·0* |
| Grey Plover | 2,000 | 20·0 |
| Knot | 67,500 | 22·5 |
| Sanderling | 320 | 3·2 |
| Dunlin | 39,500 | 7·2 |
| Black-tailed Godwit | 100* | 2·0* |
| Bar-tailed Godwit | 3,000 | 6·7 |
| Whimbrel | 215* | 2·1* |
| Curlew | 3,200 | 3·2 |
| Redshank | 2,500 (6,000†) | 2·5 (6·0†) |
| Greenshank | 115* | 2·3* |
| Turnstone | 500 | 2·0 |

Based on winter figures unless specifically mentioned
* Only autumn numbers of significance
† Autumn number

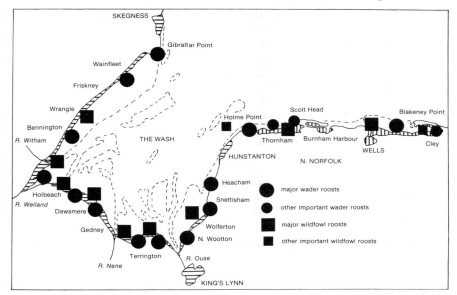

Fig. 8:3 Main concentrations of waders and wildfowl in the Wash and along the north Norfolk coast, 1969–75.

large sand dune systems and at Hunstanton there are small cliffs. The east Wash south to Snettisham is lined by a shingle beach, backed by some coastal lagoons and rough grassland but elsewhere there is a seawall separating the saltmarsh from the reclaimed land, now intensively used for agriculture. Some areas of shallow water occur off Hunstanton but there are several deep channels within the main bay.

The intertidal area of the Wash, Gibraltar Point and Holme Dunes are all Grade 1* sites in *NCR*. Gibraltar Point is also a LNR and there are bird observatories at Gibraltar Point and Holme. The Lincolnshire and South Humberside Trust for Nature Conservation has two reserves, the RSPB has one at Snettisham and the Norfolk Naturalists' Trust one at Holme.

Despite its relative isolation the Wash is one of our most threatened estuaries. The two most significant problems are the development of large bunded reservoirs for water storage on the flats off Terrington, and the continuing reclamation of saltmarshes for agriculture. Both problems have been discussed already in Chapters 4 and 5. There is some pressure from holidaymakers on the sand and shingle areas of the outer Wash, severe at times and leading to trampling of nests of Ringed Plovers and Little Terns.

The Wash is ornithologically the most important coastal site in eastern England, supporting internationally important numbers of no fewer than twelve species, see Table 8:2. Its national significance is shown in Table 8:8. It is of outstanding value for Knot, Grey Plover and Shelduck, and although only an indication is given in the table, it is the best estuary in Britain for large numbers of migrant waders in autumn. At this time of year it appears to be an important feeding and moulting ground for birds which subsequently winter elsewhere in Britain and in western Europe and Africa. Indeed the numbers of waders using the Wash has been calculated to be at least 225,000, or 40% more than the summated highest monthly counts. In addition to the species already mentioned, regionally important numbers of several species of seaduck (Scaup, Long-tailed Duck, Velvet Scoter, Red-breasted Merganser) and Red-throated Divers occur off Hunstanton and 2,000+ Mallard and 125 Pintail off the major saltmarshes. Although counts are few, about 100,000 gulls roost on the Wash. Wintering passerines are also of importance, especially Twite at somewhere in the region of 40,000 – well over half of the estimated British wintering numbers. The Wash supports an important breeding population of several species of waders and other waterfowl (Table 8:9), including the second largest Black-headed Gullery in Britain in 1974.

Virtually all sections of the Wash are of international importance (Fig. 8:3). Waders are widely distributed although perhaps slightly concentrated onto the eastern shore, particularly Knot and Sanderling. Wildfowl are mainly on the southern shore with its large saltmarshes, but even here different species have characteristic distributions. Brent Geese use mostly the south and south-western parts of the estuary while the Pink-footed Geese feed inland and roost near the Nene and off Wolferton. Major roosts can develop almost anywhere on the saltings, depending on tide height, but when tides are unusually high the southern birds move to adjacent fields and the rest to the higher sandy areas of Gibraltar Point and Thornham Harbour, where large roosts develop on the highest spring tides.

### Norfolk

*North Norfolk coast.* Here a number of small streams enter the sea in an area where extensive shingle and sand banks have been thrown up about 1½ km offshore, resulting in a complex contiguous zone of intertidal flats, saltmarshes, freshwater marshes, sand dunes, beaches, spits and islands. There are large saltmarshes between Blakeney and Wells and again between Burnham Harbour and Holme. The former area is one of the most mature and diverse in Britain. Equally the sand dune and island systems are of great value for botanical and physiographic as well as ornithological reasons. The areas of intertidal flat are relatively small and grade

*Table 8:9   Species of national importance breeding on the Wash, 1969–75*

|  | Number of pairs | %British |
|---|---|---|
| Shelduck | 300 | 2·5[3] |
| Ringed Plover | 116[1] | 2·3 |
| Redshank | 1,400 | 3·5[4] |
| Black-headed Gull | 22,000[2] | 19·8[5] |
| Common Tern | 125 | 1·7 |
| Little Tern[3] | 16 | 1·0 |

[1] 1973 census (Gribble 1976)
[2] 1974 census (Prater 1976)
[3] Steady decline probably due to severe disturbance
[4] Estimates from *Atlas of Breeding Birds in Britain and Ireland*
[5] English and Welsh

*Table 8:10  Estimated numbers and national status of waterfowl wintering on the north Norfolk coast, 1969–75*

| | Est. highest av. monthly total | % British |
|---|---|---|
| Dark-bellied Brent Goose | 2,500 | 7·6 |
| Shelduck | 1,750 | 2·9 |
| Wigeon | 2,500 | 1·2 |
| Goldeneye | 150 | 1·2 |
| Oystercatcher | 3,000 | 1·5 |
| Grey Plover | 450 | 4·5 |
| Knot | 3,000 | 1·0 |
| Sanderling | 250 | 2·5 |
| Dunlin | 6,000 | 1·1 |
| Bar-tailed Godwit | 550 | 1·2 |
| Redshank | 1,200 | 1·2 |

from muddy in the inner harbours to sandy on the outer seaward edges. Taken as a single unit the area from Cley to Holme forms one of the most diverse coastal systems in Britain.

In recognition of its value no fewer than nine separate Grade 1* sites were recognised in *NCR*; two of which, Scolt Head and Hokham, are NNRs, and three are Norfolk Naturalists' Trust reserves and one an RSPB reserve. There is one further SSSI. Scolt Head NNR, Holkham NNR, Blakeney Point SSSI and Cley and Salthouse SSSI form a site which was included in the UK list submitted on ratification of the Ramsar Convention. Thus it is well protected. The main potential problems are heavy disturbance by holidaymakers, and at times by birdwatchers, and changes in the structure of the outer sand and shingle ridges due to the natural progression of their development.

The diversity of birds and the numbers of wintering visitors, breeders, plus rare and common migrants, attracts very many birdwatchers every year. For such a well watched area it is sad that the status of the more common species of waterfowl is poorly known. However, from the incomplete counts, estimates have been obtained and some indications of the area's importance can be gleaned (Table 8:10). Estimates for the four species of international importance have been included in Table 8:2. The coast is highly important for breeding birds, too, and of international importance for terns with up to 5,000 pairs of Sandwich Terns, 2,000 pairs of Common Terns and 400 pairs of Little Terns. It is of national importance for Ringed Plover (400 pairs) and possibly for Shelduck and Redshank. The reserves on freshwater marshes have recently attracted national breeding rarities such as Avocet and Black-tailed Godwit.

All parts of the area are of importance for birds, the main concentrations being shown in Fig. 8:3, with the shore between Wells and Cley and between Holme and Scolt holding most birds. Major wader roosts can develop on any of the saltings or outer spits, and the beach at Thornham periodically receives very large numbers of birds from the Wash. The terns and Ringed Plovers are concentrated on to the sand at Blakeney Point, Scolt Head and Titchwell.

### Suffolk/Norfolk

*Breydon Water.* This is the remains of what once must have been a most impressive wetland for it is surrounded by very extensive freshwater grazing marshes. The estuary itself is embanked and muddy with a very narrow fringe of saltmarsh in its north eastern corner. It discharges to the sea through a narrow outlet and is completely separated from the sea by Great Yarmouth. Breydon Water's importance has been recognised and it is an LNR. The estuary, however, is not free from threats; there is a possible tidal barrier at Great Yarmouth and a potentially disastrous drainage scheme which could affect the adjacent grazing marshes. Further development of dock and marina facilities pose some problems, as do nutrient rich discharges from the Norfolk Broads.

At high tide the waders roost on the saltmarsh near Great Yarmouth Station but at low water feed over the whole of the mudflats. Two species are of national importance. The area supports one of the only two flocks of Bean Geese in Britain, the number averages 75, and it regularly has 50+ (2·5% British) Bewick's Swans. In addition, regionally important numbers of White-fronted Geese (80), Shelduck (490), Pintail (130), Redshank (590) and Dunlin (3,600) occur. Twenty-six species of waders and 21 of wildfowl were seen during the counts, while the diversity is even further increased by many rare species that arrive each year.

### Suffolk

*Blyth.* The Blyth is a muddy estuary connected to the sea by a narrow canalised channel. There have been numerous attempts to reclaim the mudflats and narrow saltmarshes but these have failed, leaving a mosaic of breached bunds. Part of the estuary is in the Walberswick/Minsmere National Nature Reserve, one of Britain's Ramsar Sites. The Blyth estuary is a Grade 1 site in NCR. At present there are few threats to the estuary. Three species occur in nationally important numbers, Shelduck reach 650 in winter (1·1% British) and over 350 remain in spring, and a build up of Black-tailed Godwit occurs in March and April reaching an average peak of 180 (3·6% British). About 40 (2·0% British) Bewick's Swan winter on Southwold Town Marshes. Several other species are present in regionally significant numbers: Wigeon (400), Redshank (600) and Dunlin (1,600). Twenty species of waders and 17 of wildfowl were recorded during the counts, giving a good diversity of species.

*Alde.* The outer estuary has little mud but is flanked by extensive grazing on Sudbourne and Lantern Marshes. In contrast there is a large area of mud on the inner estuary. Due to difficulty of access the estuary is protected but inadequately documented. No species is known to occur in nationally important numbers but there is a summering population of over 350 Shelduck, the number actually nesting is not known. Wintering flocks of 40+ White-fronted Geese and 30+ Bewick's Swans on Sudbourne Marshes, and up to 15 Avocets during the early autumn indicate the site's regional and, possibly, national significance. Like Butley River and the Ore there is a good variety of waders and wildfowl.

*Butley River.* Although this is a very narrow river, it and its associated marshes have a surprisingly rich bird fauna. Since it is very close to Havergate some of the species there are found in Butley River at times. This is especially true for the Avocet, over 50 regularly appearing during the period of post-breeding dispersal. The only other species of national significance is the Black-tailed Godwit which also reaches a peak in early autumn when 80+ are present. Wildfowl occur in good numbers, Wigeon exceeding 410, Teal 300 and Shelduck 160. Up to ten Bewick's Swans are regular. With 21 species of waders and 17 of wildfowl the estuary has an excellent variety of birds for its size. Fortunately the estuary is little threatened.

*Ore.* The area stretches from Orford to Shingle Street in the south and incorporates Havergate Island. The estuary mud banks are narrow but feeding for waterfowl is enhanced by the habitats managed on Havergate by the RSPB, the freshwater Boyton and Oxley Marshes and the shingle of Orford beach. Orfordness and Havergate form a Grade 1* site in *NCR* and apart from a possible future power station the area is relatively free from threats.

Three species occur in nationally important numbers; 26 Bewick's Swans winter regularly (1·3% British), 96 Shoveler (1·9% British), and about 100 pairs of Avocets nest on Havergate, small but increasing numbers also wintering here and on Butley River. There is a high diversity, with 25 species of waders and 22 of wildfowl, some being of regional significance such as 510 Wigeon, 210 Shelduck and up to 30 White-fronted Geese and 50 Brent Geese. The 2,600 pairs of Black-headed Gulls may be of national importance.

*Deben.* Like the Orwell the Deben is a long narrow estuary but on a smaller scale. There are quite extensive mud flats on the inner half but they are narrow on the outer reaches. Apart from Martlesham Creek at its northern end the estuary is largely surrounded by agricultural land with an irregular but usually narrow fringe of saltmarsh on the outer section. There is sailing and water-skiing on the estuary.

Shelduck, with a high average monthly count of 760 (1·3% British) is the only species of national importance, but of regional interest are Wigeon (870), Teal (300), Redshank (460) and Dunlin (1,210). There is quite a high diversity with 20 species of waders and 17 of wildfowl. The most important areas coincide with the mudflats and are from Kirton Creek to Woodbridge but all areas contribute towards the interest of the estuary.

*Orwell.* This is a relatively long and thin estuary with fairly even mud banks along the shore of its upper reaches but becoming more sandy at the mouth. The inner estuary is surrounded by Ipswich and its docks where further development is likely, similarly the docks at Felixstowe and the former HMS *Ganges* on either side of the mouth will probably undergo expansion or change. In between there is a long stretch of estate and farmland, including the Nacton duck decoy and near the mouth are the interesting freshwater marshes of Trimley and Shotley, much of the former however has been converted to arable. Although winter disturbance is not excessive very heavy sailing pressure in autumn limits the ornithological value of the upper reaches of the estuary at that time of year.

The most important areas for waders and wildfowl are Freston and Nacton/Levington shores and Trimley and Shotley Marshes. Wildfowl tend to be concen-

*Table 8:11   Species of national importance wintering on the Orwell, 1969–75*

|  | *Highest av. monthly count* | *% British* |
| --- | --- | --- |
| Mute Swan | 320 | 1·8 |
| Dark-belied Brent Goose | 515 | 1·6 |
| Shelduck | 1,050 | 1·7 |
| Pintail | 210 | 1·0 |
| Shoveler | 70 | 1·4 |
| Dunlin | 7,650 | 1·4 |
| Redshank | 2,100 | 2·1 |
| Turnstone | 400 | 1·6 |

trated into the first two of these although the Brent Geese move further down the estuary as the winter progresses. Only one species, Redshank, is of international importance but a further seven are of national significance (Table 8:11). These plus over 1,000 Wigeon and a total of 18 species of wildfowl indicate that the estuary is of considerable interest for this group of birds. In general the Orwell is another estuary with a good diversity of birds combined with fairly large numbers.

### Suffolk/Essex

*Stour.* The Stour is a relatively simply structured estuary with a sandy outer area and a muddier inner section. There are five main bays incorporating most of the intertidal flats; these are Seafield, Holbrook and Erwarton on the north, and Jaques and Copperas in the south. There has been piecemeal development at Harwich on the south eastern corner, but apart from some sailing, the estuary is relatively free of major problems. It is a Grade 1 site in NCR. The estuary is also an SSSI and there is a small reserve at its inner end. Most of the estuary is lined by cliff or by private land and disturbance is kept to a minimum.

*Table 8:12   Nationally important species wintering on the Stour, 1969–75*

|  | *Highest av. monthly count* | *% British* |
| --- | --- | --- |
| Mute Swan | 310 | 1·7 |
| Dark-bellied Brent Goose | 330 | 1·0 |
| Shelduck | 2,225 | 3·7 |
| Wigeon | 3,190 | 1·6 |
| Pintail | 620 | 3·1 |
| Ringed Plover | 130 | 1·1 |
| Grey Plover | 405 | 4·0 |
| Dunlin | 11,600 | 2·1 |
| Black-tailed Godwit | 685 | 13·7 |
| Redshank | 3,470 | 3·5 |

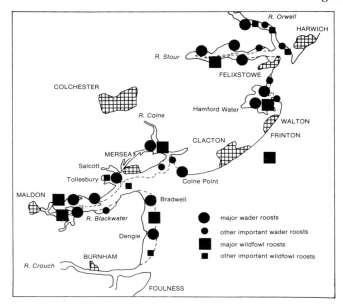

Fig. 8:4 Main concentrations of waders and wildfowl in south Suffolk and north Essex 1969–75.

Feeding birds occur on all the major bays with a tendency for most wildfowl to be on the estuary in from Holbrook Bay (Fig. 8:4). Roosts are mainly found on the quieter and well protected northern shore, the waders tending to use field roosts. Some birds which feed on Copperas Bay fly out of the estuary to roost on Pewit Island in Hamford Water. The Stour is of international significance for five species and of national importance for a further five (Table 8:12). Of these the Black-tailed Godwit flock is unique since it is the only one on the east coast of England except for the Hamford Water flock, with which it has some interchange. Wildfowl are especially numerous, relative to the British total, in the late autumn and early winter, and some species such as Redshank have a midwinter peak, a feature also of Hamford Water. An autumn gull roost of 30,000–40,000 is another feature of the estuary although only a quarter of this figure is present in winter. Since there are few areas of saltmarsh, breeding populations are limited, but about 100 pairs of Shelduck breed around the estuary, almost 1% of the national total.

### Essex

*Hamford Water*. If diversity of habitat is a criterion which indicates high value for a site, them Hamford Water would be near the top. It has a mosaic of dissected saltmarshes, islands, channels and mud flats backed by a range of brackish, fresh, and reed fringed marshes. The outer parts are severely disturbed and this, combined with egg collecting, poses a serious threat. The rapid conversion of marshland to arable poses another potential problem, as does the high wildfowling and boating pressure near Walton. The saltings are classed as a Grade 1 site in *NCR*, and they and the Naze are SSSIs. Two areas, including part of the Naze are additionally

*Table 8:13   Species of national importance wintering on Hamford Water, 1969–75*

|  | Highest av. monthly count | % British |
|---|---|---|
| Dark-bellied Brent Goose | 3,430 | 11·0 |
| Shelduck | 1,070 | 1·8 |
| Red-breasted Merganser | 75 | 1·0 |
| Ringed Plover | 385 | 2·4 |
| Golden Plover | 2,230 | 1·1 |
| Grey Plover | 695 | 6·9 |
| Sanderling | 130 | 1·3 |
| Dunlin | 12,000 | 2·2 |
| Black-tailed Godwit | 200 | 4·0 |
| Curlew | 2,500 | 2·5 |
| Redshank | 2,500 | 2·5 |

protected as reserves of the Essex Naturalists' Trust.

Because of the complexity of the site it is invidious to single out areas of special importance but the mudflats around Pewit and Horsey Islands are very rich, both islands also providing safe, major wader roosts. Stone Marsh on the Naze is also an important roost, probably at times drawing in some of the 100–200 Sanderling which winter on the Clacton-Frinton beaches. Wildfowl are concentrated on the inner parts of the estuary, especially in the south, but Teal and Wigeon abound in the north western marshes.

For its small size Hamford Water supports a remarkable number and diversity of species. Six species present in internationally important numbers are shown in Table 8:2 and those of national importance in Table 8:13. There are several other wintering species which almost reach this level, i.e. Bewick's Swan (18), Pintail (145) and Turnstone (220). Although no severe weather occurred during the study period, at such times Hamford Water does frequently hold very large numbers of duck, as in the winter of 1978/79 when 40,500 Wigeon were recorded. The breeding community is of great interest and includes three species of national importance. Passerines are of interest, too, including 2,000+ Twite. In all 32 species of wader, 27 of wildfowl and eight of divers and grebes occur, making the estuary a most valuable area for birds.

*Colne.* This smallish estuary is one of contrasts. It has an inner section which is decidedly muddy and flanked on the west by very large saltmarshes, whereas the outer parts are much more sandy with a large shingle beach at Colne Point. Two large wader roosts occur at Sandy Point and at Coopers Beach on East Mersea. Most of the wildfowl are concentrated into the inner estuary and adjacent marshlands but there are good numbers of seaduck, grebes and divers off its mouth. Fortunately, large areas of the western shore are inaccessible, but where the public have access on East Mersea and at Colne Point disturbance can be severe, despite the reserve status of the latter. Sailing is popular and several clubs exist on the east shore.

The Colne has internationally important numbers of four species and its national significance is outlined in Table 8:14. There are also several species which almost reach this level, particularly Mute Swan (170), Shoveler (45) and Turnstone (240), and autumn concentrations of Greenshank (90) and Spotted Redshank (70) are usual. The seaduck off Colne Point, especially Common Scoters, may be part of the much larger flock wintering off Clacton which reached over 2,000 in 1975. An autumn and winter gull roost of up to 250,000 small gulls occurs on East Mersea flats. Finally there are numbers of significant breeding species, including 4,000–5,000 pairs of Black-headed Gulls, 25 of Little Terns, 40 of Ringed Plover and 120 of Redshank.

*Blackwater.* The Blackwater is the second largest estuary in Essex and is a diverse and interesting example. The predominately muddy flats, the islands, creeks, river channels and some areas of adjacent freshwater marsh are deservedly classed as a Grade 1* site in NCR and it is an SSSI. There has been a considerable growth of sailing over the last decade and there is the potential danger of piecemeal reclamation encroaching further onto the important areas for birds. The estuary can be divided into two sections; the inner estuary from Thistley Creek and Stone Point and the outer estuary incorporating St Lawrence Bay in the south, and the complex of Tollesbury and Salcott channels, Mersea Fleet and the adjacent marshes in the north. In the inner section there are two large islands, Osea and Northey. No large saltmarshes remain but small ones, often ornithologically significant, are found in several places. There is a considerable amount of organic enrichment to the west of Goldhanger Creek where the Maldon Sewage Works discharge, resulting in a luxurient growth of *Enteromorpha*. At high tide waders move up to roost on Gore Saltings, Coopers Creek/Mundon Stone Point, or the saltings on Osea Island; if the tide is very high or disturbance is excessive the birds will roost on adjacent farmland. A roost, especially of passage waders, is found at Heybridge gravel pit. Wildfowl are also concentrated in the inner estuary, with Brent Geese, Wigeon and Pintail all found mainly between Osea and Northey Islands. They feed largely on *Enteromorpha* and saltmarsh grasses.

The outer estuary has fairly narrow mud banks but St Lawrence Bay and the Tollesbury area nevertheless support significant numbers of waders. Some birds from St Lawrence Bay fly out to roost on the Dengie Flats. At the north eastern

*Table 8:14   Species of national importance wintering on the Colne, 1969–75*

|  | Highest av. monthly count | % British |
|---|---|---|
| Dark-bellied Brent Goose | 1,730 | 5·2 |
| Shelduck | 1,330 | 2·2 |
| Goldeneye | 240 | 1·9 |
| Red-breasted Merganser | 75 | 1·0 |
| Ringed Plover | 140 | 1·1 |
| Grey Plover | 200 | 2·0 |
| Sanderling | 145 | 1·4 |
| Dunlin | 7,200 | 1·3 |
| Curlew | 1,490 | 1·5 |
| Redshank | 2,285 | 2·3 |

corner of the estuary the muddy Tollesbury and Salcott channels hold many Grey Plover, Dunlin and Redshank, while the importance of the area for the last species and Curlew is heightened by the existence of Old Hall and Tollesbury Wick Marshes. The former also has diverse breeding populations of waterfowl. The mouth of the estuary has an interesting sea duck, grebe and diver assemblage, particularly in the late winter.

The seven species of international importance have been summarised in Table 8:2; the national importance is shown in Table 8:15. There are also a number of species for which the Blackwater is almost of national significance: Slavonian Grebe (17), Bewick's Swan (18), Red-breasted Merganser (70), Great Crested Grebe (80), Pintail (165), Teal (590) and Wigeon (1,325), while Red-throated Diver (45) is probably of importance. Although no species is of national importance for its breeding numbers, Ringed Plover (30 pairs), Redshank (120 pairs) and Shelduck (40 pairs) are of more than local interest.

*Table 8:15  Species of national importance wintering on the Blackwater Estuary, 1969–75*

|  | *Highest av. monthly count* | *% British* |
|---|---|---|
| Dark-bellied Goose | 4,715 | 14·3 |
| Shelduck | 1,990 | 3·3 |
| Goldeneye | 180 | 1·4 |
| Ringed Plover | 245 | 1·9 |
| Grey Plover | 570 | 5·7 |
| Dunlin | 12,650 | 2·3 |
| Curlew | 1,920 | 1·9 |
| Redshank | 1,700 (2,870*) | 1·7 (2·9*) |
| Turnstone | 420 | 1·7 |

* Autumn number

*Dengie.* From Sales Point in the north to Holliwell Point in the south the Dengie Flats form an unbroken band of sand and mud. The muddy upper shore is also lined by a belt of saltmarsh, almost a kilometre in width in places and with small shell banks along its outer edge. Since public access is difficult, except from Bradwell, the area is relatively free from disturbance although where access exists it has been detrimental. For example 12 Little Tern clutches were trampled in 1968 and nine in 1969 (Blindell 1976), and the colony has been almost eliminated.

The area was classed as a Grade 1* site in *NCR* and there is an Essex Naturalists' Trust reserve at Bradwell. Brent Geese and Grey Plover occur in internationally important numbers (Table 8:1) and the national status of these and other species is shown in Table 8:16. Several other species are present in good numbers, in particular Wigeon (1,250), Shelduck (310), Pintail (140), Oystercatcher (1,845), Golden Plover (710) Curlew (935) and Bar-tailed Godwit (360). The breeding birds include 150–200 pairs of Redshank and 25–30 pairs of Ringed Plovers. Concentra-

Table 8:16   Nationally significant species on the Dengie Flats, 1969–75

|  | Highest av. monthly count | % British |
|---|---|---|
| Dark-bellied Brent Goose | 1,365 | 4·1 |
| Grey Plover | 540 | 5·4 |
| Knot | 3,360 | 1·1 |
| Dunlin | 6,575 | 1·2 |
| Turnstone | 605* | 1·0* |

* Autumn passage number

tions of roosting birds are found at Gunner's Marsh, Bradwell and between Coate and Bridgewick outfalls. Of additional and national interest are 160 Cormorants, a gull roost of up to 30,000, and as many as 2,000 Twite with small numbers of Shorelarks and Snow Bunting.

*Crouch.* This is yet another long thin and muddy estuary with much of its upper reaches flanked by reclaimed land and saltmarsh. The only significant area of saltmarsh left is Bridgemarsh Island, which is an SSSI. With little intertidal area it is not surprising that no species of wader is of national significance although Redshank (650), Dunlin (1,800) and in spring Golden Plover (525) are of interest. Wildfowl, however, are much more important, see Table 8:17, and for Brent Goose Table 8:1. In addition the 780 Wigeon, 125 Pintail and 335 Shelduck are of interest. Small roosts of waders and ducks occur along the estuary but there is a concentration at Bridgemarsh Island. The Brent Goose which build up towards the later winter are also found there and on the fields around Canewdon.

*Roach.* This long narrow estuary lies immediately behind the Foulness Islands. Its small size prohibits large numbers but it holds surprisingly good concentrations of birds. Redshank (720) almost reach national significance and there are good numbers of Dunlin (2,130) and Shelduck (275). The main roosts are on Bartonhall and Paglesham creeks and Potton Island; on this last site birds mix with others from Foulness.

*Foulness.* The complex of Foulness, Havengore, New England, Rushley and Potten Islands, combined with Maplin and Foulness Sands, form the largest

Table 8:17   Species of national significance on the Crouch, 1969–75

|  | Highest av. monthly count | % British |
|---|---|---|
| Dark-bellied Brent Goose | 800 | 2·4 |
| Teal | 920 | 1·2 |

continuous area of intertidal flats in Britain and make this area of great significance for wildlife. The area is classed as a Grade 1* site in *NCR*. Most of the land is owned and strictly administered by the Ministry of Defence so there are few of the conventional threats. The only major problems lay with the much publicised plans for a third London Airport and a new dock complex for the Port of London Authority. The first plans for an airport were dropped in 1974 and were last raised in 1979.

The intertidal flats are predominately sandy but the upper kilometre has a fairly high silt content and provides a rich feeding ground for birds. Waders and wildfowl use the whole length of foreshore with goose and ducks roosting anywhere along it. Waders, on the other hand, are concentrated into field or saltmarsh roosts at Wakering Stairs, Havengore Head, Havengore Island and Fisherman's Head and on the large shell spits at Foulness Point (Fig. 8:5).

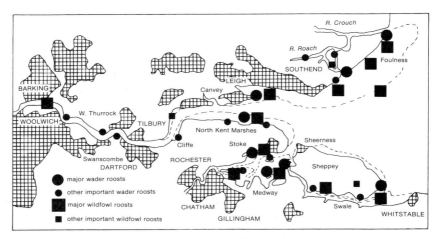

Fig. 8:5 Main concentrations of waders and wildfowl in the Thames estuary, 1969–75.

The birds of Foulness have been documented since 1961 due to the efforts of a well organised counting team. Summaries of information up to 1969 and for 1972–75 have been published by Rudge (1970) and Blindell (1978) respectively. The seven species which are of international importance are given in Table 8:2; the national status is shown in Table 8:18. Of these the Brent Goose is by far the most important, indeed regularly over 25% of all the British birds (and 12%+ of all the European) occur in early winter, although after depleting the *Zostera* beds the winter population is down to about 3,000 (9% British). Additionally, Common Scoter may be of at least national significance but the flock is rarely seen from land; one observation in December 1975 revealed 6,500, indicating the potential of the area. Quite large numbers of Shelduck (510) and Wigeon (1,200) also occur. At times very large numbers of gulls are present, particularly in autumn when, for example, Rudge (1970) estimated 180,000, although perhaps 20,000–40,000 is more regular.

The importance of Foulness does not, however, lie solely with its wintering or

*Table 8:18   Wintering species of national importance at Foulness, 1969–75*

|  | Highest av. monthly count | % British |
|---|---|---|
| Dark-bellied Brent Goose | 9,440 | 28·6 |
| Oystercatcher | 5,900 | 2·9 |
| Ringed Plover | 135 | 1·1 |
| Grey Plover | 580 | 5·8 |
| Knot | 6,690 | 2·2 |
| Dunlin | 9,570 | 1·7 |
| Bar-tailed Godwit | 2,180 | 4·8 |
| Curlew | 2,000 (2,980*) | 2·0 (3·0*) |
| Redshank | 960 (3,645*) | 1·0 (3·0*) |

* Autumn concentrations

passage birds. The protection of isolation has enabled a rich breeding community to develop. For example, it has nationally important numbers of Little Terns (60–70 pairs, 4·0% British, Blindell 1976) and 50 pairs of Ringed Plovers (1% British, Prater 1976), together with colonies of Common and Sandwich Terns and a Black-headed gullery.

*Leigh/Canvey.* Although the saltmarshes of Two Tree Island, Leigh Marsh and Canvey Point are sandwiched between the towns of Southend-on-Sea and Canvey, and the mudflats extend along the seafront of Southend as far east as Shoebury Ness, this area is of considerable significance for estuary birds. The four species of international importance have been detailed in Table 8:1, the national status is summarised in Table 8:19. The area is also of some significance in autumn for passage birds; Redshank regularly reach 2,150, Ringed Plover 400, Turnstone 270 and Wigeon 1,850. The adjacent Bowers Gifford Marshes has an interesting selection of migrant waders in spring and autumn. In view of its importance the Benfleet and Hadleigh Marshes are considered a Grade II *NCR* site and part of Leigh Marsh, together with some intertidal flats, was designated a National Nature

*Table 8:19   Species of national importance wintering at Leigh/Canvey, 1969–75*

|  | Highest av. monthly count | % British |
|---|---|---|
| Dark-bellied Brent Goose | 2,445 | 7·4 |
| Ringed Plover | 200 | 1·7 |
| Grey Plover | 320 | 3·2 |
| Dunlin | 10,300 | 1·9 |
| Redshank | 1,150 (2,150*) | 1·1 (2·1*) |

* Autumn numbers

Reserve in 1974. Apart from the creeping problem of leisure growth few threats exist for the area, although there could be some repercussions if the proposed Maplin airport scheme were to be implemented. Some ploughing has already taken place on the marshes.

### Essex/Greater London/Kent

*Inner Thames.* This long sinuous estuary runs through what was once one of the world's major ports with its concomitant industrial and urban development. Very large areas of low marshy ground have been reclaimed in historical times and today there still remain considerable pressures on parts of the habitat. For example, the Thames Barrage has removed marsh and/or foreshore at Silvertown and Aveley, while the very important wildfowl area of Woolwich Bay was reclaimed during the mid 1970s for a new town at Thamesmead. Organic and chemical pollution was a major feature of the estuary prior to 1960 but since then efforts by the Port of London Authority and the Greater London Council have resulted in massive improvements with the result that large numbers of wildfowl and waders were able to recolonise the intertidal flats. A detailed and fascinating account of this process is given in *The Thames Transformed* by Jeffery Harrison and Peter Grant (1976). The improvement in conditions has enabled estuary birds to penetrate as far as Tower Bridge but after a boom in numbers in the early 1970s there has been recently a slight falling off in bird numbers. It is not known why this should be so, but perhaps it is associated with the moving of the belt of *Tubifex* abundance up river into the narrower inner sections where little intertidal flats are exposed. Previously the large areas of the Mucking Flats and Swanscombe were available in the early 1960s, and subsequently those of Woolwich and Barking Bays.

*Table 8:20   Species of national importance on the inner Thames, 1969–75*

|  | Highest av. monthly count | % British |
|---|---|---|
| Mute Swan | 610 | 3·4 |
| Shelduck | 1,200 | 2·0 |
| Pintail | 200 | 1·0 |
| Pochard | 1,715 | 4·3 |
| Grey Plover | 110 | 1·1 |
| Dunlin | 8,775 | 1·6 |

Although no species is regularly of international importance the six of national significance are shown in Table 8:20. Several other species, especially Teal and Redshank, frequently reach the 1% level but not always in the same months. Of the less common species there are about 100 Ruff wintering on the Thames, mainly in the Swanscombe area, and this is one of the four largest flocks in Britain, averaging about 8% of the total.

At present, wildfowl are mainly found in the areas of Surrey Docks, Barking Bay, Aveley Marshes and Mucking Flats, while significant wader roosts are formed on Rainham Marshes, West Thurrock Power Station ash lagoons, Swanscombe and

Dartford Marshes and Cliffe lagoons. This last area draws in birds from Mucking Flats as well as the adjacent Higham Bay.

### Kent

*North Kent Marshes.* To a certain extent this is an artificial division since some of its birds are shared by the Medway, inner Thames and the south Essex coast. To the east it is bounded by the Isle of Grain refinery and to the west by the complex of lagoons at Cliffe, where pumped dredgings are deposited. The intertidal flats (Blyth Sands) have a high silt content. Behind the sea wall is a large area of reclaimed marshland, which still retains many slightly brackish fleets. Grazing is now giving way to arable farming on this marshland; this change of agriculture use, particularly if the fleets are reclaimed, is likely to provide a major threat since there is an important and diverse breeding bird fauna including many species of wildfowl.

*Table 8:21    Species of national importance wintering on the North Kent Marshes, 1970–76*

|  | Regular No. | % UK |  | Regular No. | % UK |
|---|---|---|---|---|---|
| White-fronted Goose | 526 | 5·3 | Grey Plover | 700 | 7·0 |
| Shelduck | 627 | 1·0 | Dunlin | 30,000 | 5·4 |
| Shoveler | 144 | 2·8 | Curlew | 1,900 | 1·9 |
| Ringed Plover | 120 | 1·0 | Redshank | 1,000 | 1·0 |

Several other threats still exist in the area, the most serious being at Cliffe where plans for a petro-chemical refinery and the reclamation of the lagoons by dredgings have been proposed; there is also the possibility of a power station.

The area around Yantlet Creek and the High Halstow Marshes are Grade 2 NCR sites and are SSSI's. Intertidal birds are distributed over the mudflats with concentrations towards high tide at Yantlet Creek, Egypt and St Mary's Bay and at Cliffe lagoons. Many birds, especially Dunlin and Knot, fly across the Thames towards the large roosts at Leigh/Canvey on the Essex coast; some, however, roost on the fields. The only full wader counts for this area have been made by the Kent Ornithological Society although wildfowl counts have been undertaken (Harrison and Grant 1976). Species of national significance are summarised in Table 8:21. Additionally, over 10,000 Lapwing and 3,000 Golden Plover occur at times on the reclaimed land.

*Medway.* This predominantly muddy estuary has the largest area of intertidal flats of any section of the Thames southern shore. Uniquely in Britain the mudflats are dotted with saltmarsh islands and there are extensive brackish grazing marshes. The oil refinery and new power station on the Isle of Grain and the port of Queensborough flank its mouth while the upper estuary is surrounded by Rochester, Chatham and Gillingham. On the north shore lies the large Kingsnorth power station. Two SSSI's have been declared, one covering the Chetney-Burnwick area;

part of this is a Grade 1 *NCR* site and Yantlett Creek is a part of a Grade 2 *NCR* site.

The inner estuary and parts of the main channel are extensively used for water borne recreation. The effects of this are felt widely on all of the islands, where it can be serious during the breeding season. Shooting too can be excessive in some areas. There are several major threats to the existence of sections of the Medway. Stoke Ooze is under pressure as an area for dumping of refuse or dredgings and reclamation. The important breeding area of Barksore Marsh and the Chetney/ Burntwick/Greenborough Marsh complex are, along with other smaller areas, continually under threats of reclamation.

Table 8:1 showed that seven species are of international importance; the national significance of these and a further five species is presented in Table 8:22. Of particular note is the concentration of dabbling duck for which the Medway ranks alongside the major estuaries in northwest England, the Wash, Lindisfarne and the Moray/Cromarty Firth. The wildfowl numbers have been considered in detail by Harrison (1972) and Harrison and Grant (1976).

*Table 8:22 Species of national importance wintering on the Medway, 1969–75*

|  | Number | % |  | Number | % |
|---|---|---|---|---|---|
| Teal | 3,900 | 5·2 | Ringed Plover | 120 | 1·0 |
| Wigeon | 7,600 | 3·8 | Grey Plover | 570 | 5·7 |
| Pintail | 650 | 3·2 | Curlew | 1,200 | 1·2 |
| Shoveler | 220 | 4·4 | Black-tailed Godwit | 315 | 6·3 |
| Shelduck | 2,375 | 4·0 | Redshank | 1,200 | 1·2 |
| Dark-bellied Brent Goose | 450 | 1·4 | Dunlin | 6,050 | 1·1 |

The saltmarsh islands and brackish grazing marshes support a diverse and rich breeding bird community. Kent Ornithological Society have undertaken regular counts since 1955, summarised in Harrison, Humphreys and Graves (1973). There is no doubt that the most important area, as shown in Fig. 8:5, incorporates the islands and peninsula of Chetney, Burntwick, Greenborough and Millfordhope. This area supports the great majority of the wildfowl and about half of the waders, as well as many breeding birds. The other 20,000 waders are found in the complex area of Stoke Ooze on the northern shore (Scott 1978), where a large gullery is also located. Nor Marsh also supports many wildfowl.

*Swale.* The Swale is basically the channel separating the Isle of Sheppey from the mainland. At the north eastern corner lies the sand and shingle spit of Shell Ness with its associated saltmarsh. There are other small areas of saltmarsh at Harty Ferry and Windmill Creek but most of the estuary is lined by dykes protecting the adjacent low lying rough grazing. A general summary of the habitat and threats can be found in *Wildlife Conservation in the North Kent Marshes* (1971).

The estuary is an SSSI and a Grade 1 *NCR* site. On the northern shore the marshland, including Shellness, has been designated a NNR and the RSPB has a nearby reserve. On the southern shore there are two LNRs and three KTNC reserves. The principal sources of disturbance are the increase of yacht moorings, wildfowlers, birdwatchers and bait digging, the latter being especially frequent near Whitstable. Kemsley paper mill introduces a certain amount of organic pollution into the inner estuary but its effects have not been fully assessed. Perhaps the main threat to the whole area remains the drainage of wet pasture for arable farming to take place.

Grey Plover, the only species of international importance, is listed in Table 8:2, but there are 13 other species which are significant at the national level, presented in Table 8:22. They show that the Swale supports a considerable diversity and number of birds outside the breeding season. The rough pasture on Sheppey also has an interesting breeding community of waders, ducks and Common Terns in addition to the numbers of wintering wildfowl which have built up in response to reserve management, particularly at the RSPB's Elmley reserve.

*Table 8:23    Species of national importance wintering on the Swale, 1969–75*

| | Number | % | | Number | % |
|---|---|---|---|---|---|
| Wigeon | 2,160 | 1·1 | Grey Plover | 725 | 7·2 |
| Shoveler | 140 | 2·8 | Curlew | 1,100 | 1·1 |
| Shelduck | 690 | 1·1 | Bar-tailed Godwit | 555 | 1·2 |
| White-fronted Goose | 450 | 4·5 | Black-tailed Godwit | 350 | 7·0 |
| Dark-bellied Brent Goose | 540 | 1·6 | Redshank | 1,115 | 1·1* |
| Oystercatcher | 3,280 | 1·6 | Knot | 3,040 | 1·0 |
| Ringed Plover | 150 | 1·2 | Dunlin | 5,715 | 1·0 |

* Autumn numbers

Figure 8:5 shows the principal concentrations of waders and ducks in the whole of the Thames estuary. The mudflats at the eastern end of the Swale form the main feeding area; birds which roost at Shell Ness and Harty, feed over the whole of the area from Whitstable to north Sheppey. Those roosting at Windmill Creek feed on the inner estuary, and White-fronted Geese on inland pasture. A general summary of wader numbers in north Kent and their movements in the Swale is given by Musson (1963) and Hori (1963). Similar numerical data for wildfowl are presented by Harrison (1972) and Harrison and Grant (1976).

*Reculver/Minnis Bay.* This area of sand and mud beaches with rocky outcrops is backed by low lying agricultural land. Few estuarine birds occur, but Sanderling regularly reach 1% of the British total, although there may be some interchange with the Foreness-Botany Bay birds.

*Pegwell Bay.* This is the estuary of the River Stour and to the south the shore is mainly sand backed by sand dunes. Around the river mouth a little saltmarsh has developed but to the north is Ramsgate and its hoverport. No species of birds occur in nationally significant numbers although 32 species of waders and 15 of wildfowl were recorded during the survey. Dunlin (1,215) and Lapwing (1,025) are the most common species. The Bird Observatory is sited at Sandwich and the area is of much interest for the great diversity of migrants recorded annually.

*South Coast areas*. On the shingle and sand beaches between Dungeness and Deal few waders are found. However, Sanderling occur in internationally important numbers (winter maxima 325) on Lade Sands between Dungeness and Hythe. The rocky promontory and beaches at Foreness and Botany Bay support 100 (1% of British) Sanderling and up to 400 (1·6% of British) Turnstones and 65 Purple Sandpipers.

CHAPTER 9

# Southern England

The coastline of southern England, defined here as Dorset, Hampshire, Isle of Wight and Sussex, can be divided into three types. From Chesil Fleet in the west to Pagham Harbour in West Sussex there are large areas of low lying coastal plains encompassing a number of large estuaries or embayments, often with considerable expanses of associated saltmarsh. The largest of these are (from west to east) Poole Harbour, Solent, Southampton Water and Portsmouth, Langstone, Chichester and Pagham Harbours. The rest of the coast is a mixture of long stretches of sand or shingle, with small rivers running down to the sea, and of chalk cliff.

The most important estuarine areas of the region are complex, either in their form or their tidal regimes. All, except Southampton Water, have narrow entrances which open into large embayments and there is relatively little fresh water flow through them. These factors result in strong tidal currents in the outer main channels and sluggish water movement in the inner regions, with the consequent accumulations of fine silt to form extensive soft mud banks. The tidal pattern is complicated. In Southampton Water and the Solent there is an approximate eight hour flood followed by a high water stand of an hour or more. The ebb is very rapid and runs for only about $3\frac{1}{2}$ hours. Moreover, the tidal range in the west Solent is only half that to the east of Southampton Water. The general effect of this pattern is to reduce the length of time the muds are exposed compared with a more conventional situation, whilst on neap tides very little mud may be exposed at low water. The effects on birds are little known. In the other major harbours, especially Poole Harbour, the narrow entrance and weather conditions can disrupt the normal pattern of tidal flow.

*Urban and industrial development and recreation*

The precise problems of each area will be discussed later but the general pattern of coastal land use and reclamation does have a strong influence on bird distribution. Urban development has been extensive around Langstone, Portsmouth and Poole Harbours and along Southampton Water, and there has been piecemeal reclamation of small creeks, bays and saltmarshes.

The proximity of so many people has resulted in a large increase of organic effluents entering the sea and estuaries. In an analysis of the botanical and bird data collected over the last 20 years Tubbs (1977) draws a correlation between organic enrichment, algal growth and changes in bird numbers. Along with the increase in the population there has been an upsurge in the use of the coast for recreation, particularly for watersports. This trend is growing and possibly forms one of the major conflicts with wildlife conservation in this region. The general aspects of this problem have already been discussed in some detail. There has been a considerable increase in development in Southampton Water related mainly to the port and petro-chemical industries. Some of these sites have become of ornithological interest with the provision of disturbance-free and artificial roosting areas. They have, however, reduced considerably the intertidal zone.

Agricultural developments, too, have had an influence on the estuaries of southern England although not quite as marked as in eastern England. In East Sussex, especially, the canalising of the river valleys of the Ouse, Cuckmere, Pevensey Haven, Waller's Haven, Brede and Rother, followed by the draining of inland marshes have reduced the value of their intertidal areas. The resulting grazing land on some of these levels is used extensively by inland waders (Lapwing, Golden Plover and Snipe) and some Curlew and Redshank.

*Main literature on the birds of southern England*

The birds occurring on the coast in this region have been summarised as follows: Dorset – Boys (1973); Hampshire – Cohen and Taverner (1972); Sussex – Shrubb (1979). In addition the annual bird reports of the Dorset Natural History and Archaeological Society, Hampshire Field Club and Archaeological Society and Sussex Ornithological Society include much information on coastal birds.

*Principal species and migration patterns*

Of the birds restricted to the estuaries the Dunlin is by far the most numerous in this region (see Table 9:1), with up to 74,000 in midwinter. In contrast no other species of shore wader has a population regularly exceeding 8,000. Of the less numerous waders the characteristic birds, of which southern England supports at least one-fifth of the numbers in Britain, are Black-tailed Godwit and Grey Plover. Less frequent species, but in a national aspect of particular interest, are the wintering flocks of Ruff and Spotted Redshank. The former have not been fully counted by estuary counts but coastal flocks during the period 1966–71 averaged 340, almost 30% of the total wintering in Britain and Ireland (Prater 1973). The 15–20 Spotted Redshank on the Beaulieu River form the largest wintering flock in Britain. After Dunlin in abundance comes, surprisingly, the Brent Goose with over 14,000 in recent years, Shelduck and Wigeon. Knot (1,260) and Bar-tailed Godwit (1,160) are of note only in that numbers are very low compared with other regions.

In southern England the migration pattern is fairly simple. There is a small but noticeable autumn (July–September) passage of most species of wader. Redshank,

*Table 9:1    Highest monthly counts of the principal species of wildfowl and waders in southern England, 1969–75*

| | | | | | |
|---|---|---|---|---|---|
| Dark-bellied Brent Goose | 11,980* | Jan | Dunlin | 73,400 | Feb |
| Shelduck | 8,620 | Feb | Lapwing | 20,970 | Jan |
| Wigeon | 8,180 | Jan | Redshank | 7,500 | Sept |
| Teal | 4,400 | Jan | Curlew | 5,350 | Sept |
| Mallard | 1,650 | Dec | Oystercatcher | 3,460 | Jan |
| Mute Swan | 1,040 | Dec | Ringed Plover | 2,190 | Aug |
| Pintail | 580 | Jan | Golden Plover | 2,090 | Jan |
| Red-breasted Merganser | 490 | Dec | Black-tailed Godwit | 1,850 | Oct |
| Goldeneye | 390 | Jan | Grey Plover | 1,850 | Oct |
| Shoveler | 190 | Feb | Snipe | 1,400 | Jan |

* Average of 1972/73–1974/75 only

Curlew and Black-tailed Godwit moult here in quite large numbers. This is followed by a very rapid increase in the numbers of the principal species (Dunlin, Brent Goose, Shelduck and Wigeon) to a midwinter peak in November. Then there follows an equally rapid decrease in numbers during late February and March. The spring migration is small in terms of numbers but migratory activity is in evidence (see Steventon 1978). There is, however, a strong passage of Bar-tailed Godwit, Common Scoter and divers eastwards along the coast between March and early May.

Quite large numbers of other birds occur in the region. Of these gulls are the most numerous but they have been less thoroughly counted than the waders and wildfowl. Large numbers use the estuaries as feeding grounds and even larger numbers as a relatively safe night-time roost. Over 15,000, mostly Black-headed Gulls, roost in Southampton Water and Langstone Harbour; few counts have been made else-where. On the Beaulieu River there is a large colony of Black-headed Gulls, which has recently reached 20,000 pairs, the second largest colony in Britain and Ireland. Sizeable colonies of this species are also found at Lymington/Keyhaven (9,000) and Newtown Marsh (500) (Gribble 1976). Few seaduck, divers and grebes are present, although the last of these groups is relatively well represented in a national context. Small flocks of Slavonian Grebes occur at times in most major estuaries but numbers rarely exceed 20; while Black-necked Grebes frequently reach 40 in Langstone Harbour they are less frequent elsewhere.

### Principal estuaries of Southern England

Seven of the estuaries or coastal sections in southern England support wader or wildfowl populations which are of international importance; the criteria defining this have already been described. Not surprisingly all of the larger estuaries support internationally important numbers of at least one species. All species of importance are presented in Table 9:2.

Chichester and Langstone Harbours clearly emerge as being of considerable importance with respectively eight and five species of significance. There have been

*Table 9:2   Percentage of the European population of the principal species of birds in southern England, 1969–75*

| | Fleet | Poole Harbour | Portsmouth Harbour | Langstone Harbour | Chichester Harbour | Climping | Goring |
|---|---|---|---|---|---|---|---|
| Brent Goose | – | – | – | 6·6 | 6·4 | – | – |
| Shelduck | – | 1·6 | – | 1·2 | 2·4 | – | – |
| Wigeon | 1·0 | – | – | – | – | – | – |
| Grey Plover | – | – | – | 1·4 | 3·3 | – | – |
| Sanderling | – | – | – | – | 1·1 | 1·7 | 1·0 |
| Dunlin | – | – | 1·1 | 1·7 | 1·9 | – | – |
| Black-tailed Godwit | – | 1·1 | 1·0 | 1·0 | 1·9 | – | – |
| Bar-tailed Godwit | – | – | – | – | 1·0 | – | – |
| Redshank | – | – | – | – | 2·5 | – | – |

many sightings of birds, particularly Black-tailed Godwits, moving between the three interconnected complexes of Portsmouth, Langstone and Chichester Harbours. The counts of these three harbours have been co-ordinated to prevent duplication of observations; if the area is considered as a single unit the number of waders exceeds 90,000 and wildfowl 15,000. This would place it about twelfth in overall importance in Europe for wintering estuarine birds.

### Sussex

*Rye Harbour.* Rye Harbour differs from other areas on the coast in that there are extensive areas of shingle and sandy beaches; behind the shingle ridge there is a complex of gravel pits. Most of the area is scheduled as an SSSI. The majority of the wildfowl are found on the gravel pits; the waders mainly feed on the beach and Camber Sands. Quite large numbers of seaduck occur offshore in Rye Bay.

There were 27 species of wader and 23 of wildfowl recorded during the counts but numbers were small. Only Sanderling (100:1·0% British) was of national importance, although 420 Pochard on the gravel pits, 220 Common Scoter in Rye Bay are regionally significant.

*Sussex coastline counts.* Between Pagham Harbour in the west and Rye Harbour in the east there are many, frequently contiguous, towns separated by some chalk cliffs. Mid-winter counts have been made at seven sites where concentrations of waders are known; few wildfowl occur. At *Climping*, at the mouth of the River Arun, and *Goring* just to the east, there are separate groups of shore waders, the only species of significance is Sanderling which at Climping averages 250 (1·7% European, 2·5% British) and at Goring averages 150 (1·0% European, 1·5% British). At the latter site up to 750 Dunlin occur. On the *River Adur* at Shoreham there is another concentration of waders including 1,100 Dunlin and 100 wintering Ringed Plovers. Further east the shore at the mouths of the *River Ouse* (Newhaven) and *Cuckmere River* (an SSSI) and the *Pett Levels* (Whinchelsea – also an SSSI) there are small concentrations of shore waders but on the fields inland large numbers of Lapwing occur especially during severe weather. *Pevensey Bay* to the east of Eastbourne also has a few (380) shore waders but here the levels, an SSSI, support large flocks of Lapwing (10,000 plus), Golden Plover (720) and Snipe.

*Pagham Harbour.* Pagham Harbour is a relatively small estuary with quite extensive areas of *Spartina* and *Halimione* marsh on its inner shores. The surrounding land is undeveloped and in places has relatively wet pasture. The main roosting areas for the birds are the relatively high central shingle banks and islands in the estuary. When the banks are covered by spring tides the displaced birds use adjacent fields, especially between Sidlesham and Church Norton. Smaller numbers roost on the outer shingle beach but there is much disturbance in this area. Small numbers of sea duck and grebes occur off the estuary mouth at times. Pagham Harbour is an LNR. No sailing or fishing takes place within the estuary.

The whole estuary is of considerable ornithological interest as it has a high species diversity, 28 species of wader and 20 of wildfowl have been recorded during the counts. Surprisingly no species is of international importance, but four are nationally important, see Table 9:3. At Sidlesham there is a flock of up to 100 Ruff in winter (10% British) which sometimes occur on the estuary. Since 1976 numbers have rapidly increased and up to 1,000 recorded in late winter. Winter and spring Avocets (2–5) are of local interest.

---

*Table 9:3   Species of national significance at Pagham Harbour, 1969–75*

|  | *Highest av. monthly count* | *% British* |
|---|---|---|
| Dark-bellied Brent Goose | 440 | 1·3 |
| Shelduck | 600 | 1·0 |
| Grey Plover | 185 | 1·8 |
| Black-tailed Godwit | 260 | 5·2 |

---

*Sussex–Hampshire*

*Chichester Harbour.* Chichester Harbour forms the largest estuary in southern England. The whole area is a Grade 1* NCR site and it is an SSSI, 950 acres form an LNR. It has a complex shape with four major arms formed by the land sinking along four small river valleys. These run into an extensive area of sand and mud flats and river channels. The Harbour has a fairly wide opening to the sea. Almost all of the shoreline is undeveloped but has restricted access, although where access is possible quite heavy disturbance results. Much sailing takes place in the Harbour. All sections of the estuary are used by waders. The largest numbers of birds roost on Thorney and Hayling Islands, the former sometimes having more than 20,000 and the latter 10,000.

On an international level (Table 9:2) Chichester Harbour supports important numbers of eight species. The twelve species of national importance are shown in Table 9:4. Of regional interest are Teal (520), Wigeon (1,000), Pintail (120), Golden Plover (670) and Knot (920); the last being the largest flock of this species anywhere

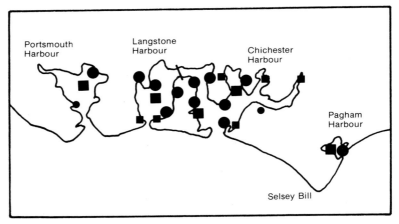

Fig. 9:1 Main concentrations of estuary birds between Pagham and Portsmouth Harbours.

on the south coast. There is a winter flock of about 10 Slavonian Grebes.

Although there are only limited data prior to 1962 it is clear that some species have increased in numbers in Chichester Harbour. Brent Geese have steadily increased in parallel with numbers in Langstone Harbour; winter 1955–56 was the first time that numbers in Chichester Harbour exceeded 100, and 1,000 was passed in 1964–65; since then it reached 3,000 in 1970–71, 4,000 in 1972–73 and a peak of 7,500 in 1973–74. Of the dabbling duck the most important three species, Teal, Wigeon and Pintail, have all shown a steady rise in numbers since 1967–68 but Shelduck has slightly declined since 1972–73 from an average of about 4,000 to about 2,700. The change may relate to the increase in organic pollution.

*Table 9:4    Species of national importance in Chichester Harbour, 1969–75*

|  | Highest av. monthly count | % British |
|---|---|---|
| Dark-bellied Brent Goose | 4,540 | 13·8 |
| Shelduck | 3,080 | 5·1 |
| Goldeneye | 120 | 1·0 |
| Ringed Plover | 140 | 1·2 |
| Grey Plover | 990 | 9·9 |
| Sanderling | 170 | 1·7 |
| Dunlin | 22,400 | 4·1 |
| Black-tailed Godwit | 780 | 15·6 |
| Bar-tailed Godwit | 880 | 2·0 |
| Curlew | 1,200* | 1·2 |
| Redshank | 2,780* | 2·3 |
| Greenshank | 100* | † |

\* Autumn
† No census but considered significant

## Hampshire

*Langstone Harbour.* Although Langstone Harbour is surrounded by urban development most of the land immediately adjacent to the shore remains relatively open. On the west there are few natural areas but to the north are the Farlington Marshes, a LNR and a Grade 1* NCR site, and to the east farmland on Hayling Island. Off Farlington Marshes is a series of low lying islands; of which South Binness and Baker's are the more important for birds, most of these and adjacent mudflats totalling 1,360 acres are an RSPB reserve. To the north-east, Langstone Harbour is joined to Chichester Harbour. The intertidal area of the harbour is a Grade 1* NCR site.

The principal roosting areas used are shown in Fig. 9:2; the most important are the islands mentioned above, Farlington Marshes and west Hayling Island. The roosting pattern is relatively simple, with most birds on the northern and western mudflats moving to the first two sites and birds on the eastern flats roosting on

*Table 9:5   Species of national importance in Langstone Harbour, 1969–75*

|  | Highest av. monthly count | % British |
|---|---|---|
| Dark-bellied Brent Goose | 4,630 | 14·0 |
| Shelduck | 1,570 | 2·6 |
| Ringed Plover | 210 | 1·7 |
| Grey Plover | 430 | 4·3 |
| Dunlin | 20,100 | 3·7 |
| Black-tailed Godwit | 390 | 7·8 |
| Redshank | 1,300* | 1·1 |

* Autumn

Hayling Island. There is some movement to roosts on east Hayling Island.

Langstone Harbour is of international importance for five species (Table 9:2). Its national status is summarised in Table 9:5. The flocks of Teal (660), Wigeon (1,280), Goldeneye (110), Red-breasted Merganser (50) and Curlew (1,100) are all just under the level of national importance but are of local significance. There is a flock of Black-necked Grebes which feeds mainly in the north-eastern section of the Harbour. The annual average peak of 30 is the largest regular concentration of this species in Britain and up to 45 have been recorded. Between 15,000–20,000 gulls have been counted coming in to roost in Langstone Harbour during the winter months.

There have been thorough counts of birds in Langstone Harbour since 1952 and they provide an almost unparalleled documentation of changes on any major British estuary. A summary of some changes are presented in Table 9:6.

Tubbs (1977) has discussed in detail the possible causes of the dramatic increase of most species and the declines of others. These include overall increases in numbers due to a series of recent good breeding seasons, combined with greatly reduced

*Table 9:6  Changes in numbers of some species of birds wintering in Langstone Harbour, 1952–75\**

| | 1952/3–1957/8 | 1958/9–1963/4 | 1964/5–1969/70 | 1970/1–1974/5 |
|---|---|---|---|---|
| Teal | 227 | 198 | 473 | 749 |
| Wigeon | 542 | 790 | 784 | 1,290 |
| Shelduck | 1,673 | 2,617 | 3,258 | 1,671 |
| Brent Goose | 368 | 823 | 2,033 | 5,013 |
| Oystercatcher | 84 | 227 | 507 | 814 |
| Ringed Plover | 560 | 158 | 193 | 141 |
| Grey Plover | 112 | 220 | 275 | 533 |
| Curlew | 875 | 1,037 | 812 | 676 |
| Black-tailed Godwit | 230 | 533 | 452 | 459 |
| Bar-tailed Godwit | 191 | 226 | 313 | 255 |
| Redshank | 975 | 1,140 | 716 | 573 |
| Knot | 243 | 313 | 243 | 576 |
| Dunlin | 8,167 | 8,917 | 15,667 | 23,920 |

\* Data from Tubbs, C. R. (in press), note that last column is slightly different from BOEE counts as it excludes 1969/70 data

hunting pressure, *Spartina* dieback increasing the area of mud, eutrophication due to the increase in organic effluent and the subsequent developments of *Entermorpha* mats. The pollution of the estuary has been described earlier; piecemeal reclamation and disturbance are the main problems of the area.

*Portsmouth Harbour.* Much of the shore of this large bay has been built up with extensive port and housing developments even though it is an SSSI. The most important roosting area is the reclaimed zone to the north of Horsea Island, in the north eastern corner (see Fig. 9:1), which draws waders from the whole of the estuary. This area is still being reclaimed by refuse disposal. Twenty per cent of the intertidal area has been reclaimed during the last decade, but to date the roosting pattern has not been seriously disrupted. Small numbers of the larger waders sometimes roost on Pewit Island and less frequently on the south western shoreline.

Wildfowl were relatively scarce here, although on average 170 of each of Shelduck and Brent Goose occurred. The number of Shelduck on Portsmouth Harbour has declined sharply in recent years from a peak count of 1,200 in 1968–69 to less than

*Table 9:7  Species of national importance in Portsmouth Harbour, 1969–75*

| | Highest av. monthly count | % British |
|---|---|---|
| Ringed Plover | 135 | 1·1 |
| Dunlin | 12,700 | 2·3 |
| Black-tailed Godwit | 365 | 7·3 |

20 in 1974–75. It is not known whether this is a long-term trend for very few observations had been made prior to 1968. Brent Geese, however, increased to 2,500 in 1978–79, and waders are abundant. Portsmouth Harbour is of international importance for wintering Dunlin and Black-tailed Godwit in autumn (Table 9:1). Its national status is shown in Table 9:7. Additionally it has 1,100 Redshank and 90 Grey Plovers at times, both of which are present in numbers only slightly below the level of national importance. Portsmouth Harbour has the third largest concentration of Knot (560) in southern England.

*Southampton Water.* This estuary is one of the most highly developed in southern England. The north eastern parts of the Rivers Test and Itchen have been dredged and docks built. At Dibden Bay there is a series of four large pans into which dredgings have been pumped. Two of the four are now almost reclaimed as freshwater marshland but the other two still have large areas of dry and wet mud. Glue (1971) demonstrated the attractiveness of these areas to roosting waders from the adjacent intertidal zone. From Hythe to Calshot Spit in the south-west there is an

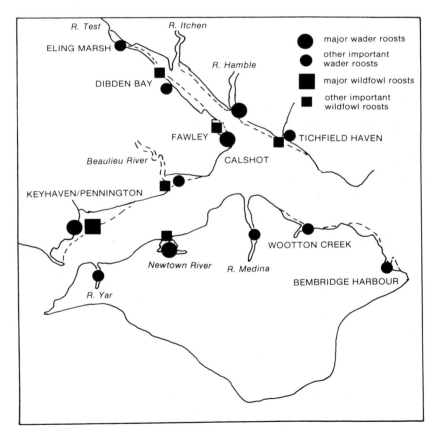

Fig. 9:2 Main concentrations of estuary birds in Southampton Water and the Solent.

oil refinery and a power station. The cooling lagoons of the latter at Fawley have provided some excellent roosting areas on high spring tides. To the seaward side of these industrial developments there is a large area of *Spartina* marsh and mud flats. On the opposite eastern side of the Southampton Water there are extensive areas of mud around the mouth of the Hamble River, and at Tichfield Haven there is an area of freshwater marsh surrounding the dammed River Meon; this plus Eling and Bury Marshes and Hythe to Calshot Marshes are SSSIs; part of Calshot is an LNR, as is Tichfield Haven. For the moment further reclamation seems unlikely and few serious problems occur.

Figure 9:2 shows that the principal roosting concentrations of estuarine birds are found at Calshot/Fawley and River Hamble, with fairly large numbers at Dibden Bay, Tichfield Haven and Eling Marsh. There is a considerable degree of movement of birds between Calshot and Hamble and Calshot and Fawley but relatively little between the other sites. The six species of birds which occur in nationally important numbers are shown in Table 9:8.

*Table 9:8   Species of national importance in Southampton Water, 1969–75*

|  | Highest av. monthly count | % British |
|---|---|---|
| Shelduck | 650 | 1·1 |
| Teal | 1,180 | 1·6 |
| Ringed Plover | 220 | 1·8 |
| Grey Plover | 225 | 2·2 |
| Dunlin | 5,800 | 1·1 |
| Black-tailed Godwit | 115 | 2·3 |

Each section has its characteristic birds. Calshot has the greatest diversity, and large numbers of all important species are present. Hamble is mainly a wader feeding area where Dunlin, Redshank and Turnstone are abundant; Tichfield Haven being primarily a wildfowl area. The number of Teal and Wigeon present in recent years (200–400 of each) was rather below those recorded in the 1950s by Atkinson-Willes (1963), but this may have been due to the increased use made of the relatively undisturbed Calshot/Fawley area; subsequently, protection at Tichfield Haven has attracted many of these back. Dibden Bay and Eling Marsh are mainly of importance for waders but up to 400 Shelduck regularly occur on the former site. Dibden Bay has recently become less attractive as the reclamation pans dry out.

About 100 pairs of Black-headed Gulls were found breeding at Calshot in 1973 (Gribble 1976). Tubbs (in litt.) notes that 30,000–35,000 gulls, mainly Black-headed and Common, have been counted roosting in Southampton Water during the winter.

*Beaulieu River.* The Beaulieu River is relatively narrow and has extensive areas of saltmarsh away from its mouth. Generally, therefore, the number of waders in the inner section is low although wildfowl are able to utilise the whole of the estuary. Much of the outer low level marshes around Needs Ore Point are of *Spartina anglica* which, like those on the adjacent Keyhaven/Lymington section, have suffered dieback. On adjacent farmland on the south west of the estuary there is a complex of freshwater pools called the Gins, and brackish pools at Warren Shore. The estuary is a Grade 1 NCR site.

Although no species of wader or wildfowl occurs on the estuary in nationally important numbers there is a good variety, with 20 species of each recorded during the counts. The most numerous species are Wigeon (660), Teal (510), Dunlin (460) and Curlew (360), although the 15–20 wintering Spotted Redshank are the largest concentration of the species in Britain.

The numbers of wildfowl have increased since those recorded in the 1950s by Atkinson-Willes (1963), when he noted regular numbers of Wigeon (470), Teal (150), Mallard (75 now 345), Shelduck (35 now 80), but he did not mention Pintail, 40 of which now occur.

The *Spartina anglica* marshes at Needs Ore Point support a very large colony of Black-headed Gulls, which has grown from 1,200 pairs in 1961 to almost 20,000 pairs in 1973 (Gribble 1976). Occasional Mediterranean Gulls and hybrid Mediterranean/Black-headed Gulls breed in the colony. Little, Sandwich and Common Terns also breed and it is of national importance for the first two species, with 2% and 1·6% respectively of the British and Irish population (Lloyd, Bibby and Everett 1975); numbers appear to be increasing. It is one of the few sites in southern England where Sandwich Terns breed.

*Keyhaven/Pennington.* This area is bounded to the west by the shingle ridge of Hurst Spit and to the east of Pitts Deep by a narrow beach. There is quite heavy pressure from leisure activities, sailing, shooting and walking. It is a Grade 1 site in NCR.

There are large expanses of intertidal flats in this north western section of the Solent. The extensive growth of *Spartina anglica* characteristic of this area ten to twenty years ago has now suffered dieback, followed by erosion, providing much more open mud than before. This may have benefitted several species of wader and wildfowl.

During the period of the counts relatively small numbers of wildfowl (1,330) and fairly large numbers of waders (9,860) regularly occurred. The species found in nationally important numbers are presented in Table 9:9. Additionally, Shelduck (450) and Brent Goose (260) are of local significance. The wintering flock of Ruff was one of the largest in Britain (9% of the total number); they occurred on the adjacent pasture at Pennington and while averaging 70 they have reached 180.

---

Table 9:9    Species of national importance in the north-west Solent, 1969–75

|  | Highest av. monthly count | % British |
|---|---|---|
| Grey Plover | 140 | 1·4 |
| Dunlin | 5,900 | 1·1 |
| Ruff | 70 | * |
| Black-tailed Godwit | 75 | 1·5 |

* Wintering number, 6% British

Unfortunately there are few data on the changes in numbers of wildfowl in this area over the last twenty years although it is only in the last five years, since its population greatly expanded, that Brent Geese have become regular in large numbers. In the early 1960s it was unusual to find more than a thousand Dunlin here but there are now regularly over 6,300 wintering. In both of these cases the dieback of *Spartina* was considered by Tubbs to have accommodated the increased number of birds. Brent Geese are now able to feed on the *Enteromorpha* growing on the eroding platforms while the mud then exposed provides feeding areas for Dunlin.

There is a large breeding colony of Black-headed Gulls on the Keyhaven/Lymington *Spartina* marshes which has grown rapidly during the 1960s from less than 1,000 pairs in 1959 to 9,000 pairs in 1973 (Gribble 1976). The breeding population of Little Terns here form 2·5% of the British and Irish numbers (Lloyd, Bibby and Everett 1975).

### Isle of Wight

*Bembridge Harbour.* This estuary of the River Yar is on the east of the Isle of Wight. Although relatively small numbers of waders and wildfowl occur here there is a fairly high species diversity, with 22 waders and 16 wildfowl recorded during the counts. The most abundant species of duck are Pochard (70) and Teal (60); of the shore waders, Dunlin regularly reach 120 and Redshank 100. The 95 wintering Sanderling form just under 1% of the British total; there is only one other flock of this species in Hampshire.

*Wootton Creek.* This small estuary supports a reasonable diversity of species but numbers are small, only Curlew (150) and Redshank (115) regularly exceed 100 individuals. There have been no counts made of the large intertidal area between Ryde and Nettlestone Point.

*River Medina.* Only small numbers of waders and wildfowl were recorded, mainly due to few counts. Part of the Medina estuary is an SSSI. Some potential problems exist with waterborne recreation and organic pollution. The few counts made have been on the inner half of the estuary, where up to 150 Shelduck, 80 Mute Swan, 400 Dunlin and 150 Redshank have been recorded.

*Newtown River.* This is the largest and most important estuary on the Isle of Wight. It is a Grade 2 NCR site and an LNR. The two main arms, Clamerkin Lake and Western Haven are separated by a large zone of flooded pasture formed in 1954 when a sea wall was breached; part is now a saltmarsh. This central area provides feeding grounds for most of the duck as well as a roosting area for birds from the estuary. A wide range of species occur on the estuary; during the last six years 26 species of wader and 11 of wildfowl. Numbers of waders are relatively low; only the Black-tailed Godwit with a regular 245 in late winter (4·9% of British) is nationally significant. No species of wildfowl exceeds 1% of the British total but locally important flocks of Teal (530), Wigeon (480), Pintail (90), Shelduck (370) and Dark-bellied Brent Goose (285) are seen regularly. All of these have increased since the 1950s (Atkinson-Willes 1963), particularly Pintail and Brent Goose which were rarely seen then. Of the waders, apart from Black-tailed Godwit, only Dunlin (1,500) were numerous. A locally important Black-headed gullery is found on the saltmarsh.

*River Yar.* This small estuary, which is also an SSSI, lies on the north-west of the Isle of Wight. Extensive salt marsh restricts the areas of mudflats and as a result waders and duck numbers are small. Teal (240) and Dunlin (310) are of local significance.

## Dorset

*Christchurch Harbour.* This small estuary, formed by the Rivers Stour and Avon, is situated on the eastern border of Dorset and like the Fleet and Poole Harbour has a very narrow eastern facing entrance, with a sand and shingle spit on the south side. Almost all of the intertidal flats are on the north side of the estuary where there is also the large freshwater/grazing area of Stanpit Marsh; this marsh is an LNR. A wide variety of species was recorded in the harbour, 18 wildfowl and 26 waders, but numbers of almost all are small. The only species of national significance is the Mute Swan with up to 320 in autumn − 1·8% of the British population. Stanpit Marsh regularly supports 440 Snipe and there is a roost of up to 5,000 gulls.

*Poole Harbour.* By far the largest and most important estuary in Dorset. Although two rivers, the Frome and Piddle enter it from the west there is relatively little freshwater inflow. The growth of Bournemouth and Poole has decreased the value of the north shore for wildfowl. On the west and southern sides, however, there remains large areas of undeveloped mudflats, islands, low lying sandy heathlands and at Wareham the flood plains of the rivers Frome and Piddle. The mudflats and saltmarshes of Poole Harbour are a Grade 1 *NCR* site; and the Arne peninsula and the adjacent heaths of Studland and Hartland are Grade 1*. All are SSSIs.

As described in the introduction to southern England the tidal pattern is very complicated, making it impossible to be sure which are the preferred feeding grounds of wildfowl and, especially, waders. In general the principal areas for feeding duck remain the Little Sea (an inland lake on the outer dune peninsula), Brands Bay, Newtown Bay and around the Arne peninsula. Many of the intertidal feeding dabbling and diving duck roost on the lakes at Brownsea Island. Waders feed

*Table 9:10   Species of national importance in Poole Harbour, 1969–75*

|  | Highest av. monthly count | % British |
|---|---|---|
| Canada Goose | 300 | 1·5 |
| Shelduck | 2,060 | 3·4 |
| Teal | 1,065 | 1·4 |
| Pintail | 325 | 1·6 |
| Shoveler | 60 | 1·2 |
| Red-breasted Merganser | 180 | 2·4 |
| Ruff | 50 | * |
| Black-tailed Godwit | 460 | 9·2 |
| Redshank | 980 | 1·0 |

* Wintering flock, 4% British

in similar areas to the ducks although the mudflats in the north-east of the estuary are also used by 1,000–2,000 feeding birds. The inner parts of Poole Harbour, including Holes and Lychett Bays, are used more extensively by waders than by ducks. Small roosts occur on many areas but, as with the duck, quite large numbers flight to Brownsea Island during high water. The other main component of the bird fauna is the diving seaduck and grebes which feed in the deeper channels and creeks of the estuary, and flight out of the Harbour at dusk to roost, presumably, on Poole Bay.

Sheplduck and Black-tailed Godwit have already been shown in Table 9:2 to be of international importance. The national status of the birds of Poole Harbour is presented in Table 9:10. Additionally, up to 15 Spotted Redshanks winter, the second largest concentration in Britain. Of probable significance although no national figures are yet available, are the Black-necked and Slavonian Grebes which feed in the Harbour. The former is the more numerous averaging about 20 birds but the latter often reach double figures. No other British estuary supports moderately large numbers of both species.

*Radipole Lake/Lodmoor.* Radipole Lake was formed by the damming of the River Wey at Weymouth, but despite the lack of tidal influence it supports a wide variety of waders when water levels are relatively low. Numbers are small apart from the inland species, Lapwing and Snipe. Most wildfowl are noticeably less abundant than they were during the 1950s when Atkinson-Willes (1963) noted maxima for Teal five times those now seen, Mallard twice, Shoveler four and Pintail ten times. Wigeon seem to have left the area and are seen only occasionally and in small numbers, whereas up to 350 used to occur. Only Tufted Duck (400) and Pochard (365) have increased, from regular winter flocks of 175 and 50 respectively. Lodmoor, just to the east of Radipole Lake has become less favourable for waterfowl although a high diversity sometimes occurs, in small numbers, when water levels are favourable. Both Lodmoor and Radipole are SSSIs.

*Portland Harbour.* There are two sections to the harbour; an outer part which exposes little mud and is protected by a large seawall, and a small inner bay at Ferrybridge where some sandy mud is exposed at low tide. The wildfowl, mainly seaduck, occur in the sheltered water of the harbour during rough weather, along with small numbers of Slavonian Grebes and a wide variety of other grebes and divers. Only Red-breasted Mergansers are regular and abundant (averaging a peak of 160: 2·1% British); these birds appear to remain separate from those on the adjacent Fleet. The waders are found on the intertidal flats just to the west of Ferrybridge. Dunlin are the most numerous wader but Ringed Plover are relatively more important, forming 0·7% of the British wintering birds.

*Fleet.* Chesil Fleet is not strictly an estuary but a long, thin embayment with a very narrow eastern entrance separated from the sea by a shingle beach. It is a Grade 1* site in *NCR*, supporting a considerable number of estuarine birds. Table 9:2 shows its international importance for Wigeon; the national significance for three species of wildfowl is presented in Table 9:11. Peak numbers of Mute Swans occur in winter but there is also an important breeding colony of 100–150 pairs. Coot regularly reach over 2,000 and if national data were available these could be of significance. A good variety of waders (25 species) was recorded during the counts but apart from

*Table 9:11   Species of national importance on the Fleet, 1969–75*

|  | Highest av. monthly count | % British |
|---|---|---|
| Mute Swan | 680 | 3·8 |
| Wigeon | 4,000 | 2·0 |
| Red-breasted Merganser | 100 | 1·3 |

1,000 Lapwing which feed in adjacent fields, and 600 Dunlin, numbers are small. During the breeding season the shingle beach is of national importance for its breeding Ringed Plover (75 pairs, 1·5% British) and Little Terns (80 pairs, 4·0% British).

The number of Mute Swans has remained relatively static since the late 1950s, although this is partly due to artificial limitation of numbers. During the years up to 1962, Wigeon regularly numbered 650 and reached 4,000 on only two occasions in 14 years; since then numbers have risen and a maximum of 6,030 was recorded in December 1972.

Most of the wildfowl are found on the western section of the Fleet, although diving duck and resting dabbling duck can occur almost anywhere. In contrast the shore waders are concentrated in the eastern parts of the area where the tidal influence exposes mud-flats at low tide.

CHAPTER 10

# South-western England

The coast of south-western England is one of the most attractive in Britain. It is cliff lined for almost the whole of Devon, Cornwall and western Somerset, cut by a number of small or moderately sized estuaries. The estuaries are almost all rias, drowned river valleys, flooded when the sea level rose and the land sank. As a result most are steep-sided and narrow, the water flow from the sea is restricted and quite high rainfall brings a considerable amount of water-borne sediment down the rivers. Intertidal flats with a high silt content have developed but because of the steep banks, there is little saltmarsh and, with the exception of some areas on the Severn and Taw/Torridge, what there is is mostly dominated by *Spartina*. A few dune systems have developed, all minor apart from that of Braunton Burrows in north Devon. Additional diversity is created by freshwater marshes, principally on the Severn, Taw/Torridge and Exe, and by coastal lagoons separated from the sea by shingle or sand beaches in south Devon and Cornwall.

The only areas outside the general pattern are the Severn and the small Hayle estuary. The former being surrounded by low lying levels (brackish or freshwater pasture) improving the estuary's attraction for inland feeding waders and wildfowl. Little offshore shallow water is found. Tide ranges are moderate over much of the region but high in the Severn, almost reaching 15 m at Avonmouth, the highest range in Britain.

*Urban and industrial development and recreation*

At present the main pressure on the estuaries of the south west comes from leisure activities and particularly waterborne recreation. The estuaries are sheltered and attractive whereas the open coast is susceptible to strong winds. Sailing, therefore, concentrates in the estuaries and there is an associated development of marinas, moorings and house building. General disturbance by holidaymakers and by research or educational parties can at times give rise to local problems. Apart from piecemeal reclamation, there is an increase in organic effluent which in these sheltered estuaries could lead to pollution problems. A number of proposals have been made for the siting of refuse tips on low areas adjacent to estuaries. This, too, may result in some reclamation, subsequent industrial development, or pollution through seepage.

The desire to harness tidal energy has led to many proposals for barrages across the Severn estuary. To date no firm recommendations have been made on its design, but this remains the principal threat to estuary birds in the south west. A fuller account of the proposals has been given in Chapter 4. Industry, too, is concentrated around Bristol on the Severn and although it produces a considerable amount of effluent its effects on birds is not yet discernable, but see Chapter 5. In Cornwall, the effluent from china clay workings and other mineral extractions can cause great turbidity and may well reduce the invertebrate biomass in the mud. A natural problem, but one enhanced by deliberate planting, is of the spread of *Spartina*. The high silt content of the mud encourages its growth and some areas have already seen it spreading steadily.

*Literature on the birds of south-western England*

The principal recent county avifaunas for this region are: Devon – Moore (1969); Cornwall – Penhallurick (1969, 1978); Somerset – Palmer and Ballance (1968). A review of the waders of the Severn, covering all counties involved, has been published by Ferns (1977). Annual bird reports are produced by the Devon Birdwatching and Preservation Society, the Cornwall Birdwatching and Preservation Society (separate reports for the mainland and the Isles of Scilly), Lundy Field Society, Somerset Ornithological Society and the Gloucestershire Naturalists' Society. Further details on the birds recorded at Slimbridge are found in the Wildfowl Trust's annual reports.

*Principal species and migration patterns*

South-western England has few large estuaries, and as a result the total number of birds is relatively low. The ten most numerous wildfowl and waders are shown in Table 10:1. With the exception of Wigeon and of the White-fronted Geese and Bewick's Swans based on Slimbridge, wildfowl are poorly represented. Perhaps this is partly a result of the small size and scarcity of saltmarshes. The wildfowl all build to a peak in midwinter, although there is the notable moulting flock of Shelduck in Bridgwater Bay during the late summer. This flock is the only one of any size (although the recently observed flock in the Firth of Forth may be of moderate size) outside the main area on the Heligoland Bight of the Federal Republic of Germany. Most of the winter build up of Shelduck occurs in the estuaries of Devon and Cornwall since winter numbers on the Severn do not reach those of late summer. There is no doubt that the mildness of the winters between 1969 and 1975 has not

*Table 10:1   Principal species on estuaries in south-western England, 1969–75*

| | | | | | |
|---|---|---|---|---|---|
| Wigeon | 12,500 | Dec | Dunlin | 54,000 | Jan |
| White-fronted Goose | 4,500 | Jan | Lapwing | 25,100 | Dec |
| Mallard | 3,800 | Jan | Golden Plover | 10,500 | Jan |
| Shelduck | 2,850 | Feb | Curlew | 8,400 | Jan |
| Teal | 1,650 | Jan | Oystercatcher | 8,400 | Sept |
| Dark-bellied Brent Goose | 450 | Jan | Redshank | 5,300 | Oct |
| Mute Swan | 350 | Dec | Ringed Plover | 4,200 | Aug |
| Bewick's Swan | 330 | Jan | Black-tailed Godwit | 1,700 | Sept |
| Pintail | 160 | Feb | Whimbrel | 1,500 | May |
| Red-breasted Merganser | 130 | Jan | Knot | 1,300 | Feb |

Figures based on the month with the highest average count for the whole region

encouraged birds to move to the region from further north and east. The importance of the south west peninsula does increase in severe weather, as was observed in 1962–63 and again in 1978–79. It would take but a small westward shift by the continental climate boundary for this region to receive regularly large numbers of wintering wildfowl.

Waders show a much more diverse pattern of occurrence than wildfowl. The most numerous species, Dunlin, and the species mainly or frequently seen inland, Lapwing, Golden Plover and Curlew, have winter peaks. However, the largest numbers of other species are seen in spring or autumn. Even though most of these are more numerous during the passage periods, numbers in winter are only slightly below these levels. Only the Ringed Plover, which exhibits a strong autumn migration, and the Whimbrel, almost only seen in late April and May, are exceptions to this rule. Knot and Bar-tailed Godwits are scarce, but up to 35% of British Black-tailed Godwits occur in the region. This pattern of abundance reflects the small size and muddy nature of the south west's estuaries. The last species, together with Lapwing and Golden Plover, are perhaps the characteristic birds of the south-west, being numerous on most larger estuaries. Few waders or wildfowl breed on the estuaries or the low coast, and grebes, divers and sea duck are generally uncommon.

*Principal estuaries of south-western England*

Five estuaries regularly support internationally important numbers of birds. These are presented in Table 10:2. The size of the Severn and the diversity of habitat within and around it make it by far the most important area in the region. The other largish estuaries, the Exe, Taw/Torridge and Tamar complex, also have their share of sigificant numbers; the only two medium-sized estuaries not supporting international numbers, are the Fal complex and the Camel, but the former only just falls outside this category. The small estuaries dotted along the south Devon and Cornish coasts are of considerable interest, for although precluded by size from supporting large numbers they do hold a great diversity of birds normally regarded as species which winter in the Mediterranean area or Africa. On the north coast of the south-western peninsula there are few estuaries, and they are separated by considerable distances, there being about 80 km intervals between Bridgwater Bay, Taw/Torridge, Camel and the Hayle estuary. This wide spacing arguably increases the need for careful consideration of development proposals in the area.

*South Devon*

*Axe.* This small estuary lies just east of Seaton, with much of its eastern shore flanked by a road. The estuary is fairly muddy, and to its west and especially its northern side, there is a moderately extensive area of brackish or fresh marshes. There is some pressure for recreational activities at present, and suggestions for changing Seaton Marshes into a large marina development were put forward in 1972. During the present counts, moderate numbers of Wigeon (170), Shelduck (50), Lapwing (1,020), Curlew (135), Dunlin (150) and Redshank (60) were recorded. A good variety of birds occurs.

*Otter.* The small estuary of the Otter enters the sea at Budleigh Salterton. An area of sand and shingle lies at its mouth and the river is flanked on the west by freshwater marshes. Disturbance can be high from walkers along the public footpaths. Most birds are found in the marsh, principally Curlew (50), Lapwing (160), Mute Swan (35) and occasional Bewick's Swans, and in summer there are 50 Shelduck. Ringed Plovers reach 40 on the shore in winter.

*Exe.* The Exe is the largest and most important estuary in the south-western peninsula. Two sandy spits or dune systems flank the entrance to the estuary. On the west the large Dawlish Warren provides a wealth of habitats used by migrant birds,

*Table 10:2   Estuaries of international importance in south-western England, 1969–75*

| | Exe | Tamar | Mounts Bay | Taw/Torridge | Severn (all) |
|---|---|---|---|---|---|
| Bewick's Swan | – | – | – | – | 3·2 |
| White-fronted Goose | – | – | – | – | 3·7 |
| Shelduck | – | – | – | – | 1·6 |
| Wigeon | 1·1 | 1·0 | – | – | – |
| Ringed Plover | 1·0 | – | – | 1·1 | 1·2 |
| Grey Plover | – | – | – | – | 1·4 |
| Lapwing | – | – | – | – | * |
| Knot | – | – | – | – | 1·1 |
| Sanderling | – | – | 1·0 | 1·0 | – |
| Dunlin | – | – | – | – | 3·9 |
| Black-tailed Godwit | 1·7 | 1·2 | – | – | 2·7 |
| Whimbrel | – | – | – | – | * |
| Curlew | – | – | – | – | 1·3 |
| Redshank | – | – | – | – | 2·0 |

(1) Only species of 1% or more included in this table.
(2) * No winter count data available but considered of international importance, see Appendix 3.

while The Point at Exmouth is a very much smaller sand bank stretching into the estuary. Behind them, flats are basically muddy, especially in the inner estuary, although patches of sand and mussel beds occur. Saltmarshes have developed behind Dawlish Warren and on the inner estuary. Exminster Marshes on the north-west side are rough grazing fields separated by large wet ditches, and a small area of marshland exists where the River Clyst enters the estuary. Most of the rest of the estuary is flanked by road, railway, urban development or estates, of which Powderham Park is the most interesting for birds. Pressure from holidaymakers can be intense, especially at Dawlish Warren and Exmouth, and is likely to increase. Planning permission for a marina near Exmouth was given some years ago but not taken up; new proposals are likely to be forthcoming. This would seriously affect the feeding grounds of some species. Other proposals elsewhere may be coming. Two natural threats exist. *Spartina* is steadily developing behind Dawlish Warren (and indeed, elsewhere in the estuary), and the dunes are being eroded by heavy storms, and require coastal protection work from time to time. A major breach here could greatly affect the sedimentation pattern of the estuary.

The Exe is a Grade 2 NCR site and is protected by an SSSI notification; the west shore from Turf Hotel to Langstone Rock is under a statutory Bird Sanctuary Order. In 1979 Dawlish Warren was declared a LNR.

Feeding grounds of birds encompass the whole estuary, but a major area for Brent Geese and Wigeon occurs near Exmouth in the zone of the marina proposals. Of the other specialities, Black-tailed Godwits are found on the east shore from Lympstone to Topsham; Avocets below Topsham and at Turf; and wintering Ruff on Exminster marshes. The Brent Goose flock on the Exe, now over 1,000 strong, is the only major concentration in the region. At high tide, the main roost is on Dawlish Warren: ducks on the inner part near the railway, with waders and Brent Geese on

---

*Table 10:3   Species of national importance on the Exe, 1969–75*

|  | Highest av. monthly count | % British |
|---|---|---|
| Dark-bellied Brent Goose | 410 | 1·2 |
| Wigeon | 4,470 | 2·2 |
| Red-breasted Merganser | 80 | 1·1 |
| Oystercatcher | 2,900 | 1·4 |
| Ringed Plover | 250 | 2·1 |
| Grey Plover | 280 | 2·8 |
| Dunlin | 7,700 | 1·4 |
| Ruff | 70 | +1 |
| Black-tailed Godwit | 670 | 16·7 |
| Bar-tailed Godwit | 680 | 1·5 |
| Curlew | 1,150* | 1·1 |
| Greenshank | 20 | +2 |
| Turnstone | 320* | 1·3 |

* Autumn numbers
+ Small wintering totals: +1 *c.* 1,000; +*c.* 300.

the outer half, although many of the latter remain off Exmouth. Exminster marshes attract good numbers, and Greenshank concentrate into Powderham Park. The species of international importance are shown in Table 10:1, while the national status is in Table 10:3. Of interest also are Avocet (at 14, the third largest wintering flock in Britain; they often float in the centre of the estuary at Turf!), Shelduck and Teal. Off shore the 20–25 wintering Slavonian Grebes are probably also of British importance. Few birds find sufficiently undisturbed areas to breed.

*Teign.* This smallish estuary is characterised by a relatively large freshwater flow. As a result, the intertidal flats in the centre section tend towards sand and gravel (which are extracted commercially) and are greatly dissected by channels. Near Newton Abbot, some saltmarsh development has occurred and the flats are muddier. At its mouth, the mussel scar of the Salty is an interesting area. Most of the estuary, the Teignmouth area excepted, is relatively undisturbed. Somewhat scattered concentrations of Oystercatchers occur on the Salty and a roost of smaller waders develops on the inner section. No species is of national importance, but of interest are 700 Oystercatchers, 275 Redshank, 100 Dunlin and 20 Red-breasted Mergansers. The Local Authority has initiated a study of the estuary which is nearly complete. Much of the upstream southern foreshore is managed as a sanctuary jointly with the Devon Trust for Nature Conservation and the Devon Wildfowlers' Association.

*Dart.* There is about fifteen miles of river between Dartmouth and Totnes, mostly with only a narrow strip of mud and a small number of waders. The river and adjacent wetter areas from Sharpham to Dartington provide habitats for the dabbling ducks. There is a considerable number of waterborne craft on the estuary, but even so the total number of birds is surprisingly small, with maxima of 190 Mallard, 120 Curlew and 100 Redshank being the most interesting.

*Kingsbridge.* Seven drowned river valleys make up the arms of this interesting estuary between Salcombe and Kingsbridge. The sluggish flow in the inner estuary has left a deep deposit of silt. Little saltmarsh development is possible with the steep grass hillsides reaching down to the high water mark. There has been a great expansion of waterborne recreation, possibly making the outer estuary poor for duck, and it is almost certain that the expansion will continue. The main areas for waders and Wigeon are Frogmore Creek and the flats between Kingsbridge and Lincombe, this latter area also holds good numbers of Shelduck in winter. No species is present in nationally important numbers, but of regional significance are 260 Shelduck, 1,160 Wigeon, 375 Redshank, 700 Golden Plover and 625 Dunlin. A good variety of waders and wildfowl have been recorded here, feeding on the fauna which are themselves of scientific interest for their diversity and numbers.

*Avon.* This delightful little estuary runs from Aveton Gifford to the sea, entering a bay near Grantham Dunes. Most of its upper reaches are narrow and muddy with some saltmarsh development, but its mouth is sandy. It is hardly surprising in view of its small size that no nationally important numbers of birds occur. However, it has a high diversity including wintering Greenshank along with other 'southern' species such as Spotted Redshank, Green Sandpiper and Common Sandpiper. Of the more numerous species, 120 Curlew, 50 Teal and 45 Mute Swans are of interest.

*Erme.* This is another attractive estuary somewhat similar in structure to the Avon, although less disturbed and with more woodland and saltmarsh. It offers a variety of habitats and is an SSSI. Duck are slightly more numerous than on the Avon, with 160 Mallard, 50 Teal and 30 Wigeon, but there are fewer waders.

*Yealm.* Unlike the two previous estuaries, the Yealm has little sand at its mouth, but towards Yealmpton it becomes quite a wide muddy estuary attractively surrounded by woodland. A small, once reclaimed area at Kitley has an additional diversity of birds, especially during severe weather. During the counts, the main species of regional interest were 45 Black-tailed Godwits, 100+ Curlew, Redshank and Mallard and 60 Shelduck. As with the Kingsbridge estuary, the intertidal fauna is of considerable interest.

### Devon/Cornwall

*Tamar complex.* From the wide rocky entrance of Plymouth Sound five separate estuaries branch out. Each has its characteristic features and birds, but since there is thought to be some movement of birds between them, the whole area is considered here. The main components are the estuaries of the Plym and Tavy in Devon, the inner Tamar straddling the border, and Lynher and St John's Lake in Cornwall. The Plym is bordered to the west by Plymouth and to the east by Saltram Estate and Chelston Meadow, an area of wet fields and a rubbish dump. The other estuaries are all relatively secluded, although Torpoint intrudes on to the outer section of St John's Lake. Like other drowned valleys in the south west, the intertidal flats are muddy and only small areas of saltmarsh have developed, although fairly extensively on the north shore of the Lynher. The outer part of the Plym and St John's Lake have slightly more sand and gravel.

Sailing is popular and is likely to increase; an area of potential impact is the Dunlin roosting marsh at Laira on the Plym. Major roosts are at Laira, Crabtree and Chelston Meadow on the Plym, at Torpoint and Sango Island on St John's Lake and possibly at night, on the Plymouth Breakwater. In the other estuaries, smaller roosts develop, depending on tide height and disturbance. The Lynher and St John's Lake

*Table 10:4  Species of national importance on the Tamar Estuary, 1969–75*

| | Highest av. monthly | % British | Plym | Tavy | Tamar | Lynher | St John's |
|---|---|---|---|---|---|---|---|
| Wigeon | 3,940 | 2·0 | – | – | – | – | 1·3 |
| Avocet | 94 | * | – | * | * | – | – |
| Golden Plover | 2,400 | 1·2 | – | – | – | – | – |
| Dunlin | 6,275 | 1·1 | – | – | – | – | – |
| Black-tailed Godwit | 475 | 9·5 | 3·8 | – | 1·1 | 2·0 | 3·0 |
| Redshank | 1,270 | 1·3 | – | – | – | – | – |

* All but about 30 British wintering Avocets are on the Tamar (64) or Tavy (30)
– Present but numbers less than 1% British
Note the unit percentages may be from different months

are each Grade 2 sites in *NCR*, and are SSSIs. The Port of Plymouth Area Recreation Study (1975) included some recommendations for restraint in the development of recreation, to protect conservation interests. The six species of national importance and their distribution is presented in Table 10:4.

### Cornwall

*Looe.* This attractive estuary has a relatively small area of intertidal flats and, being set in a steep valley, virtually no saltmarsh. Just south of its mouth is an extensive area of flattish rocks which provide a feeding ground for an interesting selection of waders and a roost for birds from the estuary. Since it is small, no species is of national importance, although in a regional context, the 50 Purple Sandpipers, 130 Turnstone, 40 Ringed Plovers and scattering of Common Sandpipers in winter are all significant.

*Fowey.* Although another small estuary with mud flats only on its inner half, the Fowey has many of the commoner waders but few wildfowl. Of regional interest are the 1,200 Lapwing, 180 Curlew and the good autumn passage of Greenshank. The area is relatively free from problems.

*Table 10:5 Species of national importance wintering on the Fal complex, 1972–75*

|  | Highest av. monthly count | % British |
|---|---|---|
| Black-tailed Godwit | 360 | 7·2 |
| Curlew | 1,600 | 1·6 |
| Spotted Redshank | 19 | * |
| Greenshank | 26 | * |

* Small numbers winter in Britain

*Fal complex.* From Falmouth the broad Carrick Roads extend northwards with four estuaries branching off it. These are the Fal/Ruan, Tresillian, Truro and Restronguet Creek. They are all, especially the first three, very muddy with only small areas of saltmarsh in sheltered corners. Its size and complexity make it the most interesting intertidal area in south Cornwall. Carrick Roads are much used by sailing dinghies, but local industries pose a far greater problem. In particular, pollution due to suspended sediments from tin extraction, to dredging and to fish processing ships; additionally, Falmouth is a primary area for oil developments off the south west, and pollution from this source is more than a possibility. At the moment, the whole of two arms, the Fal/Ruan and Truro Rivers, are SSSIs, the former including a Grade 1 *NCR* site.

The national status of the estuary is summarised in Table 10:5. The Black-tailed Godwit numbers are only just below the level of international importance; several other species are noteworthy on a regional basis, particularly 600 Wigeon, 430 Shelduck, 40 Red-breasted Mergansers, 4,650 Dunlin, 720 Redshank, 3,360 Lapwing and 55 Grey Plover; all three divers and most grebes are regularly recorded in Carrick Roads, and Falmouth has recently attracted many of the rarer gulls in winter.

*Mounts Bay.* The beach, rocks and harbours around Mounts Bay provide feeding grounds for several waders, gulls and some grebes and divers. Of most importance are 150 Sanderling (1% European, 1·5% British) and 95 Purple Sandpipers (3·1% English).

*Hayle.* For a small estuary the Hayle supports a remarkably rich and varied bird life. The estuary has two sections, a main bay to the south where the River Hayle enters, and Copperhouse Creek to the east. Some saltmarsh has developed in the south-western corner. The flats are a mixture of muddy and sandy areas. Very few birds occur on the outer sands in St Ives Bay. The estuary is surrounded by roads, railways or urban and holiday development and is under continuous threat from further reclamation. Dredging to keep a channel open to Hayle causes instability in the sediment patterns. The southern bay and Porth Kidney Sands is an SSSI.
   Although the Hayle is not of national importance for any species, Ringed Plover (115) and Golden Plover (1,750) almost reach that status. Other species of regional interest are 550 Wigeon, 100 Teal, 30 Grey Plover, 340 Curlew and 460 Dunlin. A wide range of species is recorded including several rarities. Since access is easy, it is a popular birdwatching area.

*Gannel.* A small estuary which, although attractive, supports only a few of the more common waders, Ringed Plover especially, and wildfowl.

*Camel.* The largest estuary on the north coast of Cornwall. The outer half of the estuary is sandy with some rocky sections but the flats east of Dinham are muddy with a saltmarsh developing around Burniere and the good pasture of Amble Marshes (an SSSI) on the north-eastern shore. With difficult access on its inner section, most disturbance occurs on the outer part of the estuary; here water-skiing is the main problem. Further recreation development could have repercussions for wildlife.
   Oystercatchers and Turnstones are mainly found on the outer estuary; the rest of the waders concentrate at high tide on the saltmarshes and adjacent fields. These Amble Marshes are used by the only regular flock of White-fronted Geese in Cornwall. Although in mild winters numbers are small, many more occur in severe weather. The species of national significance are presented in Table 10:6. Regionally

*Table 10:6   Nationally important species on the Camel, 1969–75*

|  | Highest av. monthly count | % British |
|---|---|---|
| Golden Plover | 3,280 | 1·6 |
| Curlew | 1,007 | 1·0 |

it is noteworthy for its 560 Wigeon, 100 Shelduck, 4,500 Lapwing and 150 Turnstone, and for its diversity of species, including regularly wintering Little Stints, wild swans and White-fronted Geese.

### North Devon

*Taw/Torridge.* These two estuaries join and are considered together. The Taw is much the larger and bordered by diverse habitats. Large saltmarshes occur on the southern shore at Penhill and Yelland and a smaller one at Crow Point. The florally interesting fresh and brackish Braunton Marsh and Horsey Island, Chivenor Airfield and the important sand dune systems of Braunton and Northam Burrows flanking the exit of the estuary to the sea, deserve special mention. The Torridge has much more urban development, and being relatively narrow has little saltmarsh development. The intertidal flats at the entrance are sandy with remnants, left after commercial exploitation, of shingle ridges. Silt increases in the inner estuary and parts are quite muddy.

The estuary is quite heavily used for recreation, particularly from Chivenor on the Taw and Bideford on the Torridge, to the mouth. This involves sailing, power-boating, angling and recreation in general, which may increase following outline planning permission for a marina at Appledore. The Devon County Council published the Taw/Torridge Estuary Study of recreational opportunities in 1979. Braunton Burrows is an NNR but the rest of the estuary has little formal protection; although SSSI notification and a Bird Sanctuary Order are being considered for the Taw.

Table 10:7   Species of national importance wintering on the Taw/Torridge Estuary, 1970–75

|  | Highest av. monthly count | % British |
|---|---|---|
| Oystercatcher | 2,500 | 1·2 |
| Ringed Plover | 280 | 2·3 |
| Golden Plover | 2,750 | 1·4 |
| Sanderling | 145 | 1·4 |
| Curlew | 1,580 | 1·6 |

The national status of birds on the Taw/Torridge is presented in Table 10:7. It is of additional regional significance for Shelduck, Wigeon, Lapwing and Redshank, while its diversity of wintering waders is notable with Ruff (20), Greenshank, Spotted Redshank, Common and Green Sandpipers and the occasional Avocet.

### Somerset/Avon/Gloucester

*Severn.* Stretching 100 km from Frampton to Bridgwater Bay, the Severn is one of the longest estuaries in Britain, with many habitat contrasts. The intertidal flats of the inner estuary and some outer ones in the centre of the channel are unstable sand. Mud predominates on the upper shore throughout the area, and has deposited rapidly in Bridgwater Bay during the last twenty years, but some sand can still be found, especially on Berrow Flats. Areas of rocky shore are exposed at Severn Beach and between the bays south of Portishead. There are small saltmarshes at Slimbridge, Chittening and in all the bays south to Bridgwater Bay where quite an extensive area of *Spartina* occurs. An important habitat associated with the Severn is the low lying pasture, the main areas being at Slimbridge (the New Grounds), at Aylburton and the Somerset Levels inland from Bridgwater Bay. A summary of the habitats and birds of the Welsh parts of the estuary is given in the next chapter.

On any estuary of this size there are bound to be many threats. The barrage and reservoir proposals are the most expansive of these and have been discussed in Chapter 4. However, others exist, particularly industrial development and the draining of low lying pasture. The Somerset Levels are greatly threatened and industrial development around Severn Beach is a possibility. Some pollution from industry in Avon occurs but there is little sign of it being detrimental to birds. Very heavy pressure is felt from holidaymakers in south Avon and Somerset.

On the English shore of the Severn there are eight SSSIs, but only that of the New Grounds is specifically for ornithological interest; Bridgwater Bay is a Ramsar and Grade 1 NCR site and an NNR; the intertidal flats of much of the area are a Grade 2 NCR site; several SSSIs and an NNR have also been scheduled in the Somerset

---

Table 10:8   *Species of national importance wintering on the Severn Estuary, 1969–75*

| | English Severn | | Whole Severn | |
|---|---|---|---|---|
| | Highest av. monthly count | % British | Highest av. monthly count | % British |
| Bewick's Swan | 320 | 16·0 | 320 | 16·0 |
| White-fronted Goose | 4,500 | 45·0 | 4,500 | 45·0 |
| Shelduck | 1,830 | 3·0 | 2,090 | 3·5 |
| Wigeon | 2,960 | 2·0 | 3,070 | 3·0 |
| Teal | – | – | 780 | 1·0 |
| Shoveler | 70 | 1·4 | 100 | 2·0 |
| Ringed Plover | 210 | 1·7 | 308 | 2·6 |
| Grey Plover | 145 | 1·4 | 420 | 4·2 |
| Lapwing | 12,150 | ** | 14,500 | ** |
| Knot | – | – | 5,400 | 1·8 |
| Dunlin | 28,100 | 5·1 | 47,000 | 8·5 |
| Black-tailed Godwit | 1,070† | 21·4 | 1,070† | 21·4 |
| Whimbrel | 1,400* | * | 1,500* | * |
| Curlew | 2,030 | 2·0 | 2,620 | 2·6 |
| Redshank | 1,180 | 1·2 | 2,200 | 2·2 |
| Turnstone | – | – | 280 | 1·1 |

\* Spring concentration } involving most of British birds – both on Bridgwater Bay
† Autumn concentration }
— Number on English shore not of national significance
\*\* No full national census but more than 10,000 on estuary

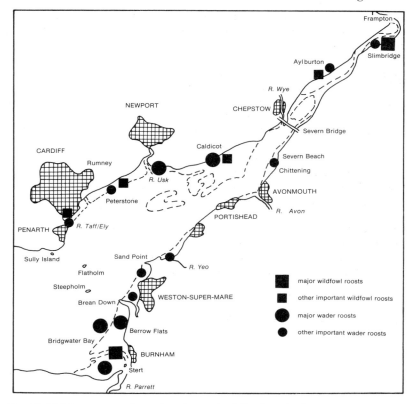

Fig. 10:1 Main concentrations of waders and wildfowl on the Severn estuary.

Levels, where the RSPB has a reserve. Waders are spread over the whole of the estuary, but wildfowl concentrate on the New Grounds, where White-fronted Geese, Bewick's Swans and many duck are attracted by the management of habitat by the Wildfowl Trust, and at Bridgwater Bay, especially known for its internationally important flock of moulting Shelduck. Waders are less abundant above the Severn Bridge, but to the south there are major concentrations at Chittening, Berrow Flats and Bridgwater Bay, with smaller numbers in Weston, Sand and Woodspring Bays and at St George's Warth. The general distribution of birds on the whole estuary is shown in Fig. 10:2. A much more detailed account of the habitats and waders of the Severn can be found in Ferns (1977).

There are seven species of international importance on the English Severn (Table 10:1) the national status is presented in Table 10:8. For the whole estuary there are twelve species of international importance, and a further five of national significance. The estuary is of major significance for White-fronted Goose, Bewick's Swan, Black-tailed Godwit and Dunlin. At passage times, Black-tailed Godwits are noteworthy in autumn, and Whimbrel in spring. Other species occur in large numbers on passage, for example, 3,800 Ringed Plovers in autumn and 1,100 in spring. Similarly, Sanderling and Dunlin on their way to and from Iceland and

Greenland, use the Severn as an important transit point on migration. During the period of counts no severe weather occurred, but it is thought that the Severn could be a major refuge. Very few breeding birds occur around the shore of the Severn, but of other species, gulls are abundant. Large breeding numbers are on Steepholm and Flatholm, and roosts of 30,000 occur on Penarth Flats and 25,000 at Frampton. Undoubtedly many more roost elsewhere around the estuary.

CHAPTER 11

# Wales

The Welsh coastline is one of contrasts, varying from the flat 'levels' of Gwent to the steep cliffs of Dyfed and Gwynedd. The coast can be divided into three sections: the south (Bristol Channel), west (Cardigan Bay) and north (Liverpool Bay) coasts. There are four estuary areas on the south coast; from east to west they are the Severn, Swansea Bay, Carmarthen Bay and Milford Haven. Each has a different character. The Severn estuary, which Gwent and South Glamorgan share with Gloucester, Avon and Somerset, is by far the largest and has a considerable area of low-lying reclaimed land (levels) behind the sea wall. Swansea Bay is small but the nearby Carmarthen Bay has four major estuaries opening into it: the Burry Inlet (Llwchwr), Gwendraeth, Tywi and Taf. Each is predominately sandy and their mouths are guarded by extensive sand dune systems. Milford Haven is the only large drowned valley in south-west Wales and mudflats have developed along its drowned tributaries. Apart from the sand dunes around Kenfig the open coast is cliffed with the height steadily increasing from Cardiff to Pembroke.

The broad sweep of Cardigan Bay has few estuaries and none of them large. The Dyfi, Mawddach and Traeth Bach are moderately sized and on the southern and northern shores of the Bay there are a number of small sites. Most of Cardigan Bay comprises of cliffs, shingle or sand beaches. The rocky Lleyn Peninsula separates Cardigan Bay from Anglesey and the north Wales coast. Most of the estuaries on this north coast are on Anglesey or Caernarvon; only the Clwyd lies to the east of Llandudno. Much of the north coast is low-lying and most of the estuaries are relatively sandy with dunes at their mouths. Most estuaries are also fairly small and enclosed although the largest one, Conwy Bay, at the north-eastern end of the Menai Straits has a wide mouth; this is the most important area away from the south coast. The Dee estuary is partly in Clwyd and although the number of birds using the Welsh section is large, the Dee is considered in its entirety under north-western England (Chapter 12).

The Severn estuary has the largest tidal range of any area in the British Isles and on spring tides exceeds 13 m. Fairly large ranges occur along the rest of the Bristol Channel and on the eastern section of the north Wales coast. In the west, however, tidal ranges are much lower and in places, especially in the north west, may only be 4–5 m on spring and 2 m on neap tides.

### Urban and industrial development and recreation

Most of the Welsh coast is relatively free from industrial development; only at Cardiff on the Severn, Swansea on Swansea Bay and Llanelli on the Burry Inlet does development materially influence the surrounding land. Although the Dee is being considered later, it should be noted here that its Welsh shore does also have some industrial development, and more is planned. Especially worrying are the plans for reservoirs and a gas terminal in this estuary. The comparative freedom elsewhere is not necessarily guaranteed for there are plans to develop the Severn estuary in particular, where threats of industrial development and a barrage loom large. Details of these have already been mentioned in Chapter 4.

Although many of the sandy beaches at the mouths of estuaries in Wales are extensively and increasingly used for recreation, this disturbance is minimal during the winter months. Relatively little shooting or sailing takes place, although in North Wales the latter activity is expanding rapidly.

### Main literature on the coastal birds of Wales

The status of coastal birds of Wales has been generally summarised by Flintshire Ornithological Society (1968) – Clwyd; Gwent Ornithological Society (1977) – Gwent; Heathcote, Griffin and Morrey Salmon (1967) – Glamorgan; Hope Jones (1974) – Merioneth; Hope Jones and Dare (1976) – Caernarvon; Ingram and Morrey Salmon (1954) – Carmarthen; Lockley, Ingram and Morrey Salmon (1960) – Pembrokeshire, and for waders by Prater (1976). In addition much information is contained in the regular bird reports of the Cambrian Ornithological Society, Cardiff Naturalists Society, Gower Ornithological Society, Gwent Ornithological Society, West Wales Naturalists' Trust, and the *Welsh Bird Report* published jointly by the Naturalists' Trusts of West Wales, North Wales and Radnor. Other local publications are included in the individual estuary summaries.

### Principal species and the migration patterns

In general the numbers of waterfowl on Welsh estuaries are relatively low. The most numerous species are presented in Table 11:1 with the month when peak numbers occur. Quite why numbers are small is not clear, although most estuaries away from the south coast are relatively small. A further 30,000 waders on the Welsh side of the Dee, are not included in these totals. Another probable reason, but one that cannot be determined critically here, is that the winters between 1969–70 and 1974–75 were relatively mild so that few birds from eastern Britain may have needed to move westwards. Included in the list of wildfowl is the Common Scoter. This is not strictly an estuarine duck but is found in shallow sandy bays; few adequate counts exist but in Carmarthen Bay, Tremadoc Bay and on the north Wales coast numbers are significant in winter. In July–August an equivalent number, mostly drakes, assembles in Carmarthen Bay for the annual moult.

1.  *Above:* The Wash at low tide from near Hunstanton – estuaries may be flat but the light reflecting from pools of water on the sand and mussel beds can be very attractive. (Michael W. Richards). *Below:* Oystercatchers flighting to roost on Bull Island, Dublin – this area within Dublin city boundaries supports an enormous number of estuary birds for its size. (Pamela Harrison).

2. Pagham Harbour, West Sussex. *Left:* The complicated creek and saltmarsh configuration typical of many southern estuaries. The outer shingle banks and the effects of training walls are clearly shown. *Right:* The strong creek patterns are still in evidence on the northern reclaimed pastures. Pagham Harbour was reclaimed in 1873 but breached in 1910, some field edges and especially drainage furrows can still be seen in the present

3. *Above:* Part (almost 1,300) of a large flock of Dunlin coming to roost at West Thurrock Power Station ash lagoons – the peripheral, undisturbed areas such as this may be used for roosting by birds from the nearby intertidal flats. (Pamela Harrison). *Below:* Almost 370 Oystercatchers plus two Shelduck coming into a roost on newly sown fields in the Netherlands – waders, especially in eastern and northern Britain, frequently use short grass or ploughed fields for roosting at times of spring tides (Pamela Harrison).

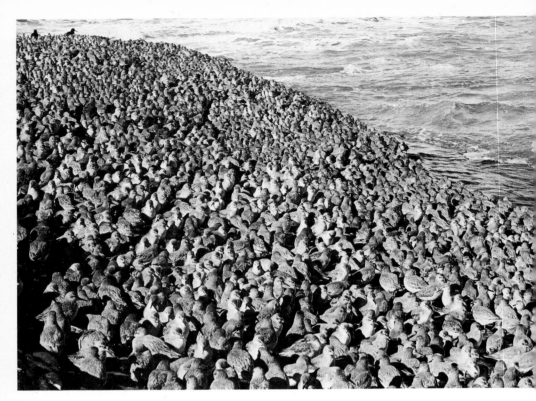

4.   *Above:* A pack of Knot on the Dee estuary – this species forms the most dense flocks of any wader. (Eric Hosking). *Below:* A subroost forming on Morecambe Bay – showing the highly aggregated Knot, widely spaced Oystercatchers and a group of gulls. (A. J. Prater).

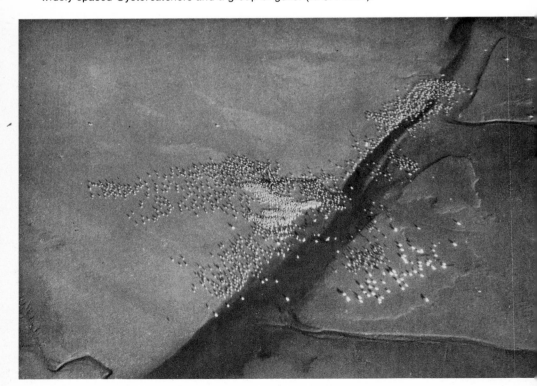

5.   *Above:* Rapidly eroding saltmarsh on the Solway Firth – a typical north-western saltmarsh, having been grazed but subject to erosion from a swinging water channel moving close to the saltmarsh and subsequently undercutting it. (Pamela Harrison). *Below:* The Medway estuary in a severe winter – the upper parts of the estuarine flats are frequently frozen when severe weather occurs and icefloes may completely cover substantial areas of the intertidal mud. (Pamela Harrison).

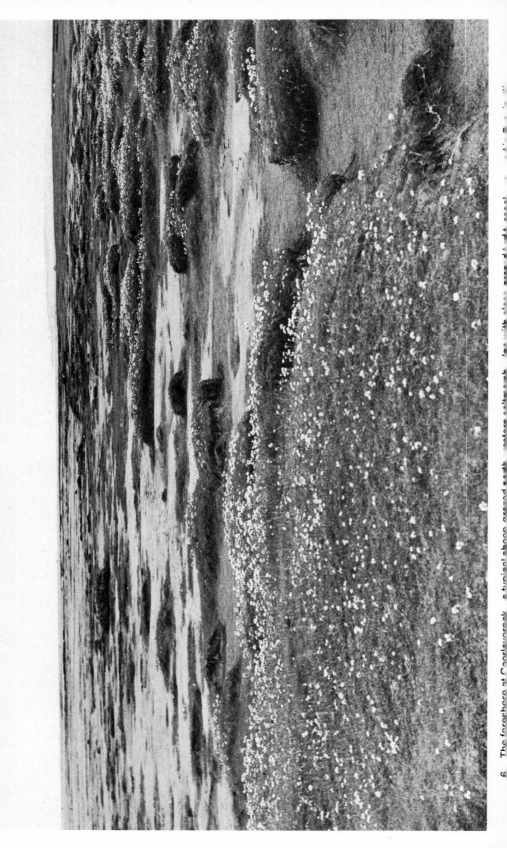

6. The foreshore at Coolmaurock, a typical boggy grazed salt-water saltmarsh, low with close-ungrazed turf and matted Puccinellia...

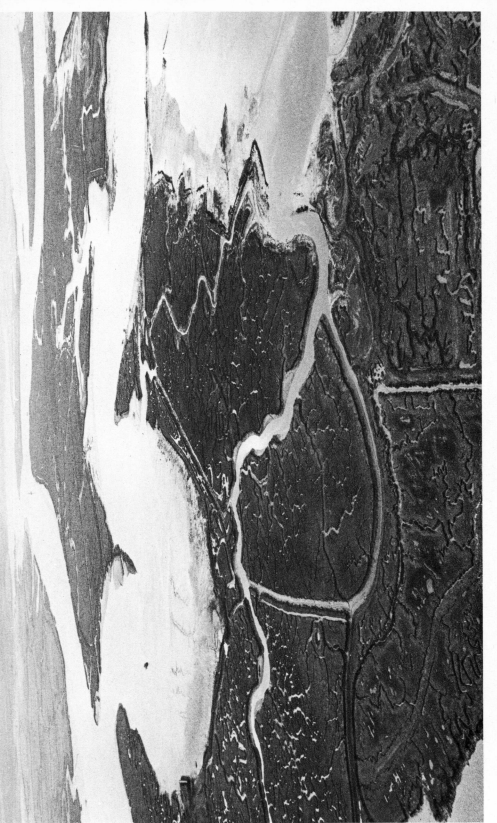

7. The Medway saltmarshes looking southeast across Greenborough from Burntwick, Chetney is in the distance to the left. The very dissected but extensive saltmarshes combined with freshwater marshes make the Medway of great significance. (Michael W. Richards/RSPB).

8. *Above:* A typical group of resting migrant Dunlin and Ringed Plovers on the Dee estuary – this is one of the most important feeding areas for spring migrants. (Eric Hosking). *Below:* Pink-footed Geese flighting to roost on sands of the Ribble estuary – several birds such as the grey geese, Lapwing and Golden Plover, flight out in the evening to roost on the intertidal mudflats of our larger more northern estuaries. (Pamela Harrison).

9. *Above:* Seven Dark-bellied Brent Geese feeding on the Swale estuary – the two plain coloured adults (centre front and back) can be easily distinguished from juveniles which have clear white edgings to their covert feathers. (Pamela Harrison). *Below:* Redshanks – one of the most ubiquitous waders. (Eric Hosking).

10.   River Adur, West Sussex near to the estuary mouth – showing river embankment, filling of creeks and the conversion of old marshes to arable, a problem on the upper reaches of many estuaries. (West Sussex County Council/Meridian Airmaps).

11.   *Above:* A Medway saltmarsh showing the effect of an oil spill – the black areas along the edge of the water courses have been completely saturated by oil from the *Seestern*. (Pamela Harrison). *Below:* A *Salicornia* saltmarsh on the Ribble Estuary – the rapidly colonising *Salicornia* plants on the mudflats provide good feeding for many wildfowl, especially Teal. (Pamela Harrison).

12. Windmill Creek on the Isle of Sheppey – to the right the area is under normal tidal innundation but the lefthand area which receives little salt

13.   *Above:* The Thames at Cross Ness – showing that numbers of waders and wildfowl can occur in industrialised areas provided that the mudflats and the food supplies remain. (Pamela Harrison).
*Below:* A Thames grain wharf – a flock of mainly immature Mute Swans congregating around the grain wharves. Birds can exploit the effluent discharges and other wastes that man creates. (Pamela Harrison).

14. *Above:* Whimbrels are passage migrants on estuaries – they usually concentrate on low-lying grassland adjacent to the shore, especially on the Severn estuary. (Eric Hosking). *Below:* Red-throated Diver – divers and grebes often appear on estuaries, particularly in northern Britain and Ireland. (Keith Atkin).

15. *Above:* A group of displaying Shelduck on the North Kent Marshes – this species is the most strictly estuarine of any of the ducks and breeds on saltmarshes and adjacent fields. (Pamela Harrison). *Below:* A colony of Sandwich Terns in north Norfolk – although nesting in a few areas, on many coasts terns are vulnerable to disturbance or high spring tides. (Eric Hosking).

16. *Left:* A Lapwing in late autumn – one of the inland birds which come onto estuaries when severe weather prevents field feeding. (Eric Hosking). *Right:*

*Table 11:1 Peak counts of the most numerous species of waterfowl on Welsh estuaries, 1969–75*

| | Highest av. monthly total | | | Highest av. monthly total | |
|---|---|---|---|---|---|
| Common Scoter | 10,000 most months | | Dunlin | 48,000 | Jan |
| Wigeon | 9,500 | Jan | Oystercatcher | 29,000 | Sept–Jan |
| Mallard | 3,300 | Nov | Lapwing | 15,000 | Jan |
| Teal | 2,150 | Oct | Knot | 12,500 | Feb |
| Shelduck | 1,850 | Mar | Curlew | 8,100 | Aug |
| Pintail | 1,500 | Jan | Golden Plover | 7,500 | Jan |
| Red-breasted Merganser | 300 | Aug | Redshank | 6,800 | Oct |
| Goldeneye | 200 | Feb | Ringed Plover | 3,150 | Aug |
| Shoveler | 180 | Jan | Bar-tailed Godwit | 1,550 | Jan |
| Mute Swan | 85 | Sept | Turnstone | 1,225 | Sept |

The general pattern of wader migration is fairly simple with a good autumn (July–September) and spring (mainly May) passage. The principal passage migrants are Ringed Plover, Dunlin and Sanderling and involve birds breeding in Iceland and Greenland. There was a small dip in numbers during October, then a rapid build-up to a midwinter peak followed by an equally rapid drop to a March low. Apart from Knot the species involved in the winter increase are primarily eastern in origin and most have spent the autumn, and moulted, on the coasts of the North Sea. Many estuaries in Wales miss the spring passage; the main areas then are the Gwent Severn and the Dyfi; the Dee is also a major staging post at this time of the year. Wildfowl show a very simple pattern with a steady build-up through the early winter to mid or late winter peaks. A few species, such as Teal, appear to pass further south in winter.

Gulls, particularly the Herring Gull, breed commonly on the Welsh coast. Nocturnal roosts form on many estuaries but the largest invariably include many Black-headed Gulls. The main roosts recorded were on the south coast with about 20,000 on the Taff/Ely and Gwent Severn, about 10,000 in Swansea Bay and 5,000–10,000 on the Burry Inlet, Milford Haven and the River Clwyd on the north coast.

Relatively few other species are found although 300+ Great Crested Grebes which join a similar number of Red-breasted Mergansers on the Lavan Sands at the north end of the Menai Straits in autumn are notworthy.

*Principal estuaries of Wales*

Three internationally important estuaries stand out, the Severn, Burry Inlet and Conwy Bay. Behind them comes a large number of nationally or regionally significant areas, particularly Taff/Ely, Swansea Bay, Gwendreath/Tywi, Taf, Milford Haven, Dyfi, Traeth Bach, S. Menai Straits, Beddmanarch Bay and the Conwy Estuary. The six estuaries which regularly support internationally important numbers of wintering birds are presented in Table 11:2, together with the percentage of the European population occurring on them. The Oystercatcher, particularly in the

Burry Inlet, is the most significant species. The flock of Common Scoter in Carmarthen Bay which regularly reaches 10,000 is another important species at 2·2% of the European population.

### Gwent/South Glamorgan

*Severn.* The Gwent and South Glamorgan coast form only a small part of the Severn Estuary. Their bird populations are, however, apparently more or less separate from those of the eastern and inner sections. Three major rivers flow into the Severn here: the Wye provides the northern boundary, the Usk enters at Newport, while the Rhymney at Cardiff provides the southern boundary. The whole of the estuary is flanked inland by the low lying Caldicot levels (between the Wye and Usk) and Wentlooge levels (between the Usk and Rhymney). These are mainly wet pasture drained by numerous reed-filled rheens (ditches), some of these feed the pills (streams) which discharge into the estuary through sluices in the sea wall. Apart from some industrial development at the mouth of the Usk, particularly the Uskmouth and Rhymney Power Stations, the whole estuary complex and the levels form an internationally important area for water birds.

Along the estuary there is a relatively narrow belt of *Spartina* marsh from Rogiet to Magor and at the eastern end of Peterstone Great Wharf. Two small areas of relatively high sheep grazed marsh occur behind the *Spartina* at Collister Pill and Rumney Great Wharf; these are used as roost sites by waders on spring tides but the swift currents are rapidly eroding them, particularly at the latter site. Large numbers of waders feed on the sand banks of the Welsh grounds and other are scattered along the narrower mud banks on the rest of the estuary. Relatively few wildfowl occur here, although Shoveler (42) and Shelduck (255) are of local significance. The waders roost mainly on the Usk–Wye section with concentrations often reaching international importance at Magor/Collister Pills and on the lagoons of the Uskmouth Power Station. On the Rhymney–Usk section, roosts develop on the west of Rumney Great Wharf and between the western end of Peterstone Great Wharf

Table 11:2   *Internationally important wintering populations of wildfowl and waders in Welsh estuaries*

|  | Welsh Severn | Swansea Bay | Burry Inlet | Gwendraeth/ Tywi/Taf | Carmarthen Bay | Conwy Bay |
|---|---|---|---|---|---|---|
| Pintail | – | – | 1·3 | – | – | – |
| Common Scoter | – | – | – | – | 2·0 | – |
| Oystercatcher | – | – | 2·5 | 1·3 | – | 1·0 |
| Ringed Plover | – | 1·0 | – | – | – | – |
| Grey Plover | 1·0 | – | – | – | – | – |
| Curlew | – | – | – | – | – | – |
| Redshank | – | – | – | – | – | 1·3 |
| Knot | – | – | 1·3 | – | – | – |
| Dunlin | 1·1 | – | – | – | – | – |
| Sanderling | – | 1·5 | – | 1·7 | – | – |

*Table 11.3    Species of national importance on the Gwent/south Glamorgan Severn, 1969–75*

|  | Highest av. monthly count | % British |
|---|---|---|
| Ringed Plover | 750 (*1) | * |
| Golden Plover | 2,000 | 1·0 |
| Grey Plover | 290 | 2·9 |
| Knot | 4,260 | 1·4 |
| Dunlin | 13,740 | 2·5 |
| Whimbrel | 120 (*2) | * |

(*1)  Autumn passage
(*2)  Spring passage

and Peterstone Pill. On spring tides or when disturbance is excessive the waders fly to roost on the fields; this happens most frequently when the fields are flooded.

The Grey Plover and Dunlin which occur in internationally important numbers are presented in Table 11:2. Table 11:3 gives the national status of birds on the Welsh Severn. The Severn is of note as a site for migrant waders; Ringed Plover and Dunlin are abundant autumn and spring migrants, while Whimbrel are significant in spring. It is unfortunately not possible to be more precise about their international importance because the international counts are not yet able to census these migrant populations.

### South Glamorgan and Mid Glamorgan

*Taff/Ely.* This small estuary, situated between Cardiff and Penarth, is almost completely surrounded by industrial and urban development. On the northern and eastern shores fairly small *Spartina* marshes have developed and it is here that wader roosts occur. On low spring tides, particularly when there is little disturbance, most waders roost on rough pasture on Penarth Moor alongside the Ely River. This roost area is slowly being reclaimed by a large rubbish tip. At other times most waders fly 5 km south to roost on Sully Island. Feeding grounds lie mainly on the outer flats, although Redshank and Shelduck frequent the inner Penarth Flats.

Although no species reached a level of national importance Redshank (565), Dunlin (3,900) and Shelduck (220), and, at times, Knot (700) and Ringed Plover (63) numbers are of regional significance. A large gull roost (20,000) develops.

*Rest of the coast.* There are no other major estuaries on the south and west Glamorgan coast, which is cliffed as far as the Ogmore River where it then consists of a narrow beach backed by sand dunes. Relatively few birds occur although about 200 Oystercatcher are on the rocky part; at Sker Point and along the Kenfig sandy beach a small winter flock of Ruff and Sanderling is present. The Kenfig dune system and lake, an SSSI, supports a few wildfowl.

*West Glamorgan*

*Swansea Bay.* Swansea Bay stretches from Port Talbot to Mumbles Head and at low tide provides a strip of sand flats over 1 km wide. The Neath River enters at the eastern end and the River Tawe in the centre of the Bay; towards the western edge a small stream, Black Pill, enters Swansea Bay. Apart from the Crymlyn Burrows at the east the whole shoreline is developed – by industry and docks in the centre and a promenade from Swansea to Mumbles.

Very few wildfowl occur, although 18 species have been recorded but there are quite large numbers of waders which feed mainly on the lower part of the shore. They roost at the mouth of the Neath River and at Black Pill, the latter site having the largest numbers. Two species, Ringed Plover and Sanderling, are of international importance (Table 11:2). Table 11:4 shows their national status. In a local context Oystercatcher (1,300), Grey Plover (80), Bar-tailed Godwit (370), Knot (340) and Dunlin (2,700) are all of significance. Black Pill also supports a moderate gull roost (10,000+) which regularly includes several Mediterranean and Ring-billed Gulls, both of which are rare.

*Table 11:4   Species of national importance on Swansea Bay, 1969–75*

|  | *Highest av. monthly count* | *% British* |
|---|---|---|
| Ringed Plover | 240 | 2·0 |
| Sanderling | 230 | 2·3 |

*West Glamorgan/Dyfed*

*Burry Inlet.* This, the combined estuary of the Afon Llwchwr (Loughor)and its tributaries Gwili, Llan, Lliw and Morlais, is the most important estuary for birds lying wholly within the Principality. Its geography, natural history (including birds), nature conservation, industry and recreational pursuits are considered in detail in Nelson-Smith and Bridges (eds) (1977). The south shore is mainly owned by the National Trust and includes an SSSI. The inner estuary, north of Loughor Bridge, is small but has relatively large areas of saltmarsh on each side. On the south (Gower) shore there are extensive areas of saltmarsh; *Spartina* is rapidly colonising the lower areas on the inner third but Llanrhidian and Landimore Marshes are, as yet, relatively unaffected. Whitford Burrows, a large sand-dune system and an NNR, guards the southern entrance to the estuary. The north (Dyfed) shore provides a striking contrast to Gower, with extensive areas of industrial and urban development from Llanelli to Burry Port. A small area of marsh at Tir Morfa and a larger area adjacent to the low sand dune system of Pembrey Burrows provides the only 'natural' habitat on this shore.

Prater (1977) described the distribution of feeding and roosting birds in the Burry Inlet. The roosts used by birds in the whole of the Carmarthen Bay complex are shown in Fig. 11:1. The principal numbers are found on the large Llanrhidian and Landimore marshes and on Whitford Burrows. Small roosts are present elsewhere

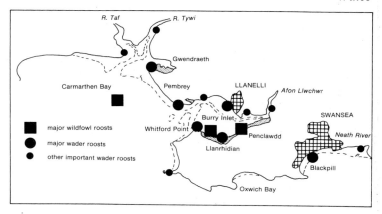

Fig. 11:1 Main concentrations of waders and wildfowl between Swansea and Carmarthen Bays.

with a notable concentration of Ringed Plover and Turnstone, but few other species, forming on Llanelli North Dock. At times in winter and during passage many Sanderling frequent the eastern end of Pembrey Burrows. Duck, especially Pintail, may be quite numerous off Penclawdd and Berthlwyd. The majority of birds feed south of the river channel, on Llanrhidian Sands, with smaller numbers near Penclawdd and on the north shore, most of which fly south to roost.

The internationally important species (Oystercatcher, Knot and Pintail) have been summarised in Table 11:2. The national significance of the Burry Inlet is presented in Table 11:5. Additionally, Shelduck (560 in winter) almost reach the national level, and of regional significance are the flock of 40–50 Eider and small numbers of grebes and divers which are found off Whitford Point. At times the outfall of the Burry Port power station attracts many migrant gulls and terns.

*Table 11:5   Species of national importance on the Burry Inlet, 1969–75*

|  | Highest av. monthly count | % British |
|---|---|---|
| Wigeon | 2,230 | 1·1 |
| Pintail | 650 | 3·2 |
| Shoveler | 90 | 1·8 |
| Oystercatcher | 14,210 | 7·1 |
| Ringed Plover | 150 | 1·2 |
| Grey Plover | 250 | 2·5 |
| Knot | 6,710 | 2·2 |
| Sanderling | 120 | 1·2 |
| Dunlin | 7,400 | 1·3 |
| Curlew | 1,000 | 1·0 |
| Black-tailed Godwit | 225 | 4·5 |
| Bar-tailed Godwit | 670 | 1·5 |
| Redshank | 1,190 | 1·2 |
| Turnstone | 300 | 1·2 |

*Table 11:6   Species of national importance on the Gwendraeth, Twyi and Taf Estuaries, 1969–75*

|  | Highest av. monthly count | % British |
|---|---|---|
| Oystercatcher | 7,480 | 3·7 |
| Sanderling | 250 | 2·5 |

## Dyfed

*Gwendraeth, Tywi and Taf.* These three estuaries, frequently referred to as the Three Rivers, are considered together as there is much interchange of their bird populations although on the Taf it may be less frequent. The Gwendraeth is the most important, mainly due to its greater diversity of habitats, and is an SSSI. The southern shore is formed by a large and complex area of saltmarsh backed by the Pembrey dune system which extends to the large sandy Tywyn Point. There are fairly extensive wet grazing areas inland in the valley of the Gwendraeth Fawr. The north shore has little marsh but there is an extensive mussel bed at Salmon Point Scar, although a large caravan park opposite this at Tanylan has brought increased disturbance. The Tywi is flanked by fairly steep hills for most of its length but there is a little marsh on the west shore and a fairly extensive low reclaimed area on the east shore at Morfa Uchaf. There are quite large cliffs in the east and inner shores of the Taf, but on the outer western part there is a large *Spartina* marsh running from Laugharne to Ginst Point. To the west Laugharne and Pendine Sands are backed by the sand-dunes of Laugharne Burrows, an SSSI; behind these is a large area of low-lying wet pasture called East and West Marsh.

Disturbance on the Gwendraeth/Tywi means that most of their birds roost on the south of the Gwendraeth, Tywyn Point or on the inland fields, but some are also to be found in the fields on the north of the Gwendraeth and on Morfa Uchaf. Waders feed mainly around the river channels and on Salmon Point Scar, although small numbers of ducks are present on the south and inner Gwendraeth and on Morfa Uchaf. On the Taf most of the waders feed between Laugharne and Ginst Point, with the majority around the mussel bed at Ginst Point. On East Marsh large flocks of Golden Plover (2,000) and Lapwing (2,500) occur at times. The only significant roost develops off Ginst Point, but when the spring tides make this untenable most birds fly to East Marsh.

The two internationally important species, Oystercatcher and Sanderling are noted in Table 11:2. The former feed mainly around Salmon Point Scar but a very variable number feed on the cockle beds elsewhere. The numbers fluctuate with cockle stocks. Sanderling are found on Pembrey beach and Tywyn Point. Of local significance are the large numbers of passage waders, particularly Greenshank (45), Spotted Redshank (15), Ruff (15) and Whimbrel (55).

*Carmarthen Bay.* Large numbers of Common Scoter occur off Pendine Sands, Tywyn Point and Burry Holms in most months of the year. Past records are summarised by Moyse and Thomas (1977) and recent aerial survey data have been supplied by R. Lovegrove (in litt.). The flock appears regularly to reach 5,000–6,000 in winter, and during the annual moult in July/August may exceed 10,000. The area is of international importance for this species, having between 1·5% and 2·5% of the European population.

*Milford Haven*. A large and deep inlet into which open six fairly small estuaries and one bay. Of these areas the three largest are on the south shore: the outermost is Angle Bay, which has two large oil storage complexes on its east shore. Next is the large and important estuary of Pembroke River, flanked on its northern side by developments of Pembroke Dock. The Carew/Cresswell estuary is, like the under-developed parts of the previous two areas, surrounded by farmland. The inner section divides into the Western and Eastern Cleddau, the former being the second most important part of this complex; both are relatively undisturbed areas. Finally, on the outer northern part are the two small estuaries of Sandyhaven Pill and Gann. All of the estuaries, except Pembroke River, are in the Pembrokeshire Coast National Park and include an SSSI at West Angle.

Each of these subdivisions has its own roost and feeding grounds, the latter covering most of the intertidal areas. The relative numbers of birds involved are shown in Fig. 11:1. No site is of international importance but the combined total of wintering Ringed Plovers on Angle Bay and Pembroke River almost reach this level. It forms 1·7% of the national total. No other species is of national importance although Curlew (700), Knot (260) and Wigeon (1,000), found mainly in Pembroke River and the Western Cleddau, are of local significance. The Western Cleddau supports the greatest variety of species.

*Gwaun*. This small estuary at Fishguard holds small numbers of waders (less than 100), mainly Oystercatcher.

*Afon Nyfer*. Another small estuary which reaches the sea at Newport. Although it holds only a few hundred waders, sixteen species were recorded. The most numerous species is Curlew (220) which roost there after feeding on surrounding farmland. It has a flock of 20–30 wintering Ringed Plovers but few wildfowl.

*Teifi*. Although larger than the two preceding estuaries this estuary, which enters the sea at Cardigan, does not, from limited counts, appear to hold many birds. The principal species are Curlew (150) Redshank (60) and Ringed Plover and Dunlin (40 each). Most Curlew join a small number (4,000) of gulls which roost on Cardigan Island.

### Dyfed/Gwynedd

*Dyfi*. The largest and most important estuary opening into Cardigan Bay, formed by the Afon Dyfi and the canalised Afon Leri which enters the main estuary in the south-western corner. The northern shore is immediately backed by steep hillside but the south has a now extensive *Spartina* marsh, behind which low, wet, grazing extends for several kilometres and incorporates the raised bog of Cors Fochno; this is a Ramsar site. There is a sand spit, part of Ynys Las dunes, at the south-western entrance. The estuary is a scheduled SSSI and the north shore is in the Snowdonia National Park. Cors Fochno is now threatened by drainage.

*Table 11:7   Species of national importance on the Dyfi, 1969–75*

|  | Highest av. monthly count | % British |
|---|---|---|
| Wigeon | 2,020 | 1·0 |
| Teal | 790 | 1·1 |
| Pintail | 270 | 1·3 |
| Red-breasted Merganser | 75 | 1·0 |
| Ringed Plover | 670* | * |

* On spring passage and of importance

Roosts of waders occur mainly on Twyni Bach area of Ynys Las dunes and at the edge of the *Spartina* marsh, with a tendency for concentrations on Traeth Maelgwyn and near Ynys-hir. Most of the wildfowl are found on the southern and especially inner parts. A small flock (25) of the Greenland race of the White-fronted Goose can be found on Cors Fochno but in much lower numbers than during the 1950s.

No species reaches international significance but Table 11:7 shows that five species are of note at the national level. The numbers of waders in winter are relatively low but in spring and autumn Ringed Plover especially, but also Sanderling and Dunlin, migrate through in at least regionally important numbers. Of local significance are the wintering Oystercatcher (1,000) and Shelduck (210). The species diversity is high with 25 waders and 21 wildfowl recorded during the counts.

*Tywyn Broadwater.* This small estuary is just to the north of the Dyfi and is formed by the Afon Dysynni. It supports several hundred wildfowl and waders but only Mallard, Oystercatcher, Lapwing, Golden Plover and Dunlin reach 100 at times. It is an SSSI.

*Mawddach.* Although quite a large estuary it supports very few birds, probably · because of its relatively coarse sand. Most birds feed upstream of the toll bridge at Penmaenpool, but on spring tides many of the waders move to the outer spit and marsh on the south-western corner.

No species reaches a national level of significance but Wigeon (500), Shelduck (130), Dunlin (440), and passage Ringed Plover (200) and Oystercatcher (320) are of regional importance.

*Afon Artro.* The estuary is a small sandy bay bounded on the west by part of Morfa Dyffryn and on the east and north sides by an airfield and low pasture. At the southern end a saltmarsh has developed where a few hundred wildfowl and up to 500 waders occur. Mallard, Wigeon, Oystercatcher, Lapwing, Golden Plover and Curlew regularly exceed 100 individuals.

*Traeth Bach.* The fairly extensive intertidal flats of the estuaries of the Afon Glaslyn and Dwyryd form the second most important complex for estuary birds in Cardigan Bay. The area is a SSSI and is partly in the Snowdonia National Park. North-east of Porthmadog there are brackish marshes, which, together with the grazed

*Puccinellia* marshes near Talsarnau, provide most of the feeding grounds for the dabbling ducks. The large dune system of Morfa Harlech to the south, fringed by *Spartina* marsh, forms a zone of little disturbance. It is along this southern shore, Traeth Bach, that most Shelduck, Pintail and waders feed and roost.

Although Traeth Bach is one of the better estuaries in Wales for wildfowl, no species occurs in internationally or nationally important numbers. Several are of regional significance, in particular Wigeon (1,270), Pintail (120), Shoveler (40), Teal (230) and Shelduck (270). Counts made between 1960 and 1969 are summarised by Gough (1969). The wader numbers are likewise of regional importance, especially Oystercatcher (730) and Curlew (530).

*Afon Wen.* Halfway between Criccieth and Pwllheli lies the small estuary of the Afon Wen. Relatively low numbers of wildfowl occur, although 160 Wigeon graze the marshes. A flock of 30–40 Common Scoter is regular, and is part of the 500+ flock which feeds in Tremadoc Bay. Slightly more waders are found, with Lapwing (600), Golden Plover (435) and Curlew (525) being of local significance on the marshes during the late winter, and Ringed Plover (125) during autumn migration.

*Pwllheli Harbour.* This relatively small area has large intertidal flats and supports a good estuarine bird fauna including about 350 ducks, most numerous of which are 120 Wigeon and 160 Mallard. A good variety (19 species) of waders has been recorded and of note in a regional context are Ringed Plover (240 in autumn) and, in winter, Knot (125) and Dunlin (1,740).

*Foryd Bay.* This sandy estuary of the Afon Gwyrfai lies at the south-eastern corner of the Menai Straits. It is an SSSI, bounded on its west side by the Morfa Dinlle dunes and rough pasture. On the western and southern sides of the estuary extensive areas of *Spartina* have developed. Up to 700 wildfowl and 1,400 waders use it, roosting mainly on the north-western and western parts. No species is present in nationally important numbers but several are of local significance in winter. These are Wigeon (635), Shelduck (220), Oystercatcher (520), Ringed Plover (80), Redshank (180) and Knot (150). Up to 10 Greenshank may winter. Bird numbers are variable, possibly due to heavy shooting disturbance.

*Conwy Bay (North-east Menai Straits).* Conwy Bay is a large area of intertidal flats situated at the north-eastern end of the Menai Straits. The southern shore between Bangor and Llanfairfechan comprises the extensive Lavan Sands backed mainly by pasture, while the Anglesey coast from Beaumaris to Penmon Port has only a narrow intertidal zone with more rocky outcrops. The Afon Ogwen enters near Bangor. A large area of Lavan Sands is scheduled as an SSSI and a LNR. The site, its birds and invertebrates have been described by Dare and Schofield (1976) and Eagle et al (1974).

The inner estuary, especially near Bangor, is predominantly muddy but the outer parts are sandy. Waders feed over most of the shore but ducks are confined mainly to the areas where freshwater enters from the Afon Ogwen, nearby at Aber and west of Llanfairfechan. Roosts of ducks are formed in these areas and waders roost all along the shore lines with concentrations at the Ogwen, between Wig and Llanfairfechan and at Beaumaris. On spring tides or when there is much disturbance the inland fields are used; several hundred Curlew and Oystercatcher, with fewer Redshanks, often spend the whole day feeding in fields.

The two species of international importance, Oystercatcher and Redshank, are noted in Table 11:1. Table 11:8 shows the five species of national importance. Mallard (490), Wigeon (560), Goldeneye (60), Shelduck (415), Knot (510) and 15–20 wintering Greenshank are of regional significance.

In addition to the important autumn flock of Red-breasted Mergansers, over 300 Great Crested Grebes also moult here; the maximum number recorded was 520 in 1976. These birds feed off Llanfairfechan at low tide and drift in to roost off Aber at high tide. Winter numbers are much lower, although still up to 100, but small numbers of Slavonian and Black-necked Grebes and Red-throated Divers also occur.

*Conwy Estuary*. This fairly narrow estuary opens in the south-east corner of Conwy Bay between Conwy and Llandudno. It falls into two sections, the outer estuary, which has extensive sandbanks, mudflats and mussel beds, is separated by the Conwy–Llandudno Junction bridge and embankment from the narrower inner estuary surrounded by pasture. Its birds and invertebrates are summarised by Thorburn and Rees (1978). There is an extensive and increasing *Spartina* marsh on the eastern side between Llandudno Junction and Glan Conwy above the Conwy bridge, and a large mud flat off Glan Conwy.

The outer estuary supports most of the feeding Oystercatchers, Ringed Plovers and Knot; they roost on the rather disturbed shores around the golf courses, particularly Deganwy, which flank the mouth of the estuary. Most of the Shelduck, Curlew, Dunlin and Redshank are upstream of the bridge; Curlew and Redshank roost on Glan Conwy and other saltings.

Although the Conwy River supports quite large numbers of waders and some duck, only Oystercatchers are of national importance at 2,160 (1·1% British). Of regional significance are Curlew (690) and Redshank (680), and Shelduck build up to 460 in spring; locally also Ringed Plover, Dunlin and Knot are noteworthy.

*Little Orme–Rhos Point*. Up to 2,000 waders are found on this open, rocky shore and mussel beds on the border of Gwynedd and Clwyd. Between 500 and 1,000 Oystercatchers, 200–300 Turnstones and small numbers (15–25) of Purple Sandpipers are the principal species; for details see Machin (1965).

*Anglesey*

*Traeth Melynog and South Menai Straits*. This is a primarily sandy area, with Traeth Melynog bounded by the sand dunes of Newborough Warren and the shingle Bar of Abermenai Point. It supports an interesting and diverse bird fauna, although only Teal (830: 1·1% British) is of national significance. Wigeon (1,300), Pintail (100), Shelduck (340), Ringed Plover (100) and Grey Plover (55) are of local importance. Most birds roost near Plas Penrhyn but others are scattered along the coastline. There is a considerable interchange of waders and wildfowl with Foryd Bay. All along the shore of the Menai Straits small flocks, rarely reaching 100 birds, of Oystercatcher, Curlew, Dunlin, Redshank, Turnstone, Red-breasted Merganser and grebes are found, but no full counts were made.

*Cefni*. Another predominantly sandy estuary although there is some mud in the

*Table 11:8   Species of national importance in Conwy Bay, 1969–75*

|  | *Highest av. monthly count* | *% British* |
|---|---|---|
| Red-breasted Merganser | 230 | 3·1 |
| Oystercatcher | 5,870 | 2·9 |
| Dunlin | 7,030 | 1·3 |
| Curlew | 1,680 | 1·7 |
| Redshank | 1,480 | 1·5 |

river channel and by the saltmarsh on the eastern side. There is a small pool at Malltraeth and wet fields to the north of the road. The only species of national importance is the Pintail (240:1·2% British), which mainly feeds near the saltmarsh. Only Shelduck (220+) are of local significance but the estuary supports a high diversity of waders and wildfowl, many of the latter feeding on the Cob Pool and adjacent flooded fields.

*Beddmanarch Bay/Alaw Estuary/Inland Sea.* This is a fairly large complex lying between Holyhead Island and the mainland of Anglesey. The main intertidal area is Beddmanarch Bay and the Alaw estuary, which are predominantly sandy and lie to the north of the main road and rail embankment. The Inland Sea, between the two bridges, has a variable but small intertidal zone, the largest area being on neap tides when the water has a chance to drain away through culverts and narrow bridges. To the south there is a small sandy creek connecting with the sea at Cymyran Bay. Apart from small sand dunes at the mouth of the Alaw the shore is a mass of small rocky or grassy promontories and islands. Many of these, especially on the eastern side of the Inland Sea are used as roosts by the waders. Diving duck and, at times, grebes are frequent in Beddmanarch Bay and the Inland Sea.

For a site with a high species diversity – 14 wildfowl and 19 waders – it is surprising that only one species, Ringed Plover (130:1·1% British), reaches a level of national importance although Wigeon (940), Shelduck (220) and Bar-tailed Godwit (260) are of note in a local context.

*Traeth Dulas.* This is a small sandy estuary with a narrow exit surrounded by pasture. Although 19 species of waders have been recorded the site is of note for the flock of Curlew which form a nightime roost on the inner estuary. Up to 2,000 (1·0% European) may occur but regularly 1,000 (1·0% British). These are mainly birds which feed during the day on fields. Only small numbers of wildfowl are present.

*Red Wharf Bay.* This is a large bay but very exposed and sandy, supporting relatively small numbers of birds. Waders predominate but only Knot (450) are of local significance. Several hundred Oystercatcher, Curlew and Dunlin are also found. Few duck occur but offshore there is a regular flock of 200+ Common Scoter which has sometimes exceeded 1,000 birds, at which level it is of national importance.

*Clwyd*

*Clwyd*. This small estuary enters Liverpool Bay at Rhyl. For most of its length it is surrounded by pasture, but Rhyl Marine Lake near the mouth forms an excellent feeding ground for waders when drained in winter.

Few wildfowl occur but up to 80 Common Scoter are regular offshore, part of a much larger flock which frequents the Abergele section of the coast. Waders are more numerous but not of national importance. Regionally wintering Redshank (400), Dunlin (1,250) and a small flock of 35 Sanderling are of note.

# CHAPTER 12

# North-western England

The coast of the north Irish Sea contains several of the largest estuaries in Britain and Ireland. There are the four large estuaries of the Dee, Mersey, Ribble and Duddon, and two large embayments, Morecambe Bay and the Solway Firth, each with several major rivers flowing into them. The two much smaller estuaries of the Alt and the Esk (Ravenglass) complete the picture. From the Point of Air on the Dee to Haverigg on the Duddon, virtually the whole coastline is either estuarine in nature or has extensive offshore sandbanks. Indeed, apart from the small section between Fleetwood and Blackpool, virtually the whole area forms a natural unit, with sand banks linking the estuaries. There have been many observations of waders moving between the Ribble, Alt, outer Mersey and Dee estuaries, and recent ringing returns show this for Sanderling and Turnstone at least. Despite the movements there is a considerable degree of stability in the numbers recorded in each section of each estuary, within and between years. The Cumbria coast contrasts with this in having a narrow shingle beach with a fairly narrow strip of shingle, sand and rocks at low water. The Esk and its sand dune system and the rocky outcrop of St Bees Head are the only major features interrupting this section until the intertidal flats of Morecambe Bay on the south Solway are reached.

Apart from the size of the intertidal flats the other main feature of this part of the coast is the area of saltmarshes. Very large ones are present on the Dee, Ribble, Morecambe Bay and Solway. Unlike most of the other saltmarshes in Britain those in north-western England have a great diversity of habitats and considerable areas are closely grazed by sheep and cattle. During the last decade *Spartina* has colonised and started to spread at an alarming rate on the eastern shore of the Dee, the southern shore of the Ribble and in some areas of the Mersey. The salt-marshes contribute materially to the importance of the region.

All of the estuaries in this region have a large tidal range. It varies from about 10 m on a spring tide to 6 m on neap tides. On the Kent estuary in Morecambe Bay there is the second largest tidal bore in Britain. Throughout the region the sediment is primarily fine sand enriched with a moderate amount of silt in the upper centimetres. Only in the Mersey, parts of the Dee, on the Alt and in small sheltered corners in the other major estuaries are there any significant areas of mud.

*Urban and industrial development and recreation*

The estuaries of north-western England have retained their importance for waterfowl despite the considerable loss of land to urban and industrial development. The major developments in the region are summarised in the accounts of the individual estuaries and only an outline is given here.

The major threats are threefold. Firstly, reclamation for water supply reservoirs; secondly, the newly discovered gas field in Morecambe Bay and thirdly, reclamation of the salt marshes for agriculture. With Morecambe Bay and, especially, the Dee under significant pressure for water storage this poses the most serious threat. The implementation of any of the reservoir schemes, however, is likely to represent a long-term rather than an immediate problem. This is not the case with the gas field. Six areas have been considered as terminals in the north-west. These involve one area in the Dee, two in the Ribble and three in Morecambe Bay. The need for the terminal to be at least 1½ km from human habitation would mean that inevitably it will be placed in one of the most important areas for birds in the estuaries concerned. At the moment there is no decision as to its location. The reclamation of salt marshes in the north-west is probably still in its infancy. The attempt on the Ribble indicates the potential scale of this problem, so we must be on our guard to ensure the continuing future of the other very large and extremely important salt marshes of the region.

In the south, in Cheshire and Merseyside, there has been considerable industrial development, with particular emphasis on the petro-chemical and heavy industries. As a result significant pollution is present on the Mersey; the inflow of domestic sewage is also very large and forms the majority of organic effluent. The sands of the outer Dee and between the Alt and Morecambe Bay attract large numbers of holidaymakers. Fortunately the associated towns have grown up mostly beside the less sensitive and narrower sandy beaches. Disturbance can be quite serious during the autumn passage but is only slight in winter and spring.

*Main literature on the birds of north-western England*

The principal works on the county avifaunas are: Cheshire – Bell (1962 and 1967); Lancashire – Oakes (1953) and Spencer (1973); Cumbria – Stokoe (1962). Additionally, records are summarised in the annual bird reports of the Cheshire Ornithological Association, the Lancashire and Cheshire Fauna Society, Lancaster and District Birdwatching Society, the Association of Cumbrian Natural History Societies, and the more irregular reports of the Merseyside Naturalists' Association. There are many publications relating to individual estuaries or sites within them, as summarised below in the respective estuary account.

*Table 12:1  Main species and peak counts of waterfowl on the coast of north-western England*

| | Highest av. monthly total | | | Highest av. monthly total | |
|---|---|---|---|---|---|
| Wigeon | 12,100 | Dec | Dunlin | 163,000 | Dec |
| Shelduck | 11,500 | Feb | Knot | 134,700 | Dec |
| Pintail | 10,100 | Dec | Oystercatcher | 87,700 | Oct |
| Teal | 8,300 | Dec | Redshank | 28,300 | Sept |
| Mallard | 7,400 | Sept | Curlew | 28,000 | Aug |
| Eider | 650 | Nov | Sanderling | 27,900 | May |
| Scaup | 560 | Feb | Lapwing | 23,900 | Jan |
| Goldeneye | 520 | Jan | Bar-tailed Godwit | 20,600 | Jan |
| Red-breasted Merganser | 410 | Jan | Ringed Plover | 10,900 | May |
| Shoveler | 84 | Jan | Turnstone | 2,900 | Aug |

*Principal species and migration patterns*

North-western England supports extremely large numbers of waders and wild-fowl. It is the most important area in the British Isles for many species, particularly waders, for most of the year. Table 12:1 presents the principal species and the levels which they reach regularly. To put the figures in perspective, the area supports over 20% of the European population of three species (Bar-tailed Godwit, Knot and Pintail) and over 10% of the European population of four others (Redshank, Curlew, Oystercatcher and Dunlin). The numbers of Sanderling in winter (2,600), while well below those during passage periods, also exceeds 15% of the European total. As mentioned earlier there are no international population figures available to enable an assessment of the importance of the migrant flocks of Ringed Plover and Sanderling. North-western England is, however, considered to be of major significance for both species.

With the great numbers of waders present all patterns of migration can be seen. There is a large influx from late July through to September of birds which use the Dee, Ribble and Morecambe Bay as staging posts on their migration to south-western Europe and West Africa. Dunlin, Ringed Plover and Sanderling (particularly the populations which have bred in Iceland, Greenland and north-eastern Canada) predominate in this movement. The other major factor at this time of year is the build up of enormous flocks of moulting waders which appear to find that the large saltmarshes and intertidal flats offer little disturbance and an abundance of food.

Late September and early October is a relatively quiet time in many areas although many waders are present on the Dee and Ribble estuaries. By early November a rapid increase of Dunlin, Knot and Bar-tailed Godwit has begun; these are birds which have spent autumn on the North Sea coasts. They reach peak numbers between late December and early February, declining rapidly as the birds return to the east. Occasionally, considerable movements of the Bar-tailed Godwit are seen.

Northward migration of Redshanks, Oystercatchers and Curlew begins as early as late February and small concentrations start to occur. Only the Redshank may show an overall increase with a distinct passage of Icelandic breeders in late March and early April. The main spring passage is only obvious initially in Morecambe Bay, the Dee and the Ribble. Later it occurs on the Alt, Duddon and Solway but is poorly represented on the Mersey. The first species to show are the Knot and Turnstone, both reach peak numbers during mid to late April. During early May there are increases of Dunlin, Ringed Plover and Sanderling, peaking in about the third week of the month. Then, suddenly, between late May and the end of the first week of June everything has gone, leaving only a few summering immatures. The populations involved in this movement are the Greenland, Canadian and Icelandic breeders which are therefore similar to those seen during the autumn migration. Some of the birds moving north will have migrated south the previous autumn through the North Sea. In general the spring passage involves few of the eastern birds which occur in autumn and the movement is rapid, being completed in about one month, with the bulk of each species occurring in a two to three week period.

The pattern for wildfowl is less complicated as most species build up numbers rapidly between October and November to an early winter peak. Only Shelduck of the more important species shows a trend which differs slightly from the national picture. There is a rapid rise in numbers during September and October, which means that many are present before the bulk of moulting birds returns from the Helgoland Bight. The reason for this influx is not known, nor its origin.

A feature of the northern estuaries of this region is their goose numbers, see Table 12:2. The Pink-footed Goose is the most widespread with 10,000–20,000 feeding on the mosslands of south Lancashire and Merseyside; many of these roost at Southport on the Ribble Estuary, and 2,000 also roost on the estuary of the Lune in southern Morecambe Bay, with a further 9,000 on the south Solway, particularly during March and April. Greylag Geese are scarce, with only small flocks on the Kent estuary in Morecambe Bay and on the south Solway. Barnacle Geese graze the saltmarshes of the inner Solway during the spring months.

Relatively few Red-throated Diver or the smaller grebes occur in the region. Apart from a notable spring concentration of up to 600 Great Crested Grebes off Formby Point, the larger grebes, too, are scarce. Gulls, however, are extremely numerous. Unfortunately very few counts are available but large roosts are known for all estuaries. Important breeding colonies of Black-headed Gulls occur on the Esk and Ribble, and of Herring and Lesser Black-backed Gulls on Morecambe Bay. Apart from the large breeding colonies of terns in Morecambe Bay, the Ribble and the Duddon, large concentrations occur during the autumn passage in the south of Liverpool Bay, with Formby Point and the Dee being favoured especially.

*Table 12:2 Principal flocks of geese in north-western England and percentage of the world population*

| | Ribble | % world | Morecambe Bay | % world | S. Solway | % world |
|---|---|---|---|---|---|---|
| Pink-footed Goose | 14,000 | 16·5 | 2,000 | 2·4 | 9,000 | 10·6 |
| Barnacle Goose | – | – | – | – | 2,400* | 4·4 |

* At times in spring virtually all of the Svalbard population may visit here

*Table 12:3 Waterfowl of international importance in winter in north-western England, 1969–75*

| | Dee | Mersey | Alt | Ribble | Morecambe Bay | Duddon | S. Solway |
|---|---|---|---|---|---|---|---|
| Bewick's Swan | – | – | – | *1 | – | – | – |
| Pink-footed Goose | – | – | – | 18·7 | 4·0 | – | 12·0 |
| Barnacle Goose | – | – | – | – | – | – | *2 |
| Shelduck | 3·3 | 1·4 | – | – | 5·1 | – | – |
| Wigeon | – | – | – | – | 1·0 | – | – |
| Teal | 1·0 | 4·3 | – | – | – | – | – |
| Pintail | 5·7 | 14·4 | – | 3·3 | 1·1 | – | – |
| Oystercatcher | 2·6 | – | – | *3 | 8·0 | 1·4 | 3·4 |
| Ringed Plover | 1·3 | – | – | – | *4 | – | 4·1 |
| Golden Plover | – | – | – | – | – | – | *5 |
| Grey Plover | 1·2 | – | – | 1·9 | – | – | – |
| Lapwing | – | – | – | – | – | – | *5 |
| Knot | 6·2 | – | 1·3 | 14·1 | 16·0 | – | 2·8 |
| Sanderling | 3·1 | – | 2·7 | 12·0 | *4 | *4 | 1·2 |
| Dunlin | 2·3 | 3·1 | – | 3·6 | 4·1 | – | – |
| Black-tailed Godwit | 1·8 | – | – | 2·7 | – | – | – |
| Bar-tailed Godwit | 5·6 | – | – | 7·9 | 9·0 | – | 4·5 |
| Curlew | 1·0 | – | – | – | 3·8+ | – | 1·8 |
| Redshank | 2·9 | 1·4 | – | 1·7 | 6·3+ | 1·7 | 2·0 |
| Turnstone | – | – | – | *5 | *5 | – | – |

*1 Now 1·0% occur
*2 At times most of Svalbard birds occur
*3 Now 2·7% occur
*4 Passage numbers only of international importance
*5 Total population not known but probably of importance
 + Many more in autumn

*Principal estuaries of north-western England*

All estuaries in north-western England, apart from the Esk, are of international importance for waders or wildfowl. Five of them are of exceptional value. They are, northwards – Dee, Mersey, Ribble, Morecambe Bay and the Solway. A summary of the internationally important wintering concentrations that each estuary supports is presented in Table 12:3. Areas of importance within each estuary and the many species which reach levels of national importance are summarised in the individual estuary accounts.

The region is of importance for migrant waders (see Table 12:4), and it is probable that these few estuaries provide the last feeding grounds before the long crossing of the north Atlantic for the majority, possibly as many as 75% of their north-western breeding populations.

Table 12:4   Waders of international importance at passage periods in north-western England

|  |  | Dee | Alt | Ribble | Morecambe Bay | Duddon | S. Solway |
|---|---|---|---|---|---|---|---|
| Ringed Plover: | autumn | 2,720 | – | 660* | 2,040 | – | 1,565 |
|  | spring | 2,095 | – | 565* | 7,280 | – | 630* |
| Sanderling: | autumn | 6,450 | 805* | 6,080 | 3,425 | – | – |
|  | spring | 6,120 | 1,100 | 6,315 | 11,860 | 2,065 | – |

* Probably of importance
– Fewer than 500 present

### Clwyd/Cheshire/Merseyside

Dee. This is a large funnel shaped estuary. On the Clwyd shore there is a small area of sand dunes guarding the mouth at the Point of Air. Most of the rest of this west side has only a small saltmarsh, reclaimed in places, with development at Tanlan (colliery), Connah's Quay (power station and urban) and Flint (urban). The river channel runs near to the shore and prevents the build up of large mud flats on the Welsh side. To the east of the canalised Dee is the large Burton saltmarsh, behind which is Shotton steel works and many associated lagoons which provide additional habitats. Further north-east in Cheshire lies part of Burton and Parkgate marshes, the latter extend into Merseyside. The marshes are contiguous. There has been a considerable spread of Spartina at the edge of the marsh and it is spreading steadily along the eastern shore towards West Kirby. At the outer eastern side, the towns of West Kirby and Hoylake reach the shore; between them lies a small group of rocks called Red Rocks, and about 1 km offshore a group of islands – Hilbre, Little Hilbre and Little Eye. The East and West Hoyle Banks extend well beyond the mouth of the estuary into Liverpool Bay and the former extend along the north Wirral coast to the mouth of the Mersey. The West Hoyle Bank is important in breaking the force of north-westerly gales and bringing sheltered conditions in the Dee.

Apart from the slight influence of the industries in Clwyd, the main adverse factor affecting the birds' distribution is human disturbance. At times at the Point of Air, West Kirby, Hoylake and the Hilbre Islands it can be severe; at the last three sites it is a problem throughout the year. A decade ago Hilbre Islands, especially Little Eye, was a major roost site but with the increase in fishermen the islands have become much less important. Even the saltmarshes are subjected to disturbance. Most of the estuary is scheduled as an SSSI and is a Grade 1* NCR site; the RSPB have recently obtained a reserve on a large area of saltmarsh and intertidal flats at the head of the Dee. The adjacent habitat of Redrocks Marsh is managed by the Cheshire Conservation Trust and that at Shotton Steel Works by the Merseyside Ringing Group.

Much has been written about the Dee estuary; a full bibliography has been prepared by the Dee Estuary Conservation Group and a copy is available at the Merseyside County Museums. Research on birds and invertebrates is being carried out by Salford University and the Dee and Clwyd Water Division. A summary of all research and its results – *The Dee Estuary Research Review* has been published by the Nature Conservancy Council.

The ten species of wader and two of duck which are of international importance have been summarised in Table 12:3. The national status is shown in Table 12:5. In most recent autumns up to 50 or 100 Spotted Redshanks occurred on the saltmarshes. Of note also are the numbers of Common Tern (up to 500+) and Little Tern (600–1,000) which are present regularly at the mouth of the Dee between July and September. The Dee is also an extremely important staging post for waders in spring and autumn and as a moulting ground in autumn. A speciality of the Hilbre islands is the flock of Purple Sandpipers.

Bird distribution in the Dee is summarised in Fig. 12:1. The main concentrations feed off the large inner saltmarshes, in the eastern sandbanks extending out to the East Hoyle Bank, and off the Point of Air. Roosts also occur in these areas but are relatively mobile, varying with the tide height and disturbance; Eades (1973) shows most of the main flight lines and interrelationships between roosts. There is some movement of wildfowl across the Wirral between the Dee and the Mersey, and the former is of greatest importance in the autumn.

### Merseyside

*Mersey.* This is the most heavily developed and polluted estuary of the region. Most of the outer two-thirds of the estuary is completely surrounded by Liverpool, Wallasey and Birkenhead; only the inner third has maintained some undeveloped areas. High saltmarshes are found at Hale, above Widnes and on the southern part where it is cut off from the surrounding land by the Manchester Ship Canal, this protects it and the Stanlow and Ince Banks from excessive disturbance. Slightly

*Table 12:5   Species of national importance wintering on the Dee Estuary, 1969–75*

|  | Highest av. monthly count | % British |
|---|---|---|
| Shelduck | 4,300 | 7·2 |
| Pintail | 2,850 | 14·2 |
| Oystercatcher | 14,400 | 7·2 |
| Ringed Plover | 320 (*1) | 2·7 |
| Grey Plover | 375 | 3·7 |
| Knot | 31,250 | 10·4 |
| Sanderling | 470 (*2) | 3·1 |
| Dunlin | 28,000 | 5·2 |
| Black-tailed Godwit | 730 | 14·6 |
| Bar-tailed Godwit | 5,060 | 11·2 |
| Curlew | 2,000 | 2·0 |
| Redshank | 3,200 | 3·2 |
| Turnstone | 250 | 1·0 |

(*1)  2,700 on passage
(*2)  6,500 on passage

*Table 12:6   Species of national importance on the Mersey, 1969–75*

|  | Highest av. monthly count | % British |
|---|---|---|
| Shelduck | 1,760 | 2·9 |
| Wigeon | 2,820 | 1·4 |
| Teal | 6,400 | 8·5 |
| Pintail | 7,200 | 36·0 |
| Golden Plover | 2,450 | 1·2 |
| Dunlin | 37,650 | 6·8 |
| Redshank | 1,500 | 1·5 |

further east lie the Frodsham lagoons, into which dredgings from the Mersey are dumped. These and the adjacent pasture form a valuable complex of brackish and freshwater habitats. The intertidal flats of Stanlow and Ince Marshes plus the adjacent saltmarsh is an SSSI.

There is a considerable literature on the birds of the Mersey. Most of it has been drawn together by Hodgson (1976), and a copy has been deposited at Salford University. The great increase in numbers of ducks using the estuary has been summarised by Allen (1974), while the demise of the geese is discussed by Williams (1962).

The three species of duck and two of wader which are of international importance have been shown in Table 12:3. The Pintail numbers should be noted as this flock constitutes almost 15% of the European winter numbers. Duck numbers increased dramatically during the 1960s; probably waders too, although earlier counts were not complete enough for comparison. The reason for this change, the most dramatic example in Britain, only rivalled by the changing fortunes of the Thames, is not known although the impression of reduced pollution may again be the explanation. However, it is possibly a response to a 'no shooting' sanctuary established by the Merseyside Naturalists' Association at Manisty. There has been a reduction in some species on the nearby Dee, an estuary with quite heavy shooting pressure at times. The national status of birds on the Mersey is shown in Table 12:6. Frodsham and Weaver Bend provide a great diversity of migrant waterbirds and excellent birdwatching.

The distribution of birds in the Mersey is fairly simple. Most waders and ducks feed in Stanlow and Ince Banks, although many Shelduck favour Oglet Bay in the east shore, and virtually everything roosts on or along the saltmarsh between Manisty and Frodsham. On large tides many of the waders leave the saltmarsh to roost on the Frodsham lagoons. Up to 6,000 waders roost at Hale, the adjacent Duck Decoy being managed by the Cheshire Conservation Trust and the Lancashire Naturalists' Trust. A few thousand small waders feed on the narrow shore at New Ferry and New Brighton and moderate sized roosts occur nearby. An enormous roost, but not accurately counted in recent years, of gulls occurs on the estuary.

*Alt.* The Alt estuary is almost a large beach and offshore sand banks with a limited, but heavily polluted, freshwater inflow. At its northern end is Formby Point and sand dunes; low dunes occur south to Hall Road and the southern boundary is at Seaforth Docks, Liverpool, at the mouth of the Mersey. Although Formby dunes are an SSSI there is much public pressure on the whole of the area, particularly in summer. The two species of wader which are of international importance are given in Table 12:3 and their national status in Table 12:7. In addition, during the autumn, large flocks of Common and Arctic Terns, Kittiwakes and other gulls feed and roost off Formby Point. Little Gulls are a feature of the Alt and over fifty can be seen at almost any time of the year. This is the largest flock in the British Isles only equalled by eastern Scotland in autumn and south-east Ireland in winter. Large numbers of Little Gulls, terns and waders roost at Seaforth Docks and Waterloo but there is some interchange with the Dee, depending on disturbance levels at the latter.

There are considerable fluctuations in the numbers of Knot and Bar-tailed Godwit on the Alt, probably due to the proximity of the East Hoyle Bank of the Dee; other species are also likely to be influenced but to a lesser extent.

### Merseyside/Lancashire

*Ribble.* This large estuary has a simple structure. Its southern and northern outer shores are sandy and attract many holiday makers to the towns of Southport, Lytham St Annes and Blackpool. The inner estuary is edged by a series of very large and varied saltmarshes. On the southern side Crossens, Banks, Hesketh Out and Longton Marshes join together to line the river channel, but on the north only the smaller Warton and Clifton Marshes remain, Clifton Sewage Works having been built on reclaimed land between them.

Inland habitats play a significant role in the importance of the Ribble to birds. The mossland (now farmland) between Southport and Maghull and the wet grazing and Wildfowl Trust reserve at Martin Mere, near Burscough, are of particular note for Pink-footed Geese and dabbling ducks respectively. The intertidal flats are predominantly sandy with some silt near the marsh edges, especially at Warton and Lytham.

The estuary is a Grade 1* site in the NCR and there are two SSSIs on the estuary, one covering most of the outer intertidal flats and the other the inner flats and saltmarshes, including the Pink-footed Goose roost off Southport. The sand dunes at Lytham St Annes are a LNR. Apart from recreation the only major threat was the sandwinning plant which operates into the latter SSSI. In recent years a major reclamation scheme was proposed for Banks and Crossens Marshes and a large area of intertidal flats. After careful consideration by conservation bodies this disastrous scheme was successfully opposed.

The birds using the Ribble estuary have been summarised by Greenhalgh (1965, 1968, 1971, 1975) and Smith and Greenhalgh (1977). Much research is being

---

*Table 12:7   Species of national importance on the Alt, 1969–75*

|  | Highest av. monthly count | % British |
|---|---|---|
| Grey Plover | 190 | 1·9 |
| Knot | 6,600 | 2·2 |
| Sanderling | 400 | 2·7 |

carried out on the area by Liverpool Polytechnic. The species of international importance have been summarised in Table 12:3 and those of national importance are in Table 12:8. Of these the Oystercatcher has, since 1975, increased greatly in numbers due to a large settlement of cockles. The average winter count for the 1975–76 and 1976–77 winters was 15,000, which now makes the Ribble of international importance for this species. Although the Ribble is of international importance for waders throughout the year, its role as a centre for moulting waders during August–October should be emphasised, in particular for Knot and Bar-tailed Godwit. For the former species the Ribble is the second most important site in Europe, on occasions supporting over 15% of the population. The other wader for which the Ribble is of great importance is the Sanderling, for not only does it have many on migration, but in winter up to 3,000 and regularly 2,000 occur. Thus it supports 13–20% of the European numbers and up to almost one third of the British birds; amost all are found in the north shore between Blackpool and Lytham. The flock of Pink-footed Geese also deserves special mention; in early winter in recent years it has built up to 20–25% of the world population. Also, recently, about 100, and up to 150, Bewick's Swans (1% world population) regularly graze the marshes in winter.

Of the other species only the breeding colonies of Black-headed Gulls and Common Terns on the marshes are important, the former up to about 10,000 pairs and 1,000 of the latter. Also on the marshes there are large numbers of breeding

Table 12:8   Species of national importance on the Ribble Estuary, 1969–75

|  | Highest av. monthly count | % British |
|---|---|---|
| Bewick's Swan | 30 (*1) | 1·5 (5·0) |
| Pink-footed Goose | 14,000 | 18·7 |
| Shelduck | 910 | 1·5 |
| Wigeon | 2,700 | 1·3 |
| Teal | 750 | 1·0 |
| Pintail | 1,650 | 8·2 |
| Oystercatcher | 3,000 (*2) | 1·5 (7·5) |
| Ringed Plover | 135 | 1·1 |
| Golden Plover | 2,300 | 1·1 |
| Grey Plover | 770 | 7·7 |
| Knot | 70,560 | 23·5 |
| Sanderling | 1,800 (*3) | 12·0 |
| Dunlin | 42,600 | 7·7 |
| Black-tailed Godwit | 1,100 | 22·0 |
| Bar-tailed Godwit | 7,080 | 15·7 |
| Redshank | 1,840 | 1·8 |
| Turnstone | 590 | 2·4 |

(*1) 100 now regular
(*2) 15,000 now occur
(*3) 6,300 on passage

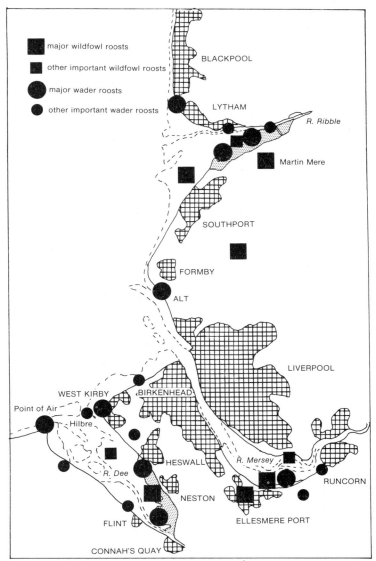

Fig. 12:1 Main concentrations of waders and wildfowl in the Dee, Mersey, Alt and Ribble estuaries.

waders, Redshank particularly.

The whole of the estuary is used by birds. A summary of the roost sites of waders is given in Fig. 12:1, from Smith and Greenhalgh (1977). Ducks and swans tend to use the estuary, particularly the southern marshes, for feeding and especially roosting; there is much interchange with Martin Mere.

*Lancashire/Cumbria*

*Morecambe Bay.* The largest and one of the most important estuaries for birds in the British Isles, formed by the estuaries of the Wyre, Lune, Keer, Kent and Leven and the mudflats which have built up behind Walney Island. Apart from the fishing port of Fleetwood and the industrial town of Barrow-in-Furness on the outer bay, the only major towns on the coast are Morecambe and Heysham. These last two are holiday centres but outside the period June–September their adverse effect is limited.

The majority of the intertidal flats consists of fine sand with a small amount of silt, although it is relatively muddy in places in the Lune and near Walney Island. Mussel beds are a major feature of Morecambe Bay with very large ones off Morecambe, Heysham and Foulney Island and smaller ones at the mouth of the Wyre. Along the west Cumbria shore there are a number of stony scars. Saltmarshes are prominent: Pilling, Cockerham, Middleton and Colloway Marshes line the Lune estuary, and Hest Bank, Carnforth, Silverdale and Meathop Marshes the Keer and Kent estuaries. There are three larger marshes at Flookburgh: East Plain, West Plain and Sandgate. Some *Spartina* occurs in the muddier upper reaches of the Lune and around Walney but most are heavily grazed and, therefore, dominated by the grasses *Puccinellia*

*Table 12:9   Species of national importance wintering on Morecambe Bay, 1969–75*

|  | Highest av. monthly count | % British |
|---|---|---|
| Pink-footed Goose | 3,000 | 4·0 |
| Shelduck | 6,640 | 11·1 |
| Wigeon | 4,120 | 2·1 |
| Teal | 950 | 1·3 |
| Mallard | 3,060 | 1·0 |
| Pintail | 560 | 2·8 |
| Eider | 630 | 1·1 |
| Common Scoter | 660 | 1·9 |
| Goldeneye | 390 | 3·1 |
| Red-breasted Merganser | 330 | 4·4 |
| Oystercatcher | 44,700 | 22·3 |
| Ringed Plover | 230 (*1) | 2·0 |
| Grey Plover | 200 | 2·0 |
| Knot | 80,200 | 26·7 |
| Sanderling | – (*2) | – |
| Dunlin | 48,700 | 8·9 |
| Bar-tailed Godwit | 8,080 | 18·0 |
| Curlew | 7,700 (*3) | 7·7 |
| Redshank | 6,900 (*4) | 6·9 |
| Turnstone | 1,670 | 6·7 |

(*1) 7,300 on passage
(*2) 11,860 on passage
(*3) 16,100 in autumn
(*4) 12,400 in autumn

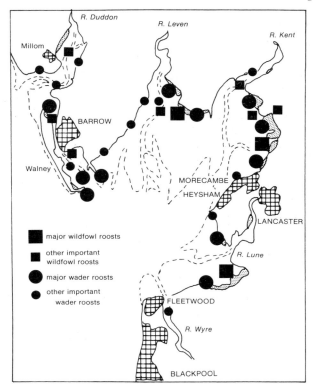

Fig. 12:2 Main concentrations of waders and wildfowl in Morecambe Bay and the Duddon estuary.

*maritima, Festuca rubra* and *Agrostis stolonifera*. The flora, intertidal fauna, sediments and general ecology of the estuary are considered by Anderson (1972), Corlett (1972) and Gray (1972).

All sections of Morecambe Bay are internationally important ornithologically and include two Grade 1* and one Grade 1 NCR sites. They are the Wyre/Lune sanctuary, the upper flats and marshes from Morecambe to the Leven estuary and the whole of the Foulney/Walney complex respectively. The RSPB has a large reserve at Leighton Moss and between Silverdale and Hest Bank. A reserve on the Wyre covering Burrows Marsh and Barnaby's Sands is administered by the Lancashire Naturalists' Trust.

Unfortunately there are several major threats to Morecambe Bay. Plans remain for massive water storage reservoirs on the north-eastern part of the Bay, and enquiries are in progress for a large gas terminal in the Lune estuary to exploit a gas field fairly close by in the Irish Sea. Less extensive though at times serious problems still arise from the disturbance in the Foulney area and the retention of Oystercatchers on the second Schedule of the Protection of Birds Act 1954.

The birds of Morecambe Bay have been partially summarised by Ruxton (1973) for ducks and more completely by Wilson (1973, 1974) for waders and generally. Additional information by Wilson and Prater is given in reports to the Central Water

Planning Unit (then the Water Resources Board) on studies carried out as part of the Morecambe Bay Barrage Feasibility Study.

The species of international importance have been summarised in Tables 12:3 and 12:4. Table 12:9 gives species of national significance. Combining these tables shows that Morecambe Bay is of considerable importance for 20 species of waterbirds, 14 at international level. Additionally south Walney Island supports the largest breeding colony of Lesser Black-backed Gulls and Herring Gulls in Britain (estimated at 25,000–30,000 pairs of each) and at least 1% of the British breeding population of each of Sandwich, Common and Little Terns can be found, particularly in the Walney area. Other breeding birds of particular interest are Eiders, 400 pairs of which occur on Walney, this being the southernmost colony on the west coast, and 40–50 pairs of Ringed Plovers (1% of the British total). The saltmarshes support many Redshank and a few pairs of Dunlin, these too being the southernmost regular coastal breeders in Britain.

Figure 12:2 shows the areas of particular interest for birds in Morecambe Bay. All sections are of international importance although the coarse sand on the outermost banks in the centre of the Bay supports few invertebrates and carries few birds. As in most estuaries the richest zone is between high water on neap tides and the mid-tide level. The flock of about 2,000 Pink-footed Geese which feed on Cockerham and Pilling Mosses roosts at night on the Wyre/Lune Sanctuary.

*Cumbria*

*Duddon.* This is a fairly large sandy estuary, with sand dunes at Haverigg, Sandscale and North Walney Island flanking its mouth. In sheltered corners, particularly between Walney and the mainland, some mud occurs. There are saltmarshes on the inner third of the estuary and also off north Walney. At Hodbarrow there is an area of disused and permanently flooded mineworkings which provide an interesting area. Most of the estuary and saltmarshes and the dune systems on the south of the estuary are scheduled as SSSIs.

The Duddon is relatively unaffected by developments, the main intrusion was the testing of hovercraft at Millom.

---

*Table 12:10   Species of national importance wintering on the Duddon, 1969–75*

|  | Highest av. monthly count | % British |
|---|---|---|
| Shelduck | 1,000 | 1·7 |
| Pintail | 450 | 2·2 |
| Red-breasted Merganser | 95 | 1·3 |
| Oystercatcher | 8,000 | 4·0 |
| Ringed Plover | 160 | 1·3 |
| Sanderling | —* | — |
| Dunlin | 6,200 | 1·1 |
| Redshank | 1,900 | 1·9 |

* 2,100 on passage

---

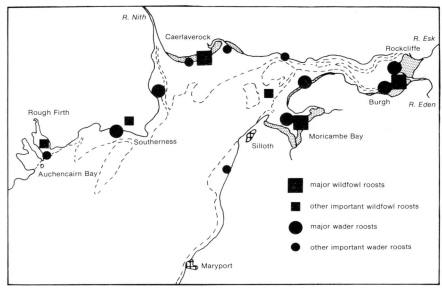

Fig. 12:3 Main concentrations of waders and wildfowl in the Solway Firth.

Little has been written about the Duddon's birds although Ruxton (1973) reported on its wildfowl numbers. Tables 12:3 and 12:4 show the species with internationally significant numbers; Table 12:10 summarises those of national importance.

Additionally about 50 pairs of Little Terns now breed on the estuary, about 2·8% of the British and Irish populations. The build up here parallels the drop in numbers at the Ravenglass colony on the Esk estuary about 30 km further north.

The distribution of birds on the Duddon is summarised in Fig. 12:2; the southern shore, particularly the outer section, provides the favoured feeding and roosting areas.

*Esk.* This estuary, the smallest in north-western England, has three arms formed by the rivers Esk, Irt and Mite. Large sand dune systems separate these arms from the sea and behind them small areas of saltmarsh have developed. Most of the flats are sandy. The northern sand dunes (Ravenglass) are a Grade 1\* NCR site, and SSSI

---

*Table 12:11   Principal species of birds breeding at the Esk Estuary*

|  | Pairs | % British |  | Pairs | % British |
|---|---|---|---|---|---|
| Black-headed Gull | 10,500 | 4·0* | Little Tern | 20 | 1·1 |
| Sandwich Tern | 600 | 4·3 | Ringed Plover | 20 | 0·4 |

\* There is no complete estimate of the British population but Sharrock (1976) assessed it as 150,000–300,000. This colony is 10% of the English and Welsh population.

*Table 12:12 Species of national importance wintering on the south Solway, 1969–75*

| | Highest av. monthly count | % British |
|---|---|---|
| Pink-footed Goose | 9,020 | 12·0 |
| Barnacle Goose | 2,400 | 42·9 (*1) |
| Shelduck | 1,010 | 1·7 |
| Scaup | 510 | 2·3 |
| Goldeneye | 150 | 1·2 |
| Red-breasted Merganser | 85 | 1·1 |
| Oystercatcher | 19,100 | 9·5 |
| Ringed Plover | 1,035 | 8·6 |
| Golden Plover | 7,800 | 3·9 |
| Lapwing | 12,300 | (*2) |
| Knot | 14,100 | 4·7 |
| Sanderling | 180 | 1·2 |
| Dunlin | 7,070 | 1·3 |
| Black-tailed Godwit | 140 | 2·8 |
| Bar-tailed Godwit | 4,080 | 9·1 |
| Curlew | 3,540 | 3·5 |
| Redshank | 2,200 | 2·2 |
| Greenshank | 70 | (*2) |
| Turnstone | 360 | 1·4 |

(*1) Of Svalbard population
(*2) Importance based on estimated numbers

and a Local Nature Reserve. Eskmeols is a Cumbria Naturalists' Trust reserve.

No species of wildfowl or wader is of international importance but, particularly in the autumn and early winter, 3,800 Oystercatchers (1·9% British) regularly occur. Breeding birds of importance are summarised in Table 12:9.

*Solway Firth, south.* The Solway is one of the great inlets of Britain and of major importance for its birds. The division of it into a southern, English, section and a northern, Scottish, section is artificial but as the administrative backgrounds are different this has been maintained. The whole complex has been put into context in an earlier chapter.

The south Solway can be divided into four sections. The inner part consists of the great marshes of Rockcliffe and Burgh, the former sandwiches between the major rivers of the Esk and Eden which flow into the Firth. Then there is a fairly long section of low coast from Glasson to Cardurnock with a narrow fringe of saltmarsh at the western end. This opens into a large embayment, Morecambe Bay, entered by the small rivers of Wampool and Waver. Large saltmarshes line Morecambe Bay and at its western edge the shingle and sand dune system of Grune Point provides a natural boundary. From Silloth south to Workington there is a sandy beach with numerous rock and mussel scars; this beach is extensive in its northern part but relatively narrow south of Mayport. Throughout the Solway sand predominates with a little mud in the sheltered corners.

On the south Solway the major saltmarshes, Rockcliffe, Burgh and Long Newton, and Grune Point are scheduled as SSSIs and considered as Grade 1 NCR sites. There are, fortunately, few threats to the area.

For an area of high international importance for birds there has been very little published; Atkinson-Willes (1963) and Stokoe (1962) are the main sources of prior information. Tables 12:3, 12:4 and 12:5 list the species of international importance. Of these the Pink-footed and Barnacle Geese deserve special mention for they do not appear to arrive in very large numbers until early March, coincidental with a decrease on the north Solway. They remain until migration time. The national importance of species on the south Solway is given in Table 12:12. Of these the Black-tailed Godwit are only present for a few weeks in the autumn.

Up to 800 Cormorants also occur, probably about 4% of the British total. Other species of note are breeding Common Terns of which 200 (1% British) are found, and up to 100,000 wintering gulls have been reported coming into roost on the estuary.

Figure 12:3 shows that important concentrations of birds occur in all areas. The only relatively small numbers are on the southern outer coast where there is little intertidal habitat.

CHAPTER 13

# Scotland

The coastline of mainland Scotland and its islands stretch for over 10,100 km. As a result it has a large range of habitats to offer, grading from the extensive outer sandy flats in the major firths to muddy inner sections. Mud, however, is relatively scarce in Scotland. Equally its successor, the saltmarsh, is quite restricted; the only large areas are on the Solway. Stony scars and shingle on flats is a much more common feature than elsewhere in Britain. The sea lochs of western Scotland and many of the islands are either heavily pounded by waves or subject to high freshwater run off and consequently have restricted areas of coarse sediment, often with quite deep water nearby. Off eastern Scotland are fairly extensive areas of shallow water, frequently enriched by organic discharges from the centres of population. However, most of the coast is taken up by rocky shores, which tend to be cliffed in the west but are often flatter in the east where the softer sedimentary rock has allowed rock shelf development with its associated rich algal growth. These and the many offshore skerries and reefs in the north form an important zone for birds. Low-lying pasture and mosslands are widespread around large and small estuaries.

*Urban and industrial developments and recreation*
During the last ten years the coast of Scotland has come under severe pressure from the North Sea oil and gas industries. Its influence is felt everywhere although perhaps the northern islands and eastern Scotland have borne the brunt of it. The problems resulting encompass the whole range of industrial development including

222

reclamation and pollution. Land based developments are platform building yards, oil and gas terminals, and repair and servicing facilities. Examples of the first of these, which also involved reclamation of intertidal areas, are Nigg Bay and Whiteness Head in the Moray Firth Basin; at the latter site the company involved showed irresponsible behaviour by extending the yard boundaries beyond those defined by the planning authority. Several other platform building yards have been built on coastal areas in north and west Scotland. Major oil terminals have been built at Sullum Voe (Shetlands), Flotta (Orkney), in the Cromarty Firth and Hound Point (Firth of Forth). Several other sites are being considered including a plan to reclaim intertidal flats at Kinneil near Grangemouth on the Firth or Forth for possible petro-chemical development. Gas development has involved fewer major problems, although pipelines bringing it ashore at St Fergus north of Peterhead did result in some habitat destruction. With the continuation of exploration to the north and west of Scotland it is quite possible that western Scotland will come under much more pressure than hitherto. Reclamation is, of course, not the only environmental impact of the oil development, pollution too is a very real threat. Scotland has internationally important seaduck, diver and grebe concentrations in the islands and firths, and auk and other seabird breeding colonies as well as large numbers of estuarine duck and waders. Spillage while unloading, due to ship accidents or due to illegal discharge of oily ballast water, could have disastrous results and with the relatively high frequency of stormy weather the emergency procedures can be more difficult to operate. Already spillages off the east coast, in the Firth of Forth and in Sullum Voe, have caused heavy mortality among seabirds. Other accidents will happen.

Although perhaps eclipsed by the oil industry there are many other instances of smaller areas of intertidal flats and shoreline being developed for industry, particularly in the Clyde and the Forth. Often reclamation is tied to refuse disposal projects. Pollution too plays a role, heavy metals are at relatively high concentrations in the major industrial areas and although they have not yet been shown to be detrimental the possibility remains. Most of the other pollution, especially that from distilleries and sewage outfalls seems to have resulted in an improvement rather than a deterioration of the habitats for seaduck. This may be a fortunate result of the large volumes of water into which they are discharged. A useful review of the relationship between discharges and birds is given by Pounder (1976).

Because relatively few estuaries are suitable for waterborne recreation this problem, which is severe in many places in Britain, is not serious except at a few localities. General disturbance is high in some areas particularly around the Clyde and the Forth–Tay area. In many places wildfowling pressure is high enough to cause concern.

### Literature on the birds of Scotland

Scotland has not received the regional treatment that is so evident in England and Wales, in fact the only recent work covered the whole country (Baxter and Rintoul 1953). Regular summaries of all Scottish birds as well as papers on them are provided in 'Scottish Birds' which incorporates the Scottish Bird Report and is published by the Scottish Ornithologists' Club. In recent years regional bird reports have been produced, the main ones being for north-east Scotland by the Aberdeen University Bird Club, for Shetland by the Shetland Bird Club, and for Orkney, Ayrshire and Clyde area and for Perthshire.

*Table 13:1 The most numerous species of wildfowl and waders on Scottish estuaries, 1969–75*

|  | Highest monthly av. |  |  | Highest monthly av. |  |
|---|---|---|---|---|---|
| Wigeon | 23,600 | Nov | Oystercatcher | 48,800 | Nov |
| Eider | 20,000 | Nov | Dunlin | 46,800 | Jan |
| Scaup | 13,600 | Jan | Knot | 39,700 | Jan |
| Common Scoter | 12,000 | Jan | Lapwing | 27,800 | Jan |
| Long-tailed Duck | 10,000 | Jan | Redshank | 26,500 | Oct |
| Mallard | 9,700 | Jan | Purple Sandpiper | 18,000 | Jan |
| Shelduck | 7,200 | Mar | Curlew | 15,400 | Sept |
| Goldeneye | 4,500 | Feb | Turnstone | 14,600 | Jan |
| Teal | 3,200 | Jan | Golden Plover | 13,500 | Jan |
| Pintail | 2,600 | Dec | Bar-tailed Godwit | 8,100 | Jan |

(1) The Pink-footed and Greylag Geese roosting on estuaries are omitted from the wildfowl
(2) Waders include estimates for coastal Purple Sandpipers and Turnstone

*Principal species and migration patterns*

Numerically, waders are the most numerous waterfowl on Scottish estuaries. However, ducks and especially seaduck form the group which is most characteristic. The ten most numerous waders and wildfowl are shown in Table 13:1. Many of the British seaduck are almost entirely confined to Scottish waters; species in this category are Eider, Long-tailed Duck, Velvet Scoter and Scaup, while almost half of the Common Scoter and Goldeneye also occur. Internationally they are less important because of the very large numbers of those species in the Baltic Sea. Wildfowl generally build up to peak numbers by midwinter but species breeding in significant numbers, i.e. Shelduck and Eider, tend to reach the highest levels in the late autumn or early spring. The more northern estuaries may have October or November peaks with birds presumably moving south in the colder winters.

Internationally, waders are more significant with Knot and Curlew each forming about 10% of the European population. Many more Purple Sandpipers and Turnstones have been recorded in Scotland than elsewhere in Europe, but should censuses be made in Norway and Iceland the numbers may not be as significant as they seem at the moment. Although most species reach their peak numbers in winter, many birds having come from moulting grounds on the Wadden Sea and the Wash, the Scottish estuaries see considerable migratory movements in spring and autumn. The position in spring is quite interesting since eastern Scotland seems to pick up proportionately more Dunlin, Ringed Plover and Sanderling than eastern England. At this time on the west coast it is only the North Solway which receives large numbers. Unfortunately one area, the Outer Hebrides, has to be left out of this account because so few counts are available. It lies in an especially favourable position for birds coming from or going to Iceland, Greenland and Canada and might be expected to be of great importance. The Firth of Forth, especially outer bays such as Aberlady Bay, were identified by Andrew (1959) on visual observations and Evans (1968) by radar as a dispersion centre in autumn, with many waders arriving from Scandinavia and subsequently striking out across country for the Clyde, Solway and Morecambe Bay.

### Principal estuaries in Scotland

In Scotland three estuarine complexes stand out as being of major significance, namely the Solway Firth, the Moray Firth and the Firth of Forth. A summary of the international significance and that of other areas is shown in Table 13:2; it must however be remembered that other coastal areas, not counted for the Estuaries Enquiry, are also of importance for seaducks and waders, particularly Shetland, Orkney and the Outer Hebrides. The three main estuaries each support large concentrations of waders while the Solway Firth has great significance for geese and the Moray Firth and Firth of Forth each has large numbers and a great diversity of seaduck. In a national context they are outstanding for their wildfowl populations.

Scotland is noteworthy for concentrations of waders and duck all along the coast, especially the east and outer islands. The fairly small number of estuaries of international importance is because of their relatively small size, all the larger ones qualifying for this status. Perhaps, too, the colder weather in midwinter limits the peak counts, for in Britain generally largest numbers are found in the December to February period. It is worth repeating here that many areas are used by concentrations of migrating birds.

### Dumfries and Galloway Region

*North Solway.* By far the largest area of intertidal flats and saltmarshes in western Scotland is found on the north Solway between the River Sark at Gretna and Mersehead to the west of Southerness Point. A relatively small area of sandy intertidal flats exists on the Scottish side of the estuary in from Annan, but there are the very extensive fine sands of Blackshaw Banks and Carse Sands around the channel of the River Nith. Several rocky scars are found off Powfoot and from Carsethorn to Southerness Point. To the west of Southerness are the sandy Mersehead sands. Further out in the channel of the Solway Firth off Mersehead Sands and Blackshaw Bank are more sand banks, but these have coarse sediment and are little used by feeding waterfowl. The large saltmarsh of Caerlaverock Merse extends from the River Nith east to Lochar Water. There are a few small saltmarshes elsewhere in the estuary. Quite large areas of low farmland are close to the estuary.

In the past, proposals for a road crossing and water storage have been put forward but now the Solway is one of the few major estuaries which is basically free from large scale threats. The Solway is recognised as an important zone for nature conservation with five contiguous Grade 1* NCR sites covering the whole of the north Solway; one of these, Caerlaverock, is a NNR and a Wildfowl Trust reserve. With the exception of the well-drained outer banks most of the intertidal flats form a rich and important feeding area for waders. The ducks are found mainly in Carse Bay and on Caerlaverock, the marshland of the latter also supporting the flocks of Svalbard Barnacle Geese. Pink-footed and Greylag Geese feed on the farmland surrounding the estuary particularly around the Nith, Caerlaverock and Southerness. Roosts of waders develop on the saltmarshes between the Nith and Powfoot, on the upper shore in west Carse Bay, the beach around Southerness and on the fields of the inner estuary up to Annan (see Fig. 13:3). Most of the birds feeding

Table 13:2   Scottish estuaries supporting at least 1% of the western European

| | All Solway | N. Solway | Wigtown Bay | Inner Clyde | Bute | Uists | Dornoch Firth | Cromarty Firth | Beauly Firth |
|---|---|---|---|---|---|---|---|---|---|
| Whooper Swan | – | – | – | – | – | – | – | – | – |
| Pink-footed Goose | 16·6 | 6·6 | 1·1 | – | – | – | – | 1·3 | – |
| Greylag Goose | – | – | – | – | 1·4 | – | – | – | 1·9 |
| Barnacle Goose | S | S | – | – | – | – | – | – | – |
| Shelduck | 1·8 | 1·1 | – | – | – | – | – | – | – |
| Wigeon | – | – | – | – | – | – | – | 1·4 | – |
| Pintail | 4·2 | 4·2 | – | – | – | – | – | – | – |
| Scaup | – | – | – | – | – | – | – | – | – |
| Eider | – | – | – | – | – | – | – | – | – |
| Long-tailed Duck | – | – | – | – | – | – | – | – | – |
| Common Scoter | – | – | – | – | – | – | (1·0) | – | – |
| Velvet Scoter | – | – | – | – | – | – | – | – | – |
| Goldeneye | – | – | – | – | – | – | – | – | – |
| Red-breasted Merganser | – | – | – | – | – | – | – | – | – |
| Goosander | – | – | – | – | – | – | – | – | 1·3 |
| Oystercatcher | 6·9 | 3·8 | – | – | – | – | – | – | – |
| Ringed Plover | 5·5 | 1·6 | – | – | – | 5·2 | – | – | – |
| Golden Plover | * | – | – | – | – | – | – | – | – |
| Lapwing | * | * | – | – | – | – | – | – | – |
| Knot | 4·3 | 1·6 | – | – | – | – | – | – | – |
| Sanderling | 1·0 | – | – | – | – | 5·0 | – | – | – |
| Purple Sandpiper | – | – | – | – | – | – | – | – | – |
| Dunlin | 1·3 | – | – | – | – | – | – | – | – |
| Bar-tailed Godwit | 5·8 | 1·8 | – | – | – | – | – | 1·1 | – |
| Curlew | 3·2 | 1·5 | – | – | – | – | – | – | – |
| Redshank | 3·7 | 2·2 | – | 7·3 | – | – | – | 1·9 | – |
| Turnstone | * | – | – | – | – | * | – | – | – |

S   = all Svalbard population (4,900)
+   = minimum roosting numbers
1·0 = used to be present but after mid 70s to Spey Bay

further up the estuary than this flight to the large saltmarshes of Rockcliffe and Burgh on the Cumbrian side of the estuary.

At the international level of importance, eleven species are significant on the north Solway and a further four are added if the whole estuary is considered, see Table 13:2. The nineteen species of national importance for the north shore and the twenty-six species for the whole of the estuary are presented in Table 13:3. The Solway has an annual average of 172,000 waders, making it numerically the third most important estuary in Britain and Ireland. It is of outstanding importance for the *population of one or more species of waterfowl in winter, 1969–75*

| | Moray Firth | All Moray Firth basin | Spey Bay | Rosehearty/ Fraserburgh | Ythan | Montrose Basin | Tay | Eden | Forth |
|---|---|---|---|---|---|---|---|---|---|
| Whooper Swan | – | 1·1 | – | – | – | – | – | – | – |
| Pink-footed Goose | – | 1·8 | – | – | 1·5 | – | 6·7+ | – | 4·9 |
| Greylag Goose | 1·2 | 3·1 | – | – | 2·2 | – | 2·1+ | – | – |
| Barnacle Goose | – | – | – | – | – | – | – | – | – |
| Shelduck | – | 1·0 | – | – | – | – | – | 1·3 | 1·2 |
| Wigeon | – | 2·9 | – | – | – | – | – | – | – |
| Pintail | – | – | – | – | – | – | – | – | – |
| Scaup | – | – | – | – | – | – | – | – | 8·6 |
| Eider | – | – | – | – | – | – | 1·3 | – | – |
| Long-tailed Duck | 1·1 | 1·2 | – | – | – | – | – | – | – |
| Common Scoter | (1·0) | 1·8 | 1·2 | – | – | – | – | – | – |
| Velvet Scoter | (1·0) | 1·4 | 1·0 | – | – | – | – | – | – |
| Goldeneye | – | – | – | – | – | – | – | – | 1·1 |
| Red-breasted Merganser | – | 1·6 | – | – | – | – | – | – | 1·0 |
| Goosander | – | 1·3 | – | – | – | – | – | – | – |
| Oystercatcher | – | 1·4 | – | – | – | – | – | – | 1·0 |
| Ringed Plover | – | 1·0 | – | – | – | – | – | – | 1·0 |
| Golden Plover | – | – | – | – | – | – | – | – | – |
| Lapwing | – | – | – | – | – | – | – | – | – |
| Knot | – | 1·1 | – | – | – | – | – | – | 3·2 |
| Sanderling | – | – | – | – | – | – | 1·3 | – | – |
| Purple Sandpiper | – | – | – | – | – | – | – | – | * |
| Dunlin | – | – | – | – | – | – | – | – | 1·0 |
| Bar-tailed Godwit | 1·8 | 3·1 | – | – | – | – | 1·2 | 1·8 | 2·0 |
| Curlew | – | – | – | – | – | – | – | – | – |
| Redshank | 1·5 | 4·1 | – | – | – | 2·4 | 1·2 | 1·1 | 2·4 |
| Turnstone | – | – | – | * | – | – | – | – | * |

\* = number exceeds provisional 1%
– = number does not reach 1%
Excludes estimates for some species for Orkney and Shetland, and Gees on Islay

Barnacle Goose holding as it does the whole of the Svalbard breeding population. It also holds almost 20% of the British Pink-footed Goose numbers in late winter and of the Oystercatcher in autumn. Wintering Pintail, Ringed Plover and Bar-tailed Godwit each make up about 10% of the national totals. The North Solway is by far the most important estuarine area for birds in western Scotland. Twenty years ago there used to be a sizeable flock of Scoters off Southerness but these have steadily decreased to leave but a few score. Rather surprisingly, breeding birds are few in number.

Table 13:3   Species of national importance wintering on the north Solway and the whole of the inner Solway, 1969–75

| | North Solway | | All inner Solway | |
| | Highest av. monthly count | % British | Highest av. monthly count | % British |
|---|---|---|---|---|
| Whooper Swan | 120 | 4·0 | 125 | 4·2 |
| Pink-footed Goose | 5,920 | 7·9 | 14,950 | 19·9 |
| Greylag Goose | – | – | 680 | 1·0 |
| Barnacle Goose | 4,900 | (*1) | (*1) | (*1) |
| Shelduck | 1,460 | 2·4 | 2,310 | 3·5 |
| Wigeon | – | – | 2,770 | 1·4 |
| Mallard | – | – | 3,000 | 1·0 |
| Pintail | 2,080 | 10·4 | 2,100 | 10·5 |
| Shoveler | 130 | 2·6 | 150 | 3·0 |
| Scaup | 385 | 1·7 | 740 | 3·3 |
| Goldeneye | – | – | 195 | 1·6 |
| Red-breasted Merganser | – | – | 110 | 1·5 |
| Oystercatcher | 19,750 | 9·9 | 38,800 | 19·4 |
| Ringed Plover | 390 | 3·2 | 1,390 | 11·6 |
| Golden Plover | 5,800 | 2·9 | 13,600 | 6·8 |
| Grey Plover | 130 | 1·3 | 140 | 1·4 |
| Lapwing | 10,300 | 1·0 | 19,600 | 2·0 |
| Knot | 7,800 | 2·6 | 21,400 | 7·1 |
| Sanderling | – | – | 150 | 1·5 |
| Dunlin | 9,700 | 1·8 | 15,600 | 2·7 |
| Black-tailed Godwit | 100 | 2·0 | 160 | 3·2 |
| Bar-tailed Godwit | 1,600 | 3·6 | 5,200 | 11·6 |
| Curlew | 3,000 | 3·0 | 6,400 | 6·4 |
| Redshank | 2,400 | 2·4 | 4,100 | 4·1 |
| Greenshank | – | – | 95 | (*2) |
| Turnstone | 250 | 1·0 | 610 | 2·4 |

(*1)  All of Svalbard breeding population
(*2)  Migrant population
—  Not at 1% national level

*Rough Firth/Auchencairn Bay.* The complex of Rough Firth (the estuary of the River Urr) and Orchardton and Auchencairn Bays lies just to the west of Southerness. The outer part of the estuary is lined by fairly high ground and the intertidal flats are predominantly sandy. The inner estuary is much muddier, with some saltmarsh in the sheltered corners and low farmland behind. Orchardton and Auchencairn Bays form an SSSI, and includes a colony of auks which adds further interest to the estuarine community.

Of the estuarine birds only Wigeon (2,500 in autumn, 1·2% of the British number) is of national significance. Several species are of regional importance:

Curlew (1,700 in autumn), Oystercatcher (1,500), Redshank (800), Shelduck (240) and Greylag Goose (165). The first three of these nearly reach the national level.

*Kirkcudbright Bay.* This smallish estuary is formed by the River Dee. The outer flats are coarse grained but on the muddier inner sections some saltmarsh development has taken place. Like most of the estuaries along this coast it is not threatened by development. It has a low species diversity of estuarine birds and supports only moderate numbers of birds, principally Redshank (500), Golden Plover (550) and Lapwing (2,250).

*Fleet Bay.* Formed by the Water of Fleet this estuary lies at the outer eastern edge of Wigtown Bay. It is relatively sandy with just a small marsh developing where the canalised Water of Fleet enters the sea. Perhaps because of its sandy nature it supports only a small estuarine bird population, but up to 50 Ringed Plovers and 60 Bar-tailed Godwits in winter, and 300 Oystercatchers and Curlew provide additional interest. Wildfowl are few, the most numerous being Wigeon (80) and Shelduck (60).

*Wigtown Bay.* The extensive sands lying on the west of Wigtown Bay comprise the largest estuarine area on the west Scottish coast between the inner Solway and the inner Clyde. The outer banks are very sandy but saltmarshes line the west bank, being particularly well-developed between the two inflowing rivers – the Cree and the Bladnoch. Unfortunately, *Spartina* is beginning to spread here. Low lying mossland is found on the west bank of the Cree. Wigtown Bay is a Grade 2 site in NCR and an SSSI; there is also a LNR proposed for the area. This last measure would be of some significance since unrestricted wildfowling causes serious disturbance and drainage schemes and plans for agricultural reclamation would, if not restricted, be detrimental to the ornithological value of the estuary.

The waders feed over much of the upper and middle shore, with ducks on the upper shore and the merse, and geese on the fields. At high tide most birds concentrate on the larger saltmarshes. In international terms only the Pink-footed Goose is of importance, see Table 13:2; the species of national importance are set out in Table 13:4.

Several other species irregularly reach this level of importance but have a lower average number: Whooper Swan (22), Wigeon (1,250), Golden Plover (1,800) and Redshank (930). At times over a thousand Knot appear for a few weeks. In the 1950s a large flock of moulting Common Scoters was recorded but there are no recent reports.

*Table 13:4   Species of national importance on Wigtown Bay, 1969–75*

|  | Highest av. monthly count | % British |
|---|---|---|
| Pink-footed Goose | 960 | 1·0 |
| Pintail | 200 | 1·0 |
| Oystercatcher | 2,350 | 1·2 |

*Table 13:5   Species of national importance in Luce Bay, 1969–75*

|  | Highest av. monthly count | % British |
|---|---|---|
| Pintail | 200 | 1·0 |
| Common Scoter | 400 | 1·2 |

*Luce Bay.* Piltanton Burn and the Water of Luce flow into the broad expanse of Luce Bay. Some mud and stony scars occur around their mouths but to the west there is a broad sandy beach backed by Torrs Warren, a large sand-dune system considered as a Grade 1 site in NCR. Piltanton Burn is quite heavily polluted by organic matter.

Birds are concentrated around the mouths of the rivers to the east of the Bay and the main roosts are there. Species of national importance are shown in Table 13:5. Common Scoters are difficult to assess since up to 1,300 have been recorded in August/September. They are irregularly recorded and as elsewhere in Britain this irregularity may mean that they sit one or more kilometres offshore and are only seen under ideal conditions. Pintail numbers apparently decreased during the period under review; up to 480 were present until 1973 but only about 150–200 during subsequent seasons. Up to 20 Red-breasted Mergansers are present in autumn but waders are relatively few, although there is a good diversity. There is a tendency for the larger wader numbers to occur in spring and autumn.

*Loch Ryan.* This very sheltered bay has only a relatively small area of rather muddy and rocky intertidal flats. The two main areas of mud are around The Wig in the north-west and between Stranraer and Leffnol Point in the south of the bay; the waders are to be found in these areas. Most diving duck and Wigeon are present along or off the southern shore, although Eiders are scattered in moderate flocks in several areas. Loch Ryan is important for its diverse and abundant duck population. During the period under review the autumn Red-breasted Merganser flock of 130, and up to 300, is of national importance (1·7% and up to 4% of British). Wigeon (1,800), Scaup (90), Goldeneye (100) and Eider (500) all occurred in numbers just below the national level.

The loch used to be an important roost for the many Greylag Geese in the area but this is no longer true. Although quite good numbers of waders are found none are of national importance, the most numerous being 1,000 Golden Plover and 750 Oystercatchers. For additional diversity Loch Ryan has small numbers of both Black-necked and Slavonian Grebes and the occasional rare seaduck.

### Strathclye Region

*Stinchar.* The very small estuary of the River Stinchar at Ballantrae, in particular the shingle beach, is of interest for biological and geological reasons. On such a limited area it is hardly surprising that no species is present in nationally important numbers. However a good variety of birds occurs, with roosting flocks of Lapwing (1,300), Golden Plover (850) and Greylag Geese (175) being the most numerous. A good range of birds breeds here.

*Turnberry/Dipple Bay.* This fairly sandy area of intertidal flats between Lochan Port and Chapeldonan is divided by (outer) rocky and (upper) stony outcrops. The number and variety of estuary birds is quite impressive for such a relatively small area. Only Goldeneye (125, 1% British) is of national importance but 330 Eiders, 140 Shelduck, 30 Red-breasted Mergansers indicate its regional significance for wildfowl, while 550 Oystercatchers, 80 wintering Ringed Plover, 220 Turnstone and 500 Curlew show that waders, too, are well represented. The mergansers and most waders tend to be more numerous in Turnberry Bay but the other sea duck are mainly south of Dipple.

*Maidens Harbour.* Maidenhead Bay is small and has only a limited area of intertidal sand, flanked by the harbour and rocks. Few wildfowl occur but waders are relatively well represented, with Dunlin (425), Turnstone (110) and 30 wintering Ringed Plovers the main species, supplemented by 720 Golden Plovers and 300 Lapwing from adjacent pasture.

*Doonfoot.* Between Ayr Harbour and the Head of Ayr there is a smallish sandy and rocky bay into which the River Doon discharges. Due to the proximity of Ayr and a holiday camp the area is at times quite heavily disturbed, even in winter. With the lack of saltmarsh there are few refuges for waders, and even duck on the sea are sometimes put up. The whole of the coast from Maidenhead Bay to the channel of the River Doon is an SSSI and a Grade 2 NCR site.

This section of the coast has a good diversity of waterfowl, 20 species of wildfowl and 22 of waders being recorded during the counts. No species reaches a level of national importance although Goldeneye (85), Mallard (360), Curlew (230) and Ringed Plover (40 in winter) are of regional interest. Additional interest is created by the 10,000+ gull roost which includes a few 'white' gulls.

*Ayr/Prestwick.* This small section of the coast is developed but the rocks, sand and outfalls are quite productive for birds. No species is of national importance but 500 Eider and 100 Goldeneye are not far below, and 150 Turnstone, 65 wintering Ringed Plover, 30 Purple Sandpiper and 60 Knot are of regional interest.

*Troon South Bay.* Apart from Troon this sandy beach is backed by golf courses set in sand dunes. Offshore is the important roost area of Meikle Craigs. There can be severe disturbance from walkers and holidaymakers at times, but is least serious in winter. The southern part of the bay is an SSSI. The most numerous species is the Curlew (1,250 in autumn) which reaches the 1% British level of importance. Other species of regional significance are Eiders (300 in autumn), Red-breasted Merganser (60 in spring), Purple Sandpiper (75) and Ringed Plover (50 in winter). The gull roost reaches 25,000 and includes several 'white' gulls.

*Troon North Bay.* Similar in nature to the South Bay, except that Stinking Rocks are a less important feature than Meikle Craigs; the North Bay is bedevilled by disturbance at any fine weekend. On high tides in winter, if permitted to by disturbance, the waders will roost on the surrounding golf courses. Species of regional significance are Knot (240), Dunlin (500), Oystercatcher (310) and Eider (150).

*Irvine Bay*. This is the only real estuary with mud flats on the Ayr coast and is formed by the Irvine and Garnock Rivers. There is a saltmarsh projecting into the estuary between the river mouths. Only a narrow channel provides the exit to the sea. Some reclamation for possible industrial development is being undertaken and because the area is outside normal planning control this represents a real threat. At times the estuary is disturbed by walkers, bait diggers and canoeists but perhaps mostly by aircraft. Whooper Swans are present in nationally important numbers (40), while regionally interesting species are Eider (330), Wigeon (180), Golden Plover (1,850), Lapwing (2,000), Redshank (500) and Knot (280).

*Table 13:6   Species of national importance on the coast between Ardrossan and Seamill, 1969–75*

|  | Highest av. monthly count | % British |
|---|---|---|
| Ringed Plover | 185 | 1·5 |
| Turnstone | 350 | 1·4 |

*Ardrossan/Ardneil Bay*. This five mile section of the coast is again a mixture of sand, stones and rocky outcrops. The largest area of flats is in North Bay at Ardrossan. The area is of some importance for waders with two species of national significance, see Table 13:6. The 980 Oystercatchers, 400 Curlew, 320 Redshank, 60 Purple Sandpipers, 300 Eider and 30 Red-breasted Merganser are of some regional interest. Many of the waders, especially Curlew roost on Horse Island and waste ground around Ardrossan dock attracts the smaller waders.

*Hunterston Sands*. Known also as Fairlie Flats this is the largest area of intertidal sand on the outer Clyde. There are some areas of stone and muddy parts too. The southern shore is now becoming increasingly industrialised by an iron-ore terminal and power station complex; this involves some intertidal reclamation. Before these developments started, Hunterston Sands was considered the best area for waders and wildfowl in the region; it still has regional significance although no species is of national importance. The main species present are Wigeon (350), Oystercatcher (680), Curlew (370), Bar-tailed Godwit (80) and Dunlin (710).

*Inner Clyde*. At first sight the Inner Clyde might seem an unlikely estuary to hold large numbers of birds. As covered in this enquiry it encompasses the Clyde from Clydebank to Inverkip, all of Gare Loch, east and inner Loch Long and from Ardentinny to Toward Point, including Holy Loch. For much of the shoreline there is only a very narrow strip of intertidal mud and rock but the mud flats of the inner section of the Clyde and of Holy Loch support many birds. A large amount of organic material enters the estuary from the Clyde and at Rhu. Because there is already much urban and industrial development on and around the estuary the inner Clyde faces many potentially serious problems. For example, plans for a major natural gas plant have been put forward for the Erskine–Langbank section, which as will be shown later is of major importance for birds. Other developments, some

*Table 13:7   Species of national importance on the Clyde, 1969–75*

|  | *Highest av. monthly count* | *% British* |
|---|---|---|
| Shelduck | 950 | 1·6 |
| Eider | 2,500 | 4·2 |
| Goldeneye | 380 | 3·0 |
| Red-breasted Merganser | 120 | 1·6 |
| Oystercatcher | 3,500 | 1·7 |
| Redshank | 8,100 | 8·1 |

involving reclamation, are possible elsewhere. Recreation too is having an impact with some marina development, as at Rhu, and uncontrolled wildfowling poses a number of disturbance problems at times. Four SSSIs are included in the estuary, at Ardmore and Rhu Points, Dumbarton Rock and the flats between Erskine and Langbank.

A substantial amount of work has been carried out on birds of the Inner Clyde (e.g. Gibson 1973, Halliday 1978, Smythe et al 1974) so that numbers and distribution are fairly well known. The most important sections are Erskine to Woodhall, where the majority of the waders feed and roost together with many dabbling and diving duck, and on the north shore all sections from Milton to Rhu support significant numbers of duck (Shelduck on the inner parts but diving duck further towards Rhu), and Oystercatcher and Redshank. Holy Loch, too, has good numbers of Oystercatcher and dabbling duck. Surprisingly only one species, Redshank, is of international importance but for this the Clyde is a major site. Table 13:7 presents the national status of birds in the Clyde. Regionally, Scaup with 140 is of importance, making the Clyde a very interesting site for diving duck. Also of regional interest are 130 Pintail, 210 Turnstone, 700 Curlew, 4,100 Dunlin and 8 wintering Greenshank. At least 35,000 gulls roost on the estuary, the bulk of them Black-headed Gulls.

*Island of Bute coast.* During these counts the whole of the coast between Ettrick Bay and Kilchatten Bay was counted, the main areas of intertidal sand, mud and rocks being Ettrick Bay, St Ninian Bay, Scalpsie Bay and Kilchatten Bay. Some areas of wet pasture found near each of these together support an interesting selection of birds. Four species are of national significance, see Table 13:8.

*Table 13:8   Species of national importance on the South Bute coast, 1969–73*

|  | *Highest av. monthly count* | *% British* |
|---|---|---|
| Greylag Goose | 1,350 | 2·0 |
| Red-breasted Merganser | 170 | 2·0 |
| Ringed Plover | 140 | 1·0 |
| Curlew | 1,100 | 1·1 |

Additionally, 380 Eider, 1,150 Wigeon, 600 Mallard, 1,050 Oystercatcher and 140 Turnstone are of regional significance. To some extent birds apparently move between the sites, so all main bays support nationally important numbers of Greylag Geese at times. These and many of the Curlew feed inland. Otherwise birds are fairly evenly shared between the sites.

*Isle of Arran coast.* Six sections of the coast of the Isle of Arran were counted. The two main bays being Lamlash and Whiting, but also Kildonan and Clecteadh on the south coast and Sannox and Catacol Bays in the north. The four southern sites had similar bird numbers; in total the areas counted included about 180 Oystercatcher, 85 Ringed Plover and Turnstone and 110 Curlew, 70 Wigeon and 50 Red-breasted Merganser, of which the last and Ringed Plover are of regional interest.

*Loch Riddon.* The head of this sea loch immediately north of Bute has quite an extensive area of mud, sand and rock. As a result it supports numbers of estuary birds which are interesting in a regional context. The most significant being 60 Red-breasted Mergansers in autumn, 170 Wigeon, 120 Teal, 100 Eider, 350 Oystercatchers and 140 Curlew. The diversity of waders is low but quite reasonable.

*Loch Crinan.* This western sea loch backed by low moorland supports an interesting selection of wildfowl, including 300 Greylag Geese, 65 Red-breasted Mergansers in autumn, 280 Wigeon and 120 Mallard. Wader numbers are, however, low being principally Curlew (120) and Oystercatcher (90).

*Other sea lochs.* Unfortunately few counts have been made at other sites but fragmentary data indicates Loch Gilp may be of some interest with 550 Oystercatcher and 255 Wigeon in October, when Loch Sween had 115 Wigeon and 55 Whooper Swans, and Loch Coalisport had 100 Oystercatcher. All had 20–30 Red-breasted Mergansers.

*Islay.* The winter birdwatching mecca of Islay has been well counted for geese and wildfowl but waders are still relatively poorly known. Birds are mainly found on the two main bays, Loch Indaal and Loch Gruinart. The geese tend to roost on the intertidal flats. In total these two areas support internationally important numbers of Barnacle Geese (14,000, about half of the Greenland population) and White-fronted Geese (being 52% and 31% of the respective Greenland populations). They also have nationally important numbers of Scaup (up to 600, 2·7% British), Red-breasted Merganser (140, 1·9% British) and Curlew (1,000, 1% British). Many other species are of regional interest with perhaps the 420 Bar-tailed Godwit, 500 Teal, 800 Wigeon, 160 Shelduck and good numbers of Slavonian Grebes and Great Northern Divers standing out.

### Western Isles Island area

Although not estuarine in nature the extensive intertidal flats and storm beaches around South and North Uist and Benbecula appear to play an important role in wader distribution in Britain. While outer beaches are sandy only a very few of the more sheltered areas become more silty. Very few counts have been made here, the only widespread ones were in August/September 1973 (Summers and Buxton 1974) and February 1975 (Hammond 1975). From these and other partial counts at least

Table 13:9    *Numbers of principal species of waders estimated on North and South Uist and Benbecula*

|  | Counted Aug/Sept 1973 | Est. Feb 1975 |
|---|---|---|
| Oystercatcher | 987 | 870 |
| Ringed Plover | 1,566* | 1,300* |
| Grey Plover | – | 4 |
| Knot | 45 | 200 |
| Sanderling | 399* | 1,300* |
| Purple Sandpiper | – | 160[†] |
| Dunlin | 385 | 2,000 |
| Bar-tailed Godwit | 648* | 1,350* |
| Curlew | 338 | 450 |
| Redshank | 734 | 750 |
| Greenshank | – | 15+ |
| Turnstone | 1,057* | 900* |

\* Of national importance
† Many hundreds, perhaps 1,000+ are present on spring migration

three species of wader are of international importance in this section of the Outer Isles, see Table 13:2. Table 13:2 shows the numbers of the principal species noted by the above authors.

The area is of major importance as a migration site for north-western breeding birds, and the flats also support many birds in winter. The waters around the Uists and in the Sound of Harris also carry large numbers of divers; in February 1975 over 750 were seen. They were probably almost all Great Northern Divers and the total probably exceeds 1,000.

Very few other parts of this region have been counted in detail, indeed on Lewis and Harris there are only two largish areas of intertidal flats, at Broad Bay and Traigh Luskentyre. The latter has up to 100 Common Scoter, 180 Wigeon, 360 Oystercatcher, 120 Ringed Plover and 120 Dunlin, the majority of birds occurring in autumn. Broad Bay has up to 250 Long-tailed Ducks, 100 Scoter but relatively few waders.

*Orkney Islands area*

Although quite a lot of survey work has been carried out in the Orkney Islands, estimates can only be made of some of the duck numbers. These give a general level of 6,000 Long-tailed Duck and Eider and 400 Velvet Scoter. Probably the most important seaduck site in Scapa Flow, where Lea (1975) found 2,400 Long-tailed Duck, 2,000 Eider, about 300 Goldeneye, 300+ Red-breasted Merganser, 200 Great Northern Divers and 60 Slavonian Grebe, all of which are nationally important. There are several other areas, such as around Raasay, Wyre, Westray and Papa Westray, and north of Kirkwall, which are almost certainly of importance. Deer Sound is one of the main wader areas in Orkney; counts have shown 3,000 Curlew (1·5% of the European and 3% British), 75 Ringed Plover, 250 Bar-tailed

Godwit, 450 Redshank and 400 Oystercatcher in winter. There may be similar numbers of most of these species in Scapa Flow and indeed elsewhere if detailed counts were available. There are estimated to be about 500 Great Northern Diver and 100 Slavonian Grebe wintering on the sea.

*Table 13:10   Estimates\* of the numbers of waders wintering in Shetland*

| Oystercatcher | <200 | Jack Snipe | <50 |
|---|---|---|---|
| Ringed Plover | 400 | Snipe | 4,000 |
| Golden Plover | <500 | Bar-tailed Godwit | <40 |
| Lapwing | 200 | Curlew | 3,000 |
| Knot | <40 | Redshank | 2,000 |
| Purple Sandpiper | 3,500 | Turnstone | 7,500 |
| Dunlin | <50 | | |

\* Mid-point of ranges given

### Shetland Islands area

As in Orkney, few detailed counts of the waders and wildfowl on intertidal bays and rocky coasts were sent in to the 'Estuaries Enquiry'. However, an estimate (see Table 13:10) has been made by members of the Shetland Bird Club (P. Kinnear in litt.) of the normal wintering numbers of waders in Shetland. The coast is impossible to cover adequately and estimates are clearly provisional.

Estimates for some other species include 2,000 Long-tailed Duck, 10,000 Eider, 400 Great Northern Diver, 30 Velvet Scoter, 250 Red-breasted Merganser and 100 Slavonian Grebe. The area is, therefore, of considerable national and international importance for many waders and ducks.

### Highland Region

*Loch Linnhe.* The area counted was from Annat to Fort William. Here there are fair sized intertidal flats where the River Lochy enters the Loch. It is surrounded by towns. One species of national significance, Red-breasted Merganser, reaches 155 (2·1% British) in autumn. Of regional interest are 55 Goldeneye, 110 Eider and 140 Oystercatcher.

*Other sea lochs.* On the west and north-west coast of the Highland Region there are many sea lochs with intertidal flats at their heads. In general, sediments are coarse and, probably as a result, bird numbers are relatively low, especially in winter. The few available counts show that Loch Carron, Loch Torridon, the Kyle of Durness, Balnakeil Bay and Kyle of Tongue support a few waders, with Oystercatcher predominating. On the west coast numbers seem to be in the region of 100–400 waders but on the large northern Lochs much smaller numbers are present, rarely reaching 100 birds in winter.

*Caithness coast.* On the north-east corner of Scotland there are a number of small sandy bays with rocky coastline in between. Of these, Dunnet Bay, Sinclair's Bay,

Gills Bay and Sandside Bay each have 100–300 waders with Oystercatcher predominating followed by Redshank and Turnstone. The rocky sections have smaller numbers, mainly Turnstone. Relatively few wildfowl are present, Eider, Goldeneye and Mallard being dominant but usually only 30–80 in total, although Gills Bay has over 100 duck.

### Moray Firth Basin

This large complex of intertidal flats, rocky coastline and shallow inshore waters is of considerable importance for waterfowl. The individual sections will be considered separately later, but a general comment on the whole area is necessary. The site stretches from Brora in the north to Burghead in the south-east. This is particularly so because of the potential and actual problems posed by the oil and petro-chemical industry. Various sites involving intertidal reclamation have already been developed but perhaps of even greater potential danger is the discovery of oil fields fairly close to the shore of the outer Moray Firth. Their exploitation could seriously threaten what is Britain's most important seaduck area, unless very careful thought is given to their design and operating procedures. A most valuable and detailed summary of sites of conservation importance within the Moray Firth area has been published by the Nature Conservancy Council (1978).

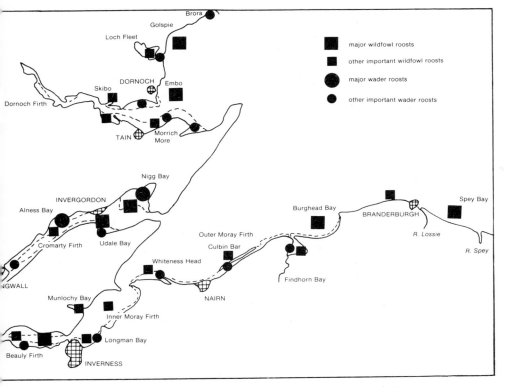

Fig. 13:1 Main concentrations of waders and wildfowl in the Moray Firth Basin.

*Table 13:11   Species of national and international importance on the Moray Firth basin, 1969–75*

|  | Highest av. monthly count | % British | % W. European |
|---|---|---|---|
| Mute Swan | 350 | 1·9 | – |
| Whooper Swan | 185 | 6·2 | 1·1 |
| Pink-footed Goose | 1,660 | 2·2 | 1·8 |
| Grey-lag Goose | 3,020 | 4·6 | 3·1 |
| Shelduck | 1,300 | 2·2 | 1·0 |
| Wigeon | 11,800 | 5·9 | 2·9 |
| Teal | 1,430 | 1·9 | – |
| Pintail | 200 | 1·0 | – |
| Eider | 2,600 | 4·3 | – |
| Long-tailed Duck | 2,200 (6,200)* | 22·0 (62·0) | – (1·2) |
| Common Scoter | 4,200 (8,100)* | 12·0 (23·1) | – (1·8) |
| Velvet Scoter | 560 (2,500)* | 16·0 (71·4) | – (1·4) |
| Goldeneye | 920 | 7·4 | – |
| Red-breasted Merganser | 650 | 8·7 | 1·6 |
| Goosander | 650 | 16·3 | 1·3 |
| Oystercatcher | 8,000 | 4·0 | 1·4 |
| Ringed Plover | 250 | 2·1 | 1·0 |
| Knot | 5,500 | 1·8 | 1·1 |
| Dunlin | 6,000 | 1·1 | – |
| Bar-tailed Godwit | 2,800 | 6·2 | 3·1 |
| Curlew | 1,800 | 1·8 | – |
| Redshank | 4,500 | 4·5 | 4·1 |
| Turnstone | 280 | 1·1 | – |

* From special survey (Mudge 1978); his figures are incorporated into national and international estimates

The bird population of the Moray Firth Basin is summarised in Table 13:11 and illustrated in Fig. 13:3. The immense value to wildfowl populations is clear; fifteen species being of national significance, two-thirds of them of international importance. Additional diversity to the seaduck present include 135 Scaup and regular rare species such as King Eider and Surf Scoter. There is some interchange with seaduck wintering in Spey Bay to the east of Lossiemouth. There is a tendency for the Moray Firth Basin to be not only an important wintering area but also a staging post on migration. The grey geese are important in spring and dabbling duck are slightly more numerous in late autumn and early winter.

*Brora/Golspie.* The waters for about a kilometre offshore are ornithologically rich in seaduck. There is a distinct seasonality in the birds' presence, with autumn and spring concentrations but fewer, though still many, in midwinter. Autumn birds include Eider and Red-breasted Merganser flocks, with Long-tailed Duck slightly later; this last species occurs frequently in May when the Loch Fleet flock is at its

*Table 13:12    Species of national importance on the Brora–Golspie coast, 1969–75*

|  | Highest av. monthly count | % British |
|---|---|---|
| Eider | 2,500 | 4·2 |
| Red-breasted Merganser | 246 | 3·3 |

peak. The beach is interesting but no species of wader reaches the national level of importance, though of interest are the 240 Knot, 45 Ringed Plover and a small but regular winter flock of 12 Sanderling. The species of national importance are shown in Table 13:2. The coast to the north of Brora is an SSSI.

*Loch Fleet.* This very interesting bay surrounded by woodland and separated from the sea by sand dunes is classed as a Grade I site in *NCR*. The intertidal flats support quite a rich bird fauna with three species of national importance (Table 13:13) and several others of regional significance. These include 800 Wigeon, 200 Common Scoter, 130 Shelduck, 970 Oystercatcher, 200 Curlew and 120 Knot. In spring spectacular numbers of Long-tailed Duck assemble in the channel near Littleferry, the average May count is 1,350.

*Table 13:13    Species of national significance on Loch Fleet, 1972–75*

|  | Highest av. monthly count | % British |
|---|---|---|
| Eider | 600 | 1·0 |
| Long-tailed Duck | 1,350 | 13·5 |
| Red-breasted Merganser | 175 | 2·3 |

*Dornoch Firth.* This, the most northerly of the large Scottish Firths, must rank among the more attractive estuaries in Britain. From the Kyle of Sutherland above Bonar Bridge, down to the Skibo estuary, is a fairly narrow, steep-sided and well-wooded estuary, with variably fine sediment. At Skibo, in the north, is a small but interesting inlet with adjacent freshwater. Opposite, on the south, from Edderton Sands out to Portmahomack and in the north from Skibo to Dornoch are large sandy flats, some areas of stony scars are also present. Above the high water mark the outer estuary is lined by sand dunes, a particularly interesting area being Morrich More. The sea at its mouth is relatively shallow with the five fathom mark running 3–5 km offshore. Two SSSIs cover much of the intertidal area, these are on the Lower Dornoch Firth (a Grade 2 *NCR* site) and Morrich More (a Grade 1* site).

Long-tailed Duck and Common Scoter at times are recorded in internationally important numbers, but like most seaduck are only irregularly seen. Flocks of these species seen off Embo, Dornoch and Portmahomack have reached 7,000 and 8,000 respectively. Species of national importance are shown in Table 13:14, which

*Table 13:14   Species of national significance on the Dornoch Firth, 1969–75*

|  | Highest av. monthly count | % British |
|---|---|---|
| Whooper Swan | 45 | 1·5 |
| Wigeon | 2,000 | 1·0 |
| Long-tailed Duck | 200 | 2·0 |
| Common Scoter | 680 | 1·9 |
| Velvet Scoter | 125 | 3·6 |
| Red-breasted Merganser | 85 | 1·1 |

includes average counts of the above species and may, therefore, involve some underestimates. 170 Scaup, 680 Teal and 180 Shelduck are the other duck which are significant at the regional level. Waders are less numerous but there is a much greater diversity than further north, with 17 species noted. The main species of regional interest are 500 Oystercatcher and 200–300 Bar-tailed Godwit, Curlew, Redshank and Dunlin as well as 170 Knot. The majority of waders are on Dornoch, Edderton and Whiteness Sands, while Edderton and Tain Sands hold most of the Scaup (though these have decreased from 300+ in the later 1960s), and Wigeon. The Skibo estuary has most of the Whooper Swans and Teal but the main wildfowl of importance are on the sea between Embo and Portmahomack. Morrich More is also an important breeding area.

*Cromarty Firth.* The narrow entrance to the Cromarty Firth is guarded by two large hills; once in the Firth it opens out into an outer section with two major bays. These are Nigg Bay, the largest area of flats in the Moray Firth Basin, and Udale Bay. The flats are basically sandy with a little silt on the upper shore and very narrow saltmarsh development; on the former the marsh was virtually destroyed by the oil terminal. The inner Firth is lined with a much narrower zone of shingle, sand and

*Table 13:15   Species of national importance on the Cromarty Firth, 1969–75*

|  | Highest av. monthly count | % British |
|---|---|---|
| Mute Swan | 270 | 1·5 |
| Whooper Swan | 140 | 4·7 |
| Pink-footed Goose | 1,200 | 1·6 |
| Wigeon | 5,600 | 2·8 |
| Goldeneye | 520 | 4·2 |
| Red-breasted Merganser | 320 | 4·3 |
| Oystercatcher | 2,750 | 1·4 |
| Ringed Plover | 145 | 1·2 |
| Bar-tailed Godwit | 1,030 | 2·3 |
| Curlew | 1,140 | 1·1 |
| Redshank | 2,120 | 2·1 |

silt, widening at Dalmore, Alness Bay and at the head of the Firth. At this last area the Conon Islands provide an additional interesting habitat. The Cromarty Firth has seen quite a considerable amount of industrial development, mainly concentrated at Invergordon where there is an aluminium smelter. In recent years parts of Nigg Bay have been reclaimed for an oil rig construction yard and further reclamation is being undertaken for oil storage facilities. Planning permission exists for an oil refinery there, and more intertidal areas are scheduled for industrial expansion. There is strong pressure for further oil-related developments in the Cromarty Firth, due mainly to its sheltered position combined with deep water. Small scale industry such as distilleries are also scattered on the shore. Two SSSIs are sited within the Firth, one covering most of the intertidal area (also a Grade 1* site in NCR), and the other the Conon Islands.

The five species of international importance have been detailed in Table 13:2, the national status is shown in Table 13:15. Of these, Wigeon is the most enigmatic, at times over 10,000 have occurred on the Cromarty Firth, mainly in Nigg Bay. Most species have a midwinter peak but there is a strong Pink-footed Goose migration through the region in March and April, the birds roosting on Nigg Bay. Several other species occur in regionally significant numbers, especially Greylag Goose, which is present all year but has a peak of 500 in the spring, Shelduck 500, Teal 300, Knot 2,000 and Dunlin 2,600; about four Greenshank winter. Nigg Bay is the most important area for dabbling ducks and waders, but Udale, Alness and Dingwall Bays are all significant. The Goldeneye and swans are concentrated around the distillery outfalls.

*Table 13:16  Species of national importance on the Beauly Firth, 1969–75*

|  | *Highest av. monthly count* | *% British* |
|---|---|---|
| Greylag Goose | 1,900 | 2·9 |
| Canada Goose | 550 | 2·7 |
| Goldeneye | 125 | 1·0 |
| Red-breasted Merganser | 120 | 1·6 |
| Goosander | 650 | 16·3 |

*Beauly Firth.* Sited at the head of the Moray Firth this very enclosed Firth has an extensive area of sand and mud flats lined by narrow saltmarsh. It is an SSSI. It has a fascinating and unique bird population, having the only large concentration of Goosander in Britain, and being the moulting ground for Canada Geese from Yorkshire. This latter species has steadily increased over recent years. The internationally important species, Greylag Goose and Goosander, have been presented in Table 13:2; the national status is shown in Table 13:16. The Goosander and merganser flock is somewhat variable, mostly it sits well out in the estuary and follows the sprat shoals. Quite frequently over 1,000 birds are seen and it may be that this is closer to the real population. Greylag Geese, although present all winter, build up in April, just after a small passage of Pink-footed Geese has gone through. Other species of regional interest are Wigeon (1,300), Teal (340) and Bar-tailed Godwit (260). In general, however, wader numbers are fairly low.

### Highland/Grampian Region

*Moray Firth.* This interesting area can be divided into two sections, an inner one including Munlochy, Longman and Ardersier Bays, and an outer part, the coastal beach area from Fort George to Burghead. The inner Firth has fairly sandy flats with areas of shingle but in Longman and Munlochy Bays some saltmarsh has developed. The outer Firth is a sandy beach which widens at Whiteness Head and Nairn/Culbin Bar and the enclosed estuary of Findhorn Bay. Behind the beach are sand dunes which, at Whiteness Head, form a long spit, while further east they form a series of isolated bars running parallel to the coast. In sheltered areas saltmarsh has developed. The five fathom line runs fairly close to the shore but extends 1½–3 km off Findhorn and in Burghead Bay. There is an oil platform yard at Whiteness and, with finds of inshore oil nearby, the potential for much more onshore development is an ever present threat. Otherwise, however, the Moray Firth is relatively unspoilt, the main exception being the reclamation, with refuse, of the saltmarsh and flats in

*Table 13:17   Species of national importance on the Moray Firth, 1969–75*

|  | Highest av. monthly count | % British |
|---|---|---|
| Greylag Goose | 1,180 | 1·8 |
| Wigeon | 2,530 | 1·3 |
| Long-tailed Duck | 2,030 (5,630)* | 20·3 (56·3) |
| Common Scoter | 3,500 | 10·0 |
| Velvet Scoter | 560 | 16·0 |
| Goldeneye | 350 | 2·8 |
| Red-breasted Merganser | 140 | 1·9 |
| Oystercatcher | 3,700 | 1·8 |
| Knot | 3,700 | 1·2 |
| Bar-tailed Godwit | 1,610 | 3·6 |
| Redshank | 1,670 | 1·7 |

* Based on Mudge and Allen (1980)

Longman Bay. SSSIs have been notified for Munlochy Bay, Whiteness Head and Culbin–Findhorn Bay.

A high diversity of birds was recorded on the Moray Firth including 25 species of waders and 27 of wildfowl. The problems of recording seaduck has already been mentioned and for this reason no regular, internationally important counts of Long-tailed Duck and Common and Velvet Scoter were obtained during the 'Estuaries Enquiry'. Occasional large numbers off Culbin, Findhorn and Burghead Bay indicated their importance; Mudge and Allen (1980) showed that Long-tailed Duck from the whole of the Moray Firth and Spey Bay gathered in internationally important numbers to roost in Burghead Bay. All sections of the Firth played a significant role for the bird populations, although Whiteness was less extensively used by waders after the rig yard's construction. For waders, Longman Bay, Whiteness, Culbin Bar and Findhorn Bay are the most important areas. The national status of the Moray Firth for birds is shown in Table 13:17. It is clearly outstanding for seaduck. Additional species of regional interest are 450 Pink-footed Geese on spring migration, 470 Shelduck, 100 Scaup and Pintail, and 3,450 Dunlin. Divers are not well counted but minimum totals of 140+ Red-throated, 65+ Great Northern and 35+ Black-throated Divers occur.

*Grampian Region*

*Spey Bay.* Between Branderburgh and Portknockie this broad sweeping bay is of considerable interest for its birds. The beach is narrow, mainly shingle and sand, but with rich rock and shingle beaches from Portgordon eastwards. The Rivers Lossie and Spey discharge into the Bay but neither has large intertidal areas at their mouths.

*Table 13:18    Species of national importance in Spey Bay, 1970–78*

|  | Average number | % British |
|---|---|---|
| Long-tailed Duck | 1,560 | 15·6 |
| Common Scoter | 5,240 | 15·0 |
| Velvet Scoter | 1,820 | 52·0 |
| Purple Sandpiper | 330 | 1·8 |
| Turnstone | 300 | 1·2 |

The main interests on the shore are the mouth of the Lossie where 400 waders are found, mostly Dunlin (200), Oystercatcher (100) and Ringed Plover (50), and the rocky coast between Portgordon and Cullen Bay. Here, there are 330 Purple Sandpipers and 300+ Turnstone, Golden Plover, Knot, Dunlin and Curlew. However, Spey Bay's importance lies in its shallow water with a seaduck flock. This was first counted in 1977–78 (Mudge and Allen 1980) when there were nationally important numbers of three species, see Table 13:18, the two of international importance are shown in Table 13:2. Additionally of interest are 300 Eider and 20 Scaup; national rarities occurred including 2 King Eider and up to 10 Surf Scoter. It seems probable that the seaduck have recently increased, having been mainly, hitherto, in the Moray Firth; this emphasises the importance of large areas of shallow water for these species.

*Coast: Cullen Bay–Cruden Bay.* This long rocky coast with occasional sandy bays and small estuaries supports a wealth of bird life. The wildfowl have been counted by the Aberdeen University Bird Club but only one full wader census has been made. Summers et al (1975) found that the total numbers wintering included 1,230 Oystercatcher, 125 Ringed Plover, 1,230 Knot, 1,510 Purple Sandpiper, 700 Dunlin, 400 Curlew, 1,350 Redshank and 2,550 Turnstone. Sites counted more regularly were the *Deveron Estuary*, where there were 100–200 each of Turnstone, Oyster-catcher and Purple Sandpiper. The *Fraserburgh–Rosehearty* coast, which revealed some dramatic numbers of birds, including three species of national importance

*Table 13:19    Species of national importance between Rosehearty and Fraserburgh, 1975–78*

|  | Average count | % British |
|---|---|---|
| Eider | 1,250 | 2·1 |
| Purple Sandpiper | 300 | 1·7 |
| Turnstone | 900 | 3·6 |

(Table 13:19) one of which was of international significance. With 600 Curlew, 80 Goldeneye and 400 Dunlin the section is of much interest.

The *Philorth estuary* is a small estuary to the east of Fraserburgh. The main species are 100 Curlew, 60 Redshank and 40 Eider. Seaduck and small flocks of waders are scattered along the coast.

*Ythan.* Due to the long-term studies by the University of Aberdeen's Culterty Field Station, the Ythan is probably the best documented estuary in Britain. It is small but has three separate sections. The inner one above the bridge is relatively muddy, the middle one has much more sand and shingle while at its mouth it is sandy. The large dune system of the Sands of Forvie, an NNR, lies between the estuary and the sea. The intertidal area is an SSSI.

Although the Ythan carries an excellent range of species, its size precludes it from being of major importance for estuarine birds. The two species of international

*Table 13:20    Species of national importance on the Ythan Estuary, 1969–75*

|  | Highest av. monthly count | % British |
|---|---|---|
| Whooper Swan | 140 | 4·7 |
| Pink-footed Goose | 1,360 | 1·8 |
| Greylag Goose | 2,160 | 3·3 |
| Eider | 1,400 | 2·3 |

importance, Greylag Goose and Pink-footed Goose, both use the estuary as a roost; and even so they roost mainly on the nearby Meikle Loch. The species of national importance are shown in Table 13:20. Other species of interest are Redshank (810), Golden Plover (1,800), Goldeneye (70) and Long-tailed Duck (50). The Sands of Forvie supports an excellent breeding community.

*Coast: Ythan–North Esk.* Between the *Ythan estuary* and *Aberdeen* there is a sandy beach backed by dunes. About 60 Sanderling winter here but offshore there are about 450 Common Scoter, 35 Velvet Scoter and 600 Eider, each forming about 1% of the British population. Entering the North Sea at Aberdeen are two rivers, the *Don* and the *Dee*, where small numbers of estuarine waders are found; each includes 20–50 of both Oystercatcher and Redshank. They are, however, of more importance for their rocky coast species such as Turnstone, Purple Sandpiper and seaduck. Each supports about 50 Goldeneye, but the Don may occasionally have as many as 4,000 Eider, and the more rocky Dee, the south shore of which extends to Girdle Ness, has fewer species and more rocky shore waders. It also is notable for its rarer gulls.

The coast from *Girdle Ness to St Cyrus* is again rocky and was censused by Summers et al (1975). They found 620 Oystercatcher, 590 Purple Sandpiper, 100 Dunlin, 180 Curlew, 620 Redshank and 1,030 Turnstone, the second and sixth of which are in, at least, nationally important numbers.

St Cyrus and its sand and shingle spits lies at the mouth of the *North Esk*. Unfortunately only autumn and spring counts are available but they indicate the potential of the estuary for wildfowl. The few counts revealed 380 Red-breasted Merganser in autumn and 400 in May (5·1% and 5·3% respectively of the British population); Goosander were also common in spring with 150 recorded (3·7% British), and up to 300 Eider also occur. The area also supports an interesting breeding community and is a Grade 1* site in *NCR* as well as being an NNR.

*Tayside Region*

*Montrose Basin.* This very enclosed smallish estuary provides a wide range of habitats. The intertidal flats grade from sand to mud and shingle; there is a saltmarsh on its inner edge and freshwater grazing fields are nearby. The area is a Grade 2 site in *NCR* and an SSSI; part is owned by the Scottish Wildlife Trust and there is a proposed LNR. At times, however, shooting pressure is heavy. It has a rich bird community, both in species and numbers, although only the Redshank reaches the level of international importance (Table 13:2). Table 13:21 presents the national

*Table 13:21   Species of national importance on Montrose Basin, 1969–75*

|  | Highest av. monthly count | % British |
|---|---|---|
| Mute Swan | 180 | 1·0 |
| Wigeon | 3,500 | 1·7 |
| Redshank | 2,670 | 2·7 |
| Knot | 4,040 | 1·3 |

status of its estuarine birds. Several other species almost reach national importance and are of regional significance. These are Pink-footed Goose (500), Greylag Goose (360), Shelduck (360), Eider (510) and Oystercatcher (1,800).

*Coast: Montrose to Carnoustie.* This is another area of soft rocky coast with a quite broad, flatish rocky platform. Summers et al (1975) surveyed it in winter 1971–72. The main species of shore wader present were Oystercatcher (830), Knot (2,730), Purple Sandpiper (325), Dunlin (275), Curlew (350), Redshank (360) and Turnstone (660).

### Tayside Region/Fife Region

*Firth of Tay.* Tentsmuir Point and Buddon Ness, two large sand dune systems guard the entrance to this large Firth. Sand banks predominate around the mouth of the estuary with there being steady accretion on Tentsmuir. Some mussel beds and stony scars occur here, too. In from Dundee and Tayport the nature of the estuary changes. It widens and large relatively muddy flats appear on the northern shore; the upper shore being lined by a dense *Phragmites* bed. The southern shore is steep sided and has only a very narrow belt of mud and shingle. The inner estuary between Perth and Newburgh is influenced by freshwater flowing down the River Tay and is much more stony. With the muddy nature of the inner flats, agricultural reclamation is always a possibility and there is, at times, quite heavy shooting pressure too. Effluent from Dundee and other towns discharges into the mouth of the Firth. The estuary is an SSSI and a Grade 1* site in NCR; Tentsmuir Point is an NNR.

The Tay is of considerable interest for its birds, there being six species of international importance (Table 13:2); of these, Pink-footed and Greylag Geese use the estuary as a roost. The national status of its birds is shown in Table 13:22; the Eider flock is of outstanding importance, and has been discussed by Milne and Campbell (1973) and Pounder (1971). The flock sits off the outer Abertay Sands and has been estimated, at times, at 16,000. Pink-footed Geese roost mainly on Abertay Sands but some are on the main inner mud banks, and Greylag Geese are mostly on Mugdrum Island in the inner estuary (Newton et al 1973). Most of the waders are

---

Table 13:22    *Species of national importance on the Firth of Tay, 1969–75*

|  | Highest av. monthly count | % British |
|---|---|---|
| Pink-footed Goose | (6,000+) | (8·0+) |
| Greylag Goose | (2,000+) | (3·0+) |
| Eider | 12,700 | 21·2 |
| Goldeneye | 230 | 1·8 |
| Oystercatcher | 2,220 | 1·1 |
| Sanderling | 190 | 1·3 |
| Bar-tailed Godwit | 1,040 | 2·3 |
| Redshank | 1,270 | 1·3 |

( ) Species only roosting on the Tay, minimum estimates

on the outer shore – Dighty Burn to Buddon Ness in the north and Tentsmuir to Tayport in the south – but Redshank predominate further inland, especially in Invergowrie Bay. Other species of interest are 850 Mallard, 50 Red-breasted Merganser and 4,100 Dunlin. Tentsmuir is an important breeding area for Shelduck and Eiders.

## Fife Region

*Eden.* Although a fairly small estuary, its outer sandy flats are contiguous with those on Tentsmuir Point and, as a result, have similar habitats. There are sand dunes at its mouth, a predominantly sandy middle section and a muddier innermost portion with an accreting saltmarsh at Guardbridge. Part of the inner estuary is a proposed LNR. The estuary is not under any major reclamation threat but there is quite widespread disturbance from leisure activities, although not noticeably from the Leuchars Airfield on the northern shore. There is continuing pressure for an expansion of leisure facilities on the estuary.

Its birds include reasonable numbers of wintering Black-tailed Godwit and Grey

*Table 13:23 Species of national importance on the Eden Estuary, 1969–75*

|  | Highest av. monthly count | % British |
|---|---|---|
| Shelduck | 1,705 | 2·8 |
| Eider | 1,570 | 2·6 |
| Oystercatcher | 4,070 | 2·0 |
| Grey Plover | 270 | 2·7 |
| Black-tailed Godwit | 110 | 2·7 |
| Bar-tailed Godwit | 1,660 | 3·7 |
| Redshank | 1,240 | 1·2 |

Plover, the former being very scarce in Scotland at any time of year, especially in winter. The three internationally important species are shown in Table 13:2. Table 13:23 presents the national position. There is a close relationship of Eiders on the Tay and Eden; the breeding population spread between the two, but most of the young are brought down to the Eden. Other species of regional significance are 1,360 Wigeon, 630 Teal, 1,730 Knot and 3,500 Dunlin. Two main roost areas are used; at Shelly Point for birds from the outer estuary, and Guardbridge saltmarsh for those from the inner flats.

## Fife/Central/Lothian Regions

*Firth of Forth.* Perhaps by virtue of its size, position and diversity of habitats the Firth of Forth is one of the most important areas for estuary birds in Scotland. Its outer shore is rocky but with flatish rocky and sandy beaches. Up the estuary as far as the Forth Road Bridge there is a series of sandy bays separated by headlands and towns. The main bays are Aberlady, Gullane, Gosford, Musselburgh and Cramond

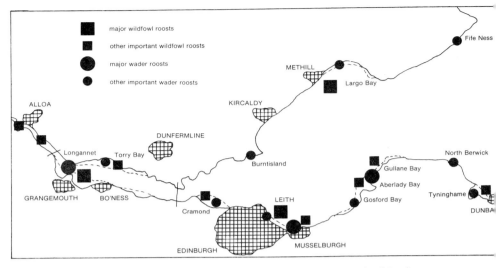

Fig. 13:2 Main concentrations of waders and wildfowl in the Firth of Forth.

on the south, and Largo and Burnt Island in the north. Set in the outer Forth are some spectacular islands famed for breeding seabirds, in particular the Bass Rock, Isle of May and Inchmickery. Above the Forth Road Bridge the habitat becomes rapidly more estuarine, with much more mud mixed with sand and shingle in Torry Bay and at Bo'ness and Grangemouth. Few saltmarshes have developed, the main one being in Aberlady Bay.

With such a large area adjacent to a major centre of population it is hardly surprising to find that it faces a number of threats. The most serious being the reclamation of the Grade 1 mudflats on either side of Grangemouth docks for possible further petro-chemical developments. In many areas the pressure of continual disturbance modifies the roosting distribution of birds, although to date no clear effect has been shown on the feeding dispersion. Excessive shooting, too, has proved a problem at times. The Forth is a heavily polluted estuary discharging organic, industrial and distillery effluent. Because of the oil terminal and various shipyards within the Forth, there is a continual danger from oil spillage, with potentially disastrous results for the massive seabird concentrations. There are 14 SSSIs covering about half of the important intertidal areas.

The birds of the Forth have been studied in some detail by amateurs and professionals from several Universities and Institutes. Of special note is Campbell (1978), which provides a detailed summary of its birds and conservation status as well as a useful reference list. Internationally 14 species on the Forth are of importance (Table 13:2). Table 13:24 presents the national status. Although not included in this survey there are at least nine species of seabirds breeding on the Forth in nationally and internationally important numbers. The Forth, too, is a regular haunt of many Red-throated and Black-throated Divers, and Great-crested, Red-necked and Slavonian Grebes; for all of these it is nationally known. While no dabbling duck appears in Table 13:24, Mallard, Wigeon and Pintail are all just under the necessary qualifying level, as are Whooper Swans. The density and diversity of species makes the Forth an outstanding estuary.

Figure 13:2 shows the main sections of the Forth with a summary of their ornithological importance. It is difficult not to mention all sites since so many do have internationally important numbers. Of special significance are the seaduck concentrations off Leith–Mussleburgh and Methil–Largo, the Shelduck and wader numbers on the inner Forth, especially Skinflats around Grangemouth, and the diversity of all species on the Aberlady Bay–North Berwick section. Campbell (1978) provides further details.

*Table 13:24   Species of national importance on the Firth of Forth, 1969–75*

|  | *Highest av. monthly count* | *% British* |
|---|---|---|
| Pink-footed Goose | 4,400 | 5·9 |
| Shelduck | 1,510 | 2·5 |
| Pochard | 1,500 | 3·7 |
| Scaup | 12,840 | 57·1 |
| Eider | 3,260 | 5·4 |
| Long-tailed Duck | 160 | 1·6 |
| Common Scoter | 1,680 | 4·8 |
| Velvet Scoter | 200 | 5·7 |
| Goldeneye | 2,220 | 17·8 |
| Red-breasted Merganser | 420 | 5·6 |
| Oystercatcher | 5,600 | 2·8 |
| Ringed Plover | 250 | 2·0 |
| Knot | 16,100 | 5·4 |
| Purple Sandpiper | 1,200 | 6·7 |
| Dunlin | 12,200 | 2·2 |
| Bar-tailed Godwit | 1,800 | 4·0 |
| Curlew | 1,530 | 1·5 |
| Redshank | 2,600 | 2·6 |
| Turnstone | 810 | 3·2 |

# CHAPTER 14

# Northern Ireland

The coast of Northern Ireland is one of contrasts with long sections of heavily waved-washed rocks and sandy bays; it has a few major inlets where the finer sediments have been deposited to form mudflats. The only significant areas of mud are in Lough Foyle and the River Bann (Co. Derry), Larne Lough (Co. Antrim), Belfast Lough (Co. Antrim/Co. Down) and Strangford Lough, Dundrum Bay and Carlingford Lough (Co. Down). The border with the Republic of Ireland runs through the first and last of these wetlands, involving Co. Donegal and Co. Louth respectively.

Hutchinson (1979) has summarised much of the available data for wetlands, including estuaries, in Northern Ireland, so the treatment here is less extensive than it would have been otherwise.

### Urban and industrial development and recreation

Fortunately few of the major problems so characteristic of British estuaries are found in Northern Ireland. This does not mean, however, that dangers do not exist. Because there are few estuaries, each of the threats is real and could, potentially, have a major impact on the birds of the province. The most serious problem is the highly damaging policy of waste disposal on the foreshore, leading to a steady loss of mudflats and, subsequently to industrial or road developments. Unless a more environmentally acceptable strategy for waste disposal is considered, the estuaries are extremely vulnerable and serious losses will continue.

Wildfowling and public disturbance can be quite heavy at times but there is no clear evidence of any major effects on bird distribution and numbers. Further sanctuary areas, particularly on Lough Foyle, Carlingford Lough and Dundrum Bay are highly desirable.

*Literature on the birds of Northern Ireland*

This area is, in terms of published material on bird numbers and distribution, one of the least well-documented of the United Kingdom. Deane (1954) and Hutchinson (1979) covering the whole area, and Marsh (1975) dealing with the north coast, are the only sources of material apart from data supplied to the Wildfowl Trust or the BTO, and scientific papers such as O'Connor and Brown (1977). There is no regular bird report although records are included in the annual Irish Bird report, now published in 'Irish Birds'.

*Principal species and migration patterns*

The most numerous species are shown in Table 14:1; totals are relatively small because of the few estuaries involved. Wildfowl are fairly well represented, particularly on Strangford Lough and Lough Foyle, which support the bulk of the Pale-bellied Brent Geese and Wigeon respectively. In international terms the Whooper Swan total is second only to the Pale-bellied Brent Goose numbers, particularly as it probably involves only Icelandic birds and forms over 12% of their population. Unlike many estuaries in Britain, the wildfowl arrive in large numbers on Northern Irish estuaries relatively early in the season, often in October and November. Subsequently, numbers decrease as birds move further south into Ireland. This pattern may be due to a major influx of birds which breed in Iceland, and other areas to the north-west, entering the British Isles through Northern Ireland; there are many ringing recoveries which indicate that this is so.

Wader numbers are relatively low and it is not surprising that the species which feed on wet pasture as well as intertidal flats are predominant: Lapwing, Curlew, Redshank and Golden Plover. Large influxes of Lapwing can take place in cold weather, so much of the variability in annual wader numbers relates to this species.

*Table 14:1   The most numerous species\* of waterfowl on estuaries in Northern Ireland, 1969–75*

| | | | | | |
|---|---|---|---|---|---|
| Wigeon | 18,800 | Oct | Lapwing | 13,900 | Jan |
| Pale-bellied Brent Goose | 9,760 | Dec | Knot | 13,600 | Jan |
| Mallard | 2,920 | Sept | Dunlin | 8,000 | Feb |
| Teal | 1,940 | Jan | Curlew | 6,330 | Aug |
| Shelduck | 1,680 | Feb | Oystercatcher | 4,600 | Oct |
| Whooper Swan | 880 | Nov | Redshank | 4,200 | Nov |
| Scaup | 645 | Jan | Golden Plover | 3,950 | Nov |
| Red-breasted Merganser | 640 | Sept | Turnstone | 470 | Nov |
| Mute Swan | 570 | Nov | Ringed Plover | 360 | Nov |
| Goldeneye | 270 | Feb | Sanderling | 160 | Aug |

\* Based on the highest average monthly counts

*Table 14:2   The percentage of the European population of the principal species of waterfowl wintering on estuaries in Northern Ireland, 1969–75*

|  | Bewick's Swan | Whooper Swan | Pale Brent Goose | Wigeon | Oyster-catcher |
|---|---|---|---|---|---|
| Strangford Lough | – | 2·5 | 64·0 | – | 2·0 |
| Belfast Lough* | – | – | – | – | – |
| Lough Foyle | 1·4 | 2·6 | – | 2·3 | – |

|  | Knot | Black-tailed Godwit | Bar-tailed Godwit | Curlew | Redshank |
|---|---|---|---|---|---|
| Strangford Lough | 2·7 | – | 1·1 | 1·1 | 1·2 |
| Belfast Lough* | – | (1·0) | – | – | – |
| Lough Foyle | – | – | 2·2 | 1·4 | – |

* Only one very incomplete count is available

It is rather surprising that the Knot is the main estuarine species in view of its very restricted distribution in Ireland, and that nearly all are concentrated on Strangford Lough. Its numbers too are very variable although the reason for this is unclear. Essentially waders build up to a midwinter peak in Northern Ireland and there is only a small autumn passage. The low level of this passage and the virtual absence of a spring movement is surprising since they are a feature of estuaries on the opposite side of the Irish Sea.

### Principal estuaries in Northern Ireland

The few estuaries and many of their birds have been described already. Strangford Lough stands out as the most important, having seven species of international importance but principally because of its huge early winter numbers of Pale-bellied Brent Geese and diversity of waders. Lough Foyle is internationally significant for five species and therefore also a major European estuary. The other estuaries are all small, or fairly small, and despite good concentrations of some scarce species they do not rank alongside the two mentioned above. Only Belfast Lough, for which virtually no counts were available, may rank higher. The species of international importance are shown in Table 14:5.

### Co. Derry

*Lough Foyle.* This large shallow embayment has extensive intertidal flats on its southern and eastern shores and, at its mouth, grades into large sandy beaches. Behind the seawall are large areas of reclaimed grazing marsh. Some land has been reclaimed for industry.

The species of international importance are shown in Table 14:2; those of national importance are in Table 14:3. The numbers of several wildfowl are difficult to estimate as the flocks of Wigeon in particular, lie well offshore during the day. In the highest average month almost 10,000 were recorded, although up to 29,000

Table 14:3  *Species of national importance on Lough Foyle, 1969–75*

|  | *Highest av. monthly count* | *% British* |
|---|---|---|
| Bewick's Swan | 140 | 15·0 |
| Whooper Swan | 450 | 7·0 |
| Wigeon | 9,280 | 4·6 |
| Teal | 1,040 | 1·4 |
| Sanderling | 120 | 1·2 |
| Bar-tailed Godwit | 1,960 | 4·4 |
| Curlew | 2,800 | 2·8 |
| Redshank | 1,400* | 1·2 |
| Greenshank | 20† | ‡ |

\* Autumn count
† Winter count
‡ More than 1% of small national wintering number

have been reported. Waders are well distributed over the intertidal area, with Sanderling and most of the Ringed Plovers at Magilligan Point in the north-east. Large numbers of Curlew, Golden Plover and Lapwing also feed inland on the grazing marshes. In addition to the species listed, others almost reaching a national level are Pale-bellied Brent Geese (120), Golden Plover (1,700), Oystercatcher (1,550) and Lapwing (3,100).

*Bann.* The long narrow estuary of the Bann has small intertidal flats and supports few estuary birds although many waders, which normally feed on adjacent grassland, use the estuary during part of the day. No species is of national significance but Lapwing (2,500), Golden Plover (1,020) and Curlew (750) occur in good numbers. Interestingly this is one of the few areas in Ireland where a small but distinct spring passage of Sanderling and Ringed Plovers is seen.

## Co. Antrim

*Larne Lough.* This sea lough has large intertidal flats which support moderate numbers of waders, although these total almost 4,000. The main species of interest is the Greenshank, approximately 20 of which winter and are of national significance. The most numerous species of wader are Lapwing (1,750), Redshank (620) and Curlew (340), Wigeon exceed 1,200 and Teal 400. Also of note are the seaduck and grebe numbers; Great Crested Grebes annually reach 70 (the largest concentration on the coast of Northern Ireland) and Goldeneye 50. Areas of the Lough are being lost from the continued dumping of rubbish, and plans for road development also threaten parts of the Lough.

## Co. Antrim/Co. Down

*Belfast Lough.* With Belfast encompassing the head of this sea lough there has been a considerable amount of industrial reclamation, this is continuing as rubbish is being dumped on the foreshore. Security restrictions have meant that virtually no counts were made during 1969–75. Sporadic observations of over 2,000 Dunlin, 400 Oystercatchers and 200 Redshank only provide a glimpse of its significance. One sighting of a flock of 400 Black-tailed Godwits shows that it might be of international significance for this species.

During the 1980–81 winter the Department of the Environment for Northern Ireland has carried out regular counts of the inner Lough between Holywood and Newtownabbey. These indicate that the Lough is of national significance with peaks of 3,760 Oystercatchers, 1,300 Redshanks, 1,045 Curlew, 125 Ringed Plover each being of importance. The 180 Scaup is only just outside the level of national significance. In general waders are well represented but wildfowl are relatively few in number.

### Co. Down

*Strangford Lough.* This large sea lough has only a very narrow channel to the sea at its southern end. It is quite unlike any other estuary in Britain, having a very indented rocky coastline and dozens of small islands. The northern section from Mahee Island to Greyabbey Bay has extensive mud and sandflats. There are

Table 14:4   *Species of national importance on Strangford Lough, 1969–75*

|  | Highest av. monthly count | % British |
|---|---|---|
| Mute Swan | 440 | 2·4 |
| Whooper Swan | 440 | 14·7 |
| Pale-bellied Brent Goose | 9,600 | † |
| Shelduck | 1,120 | 1·9 |
| Wigeon | 11,250 | 5·6 |
| Teal | 1,050 | 1·4 |
| Pintail | 200 | 1·0 |
| Shoveler | 150 | 3·0 |
| Goldeneye | 200 | 1·6 |
| Red-breasted Merganser | 310 | 4·1 |
| Oystercatcher | 2,300 | 1·1 |
| Ringed Plover | 240 | 2·0 |
| Lapwing | 6,200 | (1·2) |
| Knot | 13,450 | 4·5 |
| Black-tailed Godwit | 75 | 1·9 |
| Bar-tailed Godwit | 1,000 | 2·2 |
| Curlew | 2,300 | 2·3 |
| Redshank | 1,500 | 1·5 |
| Greenshank | 28* | † |
| Turnstone | 340 | (1·4) |

\*  Winter count
†  More than 1% of small national wintering number
( ) Based on provisional data

considerable potential problems with reclamation or disturbance, so it is particularly fortunate that much of the estuary is in the hands of the National Trust.

The large mudflats and many sheltered bays provide especially favourable feeding conditions for birds with the result that Strangford Lough is an estuary of major international importance. Of outstanding importance is the Pale-bellied Brent Goose. Approximately two-thirds of all of Ireland's individuals are found here between October and December. Species of international importance on the estuary are shown in Table 14:2 and of national importance in Table 14:4. Of the other nine species of important wildfowl, Whooper Swans and Wigeon stand out, although the latter have declined recently; the autumn concentration of Red-breasted Mergansers is notable.

The numbers of waders fluctuate, mainly due to the variations in the Lapwing and Knot flocks, but ten species are nationally important, nevertheless. The Knot is the main species but Curlew and Bar-tailed Godwit are also numerous. Of the species not tabulated, Grey Plover (75) and Dunlin (4,800) each have their largest numbers in Northern Ireland on Strangford Lough.

Finally, a good selection of seaduck, divers and grebes occur, with up to 22 Great Northern Divers being the most spectacular.

*Dundrum Bay.* A broad sandy coastal bay forms one part of this wetland and is separated from two muddy inland arms by large sand dune systems. Red-breasted Merganser (170 : 2·3%), the only nationally important species, can be found on the sea, plus a good flock of Common Scoter which averaged over 200. On the mudflats are many (340) Wigeon.

Waders are quite numerous for the small size of the estuary, the most numerous being Lapwing (700), Oystercatcher (450), Dunlin (420) and Redshank and Curlew (each 200). Of the less common species, 10 wintering Greenshank and 15 Purple Sandpipers are of interest.

*Carlingford Lough.* This lough straddles the border with the Republic of Ireland but the majority of the mudflats are on the northern shore in Northern Ireland, as is the string of small islands near its mouth. Proposals have been made for reclamation of the mudflats along the Newry River.

*Table 14:5   Species of national importance on Carlingford Lough, 1969–75*

|  | *Highest av. monthly count* | *% British* |
| --- | --- | --- |
| Scaup | 640 | 2·8 |
| Red-breasted Merganser | 135 | 1·8 |

The main importance of Carlingford Lough is its seaduck; the nationally significant species, Scaup (which have declined in numbers since the mid 1960s) and Red-breasted Mergansers, are detailed in Table 14:5. An average of 65 Goldeneye also occur together with small numbers of most seaducks, grebes and divers. The only notable dabbling ducks are Wigeon (450) and Teal (250).

Wader numbers are quite good, with the Ringed Plovers (115) in winter sometimes reaching 1% of the British total. Numerically, Dunlin (2,000), Curlew (900), Redshank (850), Oystercatcher (660) and Bar-tailed Godwit (120) are more numerous.

CHAPTER 15

# Republic of Ireland

by C. D. HUTCHINSON

The coastline of the Republic of Ireland is immensely varied. The east coast is relatively unbroken, but where estuaries occur they are generally broad and extensive with significant waterfowl populations. The most important estuaries and bays are located close to Dundalk near the Northern Ireland border, Dublin in the centre of the east coast, and Wexford at its southern extremity. In between there are relatively few shore waders or wildfowl. The south coast is totally different. From Wexford to west Cork the coastline is broken by a jagged series of estuaries, none holding as many birds as the best on the east coast, but all with sizeable concentrations and together being of considerable importance. From west Cork around the west Kerry coast the bays are deep and unsuitable for estuarine birds until Castlemaine Harbour and Tralee Bay are reached. These bays are very important, especially for wildfowl, and so is the nearby Shannon Estuary, but from there north around the west coast the shore is much indented though with remarkably limited intertidal mudflats. Lough Swilly in Donegal is perhaps the most important coastal wetland north of the Shannon Estuary.

In considering any account of the birds of estuaries in the Republic of Ireland the reader must take into account the small number of observers. During the years from 1971–72 to 1974–75 an intensive series of counts was carried out, at inland and coastal wetlands, as part of the Irish Wildbird Conservancy's 'Wetlands Enquiry'. Monthly counts were made at most of the important estuaries but only about 30 counters were involved. A major contributing factor to the success of the counts was the aerial coverage of the Shannon Estuary. But some areas, mostly on the west coast, were only counted sporadically. Few, however, are believed to be of great importance for either wildfowl or waders. Prior to the counts our knowledge of the numbers and distribution of waterfowl in Ireland was based on the standard book on the birds of Ireland (Ruttledge 1966) and, in the case of wildfowl, on the midwinter censuses carried out annually since 1966. It is fair to say that the counts in the years from 1971 to 1975 revolutionised our knowledge of the numbers and distribution of these birds (Hutchinson 1979).

We now realise more definitely Ireland's importance for certain duck species as the end of the north-west and north-east European flyways. The Republic holds some 25–45,000 Teal, 80,000 Wigeon and 7,500 Shoveler in winter. Many of these birds feed and roost on estuaries. For geese, Irish estuaries are well known as the European wintering zone of the Pale-bellied Brent Goose. But the country's significance for waders is less known. Large numbers of the common shore waders winter around the coast, but Ireland is particularly important for Lapwing and Golden Plover, which are not shore waders at all. Even in mild winters several hundred thousand Golden Plover winter in the country, many of them roosting on estuaries. In hard weather many more move into Ireland along with huge flocks of Lapwing, building up on estuaries as well as inland. Most of the Golden Plover appear to be of Icelandic origin, as are the 8–10,000 Black-tailed Godwits which winter in the country and, perhaps, many of the 9–12,000 Redshanks. The winter population of 12–16,000 Bar-tailed Godwits, with their origin in north-eastern Europe, is about 15% of the total wintering in Europe.

The threats to Irish estuaries are similar to those affecting British estuaries. Land reclamation for industrial development near Dublin and Cork, pollution in the same area and the probability of an influx of heavy industry to the Shannon Estuary are problems common to both islands. *Spartina* is also a common problem. This plant is smothering estuaries all around the coast, but is particularly prevalent in Dundalk Bay, the Shannon Estuary and Cork Harbour. In the future an oil discovery somewhere off the coast must be a probability and this would present conservation problems.

### East Coast

The coast from Carlingford Lough in the north to Dublin is a low-lying stretch of sand-dunes or low cliffs with wide sandy beaches, indented with a series of bays and estuaries, mostly at the north and south ends of the coast. The most outstanding of these, Dundalk Bay and the North Bull, are considered in detail but the other estuaries are also of importance.

The Boyne Estuary, south of Dundalk Bay, is a narrow river estuary with wildfowl and wader populations of considerable local value but none of national importance. The estuary is notable for its winter flock of up to 250 Black-tailed Godwits, the largest on this coast north of Wexford.

South of the Boyne and nearer Dublin lie a cluster of estuaries and bays, most of which have expanses of intertidal mudflats impounded behind sand-bars. Rogerstown, the most northerly, has held as many as 5,300 wildfowl and 7,800 waders in winter; Malahide, a few kilometres to the south, has substantially fewer birds; Baldoyle, the next in line, is choked with *Spartina* and no longer of significance; and the North Bull, the last of the series, is much the most important with recent maxima of 8,000 wildfowl and 36,600 waders in winter. Rogerstown holds similar wildfowl species to the North Bull. Brent Geese (400) occur in numbers of international importance and Pintail (200) and Shelduck (600) in numbers of national significance. Both Rogerstown and Malahide have a similar range of waders to the North Bull with the exception of Bar-tailed Godwits, which are quite scarce at these estuaries. Numbers, however, are far lower.

South of Dublin Bay and the North Bull a muddy creek at Kilcoole and a brackish lagoon at Broad Lough near Wicklow town are the only wetlands of importance before Wexford Harbour. These two sites hold a small flock of Greylag Geese (70) and fluctuating numbers of Bewick's Swans as well as small numbers of ducks and waders. Otherwise there are no wetlands to break the broad sweep of the bays between the east coast headlands before the great wetlands at Wexford Harbour and Slobs, which are treated in detail below.

*Dundalk Bay*. Although fed by the Castletown and Fane rivers, Dundalk Bay is not primarily an estuary but a broad bay with a very extensive and rather coarse, muddy intertidal area extending for nearly 20 km. At low tide the 4,500 ha of mudflat provide feeding for the largest concentrations of Oystercatchers and Bar-tailed Godwits in Ireland. The winter population of Oystercatchers is about 10,000 birds, representing 2% of the west European population; in autumn the peak is nearly 27,000. In European terms, however, the Bar-tailed Godwit flock is much more significant, representing 7% of the west European population. Four other wader species occur in numbers of international importance and the Golden Plover flock in autumn, which in some years exceeds 13,000, is one of the largest in Ireland (Table 15:1).

*Table 15:1   Average numbers of internationally and nationally important concentrations of individual species in the peak month at Dundalk Bay. A concentration of national importance is one which exceed 5% of the total Irish wintering population.*

|  | International |  | National |
|---|---|---|---|
| Oystercatcher | 26,700 | Knot | 3,600 |
| Curlew | 4,200 |  |  |
| Bar-tailed Godwit | 7,100 |  |  |
| Redshank | 3,700 |  |  |
| Dunlin | 12,400 |  |  |

Dundalk Bay is chiefly important as a wader site. In the Republic only the Shannon Estuary has had more waders recorded. The numbers of wildfowl are comparatively low, though the bay ranks third in importance on the east coast.

At low tide, waders spread out over the available mudflat which, despite the expansion of *Spartina* along much of the edge of the bay, is still enormous and relatively secure. At high tide there are several roosts, much the more important being on salt marsh at the South Marsh and at Lurgangreen. Smaller roosts are located on sand banks near Ballymascanlan and on shingle shore at Annagassan. Teal and Wigeon tend to congregate at the South Marsh and Lungangreen; Mallard, which number up to 700 in autumn and 300 in winter, congregate west of Ballymascanlan and of Annagassan.

Ballymascanlan Bay and part of the salt marsh at Lurgangreen are protected by an annual non-shooting Order.

*North Bull*. The North Bull is unquestionably the best documented Irish wetland.

The recently published book on the natural history of the island (Jeffery 1977) describes the extent of current knowledge of most aspects of the structure, fauna and flora of the North Bull and makes proposals for the conservation of the area. However, as a haunt of waterfowl the North Bull should not be considered in isolation, but as the roosting area for thousands of birds which feed on the mudflats of Dublin Bay.

Dublin Bay has the second largest area of sand and mudflats on this coastline, only Dundalk Bay having more. The River Liffey flows into the sea in the centre of the bay between the arms of the Bull Wall and the South Wall. North of the river, the North Bull, a low island of sand dune and salt marsh, stretches diagonally across the bay from the Bull Wall to Sutton at the base of the Howth peninsula. The area between the island and the mainland is a muddy creek fringed with salt marsh on the edge of the island. This creek is cut at mid-point by a causeway which was completed by Dublin Corporation in 1964. The creek has silted up since the construction of the causeway and now shows all the signs of salt marsh extension. A mat of *Salicornia* extends over much of the channel. More ominously, *Spartina* now grows in small clumps on the mud.

At high tide most of the waterfowl in Dublin Bay roost on the salt marsh on the island. As the tide ebbs the waders spread out across the sand and mud on both sides of the bay. The majority of the duck remain to feed in the creek between the island and the mainland, and Brent Geese feed on the *Zostera* which grows off Kilbarrack and Sutton to the north of the island. Later in the winter, when the *Zostera* is exhausted, the geese feed on the algal mats which are spreading on the flats north and south of the river.

The North Bull has substantially larger numbers of wildfowl than any other east coast wetland between Strangford Lough and the Wexford Slobs and ranks second to Dundalk Bay in numbers of waders recorded (Table 15:2). Unquestionably the density of birds supported by the available mudflat is much greater than at any other Irish estuary.

*Table 15:2   Average numbers of internationally and nationally important concentrations of individual species in the peak month at the North Bull*

| | International | | National |
|---|---|---|---|
| Shoveler | 300 | Pintail | 300 |
| Brent Goose | 1,000 | Shelduck | 400 |
| Curlew | 1,900 | Oystercatcher | 3,800 |
| Bar-tailed Godwit | 2,300 | Dunlin | 7,900 |
| Redshank | 2,400 | | |
| Knot | 6,700 | | |

The wildfowl have been counted monthly in most years since 1951 and there is no evidence of long-term decrease in numbers of any species other than Shelduck, which has declined generally along the east coast since the late 1960s. Indeed, three species, Teal, Pintail and Shoveler, have increased substantially over this period.

Although the North Bull has been protected as a Bird Sanctuary since 1931 it comes under continuing threat from local authorities. Dunlin Corporation commenced dumping domestic refuse on the salt marsh several years ago, but has halted operations pending the production of a scientific report. Dublin Port and Docks Board has proposed plans which involve converting part of the channel into an enclosed lagoon and reclaiming much of the mudflat outside the island. The utmost vigilance will be required to ensure the survival of this remarkable wetland, the value of which derives ultimately not just from the importance of the bird populations but from the area's proximity to the centre of the Republic's capital city.

*Wexford Harbour and Slobs.* Wexford Harbour is the estuary of the Slaney River. North and south of the broad estuary are the slobs, areas of alluvial mud which were reclaimed in the mid-nineteenth century and are now under arable crops or pasture. Both slobs are criss-crossed by drainage ditches and have a broad, shallow channel running through them. Out in the harbour itself most of the intertidal mudflats are on the southern side. The main wader roosts are at Rosslare Point and at Tern Island, a small and rather unstable sandy island near the mouth of the harbour.

*Table 15:3   Average numbers of internationally and nationally important concentrations of individual species at Wexford Harbour and Slobs*

| | International | | National |
|---|---|---|---|
| Pintail | 900 | Mallard | 2,500 |
| White-fronted Goose | 5,200 | Scaup | 300 |
| Brent Goose | 400 | Grey Plover | 100 |
| Bewick's Swan | 200 | Bar-tailed Godwit | 800 |
| Black-tailed Godwit | 1,200 | Redshank | 700 |

The area is undoubtedly the most important wildfowl haunt in the Republic of Ireland, supporting up to 15,400 birds in winter. Nearly half the world population of Greenland White-fronted Geese (over 5,000 birds) winter here, feeding on the slobs and flighting out to Tern Island to roost at night. White-fronted Geese appear first to have come to the slobs during the second decade of this century, but the present numbers were not reached until the late 1940s. Interestingly, they seem to have replaced the Greylag Geese which were abundant up to the 1940s and are now rare on the slobs. Pink-footed, Canada and Barnacle Geese also occur annually and a Blue Snow Goose in most years. The slobs are also of international importance for Pintail and Bewick's Swans, the latter species having increased considerably in recent years (Table 15:3).

The harbour and slobs hold the largest wader populations in Wexford. The slobs in particular are of importance as a refuge in hard weather for Lapwing and Golden Plover driven west from Britain. The diversity of habitat within the area – ranging from mudflats to brackish channels on the slobs – attracts a number of scarcer waders. The largest concentrations of Spotted Redshanks in Ireland (up to 100 in autumn) occur on the slobs.

In summer parties of Little Gulls are annual at the slobs. Tern Island holds the largest tern colony in Ireland and the largest colony of Roseate Terns in western Europe.

The main potential threat to the area is of a change in agricultural practice on the slobs. There is also the possibility of industrial development because of the close proximity of the port of Wexford. The only areas specifically protected are 100 ha of the North Slob owned, and 50 ha leased, jointly by the Forest and Wildlife Service of the Irish Department of Fisheries and Irish Wildbird Conservancy, and Tern Island and Rosslare Point which are Irish Wildbird Conservancy sanctuaries.

### South and south-west coast

The south coast is quite different from the east where the estuaries are isolated in small sections of what is a relatively unbroken coastline. From Carnsore Point in Wexford to Rosscarbery in west Cork, a series of estuaries and brackish lagoons constantly interrupts the coastline. Almost all are important for waterfowl. From Rosscarbery west and around to the mouth of the Shannon the main features are the enormous rias which divide the south-west corner of Ireland into great fingers. Most are deep and contain few wildfowl or waders, but Castlemaine Harbour and Tralee Bay are striking exceptions with extensive intertidal mudflats, sand banks and salt marshes. These two bays and the associated lagoons of west Kerry, together with the south coast estuaries, form the most important group of wetlands in the region.

The most abundant wildfowl are undoubtedly Wigeon (12–18,000) which are present in every estuary. The commonest waders are Lapwing and Golden Plover, which can number well over 10,000 each in Ballymacoda Bay and Cork Harbour, but they move inland frequently and we have little idea of the true numbers on the entire coast at any time in winter. The next most common wader is the Dunlin. Up to 35,000 winter in the area. But the most characteristic birds of the estuaries are the Black-tailed Godwits which number about 6,000 birds.

Working from east to west there are two brackish lagoons in south-east Wexford, Lady's Island Lake and Tacumshin Lake, each of which holds medium-sized concentrations of wildfowl and small numbers of waders. The flock of Bewick's Swans (average peak of 100) and the Brent Geese at Tacumshin (500) are internationally important. Farther west is the narrow muddy creek at The Cull and the large estuary at Bannow Bay which holds an internationally important flock of Brent Geese (300). This bay also holds large numbers of waders (up to 19,500). In Co. Waterford there are four important estuaries. Waterford Harbour has large numbers of Lapwing and Golden Plover but rather few shore waders. Tramore Bay and Dungarvan Harbour are much more important, holding maxima of 8,200 and 11,000 waders respectively. Dungarvan is noteworthy for its internationally important flock of Black-tailed Godwits (900). Kinsalebeg in Youghal Bay has smaller numbers of waders and some wildfowl.

Ballymacoda Bay in east Cork is a 600 ha expanse of marshy fields, salt marsh and mudflats which is of international importance for waders. Up to 29,800 have been recorded in winter. Most, however, are Lapwing and Golden Plover, though other common species are well represented. The wintering flock of Black-tailed Godwits (800) is of international importance. Between Ballymacoda and Cork Harbour lie several brackish lagoons at Ballycotton which hold small duck and wader populations, but are famous for the frequency with which scarce waders from Europe and, more particularly, North America are seen.

Cork Harbour is the most important estuary for shore waders on the south coast.

It is a large and complex area to count, as extensive mudflats are exposed on a series of narrow creeks around a large island at the south side of the harbour. The only complete count carried out during the enquiry gave a total of 27,700 waders in December 1974. From a European viewpoint Cork Harbour is probably most important for its winter population of Black-tailed Godwits (1,500–3,500), but the wintering populations of Oystercatchers (1,600), Redshanks (1,000) and Dunlin (7,700) are of national importance. Quite large numbers of duck occur, the assembly of 800 Shelduck being of national importance. Industrial development threatens the future of Cork Harbour as a habitat for wildfowl and waders: the Industrial Development Authority owns large tracts of land and its plans for the area have not been disclosed. *Spartina* grows extensively on the mud in the north of the harbour.

West of Cork Harbour are several small estuaries, the most important of which are Courtmacsherry Bay, Clonakilty Bay and Rosscarbery. Each of these has wintering flocks of Black-tailed Godwits and other waders. Mallard, Teal, Wigeon and Shelduck are the regular duck species. Farther west the inlets have very small mudflat zones, but in west Kerry the two great bays of Castlemaine Harbour and Tralee Bay have very important wildfowl flocks. Concentrations of 1,500 Mallard, 2,000 Teal, 6,800 Wigeon, 2,000 Pintail, 900 Shoveler and 4,200 Brent Geese have been recorded at Castlemaine and 1,800 Teal, 3,500 Wigeon, 500 Pintail, 200 Shoveler and 3,200 Brent Geese at Tralee Bay. All of these, except the Mallard at Castlemaine and the Wigeon at Tralee Bay, are concentrations of international importance. Wader numbers are not so important, but include up to 3,000 Bar-tailed Godwits at Castlemaine Harbour. North of Tralee Bay lies a brackish lagoon at Akeragh Lough which is famous for its annual autumn records of American waders.

### West and north-west coast

The coast of the west and north-west of Ireland from the Shannon Estuary to Lough Swilly is long and frequently broken by small inlets, but few have sufficient intertidal mud to support even small populations of waders though most of the sandy beaches hold Ringed Plover and Sanderling.

*Shannon Estuary.* The Shannon Estuary is an enormous estuarine complex, much the largest in Ireland. It stretches for approximately 80 km and varies from less than

*Table 15:4   Average numbers of internationally and nationally important concentrations of individual species at the Shannon Estuary*

| | International | | National |
|---|---|---|---|
| Teal | 2,500 | Scaup | 200 |
| Wigeon | 9,900 | Shelduck | 1,000 |
| Shoveler | 200 | Greylag Goose | 100 |
| Curlew | 3,200 | Whooper Swan | 100 |
| Black-tailed Godwit | 8,400 | | |
| Bar-tailed Godwit | 1,200 | | |
| Dunlin | 29,600 | | |

1 km to over 15 km in width. The estuary is a drowned river valley, edged with sand and mud-banks, and with many square kilometres of intertidal mudflat in the inlets on both sides of the estuary. All the small rivers flowing into the estuary deposit large quantities of silt in times of flood. In some parts, particularly on the Fergus Estuary, land has been reclaimed and is protected by embankments. On the west side of the Fergus Estuary, at Islandavanna, *Spartina* has been planted to accelerate the process of reclamation.

The estuary is internationally important (Table 15:4) for wildfowl (up to 15,400 in winter) and waders (up to 67,600 in winter). It is particularly important for its passage flocks of Black-tailed Godwits in spring. Regularly, over 6,000 (once, in 1974, a total of 16,400) occur for a brief period in March and April. The 1974 figure was much the largest concentration ever recorded in Britain or Ireland. The most important section of the estuary is the eastern half, especially the Fergus Estuary and the mudflats around Shannon Airport and Aughinish Island. This area normally holds 80% of the wildfowl and 90% of the waders.

From the Shannon Estuary north and west the coast has only a scattering of bays of ornithological importance. Galway Bay holds small numbers of duck and some Brent Geese (up to 130) as well as small numbers of the common shore waders. The total shore waders occurring might be in the region of 3–5,000 birds. The Connemara coast records few waterfowl, but several bays in north Mayo, Sligo and Donegal have small concentrations. Killala Bay in north Mayo holds some ducks and similar numbers of waders to Galway Bay. Sligo Bay, which consists of three separate estuaries, is much more important, especially in September and October when up to 2,000 Brent Geese spend a few weeks. Several hundred Barnacle Geese winter in a field by one of the estuaries. Wader numbers are similar to Galway Bay. From Sligo Bay around to Lough Swilly are a number of bays and small estuaries, all holding a few hundred waders, chiefly Oystercatchers, Curlews, Redshanks and Dunlin, and some with about 200 duck and perhaps a few Brent Geese.

Lough Swilly, the last area in our circuit of the Republic of Ireland, has much the finest coastal wetland habitat in Donegal. The lough is a 50 km long, narrow inlet gouged out by glaciation. In the southern half of the lough there are extensive intertidal mudflats and shingle banks, and two man-made lagoons. The area is chiefly important for Whooper Swans, enormous flocks of which make landfall here in October. Up to 1,500 have been counted in fields on the edge of the lough, though they move on quickly and usual winter population is in the region of 100–500 birds. The lough also holds up to 300 Greylag Geese and 80 Brent Geese as well as about 4,000 duck and appreciable numbers of waders. Midwinter totals of 500 Oyster-catchers, 900 Curlews, 500 Redshanks and 2,000 Dunlin, though small by east coast standards are quite large for the north-west coast.

# CHAPTER 16

# The estuarine birds – an introduction

It is perhaps difficult to realise that prior to the 'Birds of Estuaries Enquiry' and the IWC's 'Wetlands Enquiry' virtually nothing was known of the distribution and numbers of our waders. The Oystercatcher had been studied by MAFF and a few areas counted, some regularly but most irregularly. Wildfowl, however, were much better studied and their distribution had been summarised in *Wildfowl of Great Britain* by Atkinson-Willes (1963). The present survey therefore provides a comparison with the wildfowl counts made on estuaries in the 1950s. Some information has also been gathered on non-breeding numbers of grebes, divers, Cormorant, gulls and terns, but since these species were not the prime targets, the counts were not designed to record their numbers accurately. Much information on geese is also drawn from Ogilvie (1978). The present data indicates the known status and will no doubt be improved upon when more specific surveys are carried out. Breeding data, especially, of most species are omitted because they are dealt with by the BTO/IWC *Atlas of Breeding Birds in Britain and Ireland* (Sharrock 1976). *Ireland's Wetlands and their Birds* (Hutchinson 1979) presents greater details for each species in Ireland.

This section outlines the distribution and patterns of abundance of the main estuarine species. Unfortunately, many species occur in other habitats – for example, dabbling ducks on inland waters, seaduck scattered around the coasts or inland. The scale of these omissions is considered, but details are included for all species for which a substantial part of the population occurs in estuaries. The less important estuarine birds, or those for which the counts were not designed, are included but with much abridged accounts. Rare species are not considered. Even with all of these limitations, however, these accounts provide the most detailed documentation of birds using any British habitat throughout the year. The species are presented in the Voous (1973) order.

Within each species text there is a brief outline of breeding and wintering distribution elsewhere and of the migration pattern shown. The internationally important areas for each species are tabulated. For the major species there are four maps.

Generally, the figures quoted are average monthly counts. In the distribution maps it is these which are plotted and the relevant month or period quoted – if no month is given then the figure used is the average annual peak counts. In some species, particularly divers and grebes, additional published material is incorporated, while for geese and some sea duck other data are drawn from the Wildfowl counts. Where appropriate other sources are quoted. The histograms are all based on average monthly counts on estuaries and for some species (e.g. Scoter, Purple Sandpiper) relate only to smallish samples of the estuaries counted on a regular basis.

CHAPTER 17

# The species accounts (in Voous order)

RED-THROATED DIVER *Gavia stellata*

This is the most abundant and widespread diver species, having a Holarctic distribution in the sub-arctic and boreal zones. In winter it is found on Atlantic and Pacific coasts and also inland on large lakes and inland seas. At least 750 pairs breed in Britain and Ireland (Sharrock 1976), confined to the moorland pools and lochs of the north and west.

The winter distribution reveals clear preferences for the relatively sheltered Irish Sea and North Sea coasts; the distribution is almost complementary to that of the Great Northern Diver which is mainly northern and western. Numbers are very difficult to estimate, so the following figures should be regarded with some caution. Perhaps about 500 Red-throated Divers are found in eastern Scotland and similar numbers in eastern England. Wales and north-western England each support 250–350, and 100–150 are found in west Scotland and in southern England. Shetland supports over two hundred breeding pairs but fewer than 20 are present in winter. Allowing for some underestimating, the total British wintering population is probably about 2,500 but the habit, at times, of feeding well out from the shore means that more may be undetected.

In Ireland this is the commonest diver on the south and east coasts, occurring in smaller numbers in the north and west (Hutchinson 1979), but no total population estimate is available. Northern Ireland, in particular, holds 100–120 birds in winter.

Two recoveries in French waters suggest that British breeding birds move further south to winter, and in any case the home breeding population is too small to account for the winter numbers. There are, however, two recoveries in Britain from birds ringed in Greenland and one (possibly a migrant) from Finland, so that it is clear that our winter numbers are augmented by immigrants from these sources. The contribution of each is not clear.

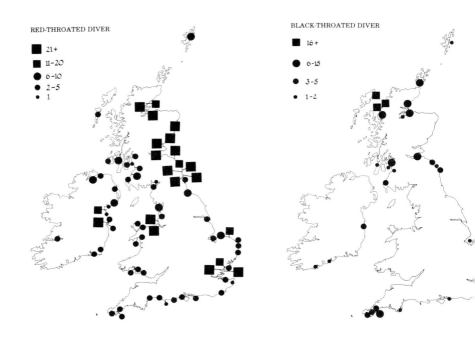

RED-THROATED DIVER

- 21+
- 11-20
- 6-10
- 2-5
- 1

BLACK-THROATED DIVER

- 16+
- 6-15
- 3-5
- 1-2

## BLACK-THROATED DIVER *Gavia arctica*

Most British wintering Black-throated Divers are found on salt water although a few birds, especially in severe winters, occur inland. Largest numbers are in Scottish waters, particularly in the north and west; few are found in Orkney and Shetland. Smaller numbers winter in England, with most in the south-west; there are very few in Ireland (Hutchinson 1979). The available data indicate that the total wintering population is about 210, although the Scottish total itself may reach this figure on occasions. Sharrock (1976) estimated the British breeding population as some 150 pairs; it would seem likely that most of these birds winter in British waters, although there have been no relevant ringing recoveries to date.

The birds which winter on the southern and south-eastern coasts of England are more likely to be of Scandinavian origin; this is inferred from the westerly breeding distribution in Scotland and from the timing and direction of their migrations. There is a marked spring passage eastwards along the southern English coast, with most moving at the end of April and early May – a time when most British breeders are on territory. This movement probably involves southern Cornish and northern French wintering birds.

# GREAT NORTHERN DIVER *Gavia immer*

This species has a mainly Nearctic breeding distribution in Alaska, Canada and Greenland; in the Palearctic it breeds regularly only in Iceland, but there are occasional records from Bear Island and from Scotland. The mainly north-western origin of the birds is reflected in the British and Irish distribution which is heavily biased towards the northern and western coasts. In winter this species is also common off the Norwegian coast and off north-western France.

A few individuals, probably storm driven, winter on lakes or reservoirs inland, but the vast majority is found offshore from rocky coasts. Sheltered inlets or bays are particularly favoured; in these areas the species can be counted easily, but many birds are found on large open stretches of water. In winter in northern Scotland the weather is frequently rough and daylight is short, under these conditions counting is extremely difficult. The remoteness of many of the wintering grounds is also a factor inhibiting survey work.

Possibly up to 1,000 occur in the Outer Hebrides (where a large concentration of up to 750 has been reported from the Sound of Harris, Hammond 1975), 500 in Orkney and 200–400 in Shetland, although in none of these main areas has a complete census been possible. A further 500 or so are found in the Inner Hebrides and elsewhere in west Scotland, and 80–100 on the eastern Scottish coast. Cornwall and Northumberland are the only English counties regularly supporting double figures. The available data suggest a wintering population for Britain of between 2,000 and 2,500.

The map for Ireland considerably understates the distribution on the northern and western coasts, where this is the commonest diver (Hutchinson 1979). Probably there are 100–150 in Northern Ireland, but no estimate is available for Ireland as a whole.

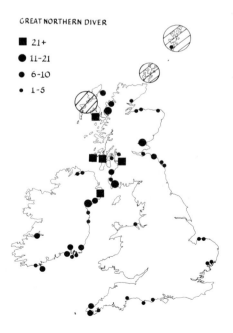

GREAT NORTHERN DIVER

■  21+
●  11-21
•  6-10
·  1-5

Only some 100–300 pairs are thought to breed in Iceland (Cramp et al 1977) so that British numbers themselves account for more than the total Icelandic population. Presumably, therefore, birds from Greenland winter here, and possibly also some from the Canadian arctic.

## LITTLE GREBE *Tachybaptus ruficollis*

The Little Grebe is our commonest breeding grebe. Sharrock (1976) estimated the breeding population to be 9–18,000 pairs. Estuary counts indicate that probably 1,500–2,500 of these winter in coastal waters; many are probably juvenile birds which tend to be more dispersive (Cramp et al 1977). Adult pairs tend to maintain a winter territory on breeding waters.

Little Grebes breeding in north-western and eastern central Europe are generally most mobile in winter, but the only evidence so far of foreign birds reaching Britain involves a Danish ringed bird found in Hertfordshire in January. British ringed birds have been found in France (2) and West Germany (1). The majority of Little Grebes wintering on the sea are found in the southern half of Britain, with few in Scotland. There are notable concentrations, of 60–90, on Strangford Lough, Wexford Harbour, the Duddon estuary and Southampton Water. There are smaller groups of 10–20 in many estuaries in eastern and southern England, but the number wintering inland is far in excess of the total estuarine population.

## GREAT CRESTED GREBE *Podiceps cristatus*

This grebe breeds on lakes and rivers across much of temperate Eurasia, showing a marked preference for salt water in autumn and winter although the larger ice-free European lakes hold many wintering birds. In Britain and Ireland persecution in the 19th century reduced the breeding stock to only 32 known pairs in 1860, but with subsequent protection there has been a continued growth in the population. A breeding season census in 1975 revealed 6,094–6,799 birds (Hughes, Bacon and Flegg 1979). There have been no attempts to assess the European population of the species.

Estuary counts total only 1,800 birds, reflecting both the difficulty of making a full count and the extensive inland wintering on larger lakes and reservoirs. There is no evidence that any British birds emigrate for the winter; indeed single recoveries of Danish and Dutch ringed birds in Kent and Suffolk show that some continental immigration occurs. This may be on a small scale inland but it is thought to be important on the eastern coasts of England and Scotland (Campbell 1980).

Spring increases occur at some of the major sites, notably Formby Point, Alt Estuary (where 100–200 winter and almost 600 are found in spring) and the Blackwater (numbers highest in March). This may be due to the presence of passage migrants, or simply to the gathering together of birds previously scattered along a longer stretch of coast. At Conwy Bay a large autumn flock of over 300 decreases to around 100 for the winter and spring, indicating that this seems to be chiefly a moulting site. In Ireland, Malahide and Carlingford Lough peak in October/November, while these sites together with Dundalk Bay and the Shannon show increases in April (Hutchinson 1979).

   The British and Irish winter distribution reflects that shown in the breeding atlas (Sharrock 1976) in that few are found in apparently suitable habitats in south Wales and south-western England and almost none in northern and north-western Scotland; this raises the possibility that most birds move only short distances, to the nearest suitable coast, although there is no evidence to suggest this. There are discrepancies in that very few are found on the north-eastern English coast and the largest Irish concentration, in Cork Harbour, is well away from the main breeding areas. Most birds are found in sheltered bays and harbours, feeding mostly in shallow inshore waters. Adjacent open coasts are also freely used.

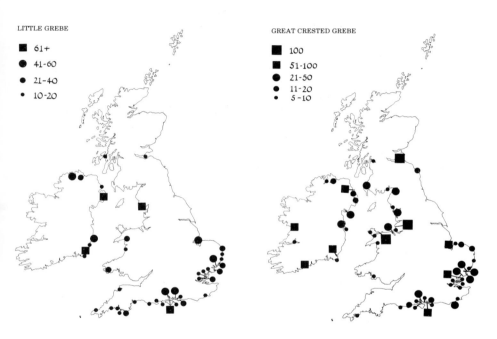

LITTLE GREBE

- ■ 61+
- ● 41-60
- ● 21-40
- • 10-20

GREAT CRESTED GREBE

- ■ 100
- ■ 51-100
- ● 21-50
- ● 11-20
- • 5-10

## RED-NECKED GREBE *Podiceps grisegena*

The only one of the five species of grebe wintering in Britain which does not breed here, the nearest breeding population being in Denmark. The Red-necked Grebe is also the rarest of the wintering grebes, with only an average 80 or so counted each year during the period 1969–75. Outside this period, the 1978–79 winter saw unprecedented influx to British waters, associated with severe weather conditions over most of western Europe.

   The origin of the Red-necked Grebes which winter in Britain is not known but the Danish or, less likely, the central European breeding population presumably provide the majority, with Finnish and Russian birds perhaps more likely to winter in the Baltic region. Red-necked Grebes start to arrive in British coastal waters at the end of July but it is not until October that the main numbers are seen; they leave during March and summering birds are rare. The Firth of Forth is the major British site for the species, where up to 50 have been recorded; it is regularly seen off the Northumberland coast. Elsewhere a few winter regularly in eastern and southern England, but generally it remains a very uncommon winter visitor to the southern half of Britain.

## SLAVONIAN GREBE *Podiceps auritus*

Slavonian Grebes maintain a small breeding population of 50–60 pairs in Britain, all in Scotland (Sharrock 1976), but many more winter here. A conservative estimate of the annual average for the period 1969–75 is about 670 (see below), making it five or six times commoner than the closely similar Black-necked Grebe *P. nigricollis*. Most are found on inshore coastal waters, generally in fairly sheltered situations, but there are probably quite significant numbers scattered in west Scottish sea lochs where censusing in winter is difficult.

Scottish birds may remain on breeding waters until September and then move off to adjacent coastlines to winter (Cramp et al 1977), but the main arrival of foreign birds occurs during October and November. Virtually the whole of the sizeable Icelandic population moves south-east after the breeding season and it is presumably these which winter in Scottish waters; up to 100 are found in each of Shetland and Orkney. Slavonian Grebes breeding in Scandinavia and further east are thought to form most of the birds in the southern North Sea in winter; although the only evidence is a Russian ringed bird found in Yorkshire.

Largest numbers of Slavonian Grebes are found in Scotland, particularly Shetland, Orkney and the Firth of Forth. There are also good numbers in southern and eastern England, where small groups (less than 20) occur from the Wash southwards around the coast to Cornwall. Most, however, occur at south coast sites, notably at Pagham and Poole Harbours, and on the Exe estuary. Very small numbers winter in Ireland (Hutchinson 1979). The species is also scarce in Wales and north-western England and, more surprisingly, it is apparently largely absent on the east coast of England between Durham and Lincolnshire. On inland waters it is scarce or absent, although birds are recorded annually, mainly during passage or in severe weather.

## BLACK-NECKED GREBE *Podiceps nigricollis*

Although breeding across much of temperate Europe, Black-necked Grebes are much commoner in eastern continental Europe. The British and Irish breeding population is currently estimated at 11 pairs (1977) but, since the species frequently forms new breeding groups in unexpected sites, some may be overlooked. Breeding records are currently confined to the central lowlands of Scotland.

In winter, singles or small groups appear at traditional localities on most coasts of Britain; occurrence in Ireland, however, is hardly annual. Black-necked Grebes are less marine than Slavonian Grebes in winter, preferring sheltered harbours and rarely being seen on open coasts. Inland wintering is not infrequent and one site (Staines Reservoir, Middlesex) regularly holds up to ten birds from August to March or April.

The total wintering population is probably about 120 birds of which half are to be found on the coast of southern and south-western England. At the main site, Langstone Harbour, the numbers tend to be erratic within each winter period; the peak count in recent years has been 41 birds.

Unless there are substantial breeding colonies overlooked in Britain and Ireland, the scale of winter numbers indicates immigration. The sources of our wintering birds are completely unknown. While the groups in southern England could arrive by movements south-westwards from continental breeding groups in Denmark and the Netherlands, this is not the case for the Dornoch Firth birds which, except for two Swedish colonies, are to the north of the known world breeding range.

## CORMORANT *Phalacrocorax carbo*

A widespread fairly common sea bird with a predominantly westerly breeding distribution in Britain and Ireland. The race concerned is the nominate *P.c. carbo*, found on north Atlantic coasts, and some 8,000+ pairs breed in Britain annually (Sharrock 1976).

Cormorants prefer shallow inshore waters and are rarely found far out at sea; they tend to return to the breeding ledges in late March and disperse widely from mid-September. There is a fairly large immature population which can be seen on many wintering grounds during the summer months. In the autumn, British birds

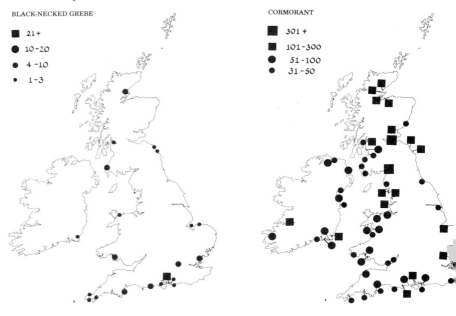

BLACK-NECKED GREBE

■ 21+
● 10-20
● 4 -10
● 1-3

CORMORANT

■ 301 +
■ 101-300
● 51-100
● 31-50

undergo an extensive southward dispersal, and there are many recoveries in northern France and Iberia. However, there is apparently little eastwards movement across the North Sea, with only three recoveries on the continental North Sea coast (all in Holland) up to 1976. Likewise, as might be expected, few continental birds are thought to reach Britain, with the majority of Dutch birds for instance wintering in the western Mediterranean.

The principal concentrations of Cormorants in midwinter in Britain are shown in the map. Estuary counts reveal at least 9,000 birds wintering on the coast. This is very likely to underestimate total numbers as the species can be difficult to count in view of its strongly diurnal and tidal movements. In addition, significant numbers of birds now feed and roost on inland waters, with counts of 100+ being made on several reservoirs in southern Britain. Coastal counts of 30–100 are widespread, while those of 100–300 come mainly from regions where there are good breeding numbers, although perhaps surprisingly also from eastern and southern England. The two largest concentrations, however, are on northern estuaries – the Solway Firth and Firth of Forth, where up to 1,200 are recorded regularly, and indeed 1,400+ were counted at a roost in the latter estuary in January 1977.

## MUTE SWAN *Cygnus olor*

One of the most familiar birds of Britain's inland waterways, Mute Swans also frequent estuarine waters in some numbers, particularly during the winter months.

Although migratory in northern Europe, Mute Swans breeding in Britain are very sedentary, with 98% of birds ringed here moving less than 80 km, and with little movement between river systems (Ogilvie 1967). There is, however, some evidence of moult movements within Britain, e.g. Midlands to the Lancashire coast (Cramp et al 1977). There are very few recoveries of foreign-ringed Mute Swans in Great Britain but small numbers of continental birds may regularly occur in south-eastern Britain in winter (Harrison and Ogilvie 1967).

Some breeding birds remain on territory throughout the year, others join winter

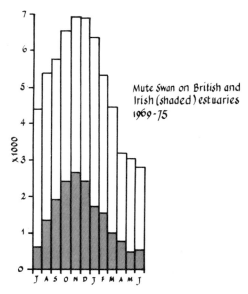

Mute Swan on British and
Irish (shaded) estuaries
1969-75

flocks, returning to breeding waters in early spring. Pre-breeders often remain in such flocks throughout the year.

Estuary counts indicate that most Mute Swans occur on coastal waters during October–January; with just under 7,000 counted on average at the peak in November. This is about 5–6% of the west European winter total; there are no British estuaries of international importance for the species (those with 1,200+). However, the counts do indicate that our estuaries are of importance for British Mute Swans, with up to a third of the population occurring in this habitat for at least four months of the year. Important sites nationally include the Fleet (Dorset), Christchurch Harbour (Dorset), Inner Thames (London), Stour (Essex/Suffolk), Orwell (Suffolk), Tweed (Northumberland), Montrose Basin (Tayside), Cromarty Firth (Highland) and Strangford Lough (Co. Down). Many of these sites are important all year round and not just in one or two months; the Thames, for example, has a flock of up to 600 non-breeding birds in summer.

## BEWICK'S SWAN *Cygnus columbianus bewickii*

Breeds in the northern USSR, east to the Taimyr Peninsula and almost the whole population winters in western Europe. In Britain, about 2,000 winter regularly, mainly in England although formerly most were found in Scotland. This is about 20% of the European total. A further 2,000 are found in Ireland with about two-thirds of these at two estuary sites – Wexford Harbour and Lough Foyle (Merne 1977).

The majority winter inland, the two most important British sites being the Ouse Washes (Cambs/Norfolk) and Slimbridge (Gloucestershire) and the surrounding area. Birds from the latter site often disperse to feed on the nearby Somerset and

Gwent levels as well as on the Severn estuary. On other estuaries there is a flock on the Ribble which now averages 150, while Breydon Water (Norfolk) and the Wash hold 30–50 regularly. Elsewhere there are scattered small flocks, mostly along the eastern and north-western coasts of England but the majority of these are of less than ten birds.

## WHOOPER SWAN *Cygnus cygnus*

The breeding distribution of the Whooper Swan is more southerly than that of Bewick's Swan, *C. columbianus bewickii*, extending into Fenno-Scandia and west to Iceland. The latter population is partially migratory, and about 75% winter in Britain (mainly Scotland) and Ireland (Cramp et al 1977). Some 4,000–6,000 Whooper Swans winter in Ireland (Hutchinson 1979), with a further 3,000 in Britain; this latter total is about 17% of the European wintering population.

Whooper Swans are more inclined to utilise coastal and marine habitat than are Bewick's Swans, but the Lindisfarne flock (*c.* 360, 2% European) is the only one of international importance on a British estuary. Other notable concentrations occur at the coastal Loch of Strathbeg, Grampian (250+), the Ythan estuary, Grampian (140+), Cromarty Firth, Highland (140+) and the North Solway Firth, Dumfries and Galloway (120+). There are many smaller coastal flocks in Scotland but few elsewhere in Britain, although Whooper Swans are regularly recorded on passage in autumn on the east coast and the small numbers occurring there could well be of Russian rather than Icelandic origin. In Ireland, Lough Foyle, Strangford Lough and Lough Swilly are the main coastal sites, all supporting internationally important numbers.

## BEAN GOOSE *Anser fabilis*

This Scandinavian and Russian breeding goose has become very scarce in Britain during the twentieth century. The number wintering in West Europe is estimated to be about 65,000. From its former wide distribution in England and Scotland, there remain only two regular haunts. Neither is strictly estuarine although a flock, averaging slightly fewer than 100, occurs on the reclaimed marshes around Breydon Water, Norfolk. The smaller flock in Kirkcudbrightshire is found on inland pasture.

## PINK-FOOTED GOOSE *Anser brachyrhynchus*

Of the four species of grey geese regularly wintering in Britain, Pink-footed Geese have the most restricted breeding range. There are two discrete populations, one in Iceland and eastern Greenland, the other in Svalbard. The Iceland/Greenlandic population winters solely in Britain, numbers having varied from 30,000 in 1950–51 to a peak of 89,000 in 1974–75, dropping to 69,000 in 1977–78. Thus, with an average British population of 75,000 in recent years, about 83% of the world population winter here. The smaller Svalbard population, numbering 12–15,000, winters mainly in the Netherlands and, more rarely, on other parts of the North Sea coast, only reaching Britain in severe winters.

Pink-footed Geese arrive in Britain from September onwards, Greenland birds join up with the Icelandic population prior to its departure. By the end of October, the whole population is present in Britain. A November count has been carried out since 1950 by the Wildfowl Trust while the birds are still concentrated in the arrival areas.

The most important areas are identified in the map; from these the geese disperse south and south-west into southern Scotland and north-western and eastern England. The spring migration involves departures from more northerly and westerly areas in Scotland and the Outer Hebrides (Williamson 1968) with the peak passage in the second half of April. Pink-footed Geese favour arable farmland and pasture for feeding, but flight to safe nocturnal roosts on estuaries and larger lochs and reservoirs. In recent years more birds have begun to move away from their former, traditional estuarine roosting sites, which are often heavily shot, to roost at inland lakes and reservoirs. On the Ribble, for instance, many fewer have been seen since the creation of the Wildfowl Trust refuge at Martin Mere and additionally, large numbers roost on farmland areas around Southport, where street lamps provide light. The average of 14,000 recorded here make this area of considerable international importance. Internationally important Scottish coastal sites in November include the Ythan (*c.* 6,500), Aberlady Bay (4,400+) and Arbroath (*c.* 4,400); important inland sites are detailed by Ogilvie (1978).

Other sites become important in late winter and early spring as birds disperse after arrival to other wintering areas, or gather before spring departure (open symbols on map). Of these, the most important is the Solway with nearly 15,000 in March, when birds have moved away from south-west Lancashire. There is a winter

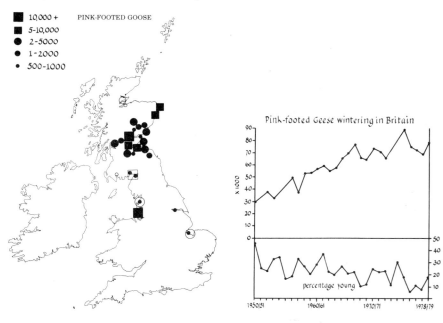

peak in the other English sites of importance, Morecambe Bay with 3,000+ in January and February, and the Wash with 3,000+ in December. Elsewhere in England the numbers have declined, on the Humber from 13,000 in the late 1950s to less than 900 now. During the spring passage the main coastal sites are in Scotland – Wigtown Bay (*c.* 1,000) and the Cromarty Firth (1,200+); count data are incomplete for north-western Scotland at this time. Few birds remain in wintering areas after mid-May.

## WHITE-FRONTED GOOSE *Anser albifrons*

### European race *A. a. albifrons*

This subspecies breeds in Arctic USSR from the Kanin peninsula (44°E) to approximately 150°E. Other subspecies breed in western Greenland (Greenland White-fronted Goose) and eastern Siberia, arctic Alaska and Canada. There are five, more or less discrete, wintering grounds in Eurasia. The British Isles form part of the Baltic–North Sea region which is thought to be visited only by birds from the western parts of the breeding range. The Baltic–North Sea population has been estimated at 120–130,000 in recent seasons. A further 175–260,000 winter in south-eastern Europe and central Turkey, and 10–40,000 in the Caspian region, plus unknown numbers in eastern Asia.

Numbers in the Baltic and North Sea areas have increased dramatically from the levels of 50,000–70,000 recorded in the 1960s. This increase has been absorbed by the Dutch and German wintering grounds and numbers in Britain have actually decreased during the 1970s. The recent mild winters have encouraged more birds to

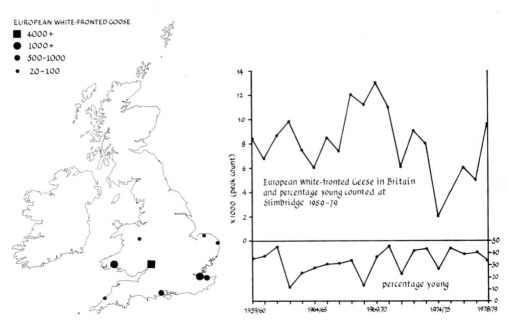

EUROPEAN WHITE-FRONTED GOOSE
- ■ 4000+
- ● 1000+
- ● 500-1000
- • 20-100

European White-fronted Geese in Britain and percentage young counted at Slimbridge 1959-79

x1000 (peak count)

percentage young

remain in the Netherlands, and there has been a concurrent increase in attractive habitat there through reclamation and the establishment of new goose refuges. Between 80,000 and 120,000 now winter in the Netherlands, and flocks in southern England and Wales are now smaller and arrive later. The lower numbers at Slimbridge have included average or higher than average proportions of young birds, showing that the decrease there is not associated with poor breeding success.

The winter habitat of European White-fronted Geese is flat grazing land. River flood plains, reclaimed grassland and coastal marshes are particularly favoured, in contrast to the preference of the Greenland race for bogs. There are now four main haunts of this subspecies in Britain. The New Grounds at Slimbridge held an average peak of 4,500 in the early 1970s but numbers subsequently fell to 1,450–4,000 in 1975–78. The Tywi valley is the second most important site, with a peak of 2,000 in 1970. As at Slimbridge, numbers have subsequently fallen. Only a few hundred geese were found here in the early 1960s. Up to 1,750 have wintered in the North Kent marshes and on the Swale; following development on the Thames marshes, the Isle of Sheppey is now the chief site. The fourth area is the lower Avon valley in Hampshire where 600–1,200 have been found regularly since the early 1960s. Elsewhere the most consistent sites are Breydon Water, Norfolk (50–100), Welshpool, Powys (less than 100), Holkham, Norfolk (50–60) and the Camel estuary, Cornwall (20–30). The Breydon Marshes were formerly a major site with up to 2,500 recorded during 1939–45. During hard weather, numbers and distribution change markedly as Dutch birds are shifted westwards and, as in 1978–79, quite large flocks of White-fronted Geese may appear at unexpected places.

## Greenland race A.a. flavirostris

This subspecies, clearly distinct from other races of the White-fronted Goose, breeds only in coastal west Greenland and winters almost exclusively in the British Isles. Flocks occur on passage in Iceland. There are almost annual records of singles or small groups in the Atlantic coast states of North America.

The population size is currently estimated at about 12,000 (Ogilvie 1978), with some recent decline, although the breeding range has been spreading northwards. There has, however, never been a complete census. The small scattered flocks in parts of Ireland and the Hebrides are among the least conspicuous of all the geese, owing to the dull dark colour of the birds and their habit of feeding in quite tall marshy vegetation. The traditional preference for bogs and marshes differentiates them from the European race and may be associated with the longer bill of the Greenland birds; many Greenland birds, however, have been attracted to arable land by the better feeding.

Half of the population winters at the Wexford Slobs, where there has been a change in feeding habit towards arable land in the last decade. Islay is the second most important site and holds about 30% of the population. Other sites regularly supporting over 100 birds are Loch Ken in Galloway (400), Kintyre (400), the Middle Shannon (300), Little Brosna River (300) and Lake Heilen in Caithness (150). Smaller flocks occur over much of central and western Ireland, and at Borth Bog in North Wales; parties are occasionally found at localities in the Outer Hebrides and on Skye and Tiree. There used to be, at least until the early 1970s, up

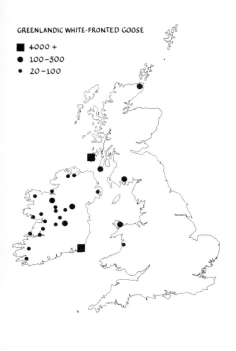

GREENLANDIC WHITE-FRONTED GOOSE

■ 4000 +
● 100–500
• 20–100

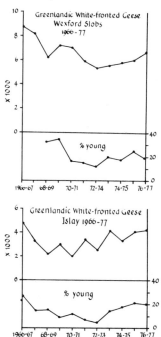

to 200 wintering in Anglesey, but during the decade they appear to have been replaced by the European race. Tregaron Bog, previously the south-eastern most site, is now deserted.

The numbers and percentage young recorded at the two main sites are shown in the diagram. Both sites show a decrease followed by a recovery, but in 1976–77 numbers were still lower than ten years previously. However, the poor correlation between the patterns of counts, and especially between the estimates of percentage young, suggests strongly that the Wexford and the Islay birds originate from different sections of the breeding grounds. Brood size in the Islay flocks is consistently lower than that recorded at Wexford.

The steady increase at Wexford since 1975 coincides with the opening of an important reserve. On Islay and the Wexford Slobs, Greenland White-fronted Geese have adapted well to drainage and reclamation which in the early 1970s was thought to be a major threat.

## GREYLAG GOOSE *Anser anser*

Greylag Geese have a very patchy distribution in the western Palearctic, which is probably mainly due to loss of habitat and persecution; in the central USSR and further east, the distribution does become more continuous. Despite this, it breeds further south than other geese and extends north beyond the Arctic Circle. Britain has a small native population, in north-western Scotland, of about 200 pairs. There are a further 500–600 pairs of feral origin breeding as far south in Britain as Kent, and in Ireland (Sharrock 1976).

Two races are recognised: *A.a. anser*, the nominate form of western and central Europe, and the eastern *A.a. rubrirostris*. All forms of intermediates occur, however, between the extreme western and eastern populations; some of the latter have been introduced and are breeding in south-eastern England.

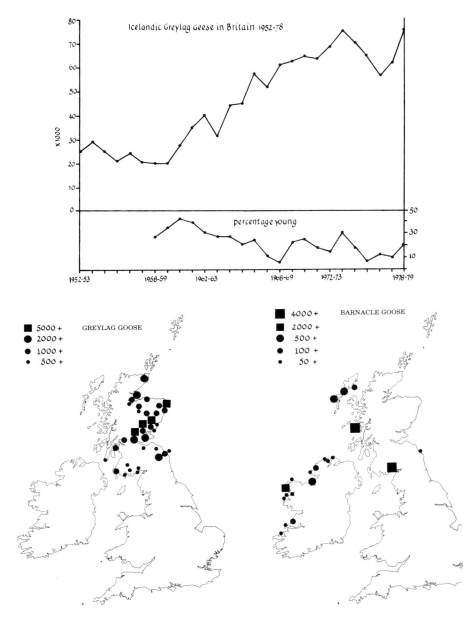

About 98,000 Greylag Geese winter in western Europe; 66,000 of these (about 67%) are found in Britain and Ireland, including almost all the Icelandic breeders. There is only one sizeable flock in Ireland, numbering about 250, and that country supports well under a thousand in total (Hutchinson 1979).

The few British breeders appear to be mainly sedentary. The main arrival of Icelandic birds occurs during the second half of October. Greylag Geese make far less use of estuaries than other geese, feeding almost exclusively on farmland and roosting mainly on inland waters. Although they occur with Pik-footed Geese *A. brachyrhynchus* in many areas of Scotland, the Greylag Goose flocks tend to be smaller and more scattered. Before departure in spring, Greylag Geese tend to concentrate in large numbers, move northwards within Britain during March, and leave in April.

As with Pink-footed Geese, many important wintering sites for Greylag Geese are inland, particularly in central and north-eastern Scotland; details are given in Ogilvie (1978). Coastal sites of international importance (those with 980+) include Stranraer (*c.* 1,900). Ythan (1,800+), Bute (1,750) and the Moray (1,350) and Beauly (980) Firths. The counts are averages for 1973–77 and indicate the lesser extent to which Greylags use estuarine and other coastal sites compared with some other goose species.

## BARNACLE GOOSE *Branta leucopsis*

Barnacle Geese have a limited Arctic distribution, breeding in eastern Greenland, Svalbard and in Russia on Novaya Zemlya and Vaiguch Island. The three populations winter in discrete areas: Greenland birds in western Scotland and Ireland, Svalbard birds entirely on the Solway Firth, and the Russian birds in the Netherlands and West Germany. Numbers wintering here have increased

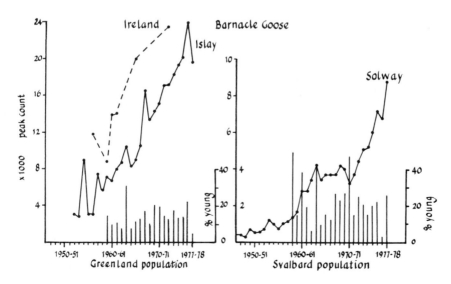

tremendously in the past 30 years, so with about 75,000 wintering on average in western Europe (the entire world population), Britain and Ireland hold almost 40%. The diagram shows that just under 20,000 birds wintered on Islay in 1977–78, and the equivalent Solway count was 6,750. These increases appear to have occurred largely as a result of increased protection on the wintering grounds.

Greenland birds arrive in the second week of October and those from Svalbard slightly earlier, from the end of September. The return in spring, however, sees the Greenland birds moving north in Britain from late March onwards, departure for the breeding grounds occurring during April, just before the Svalbard birds. In winter quarters, Barnacle Geese feed on pastureland and saltmarsh.

Sites with regular winter flocks of over 50 birds are shown in the map, with the majority of the smaller flocks in the north and west of Ireland. The main Irish flock, however, numbers 2,000+ and is on the Inishkea Islands; other sites of importance include Lissadell and Inishmurray, both in Co. Sligo, and Mutton Island, Co. Clare; each has 250–500 birds, though the first of these recorded 750 in the 1976–77 and 1977–78 winters (Hutchinson 1979). In Britain the most important site for Greenland Barnacle Geese is undoubtedly Islay which has recorded up to 24,000 in recent years (1976–77); in the Outer Hebrides up to 3,100+ have been counted (1966) with, on average, 2,300+ from seven counts made there 1957–73 (Ogilvie and Boyd 1975); the Monach Islands (650+), Sound of Harris (540+) and Shiants (350+) are the most important sites.

In 1963 it was established that all the Svalbard birds wintered on the Solway Firth; 8,800 were counted in 1978–79, having built steadily from 400 in the late 1940s (Ogilvie 1978). Virtually all of these are found at Caerlaverock (Dumfries and Galloway) early in the winter, then the birds disperse west towards Southerness as the winter progresses. In March and April large numbers are also found on the inner and southern saltmarshes of the Solway. Elsewhere, a small flock is regular on the Farne Islands, mainly in autumn, and these are probably birds of Russian origin.

## DARK-BELLIED BRENT GOOSE *Branta bernicla bernicla*

Brent Geese are high Arctic breeders and most of the birds which winter in Britain are of the nominate race *B.b. bernicla*, the dark-bellied form. They breed in the USSR from Kolgner eastwards to the Taimyr Peninsula. The entire world population of *B.b. bernicla* winters in north-western Europe. During the period 1972–75 it averaged around 70,000 birds. The population has since increased to over 150,000 (1978–80); the fluctuations in numbers wintering here and in Europe, together with annual breeding success are shown in the diagram. Numbers wintering in Britain during 1972–75 averaged about 34,400 birds or almost 50% of the world population, a slightly lower percentage (40–45%) wintered in Britain during the high numbers of the late 1970s. Virtually all of these are found in southern and eastern England between the Wash and the Exe with a few having appeared elsewhere in recent years.

Brent Geese are traditionally found wintering on mud flats, where they feed on eel-grass *Zostera*, and later in the winter on various marine algae (especially *Enteromorpha* and *Ulva*). However, many flocks have started to feed on farmland in recent years. This habit was first seen in Essex (Bennett and St Joseph 1974) but subsequently, during the late 1970s, spread to the Wash, Sussex and Hampshire. The birds feed on winter cereals, grass leys and permanent pasture and the large localised flocks can cause serious damage to the first two of these and reduce the amount of grass available for spring grazing on pasture.

Brent Geese, having moulted, leave their breeding grounds from mid-August

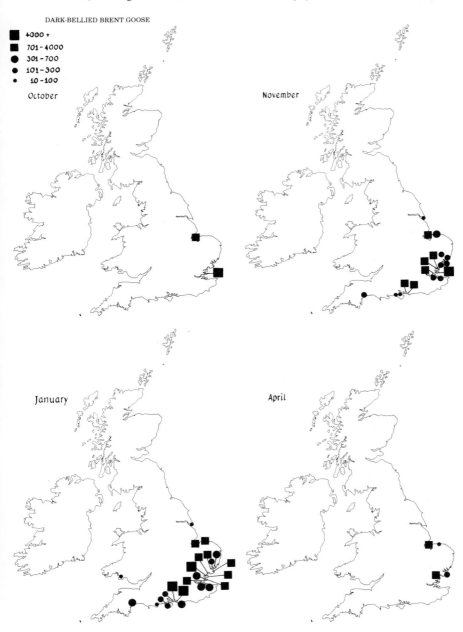

DARK-BELLIED BRENT GOOSE

4000 +
701–4000
301–700
101–300
10–100

October

November

January

April

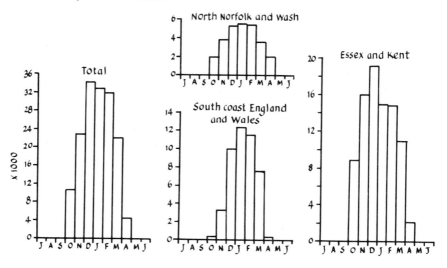

onwards and travel west along the Arctic coast, then overland to north-western Europe via the Baltic. Birds begin to arrive in England from the end of September, and by October about 11,000 are present. Numbers more than double by November and flocks are then present on many of their main wintering grounds. However, Maplin Sands/Foulness Island is a major annual site – at times in November over

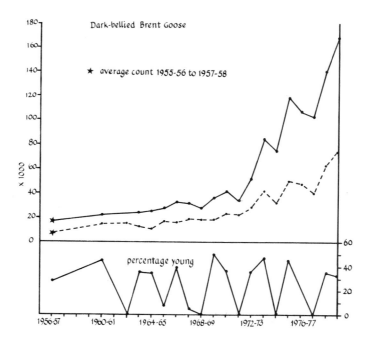

half of the Brent Geese present in Britain are found there. Other estuaries along the Essex and Kent coasts also receive early birds. The early peak at Foulness shows up clearly. In contrast the peak on the south coast occurs later, in January and February, although with the present high numbers the peak is now slightly earlier. Overall, the midwinter peak occurred in December when birds which, earlier, had stopped off in Denmark and West Germany arrived in Britain. There may also be some onward movement in early winter of birds going to France; this is the other important area for Brent Geese in north-western Europe. France and Britain, together, usually hold at least 75% and, in midwinter, often more than 90% of the total population (Ogilvie and St Joseph 1976). Although the peak occurs in December there are only slightly fewer birds in January and February. This may be due to birds going further south, or to the increased mobility of flocks when the food supply has diminished in the estuaries. In general, however, Brent Goose flocks are highly traditional, even to sub-areas within each estuary.

Table 17:1  *Principal sites for Dark-bellied Brent Goose* — Branta b. bernicla *in England, 1972–75*

| | Highest monthly count | % world population | Months above 1%* |
|---|---|---|---|
| Foulness | 9,372 | 13·4 | 10 <u>11</u> 12 1 2 3 |
| Chichester Harbour | 5,590 | 8·0 | 11 12 1 <u>2</u> 3 |
| Langstone Harbour | 5,319 | 7·6 | 11 12 <u>1</u> 2 3 |
| Blackwater | 4,715 | 6·7 | 11 <u>12</u> 1 2 3 4 |
| Wash | 3,585 | 5·1 | 10 11 <u>12</u> 1 2 3 4 |
| Hamford Water | 2,735 | 3·9 | 12 1 <u>2</u> 3 |
| Leigh/Canvey | 2,445 | 3·5 | <u>11</u> 12 1 |
| North Norfolk | 2,230 | 3·2 | 12 1 <u>2</u> |
| Colne | 1,810 | 2·6 | 12 1 <u>2</u> 3 |
| Dengie | 1,363 | 1·9 | 11 12 1 <u>2</u> 3 |
| Crouch/Roach | 809 | 1·2 | <u>2</u> |

* Month of highest count is underlined.

The large numbers present in December to February begin to diminish by the end of the latter month and especially during March when the main spring departure to the Waddensea begins. The average count for March was about 22,000+ falling to 4,500 in April. Brent Geese also leave France during this period to go to the Waddensea where, during April and May, the great majority of the population can be found. During the late 1970s the Wash had become an important site for spring flocks, when up to 5,000 were present. At the time of the 'Estuaries Enquiry', however, it was less significant.

Principal estuaries for Dark-bellied Brent in 1972–75 are listed in Table 17:1. As already mentioned, Foulness in Essex was the most important in Britain, with over 13% of the world population present in November (9,300+). In November 1973, 13,000 were counted there (15·5% of the world population), and more recently in

1979, over 19,000 were seen (12·2%). Essex, Sussex, Hampshire, Norfolk and Lincolnshire are the principal counties for Brent Geese. Only the Wash has internationally important numbers of the species for more months than Foulness, mainly because numbers were large in October and in April.

In the 1930s the Brent Goose numbers underwent a dramatic decline, apparently linked to a massive reduction of its food plant *Zostera*. As recently as the late 1950s the population was fewer than 16,000. The diagram shows that subsequently numbers rose, slowly at first to 30,000 in the late 1960s, but dramatically from 1971, so that by 1979–80 they had reached 167,000 and had become the most numerous goose in western Europe, even outstripping the White-fronted Goose. However, Dark-bellied Brent Geese have the most variable breeding success of all Palearctic geese, ranging from almost nil to nearly 50%. There have been only two failures in the last eight breeding seasons (or three out of the last eleven) compared with three successful and four failures before that. This change in climatic fortune has undoubtedly had a major influence upon the sudden increase – its effect is likely to be enhanced as the Brent Goose is a relatively long-lived species. Changes in its breeding success are not the only factors helping the increase, during the 1970s it was also given added protection against shooting in most continental European countries. Only West Germany had not protected it by 1972, but subsequently it was given some protection. The future is difficult to predict, especially with population pressures forcing birds into field feeding habits, but the likelihood of some reintroduction of shooting in Denmark and Germany may help to stabilise, or even reduce, the population level.

## PALE-BELLIED BRENT GOOSE *Branta bernicla hrota*

### North-east Canadian and Greenland Population

It had been thought that all the Irish-wintering Brent Geese came from northern and north-eastern Greenland, but ringing studies have since shown that birds from the north-eastern Canadian arctic are also involved. Birds of this race from the latter region also winter on the Atlantic coast of the USA. The boundary on the breeding grounds between American-wintering and Irish-wintering birds is unclear.

None of this race winters regularly in Europe outside Ireland; stragglers are, however, not infrequent at some sites in western Britain. Thousands occur on passage in spring and autumn in Iceland, but some flocks probably migrate direct across the Atlantic.

The size of the population was possibly as small as 7,350 in the mid-1960s, but counts of up to 16,300 have been recorded in recent seasons. Arrivals begin in late August in Co. Kerry but are not usually seen until October at Strangford Lough. Peak counts are normally in December, dropping quite steeply in the mid and late winter. This is, however, probably due to the relative ease of counting in December, when the birds are mainly in large flocks and 60–70% are at Strangford Lough, rather than to onward or return movements. Later on, the birds disperse from Strangford Lough along the eastern and southern coasts of Ireland. Most leave during March.

With counts of up to 10,800, Strangford Lough is by far the most important site.

PALE-BELLIED BRENT GOOSE

- ■ 5000 +
- ■ 1001 - 5000
- ● 501 - 1000
- ● 101 - 500
- • 50 - 100

November

Jan-February

Tralee Bay with up to 3,000, and Castlemaine Harbour (up to 2,000) are next in importance; numbers are highest in February at these sites, and in February 1974, more were counted in Tralee Bay than at Strangford Lough.

A major arrival site from which the birds disperse later in the winter parallels the strategy of Dark-bellied Brent Geese in southern England, where Foulness provides

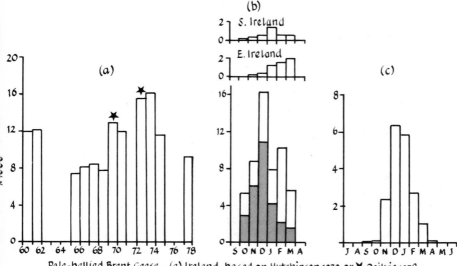

Pale-bellied Brent Geese - (a) Ireland, based on Hutchinson 1979 or ✱ Ogilvie 1978 – (b) monthly numbers in Ireland 1973/74 (Strangford Lough shaded) – (c) Svalbard population, Lindisfarne, 1969-76

an early peak count. In common with the Dark-bellied race, *B.b. hrota* has fed increasingly on inland fields since the early 1970s, even though the population size has not increased as dramatically in Ireland.

## Svalbard Population

This population of Brent Goose breeds in Svalbard and, possibly, also in the Franz Josef Islands. In winter it is only found in numbers at three localities in northern Denmark and one in north-eastern England; the winter range is the furthest north for any population of this species.

Estimates of the total number are few, but apparently there has been a decline from about 4,000–5,000 in the 1950s to a present level of less than 2,500. In October, most are in the Mariager and Randers Fjords in Denmark, having migrated down the Norwegian or Swedish coasts. A variable number then moves across the North Sea to winter at Lindisfarne; in recent seasons there were peaks of 1,714 in December 1973 and 1,000 in January 1971, but in 1974–75 only up to 300 were counted. Large influxes may take place into Britain in severe winters, for example in 1979–80 when virtually the entire population arrived at Lindisfarne and small groups were scattered over much of the coast of south-eastern England. Most British wintering birds probably return via north-western Denmark, where there is a spring peak in Nissum Fjord. Occasional Pale-bellied Brent Geese in the southern North Sea and in eastern Scotland probably originate from this 'North Sea' population rather than the 'Irish' population.

Svalbard Brent Geese have apparently declined while other European populations have been stable or increasing, and their current low level may be some cause for concern. The recent ban on shooting Brent Geese in Denmark should aid their conservation.

## SHELDUCK *Tadorna tadorna*

The number of Shelducks occurring in western Europe in recent years has been estimated at 120,000–130,000 (Atkinson-Willes 1976). Britain and Ireland support about half of this total from late December to the middle of June and form an important breeding as well as a wintering area for the species. Although the great majority of wintering Shelducks are our breeding birds they are augmented by a small, but as yet unknown, number of adults and juveniles which have bred in Sweden, West Germany and Belgium, and probably some from Denmark and the Netherlands.

Shelducks seem to be catholic in the habitats chosen. They occur in the predominantly sandy estuaries in north-western England and in the relatively muddy estuaries of eastern and southern England. The principal food item in most areas is the small gastropod snail *Hydrobia ulvae* (Olney 1965) which Shelducks obtain by moving their bills in a crescent through the muddy surface layers, or by dabbling in exposed wet or shallow water areas (Bryant and Leng 1975). Most other invertebrates in the surface mud are also taken.

The numbers occurring in Britain and Ireland are presented in the diagram.

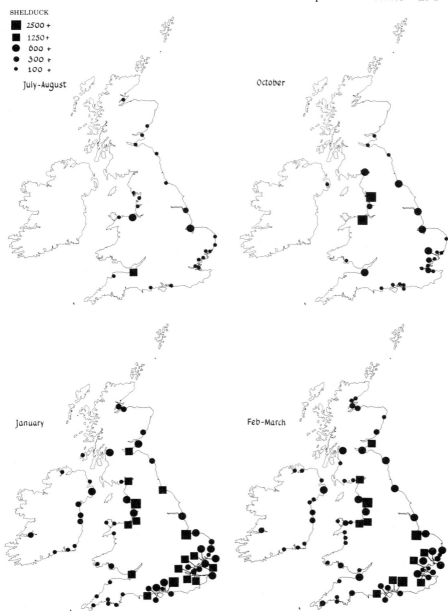

SHELDUCK
- ■ 2500 +
- ■ 1250 +
- ● 600 +
- ● 300 +
- • 100 +

July-August

October

January

Feb-March

During late June, throughout July and into early August there is a moult migration of adults, and some immatures, to the large mudflats of the Grosser Knechsand on the German Waddensea between the estuaries of the Weser and the Elbe (Coombes 1950, Goethe 1961). Birds from western Britain have been observed to leave Morecambe Bay and the Mersey (Allen and Rutter 1956) in the late evening and head eastwards, apparently en route to the Humber estuary or beyond to the Waddensea. Thus, during August and September, only juveniles and a relatively small number of adults (see later) remain in Britain and Ireland. After the completion of their moult, Shelduck start to trickle back to Britain in October but the return migration is not completed until January, coincidental with the onset of cold weather on the Waddensea. There is an apparent steady decrease in numbers during March which continues until summer. This is not, however, due to a major movement away from Britain and Ireland but results from the start of display and nest site investigations prior to breeding. The numbers recorded on estuaries do, of course, include non-breeding birds; the precise number of these is not known although it is generally assumed, based unfortunately on very few studies, to be in the order of half of the birds present.

Eastern England has peak numbers in January but in virtually all other areas they occur in February. In north-western England, however, unlike other regions, there are very large numbers in late autumn and the midwinter peak is only about 25% higher than the October count. In contrast, in eastern England it is three times higher, in southern England seven times, eastern Scotland eight times, Ireland eleven times and Wales twelve times higher. This shows the steady spread of Shelducks from the Waddensea through eastern England, then into southern, northern and, finally, western areas. Several possibilities exist which might explain the north-western anomaly; it could be the main area for recruitment of young, it might be such a good feeding area that juveniles accumulate there in autumn, or there may be an unknown moulting ground. The first possibility is unlikely in view of the south and westward dispersal of juveniles in autumn from eastern England. There is little evidence for the third, although three Scottish adults have been recovered on coasts of the north Irish Sea between August and October.

The map presents the distribution of Shelducks in Britain and Ireland during four

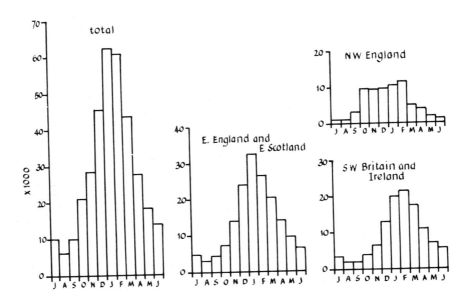

*Table 17:2  Estuaries of international importance for Shelduck, 1969–75*

| | Highest av. monthly count | % W. European | Months above 1%* |
|---|---|---|---|
| Wash | 8,660 | 6·7 | 11 12 **1** 2 3 4 5 6 |
| Morecambe Bay | 5,600 | 4·3 | 10 11 12 1 **2** 3 |
| Dee | 4,293 | 3·3 | 9 **10** 11 12 1 2 |
| Chichester Harbour | 3,074 | 2·4 | 1 **2** 3 |
| Medway | 2,385 | 1·8 | 12 1 **2** |
| Stour | 2,225 | 1·7 | **1** 2 3 |
| Poole Harbour | 2,062 | 1·6 | 12 **1** 2 3 |
| Blackwater | 1,990 | 1·5 | 12 **1** 2 3 |
| Severn | 1,824 | 1·4 | **7**                    6 |
| Mersey | 1,762 | 1·4 | **1** 2 3 |
| Eden | 1,705 | 1·3 | **3** |
| N. Kent Marshes | 1,700 | 1·3 | **1** 2 |
| Langstone Harbour | 1,567 | 1·2 | **2** |
| Firth of Forth | 1,511 | 1·2 | **12** 1 |
| Solway, north | 1,464 | 1·1 | **1**   3 |
| Teesmouth | 1,358 | 1·0 | **11** 12 1 |
| Colne | 1,330 | 1·0 | **1** |

* Underlining denotes month of highest count

different times of the year. The July/August map shows that few are present; the only really important concentration is in Bridgwater Bay on the Severn where 1,000–2,000 birds moult (Eltringham and Boyd 1963). Recently, a small number has been found moulting on the Firth of Forth (Bryant and Waugh 1976). The majority of the other birds recorded are juveniles. When numbers increase in early autumn the Irish Sea estuaries become important, but by midwinter the bulk of the population occurs from East Anglia to southern England. By mid-February, and certainly by mid-March, most Shelduck have reached their coastal breeding areas and the map for this time of year indicates the principal breeding zones. Yarker and Atkinson-Willes (1971) estimated that approximately 12,000 pairs bred in Britain and Ireland.

The principal estuaries for Shelduck are shown in Table 17:2. The Wash, with a winter peak count of over 12,000, and Morecambe Bay with a steady 3,000–6,000, are much the most important areas, although the Dee, with up to 6,000 in autumn, and Teesside, with up to 4,000 at times in winter, also support very large numbers.

The numbers of Shelducks have been steadily increasing in Britain and Ireland since wildfowl counts were started in 1948, although numbers were relatively steady from 1959–60 to 1970–71. There has been a noticeable increase since then and a dramatic increase in 1975–76; however, this latter rise is not likely to be a result of better breeding but is more probably due to the very sharp cold spell in the Wadden Sea in early February 1976.

## WIGEON *Anas penelope*

The breeding range of this sub-Arctic duck extends from Iceland and Scotland eastwards to the Pacific coast of USSR. Only 300–500 pairs are thought to breed in Britain (Sharrock 1976), mainly in upland Scotland and the northern Pennines, but some also in lowland England and Scotland. Although moorland is the typical breeding habitat, the largest single concentration in Britain is at Loch Leven in lowland Fife.

In winter, Wigeon are found around coasts and inland waters in western Europe (400,000), the Mediterranean basin (500,000), parts of North and East Africa (south to Tchad and, rarely, Tanzania), south-western Asia (500,000) and Japan. Iceland and the British Isles are the only parts of the regular breeding range which also hold wintering birds. Although small numbers summer irregularly on British estuaries, the counts from May to August were tiny compared with the winter population. Arrivals began in late August with numbers increasing rapidly to a sharp midwinter peak in December. Return movements occurred in strength from late February to late March, leaving relatively few birds in April and extremely few in May.

The regional histograms show that the patterns of counts varied with latitude. At northern localities there was a fairly low peak early in the season, in November. Three-quarters of the peak winter population was already present in October. By contrast, numbers in the south and south-west of England continued to increase until January, and only a third of the winter peak numbers were present in October. The rest of Britain and Ireland showed an intermediate timing of the peak (December) and large changes in the midwinter monthly counts, which were much less apparent elsewhere.

This pattern of change across the country is consistent with early winter birds

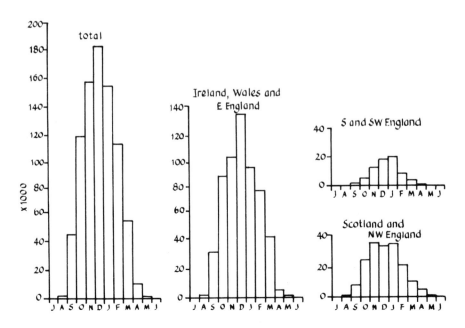

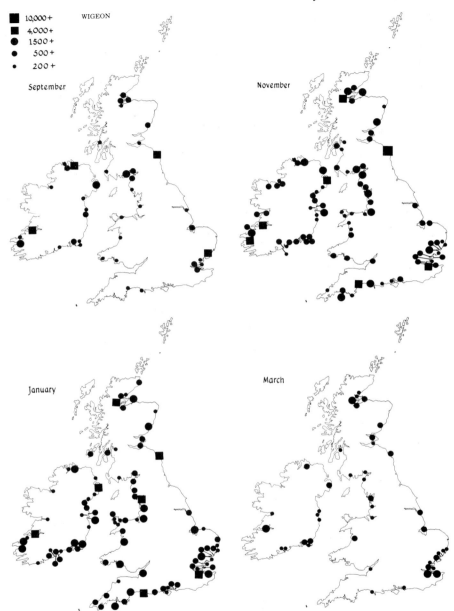

moving south from Scotland during midwinter and flocks further south also being augmented by continental arrivals at this time. Icelandic, Scandinavian and Russian birds are known to winter in Britain. Ringing recoveries show that the Icelandic birds arrive chiefly in Scotland and Ireland; continental birds migrate through the Baltic and arrive chiefly in south-eastern England from Denmark or the Netherlands (Donker 1959).

*Table 17:3   Estuaries of international importance for Wigeon*

| | Highest av. monthly count | % W. European | Months above 1% W. Europe | | | | | |
|---|---|---|---|---|---|---|---|---|
| Lindisfarne | 21,900 | 5·5 | 9 | 10 | 11 | 12 | 1 | |
| Strangford | 11,250 | 2·8 | | 10 | 11 | 12 | 1 | |
| Shannon | (10,000) | 2·5 | | | 11 | 12 | 1 | 2 |
| Foyle | 9,281 | 2·3 | 9 | 10 | 11 | | | |
| Medway | 7,541 | 1·9 | | | 11 | 12 | 1 | |
| Castlemaine | (6,500) | 1·6 | | 10 | 11 | | | |
| Cromarty | 5,609 | 1·4 | | | 11 | | 1 | |
| Exe | 4,467 | 1·1 | | | 11 | 12 | | |
| Morecambe Bay | 4,125 | 1·0 | | | | | 1 | |
| Montrose | 4,100 | 1·0 | | 10 | | | | |
| Fleet | 4,014 | 1·0 | | | | | 1 | |

*\* Underlining denotes month of highest count*

Recoveries of birds ringed in Britain in winter are widely distributed, mainly on the coasts of adjacent continental Europe and the Baltic, and interior Finland and Siberia eastwards to almost 80°E. Scandinavia apparently contributes relatively few birds to the British wintering population. The distribution of breeding season recoveries for drakes is similar to that for ducks, except that a disproportionately high percentage of the northernmost Siberian recoveries are of drakes (Mead 1974). It is likely that many British breeders remain within Britain and Ireland for the winter, but this small population must contribute less than 2% to the peak winter numbers.

Wigeon are quite distinct from other ducks in their habitat and feeding requirements, in that they are very largely vegetarian and feed chiefly on land or exposed mud. At British sites most (34·4%) feed on mudflats; inland flooded pasture (24·6%) and saltmarsh/salting pasture (20·0%) are also important (Owen and Williams 1976). It is the only duck to form tight packs of grazing birds.

Few inland sites are important, although accounting for 19% of Wigeon-days in Britain (Owen and Williams 1976). The principal inland site is the Ouse Washes, which holds numbers as high as 42,500 (or up to 21% of the British and Irish winter population). Otherwise, only Abberton Reservoir occasionally holds numbers of international importance. At such sites the birds feed chiefly on exposed grasslands near the water's edge, also on adjacent meadows and arable fields.

On the estuaries the green algae *Enteromporpha* and eel-grass *Zostera* are the major foods. At most sites, adjacent wet or dry meadows are additional feeding grounds. The internationally important estuarine sites are shown in Table 17:3.

Maps show the geographical distribution of the main sites and how the Wigeon distribution alters through the season. The increases in the relative importance of the southern and south-western sites between September and November, and between November and January are evident from the maps. March numbers are higher than for September but the distribution is less clumped into a few estuarine sites. No estuaries hold 1% of the western European population in March, whereas the September arrival produces internationally important concentrations on the eastern coast of England and in Ireland. Atkinson-Willes (1963) gives a distribution map for Wigeon sites, including those inland, which differs little from the more recent information presented here for estuaries. Numbers at the Ouse Washes have, however, increased by a factor of at least six since that date.

## GADWALL *Anas strepera*

The Gadwall is not a numerous species, breeding in small numbers in Britain and Ireland, and is only slightly more numerous on its central European breeding grounds. The north-western European wintering population is thought to be about 2,500, a small number compared to a total of 55,000 in the whole of Europe. In Britain Gadwall are most commonly seen inland in southern and eastern England, where they have increased noticeably in recent years. They occur in very small numbers, infrequently exceeding ten individuals, on estuaries in the same region.

## TEAL *Anas crecca*

This is one of the commoner surface-feeding ducks to be found in Britain. It has a circumpolar breeding distribution, although like several other Anatidae it is absent from Greenland. The North American Green-winged Teal *A.c. carolinensis* is a vagrant to Britain and the nominate *A.c. crecca* is the form breeding and wintering in north-western Europe. Nearly 90,000 pairs breed, the bulk of these in Finland; in

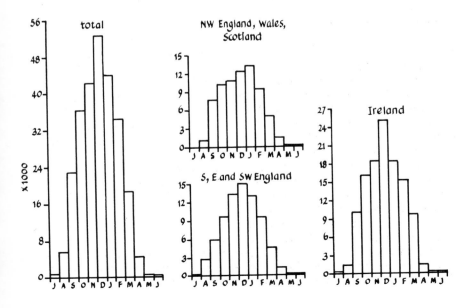

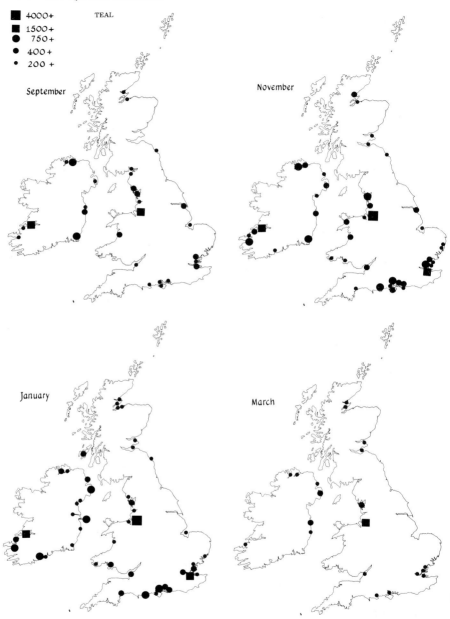

Britain about 3,500–6,000 may breed annually (Sharrock 1976). It is commoner in the north and west, where it favours rushy heath and moorland pools and streams.

Teal which winter in Britain originate from Russia, Fenno-Scandia and central Europe; Icelandic Teal winter mainly in Ireland and Scotland. British breeders tend to be largely sedentary, moving far only in severe weather.

Around 150,000 Teal winter in western Europe, mainly in Britain, the Netherlands and western France, with a few stragglers reaching North Africa. This total is small compared with numbers wintering further east: 750,000 in the Black Sea–Mediterranean region and over 600,000 in some years in the western USSR (Cramp et al 1977). The average midwinter peak on British and Irish estuaries, which occurred usually in December, revealed some 52,000+ birds, or about 35% of those in western Europe. Counts elsewhere over the same period reveal that significant numbers occur inland in Britain, probably well over 10,000.

Shallow areas of water are favoured during winter, including large estuaries, coastal lagoons, and marshes where Teal feed mainly on seeds; inland there is less dependence on man-made artefacts than in some other species, and the birds are frequently found on flooded grazing land, marshes, small ponds and decoys. Hard weather movements are liable to occur at any time during the winter, and Teal tend not to tolerate frequent disturbance by man.

As with other dabbling ducks, the males desert the females soon after their clutch is complete and undergo a moult migration. This begins in June and males moult in areas some way south of the breeding grounds, usually on larger lakes with abundant emergent vegetation such as *Phragmites* reed-beds. Birds appear in north-western Europe from late June onwards, and on moulting grounds in Denmark a peak in flightless birds occurs towards the end of July (Kortegaard 1974). A few birds move into Britain during August after moult, and numbers then build up on estuaries – 5,200 in August to 42,000 in November. The main period of movement south and south-westwards across Europe occurs in October and November (Cramp et al 1977). Numbers rise to their maximum in December, when the count in 1969–75 revealed an average of 52,300+ Teal on British and Irish estuaries. Numbers fall off somewhat in January (*c.* 44,000) – the reason for this is not entirely clear – and by the end of February some Teal begin the return migration northwards. The majority depart during March and April and by the end of April fewer than 2,000 remain, dropping further in May and June.

The principal estuaries for Teal are given in Table 17:4, which reveals that few estuaries within Britain and Ireland are internationally important for the species. However, this discounts the large number of smaller flocks which occur throughout Britain, with many estuaries having 200–700 birds during January. In north-western England the Mersey is an important site, averaging some 6,400 birds in January, but

---

*Table 17:4  Principal estuaries for Teal* Anas crecca *in Britain and Ireland, 1969–75*

|  | Peak count | % W. European | Months above 1%* |
|---|---|---|---|
| Mersey | 6,380 | 4·3 | 9 10 11 12 <u>1</u> 2 3 |
| Medway | 3,910 | 2·6 | 11 <u>12</u> 1 2 |
| Shannon | 2,000–4,000* | 1·3–2·7 | <u>12</u> |
| Castlemaine Harbour | 1,501–2,000* | 1·0–1·3 | <u>12</u> |

Underlining denotes month of highest count
* Irish data from Hutchinson (1979); no figures available for other months.

Morecambe Bay, the Dee and the Ribble also record up to 700 in this month. In the southern half of Britain the Medway is the only internationally important estuary. This holds about 4,000 in December and over 2,600 in January. However, there are many smaller flocks present on the estuaries of the south and south-east, notably Poole Harbour and Southampton Water (*c.* 1,060), the Crouch (650+), Langstone Harbour (580) and Burry Inlet (500+). In Northern Ireland, Strangford Lough regularly records over a 1,000 birds in January. Important inland sites averaging over 500 Teal during January include the Ouse Washes, Cambridge/Norfolk (3,000+) and Hickling Broad, Norfolk (*c.* 750) in the south-east; and Leighton Moss, Lancs (730+), Rosthern Mere, Cheshire (*c.* 650) and Lower Derwent Floods, Yorks (550+) in the north-west.

## MALLARD *Anas platyrhynchos*

Mallard are the most familiar and widespread ducks of the northern hemisphere, breeding as far south as the tip of North Africa and north to northern Norway; they are found throughout Iceland and the rest of the Palearctic. Mallard also breed over more than half of the USA, apart from the north-east, where they are replaced by the Black Duck *Anas rubipres*; in Greenland they are found only along the south-western coast. They breed throughout Britain and Ireland, where the total number of pairs may be as high as 150,000 (Sharrock 1976), but the picture is complicated by feral birds, and the inter-breeding of wild stock with domestic varieties in some areas.

The wintering population of western Europe is about 1,500,000; residents are augmented by birds breeding further north in Scandinavia, Iceland and the western USSR. About 300,000 (20%) winter in Britain, where the species is ubiquitous, but only about 52,000 of these winter on estuaries.

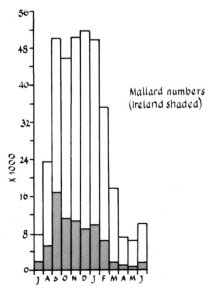

Mallard numbers
(Ireland shaded)

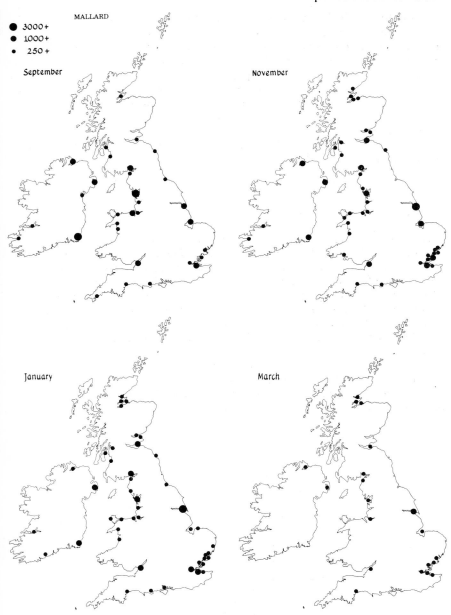

MALLARD

● 3000+
● 1000+
• 250+

September

November

January

March

Movement to winter quarters begins in August and numbers build up to reach almost 50,000 in September. Peak numbers occur in November and December, 52,000+ in the latter month. Mallard begin to return to breeding areas in early February in mild winters, and estuaries counts show a drop to 35,000+ by then, but the exodus is well under way by March (*c.* 18,000) and probably complete by April (7,200+). Flocks in April are likely to consist of unpaired birds, although break-up of breeding pairs may also be underway (Cramp et al 1977).

Coastal sites with more than 250 birds are shown in the map but there are none of international importance (1% of western Europe is the 10,000 maximum – see Appendix 2). Several estuaries record over 2,000 in autumn; Morecambe Bay (3,000+), Medway (*c.* 2,500) and North Solway (2,100+). In December, large numbers occur on the English east coast, including 2,000+ on the Wash and an enormous 6,000+ on the Humber (numbers here in December 1974 exceeded 7,700), the largest concentration recorded on any British estuary. Inland counts between 1970–71 and 1976–77 revealed that major sites include the Ouse Washes (*c.* 3,500, December), Abberton Reservoir, Essex (*c.* 3,400, September), Loch of Lintrathen, Angus (2,300+, November), Hornsea Mere, Yorkshire (*c.* 2,300, January), and Loch Leven, Kinross (*c.* 2,100, September).

## PINTAIL *Anas acuta*

Pintail have a circumpolar breeding distribution and are confined to the more northerly latitudes, few breeding south of 40°N. In North America it is one of the most numerous ducks but is virtually absent from Greenland. The majority of the European population outside Russia breed in Norway and Finland, some 20,000 pairs nesting in the latter country; the population of European Russia numbers some 316,000 pairs (Cramp et al 1977). The species is a rare but annual breeder in Britain, estimated as about 50 pairs (Sharrock 1976).

The European and Russian birds move south-west after breeding to winter in north-western Europe (*c.* 50,000), the Black Sea–Mediterranean region (*c.* 250,000) and western USSR (*c.* 184,600), with a further large number in western Africa. The origins of this last group of birds are uncertain but some 80,000 birds were counted in Senegal, January 1971 (Cramp et al 1977). Those in north-western Europe are found mainly in Britain and the Netherlands, plus a few in France and Iberia. The average number wintering on our estuaries during the 'Estuaries Enquiry' was

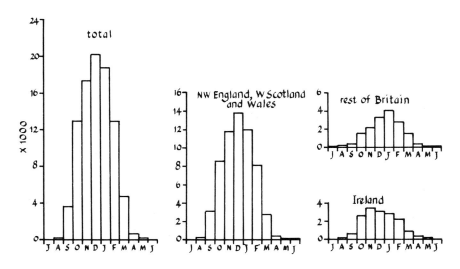

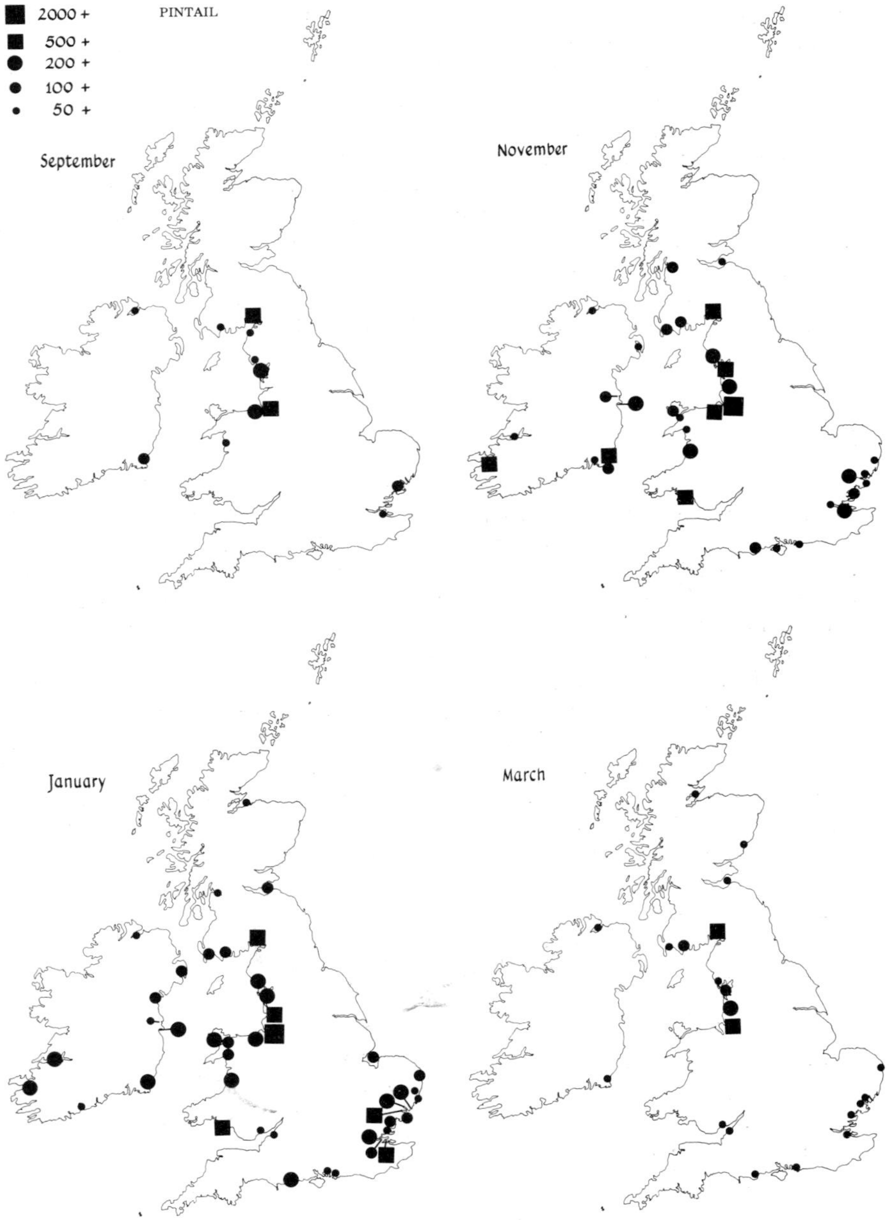

PINTAIL

2000 +
500 +
200 +
100 +
50 +

September

November

January

March

19,000–20,000, or 38–40% of those wintering in north-western Europe. The species also winters in a few sites inland (up to 3,000+ on the Ouse Washes, Cambs/Norfolk, is an exceptional concentration), so the overall total will be still higher. Hutchinson (1979) estimated the Irish wintering population to be 3,000–7,000 birds.

*Table 17:5   Estuaries of international importance for Pintail in Britain and Ireland, 1969–75*

|  | Peak count | % W. European | Months above 1%* | | | | | | |
|---|---|---|---|---|---|---|---|---|---|
| Mersey | 7,214 | 14·4 | 9 10 11 <u>12</u> 1 2 3 | | | | | | |
| Dee | 2,846 | 5·7 | <u>10</u> 11 12 | | | | | | |
| N. Solway | 2,081 | 4·2 | 9 10 11 <u>12</u> 1 2 3 | | | | | | |
| Castlemaine Harbour | 1,501–2,000† | 3·0–4·0 | <u>10</u> | | | | | | |
| Ribble | 1,646 | 3·3 | <u>12</u> 1 | | | | | | |
| Wexford Harbour | 751–1,000† | 1·5–2·0 | <u>10</u> | | | | | | |
| Medway | 671 | 1·3 | <u>12</u> 1 2 | | | | | | |
| Burry Inlet | 652 | 1·3 | 11 <u>1</u> | | | | | | |
| Stour | 620 | 1·2 | <u>10</u> 12 1 | | | | | | |
| Morecambe Bay | 555† | 1·1 | <u>11</u> | | | | | | |

\* Underlining denotes month of highest count
† Indicates full data not available
Figures for Ireland from Hutchinson (1979)

Breeding habitat in Britain includes moorland pools and lochs, lowland lakes and freshwater marshes. Wintering birds, however, are essentially estuarine though some also feed on flooded grazing land inland. Pintails seem to be a more estuarine species than other dabbling ducks, and on mud flats feed extensively on the marine snail *Hydrobia ulvae* and sometimes on *Macoma balthica*; their long, relatively slender bills being well designed to take these species. Movements between estuarine areas during winter do occur, apparently depending on the prevailing weather conditions.

Male Pintails form post-breeding flocks from late May onwards, deserting the females soon after they have completed their clutches, and undergoing a moult some way south of the breeding grounds. Up to several hundred males are recorded on the Ijsselmeer, Netherlands, at this time and peak period for moult is mid-July when the females begin to join the males. The moult may not be finished before some migration begins (Cramp et al 1977). Pintail begin to arrive in Britain from early September onwards (some 3,700+ were present by the end of this month) – males generally preceding females due to their earlier moult. Numbers then build up rapidly and distribution also alters; after being centred in the north-west, more birds appear on estuaries in the south and east. About 14,000 were present in November, but the winter peak occurred in December when over 20,000 were counted; numbers fell slightly in January to 18,700+.

As already mentioned, hard weather movements occurred and some may have moved further south into Europe at this time. Birds began to leave northwards in late February and by March the total had dropped to under 5,000. Inland sites usually also record peak numbers during December and January, and numbers fall off similarly during February and March; one or two sites have an autumn peak. By April very few remain (less than 1,000), with apparently even fewer non-breeding birds summering.

The majority of Pintail were found in north-western Britain, mainly the large flocks on the Mersey, Ribble and North Solway. The extraordinary numbers on the Mersey have appeared since 1967–68, when a mere (though still significant) 1,300 were recorded. Since then the totals have increased steadily until in 1973–74 a massive 14,800+ were counted (Allen 1974). This may have been due to a redistribution of the north-west European wintering population, caused to some extent by the changes of the Rhine delta area, and with fewer birds wintering on the Atlantic coast of France. In subsequent winters this population in the north-west has spread to surrounding estuaries such as the Ribble, Dee and South Solway, with a drop to about 7,000 on the Mersey. Since 1975 large numbers (up to 4,000) have again occurred on the Dee marshes where it was abundant many years ago. The estuaries of north-western Britain accounted for about 66% of the midwinter Pintail population during 1969–75.

Principal estuaries for the species are listed in Table 17:5. From this the international importance of north-western Britain becomes even more obvious, particularly in view of the number of months in which the 1% level of importance is exceeded. Estuaries in southern and eastern Britain hold important numbers during January, particularly the Medway and Essex/Suffolk Stour, each with 600+, although this number also occurs on the latter estuary in October. Elsewhere, Castlemaine and Wexford Harbours are important in the Republic of Ireland, but peak counts are in late autumn when up to 7,000 Pintail are estimated to be present (Hutchinson 1979). Inland, in England, the Ouse Washes, Cambridgeshire/Norfolk, regularly hold 1,500+ birds in midwinter, with over 3,200 birds in January 1975. Martin Mere, adjacent to the Ribble estuary in Lancashire, is also an important site with perhaps 1,000–2,000 in midwinter.

## SHOVELER *Anas clypeata*

Shoveler breed throughout the Palearctic and in the western half of North America. In Europe they are most numerous in the Netherlands and Finland (Cramp et al 1977); in Britain up to 1,000 pairs breed annually (Sharrock 1976). Most Shoveler populations are migratory, with European and Russian breeders wintering in western Europe, the Mediterranean basin and east to the Caspian, as well as in

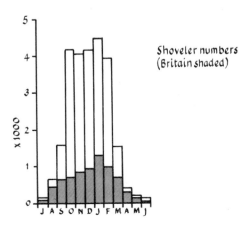

Shoveler numbers
(Britain shaded)

SHOVELER
- ■ 500+
- ● 200 +
- ● 50 +
- • 20 +

September

November

January

March

western and northern central Africa. British Shoveler winter mainly in southern France, southern Spain and Italy, with a few reaching North Africa.

About 20,000 winter in western Europe, most in the Netherlands and the British Isles, mainly from southern Fenno-Scandia and the USSR. The midwinter peak on estuaries averaged nearly 4,500 during 1969–75, or about 22% of those in western Europe. As with other dabbling duck, large numbers also winter inland in Britain, where most are found on flooded grazing land and reservoirs with abundant fringing vegetation. Male Shoveler remain with their mates longer than most other dabbling species, not deserting the females until hatching is imminent. However, few birds appear on our estuaries before October and November when the main movement across Europe occurs; most British breeders will have left by then (Cramp et al 1977). The October and November influx is apparent in the diagram when 4,000+ are recorded; the midwinter peak of almost 4,500 occurs in January. Numbers fall away quickly after the end of February, most birds departing between mid-March and mid-April; fewer than 500 are counted, on average, in the latter month.

Only one estuary in Britain, the Medway, is of international importance, recording about 220 in January. Overall, though, the largest estuarine concentrations are in Ireland, particularly at Castlemaine Harbour, Co. Kerry (900), with further sizeable flocks at North Bull, Co. Dublin (300), and Tralee Bay, Co. Kerry (200) (Hutchinson 1979). Inland counts in Britain show that important concentrations occur on the Ouse Washes, Norfolk/Cambs (400+, March); Loch Leven, Kinross (400+, October); Abberton reservoir, Essex (370+, November); Hickling Broad, Norfolk (300+, September); Fairburn Ings, Yorkshire (220+, September), and Leighton Moss, Lancashire (210+, September).

## POCHARD *Aythya ferina*

This is essentially a species of inland waters. The western European population is estimated to be 250,000, and the British and Irish breeding population to be a maximum of 400 pairs. The fleets on the reclaimed marshes of north Kent support a large percentage of the British breeders. Pochard occur in small numbers on estuaries; as with the Tufted Duck, only ten support an average monthly peak of over 100. However, it differs from the latter species in that two estuaries regularly have large flocks, these are the Inner Thames (1,800) and the Firth of Forth (1,500). In both cases very large numbers (2,500+, the 1% level of international importance) occur each winter but the timing of the influx depends on patterns of severe weather. These birds arrive from nearby freshwater reservoirs, the estuary providing vital feeding grounds during a period of stress.

## TUFTED DUCK *Aythya fuligula*

This is an abundant species which, like the Pochard, prefers inland waters. About 500,000 winter in western Europe and the British and Irish breeding population is probably between 6,000 and 8,000 pairs. Small numbers occur on estuaries; in Britain only ten estuaries had a peak count averaging over 100 birds, many of these were on small areas of water adjacent to the estuary. Four estuaries supported more than 200 birds: the Wey (380) and Poole Harbour, Dorset (250); Inner Thames (220) and Firth of Forth (220).

## SCAUP *Aythya marila*

This is a circumpolar low-arctic or sub-arctic breeding species, and is most northerly of the genus in its breeding and wintering areas. Iceland now holds only some 10,000 pairs after a drastic decline at the main site, Lake Myvatn, between 1956 and 1974. Relatively few breed in Scandinavia but the population of western arctic Siberia has been estimated at 115,000.

In winter, Scaup are found in large numbers in relatively few places. In total about 150,000 winter in north-western Europe, with most in the Baltic (80,000), the Waddensea (30,000) and the Ijsselmeer, Netherlands (25,000). Denmark supports one-third of the north-western European total. Elsewhere in the Western Palearctic 50,000 winter in the European Mediterranean and Black Sea areas, while an estimated 93,000 are found on the Black Sea and Azov coasts of the USSR.

Against this background the British and Irish figures are of minor significance. Only six sites are of national importance in holding more than 225 birds. However, one of these, the Firth of Forth, has held over 20,000 birds and thus is of considerable international importance. Its average highest monthly count was

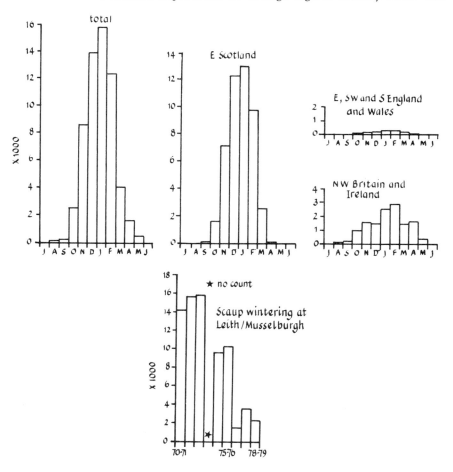

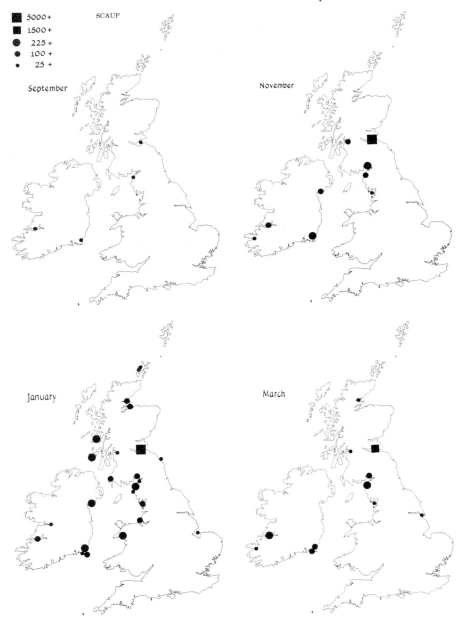

5000 +
1500 +
225 +
100 +
25 +

SCAUP

September

November

January

March

12,840 (8·6% of the western European population). The birds are attracted here by numerous industrial and sewage outfalls, chiefly at Seafield/Leith, where a mixture including sewage and distillery grain waste is discharged.

Numbers at the Seafield site increased from around 10,000 in the early 1960s, to 30,000–40,000 in 1968–69 (Milne and Campbell 1973). During the course of the

'Estuaries Enquiry' a reversion to previous levels took place and, since 1975–76, there have been further drastic decreases. These changes have been attributed to increases in grain discharges up to 1968, followed by a reduction, and to a more thorough treatment of sewage before discharge during the seasons since 1975, although other factors may be involved (L. H. Campbell pers. comm.).

Feeding at outflows is a regular feature at British and Irish sites. The flock at Loch Indaal, Islay, is apparently associated with waste grain from a distillery. This habit is potentially dangerous, as large numbers of birds are concentrated close to industrial sites where pollution could occur, either incidentally or via the outflow itself. There have been no disastrous incidents to date but a minor oil spillage at Mussleburgh in 1972 affected 200–300 Scaup (Milne and Campbell 1973).

The diagram shows a relatively short season for Scaup, with few present outside October to March. The principal eastern Scottish sites are shown separately and exhibit a rather sharp winter peak in contrast to those on the western coast of Scotland, in north-western England and Ireland. The hint of a triple peak in this group suggest spring and autumn passages together with a midwinter influx; the passage numbers are clearly proportionately much less obvious in eastern Scotland. Ruttledge (1970) believed that numbers in Ireland were higher in spring and autumn, but more recent work (Hutchinson 1979) and the 'Estuaries Enquiry' results have not borne this out.

Only Icelandic ringed Scaup have been recovered during the winter, suggesting that a major part of our population is of Icelandic origin. However, there have been recoveries of Aberdeenshire ringed birds in the Baltic (2) and USSR (2) as well as Iceland (3) and, clearly, Siberian birds also winter here. The count data may suggest a Siberian origin for the peak winter flocks, since Danish numbers increase while the eastern Scottish flocks are declining in late January and February (Milne and Campbell 1973).

Very few birds are present in summer, but moulting flocks occur in other parts of the winter range. The Ijsselmeer holds 1,000 moulting birds in late July.

The important British and Irish sites are shown in the map. No inland sites regularly hold Scaup in significant numbers, although the species is not rare inland particularly at passage times. The sites shown for September hold a high proportion of the relatively small numbers present in that month. Islay and Mull were not covered in November. Wexford Harbour held 3,000 birds until pollution decimated the mussels in 1966–67; fewer than 1,000 were present in 1967–68 (Ruttledge 1970) and now only about an average of 300 occur (Hutchinson 1979). Reductions take place at nearly all sites by March but increased numbers were counted on the Shannon and the Humber, these presumably being migrants or pre-migration gatherings of local birds.

EIDER *Somateria mollissima*

Eiders are an abundant and widespread seaduck within their Holarctic range, which extends well into the high Arctic. Large numbers are found around the northern coasts of the Nearctic and Palearctic, excepting only north-central Siberia. Within Europe they breed as far south as the Dutch Waddensea (occasionally north-western France) and are numerous in Iceland, northern Britain, Fenno-Scandia and the

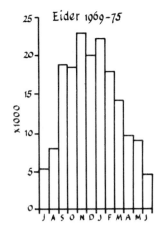

Eider 1969-75

Barcut and White Sea areas of the USSR. The Icelandic and Baltic breeding populations total some 500,000 pairs (Cramp et al 1977); the British population has been estimated at 15,000–25,000 pairs (Sharrock 1976). After Mallard *Anas platyrhynchos*, they are our most numerous breeding duck.

The wintering population of Eider in north-western Europe is probably close to 2,000,000. The most important areas are the southern Baltic and Kattegat (*c.* 750,000), Norway (250,000+) and Waddensea (*c.* 200,000). As with other seaduck, estuary counts give only a relative idea of numbers, the average peak count of 23,000 in November being less than half of the estimated total of 60,000. Of this total, some 30,000 may be in eastern Scotland (Milne and Campbell 1973); the number wintering in Ireland is not known (Hutchinson 1979) but is probably well under 5,000. Thus, Eider wintering in Britain represent about 3% of the north-western European total, and the majority are likely to be of British origin as few move further than 200 km, immatures going further than adults (Cramp et al 1977). The small numbers seen on the English southern and eastern coasts may well be of Dutch origin.

Eider prefer the sheltered parts of the coastlines where they can easily obtain their main food, molluscs – especially Mussels *Mytilus edulis*. They are usually found close inshore but during the moulting period they become flightless for a short time near the end of July and then large flocks seek comparative safety slightly further out (Pounder 1974). In the Scottish estuaries, Eider are often found near outfall areas with other sea duck and concentrations of up to 5,000 have been recorded in the Tay at such sites (Pounder 1976) although Campbell (1978) has shown that Eiders are only tenuously connected to the outfalls themselves. The variation in monthly estuary counts is shown in the diagram, and it can be seen that large numbers are present from September onwards when almost 19,000 were recorded on average. This build-up occurs as the adult population returns inshore after moulting, and at this time the estuary counts on the Firth of Tay averaged 8,300+, although well in excess of 10,000 occur at times (Milne 1965). A considerable movement along the coast may occur at this time but numbers fall only slightly in October and then peak in November (*c.* 23,000). Winter numbers fluctuate and, as with other seaduck which form large winter flocks, can be difficult to count accurately in poor

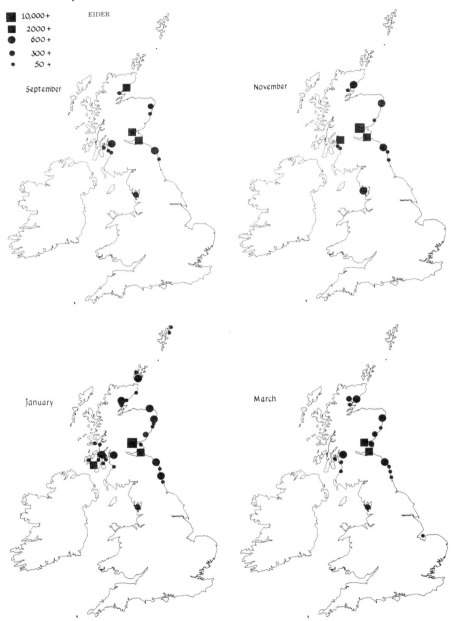

conditions. As the majority of wintering Eider occur in Scotland, bad counting conditions are not infrequent. Indeed, when calmer conditions occur, the birds may be well offshore, frustrating land based counters (Milne 1965).

The return to breeding colonies begins in March and early April, and counts fall to fewer than 10,000 by this time. In contrast to the somewhat leisurely southward

*Table 17:6   Principal estuaries for Eider in Britain, 1969–75*

| | Highest monthly av. count | % British | Months above 1%* |
|---|---|---|---|
| Firth of Tay | 12,700 | 21·2 (1·3)† | 9  10  <u>11</u>  12  1  2  3  4  5 |
| Firth of Forth | 3,258 | 5·4 | 7  8  9  10  11  12  1  2  <u>3</u>     5  6 |
| Golspie | 2,500 | 4·2 | <u>9</u>  10  11  12 |
| Inner Clyde | 2,443 | 4·1 | 8  9  10  <u>11</u>  12  1  2  3 |
| Lindisfarne | 1,707 | 2·8 | 8  <u>9</u>  10  11  12  1  2  3  4 |
| Ythan | 1,407 | 2·4 | 8     10  11  12  1  2  <u>3</u>  4 |
| Rosehearty | 1,301‡ | 2·2 | <u>12</u>  1  2 |
| Morecambe Bay | 625‡ | 1·0 | <u>11</u> |

\* Month of highest count is underlined
† Figure in brackets gives the % of the north-west European wintering total
‡ Indicates count data for other months is incomplete

movement which occurs along the eastern coast of Scotland in late autumn, the return in spring is rapid, and by June less than 5,000 were recorded, although fewer estuaries were covered in this month. Many of these may be non-breeders, as immatures do not visit breeding colonies (Cramp et al 1977).

Principal estuaries for Eider are listed in Table 17:6, which shows those where 600+ were recorded in at least one month of the year. The Firth of Tay is the only estuary of international importance for Eider (12,700+ in November). Other sites of national importance include the Firth of Forth with 3,200+, and Golspie and the Inner Clyde, each with well over 2,000. In addition the Shetlands regularly hold 6,000+ and occasionally up to 9,500 in midwinter (Shetland Bird Reports 1976–78). With the exception of the birds on Morecambe Bay (625+ in November) and a small flock on the Wash, few places outside Scotland have more than 50 on a regular basis.

## LONG-TAILED DUCK *Clangula hyemalis*

The breeding range of the Long-tailed Duck is circumpolar and extends further north on average than any other duck. Few breed outside the Arctic Circle, and most of those breeding in the Palearctic do so in the USSR, where estimates vary between 2·5 and 3·4 million pairs (Cramp et al 1977). Outside the USSR, Long-tailed Duck breed in Iceland, Fenno-Scandia, Svalbard and Bear Island, but nowhere else in Europe although breeding has been claimed in Scotland (Sharrock 1976).

Long-tailed Ducks winter in Europe mainly in the Baltic, along the northern coast of Norway, and around Iceland where the local breeders are sedentary but may occasionally move west to Greenland (Cramp et al 1977). The number wintering in western Europe is not known precisely but has been provisionally set at 500,000; in

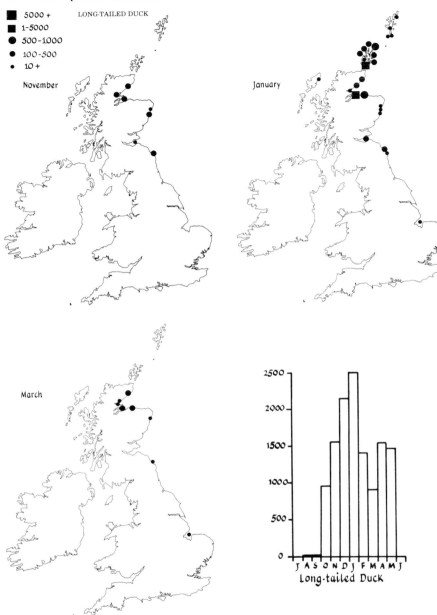

view of the size of the post-breeding population it may be substantially more (Atkinson-Willes 1976). Birds wintering in Britain are of uncertain origin and may be from Siberia (birds from there reach the Baltic) or from Fenno-Scandia.

Their great mobility and the tendency for Long-tailed Ducks to stay mainly well offshore has made accurate counts for the species impossible. It is thought that some

10,000 birds winter in Britain, so that estuary counts reflect only trends in population numbers and are very incomplete. More birds occur in Shetland, for instance, than are indicated (see maps), with some 1,100 counted in 1974 (Shetland Bird Report 1974). From this estimate about 2% of those wintering in western Europe occur in Britain and these mainly in Scotland, where some may be attracted to outfall areas where sewage or distillery waste is discharged into the sea (Pounder 1976). An important aspect, with considerable implications, is the tendency for Long-tailed Ducks to form considerable nocturnal roosts. One of these, at Burghead Bay in the Moray Firth, draws in birds from a radius of 30 km. At peak times, therefore, up to 10,000 (an internationally important number) may occur in this one small area.

Long-tailed Ducks arrive from October onwards in Britain and increase steadily through November and December; it is at this time that the main influx into the Baltic occurs (Cramp et al 1977). The peak estuary count in January recorded 2,600+, falling to less than half by February, and lower still in March as birds begin to move away. A definite spring passage occurs with 1,500+ counted in April and only slightly fewer in May; in north-eastern Scotland they often form into large inshore flocks and display vigorously. It may be that birds which have wintered slightly further south across the North Sea return northwards along the Norwegian coast via the eastern coast of Scotland, or simply that birds which have wintered locally form larger and more conspicuous flocks prior to departure.

All the important sites for Long-tailed Ducks are in Scotland although Lindisfarne regularly records 150+ in midwinter. The Moray Firth (2,000++) records most Long-tailed Ducks in midwinter, with Brora, Sutherland, having some 200–300 then, but over 1,300 in May. The Firth of Forth regularly has some 130 during January. These figures give only relative indications of the actual numbers present, but allow some comparisons to be drawn between sites. Some indication of the discrepancies between estuary counts and numbers actually present is given by considering the counts for Scapa Flow, where 2,400 were recorded in February 1975 and the total in Orkney at that time was estimated as 5,400 (Scottish Bird Report 1975). The detailed counts by Mudge and Allen (1980) on the Moray Firth indicated that up to 10,000 were present in 1977–78.

Similarly, numbers on Loch Fleet in April regularly top 2,000 (Scottish Bird Report 1975, 1976). Elsewhere in Britain the Wash is the only site in the southern half of the country to record more than ten birds regularly.

## COMMON SCOTER *Melanitta nigra*

This abundant seaduck breeds in the sub-arctic and boreal zones of Eurasia from Iceland and Ireland to the Bering Sea, and also at scattered localities in the Nearctic. Most winter on the coasts of the northern Atlantic and Pacific Oceans. The British Isles form part of a major flyway which extends from the Western Palearctic breeding grounds at least as far as Mauritania; migrant flocks are commonly observed, particularly along the English Channel coast in March–May, with 25,500 passing Dungeness in spring 1976 and 8,400 in two April days in 1977.

As a breeding species in Britain and Ireland, Common Scoter are restricted to northern and western areas in Scotland and Ireland. Co. Fermanagh holds by far the

largest concentration with 110 pairs on Lower Lough Erne in 1974. This colony grew rapidly from colonisation in 1905 to 140–150 pairs during 1967–69 but may now be in decline (Sharrock 1976). The total Irish population at the time of *The Atlas of Breeding Birds* was estimated at 130–140 pairs, with a further 30–50 pairs in Scotland (mostly in Caithness and on Islay). The wintering quarters of our breeding birds are unknown.

The size of the Western Palearctic population in winter is probably 400,000–500,000 (Atkinson-Willes 1977) although there were previous estimates suggesting a total in excess of 1½ million. The highest January count has only revealed 200,000, however, so that knowledge of the winter distribution is clearly incomplete. Danish waters are of paramount importance, holding 100,000–150,000 in winter and 150,000–200,000 (mostly males) during the late summer moult.

The wintering population of Britain and Ireland has been estimated at 35,000 but may have been as high as 50,000 in 1974. There is also a substantial moulting population, possibly about half of the winter numbers, but rather poorly documented. The diagram shows the numbers recorded by the enquiry; these are considerably lower than the real figures owing to difficulties of cover at the main sites and are further reduced by averaging for each month across seven years. Nevertheless, the pattern of counts can be seen although probably the moulting numbers are particularly under-emphasised.

The diagram includes counts from outside the 'Estuaries Enquiry', but for many coasts, even so, the information is incomplete, although best for January. There are no regular inland wintering sites but there are frequent inland records, particularly at passage times. Estuaries and coasts of international importance are shown in Table 17:7.

Carmarthen Bay has only provided large counts since about 1966. In February 1974, about 5,000 were recorded from the shore and a boat transect led to an estimate of 25,000. About 16,000 were estimated off Pembrey the following August. These developments highlight the problems of assessing distribution. The birds are, typically, too far from land to be adequately counted without seaborne or aerial surveys, and are usually dispersed in many smaller flocks; numbers in a locality are also liable to change markedly over a period of a few years.

Foulness is included in Table 17:7 although counts above the western European 1% level have only so far been recorded in one winter (1975–76). The flock, again, is a very long way from the shore and rarely countable from land. There may be some interchange between this flock and the nearby one off Clacton/Walton, which is also apparently highly variable in size.

A third problem area is the north Welsh and Cheshire coasts between Anglesey and the Mersey, where thousands are recorded erratically at a number of sites; there has been no adequate, full survey.

Numbers in Ireland were much higher before 1963, when persistent gales and cold weather along the east coast severely depleted marine life. The Dublin coast then

*Table 17:7   Sites of international importance for Common Scoter*

| | Peak | % W. European | Months above 1%* | | | | | | | | |
|---|---|---|---|---|---|---|---|---|---|---|---|
| Carmarthen Bay | 25,000 | 5·6 | 7 | 8 | | | 11 | | 1 | 2 | <u>3</u> | 6 |
| Dornoch/Moray Firths | 14,000 | 3·1 | | | 9 | <u>10</u> | 11 | 12 | <u>1</u> | 2 | 3 |
| Foulness | 7,000 | 1·6 | | | | | | 12 | | <u>2</u> |

* Underlined is month of peak count

held 2,000–3,000, while 500+ were off Co. Wexford and 1,000+ in Dundrum Bay (Ruttledge 1970). It should be noted that the maps are incomplete for Ireland, although that for January shows data from Hutchinson (1979). Possibly most of these Irish birds have now switched to the Carmarthen Bay site.

Similarly, the very large numbers at Southerness (North Solway) which were present up to the late 1960s have not been recorded since. Only Wigtown and Luce Bays on that coast now hold important numbers, particularly during the moult. There is at present no indication as to why this redistribution should have taken place.

More moulting flocks probably remain to be discovered, but at present the number of sites is thought to be low compared with the more widespread winter distribution. Males form a high proportion of the late summer flocks. They arrive from the breeding grounds mainly in July and August to join the non-breeding birds. After the moult, the males disperse and some may leave the British Isles. The overall numbers are swelled by fresh arrivals of females and juveniles from the breeding grounds in September and October, and of moulted birds from the Baltic, chiefly from November to early January. Return movements occur from late February to early May.

Ringing has shown that some Icelandic birds winter in the British Isles, but the implication from the large numbers indicates a mainly Scandinavian/Siberian origin of winter flocks.

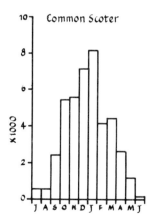
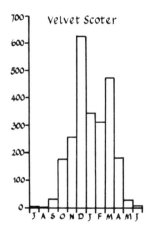

VELVET SCOTER *Melanitta fusca*

Moulting flocks of adult males of this species number 45,000 in Denmark in late summer, and extrapolation from this gives a figure of 150,000–200,000 for the expected western European winter population. January counts have, however, never exceeded 25,000 for the whole region, so we are unable to account for very large numbers, assuming the calculations are correct. Known concentrations are in the Limfjorden and Kattegat in Denmark (20,000+), southern Atlantic Norway (2,800 in 1972, but largely unsurveyed) and eastern Scotland (2,000+). Smaller numbers are found on the Atlantic, Mediterranean and Black Sea coasts of Europe, and on some of the larger central European lakes (Atkinson-Willes 1977, Cramp et al 1977). Difficulties in surveying for winter flocks are compounded by the relatively marine habit, rather than inshore, and by marked changes in counts between years.

The breeding range extends from Norway to Kamchatka in the Palearctic and across most of the Western Nearctic. Breeding numbers in the Western Palearctic are

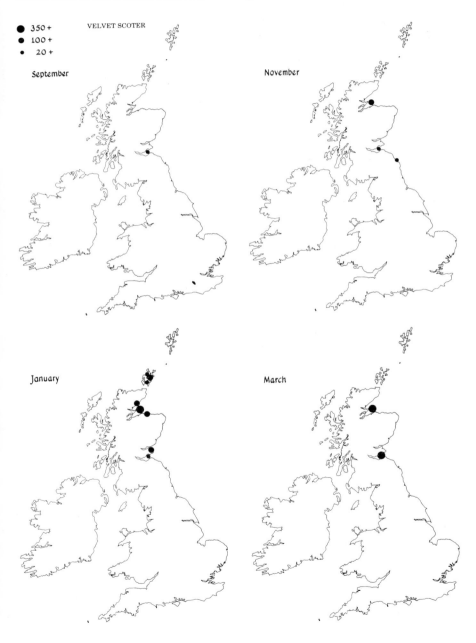

Table 17:8   *Sites of national importance for Velvet Scoter (35 as provisional 1%)*

|  | Peak | % British and Irish | Months above 1%* |
|---|---|---|---|
| Moray Firth | 560 | 16·0 | 10 11 <u>12</u> 1 2 3 4 |
| Eden | 293 | 8·4 | (Jan count only) |
| Firth of Forth | 204 | 5·8 | 10 11    1 2 <u>3</u> 4 |
| Orkney | 203 | 5·8 | (Jan count only) |
| Brora | 194 | 5·5 | (Jan count only) |
| Lossiemouth/Burghead | 184 | 5·3 | (Jan count only) |
| Dornoch Firth | 125 | 3·6 | <u>2</u> |

* Underlining denotes month of highest count

everywhere quite low, with recent declines in Sweden and inland Finland.

The map shows that the main British and Irish haunts in January are all in eastern Scotland. Much smaller numbers are found on most coasts of Britain and Ireland (although generally the species avoids exposed Atlantic coasts); of non-Scottish coasts only Lindisfarne (26 in November) and the Wash (25 in April) regularly hold more than 20 birds. Velvet Scoters are usually found with Common Scoters but often form single species parties within the flocks. Some minor sites, such as the Blackwater and Portland Harbour, regularly hold singles or small parties of Velvet Scoter in the absence of a regular Common Scoter flock. Sites of national importance are shown in Table 17:8, but all are likely to be under-estimates. The average daily count for the Moray Firth/Dornoch region was 2,480 in 1977–78 (Mudge and Allen 1980), although less intensive shore-based counts revealed an average of only a fifth of this figure. There is an apparently exceptional count of 1,500 in the Firth of Forth (February 1972).

The monthly pattern of counts is shown in the diagram. Small numbers are present in summer with non-breeding/moulting flocks of Common Scoter, for example at Dunwich (Suffolk) as well as with the more important concentrations. Main arrivals begin in October. The relatively low midwinter counts are probably the result of surveying difficulties rather than a real decline at this time. Most wintering birds have left by the end of April. A regular spring passage is noted at Channel coast observatories between March and May, but the movement is rapid and these birds do not appear on coastal counts.


GOLDENEYE *Bucephala clangula*

Goldeneye breed in the sub-arctic forest-taiga zones of Eurasia and the New World. They are abundant in Scandinavia, and in western USSR the breeding population is estimated at 120,000 pairs. None breed in Iceland where the species is replaced by Barrow's Goldeneye. Recently a small population has become established in Scotland but this is probably, still, of fewer than 20 pairs.

The main wintering grounds of western birds are in the Danish and Swedish

Baltic, where up to 170,000 occur. A large concentration, numbering 52,000, is found on the USSR coasts of the Black and Caspian Seas. The larger central European lakes hold 20,000 or more and the freshwater Ijsselmeer up to 17,000. In Britain and Ireland about 10–15,000 winter, over 7,000 at coastal or estuarine sites.

Appreciable numbers are present only from October to April, with a peak in January and February. In some other parts of the winter range there are large moulting flocks; for example, in Limfjorden (Denmark) where 10,000 are present in late summer. The eastern Scottish region holds up to 54% of the passage numbers but proportionately fewer (43%) of the midwinter peak. Each region shows a broadly similar pattern of numbers through the year, but the timing of the peak varies locally between January and February.

The Firth of Forth is the main site. Internationally important numbers have occurred there in February (2,000 or 1·1% of the western European population) and nationally important numbers from October to April (Table 17:9). The attraction of this site is the presence of numerous outflows of sewage and industrial waste, particularly at Seafield which has supported up to 35% of the eastern Scottish population (Campbell and Milne 1977). Several other eastern Scottish sites are also associated with outflows and this species, like Scaup *Aythya marila*, may actually benefit from limited organic pollution. The reason for the recent decline of the Forth numbers (since 1977) is not known but may be associated with a more thorough treatment of sewage before discharge. Goldeneye which have been displaced are most likely to winter in Denmark, where they are threatened by pollution and by shooting (the annual bag in Denmark is estimated to be a staggering 25,000 birds).

The preference for relatively sheltered waters is well illustrated by the distribution maps, which show the absence of important sites on exposed westerly coasts. Their predominance in the deep firths of eastern Scotland is clear throughout. South-eastern England is much more important in spring (March) than in autumn (November).

Although usually considered a 'seaduck', Goldeneye also winter inland in

---

*Table 17:9  Estuaries and coastal sites of national importance for Goldeneye*

| | Peak | % British | Months above 1%* |
|---|---|---|---|
| Firth of Forth | 2,222 | 17·8 | 10 11 12 1 _2_ 3 4 |
| Cromarty Firth | 522 | 4·2 | 11 12 _1_ 2 3 4 |
| Morecambe Bay | 390 | 3·1 | 11 12 _1_ 2 3 |
| Inner Clyde | 380 | 3·0 | 11 12 _1_ 2 3 |
| Moray Firth | 346 | 2·8 | 12 _1_ 2 3 |
| Wash | 257 | 2·1 | 1 _2_ 3 |
| Colne | 240 | 1·9 | 12 1 _2_ 3 |
| Tweed | 205 | 1·6 | 12 1 _2_ |
| Strangford Lough | 195 | 1·6 | 11   1 _2_ 3 |
| Blackwater | 180 | 1·4 | 12 1 _2_ |
| South Solway | 153 | 1·2 | _3_ |

* Underline denotes month of highest count

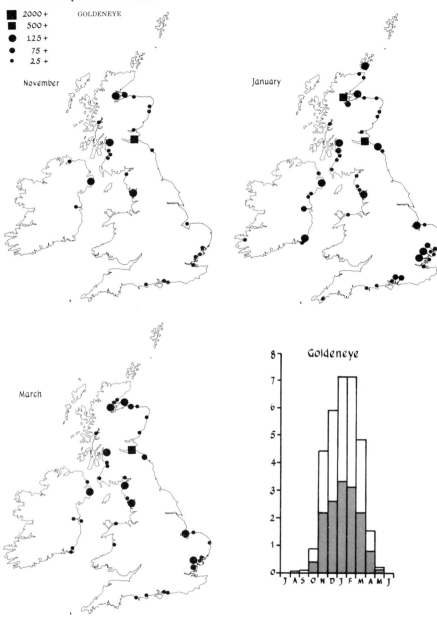

appreciable numbers. Larger reservoirs and reservoir complexes with adequate refuge areas are consistently occupied, as are the larger natural lakes. By far the most important site is the Lough Neagh basin, where counts between 1964 and 1968 showed a March peak averaging 5,000 birds (Hutchinson 1979). The next most important are Abberton Reservoir (Essex) where the peak averaged 376 between

1970–71 and 1976–77, and Loch Leven (Kinross) averaging 371.

Goldeneye flocks show interesting local variations in the proportions of adult males (Pounder 1976) but there is no evidence that the distribution of adult males differs on the national scale from that of females and immatures. Campbell (1977) suggests that such differential use of feeding areas may reflect differences in the relative importance, to adult males and to others, of factors such as shelter and disturbance at different sites.

## RED-BREASTED MERGANSER *Mergus serrator*

Red-breasted Mergansers have an Holarctic distribution reaching a latitude of 75°N in the USSR. In Europe they breed from Iceland through north-western Britain and Ireland, Denmark and Fenno-Scandia into Russia, where they are birds of the tundra and scattered coastal islands. An estimate of the British breeding population is 2,000–3,000 pairs (Sharrock 1976), and although some birds are found far up river or on remote moorland burns, the majority favour sheltered coastal waters.

About 40,000 Mergansers are thought to winter in north-western Europe, with most in the Baltic and further west or south-west into the Netherlands and Britain (Cramp et al 1977). The number wintering in Britain and Ireland is about 7,500 and 10% of the European total. Peak numbers recorded by the 'Estuaries Enquiry' averaged 3,700+ in December, so approximately half of them would appear to use the estuarine habitat.

Red-breasted Mergansers are almost exclusively birds of inner coastal waters in winter, only exceptionally present on fresh water lakes and reservoirs. The species occurs in well-scattered smaller flocks and in north-western Scotland, particularly, may easily be missed. Another counting problem occurs on the eastern coast of Scotland in the Beauly-Moray Firth area, where many Goosander *Mergus merganser* also winter (1,200 January 1975). This is probably the only place where large numbers of both species are found wintering together regularly; elsewhere Goosander winter on freshwater. Difficulties obviously arise in bad counting conditions with distant flocks, particularly with the relatively similar females for the two species.

The British wintering population is largely composed of local breeders, but is augmented to some extent by Icelandic birds in the north-west and continental ones in the south and east. Males gather offshore to moult from early June onwards and at moulting grounds in northern Denmark a peak of about 20,000 occurs in mid-July (Joensen 1973). Some 1,500 were recorded on average in July and August, rising to 2,750+ in September when the distribution probably reflects that of the

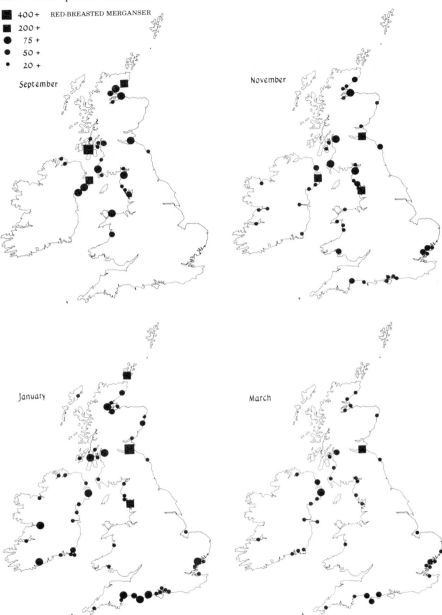

British post-breeding population. The distribution of counts further suggests that the few continental and Icelandic birds which arrive in Britain do not appear much before the end of October or early November; peak movement through the Baltic does not occur until mid- or late October (Cramp et al 1977). By November more birds have appeared on the southern and eastern coasts of England and numbers peak in December (3,700+).

Red-breasted Mergansers may make hard weather movements, such as were seen in mid-February 1979, when spectacular numbers of other normally scarce species (e.g. Red-necked Grebe *Podiceps grisegena*) were also seen in Britain. However, the counts indicate a fall-off in numbers from December although the February count (3,000+) is not much below the peak. The return to breeding areas begins at the end of February, but mainly during March when the count averaged 2,200+. By April, fewer than 2,000 were counted and lowest numbers of the year occurred in June (less than 500).

Two internationally important sites were identified by the 'Estuaries Enquiry', namely the North Esk and Firth of Forth, each holding 1% of the north-western European total, the former in May and the latter in October. More recently, a site not covered by the 'Estuaries Enquiry' at Tayinloan, Argyll, has recorded annually up to 1,400 (3·5% north-western Europe) from mid-June onwards into July and August (Scottish Bird Reports). These are no doubt local breeders which have gathered to moult there; other important moulting areas include Loch Linnhe, Argyll, and Kinnaber, Angus, each with 400+ in July/August. Elsewhere in Scotland, northern and north-western Britain and Wales, there are many smaller flocks of 100–300. In the southern half of England, Poole Harbour and Portland regularly hold 100+ in midwinter and in Ireland, Strangford Lough records 200–300 from September through to February.

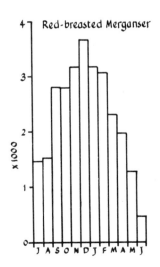

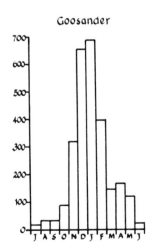

## GOOSANDER *Mergus merganser*

The breeding distribution of the Goosander is similar to that of the Red-breasted Merganser *Mergus serrator* though it tends to be more southerly; it is also absent from Greenland. In Britain it is a relatively recent colonist and latest estimates suggest some 900–1,250 pairs breed here annually (Meek and Little 1977a), the majority in Scotland and north-west England. Goosanders are much less marine than Red-breasted Mergansers, with the result that few (with one major exception)

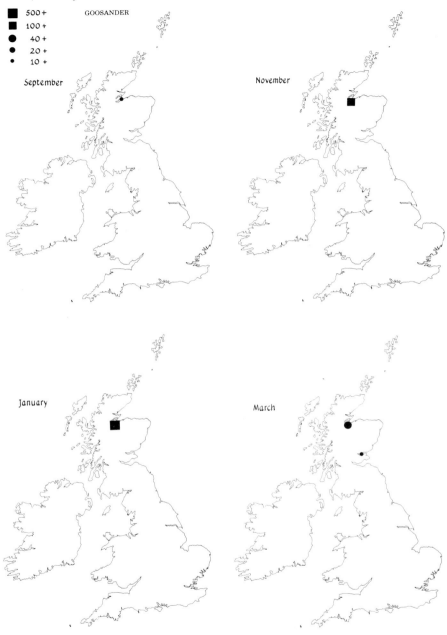

are recorded on estuaries. Some 4,000 winter in Britain, mostly on the larger inland water bodies. With an estimated north-western European wintering population of 50,000, the total in Britain and Ireland represents about 8%.

*Table 17:10   Peak counts of Goosander wintering on the Beauly Firth, Highland Region*

| Winter | Peak count | Month | % N.W. Europe |
|--------|-----------|-------|---------------|
| 1970/71 | 893 | Dec | 1·8 |
| 1971/72 | 324 | Feb | 0·6 |
| 1972/73 | 371 | Feb | 0·7 |
| 1973/74 | 1,080 | Jan | 2·2 |
| 1974/75 | 1,290 | Jan | 2·6 |

British breeders tend to disperse between north and west-south-west in autumn and winter, with recoveries as far north as Fenno-Scandia. Recovery dates of some birds introduces the intriguing possibility that part of the British population might move to the north Norwegian fjords to moult (Meek and Little 1977b). However, groups of moulting birds have been seen in Scottish waters in late August and early September in 1975 and 1976 (Scottish Bird Reports). Birds ringed in Fenno-Scandia have also been recovered in Britain while wintering on reservoirs in south-eastern England.

The fluctuations in numbers present are shown in the diagram and the totals are almost wholly due to the flocks wintering uniquely on the Beauly and Moray Firths. This is an internationally important area for the species with some 1·3% of the north-western European total, on average, in December and January, and even more in some years if peak counts only are considered (Table 17:10). Although males leave the breeding grounds to moult after mating, no concentrations appear there before November when an average of 300+ have been recorded. Numbers increase overall to a peak of just under 700 in January, but the peak may be earlier or later in some years. Some inland waters record most during spring migration in late March when the majority are returning to breeding areas. At this time a small flock is seen on the Firth of Tay but the estuary count has fallen to about 130 and, despite a small increase in April when good numbers are also recorded on the north Esk, numbers tail off during the next two months. Twos and threes may be seen elsewhere on east and south coast estuaries in winter and spring but the larger flocks are more familiar at this time to reservoir observers.

## OYSTERCATCHER *Haematopus ostralegus*

The Oystercatcher is a common breeding bird in northern Britain, where it nests both inland and on the coast. In the southern half of England, Wales and Ireland, however, relatively small numbers breed along the coast. Dare (1966) estimated the British and Irish breeding population in 1960–65 at over 19,000 pairs and possibly as high as 30,000–40,000 pairs. There has been no subsequent census although Sharrock (1976) shows that there has been a marked and continuing increase in range, especially inland in Scotland (cf. Buxton 1961). In autumn and winter the native birds are augmented by large numbers from Iceland, the Faeroes and Norway,

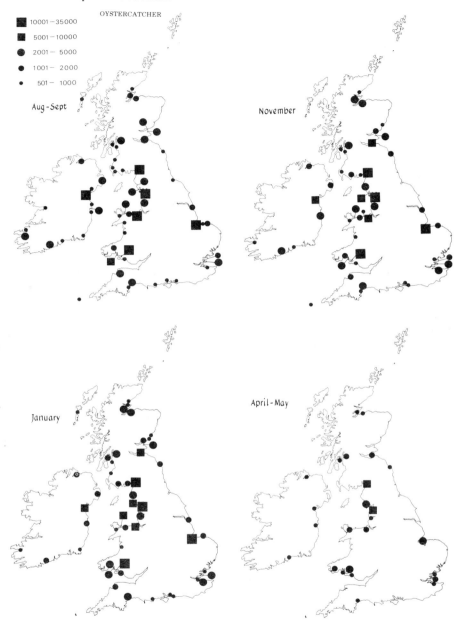

and small numbers – especially on the southern and south-eastern coasts of England – from the Netherlands, Sweden and western USSR (Dare 1970, Anderson and Minton 1978).

The average number of Oystercatchers wintering in Europe during 1966–75 was 560,000 (Prater 1976a). The British and Irish wintering numbers of 200,000 birds form about 36% of the European wintering population. Fewer than 5,000 birds winter in north Africa and none occur to the south of the Sahara. The main continental European haunts of the species are the Wadden Sea, the Delta region of the Netherlands, and western France.

Oystercatchers normally do not breed until they are four (females) or five (male) years old (Harris 1967). Those present on estuaries between late May and early July are mainly immature birds. In late July and through August, numbers steadily increase as post-breeding adults and juveniles gather on the shore. Peak numbers occur in September when just over 250,000 are present in our estuaries. Many British and Irish juveniles, and a small number of adults, migrate south to France and Iberia during August and September. This exodus contributes to the October decrease but there is also a movement of birds onto fields adjacent to the coast, primarily in the area of the Irish Sea, with the onset of winter rains. Overall numbers decrease slightly through the winter but small increases may occur when cold weather forces inland feeders off the fields. Oystercatchers return to their breeding territories from late January in southern areas, from mid-February in Scottish coastal areas, from March in inland sites and from late March in Norway (Dare 1970). Thus the rapid decrease in numbers on estuaries in late February and March is almost certainly due mainly to the return of adults to their territories. Most birds remaining in late April and May are the non-breeding summering individuals.

The map also shows that the largest numbers were around the Irish Sea where about half of the British and Irish birds occur. The pattern of occurrence is similar throughout Ireland and western Britain. On the eastern and southern coasts there may be a small influx in midwinter and a relatively slower fall in numbers through March. This may be associated with the different origins of these birds. Dare (1970) showed that most of the western Oystercatchers breed in Scotland, the Faeroes and Iceland with relatively few from Norway. In contrast, eastern birds are almost exclusively of Norwegian origin, although there are small numbers of birds from

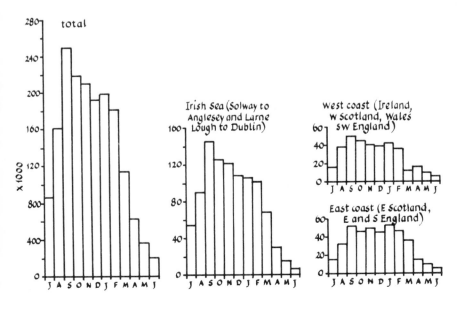

*Table 17:11  Estuaries of international importance for Oystercatcher, 1969–75*

|  | Highest av. monthly count | % W. European | Months above 1%* |
|---|---|---|---|
| Morecambe Bay | 44,710 | 8·0 | 7 8 9 <u>10</u> 11 12 1 2 3 4 5 |
| Solway Firth | 38,794 | 6·9 | 7 8 <u>9</u> 10 11 12 1 2 3 4 |
| Dundalk Bay† | 27,000 | 4·8 | <u>9</u> 10 11 12 1 |
| Wash | 17,658 | 3·2 | 8 <u>9</u> 10 11 12 1 2 3 |
| Dee | 14,400 | 2·6 | 7 8 <u>9</u> 10 11 12 1 |
| Burry Inlet | 14,211 | 2·5 | 8 9 <u>10</u> 11 12 1 2 3 |
| Duddon | 7,976 | 1·4 | 10 <u>11</u> 12 1    3 |
| Gwendraeth | 6,033 | 1·1 | <u>9</u> |
| Foulness | 5,900 | 1·1 | <u>1</u> |
| Conwy Bay | 5,867 | 1·0 | <u>12</u> |

\* Underlining denotes month of highest count
† Limited data, figure from Hutchinson (1979)

other countries in northern and western Europe. The winter peak may be of birds forced by cold weather from the strongholds in the Netherlands, and the slower emigration in the spring may be due to their later appearance on northern breeding grounds.

The diagram and Table 17:11 summarise the important sites for Oystercatchers in Britain and Ireland. Their relative abundance is fairly similar throughout the year at each site although one notable autumn concentration of 26,000 at Dundalk Bay was not maintained through to the winter. The most important sites are similar to those recorded by Dare (1966).

The Oystercatcher is the only species of wader for which detailed counts (Dare 1966) were made in some areas prior to the 'Estuaries Enquiry'. Dare's survey was not quite as comprehensive as the present counts, as it was not possible to make monthly counts on all sites and some estimates had to be included. The comparisons

*Table 17:12  Wintering numbers of Oystercatchers in Britain and Ireland in 1963–65 (Dare) and 1969–75 (present study)*

|  | Dare (1966) | | Present study |  |
|---|---|---|---|---|
| Region (see map) | Range | median | mean |  |
| Irish Sea | 41,000–70,000 | 55,500 | 105,750 |  |
| West coast | 28,200–52,700 | 40,500 | 40,750 |  |
| South/east coast | 26,500–52,000 | 39,250 | 52,300 |  |
|  | | 135,250 | 198,800 | (206,600*) |

\* Dare (1966) notes 5,100–10,500 (median 7,800) birds on coastal areas and islands not counted during present study, this figure is added here.

Table 17:13  Changes in the numbers of Oystercatchers wintering on the eastern and northern parts of Morecambe Bay between 1960 and 1980

| Winter | Number | Reference |
|---|---|---|
| 1960–61 | 120,000 | Dare, 1966 |
| 1961–62 | 55,000 | ,, |
| 1962–63 | 35,000 | ,, |
| 1963–64 | 11,000 | ,, |
| 1964–65 | 13,500 | ,, |
| 1965–66 | No count | |
| 1966–67 | 17,000 | Wilson, 1973 |
| 1967–68 | 20,000 | ,, |
| 1968–69 | 25,500 | ,, |
| 1969–70 | 30,500 | ,, |
| 1970–71 | 42,000 | This study* |
| 1971–72 | 40,500 | ,, |
| 1972–73 | 36,000 | ,, |
| 1973–74 | 32,500 | ,, |
| 1974–75 | 36,000 | ,, |
| 1975–76 | 53,500 | ,, |
| 1976–77 | 46,250 | ,, |
| 1977–78 | 41,600 | ,, |
| 1978–79 | | |
| 1979–80 | 44,500 | ,, |

* During the present counts total figures for Morecambe Bay have been received, thus 2,000 has been subtracted from the total to account for the numbers wintering in the south of the Bay.

Table 17:14  Numbers of Oystercatchers summering (May/June) at selected estuaries in 1963–65 and 1969–75

| | 1963–65 (Dare 1966) | 1969–75 (present study) |
|---|---|---|
| Morecambe Bay | 3,000 | 5,100* |
| Burry Inlet | 2,000 | 2,800 |
| Wash | 750 | 2,400 |
| Conwy Bay† | 1,250 | 1,350 |
| Dee | 750 | 1,100 |
| Swale | 350 | 350* |
| Exe | 850 | 500 |

* May count only available
† Conwy Bay and Conwy River combined

between that census (1963–65) and the present counts shows that there has been an increase in winter numbers from 135,000 to 206,000 (Table 17:12). The increase has taken place mainly around the Irish Sea where 50,000 additional birds are now present. Table 17:13 shows that Morecambe Bay accounts for about 20,000 of this increase. However, numbers there are still well below the enormous counts made prior to the collapse of the cockle stocks in the cold winter of 1962–63. Dare (1966) also presented data for the numbers summering in a few estuaries, the limited data for recent years for these are also included in Table 17:14. In almost all areas there has been an increase in the non-breeding birds, presumably reflecting the higher overall numbers. The index since 1969 is presented in the graph and this shows a continuing upward trend in numbers.

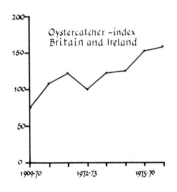

## AVOCET *Recurvirostra avosetta*

In the winter immediately after the Avocet recolonised Britain as a breeding species in 1947, small numbers began wintering on the Tamar estuary, Devon. Since then there has been a steady increase in numbers of birds wintering there and on the nearby Tavy; they reached a peak of 86 in the 1973–74 winter in which year a further 15 birds wintered on the Exe estuary, also in Devon (Prater 1976b). Since 1968–69, a small but increasing number has also begun to winter in East Anglia (Cadbury and Olney 1978), culminating in a maximum of 26 birds at Havergate in 1976–77 (*Trans. Suff. Nat. Hist. Soc.* 1978). Other estuaries in the south of England, particularly Pagham and Poole Harbours, have also had one or two Avocet in recent years. In Ireland the species is still a vagrant, though now of almost annual occurrence, mainly in winter (Hutchinson 1979). The increase in numbers wintering has closely paralleled the steady rise (averaging about 10% per annum) in the British breeding stock.

In international terms there are no British estuaries where numbers reach the 1% level of importance (230), but in terms of British bred Avocets wintering in south-western England, the Tamar/Tavy complex must be of significance. Evidence that some of our birds winter here has been provided by the sighting of birds

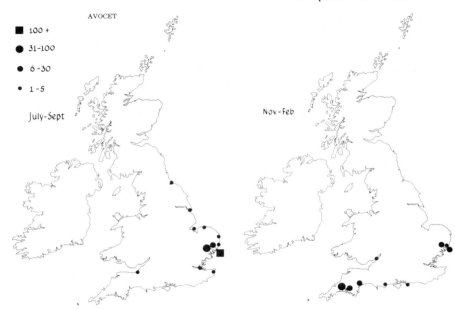

AVOCET

■ 100 +
● 31-100
● 6-30
• 1-5

July-Sept

Nov-Feb

colour-ringed at Minsmere, Suffolk, on the Tamar in 1971 (Cadbury and Olney 1978) and in 1973. Numbers wintering in Britain have varied from less than 25% to 47% of our post-breeding population of adults and immatures (Cadbury and Olney 1978). Ringing recoveries, Table 17:15, indicate that a proportion of our birds winter in Iberia along with the continental population. In complete contrast some continental Avocets have been observed wintering alongside Suffolk breeders on the estuaries of Devon and Cornwall.

The patterns of occurrence in south and south-west Britain, and eastern Britain are quire different. The wintering population in the south and south-west peaks in January (115 birds) falling in February, perhaps as some birds move to the continent. Numbers continue to drop in the south-west through February and March but birds begin returning to breeding localities in eastern England during the latter month. The exodus from the south-west is almost complete by April when numbers are approaching a peak in eastern England (125 were present on the Ore –

Table 17:15    *Foreign recoveries of British ringed Avocets*

| Date ringed | Recovered | Ringed | When ringed | Recovery |
|---|---|---|---|---|
| 18.7.70 | 21.6.77 | Orford | 1st summer | Lisbon, Portugal |
| 28.7.70 | 22.10.70 | Minsmere | pullus | Treto, N. Spain |
| 15.6.71 | 1.12.72 | Havergate | pullus | Cadiz, S.W. Spain |
| 18.6.71 | 18.8.73 | Minsmere | pullus | Fuzeta, S. Portugal |
| 16.7.71 | 12.11.76 | Minsmere | pullus | Honfleur, N. France |

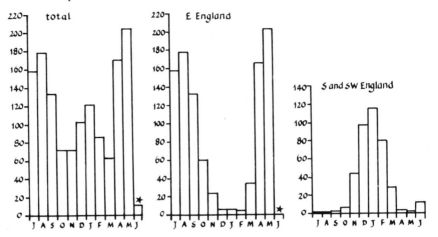

which includes Havergate Island – on average during 1969–75). Immatures arrive later on the breeding grounds (Cadbury and Olney 1978), helping to boost the peak count (200) in May. There are no complete figures from eastern England for June.

Immature birds also leave sooner than adults in the autumn, often by mid-June, and these may account for some of the records on the south coast at this time. Post-breeding adults leave their breeding areas from July onwards, and by August numbers on the adjacent estuaries reach their autumn peak of 180. At this time many birds cross over to the continent, so numbers decrease rapidly through September and October. Adults undergo a moult in the autumn, the majority moulting through August to early November and concentrating in the Waddensea. From November, numbers begin to build up on the south-western estuaries. Presumably once adults have completed their moult they continue to move further south into southern France and Iberia, but a few return to British estuaries. Numbers increase in the south-west through December, to reach a peak in January.

## RINGED PLOVER *Charadrius hiaticula*

Ringed Plovers are widely distributed on the coasts of Britain, Ireland and continental Europe; they are, however, not abundant in winter when a total of only 20,000–25,000 is present in the whole of Europe. Almost exactly half of these occur in Britain and Ireland. The species is a common winter visitor to the African coasts; in Morocco and Mauritania alone there are a further 23,000 birds (Prater 1976a and unpublished).

Three groups of Ringed Plovers occur in Britain. The wintering birds are primarily local breeders although augmented by birds which breed from the Netherlands to southern Sweden and the German Democratic Republic. During migration periods large numbers which breed in Iceland, Greenland and Scandinavia may be present, although relatively few occur from the last area, and even then mainly in autumn.

The sandier parts and the upper shore of estuaries hold the largest numbers of feeding Ringed Plovers. They are also found, but usually in small numbers, along sandy or shingle beaches and are extremely uncommon inland during the winter. Ringed Plover feed on a wide range of food items, mainly those found in the surface centimetre of the sand, but they are also adept at catching polychaete worms when they approach the surface.

The diagram shows the numbers of Ringed Plovers recorded in Britain and Ireland each month. There is a rapid build up in numbers during August and a peak is reached usually in the last week of August or the first week in September. The timing of this peak is similar in all regions although numbers decrease much more rapidly in the western coast than on the eastern and southern coasts. During late September there is a rapid decrease to a fairly stable winter level by the end of October. Only in Ireland are as many birds likely to be present in winter as in autumn, although autumn counts are not as comprehensive as in January.

The first Ringed Plovers start displaying on territories in late February, and the majority of coastal breeders in the British Isles have returned by the end of March. Counts show an abrupt drop during February to reach a March/April low coincidental with this return to territories. Spring migrants are in evidence from mid or late April but peak numbers do not occur until the third week of May, and many remain into the first week of June. The spring passage appears to involve an average of about 15,000 birds.

In the autumn, large numbers of Ringed Plovers occur in all parts of Britain but, rather surprisingly, this does not seem to be a feature in Ireland. The passage is strongest in Britain in the west, where the largest concentrations are on the Severn (3,800), the Dee (2,700) and Morecambe Bay (2,050). By November the winter distribution has been established with many moderately sized flocks, only the Uists and the Solway reaching a thousand individuals. Ringed Plover are widespread but still not numerous, in Ireland throughout the winter. The spring migration is a major feature of the estuaries in Britain which border the Irish Sea; the path of this movement appears to be extremely narrow for the south-west, and Ireland seems to miss it and very few are seen on the east coast of Britain. Morecambe Bay (7,300),

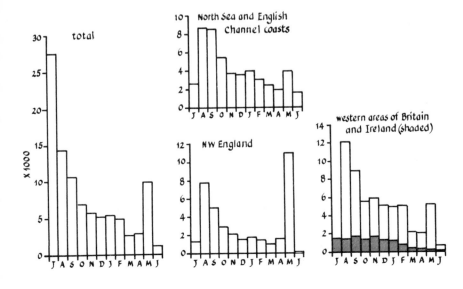

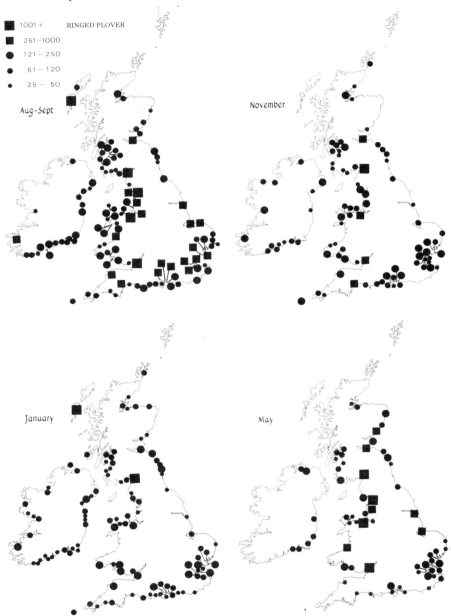

the Solway (2,250), and the Dee (2,100) support the largest numbers.

By mid-June and in July the only Ringed Plovers remaining are our breeding birds. Their numbers and distribution are described by Prater (1976c), who found that there were between 5,800 and 6,300 pairs in Britain, mostly in eastern England and the northern and western islands of Scotland. Many of those breeding in Norfolk move across the country to the Irish sea for the winter, but judging by the very large numbers found in the Uists in winter, many of the birds from the Outer Hebrides are likely to remain there.

The principal estuaries for non-breeding Ringed Plovers are presented in Table 17:11. The largest numbers occur during passage periods but, because the European population is not known at this time of the year, a provisional level of significance of 500 birds has been used. It is, however, certain that the last five of these areas would be of international importance. Because the numbers wintering in Europe are known it is possible to be more precise about international importance at this time of the

Table 17:16 *Internationally important estuaries for Ringed Plover in Britain and Ireland, 1969–75*

(A) *In winter (October–March: 1% = 250)*

| | Highest av. monthly count | % W. Eurpean | Months above 1%* |
|---|---|---|---|
| Solway, south | 1,364 | 5·5 | 10 <u>11</u> 12 1 2 3 |
| Uists† | 1,000 | 4·0 | <u>2</u> |
| Solway, north | 467 | 1·9 | <u>10</u> 11 |
| Blackwater | 375 | 1·5 | <u>10</u> |
| Medway | 366 | 1·5 | <u>10</u> |
| Taw/Torridge | 360 | 1·4 | <u>10</u> 12 2 |
| Southampton Water | 345 | 1·4 | <u>10</u> |
| Dee | 335 | 1·3 | <u>10</u> 11 |
| Morecambe Bay | 335 | 1·3 | <u>10</u> |
| Severn | 316 | 1·3 | <u>10</u> |
| Swansea Bay | 311 | 1·2 | <u>10</u> |
| Hamford Water | 310 | 1·2 | <u>10</u> 2 |
| Firth of Forth | 282 | 1·1 | <u>10</u> |
| Exe | 254 | 1·0 | <u>11</u> 12 |

* Underlining denotes month of peak count
† Only February count

(B) *On passage (July–September, April–May: 1% = 500)*

| | Autumn | Spring |
|---|---|---|
| Morecambe Bay | 2,042 | 7,280 |
| Severn | 3,791 | 1,088 |
| Dee | 2,721 | 2,093 |
| Solway, north | 688 | 1,624 |
| Uists | 1,566 | ND |
| Solway, south | 1,564 | 631 |
| Medway | 778 | (185) |
| Southampton Water | 702 | (160) |
| Dyfi | 581 | 668 |

year. The Solway and the Uists clearly stand out but quite a number of other areas reach the 1% level.

Although the numbers of wintering Ringed Plovers have fluctuated over the last seven years no clear trend is evident. This is probably because the population monitored breeds in temperate latitudes, where extremes of climate, and hence of breeding success, are rare.

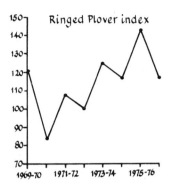

GOLDEN PLOVER *Pluvialis apricaria*

As a breeding bird the Golden Plover is restricted to the north-western Palearctic from Iceland and the British Isles in the west, through Scandinavia to central Siberia. The wintering range includes most of western and south-western Europe with a few birds reaching north-west Africa. Two races are recognised: the 'northern' *P.a. altifrons* (Iceland, northern Scandinavia to central USSR) and the nominate 'southern' race *P.a. apricaria* (Ireland to southern Finland). In Britain, where the species is characteristic of moorland in the north and west, the majority of breeders are *apricaria* though some *altifrons* occur in Scotland, particularly at higher elevations (Ratcliffe 1976b). The number of breeding pairs in Britain has been estimated at 30,750+, although the species has declined substantially over the past century (Ratcliffe 1976b).

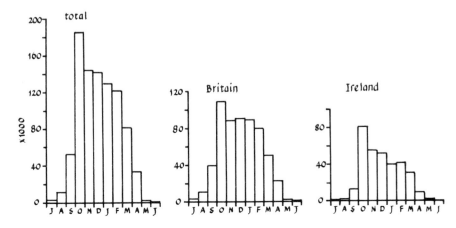

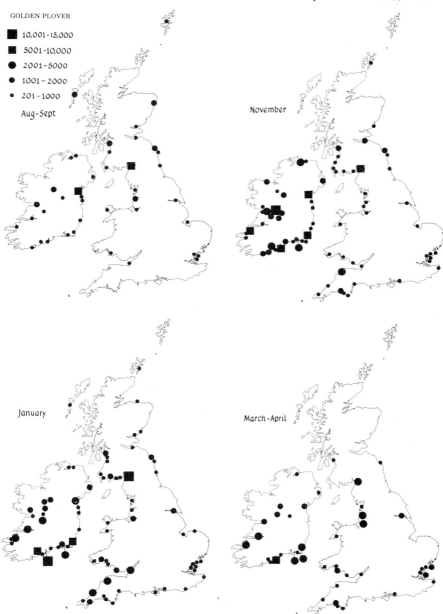

Golden Plovers, typically, winter inland in Britain and make great use of permanent pasture for feeding, and ploughed fields for roosting (Lloyd 1978, Fuller and Youngman 1979). They are not a typical estuarine species but in hard weather they will rapidly seek out coastal saltings and muddy foreshores, moving south and west in Britain and Ireland at such times.

Table 17:17    Areas recording 5,000 or more Golden Plovers in at least one month

|  | Peak count | Peak month | Other months with 5,000+ |
|---|---|---|---|
| Ballyforan | 11,900 | Oct | * |
| Ballymacoda | 10,200 | Jan | 10–12  2  3 |
| South Solway | 7,783 | Jan | 9  12 |
| Dundalk Bay | 7,250 | Nov | 9  12 |
| Wexford Harbour | 7,015 | Jan | 12 |
| Cork Harbour | 6,250 | Dec | 12 |
| North Solway | 5,782 | Jan | — |
| Little Brosna | 5,556 | Oct | — |
| Barrow Harbour | 5,000 | Oct | * |

* Count data incomplete for other months

The highest numbers are recorded in October and the average estuaries count at this time is almost 186,000. However, the numbers in winter are somewhat lower, in the region of 130,000, with probably double this number inland. Thus, the total wintering in Britain and Ireland is about 400,000; estimates of the total wintering population of western Europe and north Africa have not been published but it is probably in the region of 750,000–1,000,000 birds. Thus, 40–50% of these winter in Britain and Ireland, 13–17% on estuaries.

British birds leave their breeding grounds in July and probably winter in the surrounding lowlands, not moving far unless forced to do so by severe weather. Not many of these reach estuaries in the autumn and there is little increase until October when Icelandic and continental birds arrive. Although *altifrons* and *apricaria* can be separated in breeding plumage in most cases (intermediates do occur) this is not possible in winter plumage; the biometrics of the two forms are also similar (Prater, Marchant and Vuorinen 1977). Thus it is impossible to define the exact limits of winter distribution of the two forms. However, the majority of birds in Ireland originate from Iceland as over half of the Icelandic foreign recoveries have been in Ireland (Hutchinson 1979). British breeders stay mainly in central and southern Britain, a few reaching Iberia and north Africa, while northern European birds seem to occur mainly in eastern Britain (e.g. one Norwegian juvenile recovered in Lincolnshire). The seasonal changes in distribution are shown in the maps.

Following the October influx, the large flocks recorded on some estuaries break up and move inland, and counts fall off through the winter. Several British estuaries do record a midwinter peak, however, notably the Solway (13,500+ in January). Birds move off early in the spring and some British breeders are back on territory in January, though they will temporarily vacate them in severe weather. The majority of wintering birds have dispersed by March and April, a time when some British breeders are on eggs. Some estuaries record small spring peaks in these months (Burry Inlet, Foulness, Humber, Mersey) evidencing the return movement north and north-east of *altifrons* which have wintered further south. Few summering birds remain on our estuaries, less than 500 overall in May and fewer still in June.

Only three areas are of international importance with more than 8,000 (the provisional 1% level) present in any month. Two of these areas were in Ireland – Ballyforan (11,900 in October) and Ballymacoda (10,200 in January) – but the largest number (13,500) is on the Solway in January. Other estuaries recording at least 5,000 birds in any month are given in Table 17:17. The numbers recorded by the 'Estuaries Enquiry' have fluctuated erratically with a peak in 1971–72 followed by two decreases, so that the 1973–74 value was about 50% of this peak; since then there have been rises in 1974–75 and 1975–76. The numbers present on estuaries in midwinter, however, depend mainly on weather conditions.

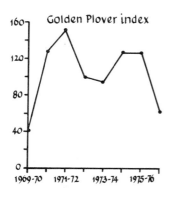

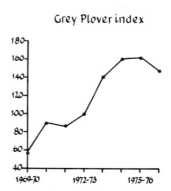

## GREY PLOVER *Pluvialis squatarola*

Grey Plovers breed in a belt along the arctic tundra from north-western USSR to eastern Canada. They do not, however, penetrate into Greenland nor to the islands in the north-east of Canada. The birds which are seen in western Europe originate only from the breeding area between the White Sea and the Taimyr peninsula (Branson and Minton 1976).

The Grey Plover has one of the widest wintering ranges of any wader. In the Old World it is found from Scotland south to South Africa, and east to Japan and New Zealand. It is also common along the coasts of North and South America. International wader counts have shown there to be 30,000–40,000 in western Europe and a further 15,000 in north-west Africa; an unknown number winter to the south of the Sahara. In Europe, Britain and France each support about a third (10,000–12,000) of the total; most of the rest are in the Netherlands and Iberia. Ireland has relatively few Grey Plover.

The maps show the seasonal variation in the number present in Britain and Ireland. Overall the picture is fairly simple: numbers build up rapidly through late July and August to reach peak numbers in September and October. Initially, judging by their incomplete summer plumage, most are immature non-breeding birds, but during August there is a rapid increase in the number of adults in their striking grey and black summer plumage. From late August, many juveniles arrive on our estuaries. Although Grey Plovers have a long and complex moult in autumn (Branson and Minton 1976), most active feather growth ceases by November. At this time numbers decrease slightly – ringing returns indicate that this is due to a small southerly movement. There is a small rise into January and numbers are maintained through February before dropping steadily during spring. The birds forming the winter peak are probably those which moulted in the autumn on the Waddensea, and the decrease is due to birds returning there before migrating to the north-eastern breeding grounds.

Regionally, however, the picture is not quite so clear. Eastern England contributes most birds to the national picture and follows it most closely; a similar picture emerges from southern England, too. The most noticeable departure is seen in western Britain and Ireland. Not surprisingly, as the species arrives from the east, there is relatively little autumn passage; numbers, however, build up very steadily during the winter and there is a February peak. This peak is seen clearly in most sub-regions and in most years. It is not clear if this is due to a steady movement westwards during the winter or to some northerly movement from Europe, probably the former. Spring passage is unremarkable except for birds moving east along the coasts of southern England during April and May; like the Bar-tailed Godwit passage, this is likely to originate mainly from the African wintering population. Only small numbers of winter-plumaged or partially summer-plumaged Grey Plovers remain on British estuaries through June.

The distribution within Britain and Ireland is essentially south-eastern at all seasons, the sector from the Wash to the Solent supporting most birds. Grey Plovers are always scarce in Scotland and, apart from a handful of sites, they are also scarce in Ireland. Grey Plover are most frequently found on the muddier estuaries of Britain and Ireland; it is not entirely clear whether the distribution is most closely related to substratum type, to the distribution of food supply, to climatic preferences or to other factors. Where there are adjacent estuaries which have greatly differing numbers of Grey Plover it is usually the case that they are in the muddier estuary or the muddier part of it. The Wash is outstanding at all times of the year; it supports in excess of 1,000 Grey Plover except during midsummer, and over 4,000 have been seen at the peak of the autumn migration. In autumn the Humber has a large flock but, as with a number of species there, numbers drop rapidly into winter. Two areas at the mouth of the Thames, Foulness and the Swale, have surprisingly few Grey Plover in autumn considering the winter numbers. In winter, numbers in the western

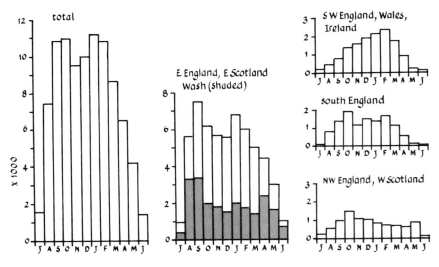

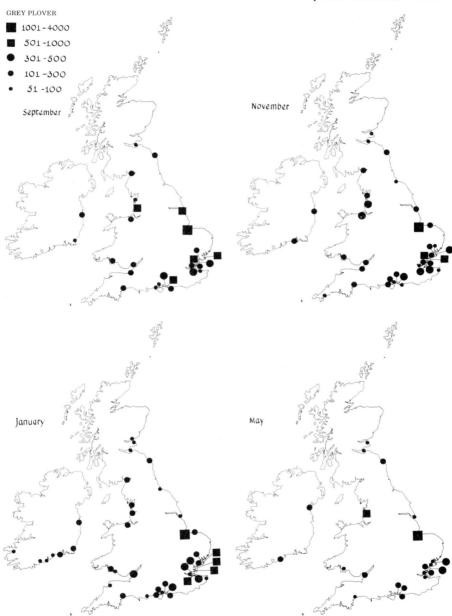

GREY PLOVER

- 1001–4000
- 501–1000
- 301–500
- 101–300
- 51–100

September

November

January

May

estuaries are slightly higher. In spring only the Ribble, apart from the Wash and the Essex coast, has internationally significant numbers. All estuaries supporting internationally important flocks are presented in Table 17:18. Eight estuaries in south-eastern England (apart from the Ribble) support very large numbers for six or more months of the year and are consistently of high value for this species.

*Table 17:18   Estuaries of international importance for Grey Plover, 1969–75*

| | Highest av. monthly count | % W. European | Months above 1%* | | | | | | | | | | | |
|---|---|---|---|---|---|---|---|---|---|---|---|---|---|---|---|
| | | | 7 | 8 | 9 | 10 | 11 | 12 | 1 | 2 | 3 | 4 | 5 | 6 |
| Wash | 3,364 | 11·2 | 7 | 8 | **9** | 10 | 11 | 12 | 1 | 2 | 3 | 4 | 5 | 6 |
| Chichester Harbour | 988 | 3·3 | | 8 | 9 | **10** | 11 | 12 | 1 | 2 | 3 | | | |
| Ribble | 771 | 2·6 | | 8 | 9 | 10 | 11 | 12 | | 2 | 3 | 4 | **5** | |
| Hamford Water | 750 | 2·5 | | | **9** | 10 | 11 | 12 | 1 | 2 | 3 | 4 | | |
| Dengie | 725 | 2·4 | | **8** | 9 | 10 | 11 | 12 | 1 | 2 | 3 | 4 | | |
| Swale | 723 | 2·4 | | | | 10 | 11 | **12** | 1 | 2 | 3 | | | |
| Blackwater | 720 | 2·4 | | 8 | **9** | 10 | 11 | 12 | 1 | 2 | 3 | | | |
| Foulness | 580 | 1·9 | | | | | | | | 1 | 3 | | | |
| Humber | 579 | 1·9 | | | **9** | 10 | | | | | | | | |
| Medway | 577 | 1·9 | | 8 | 9 | 10 | 11 | 12 | 1 | **2** | 3 | | | |
| Langstone Harbour | 426 | 1·4 | | | 9 | 10 | | | | **2** | | | | |
| Stour | 405 | 1·3 | | | | 10 | | | | **2** | | | | |
| North Bull | 389 | 1·3 | | | | | | | | **2** | | | | |
| Severn | 379 | 1·3 | | | | | **11** | | 1 | 2 | | | | |
| Dee | 375 | 1·3 | | | | 10 | **11** | | | | | | | |
| Leigh/Canvey | 320 | 1·1 | | | | | | | **1** | | | | | |
| Exe | 304 | 1·0 | | | | | | | | **2** | | | | |

* Underlining denotes month of highest counts

Grey Plovers have changed their status in a number of areas during the last thirty years, from fairly scarce passage migrant to common winter visitor (Prater 1976a). During the 'Estuaries Enquiry' the numbers have steadily risen in Britain, no doubt reflecting the increased frequency of good breeding seasons and a reduction in shooting pressure – factors which operate similarly for the Dark-bellied Brent Goose.

## LAPWING *Vanellus vanellus*

Lapwings have a breeding range which stretches eastwards across the Palearctic from western Europe right across the USSR, mainly between latitudes 40°N and 60°N (Voous 1960). There are no subspecies, probably because of extensive mixing of different sub-populations (Mead, Flegg and Cox 1968).

In Britain and Ireland they are ubiquitous as a breeding species with at least 200,000 pairs breeding annually (Sharrock 1976). Lapwings exhibit a complex pattern of dispersion and migration (Imboden 1974) and very large numbers winter in western Europe (no doubt several million birds). The British and Irish total must be at least one million; many of these frequent inland areas, occurring on estuaries only during severe weather when feeding grounds on arable fields and grassland are frozen over. As with a few other species which winter predominantly inland (e.g.

Golden Plover *Pluvialis apricaria*), estuary counts for Lapwing show the general pattern of occurrence but do not provide comprehensive monthly totals.

Britain and Ireland are important wintering areas for Scandinavian Lapwings (Imboden 1974). Birds from the low countries, central and eastern Europe and Russia also reach Britain. Many British breeders winter close to their area of origin but many also move south-west to the continent, or west to Ireland; the percentage of non-migratory birds is greater in England than in Scotland (Imboden 1974).

Lapwing numbers begin to increase from June onwards in Britain and at this time there is a partial summer migration to the west involving more adults than juveniles (Imboden 1974). This western bias in distribution is strikingly evident in August and September; during the latter month the estuaries count averaged some 70,000 birds. Lapwing from east and central Europe also move west and north-west from June–July onwards, some reaching Britain, and this partial summer migration apparently merges into the main autumn movement, which occurs during October for Scandinavian birds, and November–December for the eastern/central European birds (Imboden 1974). Britain thus continues to receive immigrants from the north and east, from early summer through to December, with peak numbers in January (145,000+).

The pattern of counts for western Britain differs from that for eastern/southern Britain. There is a distinct peak in September in the west, presumably due mainly to the westward movement of British birds. In the east and south, however, there is a gradual build up from June through until January, perhaps due to continental immigrants, particularly in the winter months. A second peak occurs in the west in December and January when severe weather is most likely to cause birds wintering in Europe, and also inland in Britain, to seek ice-free feeding areas. The distribution map for January is the most complete, and clearly shows the concentrations inland and on the coast in the south and west.

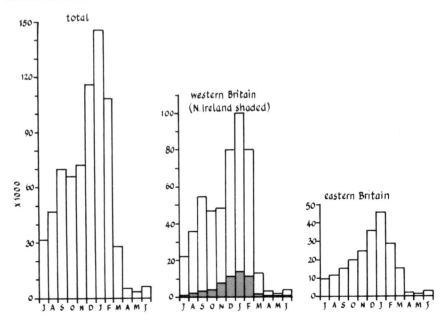

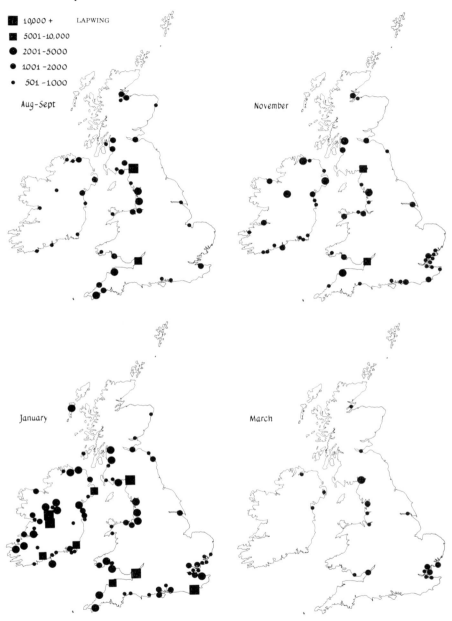

Departure in spring takes place from late January onwards and numbers drop rapidly through February and into March, the peak period for spring migration. There are fewer than 30,000 by then on estuaries, and only just over 5,000 in April. A small non-breeding population remains on the wintering areas and the lowest count of the year occurs in May (less than 3,000).

The index constructed from estuary counts shows a continuing upward trend despite declines in 1972–73 and 1974–75. Lapwings were one of the species hit hardest in Britain by the severe winter of 1962–63 when many died, despite having moved in large numbers to south-western England and western Ireland (Dobinson and Richards 1964); continental birds presumably fared similarly. The increase in the index since 1969–70 may well be a reflection of the continuing recovery of the population.

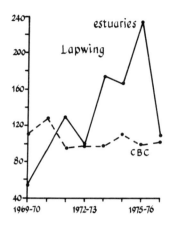
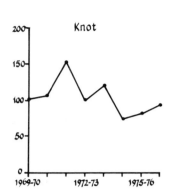

KNOT *Calidris canutus*

Virtually all of the Knot which occur in Britain and Ireland breed in northern Greenland and north-eastern Canada; only a small proportion (probably less than 10%), mainly in autumn, are of Siberian origin (Dick et al 1976, Prater 1974). In winter, Britain and Ireland support about 65% of the European and north-west African population of the species; the other principal wintering areas are in the Netherlands, France and Mauritania (Prater 1976a).

The pattern of occurrence of Knot shows a large influx in August and relatively stable numbers (around 170,000) up to October; this is the period when Knot moult. There is rapid rise in early winter to reach a January peak of 301,000. There is an even more rapid departure during March and April to leave only a few thousand immature birds after mid-May. The regional breakdown of counts shows that the Irish Sea, principally Dublin Bay to Strangford Lough, and the Dee to the Inner Solway, support more Knot than any other area. Few Knot are found in southern and south-western areas. The four principal estuaries (Morecambe Bay, the Ribble and the Dee on the Irish Sea, and the Wash on the North Sea coast) support at least 75% of all Knot in Britain and Ireland except during the midwinter period of November to February. During these months large numbers, which have moulted on the Waddensea, move into the British Isles and, when added to those already here, result in the midwinter peak. This influx is seen on the east and west coasts, although ringing recoveries have shown that some of the winter influx in the west results from a movement of Knot which moulted in the Wash. The decrease in late winter is due to birds moving back to the Waddensee, where they put on weight for the return

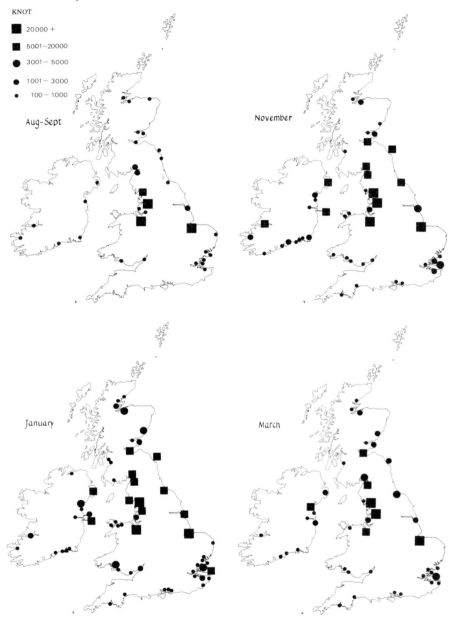

movement to the breeding grounds.

The seasonal distribution in Britain and Ireland is presented in the maps. This emphasises their restricted distribution with just a few internationally important concentrations in the major estuaries. Knot occur most widely in midwinter, and large numbers are found in many east coast and Irish estuaries where there are few in

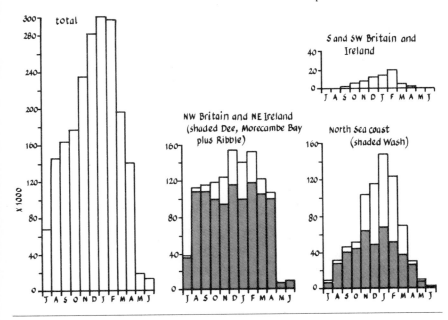

Table 17:19   *Estuaries of international importance for Knot, 1969–75*

| | Highest av. monthly count | % W. European | Months above 1%* |
|---|---|---|---|
| Morecambe Bay | 80,206 | 16·0 | 8 9 10 11 12 1 2 3 4̲ |
| Ribble | 70,556 | 14·1 | 7 8̲ 9 10 11 12 1 2 3 4 5 6 |
| Wash | 67,492 | 13·5 | 7 8 9 10 11 12 1̲ 2 3 4 5 |
| Dee | 31,238 | 6·2 | 7 8 9 10̲ 11 12 1 2 3 |
| Humber | 22,059 | 4·4 | 12 1 2̲ 3 |
| Firth of Forth | 16,117 | 3·2 | 11 12 1̲ 2 3 |
| Solway, south | 14,070 | 2·8 | 11 12̲ 1 2 3 |
| Strangford Lough | 13,443 | 2·7 | 11 12 1̲ 2 |
| Lindisfarne | 9,250 | 1·8 | 11 12 1̲ |
| Solway, north | 7,800 | 1·6 | 11 12 1 2̲ |
| Teesmouth | 7,367 | 1·5 | 11 12̲ 1 2 |
| Burry Inlet | 6,722 | 1·3 | 2̲ |
| North Bull | 6,700 | 1·3 | 11 12 1̲ 2 |
| Foulness | 6,690 | 1·3 | 12̲ 1 2 |
| Alt | 6,567 | 1·3 | 10̲ |

* Underlining denotes month of highest count

autumn or spring. The reasons are not known for this apparent winter filling up of what may be sub-optimal habitats. All the estuaries, and the main sections of each estuary where large numbers occur, have extensive areas of sand with some finer sediment on the surface. Most Knot feed in this habitat although smallish flocks also occur on biologically productive rocky coasts, especially in north-eastern England and eastern Scotland.

The principal estuaries for Knot are presented in Table 17:19. There are three major estuaries which support 10% or more of the European population; Morecambe Bay does so for five months in winter and spring, the Wash for three months in winter, and the Ribble for two months in autumn. No other estuary has 50,000 or more Knot in any month, although the Dee has 20,000+ for seven months from August to February.

The Knot is the only species which has decreased markedly during the period of the 'Estuaries Enquiry'. At its peak, 1971–72, almost 400,000 were present, but only just over 230,000 were found in 1973–74. A large decrease has also occurred in the French wintering population since the late 1960s and early 1970s, from 110,000 to fewer than 20,000 by 1976 (R. Maheo in litt.). The population changes of the British and Irish wintering birds is shown in the diagram. The fluctuations correspond with the breeding success of the Irish wintering Pale-bellied Brent Geese, which breed in the same area of Canada as the Knot. The main cause of the Knot's decrease therefore appears to be the increasing frequency of bad breeding seasons in the Canadian Arctic, although the loss of wintering areas to many reclamation schemes will not have helped to maintain numbers.

## SANDERLING *Calidris alba*

Sanderlings breed in relatively restricted areas of high Arctic Alaska, Canada, Greenland, Svalbard and Siberia. At these high latitudes the breeding season is short and closely related to the timing of migrations. There is only about eight weeks between the late spring and early autumn migration peaks. It is a measure of this numerical status and migration ability that they can be found outside the breeding season on coasts in almost all temperate and tropical parts of the world.

The non-breeding habitat is almost exclusively sandy coasts, including the sandy parts of estuaries. Few large winter concentrations are known, so apparently Sanderlings are widely but thinly distributed over much of their world range. In Britain there are long stretches of apparently suitable sandy beaches which are not

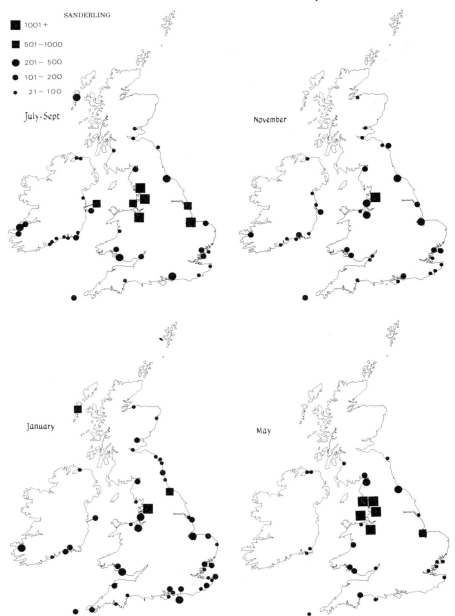

used, and virtually all large concentrations are associated with estuaries (Prater and Davies 1978). Thus, here at least, there may be a preference for estuarine sand.

The maps and histograms show only the results of the 'Estuaries Enquiry', not the full numbers and distribution in Britain. Prater and Davies (1978) give the major non-estuarine localities and estimate the average wintering numbers at 10,300 birds;

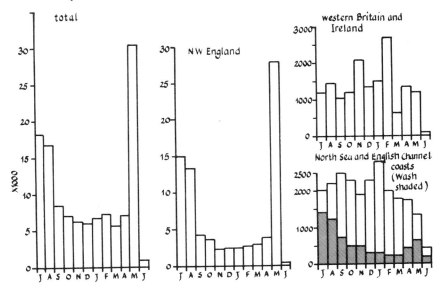

probably in excess of 2,000 winter in Ireland (Hutchinson 1979). Elsewhere in western Europe only 4,000 are known, with a further 16,000 in Morocco and Mauritania (Prater 1976). Thus Britain and Ireland are of particular importance, supporting about 63% of European wintering Sanderling.

Ringing recoveries and colour-ring sightings have shown that Siberian and Greenland birds occur in Britain at passage times, but at present the origins of our wintering birds are not fully known. Most recoveries and observations support the hypothesis that wintering birds are of Siberian origin, but there are recent sightings of single Greenland-marked birds wintering in Scilly (three consecutive winters) and being present in Ireland and north-eastern England in early March. A situation somewhat more complex than was thought at first.

Although the wintering population is internationally important, the numbers are dwarfed by the very large autumn and, particularly, spring passages. The diagram shows that numbers are relatively constant from September to April, but that migration peaks sharply in July–August and in May. The peaks are almost entirely due to the numbers recorded in north-western England; elsewhere passage numbers are comparable with or even lower than the wintering figures. June numbers are very low (partly due to incomplete cover) but as in other parts of the winter range, some non-breeders stay for the summer.

There is little difference between the November and January distributions. The north-west English sites hold 35–40% of the 'Estuaries Enquiry' total and probably 19–24% of all the British and Irish winter total.

In July–September, Sanderling are similarly distributed but with some large concentrations. North-western England holds 83% of the July estuary numbers, falling to 55% in September. The other main sites are the Wash, Humber and North Bull. The May map shows the highly localised distribution at this season. Away from the north-west English coast, only the Wash and the Tees carry more than 200 birds.

*Table 17:20   Estuaries of international importance for Sanderling in Britain and Ireland, 1969–75*

(A) *For Passage Birds (April–October, 1% = 500 birds)*

|  | Highest av. monthly count | % W. European | Months above 1%* |
|---|---|---|---|
| Morecambe Bay | 11,857 | 23·7 | 4 <u>5</u> 7 8 9 |
| Dee | 6,452 | 12·9 | 4 5 <u>7</u> 8 9 10 |
| Ribble | 6,316 | 12·6 | 4 <u>5</u> 7 8 9 10 |
| Duddon | 2,066 | 4·1 | <u>5</u> |
| Wash | 1,238 | 2·5 | 5 <u>7</u> 8 9 |
| Alt | 1,101 | 2·2 | <u>5</u> 7 8 |
| Humber | 640 | 1·3 | <u>9</u> 10 |
| North Bull | 518 | 1·0 | <u>7</u> |

(B) *For Wintering Birds (November–March, 1% = 150 birds)*

|  | Highest av. monthly count | % W. European | Months above 1%* |
|---|---|---|---|
| Ribble | 1,771 | 11·8 | 11 12 1 2 <u>3</u> |
| Uists | 1,397 | 9·3 | <u>2</u> |
| Teesmouth | (600) | 4·0 | 11 12 <u>1</u> 2 3 |
| Dee | 471 | 3·1 | 11 12 1 2 <u>3</u> |
| Alt | 396 | 2·6 | 11 12 1 <u>2</u> 3 |
| Castlemaine Harbour | 340 | 2·3 | 12 1 <u>2</u> |
| Wash | 321 | 2·1 | <u>11</u> 12 1 2 3 |
| Climping | 251 | 1·7 | 12 <u>1</u> |
| Gwendraeth | 250 | 1·7 | <u>11</u> |
| Waterford Harbour | 244 | 1·6 | <u>2</u> |
| Swansea Bay | 228 | 1·5 | 11 12 <u>1</u> 2 |
| Firth of Tay | 189 | 1·3 | <u>1</u> |
| Humber | 182 | 1·2 | <u>11</u>   2 |
| S. Solway | 180 | 1·2 | <u>3</u> |
| Tramore | 178 | 1·2 | 12 1 <u>2</u> |
| Chichester Harbour | 167 | 1·1 | <u>2</u> |
| Dublin Bay | 165 | 1·1 | <u>11</u> |
| Goring | 154 | 1·0 | <u>1</u> |
| Duddon | 151 | 1·0 | <u>3</u> |

* Underlining denotes months with highest counts

There is no evidence of any spring passage in Ireland (Hutchinson 1979).

Ringing recoveries show that these May flocks have wintered at least as far south as Mauritania and Ghana, but there is, as yet, no evidence as to their destination. That the flocks are concentrated on the west coast may indicate that it is Greenland, especially as they are in company with Dunlin and Ringed Plovers known to be of Greenland stock, but some Siberian species are also known to occur on passage in these estuaries.

The sites exceeding the 1% level of international importance are shown in Table 17:20, for the winter and the migration periods. The massive May peak in Morecambe Bay represents nearly a quarter of the total known to be present in western Europe; remarkably, the winter numbers rarely exceed 100. The 135 km of the north-west English coast supports about 55% of the birds seen in Europe in spring. Elsewhere in Britain only the Wash has an important spring passage. It is probable, however, that the Uists are important during both passage periods.

For wintering birds the Ribble is the most important site; this estuary is of international importance for Sanderling throughout the year except for the breeding month of June. Incomplete cover of the Uists and Benbecula for the 'Estuaries Enquiry' nevertheless shows the value of this area. No other areas hold comparable winter numbers, but 17 sites carry between 1% and 4% of the west European total.

On isolated beaches the numbers of Sanderlings present throughout a winter can be remarkably stable. However, where beaches are interconnected Sanderling may move about to a considerable extent. For example, the outer areas of the Ribble, Alt, Mersey and Dee estuaries are all fairly close together, and ringing studies have shown movement between these sites. This mobility is probably the reason why every winter there are over 3,000 Sanderlings recorded on the Ribble but that this number is not consistently recorded.

The Index of Sanderling numbers is highly variable as befits a high Arctic breeder, but its mobility in certain areas may be the major cause of (apparently) fluctuating fortunes. The general trend has been one of shallow increase.

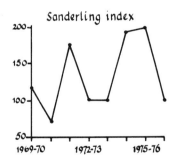

## LITTLE STINT *Calidris minuta*

The breeding grounds of the Little Stint are on the high Arctic tundra between 20° and 130°E; in winter they are found chiefly on the coasts and inland lakes of Africa and south-west Asia. The small but regular spring and autumn passages of this species through the British Isles are of little international importance, but none the less of considerable interest.

Fresh and brackish water sites at estuaries, such as feeder streams and adjacent pools and scrapes, are extensively used at passage periods, greatly facilitating counting. A high proportion of passage birds occur at similar localities inland. The

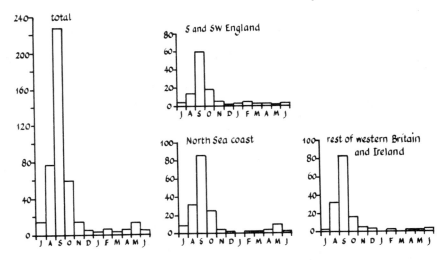

small number of wintering birds apparently show a greater preference for a muddy estuarine habitat, which makes the birds harder to detect among flocks of Dunlin and partly explains the irregularity of the winter records.

Autumn passage arrival, initially of adults but later involving much larger numbers of juvenile birds, begins in late July and continues into October. In all regions there is a large peak in September. However, in southern and western areas (including Wales and Ireland) the mean passage date is later, with proportionately more birds in October than elsewhere. The largest numbers are on the east coast.

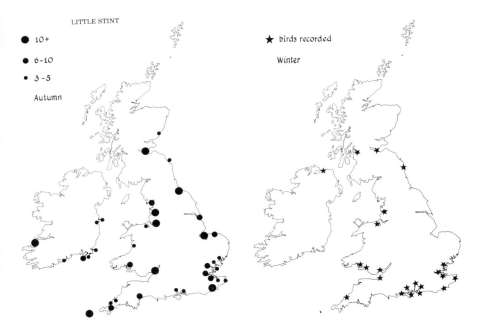

Onward movements cease in early November so that records between mid-November and mid-April refer to wintering birds. All regions except the Irish Republic provided winter records during the course of the 'Estuaries Enquiry', but records were most regular in southern England. No less than 21 sites were involved. The Camel River in Cornwall was the most consistently occupied site in winter, in spite of relatively low autumn passage numbers. However, it is probable that more birds wintered in the Sussex and Hampshire estuaries, here up to four were seen on count dates but casual records at other times indicates that perhaps as many as 10–20 could be present. The British Isles lie well to the north of the main wintering concentrations of western birds in Morocco and Mauritania, but small numbers (*c.* 100) also occur in winter in France and rather more (1,000+) in Iberia.

The spring passage begins in late April in Britain, with a peak in May and a few are still present in early June. Only the English east coast sees a regular spring migration, with the most regular sites at this season being the Humber, Blackwater and Orwell estuaries.

Major autumn passage estuaries are shown in the map. In most cases these are the larger estuaries, but the Solway in particular provided few records. Rye Harbour and the Isle of Scilly, on the other hand, are relatively important sites in spite of their small size.

## CURLEW SANDPIPER *Calidris ferruginea*

This high Arctic breeder is almost exclusively a passage bird in Britain and Ireland, although an occasional individual is reported in winter. Winter quarters are in Africa (mainly south of the Sahara), India, south-eastern Asia and Australasia. Migrants in western Europe are probably en route to the large concentration on the Banc d'Arguin, Mauritania, or further south along the West African coast.

The autumn's first arrivals in Britain are seen on the English east coast from mid-July and into August. These early migrants are almost all adults in summer plumage or in early stages of body moult. An important site, not covered by

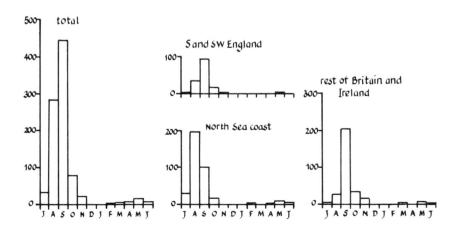

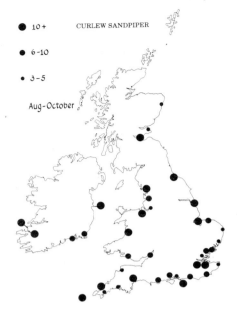

● 10 +   CURLEW SANDPIPER

● 6-10

• 3-5

Aug-October

'Estuaries Enquiry', is Wisbech sewage farm (close to the Wash) where up to 150 adults have been counted in August.

Away from eastern England, July records are scarce and peak numbers occur in September. After mid-August, arrivals are nearly all of juvenile birds. In 1969, the first year of counts for the 'Estuaries Enquiry', there was an unprecedented influx of juveniles beginning in mid-August; by the end of that month a minimum of 3,500 birds was estimated to be present, many at inland localities (Stanley and Minton 1972). This exceptional season has contributed a large proportion of the numbers recorded by the 'Estuaries Enquiry' but the geographical distribution of records was similar to that in other seasons. Thus the map gives an unbiased picture of the autumn distribution.

October numbers are much lower and normally very few stragglers remain by early November. Winter records came from five sites but none of them was occupied in more than one winter.

A small spring passage begins in late April but only in eastern England does any estuary hold more than one or two birds. Spring migration reaches its peak in late May or early June.

Curlew Sandpipers usually choose particularly rich feeding areas in muddy parts of estuaries, and roost communally with other calidrids. The chief British sites in autumn are the Humber, Wash and Medway; in spring they are most regular on the Medway and the Orwell.

## PURPLE SANDPIPER *Calidris maritima*

Purple Sandpipers breed in the Arctic from western Canada to central USSR, being replaced in the Pacific region by Rock Sandpiper (*C. ptilocnemis* – which may be conspecific). The winter quarters are exclusively on rocky marine shores, from western Greenland to New Jersey on the western coast of the Atlantic, and in Europe from Iceland and northern Norway to northern France; this is, in fact, the most northerly wader species in winter, and is found in all coastal parts of its range which remain ice-free. The winter habitat is exclusively maritime with preference for rocky shores and skerries, although harbour walls and jetties are occasional substitutes. Turnstone is a frequent congener, particularly in the southern parts of the range. Many wintering areas are exclusive to these two species and outside the scope of 'Estuaries Enquiry' counts, so that its data are incomplete.

It may be possible, however, to deduce the monthly pattern of numbers using only those sites counted in every month. Most adults moult on or near the breeding grounds, not reaching Britain until September or October; juveniles occur from mid-August in small numbers. Arrivals continue until the winter peak in January. The return movement begins in February but most birds depart during late April and May. The summering population is proportionally larger than shown, but most birds are on the more remote northerly coasts not providing monthly counts. It should be remembered that the histogram is based on less than 5% of the estimated British population.

No monthly counts are available from Ireland, but there is some evidence of larger numbers in March/April (Hutchinson 1979). Spring increases also occur at some south-western sites, possibly indicating the route of northward passage from the northern coast of France.

The origin of British wintering birds is indicated by four recoveries between

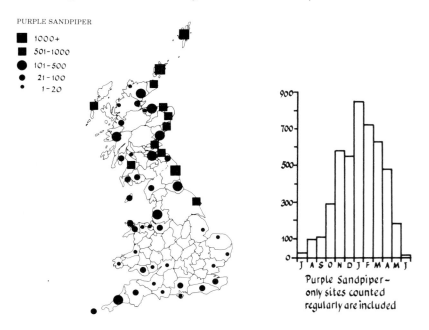

PURPLE SANDPIPER

- ■ 1000+
- ■ 501–1000
- ● 101–500
- ● 21–100
- • 1–20

Purple Sandpiper –
only sites counted
regularly are included

*Table 17:21    Sites of national importance for Purple Sandpipers*

|  | Average peak | % British total |
|---|---|---|
| Shetland | (3,500) | 19·4 |
| Collieston–Buckhaven (Aberdeen) | 582 | 3·2 |
| Tyninghame–Gullane (E. Lothian) | 504 | 2·8 |
| Portgordon–Cullen Bay (Banff) | 331 | 1·8 |
| St Combs–Lions Head (Aberdeen) | 329 | 1·8 |
| Scarborough, South Bay (Yorks) | 300 | 1·7 |
| Papa Westray (Orkney) | 300 | 1·7 |
| Beadnell–Bamburgh (Northumberland) | 250 | 1·4 |
| Sanday (Orkney) | 200 | 1·1 |
| North Rona (Outer Hebrides) | 200 | 1·1 |
| Newtonmill–Girdleness (Kincardine) | 199 | 1·1 |
| Whitehills–Gordonstown (Banff) | 192 | 1·1 |
| Thorntonloch–Dunbar (E. Lothian) | 184 | 1·0 |

eastern Scotland and the Norwegian breeding grounds. A bird from the Icelandic population has been found in the Netherlands, however, so that it is very likely that these birds also visit Britain. In addition, a bird ringed at Hilbre was recovered in southern Greenland on 27 October, five years later, possibly on route from the west Greenland breeding grounds.

The maps show the predominantly north-easterly distribution in Britain and Ireland. The data for Britain are from a special enquiry (Atkinson, Davies and Prater 1978) which provided an estimate of 14,500–23,000 birds. No estimate is available for the Irish population but numbers of less than 100 occur quite widely, as do spring flocks of up to 175 (Hutchinson 1979). In eastern Britain all suitable coasts are occupied; south of Yorkshire and along the south coast there is little habitat for this species. In the west, however, numbers are generally lower and some stretches of rocky coast hold surprisingly few birds. The prevalence of flat rock shelves on eastern coasts may be an important factor here; many western coasts slope steeply and provide little intertidal area for feeding.

The main sites are shown in Table 17:22. Estimates for Shetland range between 2,000 and 5,000 (P. Kinnear, R. J. Tulloch) but the mean figure represents 19·4% of the British total and 2·3% of European birds; no site data are available. Elsewhere, nationally important concentrations are confined to the Northern Isles and the mainland east coast south to Yorkshire.

Colour-ringing studies in eastern Scotland have revealed high site fidelity by wintering birds within and between winters.

360    *The species accounts*

DUNLIN *Calidris alpina*

This is perhaps the most familiar estuarine species, occurring almost throughout Britain and Ireland, in all seasons in moderate or large numbers. Flocks feed particularly on extensive muddier areas of estuaries; many fewer are found on sandy and stony areas. Saltmarshes and shingle beaches are usually the preferred roosting sites, but when these are covered by spring tides or are heavily disturbed, roosts are often inland on pasture or plough.

The Dunlin is a circumpolar species, breeding mostly in the Arctic but extending to much lower latitudes in western Europe. About 4,000–8,000 pairs nest in northern and western Britain and Ireland, with those on Dartmoor the most southerly in the world (Sharrock 1976). British breeders are of the race *C.a. schinzii*, which also breeds in south-eastern Greenland, Iceland, the Baltic region and the Netherlands.

Outside the breeding season the British Isles are also important as a moulting and wintering ground for the nominate race *C.a alpina* (from northern Scandinavia and the USSR), as a staging post for *C.a arctica* (which breeds in north-eastern Greenland) and for *C.a schinzii*. *C.a alpina* also winter on coasts south to Morocco, and *C.a artica* and *C.a schinzii* winter largely in Mauritania and Morocco.

Typical British breeding grounds are on upland mosses and peat flows, comparable with breeding habitat in the arctic, but in western Scotland and Ireland damp lowland grassland is the usual habitat; in north-western England a few pairs nest on the extensive saltmarshes. Adults are present from late April to the end of July, although dispersal begins in June. Passage of adult *C.a schinzii* at estuaries is evident from mid-June to the end of August, although there are few birds before July. The juveniles move through in August, mainly, and there are few after early October. The vast bulk of this movement originates from Iceland and the Baltic, where the

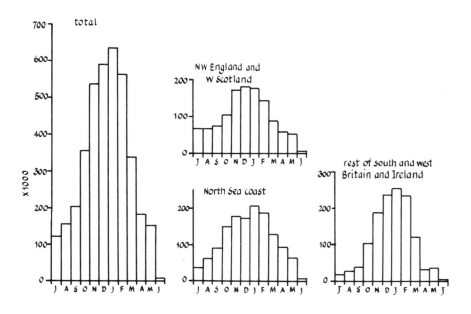

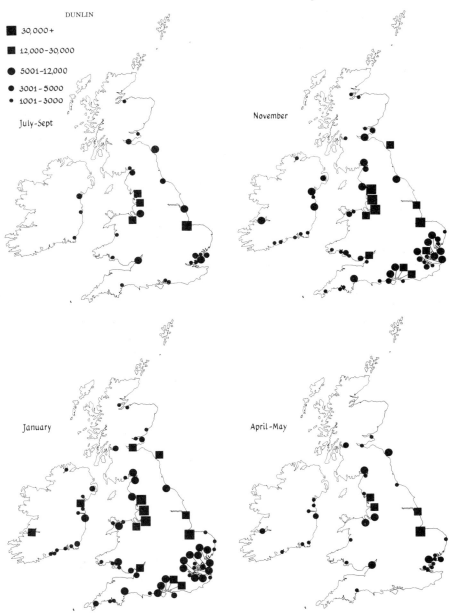

DUNLIN

- ■ 30,000+
- ■ 12,000–30,000
- ● 5001–12,000
- ● 3001–5000
- • 1001–3000

July–Sept

November

January

April–May

numbers are very much larger than the small British and Irish breeding population. Adult *C.a schinzii* move shortly after breeding to moult and winter in Africa; a small number start wing moult on British estuaries. Greenlandic Dunlin, *C.a arctica*, join this passage and have similar timing of migration in autumn. Probably most migrate through the British Isles. Adult *C.a alpina* arrive in Britain mainly from late October

Table 17:22   *Estuaries of international importance for Dunlin*

| | Peak | % W. European | 7 | 8 | 9 | 10 | 11 | 12 | 1 | 2 | 3 | 4 | 5 |
|---|---|---|---|---|---|---|---|---|---|---|---|---|---|
| Morecambe Bay | 48,722 | 4·1 | 7 | 8 | 9 | 10 | 11 | 12 | 1 | 2 | 3 | 4 | 5 |
| Ribble | 42,614 | 3·6 | 7 | 8 | 9 | 10 | 11 | 12 | 1 | 2 | 3 | 4 | |
| Wash | 40,154 | 3·3 | 7 | 8 | 9 | 10 | 11 | 12 | 1 | 2 | 3 | 4 | 5 |
| Mersey | 37,654 | 3·1 | | | | 10 | 11 | 12 | 1 | 2 | | | |
| Shannon | 30,000 | 2·5 | | | | | 11 | 12 | 1 | 2 | | | |
| Severn | 28,107 | 2·3 | | | | 10 | 11 | 12 | 1 | 2 | 3 | | |
| Dee | 27,991 | 2·3 | 7 | 8 | 9 | 10 | 11 | 12 | 1 | 2 | 3 | | |
| Chichester Harbour | 22,409 | 1·9 | | | | 10 | 11 | 12 | 1 | 2 | 3 | | |
| Langstone Harbour | 20,067 | 1·7 | | | | | 11 | 12 | 1 | 2 | | | |
| Humber | 17,438 | 1·5 | | | | 10 | 11 | 12 | 1 | 2 | 3 | 4 | 5 |
| Dundalk Bay | 14,750 | 1·2 | | | | | | 12 | | 2 | | | |
| Lindisfarne | 13,900 | 1·2 | | | | | 11 | 12 | 1 | | | | |
| Portsmouth Harbour | 12,722 | 1·1 | | | | | | 12 | | 2 | | | |
| Blackwater | 12,650 | 1·1 | | | | | 11 | | | 2 | | | |
| Firth of Forth | 12,206 | 1·0 | | | | | | | 1 | | | | |
| Hamford Water | 12,000 | 1·0 | | | | | | | 1 | | | | |

\* Underlining denotes months with highest counts

having moulted in the Waddensea, although quite a significant component moults in Britain, especially on east coast estuaries such as the Wash. The juveniles also arrive quite late, from the end of August through to November.

The diagram shows the monthly numbers; they represent the sum of the various populations and do not in themselves give a clear picture of the migrations. There is a sharp winter peak in all regions, especially southern Britain, Wales and Ireland due to continuing arrivals from continental Europe, where the winters are much more severe. In north-western England and western Scotland, however, there is a much less well marked midwinter influx, and a much flatter peak which occurs in December rather than January. The return movement of these birds begins in February and continues into early April, again many passing through the Waddensea. They are partially replaced from April to May by *C.a schinzii* and *C.a arctica* returning from Africa. Continental *C.a schinzii* are mostly on or close to the breeding grounds by early May, and so flocks seen on favoured estuaries in May (such as the Dee, Morecambe Bay or the Ribble) are a mixture of Icelandic *C.a schinzii* and *C.a arctica*.

Passage numbers at both seasons are swamped by the very large wintering population. There are low numbers everywhere in June, because even though many immature Dunlin do not breed in their first summer, most attain summer plumage and migrate close to or even onto the breeding grounds. The Banc d'Arguin is exceptional in that it holds an estimated 10,000 summering Dunlin, possibly because it is less advantageous for non-breeding birds to migrate back to the breeding areas than to remain on the wintering grounds.

The sites used in spring and autumn passage periods are quite similar; the Wash, the Humber and the north-western English estuaries being particularly important. In winter, large numbers are much more widespread. Sites in southern, south-eastern England, south Wales and south-eastern Scotland hold many birds. There is little change in distribution between November and January but more Dunlin are seen on the large majority of sites as Waddensea birds continue to arrive. Ringing studies in all major estuaries indicate that when Dunlin have settled in an estuary in winter they are highly sedentary, very few moving even a few kilometres within that estuary. Similarly there is a high site-fidelity in consecutive winters.

Estuaries of international importance are shown in Table 17:21. The main passage sites are those holding 1% or more during July to September and April to May; of these, the Humber is unusual since it is much more important in spring than in autumn. The peak on the Wash is in September as passage numbers are swelled by the moulting population of *C.a alpina*. All the other internationally important sites show a peak in winter, between November and February.

The numbers have apparently increased steadily up to about 1973 but subsequently they have levelled off. Total numbers passing through Britain are not known but considerably exceed the estuary count figures, perhaps by 20–25%. There is no doubt that estuaries in Britain and Ireland are of great importance for all of the Western Palearctic populations of Dunlin.

Dunlin index

## RUFF *Philomachus pugnax*

Ruff have a breeding distribution which extends from northern central Europe in a broad belt eastwards across Asia. In Europe Ruff nest in small numbers in Britain, France and Belgium, more commonly in the Netherlands and through Germany, Czechoslovakia and Poland to Russia. The species was virtually extinct as a regular breeding bird in Britain by the end of the last century, but recolonisation began in the early 1960s; breeding was proved on the Ouse Washes in 1963 (Cottier and Lea 1969) following a period during which increasing numbers wintered here (Prater 1973).

Most of the Ruff which pass through Britain in autumn are en route to winter quarters in central and southern Africa where an unknown number, but certainly well over 1,000,000 winter. Relatively few (c. 1,600 – Prater 1976a) remain in Europe and North Africa. The first wintering records for Britain were in Cambridgeshire in 1934–35 and small numbers (up to 30) were recorded in subsequent winters. The winter of 1954–55 was an exceptional year for late summer visitors

and passage migrants (Barnes 1966) and the unprecedented number of 110 Ruffs wintered. Since then numbers have further increased, with average winter populations of 357 (1960–65) and over 1,200 (1966–71) (Prater 1973). These birds are mainly males, which generally winter further north than females.

Counting efficiency will have been lower for Ruff than for more typically estuarine species, because many of the wintering birds frequent inland sites. They feed on flooded grazing land, sewage farms, reservoirs and even ploughed fields on occasions. To make counting difficult, birds may also delay their return to a roost from feeding sites until dusk.

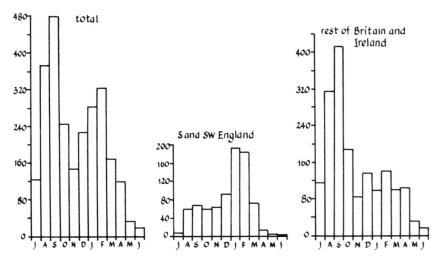

The main migration months are August and September, with a peak in the latter month. At this time the east coast estuaries such as Teesmouth, the Humber and the Wash are important; the Ribble and Mersey in the north-west also record their best figures during these two months. Peak numbers are recorded at about the same time in Ireland where the species is mainly a passage migrant (Hutchinson 1979). Estuary counts at this time are also likely to underestimate the total passage since many, probably most, are inland.

As the autumn passage declines, numbers begin building up on estuaries in the south (particularly on the Solent and at Christchurch, Chichester and more recently Pagham Harbours), south-west (Exe and Taw/Torridge) and south-east (Inner Thames), where subsequently most birds winter. Smaller numbers winter in north-western England (Ribble/Mersey/Dee) and at some inland sites, especially the Ouse Washes (Norfolk/Cambridgeshire). The peak winter numbers in Britain and Ireland occur in January and February, average estuarine counts during 1969–75 being 290 and 325, respectively. These represent about 25% of the total in Britain. The increase which occurs over the course of the winter may be due to immigrants from the continent moving north and west in early January (Prater 1973). These birds have moved away by mid-March, perhaps going northwards very early, before the rest of the spring migrants return from Africa. British breeders begin to arrive on 'territories' from the end of March and usually all will have returned by mid-April. Estuarine counts at this time fall off considerably with only a few non-breeding birds summering.

The number of birds wintering here increased rapidly over the period 1960–71 (Prater 1973). In many areas, especially Hampshire and south-western Britain, there has been a decrease during the mid-1970s. Numbers on the Ribble, Ouse Washes and particularly in Sussex however, have increased. In the last county there has been a spectacular increase, mainly at Pagham Harbour where over 1,000 Ruff were counted flying in to roost in January 1979.

## SNIPE *Gallinago gallinago*

Snipe are present on most estuaries but because they remain hidden in saltmarshes or along borrow-dykes and wet patches inland, the counts received are at best a guide to the numbers present. It is one of the very few species which can be seen in or flushed from *Spartina* marshes. Fifteen estuaries regularly recorded 100+ Snipe, mostly in the south and south-east of England. The largest numbers were on the Pevensey Levels, Sussex (645); Christchurch Harbour, Dorset (370); Dee, Cheshire/Clwyd (350), and the Taw/Torridge, Devon (300).

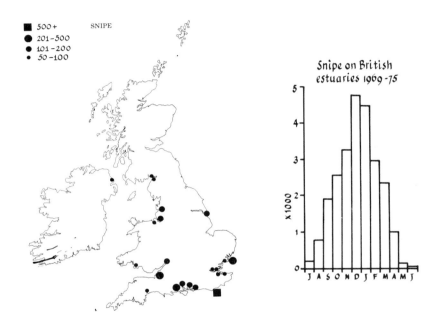

## BLACK-TAILED GODWIT *Limosa limosa*

The Black-tailed Godwit maintains only a toe-hold in Britain as a breeding species, with probably between 50 and 100 pairs in most years. The numbers wintering here, however, have increased steadily over the past forty years although recently there have been indications that a peak has been reached (Prater 1975). Those birds breeding in Iceland, 1,300 km from the nearest continental birds, belong to a distinct sub-species, *L.l. islandica*; it is this race which winters in Britain, Ireland and France and, probably, also predominates in Iberia and Morocco. The bulk of the nominate race, *L.l. limosa*, winters south of the Sahara in west Africa.

The total of Black-tailed Godwits wintering in Britain and Ireland during the study period averaged almost 10,300 birds; over 6,000 of which were in Ireland. With the total European population estimated at 40,000 (Prater 1975) about 26% were in Britain and Ireland in midwinter. However, if December is considered, the average monthly counts over the same period revealed nearly 14,400 birds, or 36% of the total wintering population. At times in spring and autumn, even greater numbers have been recorded; for example, in April almost 50% of the European wintering population have been recorded in Ireland alone.

Black-tailed Godwits prefer muddy estuaries and, like many waders, form tightly-packed roosts at traditional sites; they usually remain in a distinct and separate flock, even when roosting with other waders. Roosts may often form inland on grassland, especially wet pasture, a habitat only occasionally chosen by the Bar-tailed Godwit. The very varied roosting habitats used by Black-tailed Godwits make them a difficult bird to census in some estuaries. They may move between adjacent estuaries, often within a few days, and counts can show relatively greater fluctuations than for most species.

The majority of breeding Black-tailed Godwits in Britain (those in East Anglia) are undoubtedly of continental origin. A female found dead on a nest with recently hatched young on the Ouse Washes in 1966 was of the nominate race, *L.l. limosa* (Cottier and Lea 1969). These birds prefer a similar habitat to the continental birds, usually nesting on wet lowland grazing meadows. The small number of birds which breeds in north-western Scotland are considered to be of the race *L.l. islandica* on the basis of plumage characteristics.

In Britain and Ireland, the autumn passage starts in July and numbers increase rapidly throughout August to reach a peak in September, when over 16,500 are present on British and Irish estuaries (there are also some inland in Ireland). The vast majority of these birds are *L.l. islandica*; most of those in Ireland stay to complete their wing moult (Hutchinson 1979). Very few *L.l. limosa* pass through Britain, with

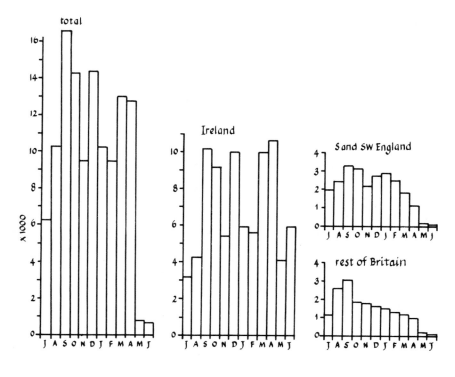

BLACK-TAILED GODWIT

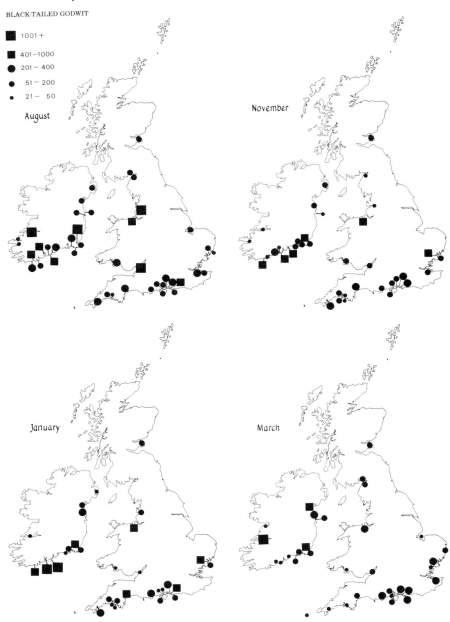

the Dutch breeding population, for instance, having departed for southern Europe and Africa by mid-July (Mülder 1972).

The autumn peak occurs on almost all British estuaries. Numbers fall in October as birds pass on to winter further south in Europe. In Ireland, however, changes in numbers are not so clear, mainly due to the lack of comprehensive counts. Indeed,

*Table 17:23  Principal estuaries in Britain and Ireland for Black-tailed Godwits, 1969–75*

| | Highest av. monthly count | % W. European | Months above 1%* |
|---|---|---|---|
| Shannon | 8,425 | 21·1 | 7 8 9 10  12  2 3 <u>4</u> |
| Little Brosna | 4,150 | 10·4 | 1 2 <u>3</u> |
| Cork Harbour | 1,975 | 4·9 | 9 10  12 <u>1</u> |
| Wexford Harbour | 1,290 | 3·2 | 9 10 11 <u>12</u>  3 4 |
| Ribble | 1,095 | 2·7 | 8 <u>9</u> |
| Severn | 1,070 | 2·7 | <u>7</u> 8 9 |
| Ballymacoda Bay | 1,050 | 2·6 | 8 9 10 11 12 <u>1</u> |
| Dungarvan Harbour | 885 | 2·2 | 10 11 <u>12</u> |
| Clonakilty | 840 | 2·1 | 8 <u>9</u> 10 11 12 1 |
| Chichester Harbour | 775 | 1·9 | 9 <u>10</u>  12 1 |
| Dee | 730 | 1·8 | 8  10 <u>11</u> 12 1 2 |
| Stour (Essex/Suffolk) | 685 | 1·7 | 8 <u>9</u> 10 11 12 1 2 |
| Exe | 670 | 1·7 | 12 <u>1</u> |
| Dundalk Bay | 600 | 1·5 | <u>3</u> |
| Poole Harbour | 460 | 1·1 | <u>2</u> |
| Courtmacsherry Bay | 400 | 1·0 | <u>10</u> |

* The month in which the highest average count occurred is underlined in the last column of the table

the autumn, December and March counts are all just over 10,000 birds, so it is quite possible that this number are present for the whole period and the observed fluctuations result from internal movements.

An unexplained increase occurs in southern and south-western England in December after a low November count. This is not a result of northerly concentrations moving south, nor is it due to a northward movement of birds from France; nor, indeed, is it better coverage. There must be some subtle change in behaviour or habits which alters the birds' distribution. To some extent Black-tailed Godwits do move in response to severe winters. In 1962–63 they were especially scarce even in their normal strongholds in southern and south-western England. No equivalent conditions occurred during the years of the 'Estuaries Enquiry' to distort the pattern. However, very cold weather would not be expected to occur in or affect the November distribution.

In April there is a distinct increase in the numbers of Black-tailed Godwits in Ireland; in contrast, the numbers are lower in western and southern Britain, implying that some British birds move to Ireland before migrating north to Iceland. This suggestion is, however, rather over-simplifying the position because the large numbers of this population from France and Iberia are not obviously recorded on their way north. It is possible that the concentrations in Ireland are made up of birds moving through, and thus they involve more birds than those counted. At this time of year, a few estuaries in south-eastern England, where few birds winter, also support several hundred Black-tailed Godwits – of special note are Pagham Harbour, Medway/Swale and the Blyth estuary in Suffolk.

Table 17:23 details the principal estuaries for Black-tailed Godwits in Britain and Ireland throughout the year. The average April count of 8,425 for the Shannon emphasises the importance of this estuary for spring passage Black-tailed Godwits; in 1974 over 16,400 were seen during the April count. However, it should be noted that the 1% level of importance was exceeded in at least seven other months on this estuary. The Little Brosna (4,150), Cork and Wexford Harbours (1,975 and 1,290 respectively) and Ballymacoda Bay (1,050) further underline the importance of Irish wetlands to the species. In Britain, the recently reprieved Ribble estuary provided the highest average monthly count (1,095), and the count of 1,210 Black-tailed Godwits on the nearby Dee, in January 1973, was the largest wintering concentration ever recorded in Britain (Prater 1975). Chichester Harbour, the Dee, Stour, Exe and Poole Harbour also were of international importance in at least one month. Several estuaries were only just below this level, especially Langstone and Portsmouth Harbours and the Fal estuary. These support internationally important numbers each year but, because Black-tailed Godwits are relatively mobile, no average monthly count exceeds the critical level.

Gudmundsson (1951) describes the increase and spread of Black-tailed Godwits in Iceland over the last 50 years, apparently due largely to a climatic amelioration. A parallel increase in numbers wintering in Britain has taken place (Prater 1975). Conditions have since deteriorated slightly in Iceland and a decline in the wintering population of Black-tailed Godwits might be expected. During recent years there has been an apparent stability in numbers in Britain, and some indication of a decrease so that it is possible that the peak has now passed.

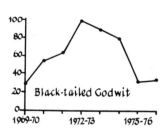
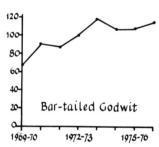

## BAR-TAILED GODWIT *Limosa lapponica*

The breeding distribution of the Bar-tailed Godwit stretches from northern Scandinavia eastwards through the Soviet Union to the Bering Straits and into the extreme north-west of Alaska. This is a much more northerly distribution than the Black-tailed Godwit *L. limosa*, which it replaces. Unlike many of our other waders the Bar-tailed Godwit is absent as a breeding bird from Iceland, Greenland and Canada. Two races are recognised: the nominate *L.l. lapponica* (Scandinavia, western USSR) and *L.l. baueri* (eastern USSR, Alaska); *L.l. lapponica* is the race which occurs in Britain; *L.l. baueri* has not been recorded in Europe and winters in Australasia.

The average number of Bar-tailed Godwits wintering in Britain and Ireland in the period 1969–75 was over 58,000. Prater (1976a) gives the total wintering population of western Europe as some 89,000. The proportion wintering in Britain is,

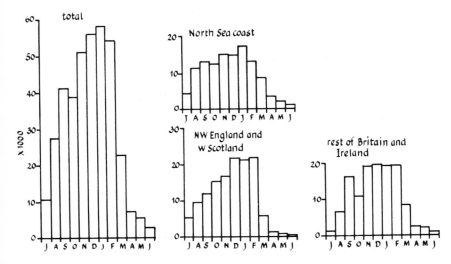

therefore, approximately 65%, and our estuaries are thus extremely important for the species. In addition to this wintering population in western Europe, large numbers winter in Mauritania, on the Banc d'Arguin (210,000), with smaller numbers (c. 5,000) in Morocco. There is no evidence to show if these two wintering populations have a different origin. International counts and observations indicate that the population wintering in Africa does not frequent British and Irish estuaries.

Bar-tailed Godwits prefer the sandier parts of the large estuaries and this may explain their distribution in Britain and Ireland, which is distinctly western. Apart from the large concentrations which occur on some of the north-western estuaries (Table 17:24) there are also scattered, small flocks on many of the western beaches and bays, especially in Ireland and Scotland; this is apparently not the case for similar areas in England.

From the end of July to mid-August large flocks are seen migrating south-west past Ottenby in the Baltic. Many of these stop on the Atlantic coasts, especially the Waddensee, where they moult their wing feathers. The bulk of these birds passes through rapidly, however, continuing southwards to wintering grounds in North Africa. In Britain the autumn passage is small when compared with the Waddensea; the largest numbers are at favoured moulting grounds such as the Wash (5,600+) in the east, and on the Ribble (5,000) and Morecambe Bay (2,400) in the north-west. Numbers continue to rise as juveniles enter Britain during September, reaching 41,000 birds for Britain and Ireland. Some birds move southwards in October, but from November onwards numbers increase as birds which have moulted on the Waddensea arrive to winter in Britain. The midwinter peak was usually reached in January (occasionally December) when an average of 58,000+ birds were present.

The departure in spring begins in February and numbers drop dramatically as the exodus continues through March. A parallel increase on the Waddensea at this time indicates that our wintering birds move there to fatten up before leaving for their breeding grounds.

At the end of April and beginning of May, a month after most of the wintering population has left, a strong passage of Bar-tailed Godwits is seen moving eastwards

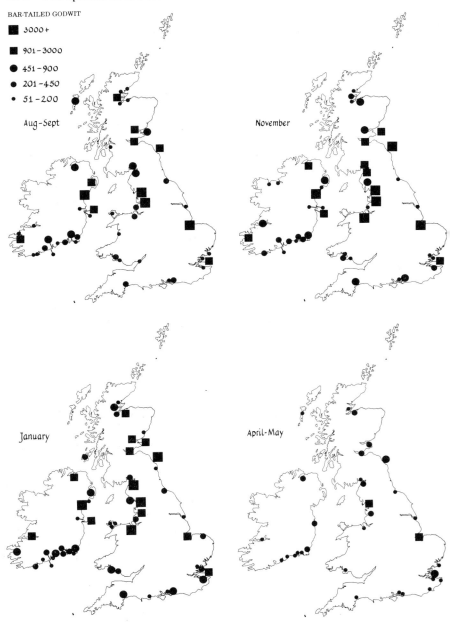

BAR-TAILED GODWIT

■ 3000+

■ 901–3000

● 451–900

● 201–450

· 51–200

Aug–Sept

November

January

April–May

along the southern coast of Britain. In 1976, about 6,500 were seen passing Beachy Head, Sussex, mostly between 20 and 29 April, and in 1973 over 8,000 were recorded at Dungeness, including 4,188 on 26 April. These birds are those returning from winter quarters in Mauritania and Morocco and they assemble on the Waddensea, where peak numbers for spring occur in May.

Table 17:24  Principal estuaries for Bar-tailed Godwit in Britain and Ireland, 1969–75

| | Highest av. monthly count | % W. European | Months above 1%* |
|---|---|---|---|
| Morecambe Bay | 8,076 | 9·1 | 7 8 9 10 11 12 <u>1</u> 2 3 |
| Ribble | 7,082 | 7·9 | 7 8 <u>9</u> 10 11 12 1 2 3 |
| Dundalk Bay† | 6,000–7,000 | 6·7–7·8 | — |
| Wash | 5,616 | 6·3 | 7 <u>8</u> 9 10 11 12 1 2 3 4 |
| Dee | 5,061 | 5·7 | 10 11 12 <u>1</u> 2 3 |
| Lindisfarne | 4,374 | 4·9 | 8 9 10 11 <u>12</u> 1 2 3 |
| Solway, south | 4,078 | 4·6 | 10 11 12 <u>1</u> 2 |
| Foulness | 2,370 | 2·7 | 8 9 10 11 12 <u>1</u> 2 3 |
| Lough Foyle | 1,957 | 2·2 | 11 12 1 <u>2</u> |
| Firth of Forth | 1,793 | 2·0 | 9 10 11 12 1 <u>2</u> 3 |
| Eden | 1,659 | 1·9 | 11 12 <u>1</u> 2 3 |
| Moray Firth | 1,609 | 1·8 | <u>1</u> 2 |
| Solway, north | 1,608 | 1·8 | <u>10</u> 11 12 |
| Uists | 1,367 | 1·5 | <u>2</u> |
| Firth of Tay | 1,037 | 1·2 | <u>9</u>    1 |
| Cromarty Firth | 1,032 | 1·2 | <u>8</u>  10 |
| Strangford Lough | 937 | 1·1 | 9  <u>12</u> |

\* Underlinings denote month of highest counts
† Figure taken from Hutchinson (1979)

Very few birds are present during April/June on British estuaries with the majority occurring on the Wash, Lindisfarne, Solway Firth and Eden. The lowest numbers of the year are in June (less than 300), almost all are immatures in winter plumage.

The principal estuaries for Bar-tailed Godwits are listed in Table 17:24; from this it is clear that the greatest numbers occur on a few of the large estuaries. Some of these are favoured during the autumn moult period (e.g. the Wash), and others are wintering sites (e.g. Morecambe Bay). However, a clearer indication of the importance of these sites is gained by considering the number of months in which the 1% level of international importance (900) is exceeded; for seven of the estuaries in Table 17:24 (Wash, Morecambe Bay, Lindisfarne, Foulness, Ribble, Firth of Forth and Dee) this is six or more months and serves to emphasise how important some sites are for this species. Despite being relatively numerous, if individuals are restricted to a few favoured areas, the species could be particularly vulnerable to development.

The Bar-tailed Godwits wintering in Britain and Ireland increased slowly to a peak in 1973–74, after which numbers decreased a little.

WHIMBREL *Numenius phaeopus*

The Whimbrel has virtually a circumpolar, albeit a discontinuous, distribution. Three races are recognised: the nominate *N.p. phaeopus* (Iceland, east to western USSR), *N.p. variegatus* (central to eastern USSR) and *N.p. hudsonicus* (Nearctic). To a certain extent this distribution is complementary with that of the Curlew, *N. arquata*, although because the latter has spread further north this century, overlap now occurs. Whimbrels tend to breed at higher elevations on mountain slopes though, with Curlew, preferring the damper environs of river valleys. Even in Britain, where the breeding population is less than 200 pairs (Sharrock 1976), this separation by habitat appears to hold true. Birds passing through Britain are all *N.p. phaeopus* (although *N.p. hudsonicus* has been recorded) and the vast majority winters in Africa south of the Sahara, some down to Cape Province. There is a small concentration (*c.* 3,500, Prater 1976a) which winters on the Banc d'Arguin, Mauritania, and singletons have been found wintering in Britain. However, recent counts have suggested that some 30,000–40,000 Whimbrel pass through western Europe to winter mainly in West Africa. Ringing recoveries provide some evidence of the destinations and origins of birds occurring in Britain, with recoveries in February of a Shetland ringed chick in Ghana, and an adult in Nigeria in May, ringed in the previous autumn in Britain. In addition, other birds ringed here in August have been recovered on their breeding grounds in Finland (1) and Archangel, USSR (2).

Whimbrel occur in a wide range of habitats – on grazing land, saltmarsh and coastal lagoons and marshes as well as on estuaries. Feeding and roosting sites may be widely separated. Birds which have spent the day feeding inland in scattered flocks on the Somerset Levels, for instance, return to an evening roost on Steart Island in the Severn (Somerset Bird Report 1978). On estuaries where smaller numbers occur, Whimbrel will also roost with other species, notably Curlew.

The autumn passage begins in July, the numbers building to an August peak, when

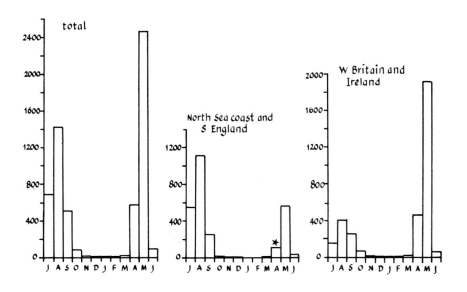

the average estuaries counts for 1969–75 was over 1,500 for Britain and Ireland. The timing of the peak may vary slightly according to conditions on the breeding grounds, although Gudmundsson (1957) recorded that the main exodus of the post-breeding population from Iceland takes place during August. The peak for Britain and Ireland has occurred in this month every year during 1969–75. The majority of birds will have left by the end of September, a few lingering into October and November. Occasional birds have been found wintering in south-western Britain and Ireland but there are no signs of this increasing.

The return movement in spring begins in earnest during April and the peak count for the year (*c.* 2,500) occurs in May. This total is largely due to a spectacular roost on Steart Island, Somerset, at this time, where 1,500–2,000 have been regularly recorded in recent years (Ferns, Green and Round 1979). This spring passage is small in comparison with that for the Netherlands, West Germany and Belgium, where 30,000+ were counted at evening roosts in spring 1978 (van Dijk 1979). The majority of birds have moved north by the end of the month and few remain in June.

Few Whimbrel occur in Britain away from southern England (apart from the Scottish breeding population) and the only site of international importance is Steart Island in the Severn estuary, the spring roost there being unprecedented throughout Britain. Elsewhere, fair numbers occur on the Gwent Levels (also in the Severn estuary) and in August on the Wash (200+), with smaller numbers (60–100) regular at Pagham, Chichester and Langstone Harbours, and on Hamford Water, Morecambe Bay, the Humber and the Blackwater.

It is interesting to compare the counts from the 'Estuaries Enquiry' with those from the 'Inland Wader Enquiry' carried out during 1971–74 (Mason 1971, Smallshire 1974). Totals for July, August and September have been added for each of these years and, despite the difficulties involved in counting, the trends revealed by each scheme are gratifyingly similar. The large influx in autumn 1973 followed a good breeding season for Whimbrel, and indeed other waders (Grey Plover *Pluvialis squatarola*) also breeding at high latitudes. Numbers on passage in Britain depend to a large extent on the success of the previous breeding season, bad weather depressing success or virtually curtailing breeding altogether in some years.

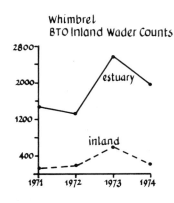

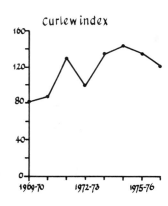

## CURLEW *Numenius arquata*

Curlews have an almost trans-Palearctic breeding distribution, from Britain and Ireland in the west, through Fenno-Scandia and Central Europe to eastern USSR and Mongolia. Their range extends further south in Europe than that of the closely related Whimbrel *N. phaeopus*; it is absent from Iceland, though breeding at more northerly latitudes in Norway. The nominate *N.a. arquata* breeds in Europe; the eastern form *N.a. orientalis* does so east of the Urals.

In Britain the Curlew is widespread as a breeding species, though largely absent from the extreme south-east of England. Some 40,000–70,000 pairs are thought to breed annually in Britain and Ireland (Sharrock 1976). Originally a bird of the upland moors they are now found, too, in more lowland regions and river valleys, damp pasture, heaths and even in fields of arable crops.

The nominate race winters largely in western Europe; the eastern race moves south into Arabia and India. The average number of birds wintering on estuaries in Britain and Ireland during 1969–75 exceeded 90,000, although perhaps as many as 125,000 are present in all habitats. The total for western Europe has been estimated at about 200,000, with a further 5,500 in Morocco and on the Banc d'Arguin (Prater 1976a). Thus more than 38% of the Curlews wintering in Europe do so on British and Irish estuaries.

Curlews favour extensive estuarine mud flats for feeding where they can best use their extremely long, decurved bills. Feeding birds are usually well dispersed over an estuary, but fly to communal roosts on salt marshes and sand banks; others also move inland to roost. Some birds feeding inland never go to the coast; they roost on artificial wet areas (settling beds are favoured). Curlews are a quarry species on the intertidal habitat between 1 September and 21 February. The start of the shooting season coincides with, or may be reason for, a dispersion of the autumn flocks and the apparent decrease in numbers in October, which seems to be due to many birds moving inland (Bainbridge and Minton 1978).

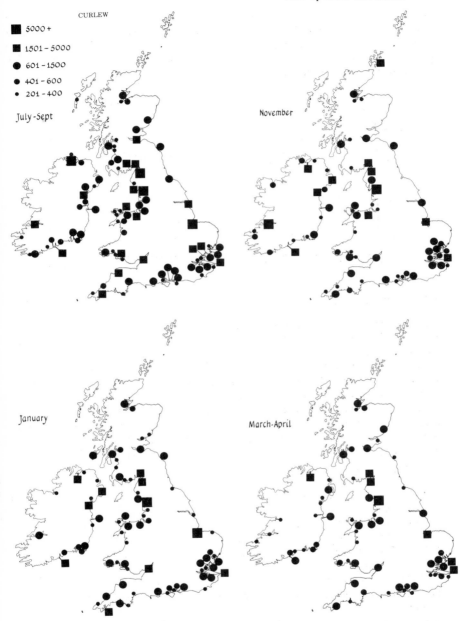

CURLEW

- ■ 5000+
- ■ 1501–5000
- ● 601–1500
- ● 401–600
- • 201–400

July-Sept

November

January

March-April

Curlews begin to arrive from their northern breeding grounds in late June and July when the majority start their 70–80 days post-nuptial moult (Sachs 1968). All of these birds are at least one year old; the main arrival of juveniles does not take place until the second half of September. Birds continue to arrive through August and peak numbers for the year (107,000) occur in September. Bainbridge and Minton (1978) have demonstrated a clear difference in the winter quarters of British breeders from separate regions; birds from Scotland winter in western Britain and in Ireland; those from southern England winter in south-western Britain or may move south into France and Spain. Birds breeding in the northern counties of England may winter in either area. As the autumn peak in Ireland did not occur until November (although count data was incomplete), it may be that some of the birds which moulted earlier in north-western Britain moved to Ireland at this time. However, there are no ringing recoveries to support this, and continental birds are certainly capable of reaching Ireland earlier in the autumn, moulting and then moving onto the estuaries to winter there.

The count data show that overall a drop in numbers occurs as the autumn progresses, with numbers at important sites such as Morecambe Bay and the Wash falling until December. At Morecambe Bay, the August peak of over 16,000 will have dwindled to less than 7,000 by December; on the Wash there was a proportionately similar change from nearly 6,000 to little more than 2,000. Birds may leave estuarine areas at high tide (the counting period) to feed, as well as to avoid being shot, and this undoubtedly affects the counts. The midwinter peak occurs slightly later, in February, when an average of 90,000+ were counted during 1969–75. January numbers are slightly lower and it may be that numbers peak slightly later than for some other waders because of a number of factors: the cessation of shooting towards the middle of February, more agricultural activity inland and, also, flocks beginning to congregate prior to the spring departure. However some British lowland breeders are back on their breeding grounds by the end of February.

Evidence for the origins of non-British birds wintering here is amply provided by recoveries of foreign ringed birds: Bainbridge and Minton (1978) found that Finland (103), Sweden (64), Holland (24) and Norway (16) provided the bulk of these. Birds from the discrete breeding population in Norway tend to winter in northern Britain and Ireland; Swedish and Finnish birds occur over the whole area; and central western European breeders in the southern half of England and southern Wales. Birds leave from February onwards and numbers fall rapidly through March and April, leaving a small summering population of some 7,500 birds in May; since most

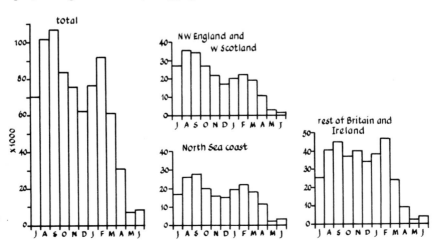

*Table 17:25  Principal estuaries for Curlew in Britain and Northern Ireland, 1969–75*

| | Highest av. monthly count | % W. European | Months above 1%* |
|---|---|---|---|
| Morecambe Bay | 16,065 | 8·0 | 7 <u>8</u> 9 10 11 12 1 2 3 4 |
| Wash | 5,950 | 3·0 | 7 8 <u>9</u> 10 11 12 1 2 3 4 |
| Solway, South | 5,760 | 2·9 | 7 <u>8</u> 9 10 11 12 1 2 3 |
| Lough Foyle | 3,830 | 1·9 | <u>8</u>              2 3 |
| Dee | 3,520 | 1·8 | 7 8 <u>9</u> 10 11 |
| Deersound, Orkney† | 3,000 | 1·5 | <u>11</u> |
| Foulness | 2,980 | 1·5 | 7 8 <u>9</u> |
| Solway, north | 2,960 | 1·5 | 7 8 9 10 <u>11</u> 12 1 2 |
| Hamford Water | 2,500 | 1·3 | <u>2</u> |
| Colne | 2,400 | 1·2 | <u>8</u> |
| Strangford Lough | 2,300 | 1·2 | <u>2</u> |
| Conwy Bay | 2,135 | 1·1 | <u>7</u> |
| Firth of Forth | 2,125 | 1·1 | <u>9</u> |
| Fal | 2,100 | 1·1 | <u>9</u> |
| Humber | 2,100 | 1·1 | <u>9</u> |
| Severn | 2,030 | 1·0 | <u>1</u> |

\* Underlinings denote month of highest counts
† Incomplete counts for rest of year

birds aged two years or more return to the vicinity of their natal area, these are likely to be one-year-old birds.

Principal estuaries for Curlew are shown in Table 17:25. The massive 16,000+ concentration at Morecambe Bay in August is by far the largest for any British estuary. The Wash, the whole of the Solway, Lough Foyle, Dee and Deersound on Orkney, each recorded 3,000+ in at least one month. It is noteworthy that the Wash and Morecambe Bay are internationally important for the species in no fewer than 10 months of the year, and the Solway in nine. Despite the large numbers occurring on the big estuaries, there are also numerous flocks of 600–1,500 at estuaries throughout Britain, particularly in the south and south-east. Although not censused, there is also a number of flocks of Curlew inland in Britain, particularly to the north and west of a line from Teesmouth and the Exe. They coalesce to form sizeable nocturnal roosts of up to 500–1,000 birds.

The total of birds wintering here has increased since the enquiry began and, with the exception of a dip in the 1972–73 winter, the index shows a continuing upward trend.

SPOTTED REDSHANK *Tringa erythropus*

Spotted Redshanks breed in the boreal zone of Eurasia, from northern Scandinavia eastwards across the USSR. Most birds winter in the northern sub-tropics, although some travel as far as Cape Province. The western populations winter south from the Mediterranean region, but West Africa (Senegal–Nigeria) is the main wintering area. In the British Isles it is mainly a double passage migrant, but there is also a fairly substantial wintering population.

Spotted Redshanks feed mainly in water, so feeding birds on estuaries are usually localised around features such as river channels and oyster beds, or especially on adjacent fresh or brackish lakes, pools and streams. Many migrants are recorded inland at reservoirs, gravel pits and sewage farms, but in winter they are rare away from the immediate vicinity of the coast.

The 'Estuaries Enquiry' numbers show an increasing trend with a particularly good season in 1972–73. The 'Inland Wader Enquiry' recorded quite strong autumn passages in 1972 and 1973.

The autumn is dominated by the large September peak, with much smaller numbers recorded in winter and spring. Autumn movement begins in late June when the earliest adults return from the breeding grounds. These birds include failed breeders and also post-breeding females, some of which leave the breeding grounds immediately after or even during incubation. Most birds recorded in late May and June are, however, non-breeding summering individuals. Juveniles arrive mostly from mid-August to early October. Onward passage continues into early November. From then until mid-April the records refer to wintering birds. The spring passage which involves relatively few birds, occurs in the second half of April and in early May.

Eastern England is by far the most important region for this species. There is a

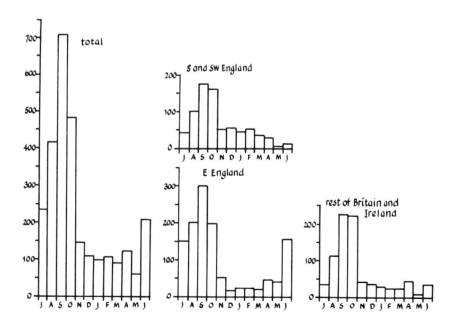

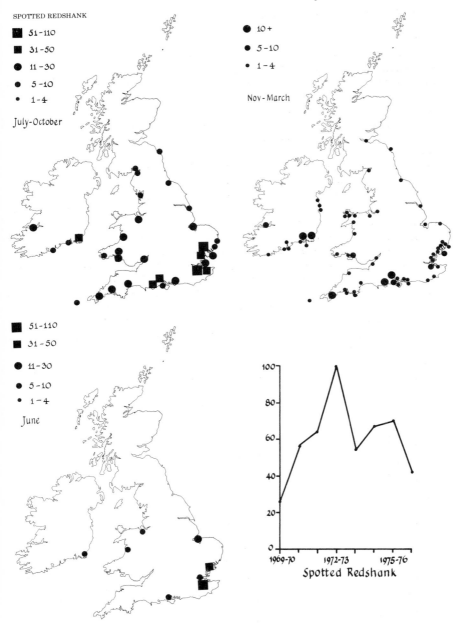

Spotted Redshank

strong autumn passage involving more than 40% of the national total, and only this region holds substantial numbers in June and July. There is a well-marked spring increase in April.

The southern and south-western coasts of England hold the bulk of the wintering population but are relatively less important at passage times. The median date of autumn migration is later here than on the east coast.

No estuaries reach the 1% criterion of international importance. In June, 85 birds on the Medway, 40 on the Colne and 25 on the Wash are the only totals in double figures. Thus the distribution is strongly clumped. In autumn, migrants are more widespread in England, Wales and the southern half of Ireland, but the Medway and Colne are again the major sites. Wexford Harbour in south-eastern Ireland regularly has 70 birds in autumn and is the only major Irish site for the species. The North Solway is the only Scottish site regularly holding more than five birds.

In winter, a large number of sites as far north as the Forth hold one or two birds – a pattern contrasting with the strongly clumped summer distribution. The Fal (19), Beaulieu River (15), Wexford and Waterford Harbours (10) and Poole Harbour (11) are the only sites at which double figures are regularly found between December and March.

## REDSHANK *Tringa totanus*

Generally the commonest of the *Tringa* species, the Redshank is widely distributed across the middle latitudes of the Palearctic and is an abundant breeder in Western Europe. Most populations are fairly short-distance migrants and presumably there is a direct connection between this and the complex taxonomy of the species (Hale 1971, 1973). Two races are currently recognised in Europe: *T.t. robusta*, breeding in Iceland, and nominate *T.t. totanus*, described from Spain and from Scandinavia. Elsewhere in Europe (including the British Isles) there is apparently a broad zone of intermediates between these two forms.

The breeding habitat is typically wet lowland meadow, and low moorland, although marshes (especially by lakes) and saltmarshes are frequent sites. In Britain many inland sites are subject to, or threatened by drainage schemes. Redshanks can use quite small and isolated patches of suitable breeding habitat but, largely as a result of drainage in lowland England, there has been a marked reduction in inland breeding. Saltmarshes have become especially important; on the Wash, for example, 1,500 pairs (c. 2% British) have been estimated.

There is a trend for birds breeding further north in Britain to migrate, whereas the southern breeders are almost sedentary. Birds in their first winter move further than adults; some wintering in France and a few in Iberia. Numbers in Britain and Ireland are swelled by the Icelandic population which winters almost exclusively on these

*Table 17:26 Estuaries of international importance for Redshank in Britain, 1969–75*

| | Highest av. monthly count | % W. European | Months above 1%* |
|---|---|---|---|
| Morecambe Bay | 12,420 | 9·9 | 7 8 <u>9</u> 10 11 12 1 2 3 4 |
| Inner Clyde | 8,073 | 6·5 | 7 8 9 <u>10</u> 11 12 1 2 3 4 |
| Wash | 6,003 | 4·8 | 7 8 <u>9</u> 10 11 12 1 2 3 4 |
| Dee | 5,741 | 4·6 | 7 8 <u>9</u> 10 11 12 1 2 3 4 |
| North Solway | 4,378 | 3·5 | 8 9 <u>10</u> 11 12 1 2 3 |
| Ribble | 4,237 | 3·4 | 8 <u>9</u> 10 11 |
| Forth | 3,759 | 3·0 | 8 <u>9</u> 10 11 12 1 2 3 4 |
| Foulness | 3,645 | 2·9 | 8 <u>9</u> 10 |
| Stour | 3,470 | 2·8 | 7 8 9 <u>10</u> 11 12 1 2 3 4 |
| South Solway | 3,444 | 2·8 | 8 <u>9</u> 10 11 12 1 2 3 |
| Blackwater | 2,870 | 2·3 | 7 8 <u>9</u> 10 11 |
| Chichester Harbour | 2,784 | 2·2 | 8 <u>9</u> 10 |
| Montrose | 2,666 | 2·1 | 8 9            2 <u>3</u> |
| Hamford Water | 2,500 | 2·0 | 9 10 11 12 1 <u>2</u> 3 |
| Colne | 2,285 | 1·8 | 8 9 10 11 12 <u>1</u> 2 |
| Duddon | 2,188 | 1·8 | 8    10 <u>11</u> 12 1 2 |
| Leigh | 2,150 | 1·7 | 7 8 <u>9</u> |
| Cromarty Firth | 2,117 | 1·7 | 9      11 12 <u>1</u>    3 |
| Orwell | 2,100 | 1·7 | 11 <u>12</u> 1 2 |
| Humber | 2,024 | 1·6 | 9 10 11       2    <u>4</u> |
| Tay | 1,706 | 1·4 | <u>8</u> 9 10            4 |
| Moray Firth | 1,673 | 1·3 | 10 <u>11</u>    1 2 3 |
| Strangford Lough | 1,639 | 1·3 | 9 <u>10</u> 11 |
| Conwy Bay | 1,637 | 1·3 | 9 <u>10</u> 11 12 |
| Severn | 1,535 | 1·2 | 7 <u>8</u>    10 |
| Medway | 1,448 | 1·2 | 8 <u>9</u> |
| Eden | 1,431 | 1·1 | <u>9</u> |
| Lough Foyle | 1,387 | 1·1 | <u>9</u> |
| Langstone Harbour | 1,312 | 1·0 | <u>7</u>    9 |

* Underlinings denotes month of highest counts

coasts and those adjacent in continental Europe. Icelandic birds appear to form about 50% of the British wintering population. Birds from Scandinavia have the longest migration of the birds in this group, moving to winter largely in Iberia, the western Mediterranean and North Africa. Few birds from this population occur in Britain, but some reach eastern England during the autumn passage.

Redshanks detect their food mainly by sight in the estuarine habitat, and hence feed mainly during the day. Feeding territories are established and defended, and in many sites this leads to a low density distribution over most of the estuary. There is some preference, however, for the upper shore and for muddy river channels; many feeding territories are associated with saltmarshes. Particularly during daytime high tides, Redshanks may feed inland, and wet grassland adjacent to estuaries may occasionally hold large numbers.

Although there are some problems when censusing Redshanks (in scattered flocks, including some on coastal farmland) the number wintering in Europe is about 125,000, Britain having 80,000 (64%) and Ireland 15,000 (12%). In autumn, almost all of these birds are in Britain and Ireland, birds on the continental coasts being those which finally winter in north-west Africa and the southernmost parts of Iberia.

The seasonal patterns of occurrence on estuaries are shown in Table 17:26. British breeders can be found on estuaries all the year round, as many wintering sites also hold suitable habitat for breeding. Thus the presence of some thousands on estuaries in May and June is not evidence for a substantial non-breeding population.

The return movement of inland British breeders to the coast begins in early July; then numbers are also swelled by locally fledging juveniles. Icelandic birds begin to arrive on all coasts in August and arrivals continue into October. Autumn numbers reach a peak in September/October as the last immigrants arrive. There is a tendency for the autumn peak to be later on the western coasts than in the east, possibly because a slightly greater proportion of west coast birds are from the late-arriving Icelandic population. In south-western and southern England there are very low autumn counts compared with the July levels and the wintering numbers: it is likely, however, that passage is no less active here than elsewhere, but that onward movements are almost matching the autumn arrivals.

In each region the counts decrease from the autumn peak to December/January. A degree of onward passage is implicated here, but the main part of this decrease is probably accounted for by mortality and more especially by difficulties in counting the birds as they spread their feeding areas increasingly over the estuary and surrounding land.

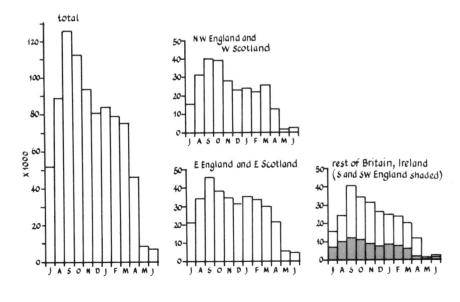

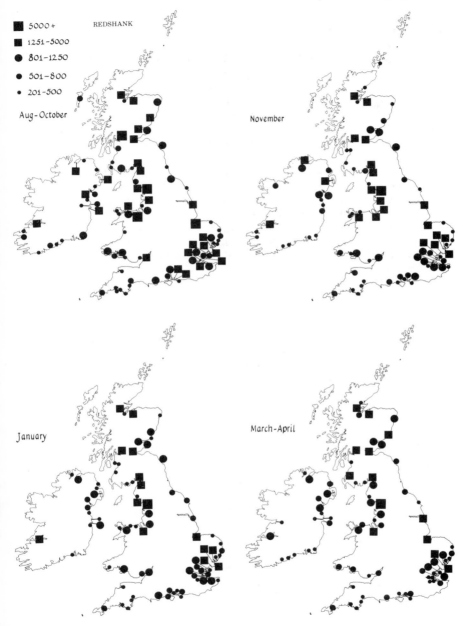

The maps show the relatively even distribution of this species around the British Isles throughout the non-breeding period. Though clearly there are more birds present in August to October, the only marked change in the balance of distribution between then and the winter and spring periods is in Ireland, where incomplete cover has probably affected the picture. Passage numbers in the Western Isles are not maintained for the winter, but here again cover was not complete. This pattern of distribution supports the idea that Redshank is a particularly successful species on estuaries, finding suitable habitat widespread and exploiting it evenly.

There has been a slow increase in the numbers of Redshank in Britain and Ireland during the period 1969–70 to 1975–76. A part of this, during the early years of the 'Estuaries Enquiry', was due to the improving coverage of each estuary – the Redshank being a species which may form many small roosts.

British breeding birds start to leave for the breeding grounds in January although most territories are set up in February and March. There is relatively little decrease in overall numbers on estuaries during this time, presumably as departures are counterbalanced by passage arrivals from France and Iberia. The Icelandic population leaves between late March to early May. By April a high proportion of Redshank flocks on estuaries are *T.t. robusta*.

Redshank index

## GREENSHANK *Tringa nebularia*

This species breeds across Eurasia from Ireland to Kamchatka, overlapping in range with the boreal Spotted Redshank and the more southerly Redshank, but intermediate in mean latitude. The winter range includes much of inland and coastal Africa, the Mediterranean, southern Asia, and Australasia south to Tasmania and New Zealand, while the British Isles form a rather isolated wintering area.

British breeding densities are highest in the flows of Sutherland, but more broken ground and even the interiors of open canopy pine woods are also used. The Scottish breeding range extends as far south as mid-Argyll (Sharrock 1976) while in 1972 and 1974 a pair was proved to breed in Connaught. Nethersole-Thompson and Nethersole-Thompson (1979) estimate the current breeding population as 805–905 pairs, but they emphasise that numbers are rather variable from year to year.

Outside the breeding season most birds are found on estuaries, although there is a strong inland passage particularly in autumn. The favoured feeding places are around deep water sites such as river channels and fresh or brackish pools and lakes. Greenshanks are less dependent on these habitats than the Spotted Redshank, however, and will feed readily on open mud. At most sites birds spend the high tide period at non-tidal feeding areas nearby; Greenshanks will roost with other waders, and at the peak of autumn passage there can be large single species roosts on saltmarshes.

The diagram shows the wintering numbers to be around 600, the large autumn passage peaking at 2,000 in September and the relatively low numbers of about 200 during April–June. Autumn passage is most marked in eastern England (with an August peak) and in Ireland (peaking in September). Only eastern England holds appreciable numbers in July. Spring passage birds outnumber winter birds only in eastern England and north-western England, where there are May peaks.

Ringing recoveries of southern and eastern England passage migrants from France (7), Italy, Denmark and Norway suggest, perhaps, a mainly Scandinavian rather than Scottish origin, but there are no breeding season or winter recoveries as yet.

Most of the wintering population is in the south and west, including Wales and Ireland. Interestingly there are twice as many in western Scotland, mainly on the firths and sea lochs of the Hebrides, than on the whole eastern coast of England and Scotland. More than half are in Ireland. The origins of the British and Irish winterers are unknown but there is circumstantial evidence to suggest that they are of Scottish origin.

In particular, the winter birds begin to move off in late March, simultaneously with the first returns to Scottish breeding sites, and all have left by late April. First records in Scandinavia are usually, also, in late April and the breeding sites are not occupied until mid-May. There has been a single recovery of a Scottish ringed pullus, in Co. Cork in mid-October. This bird may have been on passage and indeed count data indicate that possibly 75% or more (allowing for recruitment) of Scottish Greenshank must move south, probably as far as north-west Africa. The total numbers wintering in Europe may be about 800 birds, over 75% of which are in Britain and Ireland.

The diagram illustrates on a site basis how the distribution withdraws westwards following the autumn passage period and how few birds are present in April and May. One can speculate whether the concentration in south-western England, particularly in April, represents the return passage of Scottish rather than Scandinavian birds.

The 'Inland Wader Enquiry', reported by Prater in Nethersole-Thompson and Nethersole-Thompson (1979), shows a clear double peak for the autumn passage, using data for five day periods at 50 major sites. A small peak at the end of July in each year (1971–73) refers mainly to adult birds, while the second, larger peak at the end of August is composed mostly of juveniles.

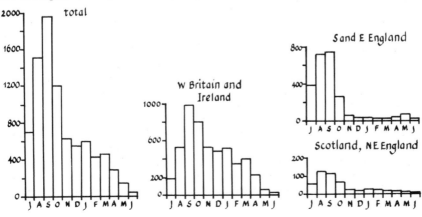

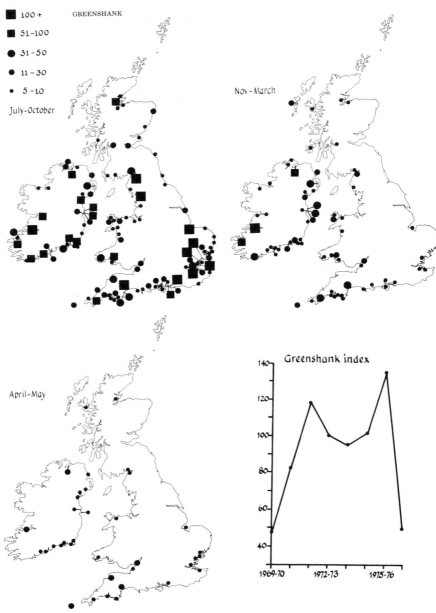

No British or Irish sites are of international importance for this species. Autumn concentrations over 70 are found on the Wash (116), Chichester Harbour (100), Colne (90), Blackwater (80) and South Solway (72). In winter, groups exceed 25 on the Shannon (55), Castlemaine Harbour (38), Lough Foyle (36), Lough Crusin (30), Strangford Lough (28) and the Fal (26).

If records for the 1920–50s are examined, the Greenshank appears to have become more numerous, and there was a further slight increase over the first six years of the 1970s.

## GREEN SANDPIPER *Tringa ochropus*

Few Green Sandpipers breed in Britain and none in Ireland so that almost all of those seen are of Scandinavian origin. The numbers on British and Irish estuaries are presented in the diagram; this indicates that numbers build rapidly from late June to an August peak. In autumn, concentrations of over 50 occur at times on marshes adjacent to the Thames. It is a species which is found commonly, although usually as groups of fewer than twenty birds, on inland lakes, reservoirs, sewage farms and flooded meadows. Even in autumn it is a relatively scarce bird in the northern and western parts of the British Isles.

Numbers fall rapidly to a steady wintering level on estuaries of 25–30 birds by

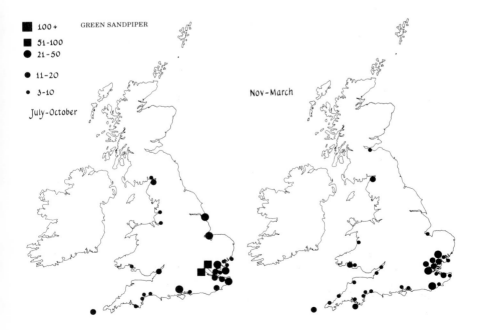

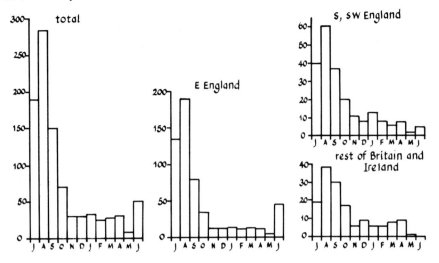

November. Because of the birds' mobility it is very difficult to assess the total numbers wintering but they are also widely scattered inland over the southern half of England and Wales. A provisional estimate of the total would be in the order of 150–250. The species is scattered elsewhere in southern Europe in winter, but most birds probably winter south of the Sahara.

## WOOD SANDPIPER *Tringa glareola*

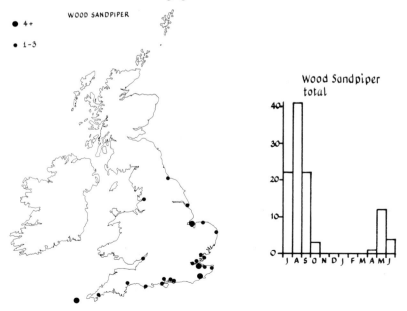

This is an uncommon migrant from Scandinavia and occurs in small numbers on saltmarsh pools on the eastern and southern coasts of England in autumn. It is rare elsewhere on the coast but small numbers are found on inland sewage farms and reservoirs in the southern half of England. It is absent in Britain and Ireland in winter, nor does it winter in Europe. There is a small, May return passage in eastern England.

## COMMON SANDPIPER *Actitis hypoleuca*

Because the Common Sandpiper is primarily a bird of rivers and lake sides it is not surprising that it is a relatively scarce bird on British and Irish estuaries. The origin of the autumn passage birds is unknown, but in view of a number of ringing recoveries of Norwegian and Swedish birds in eastern England, the large numbers on that coast may be predominantly from Scandinavia. Elsewhere, particularly in autumn, there is likely to be a mixture of our breeding stock and immigrants. There is no evidence as to the origin of the wintering birds. In winter, Common Sandpipers occur singly or in small groups throughout southern and western Europe and north Africa, but most of the population is south of the Sahara.

The monthly pattern of occurrence of Common Sandpipers on estuaries is shown in the diagram and the distribution of birds in autumn, winter and spring in the maps. There is a strong autumn passage from mid-July to early September. Even at this time, however, surprisingly few birds are recorded from northern and western Britain and Ireland. By the end of September few birds remain and there is a fairly stable wintering population on estuaries of about 50 individuals. Some individuals also occur outside estuaries and it is unlikely that the total wintering in Britain and Ireland ever exceeds about 100 birds. In winter, south-western England supports almost two-thirds of the total number present. Common Sandpipers have been known to occur in winter for many years but the indications are that the wintering habit has become slightly more prevalent since the 1950s. In Ireland, too, it is only

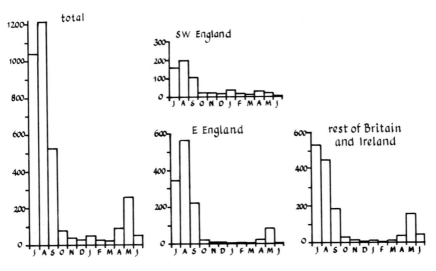

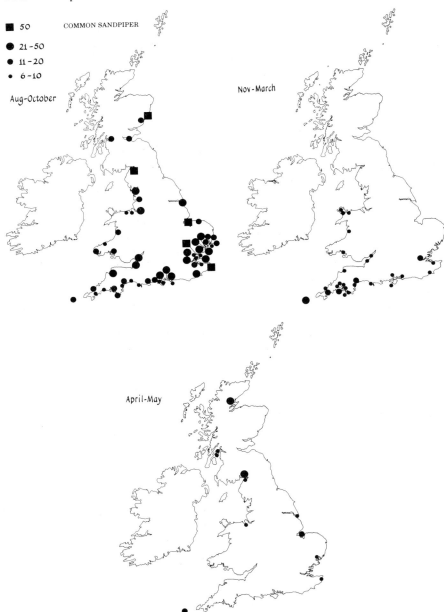

the south-western corner which has any winter birds and even there they are scarce. Judging by the small numbers recorded on the coasts in spring, the birds either fly directly inland or move through extremely rapidly; the few that are seen are mainly in eastern England and Scotland.

In autumn the majority of Common Sandpipers are on inland water bodies. On the coast they occur widely on inflowing rivers, saltmarsh pools and gutters, shingle banks and on borrow dykes behind the sea wall. Exceptional gatherings of up to 50 birds may occur. Very few feed out on the mudflats. In winter, however, they prefer the inner estuaries where the freshwater flow forms smaller mudflats broken with eroded marsh and small stony areas.

TURNSTONE *Arenaria interpres*

Breeding distribution of Turnstone is circumpolar and mainly coastal. It is among the world's most northerly breeding birds and a great long-distance migrant, reaching southern South America and Australasia outside the breeding season. Turnstones do not breed in Britain on a regular basis, although they may have done so in 1976.

The race seen in Britain is the nominate *A.i. interpres* which breeds in north-eastern Canada, Greenland and the Palearctic; the Nearctic form, *A.i. morinella* occurs here only as a vagrant. Turnstones wintering in Britain are almost all of the Greenland/Canadian population; and although those breeding in northern Europe (mainly Finland) occur on passage in fair numbers in the autumn, they use Britain only as a staging post before leaving to winter further south in, mainly, West Africa (Branson et al 1978). There is no evidence of any central Russian birds occurring in western Europe.

Counts of Turnstone on estuaries provide a very incomplete estimate of the total number in Britain, because the birds occur in small scattered flocks on rocky shores and other similar areas often inaccessible to recorders. The maps show the general pattern of occurrence at well-covered estuaries. Although the January count is close to 10,800, county bird reports and single counts from poorly covered estuaries reveal at least another 12,300; the overall winter population is probably of the order of 25,000. This does not include those in Ireland where numbers are unknown, but likely to be well in excess of 5,000 (Hutchinson 1979). The known western

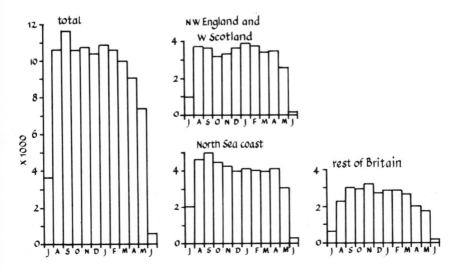

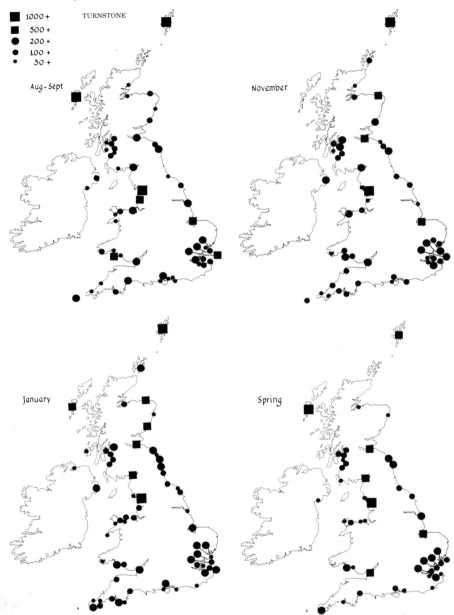

European wintering total is at least 32,000 but very large numbers winter on the Norwegian and Icelandic coastlines; the totals for these areas are as yet unknown, but undoubtedly number many tens of thousands – possibly 100,000+.

The first adults arrive during July from the breeding grounds but the real influx occurs during August and September, with a peak of 11,600+ in the latter month.

Birds of both populations occur then, with the Greenland/Canadian birds remaining to moult and over-winter and most of the Scandinavian birds moving further south into Iberia and Africa after a 'fattening-up' period. Autumn and spring ringing recoveries show that of the Greenland/Canadian birds found in Europe, 50% occur in Britain and Ireland, compared with only 9% of Scandinavian breeders (Branson et al 1978). A fairly steady winter population of 10,600 or so is left after the departure of the Scandinavian birds.

Return passage in spring takes place in April and May; some birds return via Iceland to Greenland and Canada, others may go direct. This latter group remain until the end of May before leaving (Clapham 1979), and there may also be some northerly movement within Britain before the final departure (Branson et al 1978). A small population of Greenlandic first summer birds remains in Britain and Ireland, they begin to moult in June; at least some Turnstone return to their breeding grounds in their first summer, although it is not known if they breed (Clapham 1979). A few first summer Scandinavian Turnstones may also remain here, but the bulk of the adult population returns along the continental European coast (Branson et al 1978).

Turnstones are present on virtually all of Britain's coastlines and the major sites are shown in the map. Morecambe Bay had an average September count of nearly 1,900 and held over 1,300 birds in nine other months of the year. Recent estimates for the Shetlands reveal a massive January population of about 7,500 and there are probably 600–1,000 on the Uists at this time. The Wash (Lincs/Norfolk) and Rosehearty (Grampian) have peaks of nearly 1,000 in September and November respectively; the Firth of Forth (800+), Burry Inlet (650+), Dengie Flats (600+) and the Ribble (585) also held good numbers.

The index in numbers calculated from a sample of estuaries counts shows an upward trend. The sharp dip which occurred between 1971–72 and 1972–73 was due to the poor breeding season for Turnstones breeding in Arctic Canada and Greenland in the summer of 1972. Similar sharp drops occurred in populations of other species also breeding in this region, notably Knot *Calidris canutus* and Pale-bellied Brent Goose *Branta bernicla hrota*. The 1975–76 index for Turnstone, however, surpassed the previous peak of 1971–72.

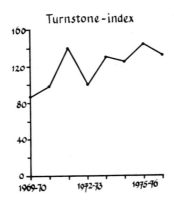

Turnstone-index

## GULLS *Laridae*

This ubiquitous and very successful group of birds occurs abundantly on British and Irish estuaries. The counting methods employed for the other species of estuary birds were not designed to assess accurately the feeding and roosting numbers of gulls using this habitat. Gulls also occur widely inland, along the coasts between estuaries and out at sea. Despite the limitations of the counts it has been felt that the information gathered should be included. The majority of large counts are of birds gathering at dusk before roosting. Many birds come from inland or marine feeding grounds to roost on the intertidal flats and sheltered waters of estuaries. Censuses of inland roosting gulls in England and Wales have been carried out (Hickling 1977 recorded almost one million gulls in January 1973) but undoubtedly very much larger numbers roost on the coast where they are, unfortunately, much more difficult to count comprehensively. During the 'Wetlands Survey' in Ireland, gulls were not counted as widely as in Britain and therefore the distribution there is not presented in the maps.

Most major estuaries have a large gull roost and in addition many gulls, especially Black-headed Gulls *Larus ridibundus*, feed on the intertidal flats during the day. Several estuaries are known to receive 100,000 or more gulls during peak periods. These include the Thames, Wash, Severn, Morecambe Bay and the Solway Firth. Additionally, the Mersey also exceeds this figure, although no accurate counts were made during the 'Estuaries Enquiry'.

The Little Gull *L. minutus* was the scarcest of gulls occurring widely on British and Irish estuaries. The largest numbers were seen in autumn on the Fife/Angus coast of eastern Scotland or in winter on the Alt, Ribble or outer Mersey, and on the coasts of Co. Wicklow and Co. Wexford in Ireland. Each area supported up to 120 birds at these times. Elsewhere up to ten birds were seen regularly. The Irish and Liverpool

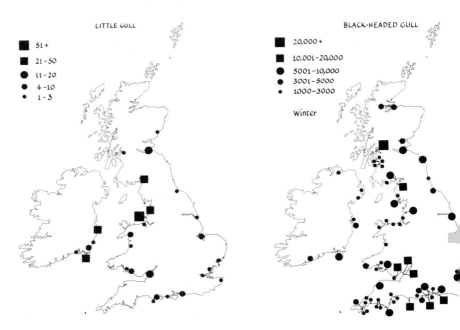

LITTLE GULL

| | |
|---|---|
| ■ | 51+ |
| ■ | 21–50 |
| ● | 11–20 |
| ● | 4–10 |
| • | 1–3 |

BLACK-HEADED GULL

| | |
|---|---|
| ■ | 20,000+ |
| ■ | 10,001–20,000 |
| ● | 5001–10,000 |
| ● | 3001–5000 |
| • | 1000–3000 |

Winter

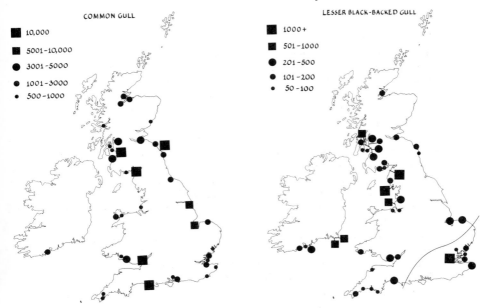

Bay birds may be part of the same pelagic flock, for numbers fluctuate considerably. Detailed maps and a discussion on the species' migration and recent increase in numbers is given by Hutchinson and Neath (1978).

The most numerous species was the Black-headed Gull, although it was relatively scarce north of a line between the Firth of Forth and the Firth of Clyde. Four estuaries had an average annual peak of over 20,000: the Severn (42,000), the Wash (31,000), the Firth of Clyde (27,000) and the Solway Firth (21,000). This species is the most numerous inland wintering species, 584,000 being counted in January 1973 (Hickling 1977).

The Black-headed Gull is also an important component in the breeding community of estuaries in England. All the major Black-headed gulleries are on saltmarshes or dune systems; they are (the figures based on a census in 1973 by Gribble 1976) Beaulieu River, Hants (18,500 pairs), Ravenglass, Cumbria (10,480 pairs), Solent, Hants (9,800 pairs), the Wash (7,800 pairs), and Ribble (7,150 pairs). Other important colonies are on the Colne, Essex (3,750 pairs), and the Medway (3,025 pairs). About 75,000 pairs out of a total 105,000 pairs (74%) bred on coastal marshes. As the species is continuing to expand the numbers have risen since 1973 and at times over 20,000 pairs have bred in the Wash, and over 10,000 on the Ribble.

Common Gulls *L. canus* are characteristic birds of inland pastures and are more frequently seen roosting inland than on the coast; a total of 142,000 was seen inland in January 1973. On the coast, large numbers are scattered around the country, but especially in the north and west. Four estuaries had an average of over 10,000: the Solway Firth (54,000), Troon, Ayr (25,000), The Severn (20,000+) and Lindisfarne (15,000).

The Lesser Black-backed Gull *L. fuscus* is mainly a migratory species with the

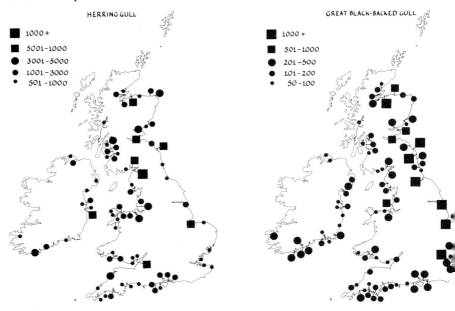

British breeding population wintering off Iberia and north-west Africa. In recent years, however, there has been a trend for larger numbers to winter here. The distribution reflects two patterns. Firstly, the large numbers in southern Scotland and north-western England occur in autumn when there is the dispersal of the large breeding colonies on or near estuaries. Important numbers, over 1,000, are seen on the Firth of Forth, Solway Firth, Duddon estuary and Morecambe Bay (here 19,100 pairs bred in 1978). Secondly, there is a group of birds centred on the Thames which reaches its peak in winter. Some of these may be our breeders but many are of the nominate Scandinavian race.

Herring Gulls *L. argentatus* are widespread but most are northern and western, reflecting their essentially sedentary nature and choice of sea cliffs as nesting sites. The largest concentrations are at Morecambe Bay (where 21,900 pairs bred in 1978) and 17,800 on the Solway Firth.

Great Black-backed Gulls *L. marinus* were also found widely, small groups occurring on all western and northern estuaries near to breeding areas. However, in most estuaries along the North Sea coasts of England and Scotland largest numbers were observed in winter, particularly during stormy weather. These were presumably birds from the British and Scandinavian populations which feed pelagically. The largest concentrations were 2,900 in Teesmouth and the Wash, 2,500 at Foulness, 1,900 at Pegwell Bay and 1,500 on the Humber and Lindisfarne.

Kittiwakes *Rissa tridactyla* are seen passing along most coasts. They appear in small numbers in many, particularly eastern, estuaries. Shoals of sprats sometimes occur in early winter in estuaries between the Moray Firth and Teesmouth, and as a result large flocks of Kittiwakes may be seen. The largest flocks, 1,000–3,000, are in the Moray Firth, off the North Esk and in the Firth of Forth.

Several very scarce species of gulls were recorded during the counts, as were all four species of skuas, but the numbers were so small and the birds did not really use the estuaries, that their occurrences are not given.

## TERNS *Sternidae*

This group of species occurs mainly between April and September, when they are a frequent sight feeding in shallow waters of estuaries. They breed on sand and shingle beaches and small islands along the coast. In most cases no special efforts were made to count feeding or roosting birds, but no account of estuary birds can be complete without some reference to them.

The species involved are Sandwich Tern *Sterna sandvicensis*, Roseate Tern *S. dougallii*, Common Tern *S. hirundo*, Arctic Tern *S. paradisaea* and Little Tern *S. albifrons*. Details of the population size and distribution of their breeding colonies is given in Cramp et al (1974) and updated by Lloyd et al (1975).

Outside the breeding season, largest numbers are seen in autumn when flocks are roosting on beaches of most of the major estuaries. Several thousand birds form mixed flocks which are most noticeable in eastern England and eastern Scotland although large flocks also can be found in Liverpool Bay and eastern Ireland. One very important concentration of Little Terns is present around the mouths of the Dee and the Alt, where a peak of between 500 and 1,200 is observed annually.

## OTHER SPECIES

Although the estuary counts provided an assessment of the species which fed intertidally, a number of other species of waterbirds, raptors and passerines occur on estuaries. Some occur in nationally significant numbers on estuaries, especially the saltmarshes, and any full assessment should take these into account. The more characteristic species are briefly outlined below.

Herons *Ardea cinera* are found in many estuaries, where they feed along the lower water channels and wider ditches. Woods adjacent to estuaries are often used as

heronries; Northward Hill, Kent, is the largest colony in Britain. Several birds of prey hunt over saltmarshes, especially Hen Harriers *Circus cyaneus*, Merlins *Falco columbarius* and Short-eared Owls *Asio flammeus*; Peregrines *F. peregrinus* are frequent winter visitors to high tide wader roosts. All the raptors prefer the large saltmarshes of our major estuaries.

Water Rails *Rallus aquaticus* inhabit many *Spartina* saltmarshes and up to 200 have been flushed from those on the Dee by high spring tides. Coot *Fulica atra* congregate among grazing duck on some estuaries and adjacent brackish pools, especially in southern and south-eastern England. Numbers may reach 1,000 at times, but this is well below the level of international importance.

Two groups of passerines are significant components of saltmarshes, one group breeds there, the other takes advantage of the seed production on high-level mixed marshes and winters in considerable numbers. Of the breeding birds, Skylark *Alauda arvensis*, Meadow Pipit *Anthus pratensis* and Reed Bunting *Emberiza schoeniclus* are characteristic. The wintering species, however, tend to be more significant at the national level. The principal species are Shore Lark *Eremophila alpestris*, Twite *Carduelis flavirostris*, Lapland Bunting *Calcarius lapponicus* and Snow Bunting *Plectrophenax nivalis*. These mainly winter on estuaries along the North Sea, although the last mentioned species occurs in a number of areas away from estuaries. Twite populations on the Wash are important, up to 30,000 are estimated to winter here (Wilson 1976); this is probably about three-quarters of all in England and Wales and includes many English breeders. Most of the rest of the Twite are in Norfolk, Suffolk, Essex and Kent. No accurate estimates of the numbers of the other species have been made. Other finches are frequent along tidelines, especially Greenfinches *C. chloris*, Linnets *C. cannabina* and Chaffinches *Fringilla coelebs*. In some, especially western and northern, estuaries Crows *Corvus corone* scavenge in large numbers on the intertidal flats.

APPENDIX 1

# List of highest average monthly counts of main species for each estuary

SOUTH-WESTERN ENGLAND

| | Severn | Taw/Torridge | Camel | Gannel | Hayle | Fal | Fowey | Looe | St John's & |
|---|---|---|---|---|---|---|---|---|---|
| Mute Swan | 6 | 73 | 17 | + | 8 | 19 | 7 | 26 | |
| Bewick's Swan | (320) | + | 1 | – | – | – | – | – | |
| Whooper Swan | + | – | 1 | – | – | – | – | – | |
| Pink-footed Goose | + | – | – | – | – | – | – | – | |
| White-fronted Goose | (4500) | – | 16 | – | – | – | – | – | |
| Greylag Goose | + | – | – | – | – | – | – | – | |
| Barnacle Goose | + | – | + | – | – | – | – | – | |
| Dark Brent Goose | 1 | 8 | – | – | + | – | – | – | |
| Pale Brent Goose | – | + | + | – | – | – | – | – | |
| Shelduck | 1824 | 221 | 102 | – | 23 | 430 | 21 | 12 | 1 |
| Wigeon | 2957 | 485 | 555 | 5 | 545 | 599 | – | – | 25 |
| Gadwall | 5 | 1 | 2 | – | 1 | 1 | – | – | |
| Teal | 591 | 103 | 82 | 4 | 97 | 113 | – | – | 1 |
| Mallard | 1957 | 107 | 16 | 2 | + | 238 | 42 | 33 | |
| Pintail | 124 | 5 | 17 | – | + | 1 | – | – | |
| Shoveler | 67 | 1 | 3 | – | + | 3 | – | – | |
| Pochard | 10 | 59 | – | – | + | 32 | – | – | |
| Tufted Duck | 3 | 8 | – | – | – | 90 | – | – | |
| Scaup | 1 | + | – | – | – | + | – | – | |
| Eider | 6 | 1 | – | – | – | 6 | – | – | |
| Long-tailed Duck | + | – | – | – | + | – | – | – | |
| Common Scoter | 1 | + | – | – | – | – | – | – | |
| Velvet Scoter | – | – | + | – | – | – | + | – | |
| Goldeneye | 3 | 1 | 2 | – | 1 | 32 | – | – | |
| Red-breasted Merg. | + | 2 | 1 | – | 1 | 39 | – | – | |
| Goosander | + | + | + | – | 1 | – | – | – | |
| Oystercatcher | 400 | 2500 | 300 | 30 | 50 | 500 | 100 | 30 | 3 |
| Avocet | 3 | – | – | – | – | – | – | – | |
| Ringed Plover | 3000 | 400 | 30 | 15 | 110 | 60 | 7 | 40 | |
| Golden Plover | 2000 | 3000 | 3000 | – | 1700 | 1500 | – | – | |
| Grey Plover | 145 | 70 | 50 | 2 | 30 | 55 | 8 | 20 | |
| Lapwing | 12000 | 5500 | 5000 | – | 1300 | 4000 | 1200 | – | 4 |
| Knot | 500 | 250 | 15 | 1 | 10 | 10 | – | – | 6 |
| Sanderling | 145 | 145 | 15 | – | 15 | – | 1 | – | |
| Purple Sandpiper | 5 | – | 2 | – | – | – | – | 50 | |
| Dunlin | 28000 | 4000 | 500 | 30 | 500 | 5000 | 30 | 50 | 30 |
| Ruff | 10 | 20 | 10 | – | 1 | 10 | – | 5 | |
| Snipe | 155 | 300 | 45 | 3 | 20 | 20 | 4 | 25 | |
| Black-tailed Godwit | 1100 | 10 | 5 | – | 3 | 400 | 2 | – | 1 |
| Bar-tailed Godwit | 110 | 25 | 30 | 2 | 12 | 15 | 8 | – | |
| Whimbrel | 1400 | 25 | 40 | – | 5 | 4 | – | 2 | |
| Curlew | 2000 | 1600 | 1000 | 60 | 350 | 2000 | 200 | 50 | 2 |
| Spotted Redshank | 20 | 5 | 2 | – | 2 | 20 | – | 1 | |
| Redshank | 1500 | 750 | 100 | 7 | 60 | 800 | 70 | 100 | 6 |
| Greenshank | 20 | 25 | 20 | 1 | 4 | 40 | 15 | 3 | |
| Turnstone | 330 | 140 | 150 | 2 | 90 | 50 | – | 150 | 1 |

SOUTH-WESTERN ENGLAND

| *Lymher* | *Upper Tamar* | *Tavy* | *Plym* | *Yealm* | *Erme* | *Avon* | *Kingsbridge* | *Dart* | *Teign* | *Exe* | *Otter* | *Axe* |
|---|---|---|---|---|---|---|---|---|---|---|---|---|
| 4 | 6 | 3 | 2 | 28 | 16 | 44 | 30 | 17 | 19 | 80 | 35 | 23 |
| – | – | – | – | – | – | + | – | – | – | 1 | 2 | – |
| – | – | + | – | – | – | – | – | – | – | 1 | – | – |
| – | – | – | – | – | – | – | – | – | – | – | – | – |
| – | – | – | – | – | – | – | – | – | – | 1 | – | + |
| – | – | – | – | – | – | – | – | – | 7 | – | – | + |
| – | – | – | – | – | – | – | – | – | – | + | – | – |
| – | – | – | – | – | – | – | – | – | – | 410 | – | – |
| – | – | – | – | – | – | – | – | – | – | – | – | – |
| 250 | 126 | 59 | 65 | 57 | 20 | 23 | 270 | 43 | 45 | 370 | 55 | 48 |
| 1425 | 15 | 39 | – | 32 | 29 | 17 | 1160 | 44 | 1 | 4470 | – | 170 |
| – | – | – | – | – | – | + | – | – | – | – | – | – |
| 120 | 13 | 2 | 10 | 55 | 55 | 50 | 14 | 15 | + | 460 | – | 34 |
| 53 | 125 | 13 | 85 | 175 | 160 | 55 | 7 | 190 | 19 | 970 | 6 | 37 |
| 10 | + | – | – | – | – | 1 | 8 | – | – | 38 | – | + |
| + | 1 | – | – | – | – | – | 3 | – | – | 5 | – | – |
| – | + | – | – | 5 | – | + | – | 1 | – | 10 | – | – |
| 1 | – | – | – | – | – | – | 28 | 91 | 1 | 6 | – | – |
| – | – | – | – | + | – | – | 1 | + | – | 2 | – | – |
| – | – | – | – | – | – | 1 | 3 | – | – | 12 | – | – |
| – | – | – | – | – | – | – | – | – | – | – | – | – |
| – | – | – | – | – | – | – | – | – | – | 9 | – | – |
| – | – | – | – | – | – | – | – | – | – | + | – | – |
| + | 1 | – | – | + | + | – | 20 | + | 1 | 25 | – | + |
| 1 | – | – | – | 1 | – | – | 17 | – | 18 | 80 | – | + |
| – | – | – | 1 | – | – | – | – | – | – | 1 | – | – |
| 50 | 16 | 25 | 150 | 30 | 20 | 55 | 350 | 20 | 700 | 3000 | 14 | 14 |
| – | 64 | 30 | – | – | – | – | – | – | – | 14 | – | – |
| 10 | + | – | 30 | – | 2 | 25 | 10 | 4 | 15 | 500 | 45 | 26 |
| – | 1500 | 500 | 800 | 1 | – | – | 700 | – | – | 500 | – | – |
| 1 | + | – | 3 | – | – | – | 40 | – | – | 300 | 7 | 4 |
| 500 | 750 | 300 | 90 | 400 | 150 | 55 | 500 | 200 | 250 | 600 | 160 | 1000 |
| 100 | – | – | 20 | – | – | – | 30 | – | – | 500 | – | – |
| – | – | – | – | – | – | 2 | – | – | – | 100 | – | – |
| – | – | – | – | – | – | – | – | – | – | 20 | – | – |
| 500 | 600 | 700 | 2300 | 120 | 2 | 25 | 700 | 40 | 1000 | 9000 | 25 | 150 |
| – | – | – | 2 | – | – | – | – | – | – | 70 | – | 2 |
| – | 4 | – | 15 | – | 1 | 15 | – | – | 12 | 80 | 3 | 50 |
| 100 | 55 | 40 | 190 | 45 | – | 1 | 4 | – | – | 700 | – | 5 |
| 30 | + | – | 10 | 7 | – | 6 | 7 | – | 3 | 700 | – | 4 |
| – | 1 | 3 | – | 2 | – | 12 | 3 | – | – | 30 | – | – |
| 150 | 210 | 200 | 250 | 150 | 70 | 120 | 300 | 120 | 100 | 1100 | 50 | 150 |
| 20 | – | 1 | – | – | – | 3 | 2 | – | – | 14 | – | – |
| 500 | 420 | 200 | 400 | 120 | 20 | 60 | 400 | 100 | 300 | 600 | 20 | 60 |
| 10 | 2 | 2 | – | 20 | 3 | 10 | 20 | – | 3 | 50 | – | 2 |
| – | 8 | – | 8 | 1 | – | 40 | 20 | 10 | 30 | 300 | 11 | – |

SOUTHERN ENGLAND

| | The Fleet | Portland Harb. | Rivers Wey & Lodmoor | Poole Harb. | Christchurch Harbour | West Yar | R. Newtown | R. Medina |
|---|---|---|---|---|---|---|---|---|
| Mute Swan | 680 | 1 | 160 | 70 | 320 | 6 | 17 | 55 |
| Bewick's Swan | – | – | 1 | – | 1 | – | – | – |
| Whooper Swan | – | – | – | + | – | – | – | – |
| Pink-footed Goose | – | – | – | – | – | – | – | – |
| White-fronted Goose | – | – | + | – | – | – | – | – |
| Greylag Goose | – | – | + | 10 | – | – | – | – |
| Barnacle Goose | – | – | – | – | – | – | – | – |
| Dark Brent Goose | 2 | + | + | 65 | – | – | 290 | – |
| Pale Brent Goose | – | – | – | – | – | – | – | – |
| Shelduck | 60 | – | 10 | 2100 | 75 | 22 | 375 | 145 |
| Wigeon | 4000 | – | 1 | 1000 | 25 | 23 | 380 | 90 |
| Gadwall | 15 | – | 1 | 15 | 1 | – | – | – |
| Teal | 80 | – | 160 | 1100 | 23 | 230 | 450 | 1 |
| Mallard | 100 | – | 200 | 500 | 37 | 7 | 45 | 14 |
| Pintail | 40 | – | 3 | 325 | 1 | 1 | 75 | – |
| Shoveler | 17 | – | 33 | 60 | 2 | – | 1 | – |
| Pochard | 110 | – | 300 | 60 | 2 | 1 | – | – |
| Tufted Duck | 45 | – | 380 | 250 | 1 | + | – | 3 |
| Scaup | 2 | – | 1 | 45 | 1 | – | – | – |
| Eider | + | 9 | – | 7 | 1 | – | – | – |
| Long-tailed Duck | 5 | 2 | + | 3 | – | – | – | – |
| Common Scoter | – | 1 | 2 | 5 | + | – | – | – |
| Velvet Scoter | – | 1 | + | 1 | – | – | – | – |
| Goldeneye | 45 | 5 | 1 | 75 | 6 | – | 5 | 4 |
| Red-breasted Merg. | 100 | 120 | – | 180 | 1 | – | 30 | – |
| Goosander | – | – | – | 1 | – | – | – | – |
| Oystercatcher | 13 | 6 | 2 | 700 | 75 | 3 | 20 | 20 |
| Avocet | – | – | – | 2 | 1 | – | – | – |
| Ringed Plover | 80 | 150 | 3 | 100 | 110 | 10 | 20 | 30 |
| Golden Plover | – | – | – | 34 | + | – | 400 | – |
| Grey Plover | 10 | 4 | – | 55 | 3 | 1 | 30 | 2 |
| Lapwing | 900 | – | 200 | 800 | 320 | 200 | 1300 | 160 |
| Knot | 10 | – | – | 20 | 1 | – | 10 | – |
| Sanderling | 25 | 3 | – | 10 | 9 | – | – | – |
| Purple Sandpiper | – | – | – | – | 1 | – | – | – |
| Dunlin | 400 | 250 | 20 | 3000 | 900 | 300 | 2000 | 400 |
| Ruff | – | – | 4 | 50 | 1 | – | 1 | – |
| Snipe | 2 | – | 40 | 30 | 370 | 20 | 6 | 3 |
| Black-tailed Godwit | 3 | – | – | 500 | 1 | 6 | 250 | 30 |
| Bar-tailed Godwit | 30 | 13 | – | 100 | 3 | – | 2 | – |
| Whimbrel | 10 | – | – | 10 | 5 | – | 3 | 1 |
| Curlew | 3 | – | 1 | 725 | 3 | 15 | 150 | 70 |
| Spotted Redshank | – | – | 1 | 30 | 1 | – | 2 | – |
| Redshank | 50 | 1 | 3 | 1000 | 55 | 40 | 200 | 150 |
| Greenshank | 6 | 2 | 2 | 20 | 2 | – | 8 | – |
| Turnstone | 10 | 13 | 3 | 30 | 18 | 1 | 20 | 10 |

* Wader counts only.

SOUTHERN ENGLAND

| Brading Harb. | NW Solent | R. Beaulieu | Southampton Water | Portsmouth Harb. | Langstone Harb. | Chichester Harb. | Pagham Harb. | *Climping | *Goring | *R. Adur | *Newhaven/Cuckmere | *Pevensey Bay |
|---|---|---|---|---|---|---|---|---|---|---|---|---|
| 15 | 17 | 2 | 50 | 26 | 30 | 75 | 4 | | | | | |
| 3 | – | – | – | – | – | 1 | – | | | | | |
| – | – | 1 | 1 | – | – | 1 | + | | | | | |
| – | – | – | – | – | – | – | – | | | | | |
| – | – | 10 | – | – | 4 | 7 | – | | | | | |
| – | – | + | – | – | + | – | – | | | | | |
| + | – | + | – | – | – | – | – | | | | | |
| + | 255 | 7 | 9 | 125 | 4630 | 4540 | 440 | | | | | |
| – | – | – | – | – | – | – | – | | | | | |
| 11 | 380 | 80 | 660 | 140 | 1570 | 3100 | 570 | | | | | |
| 2 | 140 | 500 | 350 | 11 | 870 | 1000 | 70 | | | | | |
| – | – | + | – | 1 | – | – | – | | | | | |
| 50 | 210 | 300 | 1200 | 9 | 660 | 450 | 330 | | | | | |
| 32 | 30 | 260 | 260 | 5 | 60 | 200 | 100 | | | | | |
| 1 | 2 | 30 | 8 | – | 80 | 100 | 50 | | | | | |
| 3 | 2 | 12 | 22 | + | 40 | 1 | 26 | | | | | |
| 70 | 40 | 5 | 80 | + | 8 | 45 | 22 | | | | | |
| 22 | 1 | + | 160 | + | – | 60 | 25 | | | | | |
| + | – | – | – | 1 | + | 2 | + | | | | | |
| 1 | 5 | 1 | 3 | – | + | 3 | 30 | | | | | |
| 2 | – | + | + | – | 1 | 1 | – | | | | | |
| – | 15 | + | + | – | – | + | + | | | | | |
| – | + | – | – | – | – | + | + | | | | | |
| – | 6 | 3 | 20 | 45 | 100 | 120 | 2 | | | | | |
| 4 | 30 | 7 | 2 | 6 | 45 | 32 | 4 | | | | | |
| – | + | – | + | – | – | 1 | + | | | | | |
| 30 | 90 | 100 | 500 | 400 | 750 | 800 | 200 | 130 | 20 | – | 1 | 4 |
| – | – | – | 4 | – | – | – | 3 | – | – | – | – | – |
| 30 | 120 | 30 | 700 | 250 | 300 | 250 | 200 | 4 | 120 | 175 | 25 | 30 |
| 1 | 110 | 200 | 200 | – | 1 | 550 | 100 | – | – | – | 1 | 800 |
| 2 | 140 | 30 | 230 | 100 | 450 | 1000 | 200 | 10 | 40 | – | 1 | 5 |
| 150 | 1200 | 1500 | 1300 | 150 | 900 | 1100 | 500 | 130 | – | 1350 | 900 | 10000 |
| – | 10 | 2 | 20 | 450 | 400 | 500 | 10 | – | – | 5 | – | 2 |
| 50 | 3 | 6 | 2 | – | 2 | 350 | 25 | 250 | 150 | – | 1 | 10 |
| – | – | – | – | – | – | – | 2 | 4 | 6 | – | 25 | 15 |
| 80 | 6000 | 400 | 6000 | 13000 | 20000 | 23000 | 4000 | 8 | 750 | 1100 | 70 | 200 |
| – | 70 | 6 | 7 | – | 6 | 30 | 6 | – | – | – | – | 2 |
| 20 | 40 | 25 | 130 | – | 150 | 150 | 25 | – | – | – | 40 | 700 |
| – | 100 | 100 | 120 | 400 | 400 | 800 | 300 | – | – | – | – | – |
| 1 | 15 | 10 | 20 | 10 | 200 | 900 | 10 | – | – | 5 | – | – |
| – | 10 | 5 | 10 | 15 | 70 | 90 | 100 | – | – | 2 | – | – |
| 4 | 300 | 300 | 700 | 700 | 1000 | 1200 | 300 | – | – | 1 | 20 | 10 |
| – | 10 | 30 | 4 | – | 4 | 30 | 2 | – | – | – | – | 1 |
| 100 | 600 | 150 | 800 | 1000 | 1300 | 3000 | 350 | 5 | 15 | 90 | 30 | 20 |
| – | 20 | 6 | 20 | 7 | 50 | 100 | 15 | – | – | – | – | – |
| 5 | 70 | 30 | 250 | 100 | 70 | 150 | 120 | 6 | 4 | – | – | 100 |

|  | SOUTHERN ENGLAND | | | | | | | | |
|---|---|---|---|---|---|---|---|---|---|
|  | * Pett Levels | Rye Harb. | Peguell Bay | Minnis Bay | Swale | Medway | * N. Kent Marshes | Inner Thames | *Langle* |
| Mute Swan |  | 35 | 5 | 1 | 40 | 25 |  | 610 |  |
| Bewick's Swan |  | + | – | – | 2 | 6 |  | – |  |
| Whooper Swan |  | – | – | – | 2 | + |  | – |  |
| Pink-footed Goose |  | + | 1 | – | – | + |  | – |  |
| White-fronted Goose |  | 12 | – | 5 | 450 | 81 |  | – |  |
| Greylag Goose |  | + | – | – | 22 | 57 |  | – |  |
| Barnacle Goose |  | – | – | – | + | – |  | – |  |
| Dark Brent Goose |  | 1 | 29 | + | 540 | 460 |  | – | 24 |
| Pale Brent Goose |  | – | – | – | – | – |  | – |  |
| Shelduck |  | 25 | 60 | 9 | 700 | 2500 |  | 1200 |  |
| Wigeon |  | 50 | 60 | 1 | 2200 | 7550 |  | 45 | 18 |
| Gadwall |  | 10 | – | – | – | 6 |  | 2 |  |
| Teal |  | 70 | 45 | 1 | 390 | 4000 |  | 560 | 1 |
| Mallard |  | 150 | 150 | 33 | 500 | 2500 |  | 1200 |  |
| Pintail |  | 1 | 3 | – | 20 | 700 |  | 200 |  |
| Shoveler |  | 10 | 9 | – | 140 | 220 |  | 7 |  |
| Pochard |  | 390 | 6 | – | 60 | 110 |  | 1800 |  |
| Tufted Duck |  | 100 | 9 | + | + | 90 |  | 220 |  |
| Scaup |  | 4 | – | – | – | 20 |  | – |  |
| Eider |  | 1 | 1 | – | 10 | 9 |  | – |  |
| Long-tailed Duck |  | 1 | – | + | – | 1 |  | – |  |
| Common Scoter |  | 200 | 7 | 40 | 100 | 9 |  | – |  |
| Velvet Scoter |  | – | – | 1 | – | + |  | – |  |
| Goldeneye |  | 2 | 1 | + | 6 | 70 |  | – |  |
| Red-breasted Merg. |  | 2 | – | 1 | 35 | 22 |  | – |  |
| Goosander |  | 8 | – | – | – | – |  | – |  |
| Oystercatcher | 15 | 300 | 500 | 10 | 3300 | 650 | 40 | 6 | 2 |
| Avocet | – | 6 | 3 | – | – | 1 | 1 | – |  |
| Ringed Plover | 3 | 200 | 150 | 40 | 200 | 800 | 70 | 250 | 4 |
| Golden Plover | 100 | 50 | 500 | 15 | 1100 | 200 | 300 | – |  |
| Grey Plover | 6 | 20 | 60 | 20 | 500 | 600 | 100 | 110 | 3. |
| Lapwing | 800 | 1000 | 1000 | 30 | 2500 | 2000 | 400 | 600 | 5 |
| Knot | – | 15 | 400 | 3 | 3000 | 1100 | 200 | 10 | 20 |
| Sanderling | – | 90 | 100 | 110 | 20 | – | – | – |  |
| Purple Sandpiper | – | – | – | – | 1 | – | – | – |  |
| Dunlin | 10 | 250 | 1200 | 40 | 6000 | 6000 | 3000 | 9000 | 110 |
| Ruff | – | 3 | 4 | 3 | 7 | 13 | 3 | 50 |  |
| Snipe | 30 | 15 | 80 | – | 100 | 90 | 10 | 120 | 1 |
| Black-tailed Godwit | – | 1 | 5 | – | 350 | 300 | 2 | – |  |
| Bar-tailed Godwit | – | 100 | 100 | – | 550 | 60 | 10 | – |  |
| Whimbrel | – | 50 | 20 | – | 20 | 50 | 10 | 8 |  |
| Curlew | 300 | 400 | 300 | 2 | 1100 | 1200 | 600 | 15 | 6 |
| Spotted Redshank | – | 2 | 2 | – | 30 | 110 | 1 | – |  |
| Redshank | 4 | 100 | 250 | 20 | 1100 | 1500 | 500 | 900 | 22 |
| Greenshank | – | 5 | 10 | – | 20 | 50 | 3 | 7 |  |
| Turnstone | 10 | 60 | 25 | 150 | 400 | 70 | 50 | 2 | 3 |

* Wader counts only.

## EASTERN ENGLAND

| *Foulness* | *Roach* | *Crouch* | *Dengie Flats* | *Blackwater* | *Colne* | *Hamford Water* | *Stour* | *Orwell* | *Deben* | *Ore* | *R. Butley* | *Alde* |
|---|---|---|---|---|---|---|---|---|---|---|---|---|
| 60 | 20 | 13 | – | 110 | 170 | 18 | 310 | 320 | 54 | 13 | 17 | 20 |
| – | 3 | – | 7 | 18 | 11 | 18 | – | – | 5 | 26 | 10 | 3 |
| – | – | – | 4 | – | – | 5 | – | – | – | – | – | – |
| – | – | – | – | – | – | 9 | – | – | – | – | – | – |
| 4 | – | 5 | 10 | 18 | 13 | 12 | – | – | – | 20 | – | – |
| – | – | – | – | – | – | 2 | – | – | – | + | – | – |
| – | – | – | – | – | – | – | – | – | – | + | + | – |
| 9500 | 13 | 800 | 1400 | 4800 | 1800 | 3500 | 330 | 520 | – | 13 | – | 3 |
| – | – | – | – | – | – | – | – | – | – | – | – | – |
| 510 | 280 | 340 | 310 | 2000 | 1350 | 1100 | 2250 | 1050 | 760 | 210 | 170 | 350 |
| 1180 | 120 | 780 | 1250 | 1330 | 130 | 440 | 3200 | 1030 | 870 | 520 | 420 | 270 |
| 2 | – | 8 | – | 12 | 8 | 3 | – | 8 | – | 7 | 7 | 4 |
| 270 | 280 | 920 | 320 | 590 | 300 | 350 | 120 | 130 | 300 | 350 | 300 | 33 |
| 250 | 300 | 340 | 1100 | 880 | 670 | 370 | 760 | 380 | 170 | 400 | 80 | 450 |
| 20 | – | 125 | 140 | 170 | 11 | 145 | 620 | 210 | 250 | 65 | 1 | 55 |
| 22 | 17 | 45 | 5 | 45 | 45 | 15 | 20 | 70 | 1 | 100 | 9 | 1 |
| 55 | 30 | 3 | – | 120 | 250 | 45 | 4 | 120 | 5 | 30 | 3 | 10 |
| 13 | 21 | 6 | – | 70 | 40 | 7 | 18 | 80 | 15 | 6 | 30 | 6 |
| 1 | – | – | – | 3 | – | – | – | 4 | + | + | – | 7 |
| 15 | – | 2 | 50 | 17 | 20 | 8 | – | 10 | + | + | – | – |
| 6 | – | 2 | + | 6 | 10 | 4 | – | 2 | + | + | + | – |
| 280 | – | – | 75 | 16 | 100 | 70 | – | 12 | 1 | 10 | – | – |
| 1 | – | – | 2 | 3 | 1 | 1 | – | 4 | – | – | – | – |
| 3 | 3 | 2 | 30 | 180 | 240 | 45 | 45 | 80 | 40 | 1 | 3 | 7 |
| 5 | 10 | 2 | 20 | 70 | 75 | 75 | – | 8 | – | + | + | 1 |
| – | – | – | – | – | – | – | – | – | – | – | – | 1 |
| 6000 | 30 | 50 | 1900 | 600 | 400 | 400 | 150 | 400 | 60 | 50 | 60 | 100 |
| – | – | – | – | – | – | – | – | – | – | 200 | 50 | 15 |
| 320 | 70 | 50 | 200 | 600 | 400 | 700 | 150 | 300 | 25 | 70 | 10 | 40 |
| 1300 | 30 | 500 | 700 | 650 | 400 | 2200 | 100 | 7 | 100 | 30 | 3 | 3 |
| 600 | 15 | 20 | 750 | 720 | 200 | 750 | 300 | 60 | 6 | 20 | 2 | 10 |
| 800 | 1000 | 1800 | 700 | 1700 | 1100 | 2000 | 700 | 800 | 250 | 200 | 200 | 500 |
| 6700 | – | 25 | 3400 | 550 | 60 | 250 | 1000 | 300 | 25 | 50 | 7 | 30 |
| 150 | – | – | 200 | – | 160 | 150 | – | 7 | – | 3 | – | 4 |
| – | – | – | – | – | 1 | 4 | – | – | – | – | – | – |
| 10000 | 2200 | 2000 | 8000 | 13000 | 7200 | 12000 | 12000 | 8000 | 1200 | 400 | 400 | 1200 |
| 2 | 4 | 5 | 8 | 14 | 6 | 15 | – | 2 | – | 4 | 2 | – |
| 12 | 40 | 35 | 7 | 70 | 60 | 200 | 20 | 40 | 20 | 5 | 7 | 20 |
| 2 | 3 | 3 | 4 | 30 | 4 | 200 | 700 | 13 | 20 | 25 | 90 | 8 |
| 2500 | 6 | 20 | 400 | 200 | 30 | 130 | 10 | 20 | 7 | 50 | 2 | 10 |
| 20 | 15 | 15 | 20 | 75 | 25 | 70 | 10 | 30 | 5 | 10 | 1 | 10 |
| 3000 | 300 | 300 | 700 | 2000 | 2500 | 2500 | 700 | 500 | 150 | 90 | 100 | 150 |
| 10 | 1 | 4 | 1 | 50 | 40 | 15 | 4 | 3 | 2 | 3 | 1 | 5 |
| 3700 | 1000 | 700 | 600 | 3000 | 2300 | 2500 | 3500 | 2000 | 500 | 150 | 200 | 300 |
| 50 | 20 | 6 | 10 | 80 | 90 | 12 | 15 | 6 | 4 | 7 | 2 | 5 |
| 150 | 2 | 4 | 600 | 450 | 250 | 220 | 200 | 400 | 1 | 5 | – | 6 |

## EASTERN ENGLAND

| | Blyth | Breydon Water | Wells/Stiffkey | Wash | Humber | *Cornelian Bay | Teesmouth | Whitburn Coast | |
|---|---|---|---|---|---|---|---|---|---|
| Mute Swan | 7 | 70 | 17 | 70 | 7 | | 12 | – | |
| Bewick's Swan | 15 | 50 | 1 | 30 | 7 | | 5 | – | |
| Whooper Swan | – | – | – | 5 | 3 | | 1 | – | |
| Pink-footed Goose | – | 2 | – | 3200 | 830 | | – | – | |
| White-fronted Goose | – | 81 | – | 10 | 3 | | 3 | – | |
| Greylag Goose | + | – | – | 7 | + | | + | – | |
| Barnacle Goose | – | 2 | – | 3000 | + | | 1 | – | |
| Dark Brent Goose | + | 9 | 4000 | 3000 | 40 | | – | – | |
| Pale Brent Goose | – | – | – | – | – | | – | – | |
| Shelduck | 650 | 500 | 670 | 8750 | 1100 | | 1360 | – | |
| Wigeon | 400 | 630 | 180 | 4000 | 1300 | | 160 | 33 | |
| Gadwall | 1 | 1 | – | 2 | 1 | | + | – | |
| Teal | 10 | 40 | 100 | 320 | 670 | | 120 | 18 | |
| Mallard | 65 | 70 | 55 | 2100 | 6100 | | 560 | 145 | |
| Pintail | 2 | 130 | 4 | 130 | 200 | | 19 | – | |
| Shoveler | 2 | 11 | 2 | 27 | 16 | | 20 | – | |
| Pochard | – | 5 | 1 | 50 | 19 | | 24 | – | |
| Tufted Duck | + | 6 | – | 17 | 21 | | 6 | – | |
| Scaup | + | 15 | 9 | 65 | 30 | | 1 | 1 | |
| Eider | – | – | 5 | 60 | 5 | | 7 | 2 | |
| Long-tailed Duck | + | – | 1 | 40 | 3 | | 1 | – | |
| Common Scoter | + | + | 100 | 460 | 30 | | – | 5 | |
| Velvet Scoter | – | – | – | 25 | + | | + | – | |
| Goldeneye | 1 | 30 | 80 | 260 | 7 | | 11 | 2 | |
| Red-breasted Merg. | + | – | 20 | 70 | 1 | | 2 | 1 | |
| Goosander | – | – | – | 1 | 3 | | – | – | |
| Oystercatcher | 80 | 40 | 2000 | 18000 | 1600 | 300 | 500 | 30 | |
| Avocet | 1 | 1 | – | 2 | 1 | – | 2 | – | |
| Ringed Plover | 80 | 100 | 150 | 600 | 350 | 7 | 200 | 15 | |
| Golden Plover | – | 30 | 250 | 800 | 1300 | – | 200 | 30 | 100 |
| Grey Plover | 20 | 50 | 200 | 4000 | 600 | 3 | 70 | 2 | |
| Lapwing | 100 | 300 | 350 | 600 | 2700 | – | 800 | 2 | 4( |
| Knot | 30 | 400 | 3000 | 68000 | 22000 | 250 | 8000 | 2 | 8 |
| Sanderling | – | 40 | 160 | 1200 | 650 | 10 | 500 | 50 | |
| Purple Sandpiper | – | – | – | 2 | 1 | 250 | 10 | 10 | |
| Dunlin | 2000 | 4000 | 4000 | 40000 | 18000 | 1100 | 6000 | 80 | 8( |
| Ruff | – | 4 | – | 40 | 30 | – | 20 | 1 | |
| Snipe | 2 | 10 | 1 | 40 | 120 | – | 100 | – | |
| Black-tailed Godwit | 180 | 2 | 1 | 100 | 6 | – | 1 | – | |
| Bar-tailed Godwit | 20 | 30 | 450 | 6000 | 200 | 10 | 350 | 2 | |
| Whimbrel | 10 | 10 | 1 | 200 | 70 | 1 | 60 | 1 | |
| Curlew | 20 | 60 | 350 | 6000 | 2000 | 20 | 750 | 1 | 5 |
| Spotted Redshank | 10 | 2 | 1 | 25 | 8 | – | 6 | – | |
| Redshank | 600 | 600 | 700 | 6000 | 2000 | 600 | 1000 | 20 | 4( |
| Greenshank | 7 | 3 | 1 | 100 | 13 | – | 6 | 1 | |
| Turnstone | 1 | 7 | 100 | 1000 | 400 | 200 | 150 | 20 | |

| | | | | EASTERN | ENGLAND | | | | | | | |
|---|---|---|---|---|---|---|---|---|---|---|---|---|
| *Whitley Bay | *Blyth | *Wansbeck | *N. Druridge Bay | Coquet | *Almouth Bay–beach | *Alnmouth Bay | *Alnmouth–Boulmer | *Boulmer–Howick | Beadnell Shore | *Beadnell–Budle Point | Lindisfarne | *Goswick–Berwick |
| | | | | 24 | | | | | 6 | | 35 | |
| | | | | – | | | | | – | | 7 | |
| | | | | 1 | | | | | – | | 360 | |
| | | | | – | | | | | – | | 60 | |
| | | | | – | | | | | – | | 3 | |
| | | | | – | | | | | – | | 340 | |
| | | | | – | | | | | – | | 50 | |
| | | | | – | | | | | – | | – | |
| | | | | – | | | | | – | | 650 | |
| | | | | 24 | | | | | 18 | | 610 | |
| | | | | 1 | | | | | 40 | | 21900 | |
| | | | | – | | | | | – | | + | |
| | | | | 10 | | | | | 1 | | 520 | |
| | | | | 5 | | | | | 1 | | 830 | |
| | | | | – | | | | | – | | 50 | |
| | | | | – | | | | | – | | 3 | |
| | | | | + | | | | | – | | 13 | |
| | | | | 1 | | | | | – | | 18 | |
| | | | | 1 | | | | | – | | 40 | |
| | | | | 155 | | | | | 220 | | 1700 | |
| | | | | + | | | | | – | | 170 | |
| | | | | + | | | | | – | | 600 | |
| | | | | – | | | | | – | | 26 | |
| | | | | + | | | | | 5 | | 60 | |
| | | | | 1 | | | | | 5 | | 65 | |
| | | | | + | | | | | – | | 2 | |
| 150 | 30 | – | 65 | 50 | 50 | 12 | 25 | 90 | 200 | 150 | 1500 | 50 |
| – | – | – | – | – | – | – | – | – | – | – | – | – |
| 40 | 8 | 7 | 40 | 25 | 110 | 40 | 140 | 12 | 100 | 90 | 250 | 50 |
| 200 | – | – | – | 10 | – | – | 6 | 250 | 300 | – | 1600 | – |
| – | – | – | 3 | 3 | 5 | – | 3 | 30 | 2 | 10 | 200 | 3 |
| 120 | – | 240 | – | 40 | – | 150 | – | 300 | 30 | 16 | 2500 | – |
| 1800 | – | – | 10 | 100 | – | – | – | – | 150 | 160 | 9000 | 3 |
| 150 | – | – | 20 | 2 | 10 | – | – | 1 | 4 | 60 | 130 | – |
| 160 | 30 | – | 40 | 10 | 12 | – | – | 4 | 75 | 260 | 30 | 10 |
| 200 | – | 2 | 120 | 600 | 300 | 100 | 1100 | 550 | 200 | 800 | 14000 | 35 |
| – | – | – | – | – | – | – | – | – | – | – | 10 | – |
| 5 | – | – | – | 2 | – | 10 | – | 4 | 2 | – | 30 | – |
| – | – | – | – | – | – | – | – | – | – | – | 3 | – |
| 1 | – | – | – | 2 | – | – | 5 | 12 | 20 | 75 | 5000 | 1 |
| – | – | – | – | – | – | – | – | 1 | – | – | 30 | – |
| 35 | – | – | 2 | 25 | – | 6 | 7 | 30 | 60 | 1000 | 20 | 20 |
| – | – | – | – | – | – | – | – | 2 | – | – | 10 | – |
| 120 | 70 | 70 | 45 | 125 | 30 | 110 | 70 | 100 | 200 | 100 | 1200 | 31 |
| – | – | – | – | 1 | – | 2 | – | 1 | – | – | 5 | – |
| 200 | 13 | 20 | 80 | 40 | 50 | 15 | 500 | 250 | 350 | 300 | 250 | 70 |

EASTERN SCOTLAND

| | Tweed | Forth | Eden | Tay | Montrose Basin | N. Eskmouth | Dee | Don | |
|---|---|---|---|---|---|---|---|---|---|
| Mute Swan | 350 | 77 | 1 | 12 | 180 | 12 | 4 | 1 | |
| Bewick's Swan | – | 2 | – | 3 | – | – | – | – | |
| Whooper Swan | – | 21 | + | 1 | – | – | – | – | 1 |
| Pink-footed Goose | – | 850 | 60 | 275 | 490 | – | – | – | 1 |
| White-fronted Goose | – | + | – | – | – | – | – | – | |
| Greylag Goose | – | 32 | 8 | 250 | 360 | – | – | + | 2 |
| Barnacle Goose | – | + | – | 2 | + | – | – | – | |
| Dark Brent Goose | – | 1 | – | – | – | – | – | – | |
| Pale Brent Goose | – | – | – | – | – | – | – | – | |
| Shelduck | – | 1520 | 1700 | 30 | 360 | 30 | – | 1 | |
| Wigeon | – | 1230 | 1400 | 30 | 4100 | – | – | 2 | |
| Gadwall | – | + | – | – | – | – | – | – | |
| Teal | – | 350 | 630 | 100 | 50 | 2 | – | 50 | |
| Mallard | – | 2000 | 500 | 850 | 860 | 11 | 80 | 120 | |
| Pintail | – | 150 | 50 | 1 | 70 | – | – | – | |
| Shoveler | 2 | 8 | 2 | – | – | – | 1 | + | |
| Pochard | + | 1500 | – | 5 | – | – | – | 4 | |
| Tufted Duck | 5 | 220 | – | 75 | – | – | – | 140 | |
| Scaup | – | 13000 | 3 | 1 | 1 | – | – | 25 | |
| Eider | 2 | 3300 | 1600 | 12700 | 520 | 300 | 200 | 20 | 1 |
| Long-tailed Duck | – | 160 | – | – | – | – | – | + | |
| Common Scoter | – | 1700 | 120 | – | – | – | + | – | |
| Velvet Scoter | – | 210 | 5 | + | + | 2 | – | – | |
| Goldeneye | 250 | 2250 | 22 | 70 | 30 | 15 | 40 | 55 | |
| Red-breasted Merg. | – | 420 | 20 | 50 | 12 | 400 | + | 1 | |
| Goosander | – | 4 | + | 12 | 5 | 150 | 2 | 6 | |
| Oystercatcher | 65 | 5500 | 4000 | 2200 | 1800 | 90 | 75 | 25 | |
| Avocet | – | – | – | – | – | – | – | – | |
| Ringed Plover | 200 | 450 | 200 | 70 | 300 | 70 | 3 | 4 | |
| Golden Plover | – | 1000 | 200 | 300 | 120 | – | – | – | |
| Grey Plover | 15 | 150 | 300 | 90 | 20 | 2 | – | – | |
| Lapwing | 700 | 1400 | 200 | 700 | 550 | 20 | – | 20 | |
| Knot | 10 | 16000 | 1750 | 400 | 4000 | – | 6 | – | |
| Sanderling | 100 | 80 | 80 | 200 | – | 12 | – | 10 | |
| Purple Sandpiper | 12 | 120 | 115 | – | – | – | 65 | – | |
| Dunlin | 200 | 13000 | 3500 | 4000 | 1500 | 15 | 2 | 6 | |
| Ruff | – | 10 | 5 | 1 | 4 | – | – | – | |
| Snipe | 3 | 30 | 1 | 15 | 20 | – | – | 4 | |
| Black-tailed Godwit | – | 10 | 110 | 1 | 1 | – | – | – | |
| Bar-tailed Godwit | 4 | 1800 | 1700 | 1100 | 150 | 1 | – | – | |
| Whimbrel | – | 20 | 10 | 1 | 1 | – | – | 1 | |
| Curlew | 20 | 2100 | 320 | 620 | 900 | 6 | 7 | – | |
| Spotted Redshank | – | 2 | – | 1 | – | – | – | 1 | |
| Redshank | 120 | 2600 | 1500 | 1700 | 2700 | 15 | 50 | 20 | |
| Greenshank | – | 15 | 5 | 2 | – | – | – | – | |
| Turnstone | 200 | 800 | 90 | 45 | 30 | 45 | 75 | 2 | |

| | EASTERN SCOTLAND | | | | | | | | | WESTERN SCOTLAND | | |
| Philorth | Deveron | Spey | Moray Firth | Beauly Firth | Cromarty Firth | Dornoch Firth | Loch Fleet | Brora/Golspie | Loch Linnhe | Loch Crinan | Loch Riddon | Arran Coast |
|---|---|---|---|---|---|---|---|---|---|---|---|---|
| + | 2 | 22 | 54 | 14 | 268 | 56 | 4 | – | 30 | 9 | 10 | 1 |
| – | – | – | – | – | – | – | – | 1 | – | – | + | – |
| – | – | 1 | 9 | 9 | 140 | 45 | 10 | 1 | – | – | 1 | – |
| 3 | – | – | 450 | 160 | 1200 | – | – | – | – | 1 | – | – |
| – | – | – | 2 | – | – | – | – | – | – | 5 | – | – |
| + | – | + | 1200 | 1900 | 500 | 20 | – | 1 | 23 | 275 | + | – |
| – | – | – | + | – | – | + | – | – | – | + | – | – |
| – | – | – | 9 | – | 1 | – | – | – | – | – | – | – |
| – | – | – | – | – | – | – | – | – | – | – | – | – |
| 10 | – | 16 | 470 | 95 | 500 | 140 | 140 | 8 | + | 25 | 30 | 18 |
| 1 | – | 130 | 2550 | 1300 | 5600 | 2030 | 810 | 1 | 75 | 280 | 170 | 70 |
| – | – | – | 1 | – | – | 1 | + | – | – | – | – | – |
| 3 | – | 40 | 360 | 340 | 310 | 680 | 90 | – | 5 | 45 | 125 | 4 |
| 2 | 1 | 50 | 600 | 800 | 500 | 400 | 310 | 10 | 30 | 120 | 50 | 40 |
| – | – | – | 100 | 40 | 80 | 45 | + | – | – | – | – | – |
| – | – | – | + | 1 | + | – | – | – | – | – | – | – |
| – | – | – | 2 | – | 8 | 14 | 5 | – | – | – | – | – |
| – | – | + | 4 | 150 | 1 | 140 | 1 | – | 1 | – | – | – |
| – | – | – | 80 | 11 | 6 | 125 | + | – | – | – | – | – |
| 40 | 40 | 2 | 35 | – | 2 | 260 | 600 | 2500 | 110 | 30 | 100 | 55 |
| 1 | 2 | 180 | 2100 | – | – | 210 | 1350 | 300 | – | – | – | – |
| 1 | – | – | 3500 | – | – | 2000 | 200 | 65 | – | – | – | – |
| – | – | – | 560 | – | – | 125 | + | 7 | – | – | – | – |
| 7 | 75 | 80 | 350 | 120 | 525 | 40 | 30 | 7 | 55 | 5 | 6 | 2 |
| 3 | + | 8 | 140 | 120 | 320 | 90 | 180 | 250 | 160 | 70 | 60 | 50 |
| – | 1 | 1 | 8 | 655 | 3 | 1 | + | – | 2 | – | – | – |
| 30 | 75 | 25 | 3800 | 350 | 2500 | 500 | 1000 | 300 | 140 | 100 | 360 | 200 |
| – | – | – | – | – | – | – | – | – | – | – | – | – |
| 10 | – | 25 | 250 | 10 | 200 | 40 | 50 | 50 | 10 | 20 | 3 | 100 |
| 15 | 55 | – | – | – | 60 | 200 | 12 | 40 | – | – | – | – |
| 3 | – | – | 30 | – | 2 | 10 | – | – | – | 2 | – | – |
| 15 | 2 | 6 | 1000 | 700 | 1300 | 400 | 150 | 200 | 6 | 40 | 40 | 100 |
| – | 100 | 1 | 4000 | 100 | 2000 | 200 | 120 | 250 | – | 2 | – | – |
| 2 | – | 2 | 30 | – | 2 | 4 | – | 15 | – | – | – | – |
| – | 50 | – | 25 | – | – | 10 | 7 | 45 | – | – | – | 4 |
| 40 | 15 | 20 | 3500 | 450 | 2500 | 300 | 80 | 300 | 20 | 15 | 2 | 20 |
| – | – | 1 | 2 | – | 1 | – | – | – | – | – | – | – |
| 10 | – | 1 | 4 | 4 | 2 | 1 | 1 | – | 1 | 2 | 1 | 1 |
| – | – | – | 2 | 10 | 20 | – | – | 125 | – | – | – | – |
| 4 | – | – | 1600 | 300 | 1050 | 250 | 13 | – | – | 2 | – | – |
| – | 1 | 7 | 1 | 1 | 2 | 1 | – | – | – | – | 2 | – |
| 100 | 8 | 85 | 750 | 350 | 1100 | 220 | 200 | 70 | 25 | 130 | 150 | 110 |
| – | – | – | 3 | 1 | – | – | – | – | – | – | – | – |
| 60 | 20 | 30 | 1600 | 650 | 2100 | 250 | 150 | 260 | 15 | 20 | 25 | 50 |
| – | – | – | 4 | 4 | 45 | 3 | – | – | – | 4 | 1 | 1 |
| 15 | 70 | 25 | 115 | 30 | 50 | 50 | 7 | 75 | 5 | – | – | 75 |

WESTERN SCOTLAND

| | Bute Coast | Inner Clyde | Islay | Hunterston | Ardrossan/Seamill | Irvine Flats | Barassie/Troon | S. Bay, Troon |
|---|---|---|---|---|---|---|---|---|
| Mute Swan | − | 50 | − | 4 | 3 | 9 | − | 5 |
| Bewick's Swan | − | − | − | − | − | − | − | − |
| Whooper Swan | − | 2 | − | 8 | − | 36 | − | − |
| Pink-footed Goose | − | 2 | − | − | − | − | − | − |
| White-fronted Goose | 11 | − | − | − | − | − | − | − |
| Greylag Goose | 1350 | 60 | − | 50 | 9 | 3 | − | − |
| Barnacle Goose | − | + | − | − | − | 1 | − | − |
| Dark Brent Goose | + | + | − | − | − | − | − | − |
| Pale Brent Goose | | | − | − | − | − | − | − |
| Shelduck | 75 | 950 | − | 17 | 21 | 50 | 5 | 7 |
| Wigeon | 1150 | 390 | − | 350 | 60 | 180 | 1 | − |
| Gadwall | − | − | − | − | − | − | − | − |
| Teal | 150 | 70 | − | 1 | − | 80 | − | 10 |
| Mallard | 600 | 750 | − | 12 | 3 | 100 | 250 | 7 |
| Pintail | − | − | − | − | − | 1 | − | − |
| Shoveler | 3 | 1 | − | − | − | − | − | − |
| Pochard | − | 70 | − | − | − | − | − | − |
| Tufted Duck | 1 | 150 | − | − | − | − | − | − |
| Scaup | − | 90 | − | − | − | − | 7 | − |
| Eider | 380 | 2500 | − | 150 | 300 | 330 | 150 | 300 |
| Long-tailed Duck | − | 1 | − | − | 1 | 2 | − | 1 |
| Common Scoter | − | 2 | − | − | − | + | − | 30 |
| Velvet Scoter | − | + | − | − | − | − | − | − |
| Goldeneye | 15 | 380 | − | 1 | 6 | 3 | 21 | 40 |
| Red-breasted Merg. | 170 | 120 | − | 20 | 30 | 12 | 1 | 60 |
| Goosander | − | + | − | − | − | − | − | − |
| Oystercatcher | 1000 | 3400 | 300 | 700 | 1000 | 300 | 350 | 200 |
| Avocet | − | − | − | − | − | − | − | − |
| Ringed Plover | 130 | 100 | 100 | 80 | 200 | 30 | 100 | 100 |
| Golden Plover | 70 | 400 | 200 | 1 | 100 | 2500 | 200 | 450 |
| Grey Plover | 4 | 3 | 10 | 1 | − | 10 | 3 | 2 |
| Lapwing | 600 | 3500 | 1000 | 250 | 300 | 2000 | 8 | 5 |
| Knot | 7 | 35 | 25 | 15 | 20 | 300 | 250 | 30 |
| Sanderling | − | − | 8 | − | − | − | 5 | 50 |
| Purple Sandpiper | 6 | 4 | 15 | − | 65 | 10 | 4 | 75 |
| Dunlin | 200 | 4100 | 200 | 700 | 650 | 450 | 650 | 300 |
| Ruff | − | 1 | − | − | 1 | 1 | − | − |
| Snipe | 30 | 20 | 10 | 1 | 4 | 30 | − | 2 |
| Black-tailed Godwit | − | 5 | − | − | 1 | 1 | 2 | − |
| Bar-tailed Godwit | 35 | 12 | 420 | 100 | 3 | 1 | 10 | 4 |
| Whimbrel | 1 | 1 | − | − | − | 1 | 1 | 7 |
| Curlew | 1100 | 700 | 1000 | 300 | 450 | 200 | 150 | 1300 |
| Spotted Redshank | − | 1 | − | − | − | − | − | 1 |
| Redshank | 200 | 8000 | 200 | 200 | 250 | 500 | 200 | 90 |
| Greenshank | 2 | 15 | 3 | 2 | 2 | 1 | 1 | 1 |
| Turnstone | 150 | 210 | 100 | 20 | 350 | 40 | 30 | 110 |

WESTERN SCOTLAND

| Doon | Maiden's Harb. | Turnberry/Dipple | Stinchar | Loch Ryan | Luce Bay | Wigtown/Loch Cree | Fleet Bay | Kirkcudbright Bay (R. Dee) | Rough Firth | N. Solway |
|---|---|---|---|---|---|---|---|---|---|---|
| 18 | 1 | 6 | 11 | 50 | 1 | 10 | 6 | 14 | – | 70 |
| – | – | – | – | – | – | 2 | – | – | – | 12 |
| + | – | + | – | 6 | 2 | 22 | – | 4 | – | 125 |
| – | – | + | – | – | – | 1000 | – | – | – | 6000 |
| – | – | – | – | – | – | 20 | – | – | – | 2 |
| 2 | – | – | 180 | 25 | 7 | 3 | 50 | 75 | 170 | 500 |
| – | – | – | – | – | – | + | – | – | – | 5400 |
| – | – | – | – | + | – | – | – | – | – | + |
| + | 1 | – | – | – | – | – | – | – | – | – |
| 16 | 3 | 145 | 5 | 18 | 40 | 120 | 60 | 90 | 240 | 1500 |
| 90 | – | 23 | 13 | 1800 | 100 | 1220 | 90 | 130 | 2500 | 1310 |
| – | – | – | – | – | – | – | – | – | – | 2 |
| 4 | – | 2 | 1 | 9 | 17 | 25 | 3 | – | 3 | 370 |
| 360 | 4 | 130 | 50 | 12 | 70 | 60 | 3 | 10 | 110 | 2150 |
| 1 | – | + | – | – | 190 | 200 | – | – | 1 | 2100 |
| 1 | – | + | – | – | – | 15 | – | – | 22 | 130 |
| + | – | 1 | – | – | – | – | – | – | – | 4 |
| 1 | – | 1 | – | – | – | – | – | – | – | 3 |
| 6 | – | + | – | 35 | – | – | – | – | – | 390 |
| 2 | 11 | 330 | 6 | 200 | – | – | – | – | – | 5 |
| + | – | 1 | – | 1 | – | – | – | – | – | – |
| + | 8 | + | – | 2 | 400 | – | – | – | – | 40 |
| – | – | – | – | + | – | – | – | – | – | + |
| 85 | 1 | 125 | 11 | 60 | 8 | + | 4 | 11 | 15 | 70 |
| 5 | 2 | 30 | 12 | 130 | 35 | 3 | 6 | 5 | – | 35 |
| + | – | – | – | 1 | – | – | – | – | – | 6 |
| 250 | 100 | 550 | 120 | 950 | 520 | 2500 | 350 | 300 | 1500 | 22000 |
| – | – | – | – | – | – | – | – | – | – | – |
| 80 | 90 | 160 | 70 | 40 | 130 | 50 | 50 | 130 | 80 | 1650 |
| 350 | 730 | 360 | 850 | 1000 | 800 | 1800 | 250 | 550 | 320 | 5800 |
| 1 | – | 1 | 1 | – | 1 | 4 | 4 | 13 | – | 150 |
| 600 | 300 | 350 | 1300 | 800 | 650 | 2500 | 600 | 2300 | 1800 | 11000 |
| 9 | 4 | 4 | 9 | 100 | 70 | 720 | 11 | 200 | 250 | 7800 |
| 16 | – | 17 | 2 | – | 1 | – | – | – | – | 100 |
| 1 | – | 3 | 10 | – | – | – | – | – | – | 18 |
| 170 | 430 | 200 | 45 | 180 | 320 | 1100 | 520 | 730 | 1350 | 9700 |
| – | 2 | – | – | – | – | – | – | – | – | 8 |
| 13 | 1 | 1 | 30 | 4 | 20 | 12 | 15 | – | 5 | 80 |
| – | – | – | – | – | – | – | – | – | – | 100 |
| 3 | 16 | 20 | 8 | 1 | 35 | 25 | 60 | – | – | 1700 |
| – | – | 3 | – | – | 2 | – | – | – | – | 15 |
| 250 | 8 | 500 | 25 | 90 | 200 | 700 | 310 | 60 | 1700 | 3000 |
| – | – | – | 1 | 1 | 1 | 3 | – | – | – | 9 |
| 120 | 70 | 300 | 50 | 330 | 160 | 950 | 100 | 500 | 800 | 3500 |
| 1 | 1 | – | – | – | 4 | 11 | 2 | – | – | 30 |
| 50 | 110 | 230 | 50 | 50 | 80 | 40 | 30 | 10 | 1 | 420 |

NORTH-WESTERN ENGLAND

| | S. Solway | Esk | Duddon | Morecambe Bay | Ribble | Alt | Mersey | Dee |
|---|---|---|---|---|---|---|---|---|
| Mute Swan | 33 | 3 | 2 | — | 1 | 1 | 2 | 2 |
| Bewick's Swan | 2 | — | — | — | 29 | — | 11 | 2 |
| Whooper Swan | 7 | + | 4 | — | 1 | — | + | — |
| Pink-footed Goose | 9000 | 7 | 12 | 3100 | 3100 | 220 | — | + |
| White-fronted Goose | 3 | — | — | — | — | — | — | 2 |
| Greylag Goose | 280 | 55 | 66 | — | — | — | — | — |
| Barnacle Goose | 2400 | + | + | — | — | — | — | — |
| Dark Brent Goose | 3 | — | — | — | 1 | — | + | + |
| Pale Brent Goose | | — | — | — | — | — | — | — |
| Shelduck | 950 | 90 | 1000 | 6700 | 950 | 70 | 1770 | 4300 |
| Wigeon | 1900 | 1050 | 710 | 4200 | 2700 | 6 | 2850 | 620 |
| Gadwall | — | — | — | — | 1 | — | 1 | — |
| Teal | 250 | 70 | 550 | 950 | 750 | + | 6400 | 670 |
| Mallard | 1000 | 350 | 480 | 3100 | 730 | 100 | 1000 | 1400 |
| Pintail | 70 | 1 | 450 | 560 | 1650 | 30 | 7300 | 3000 |
| Shoveler | 50 | 2 | — | 45 | 50 | — | 20 | 30 |
| Pochard | 35 | 4 | 120 | — | 3 | 12 | 25 | 22 |
| Tufted Duck | 5 | — | 70 | — | — | 4 | 2 | 7 |
| Scaup | 520 | 3 | — | 100 | + | 5 | — | 15 |
| Eider | — | — | 21 | 630 | — | — | — | + |
| Long-tailed Duck | 1 | — | — | — | + | + | — | 1 |
| Common Scoter | 15 | 2 | 2 | 660 | 11 | 4 | — | 16 |
| Velvet Scoter | — | — | — | — | — | — | — | + |
| Goldeneye | 155 | 23 | 45 | 390 | 1 | 3 | 1 | 13 |
| Red-breasted Merg. | 90 | 40 | 95 | 330 | 1 | 1 | + | 12 |
| Goosander | 20 | — | — | — | — | — | — | + |
| Oystercatcher | 2000 | 3800 | 8000 | 45000 | 3000 | 350 | 100 | 15000 |
| Avocet | — | — | — | — | — | — | — | — |
| Ringed Plover | 1800 | 100 | 270 | 2100 | 660 | 150 | 450 | 3000 |
| Golden Plover | 8000 | 120 | — | 950 | 2300 | 210 | 2500 | 210 |
| Grey Plover | 80 | 1 | 60 | 200 | 800 | 190 | 100 | 400 |
| Lapwing | 12500 | 1400 | 770 | 3300 | 5700 | 20 | 2500 | 3000 |
| Knot | 10500 | 170 | 1500 | 80000 | 71000 | 6600 | 120 | 32000 |
| Sanderling | 400 | 3 | 2100 | 12000 | 6400 | 1200 | 1 | 6500 |
| Purple Sandpiper | 8 | 5 | — | — | — | — | — | 55 |
| Dunlin | 7100 | 400 | 6200 | 49000 | 43000 | 810 | 38000 | 28000 |
| Ruff | 4 | 1 | — | 1 | 40 | 1 | 30 | 6 |
| Snipe | 80 | 9 | 13 | — | 250 | 3 | 160 | 350 |
| Black-tailed Godwit | 150 | 1 | — | 2 | 1100 | 4 | 20 | 750 |
| Bar-tailed Godwit | 4100 | 6 | 75 | 8100 | 7100 | 400 | 40 | 5100 |
| Whimbrel | 16 | 6 | 5 | 65 | 17 | 3 | 2 | 7 |
| Curlew | 6000 | 320 | 1700 | 16000 | 860 | 600 | 1000 | 3400 |
| Spotted Redshank | 7 | 3 | — | 6 | 3 | 1 | 2 | 30 |
| Redshank | 5000 | 520 | 1900 | 12000 | 4300 | 300 | 1500 | 6000 |
| Greenshank | 75 | 6 | 1 | 60 | 7 | 3 | 6 | 8 |
| Turnstone | 400 | 20 | 90 | 2000 | 600 | 80 | 10 | 250 |

* Wader counts only.

WALES

| Cluyd | *Rhos Point/ Little Orme | R. Conwy | Conwy Bay | Red Wharf Bay | Traeth Dulas | Inland Sea | Afon Cefni | S.W. Menai (Traeth Melynog) | Pwllheli Harb. | Afon Wen | Traeth Bach | Mawddach |
|---|---|---|---|---|---|---|---|---|---|---|---|---|
| 15 | | 2 | 10 | – | – | 9 | 15 | 1 | 48 | 4 | 10 | – |
| + | | 1 | – | – | – | – | 22 | – | – | 2 | – | – |
| – | | – | – | – | – | – | – | – | – | – | 14 | – |
| 4 | | – | + | – | – | – | – | – | – | – | – | – |
| – | | – | – | – | – | – | – | – | – | – | + | – |
| – | | – | – | – | – | 2 | 4 | – | – | 2 | – | – |
| – | | – | – | – | – | – | – | – | – | – | – | – |
| – | | – | – | – | – | – | – | 1 | – | – | – | – |
| – | | – | – | – | – | – | – | – | – | – | – | – |
| 50 | | 460 | 420 | 50 | 20 | 220 | 220 | 350 | 45 | 15 | 250 | 140 |
| 17 | | 90 | 560 | 200 | 50 | 950 | 380 | 800 | 120 | 170 | 1300 | 470 |
| – | | – | – | – | – | – | – | 4 | – | 1 | + | – |
| 50 | | 60 | 80 | 1 | 14 | 23 | 150 | 840 | 20 | 4 | 260 | 80 |
| 20 | | 180 | 590 | 18 | 2 | 250 | 90 | 280 | 170 | 70 | 450 | 190 |
| – | | 4 | 11 | – | – | 14 | 240 | 120 | – | 1 | 120 | 40 |
| 1 | | – | 3 | – | 1 | 50 | – | 3 | – | – | 40 | – |
| 3 | | – | – | – | 2 | – | – | 5 | – | 5 | + | – |
| – | | – | 11 | – | – | 4 | – | – | 1 | 4 | 3 | – |
| – | | – | 1 | – | + | – | – | – | + | – | 1 | – |
| – | | – | – | – | – | 10 | – | – | – | – | – | – |
| – | | – | + | – | – | – | – | 1 | – | – | 1 | – |
| 80 | | – | 20 | 6 | – | 2 | – | – | – | 35 | – | – |
| – | | – | – | – | – | – | – | – | – | – | – | – |
| 1 | | 4 | 60 | – | + | 55 | 15 | 9 | 4 | 2 | 15 | 9 |
| 4 | | 2 | 225 | 22 | 17 | 11 | 14 | 15 | 23 | 34 | 14 | 24 |
| – | | – | – | – | – | 4 | – | – | – | – | – | – |
| 120 | 470 | 2200 | 5900 | 390 | 70 | 250 | 560 | 400 | 110 | 130 | 730 | 320 |
| – | – | – | – | – | – | – | – | – | – | – | – | – |
| 70 | 5 | 65 | 150 | 75 | 60 | 180 | 70 | 110 | 250 | 130 | 50 | 200 |
| 120 | – | – | – | 40 | – | 270 | 400 | 100 | – | 450 | 1 | – |
| 5 | 1 | – | 30 | 9 | 2 | 7 | 40 | 90 | 3 | – | 9 | 12 |
| 1150 | – | 170 | 580 | 160 | 100 | 720 | 860 | 1100 | 70 | 610 | 350 | 140 |
| 80 | 3 | 240 | 520 | 460 | 3 | 60 | 1000 | 40 | 130 | 10 | 25 | 3 |
| 40 | – | 2 | 3 | 2 | 3 | 4 | 1 | – | 1 | – | – | – |
| – | 6 | – | – | – | – | – | – | – | – | 1 | – | – |
| 1300 | 15 | 3000 | 7000 | 500 | 190 | 630 | 1900 | 750 | 1750 | 50 | 400 | 450 |
| 2 | – | – | – | – | – | – | 1 | – | – | – | – | – |
| 30 | 1 | 20 | 12 | 1 | 40 | – | 90 | 1 | 15 | 7 | 32 | – |
| – | – | – | 2 | – | – | 10 | – | – | 15 | 2 | 2 | – |
| 3 | – | 2 | 100 | 60 | – | 280 | 20 | 110 | 25 | 12 | – | 18 |
| 10 | – | 2 | 7 | 5 | 6 | – | 1 | – | 10 | 13 | 5 | – |
| 200 | 60 | 700 | 2200 | 370 | 1000 | 280 | 820 | 330 | 170 | 530 | 530 | 180 |
| 2 | – | – | 1 | – | – | 1 | 1 | 1 | – | – | 1 | 2 |
| – | 65 | 680 | 1700 | 170 | 140 | 290 | 420 | 260 | 130 | 30 | 180 | 160 |
| 400 | – | 2 | 13 | 2 | 2 | 9 | 11 | 7 | 3 | 6 | 5 | 5 |
| 75 | 90 | 70 | 230 | 25 | 40 | 90 | 17 | 180 | 6 | 70 | 2 | – |

WALES

| | Dyfi | *Teifi | Nyfi | *Gwaun | Milford Haven | Taf | Guendraeth/Tywi | Burry Inlet | |
|---|---|---|---|---|---|---|---|---|---|
| Mute Swan | 1 | | – | | 12 | 1 | 2 | + | |
| Bewick's Swan | 1 | | – | | – | – | – | – | |
| Whooper Swan | 1 | | – | | 1 | – | – | 1 | |
| Pink-footed Goose | – | | – | | – | – | – | – | |
| White-fronted Goose | 25 | | – | | 5 | 4 | 4 | 2 | |
| Greylag Goose | + | | – | | 1 | + | – | + | |
| Barnacle Goose | 2 | | – | | + | – | – | 3 | |
| Dark Brent Goose | – | | – | | 1 | – | – | 38 | |
| Pale Brent Goose | – | | – | | | – | – | 2 | |
| Shelduck | 210 | | 3 | | 280 | 170 | 45 | 560 | |
| Wigeon | 2000 | | 13 | | 1000 | 125 | 250 | 2200 | |
| Gadwall | – | | – | | + | – | – | + | |
| Teal | 800 | | – | | 300 | 1 | 100 | 500 | |
| Mallard | 900 | | 5 | | 230 | 180 | 300 | 150 | |
| Pintail | 270 | | – | | 11 | 70 | 5 | 650 | |
| Shoveler | 5 | | – | | 20 | 4 | 20 | 100 | |
| Pochard | 1 | | – | | + | – | + | – | |
| Tufted Duck | – | | – | | + | – | – | – | |
| Scaup | 1 | | – | | + | – | 1 | 7 | |
| Eider | – | | – | | – | 3 | 50 | 45 | |
| Long-tailed Duck | 1 | | – | | + | + | – | 1 | |
| Common Scoter | – | | – | | 1 | 2 | 3 | 11 | |
| Velvet Scoter | – | | – | | + | – | – | + | |
| Goldeneye | 30 | | 2 | | 11 | – | 3 | 3 | |
| Red-breasted Merg. | 55 | | 2 | | 9 | 2 | 50 | 18 | |
| Goosander | + | | – | | – | – | – | – | |
| Oystercatcher | 900 | 21 | 31 | 44 | 360 | 2200 | 6000 | 15000 | 13( |
| Avocet | – | – | – | – | – | – | – | – | |
| Ringed Plover | 670 | 40 | 30 | – | 210 | 50 | 170 | 200 | 5( |
| Golden Plover | 45 | – | – | – | 580 | 2000 | 480 | 1200 | |
| Grey Plover | 20 | 1 | 1 | – | 45 | 3 | 20 | 250 | 1( |
| Lapwing | 380 | 7 | 4 | – | 2200 | 2600 | 1700 | 3000 | 1( |
| Knot | 45 | 4 | 2 | – | 260 | 8 | 90 | 6800 | 3. |
| Sanderling | 150 | 2 | 4 | – | 2 | – | 250 | 160 | 3. |
| Purple Sandpiper | – | 2 | – | – | – | – | – | 4 | |
| Dunlin | 2700 | 50 | 50 | – | 3000 | 450 | 2400 | 7500 | 26( |
| Ruff | 1 | – | – | – | 1 | – | 11 | – | |
| Snipe | 25 | 2 | 2 | – | 40 | 35 | 20 | 60 | |
| Black-tailed Godwit | 4 | – | 1 | – | 1 | 17 | 9 | 250 | |
| Bar-tailed Godwit | 70 | – | 20 | – | 22 | 9 | 100 | 670 | 4( |
| Whimbrel | 8 | – | 3 | – | 5 | – | 60 | 50 | |
| Curlew | 440 | 150 | 220 | 2 | 870 | 290 | 320 | 1600 | 3. |
| Spotted Redshank | 11 | – | – | – | 6 | – | 12 | 11 | |
| Redshank | 210 | 60 | 17 | 4 | 820 | 130 | 530 | 1200 | 2' |
| Greenshank | 13 | – | 1 | – | 30 | 4 | 45 | 6 | |
| Turnstone | 4 | 20 | 15 | 17 | 140 | – | 170 | 660 | 1( |

* Wader counts only

| *Sker–Port Talbot | *Ogmore–Llantwit | *Aberthaw | *Barry | Taff/Ely | Severn (Welsh) |
|---|---|---|---|---|---|
| | | | | − | 1 |
| | | | | − | 4 |
| | | | | − | + |
| | | | | − | + |
| | | | | + | 2 |
| | | | | − | − |
| | | | | − | − |
| | | | | − | − |
| | | | | − | − |
| | | | | 200 | 260 |
| | | | | + | 150 |
| | | | | − | − |
| | | | | 32 | 175 |
| | | | | 100 | 270 |
| | | | | − | 21 |
| | | | | − | 45 |
| | | | | − | + |
| | | | | − | + |
| | | | | − | 4 |
| | | | | − | − |
| | | | | − | − |
| | | | | − | 6 |
| | | | | − | − |
| | | | | − | + |
| | | | | − | 1 |
| | | | | − | − |
| 40 | 200 | 60 | 7 | 20 | 40 |
| − | − | − | − | − | − |
| 40 | − | 2 | 4 | 70 | 800 |
| 1200 | − | − | − | − | 2000 |
| − | − | − | − | 13 | 340 |
| 1000 | − | − | − | 130 | 4800 |
| − | − | − | − | 1100 | 5000 |
| 30 | − | − | − | 5 | 5 |
| 3 | − | − | − | − | − |
| 10 | 2 | 100 | 100 | 4000 | 15000 |
| 1 | − | − | − | − | 1 |
| − | − | − | − | 5 | 50 |
| − | − | − | − | − | 7 |
| 1 | − | − | − | 1 | 70 |
| − | − | − | − | 10 | 140 |
| 70 | 10 | − | − | 130 | 650 |
| − | − | − | − | − | 5 |
| 7 | 3 | 5 | 1 | 600 | 500 |
| − | − | − | − | − | 13 |
| 20 | 7 | 3 | 4 | 10 | 200 |

# Criteria of international importance for species

This table sets out the criteria which were used to assess the international significance of wetlands for wildfowl and waders. There were not adequate data for the other species. Chapter 6 discusses the basis of these criteria. They refer to the years 1970–75. In order to help with current assessments the population data for the period 1976–80 are also indicated.

*Explanatory notes:*

(1) All data are based on average counts, using between three and five years.
(2) 1% column refers only to W. Europe, except where indicated.
(3) If it is placed in parenthesis it is a provisional figure.
(4) Most wildfowl winter within the region and, therefore, figures relate to the whole year, but for waders different criteria apply during passage periods. Appropriate comments are made in the notes.
(5) Where there are separate populations, often forming sub-species, the 1% figure for these, their breeding areas and their main wintering areas are indicated in the notes.
(6) No separate account is taken of summering immature birds, the information on them is incomplete but the loss of major summering areas could affect subsequent population levels.

| Species | 1% W. Europe pop. 1969–75 | 1% W. Europe pop. 1975–80 | Notes |
|---|---|---|---|
| Mute Swan *Cygnus olor* | 1,200 | 1,200 | |
| Bewick's Swan *C. columbianus bewickii* | 100 | 120 | |
| Whooper Swan *C. cygnus* | 175 | 70 | Iceland (winter Ireland/Britain) |
| | | 150 | Scandinavia (winter Britain/ continent Europe) |
| Bean Goose *Anser fabalis* | 650 | 700 | |
| Pink-footed Goose *A. brachyrhynchus* | 750 | 750 | Iceland/Greenland (winter Britain) |
| | 155 | 300 | Svalbard (winter continent Europe) |
| White-fronted Goose *A. albifrons albifrons* | 1,070 | 2,000 | USSR (Europe, England, S. Wales) |
| *flavirostris* | 130 | 150 | Greenland (Ireland, West Scotland, N.W. Wales) |
| Greylag Goose *A. anser* | 660 | 700 | Iceland/Britain (winter Scotland) |
| | 300 | 400 | USSR/Scandinavia (winter continent Europe) |
| Canada Goose *Branta canadensis* | 200 | 250 | Britain (winter Britain) |
| | 150 | 150 | Scandinavia (winter continent Europe) |

| Species | 1% W. Europe pop. 1969–75 | 1% W. Europe pop. 1975–80 | Notes |
|---|---|---|---|
| Barnacle Goose | | | |
| B. leucopsis | 300 * | 300 * | Greenland (winter W. Britain) Svalbard, all 5,000+ winter on the Solway |
| | 420 | 500 | USSR (winter continent Europe) |
| Brent Goose dark | | | |
| B. bernicla bernicla | 700 | 1,250 | USSR (winter S. England, continent Europe) |
| Brent Goose pale | | | |
| B. bernicla hrota | 150 | 150 | Greenland/Canada (winter Ireland) |
| | 25 | 25 | Svalbard (winter continent Europe, Lindisfarne) |
| Shelduck | | | |
| Tadorna tadorna | 1,300 | 1,300 | |
| Wigeon | | | |
| Anas penelope | 4,000 | 5,000 | |
| Gadwall | | | |
| A. strepera | 100 | 550 | W. European birds now considered to belong to Mediterranean/Black Sea population |
| Ruff | | | |
| Philomachus pugnax | 100 | (50) | Winter in Europe |
| | — | (10,000) | Over 1·0 million winter in Africa |
| Snipe | | | |
| Gallinago gallinago | — | (10,000) | No count but probably over 1 million occur |
| Black-tailed Godwit | | | |
| Limosa limosa | 400 | 400 | Iceland breeders (winter N.W. Europe) |
| | 3,000 | 3,500 | Continental Europe breeders (winter W. Africa) |
| Bar-tailed Godwit | | | |
| L. lapponica | 900 | (5,500) | Provisional due to inclusion of remarkable W. African counts. 900 is 1% of N.W. European wintering birds |
| Whimbrel | | | |
| Numenius phaeopus | 300 | 500 | Passage periods only in Europe |
| Curlew | | | |
| N. arquata | 2,000 | 3,000 | |
| Spotted Redshank | | | |
| Tringa erythropus | 100 | ( — ) | Fewer than 1,000 present in N.W. Europe in winter, now treated as passage |
| | 200 | 500 | Provisional: passage periods (May–Oct) |

| Species | 1% W. Europe pop. 1969–75 | 1% W. Europe pop. 1975–80 | Notes |
|---|---|---|---|
| Teal *A. crecca* | 1,500 | 2,000 | |
| Mallard *A. platyrhynchos* | 10,000 | 10,000 | Total 1·5 million but 10,000 maximum rule applies |
| Pintail *A. acuta* | 500 | 750 | |
| Shoveler *A. clypeata* | 200 | 1,000 | Increase due to changes of boundaries for birds relating to N.W. Europe |
| Pochard *Aythya ferina* | 2,500 | 2,500 | |
| Tufted Duck *A. fuligula* | 5,000 | 5,000 | |
| Scaup *A. marila* | 1,500 | 1,500 | |
| Eider *Somateria mollissima* | 10,000 | 10,000 | Total 2·0 million but 10,000 maximum rule applies |
| Long-tailed Duck *Clangula hyemalis* | 5,000 | 5,000 | Some authors estimate at least 1 million migrate into the Baltic and around N. Norway from USSR so the 1% may have to be 10,000 when more data available |
| Common Scoter *Melanitta nigra* | 4,500 | 10,000 | Revision due to inclusion of African birds |
| Velvet Scoter *M. fusca* | 1,750 | 2,000 | |
| Goldeneye *Bucephala clangula* | 2,000 | 2,000 | |
| Smew *Mergus albellus* | 200 | 200 | Almost all 20,000 in one site – the Ijsselmeer |
| Red-breasted Merganser *M. serrator* | 400 | 400 | |
| Goosander *M. merganser* | 500 | 750 | |
| Oystercatcher *Haematopus ostralegus* | 5,600 | 7,500 | |
| Avocet *Recurvirostra avosetta* | 230 | 260 | (or 115 pairs) |

| Species | 1% W. Europe pop. 1969–75 | 1% W. Europe pop. 1975–80 | Notes |
|---|---|---|---|
| Ringed Plover | | | |
| *Charadrius hiaticula* | 250 | 400 | Wintering (October–March) European birds |
| | (500+) | 1,000 | Migration periods (July–Sept and April–May) |
| Golden Plover | | | |
| *Pluvialis apricaria* | 8,000 | 10,000 | |
| Grey Plover | | | |
| *P. squatarola* | 300 | 800 | Wintering – increase due to inclusion of birds in W. Africa |
| Lapwing | | | |
| *Vanellus vanellus* | 20,000 | 20,000 | No count data but probably in excess of 2·0 million in winter so 20,000 maximum rule applies |
| Knot | | | |
| *Calidris canutus* | 5,000 | 3,500 | Greenland/Canadian (winter W. Europe) |
| | — | 3,000 | Siberian (winter W. Africa) |
| Sanderling | | | |
| *C. alba* | 150 | 150 | Winter (October–March) |
| | 500 | 500 | Migration periods (July–Sept and April–June) |
| Purple Sandpiper | | | |
| *C. maritima* | (500) | (500+) | No real census but probably 50,000+ occur |
| Dunlin | | | |
| *C. alpina* | 12,000 | 20,000 | Estimate of 1·5 million USSR birds in winter in Europe, 0·7 million Scandinavia/Britain/Iceland/Greenland and N.W. Africa but separation of subspecies not yet clear and 20,000 maximum rule applies |
| Redshank | | | |
| *Tringa totanus* | 1,250 | 2,000 | British/Icelandic breeders (winter France northwards) |
| | 1,500 | 2,000 | Continental Europe breeders (winter Iberia, W. Africa) |
| Greenshank | | | |
| *T. nebularia* | 100 | ( ? ) | European (Britain/Ireland) winterers *may* all belong to Scottish population but not known for certain – provisionally treat as passage |
| | 200 | (500) | Provisional: passage periods (April–Oct) |
| Turnstone | | | |
| *Arenaria interpres* | (500) | (500) | No full count: provisional |

# Criteria of national (British) importance for species

(1)   These data apply to the period 1970–75, although for most species they are still correct – any changes are indicated.

(2)   National criteria are discussed in Chapter 6.

(3)   The figures represent the average numbers at the relevant times of year. To use them correctly the averages of annual observations should be compared, preferably using a period of at least three, and preferably four, years.

(4)   Since national populations are involved, several species are present at low levels. Where the number is small or the species is found in very few sites it is indicated by an asterisk (*). For these strictly using the 1% level might give misleading implications to the importance of sites.

(5)   Wintering wader and wildfowl data are based on the counts of the 'Birds of Estuaries Enquiry', and 'Wildfowl Counts' and special surveys. Diver and grebe numbers on estimates made of numbers by local ornithologists, literature surveys and the 'Birds of Estuaries Enquiry'.

| Species | 1% of non-breeding numbers | Notes |
|---|---|---|
| Red-throated Diver<br>*Gavia stellata* | Provisional estimate 25 | Total estimated as *c.* 2,500 |
| Black-throated Diver<br>*G. arctica* | * | Total estimated as *c.* 210 |
| Great Northern Diver<br>*G. immer* | Provisional estimate 25 | Total estimated as *c.* 2,500 |
| Great Crested Grebe<br>*Podiceps cristatus* | Provisional estimate 100 | No winter census |
| Red-necked Grebe<br>*P. grisegena* | * | Rare (total *c.* 80) |
| Slavonian Grebe<br>*P. auritus* | Provisional estimate 10 | Total estimated as *c.* 670 |
| Black-necked Grebe<br>*P. nigricollis* | * | Rare. Total estimated as *c.* 120 |
| Cormorant<br>*Phalacrocorax carbo* | Provisional estimate 150 | Based on resident breeders |
| Shag<br>*P. aristotelis* | Provisional estimate 600 | Based on resident breeders |
| Mute Swan<br>*Cygnus olor* | 180 | |
| Bewick's Swan<br>*C. columbianus*<br>*bewickii* | 20 | |
| Whooper Swan<br>*C. cygnus* | 30 | |
| Bean Goose<br>*Anser fabalis* | * | Only *c.* 150 present in two flocks (Suffolk/Solway) |

| Species | 1% of non-breeding numbers | Notes |
|---|---|---|
| Pink-footed Goose *Anser brachyrhynchus* | 750 | |
| White-fronted Goose *A. albifrons flavirostris* | 150 | Greenland breeders (in Ireland, Scotland, N.W. Wales) |
| *albifrons* | 100 | USSR breeders (in England, S. Wales) |
| Greylag Goose *A. anser* | 660 (Oct–April) 50 (May–Sept) | Iceland breeders British breeders |
| Canada Goose *Branta canadensis* | 200 | |
| Barnacle Goose *B. leucopsis* | 240 | W. Scottish population (from Greenland) |
| | * | Solway is only area for other population (from Svalbard) |
| Brent Goose (dark) *B. bernicla bernicla* | 330 | Now *c.* 650 |
| Brent Goose (pale) *B. bernicla hrota* | * | Only *c.* 500 present in one flock (Lindisfarne) |
| Shelduck *Tadorna tadorna* | 600 | |
| Wigeon *Anas penelope* | 2,000 | |
| Gadwall *A. strepera* | 30 | |
| Teal *A. crecca* | 750 | |
| Mallard *A. platyrhynchos* | 3,000 | |
| Pintail *A. acuta* | 200 | |
| Shoveler *A. clypeata* | 50 | |
| Pochard *Aythya ferina* | 400 | |
| Tufted Duck *A. fuligula* | 450 | |
| Scaup *A. marila* | 225 | |
| Eider *Somateria mollissima* | 600 | |
| Long-tailed Duck *Clangula hyemalis* | 100 | |

| Species | 1% of non-breeding numbers | Notes |
|---|---|---|
| Common Scoter *Melanitta nigra* | 350 | |
| Velvet Scoter *M. fusca* | 35 | |
| Goldeneye *Bucephala clangula* | 125 | |
| Smew *Mergus albellus* | * | Rare only *c.* 50 present |
| Red-breasted Merganser *M. serrator* | 75 | |
| Goosander *M. merganser* | 40 | |
| Oystercatcher *Haematopus ostralegus* | 2,000 (July–April) | Now 3,000 |
| Avocet *Recurvirostra avosetta* | * | Only at a few sites in low numbers – total less than 150 |
| Ringed Plover *Charadrius hiaticula* | 300 (July–Oct; April–May) 120 (Nov–March) | |
| Golden Plover *Pluvialis apricaria* | 2,000 | Census winter 1976–77 and 1977–78 |
| Grey Plover *P. squatarola* | 100 | |
| Lapwing *Vanellus vanellus* | Provisionally 5,000 | No census data |
| Knot *Calidris canutus* | 3,000 (July–April) | Now 2,500 |
| Sanderling *C. alba* | 300 (July–Sept and May) 100 (Oct–April) | |
| Purple Sandpiper *C. maritima* | 180 | |
| Dunlin *C. alpina* | 5,500 (Oct–March) 2,000 (April–Sept) | |
| Ruff *Philomachus pugnax* | * | Only small numbers winter (*c.* 1,100) |
| Snipe *Gallinago gallinago* | * | No data available, but 100,000+ occur |
| Black-tailed Godwit *Limosa limosa* | 50 | |

| Species | 1% of non-breeding numbers | Notes |
|---------|---------------------------|-------|
| Bar-tailed Godwit *L. lapponica* | 450 | |
| Whimbrel *Numenius phaeopus* | 100 (July–Sept, April–May) | Rare in winter |
| Curlew *N. arquata* | 1,000 | Including estimated 15,000–20,000 inland |
| Spotted Redshank *Tringa erythropus* | 50 (June–Oct) * (winter) | Total 100 present |
| Redshank *T. totanus* | 1,200 (August–Oct) 1,000 (Nov–April) | |
| Greenshank *T. nebularia* | 50 (July–Oct) * (Nov–April) | Total 300 in winter |
| Turnstone *Arenaria interpres* | 250 | |

# References

Alexander, W. B., Southgate, B. A. and Bassindale, R. (1935). Survey of the River Tees. Part II – the estuary, chemical and biological. DSIR Water Pollution Res. Tech. Paper No. 11: 1–609.

Allen, R. H. (1974). The Mersey Ducks since 1950. Cheshire Bird Report 1973: 31–33.

Allen, R. H. and Rutter, G. (1956). The moult migration of the Shelduck in Cheshire in 1955. Brit. Birds 49: 221–225.

Anderson, S. A. (1972). The Ecology of Morecambe Bay. II. Intertidal invertebrates and factors affecting their distribution. J. Appl. Ecol. 9: 161–178.

Andrew, D. G. (1959). Migrations of the oystercatcher. Brit. Birds 52: 216–220.

Ash, J. S. and Sharpe, G. I. (1964). Post-mortem and pesticide examinations of birds in the cold spell of 1963. Bird Study 11: 227–239.

Atkinson, N. K., Davies, M. and Prater, A. J. (1978). The winter distribution of Purple Sandpipers in Britain. Bird Study 25: 223–228.

Atkinson-Willes, G. L. (ed.) (1963). *Wildfowl in Great Britain*. Nature Conservancy Monograph No. 3. London.

Atkinson-Willes, G. L. (1976). The numerical distribution of ducks, swans and coots as a guide in assessing the importance of wetlands. Proc. Int. Conf. Wetlands and Waterfowl, Heiligenhafen, 1974: 199–254.

Atkinson-Willes, G. L. (1978). The numbers and distribution of sea-ducks in north-west Europe, January 1967–1973. Proc. IWRB/NSEPB Symp. on Sea Ducks, Stockholm 1975: 28–67.

Bainbridge, I. P. and Minton, C. D. T. (1978). The Migration and Mortality of the Curlew in Britain and Ireland. Bird Study 25: 39–50.

Barnes, R. S. K. (1974). *Estuarine Biology*. London.

Baxter, E. V. and Rintoul, L. J. (1953). *The Birds of Scotland*. Vol. 2. Edinburgh.

Beeftink, W. G. (1975). The ecological significance of embankment and drainage with respect to the vegetation of the South-west Netherlands. J. Ecol. 63: 423–458.

Bell, T. H. (1962). *The Birds of Cheshire*. Altringham.

Bell, T. H. (1967). *A supplement to The Birds of Cheshire*. Manchester.

Bennett, T. J. and St Joseph, A. K. M. (1974). Brent Geese feeding inland in S.E. England. Wildfowl Trust: cyclostyled report.

Binnie and Partners (1965). *The Water Resources of the Great Ouse Basin*. London.

Binnie and Partners (1971). Dee Estuary Scheme, Phase IIa. Vol. 1. HMSO. London.

Binnie and Partners (1974). Dee Estuary Scheme, Phase IIa. Supplementary Report. Welsh Office and Dept of Environment.

Binnie and Partners (1978). Regional Water Resources Studies – Storage in Morecambe Bay. Report to North West Water Authority.

Blindell, R. M. (1975). The status of the Little Tern, *Sterna albifrons* in Essex, 1950–1974. Essex Bird Report 1974: 69–75.

Blindell, R. M. (1976). The estuarine bird population of the region, Orwell–Thames, 1972–1975. Essex Bird Report 1976: 71–102.

Boaden, P. J. S., O'Connor, R. J. and Seed, R. (1975). The composition and zonation of a *Fucus serratus* community in Strangford Lough, Co. Down. J. exp. mar. Biol. Ecol. 17: 111–136.

Boys, J. V. (1973). *Check List of the Birds of Dorset*. Dorchester.

Branson, N. J. B. A. and Minton, C. D. T. (1976). Moult, Measurements and Migrations of the Grey Plover. Bird Study 23: 257–266.

Branson, N. J. B. A., Ponting, E. D. and Minton, C. D. T. (1978). Turnstone migrations in Britain and Europe. Bird Study 25: 181–187.

Brown, R. A. and O'Connor, R. J. (1974). Some observations on the relationships between Oystercatchers *Haematopus ostralegus* L. and Cockles *Cardium edule* L. in Strangford Lough. Irish Nat. J. 18: 73–80.

Bryant, D. M. (1979). Effects of Prey Density and Site Character on Estuary Usage of Overwintering Waders (Charadrii). Estuarine and Coastal Marine Science 9: 369–384.

Bryant, D. M. and Leng, J. (1975). Feeding distribution and behaviour of Shelduck in relation to food supply. Wildfowl 26: 20–30.

Bryant, D. and Waugh, D. R. (1976). Flightless Shelducks on the Forth. Scott. Birds, 9: 124–125.

Butterworth, J., Lester, P. and Nickless, G. (1972). Distribution of heavy metals in the Severn estuary. Mar. Poll. Bull., 3: 72–74.

Buxton, N. E., Gillham, R. M. and Pugh-Thomas, M. (1977). The Ecology of the Dee Estuary. Unpublished Report to Central Water Planning, Dee and Clwyd River Division and Welsh National Water Development Authority.

Buxton, N. and Summers, R. (1974). Autumn waders in the outer Hebrides. Tay R.G. Report 1973: 14–17.

Cadbury, C. J. and Olney, P. J. S. (1978). Avocet population dynamics in England. Brit. Birds 71: 102–121.

Calder, W. A. (1974). Consequences of body size for avian energetics. In Paynter, R. A. (ed.) Avian Energetics. Cambridge, Mass. 86–143.

Campbell, L. H. (1977). Local variations in the proportion of adult males in flocks of Goldeneye wintering in the Firth of Forth. Wildfowl 28: 77–80.

Campbell, L. H. (1978a). Report of the Forth Ornithological Working Party. Cyclostyled report. NCC.

Campbell, L. H. (1978b). Patterns of distribution and behaviour of flocks of seaducks wintering at Leith and Musselburgh, Scotland. Biol. Conserv. 14: 111–124.

Campbell, L. H. (1980). The impact of an oilspill in the Firth of Forth on Great Crested Grebes. Scott. Birds 11: 43–47.

Campbell, L. H. and Milne, H. (1977). Goldeneye Bucephala clangula feeding close to sewer outfalls in winter. Wildfowl 28: 81–85.

Central Water Planning Unit (1976). The Wash water storage scheme feasibility study: a report on the ecological studies. N.E.R.C. Publ. Ser. C. No. 15.

Chislett, R. (1954). Yorkshire Birds. London.

Clapham, C. R. (1979). The Turnstone populations of Morecambe Bay. Ringing and Migration 2: 144–150.

Cohen, E. and Tavener, J. J. (1972). A revised list of Hampshire and Isle of Wight Birds. Oxford.

Coles, S. M. and Curry, M. (1976). Algal studies in the Wash. Wash Feasibility Study: Scientific study.

Coombes, R. A. H. (1950). The moult migration of the Shelduck. Ibis 92: 405–418.

Corlett, J. (1972). The ecology of Morecambe Bay. I. Introduction. J. Appl. Ecol. 9: 153–159.

Cornwallis, R. K. (1969). Supplement to the Birds of Lincolnshire 1954–1968. Lincoln.

Cottier, E. J. and Lea, D. (1969). Black-tailed Godwits, Ruffs and Black Terns breeding in the Ouse Washes. Brit. Birds 62: 259–270.

Cramp, S., Bourne, W. R. P. and Saunders, D. (1974). The Seabirds of Britain and Ireland. London.

Cramp, S. and Simmons, K. E. L. (eds) (1977). The Birds of the Western Palearctic. Vol. 1. Oxford.

Dare, P. J. (1966). The breeding and wintering populations of the oystercatcher (Haematopus ostralegus Linnaeus) in the British Isles. Fishery Invest. Lond. Ser. II 25 No. 5.

Dare, P. J. (1969). The movements of Oystercatchers Haematopus ostralegus L. visiting or breeding in the British Isles. Fishery Invest. Lond. (Ser II) 25: 1–137.

Dare, P. J. and Schofield, P. (1976). Ecological survey of Lavan Sands: Ornithological Survey, 1969–74. Cambrian Ornithological Society. Cyclostyled.

Deane, C. D. (1954). Handbook of the Birds of Northern Ireland. Belfast Museum and Art Gallery Bulletin 1, 6: 121–190.

Dick, W. J. A., Pienkowski, M. W., Waltner, M. and Minton, C. D. T. (1976). Distribution and geographical origins of Knot Calidris canutus wintering in Europe and Africa. Ardea 64: 22–47.

Dobinson, H. M. and Richards, A. J. (1964). The effects of the severe winter of 1962/63 on birds in Britain. Brit. Birds 57: 373–434.

Donker, J. K. (1959). Migration and distribution of the Wigeon Anas penelope L. in Europe, based on ringing results. Ardea 47: 1–27.

Drinnen, R. E. (1957). The winter feeding of the Oystercatcher (*Haematopus ostralegus*) on the edible cockle (*Cardum edule*). J. Anim. Ecol. 26: 441–469.

Driver, P. A. (1977). Fishery problems of Morecambe Bay. In 'Problems of a Small Estuary', Nelson-Smith, A. and Bridges, E. M. (eds) 9: 4/1–4/11. Swansea.

Dunthorn, A. A. (1971). The predation of cultivated mussels by Eiders. Bird Study 18: 107–112.

van Dyk, A. J. (1979). Onderzoek naar het voorkomen van de Regenwulp – *Numenius phaeopus* – in Nederland. Watervogels 4: 7–13.

Eagle, R. A., Hartley, J. P., Rees, E. I. S., Rees, L. J. and Walker, A. J. M. (1974). Ecological survey of the Lavan Sands: Invertebrate Macrofauna. Marine Science Laboratories, Menai Bridge. Cyclostyled.

Eltringham, S. K. and Boyd, H. (1963). The moult-migration of the Shelduck to Bridgwater Bay, Somerset. Brit. Birds 56: 433.

Evans, M. E. (1979). Aspects of the life cycle of the Bewick's Swan, based on recognition of individuals at a wintering site. Bird Study 26: 149–162.

Evans, M. E., Wood, N. A. and Kear, J. (1973). Lead shot in Bewick's Swans. Wildfowl 24: 56–60.

Evans, P. R. (1966). Wader Migration in north-east England. Trans. N.H.S. Northumb., Durham & Newcastle-upon-Tyne. Vol. 16, No. 2: 126–151.

Evans, P. R. (1968). Autumn movements and orientation of waders in north-east England and southern Scotland, studied by radar. Bird Study 15: 53–64.

Evans, P. R. (1976). Energy balance and optimal foraging strategies in shorebirds: some implications for their distributions and movements in the non-breeding season. Ardea 64: 117–139.

Evans, P. R. and Smith, P. C. (1975). Studies of shorebirds at Lindisfarne, Northumberland. 2. Fat and pectoral muscle as indicators of body condition in the Bar-tailed Godwit. Wildfowl 26: 64–76.

Feare, C. J. (1971). Predation of Limpets and Dogwhelks by Oystercatchers. Bird Study 18: 121–129.

Ferns, P. N. (1977). *Wading birds of the Severn Estuary*. Cardiff.

Ferns, P. N., Green, G. H. and Round, P. D. (1979). Significance of the Somerset and Gwent Levels in Britain as feeding areas for migrant Whimbrels *Numenius phaeopus*. Biol. Conserv. 16: 7–22.

Firth, J. N. M. (1975). Pollution. In Shaw, T. L. (ed.). An environmental appraisal of the Severn Barrage. Cyclostyled report. Bristol.

Flintshire O.S. (1968). *The Birds of Flintshire*. Rhyll.

Franklin, A. (1977). The Burry Inlet Cockle Fishery. In Nelson-Smith, A. and Bridges, E. M. (eds). Problems of a small estuary 3: 1/1–1/5. University of Swansea.

Fuller, R. J. and Youngman, R. E. (1979). The utilization of farmland by Golden Plovers wintering in southern England. Bird Study 26: 37–46.

Furness, R. W. (1973). Roost selection by waders. Scott. Birds 7: 281–287.

Galloway, B. and Meek, E. R. (1978). Northumberland's Birds. Part 1. Nat. Hist. Soc. of Northumbria.

Gibson, I. (1973). Inner Clyde – Report for 1972/73. Cyclostyled report B.T.O.

Gillham, E. H. and Homes, R. C. (1950). *The Birds of the North Kent Marshes*. London.

Glue, D. E. (1971). Saltmarsh Reclamation Stages and their associated bird-life. Bird Study 18: 187–198.

Goethe, F. (1961). The moult gatherings and moult migrations of Shelduck in north-west Germany. Brit. Birds 54: 145–161.

Goss-Custard, J. D. (1969). The winter feeding ecology of the Redshank, *Tringa totanus*. Ibis 111: 338–356.

Goss-Custard, J. D. (1970a). Feeding Dispersion in Some Overwintering Wading Birds. In Crook, J. H. (ed.) *Social Behaviour in Birds and Mammals*. London, 1–35.

Goss-Custard, J. D. (1970b). The responses of redshank (*Tringa totanus* (L)) to spatial variations in the density of their prey. J. Anim. Ecol. 39: 91–114.

Goss-Custard, J. D. (1975). Beach Feast. Birds, Sept/Oct: 23–26.

Goss-Custard, J. D. (1976). Variation in the dispersion of Redshank *Tringa totanus* on their winter feeding grounds. Ibis, 118: 257–263.

Goss-Custard, J. D. (1977a). Optimal foraging and the size selection of worms by Redshank, *Tringa totanus*, in the field. Anim. Behav. 25:10–29.

Goss-Custard, J. D. (1977b). The energetics of prey selection by Redshank, *Tringa totanus* (L), in relation to prey density. J. Anim. Ecol. 46: 1–19.

Goss-Custard, J. D. (1977c). Predator responses and prey mortality in Redshank, *Tringa totanus* (L), and a preferred prey, *Corophium volutator* (Pallas). J. Anim. Ecol. 46: 21–35.

Goss-Custard, J. D. (1977d). The Ecology of the Wash. III. Density-related behaviour and the possible effects of a loss of feeding grounds on wading birds (Charadrii). J. Appl. Ecol. 14: 721–739.

Goss-Custard, J. D. (in press). Role of winter food supplies in the population ecology of common British wading birds. Proc. I.W.R.B. Symp. Gwatt, Switzerland.

Goss-Custard, J. D., Jenyon, R. A., Jones, R. E., Newberry, P. E. and Williams, R. le B. (1977). The Ecology of the Wash. II. Seasonal variation in the feeding conditions of wading birds (Charadrii). J. Appl. Ecol. 14: 701–719.

Goss-Custard, J. D., Jones, R. E. and Newberry, P. E. (1977). The Ecology of the Wash. I. Distribution and Diet of Wading Birds (Charadrii). J. Appl. Ecol. 14: 681–700.

Goss-Custard, J. D., Kay, D. G. and Blindell, R. M. (1977). The density of migratory and overwintering Redshank, *Tringa totanus* (L) and Curlew, *Numenius arquata* (L), in relation to the density of their prey in south-east England. Estuarine and Coastal Marine Science 5: 497–510.

Gray, A. J. (1972). The Ecology of Morecambe Bay. V. The salt marshes of Morecambe Bay. J. Appl. Ecol. 9: 207–220.

Greenhalgh, M. E. (1965). Shelduck numbers on the Ribble estuary. Bird Study 12: 225–256.

Greenhalgh, M. E. (1968). The autumn Migration of waders through the inner Ribble marshes, Lancashire. The Naturalist No. 906: 79–84.

Greenhalgh, M. E. (1971). The Breeding Bird Communities of Lancashire Saltmarshes. Bird Study 18: 199–212.

Greenhalgh, M. E. (1975). *Wildfowl of the Ribble estuary*. WAGBI Conservation Publ. Chester.

Gribble, F. C. (1976). Census of Black-headed Gull colonies in England and Wales in 1973. Bird Study 23: 139–149.

Groves, S. (1978). Age-related differences in Ruddy Turnstone foraging and aggressive behaviour. Auk 95:95–103.

Gudmundsson, F. (1951). The effects of the recent climatic changes on the Bird Life of Iceland. Proc. Xth Int. Orn. Congr. Uppsala, 502–514.

Gundmundsson, F. (1957). Icelandic Birds XV. The Whimbrel (*Numenius phaeopus*). In Icelandic, English summary. Natturufraedingurinn 27: 113–125.

Gwent, O. S. (1977). *The Birds of Gwent*. Pontypool.

Hale, W. G. (1971). A revision of the taxonomy of the Redshank *Tringa totanus*. Zoo. Journ. Linn. Soc. 50: 3: 199–268.

Hale, W. G. (1973). The distribution of the Redshank *Tringa totanus* in the winter range. J. Linn. Soc. 53: 177–236.

Halliday, J. B. (1978). The feeding distribution of birds on the Clyde estuary tidal flats 1976–77. Cyclostyled report. NCC.

Hammond, N. (1975). Outer Hebrides expedition February 1975. Cyclostyled report. RSPB Cumbria group.

Harris, M. P. (1967). The biology of Oystercatchers *Haematopus ostralegus* on Skokholm Island, S. Wales. Ibis 109: 180–193.

Harris, P. R. (1979). The winter feeding of the Turnstone in North Wales. Bird Study 26: 259–266.

Harrison, J. G. (1972). Wildfowl of the North Kent Marshes. Conservation Publication. WAGBI.

Harrison, J. G. and Buck, W. F. A. (1967). Peril in Perspective. Kent OS, special supplement.

Harrison, J. G. and Grant, P. J. (1976). *Thames Transformed*. London.

Harrison, J., Humphreys, J. N. and Graves, G. (1972). Breeding birds of the Medway estuary. Supplement to Kent Bird Report 1972.

Harrison, J. G. and Ogilvie, M. A. (1967). Immigrant Mute Swans of South-east England. Wilf. Trust Ann. Rep. 18: 85–87.

Harrison, J. M. (1953). *The Birds of Kent*. London.

Hauser, B. (1973). Bestandsünderangen der makrofauna an einer station im ostfriesischen Walt. Jber. Forschst. Norderney 24: 171–203.

Heathcote, A., Griffin, D. and Salmon, H. M. (1967). *The birds of Glamorgan*. Cardiff.

Heppleston, P. B. (1971). The feeding ecology of Oystercatchers (*Haematopus ostralegus* L.) in winter in northern Scotland. J. Anim. Ecol. 40: 651–672.

Hickling, R. A. O. (1977). Inland wintering of gulls in England and Wales, 1973. Bird Study 24: 79–88.

Hodgson, D. (1976). Mersey Birds. M.Sc. Thesis. University of Salford.

Hope-Jones, P. (1974). Birds of Merioneth. Cambrian OS.

Hope-Jones, P. and Dare, P. J. (1976). Birds of Caernarvonshire. Cambrian OS.

Hori, J. (1963). The winter roosting and movements of waders in the Swale. Kent Bird Report No. 11: 60–65.

Horwood, J. W. and Goss-Custard, J. D. (1977). Predation by the Oystercatcher, *Haematopus ostralegus* (L), in relation to the cockle, *Cerastoderma edule* (L), fishery in the Burry Inlet, South Wales. J. Appl. Ecol. 14: 139–158.

Hudson, R. and Pyman, G. A. (1968). *A Guide to the Birds of Essex*. Essex Bird-watching and Preservation Society.

Hughes, S. W. M., Bacon, P. and Flegg, J. J. M. (1979). The 1975 census of the Great Crested Grebe in Britain. Bird Study 26: 213–226.

Hutchinson, C. D. (1979). *Ireland's wetlands and their birds*. Dublin.

Hutchinson, C. D. and Neath, B. (1978). Little Gulls in Britain and Ireland. Brit. Birds 71: 563–582.

Imboden, C. (1974). Zug, Fremdansiedlung und Brut periode des Kiebitz *Vanellus vanellus* in Europa. Der. Orn. Beob., 71: 5–134.

Ingram, G. C. S. and Salmon, H. M. (1954). A hand list of the birds of Carmarthenshire. West Wales Field Society.

Jeffrey, D. W. (ed.) (1977). *North Bull Island Dublin Bay – a modern coastal natural history*. Dublin.

Joensen, A. H. (1973). Moult migration and wing-feather moult of Seaducks in Denmark. Dan. Rev. Game Biol. Vol. 8, No. 4. 42 pp.

Kerr, A. (1974). In Caerlaverock: Conservation and Wildfowling in Action: 43–60. WAGBI Conservation Publ. Rossett.

Knight, P. J. and Dick, W. J. A. (1975). Recensement de Limicoles au Banc d'Arguin (Mauritanie). Alauda 43: 363–385.

Krebs, J. R. (1978). Optimal foraging: decision rules for predators. In Krebs, J. R. and Davies, N. (eds) Behavioural Ecology: an evolutionary approach. Oxford. 23–63.

Little, C. (1975). Possible biological effects. In Shaw, T. L. (ed.) An environmental appraisal of the Severn Barrage. 55–65. Cyclostyled report. Bristol.

Lloyd, C. S., Bibby, C. J. and Everett, M. J. (1975). Breeding Terns in Britain and Ireland in 1969–74. Brit. Birds, 68: 221–237.

Lloyd, D. (1978). Golden Plover Survey. BTO News No. 95: 6.

Lockley, R. M., Ingram, G. C. S. and Salmon, H. M. (1960). The Birds of Pembrokeshire. West Wales Field Society.

Longbottom, M. R. (1970). The distribution of *Arenicola marina* (L) with particular reference to the effects of particle size and organic matter of the sediments. J. Exp. mar. Biol. Ecol. 5: 138–157.

McLusky, D. S. (1971). *Ecology of Estuaries*. London.

Marsh, P. J. (1975). Birds of the north coast region. Cyclostyled report.

Mason, C. F. (1971). Report on the pilot survey of the Inland Wader Enquiry, autumn 1971. Cyclostyled report. BTO.

Matthews, G. V. T. (1960). An examination of basic data from wildfowl counts. Proc. Int. Orn. Congr. 12: 483–491.

Mead, C. J. (1974). *Bird Ringing*. BTO Guide No. 16. Tring.

Mead, C. J., Flegg, J. J. M. and Cox, C. J. (1968). A factor inhibiting subspecific differentiation in the Lapwing. Bird Study 15: 105–106.

Meek, E. R. and Little, B. (1977a). The spread of the Goosander in Britain and Ireland. Brit. Birds 70: 229–237.

Meek, E. R. and Little, B. (1977b). Ringing studies of Goosanders in Northumberland. Brit. Birds 70: 273–283.

Merne, O. M. (1977). The changing status and distribution of the Bewick's Swans in Ireland. Irish Birds 1: 3–15.

Milne, H. (1965). Seasonal movements and distribution of Eiders in North-east Scotland. Bird Study 12: 170–180.

Milne, H. and Campbell, L. H. (1973). Wintering Sea-ducks off the East Coast of Scotland. Bird Study 20: 153–172.

Milne, H. and Dunnet, G. M. (1972). Standing Crop, Productivity & Trophic Relations of the Fauna of the Ythan Estuary. In Barnes, R. S. K. and Green, J. (eds) *The Estuarine Environment*. London.

Minton, C. D. T. (1976). The Waders of the Wash – Ringing and Biometric studies. Wash Feasibility Study: Scientific Study G.

Moore, R. (1969). *The Birds of Devon*. Newton Abbot.

Moreau, R. E. (1972). *The Palaearctic African Bird Migration Systems*. London.

Moyse, J. and Thomas, D. K. (1977). Sea-duck of Carmarthen Bay. In Proc. Burry Inlet Symp.: Nelson-Smith, A. and Bridges, E. M. (eds): 5: 3/1–3/13.

Mudge, G. (1979). The feeding distribution of wintering wading birds (Charadriiformes) in the Severn estuary in relation to barrage proposals. Cyclostyled report. NCC.

Mudge, G. P. and Allen, D. S. (1980). Wintering seaducks in the Moray and Dornoch Firths, Scotland. Wildfowl 31: 123–130.

Mulder, T. (1972). De Grutto in Nederland. Wetenschappelijke mededelingen K.N.N.V. nr 90: 52 pp.

Musson, D. F. (1963). Status of waders in North Kent. Kent Bird Report No. 11: 49–59.

Nature Conservancy (1971). *Wildlife Conservation in the North Kent Marshes*. Wye.

Nature Conservancy Council (1978). Nature Conservation within the Moray Firth area. NCC, North West Scotland Region.

Nelson-Smith, A. and Bridges, E. M. (eds) (1977). Problems of a small estuary. Swansea University.

Nethersole-Thompson, D. and Nethersole-Thompson, M. (1979). *Greenshanks*. Berkhamsted.

Newton, I. (1968). The temperatures, weights and body composition of moulting Bullfinches. Condor 70: 323–332.

Newton, I., Thom, V. M. and Brotherston, W. (1973). Behaviour and distribution of wild geese in south-east Scotland. Wildfowl 24: 111–121.

Norton-Griffiths, M. (1967). Some ecological aspects of the feeding behaviour of the Oystercatcher *Haematopus ostralegus* on the edible mussel *Mytilus edulis*. Ibis 109: 412–424.

Oakes, C. (1953). *The Birds of Lancashire*. Edinburgh and London.

O'Connor, R. J. and Brown, R. A. (1977). Prey depletion and foraging strategy in the Oystercatcher *Haematopus ostralegus*. Oecologia 27: 75–92.

Ogilvie, M. A. (1967). Population changes and mortality of the Mute Swan in Britain. Wildf. Trust Ann. Rep. 18: 64–73.

Ogilvie, M. A. (1978). *Wild Geese*. Berkhamsted.

Ogilvie, M. A. and Boyd, H. (1975). Greenland Barnacle Geese in the British Isles. Wildfowl 26: 139–147.

Ogilvie, M. A. and St Joseph, A. K. M. (1976). The Dark-bellied Brent Goose in Britain and Europe. Brit. Birds 69: 422–439.

Olney, P. J. S. (1965). The food and feeding habits of the Shelduck *Tadorna tadorna*. Ibis 107: 527–532.

Owen, M. (1975). Implications for Wildfowl. In Shaw, T. L. (ed.) An environmental appraisal of the Severn Barrage, 73–77. Cyclostyled report. Bristol.

Owen, M. and Williams, G. (1976). Winter distribution and habitat requirements of Wigeon in Britain. Wildfowl 27: 83–90.

Palmer, E. M. and Ballance, D. K. (1968). *The Birds of Somerset*. London.

Payn, W. H. (1978). *The Birds of Suffolk*. Ipswich.

Penhallurick, R. (1969). *Birds of the Cornish Coast*. Truro.

Penhallurick, R. (1978). *The Birds of Cornwall and the Isle of Scilly*. Penzance.

Pilcher, R. E. M., Beer, J. V. and Cook, W. A. (1974). Ten years of intensive late winter surveys for waterfowl corpses on the north-west shore of the Wash, England. Wildfowl 25: 149–154.

Ploeger, P. L. (1968). Geographical differences in Arctic Anatidae as a result of isolation during the last glacial. Ardea 56: 1–159.

Portsmouth Polytechnic (1976). Langstone Harbour Study: the effects of sewage effluent on the ecology of the Harbour.

Pounder, B. (1971). Wintering Eiders in the Tay estuary. Scott. Birds 6: 407–419.

Pounder, B. (1974). Breeding and moulting Eiders in the Tay region. Scott. Birds 8: 159–176.

Pounder, B. (1976). Waterfowl at effluent discharges in Scottish coastal waters. Scott. Birds 9: 5–36.

Prater, A. J. (1972). The Ecology of Morecambe Bay. III. The Food and Feeding Habits of Knot in Morecambe Bay. J. appl. Ecol. 9: 179–194.

Prater, A. J. (1973). The Wintering Population of Ruffs in Britain and Ireland. Bird Study 20: 245–250.

Prater, A. J. (1974). The population and migration of Knot in Europe. Proc. IWRB Wader Symp. Warsaw 1973: 99–113.

Prater, A. J. (1975). The wintering population of the Black-tailed Godwit. Bird Study 22: 169–176.

Prater, A. J. (1976a). The distribution of coastal waders in Europe and North Africa. Proc. Int. Conf. on Conservation of Wetlands and Waterfowl, Heiligenhafen 1974: 255–271.

Prater, A. J. (1976b). The midwinter estuarine population of waders in Wales, 1971–74. Nature in Wales 15: 2–7.

Prater, A. J. (1976c). Breeding population of the Ringed Plover in Britain. Bird Study 23: 155–161.

Prater, A. J. (1977). The birds of the Burry Inlet. Proc. Burry Inlet Symp. 5: 1/1–1/12. Swansea University.

Prater, A. J. (1978). The effect of estuarine engineering schemes on birds. Hydrobiological Bull. 12: 322–332.

Prater, A. J. (1979). Trends in accuracy of counting birds. Bird Study 26: 198–200.

Prater, A. J. and Davies, M. (1978). Wintering Sanderlings in Britain. Bird Study 25: 33–38.

Prater, A. J., Marchant, J. H. and Vuorinen, J. (1977). Guide to the identification and ageing of Holarctic Waders. BTO Guide No. 17: 168 pp.

Prato, S. Da and Prato, S. R. D. Da (1979). Counting wintering waders on rocky shores in East Lothian, Scotland. WSG Bull. 25: 19–23.

Pyke, G. H., Pulliam, H. R. and Charnov, E. L. (1977). Optimal foraging: a selective review of theory and tests. Q. Rev. Biol. 52: 137–154.

Ratcliffe, D. A. (1976a). Thoughts towards a philosophy of Nature Conservation. Biol. Conserv. 45–54.

Ratcliffe, D. A. (1976b). Observations on the Breeding of the Golden Plover in Great Britain. Bird Study 23: 63–116.

Reading, C. J. and McGrorty, S. (1978). Seasonal variations in the burying depth of *Macoma balthica* (L.) and its accessibility to wading birds. Estuarine and Coastal Marine Sce. 6: 135–144.

Rees, E. I. S. (1978). Observations on the ecological effects of pipeline construction across Lavan Sands. Marine Science Laboratories, Menai Bridge, Cyclostyled.

Roberts, L. (1974). In Caerlaverock: Conservation and Wildfowling in Action: 61–73. WAGBI Conservation Publ. Rossett.

Rudge, P. (1970). The birds of Foulness. Brit. Birds 63: 49–66.

Ruttledge, R. F. (1966). *Ireland's Birds*. London.

Ruttledge, R. F. (1970). Winter distribution and numbers of Scaup, Long-tailed Duck and Common Scoter in Ireland. Bird Study 17: 241–246.

Ruxton, J. (1973). *Wildfowl of Morecambe Bay*. WAGBI Conservation Publ. Chester.

Sachs, G. (1968). Die Mauser des Grossen Brachvogels, *Numenius arquata*. J. Orn. 109: 485–511.

Schneider, D. (1978). Equalisation of prey numbers by migrating shorebirds. Nature, Vol. 271, No. 5643: 353–354.

Scott, R. E. (1978). Winter bird populations of Stoke Ooze. Kent Bird Rep. 25: 90–91.

Seago, M. J. (1977). *Birds of Norfolk*. Norwich.

Seed, R. and Brown, R. A. (1978). Growth as a strategy for survival in two marine bivalves, *Cerastoderma* and *Modiolus modiolus*.

Sharrock, J. T. R. (1976). *The Atlas of Breeding Birds of Britain and Ireland*. Berkhamsted.

Shevareva, T. (1970). Geographical distribution of main dabbling duck populations in the USSR and the main directions of their migrations. Proc. Int. Conf. on Conservation of Wildfowl Resources, Leningrad 1968: 46–55.

Shrubb, M. (1979). *The Birds of Sussex*. Woking.

Smallshire, D. (1974). The inland wader enquiry, 1971–74. Cyclostyled report. BTO.

Smith, A. E. and Cornwallis, R. K. (1955). *The Birds of Lincolnshire*. Lincoln.

Smith, P. H. and Greenhalgh, M. E. (1977). A four-year census of wading birds in the Ribble estuary, Lancashire/Merseyside. Bird Study 24: 243–258.

Smith, P. S. (1975). A study of the winter feeding ecology and behaviour of the Bar-tailed Godwit (*Limosa lapponica*). Ph.D. thesis, University of Durham.

Smyth, J. C., Curtis, D. J., Gibson, I. and Wilkinson, M. (1974). Intertidal Organisms of an industrialised Estuary. Marine Poll. Bull. Dec 74, Vol. 5, No. 12.

Spencer, K. G. (1973). *The status and distribution of birds in Lancashire*. Burnley.

Stanley, P. I. and Minton, C. D. T. (1972). The unprecedented westward migration of Curlew Sandpipers in autumn 1969. Brit. Birds 65: 365–380.

Steventon, D. J. (1977). Dunlin in Portsmouth, Langstone and Chichester Harbours. Ringing and Migration 1: 141–147.

Stokoe, R. (1962). *Birds of Cumberland*. Carlisle.

Summers, R. W., Atkinson, N. K. and Nicoll, M. (1975). Wintering wader populations on the rocky shores of eastern Scotland. Scott. Birds 8: 299–308.

Tanner, M. F. (1973). Water Resources and recreation. Sports Council, Study 3. London.

Thorburn, I. W. and Rees, E. I. S. (eds) (1978). An ecological survey of the Conwy estuary. Marine Science Laboratories, Menai Bridge. Cyclostyled.

Tjallingii, S. J. (1972). Habitat selection of the Avocet (*Recurvirostra avosetta*) in relation to feeding. Proc. XV Int. Orn. Congr.: 696.

Tubbs, C. R. (1977). Wildfowl and waders in Langstone Harbour. Brit. Birds 70: 177–179.

Voous, K. H. (1960). *Atlas of European Birds*. Amsterdam.

Voous, K. H. (1973). List of Recent Holarctic bird species. Non-passerines. Ibis 115: 612–638.

Ward, P. and Zahavi, A. (1973). The importance of certain assemblages of birds as 'information-centres' for food-finding. Ibis 115: 517–534.

Water Resources Board (1966). *Morecambe Bay Barrage: desk study: report of consultants*. London.

Water Resources Board (1970). *The Wash: Estuary Storage*. London.

Water Resources Board (1972). Morecambe Bay estuary storage. Report by Water Resources Board Publ. No. 12. HMSO. London.

Water Resources Board (1973). Water Resources in England and Wales. HMSO. London.

West, A. B. (1977). Fauna of intertidal flats and beach. In Jeffrey, D. W. (ed.) North Bull Island Dublin Bay, 38–45. Dublin.

Williams, T. S. (1962). The wild geese of Mersey and Dee. Birds of the Wirral Peninsula 1961: 21–26. Liverpool Ornithologists' Club.

Williamson, K. (1968). Goose emigration from western Scotland. Scott. Birds 5: 71–89.

Wilson, J. (1973). Wader Populations of Morecambe Bay, Lancashire. Bird Study 20: 9–23.

Wilson, J. (1974). *The Birds of Morecambe Bay*. Lancaster.

Wilson, P. J. (1976). Wash wintering Twite population Study. Wash Feasibility Study: Scientific Study O.

Yarker, B. and Atkinson-Willes, G. L. (1971). The numerical distribution of British breeding ducks. Wildfowl 22: 63–70.

Zwarts, L. (1978). Intra- and inter-specific competition for space in estuarine bird species in a one-prey situation. Proc. Int. Orn. Congr. Berlin.

# Index